HISTORICAL INTRODUCTION TO PHILOSOPHY

Albert Hakim
Seton Hall University

Macmillan Publishing Company
New York

Collier Macmillan Publishers
London

Dedicated with affection to my wife

Irene, loving and wise

and to our children

Michael, William, and Katherine

Copyright 1987, Macmillan Publishing Company, a division of Macmillan, Inc.

Printed in the United States of America

Macmillan Publishing Company
866 Third Avenue, New York, New York 10022

Collier Macmillan Canada, Inc.

Library of Congress Cataloging in Publication Data

Hakim, Albert.
    Historical introduction to philosophy.

    Bibliography: p.
    1. Philosophy   2. Philosophers.   I. Title.
BD41.H29 1987 190 86-33288
ISBN 0-02-348790-9

Printing: 1 2 3 4 5 6 7 8   Year: 7 8 9 0 1 2 3 4 5 6

ISBN   0-02-348790-9

Preface

Historical Introduction to Philosophy is designed to lead beginning students to an appreciation of philosophy by developing in them a sense of its history, a grasp of the problems it has dealt with, and a familiarity with major philosophers and their works. To bring this about, the historical approach and the problem or thematic approach have been blended, allowing students to study major philosophical problems and to read key philosophers within a historical setting.

The book spans 2000 years of Western philosophy, extending from the predecessors of Socrates down to our own day. Introductions to each of the four parts — ancient, medieval, modern, and contemporary —provide a synopsis of each age, describes its intellectual milieu, and traces the development of philosophy throughout the period. Each chapter is devoted to a single philosopher and begins with an introduction to his life and thought. The readings that follow offer a representative profile of his work, his concerns and contributions as a philosopher. Selections are substantial and broad-ranging in order to give students the full flavor of a philosopher's writings, and to allow professors to tailor the course as they wish. Questions for discussion or review come at the end of each chapter. Included at the end of the book are a glossary of key terms and a bibliography of titles for further reading. An alternate table of contents—the Table of Problems—provides a separate reference to the philosophical problems covered in the readings and can be used to pursue a particular theme or subject of interest. *Historical Introduction to Philosophy* thus lends itself as a practical and pliable text to instructors and students in any number of teaching styles, course objectives and classroom contexts.

I take this opportunity to express my gratitude to all those who made suggestions to me as the book was in progress: to my colleagues in the Department of Philosophy at Seton Hall University, especially Dr. David O'Connor, who read through the book as a whole and made many perceptive recommendations which I incorporated; to Robert Durrant who, as Chairman of the Department of Philosophy at the University of Otago, New Zealand, generously facilitated my work during my sabbatical there; to those who reviewed the manuscript in various stages, R. Puligandla (The University of Toledo), Sidney A. Gross (Elmhurst College), and John M. Koller (Rensselaer Polytechnic Institute); to

Helen McInnis, Executive Editor of the College Division of Macmillan, whose guidance and confidence in my writing persisted to the end; and to that student whose surreptitiously recorded tapes of my lectures became the occasion of my whiling away the hours of a long hospitalization by transcribing several notebooks full of my own voice.

A.H.

Introduction

The purpose of this book is to introduce you, as a beginning student, to philosophy. By the time you reach the end, you will have seen philosophers at work, discussed their ideas, and developed a feeling for the spirit of philosophical inquiry — which feeling is by far the best introduction to philosophy you can have. But even now it would be useful to have some basic notion of the ways in which philosophy differs from other areas of knowledge. Often, in undertaking a new study, a start can be made with a definition; in this case, however, a definition does not immediately come to hand, for there is none to be found which states absolutely and simply what philosophy is. But we can develop a sense for what takes place when we "philosophize" or "do philosophy," and accordingly describe it.

First, let's look at the kind of question we ask when we think about things, for the kind of question is in itself a key to the truth we seek. Take the simple example of an apple. We can ask questions like, what is its shape? its color? its taste? How much does it cost? How much does it weigh? Where does it grow? How is it shipped? What is its best perspective for a painting? and so on. But we can also ask question of another kind: Why does the apple exist rather than not? Is it caused, or is it just there? What's in its make-up to distinguish it from a stone, a dog, a man? Is there a reason why it exists? a purpose? an end? The questions of the first kind differ from those of the second in that they are questions of fact. They are questions we ask as merchants, farmers or artists. They arise from experience, but they are not an inquiry into the experience itself. The questions of the second kind, however, ask for more than a mere statement of fact, for things not given in the experience; they arise from experience, but they invite us to probe the possibility as to whether there is more in experience than what we first meet. They summon us to reflect on what, if anything, is required beyond the experience to warrant our having it to begin with. Thus, *reflection on experience* is a good description of what philosophy is.

Take another example of experience, perhaps one you have as a spectator in an art gallery, attracted by a painting you never saw before. You call it beautiful; you enjoy it; you experience it. You don't have to ask yourself *why* it is beautiful, yet if you do, you are asking a question which opens up further understanding of the experience. Thus, given the experience of this work of art as beautiful, the effort to discover why this is so is what the philosophy of art is all about.

An example of an entirely different texture is had in language — our ordinary, everyday use of words. Our experience is generally one of satisfaction that by the words we use and the sentences we fashion we can communicate with others in speech and writing. The questions we raise usually refer to grammar or style. But further questions can be raised, like those pertaining to the relationship between language and the world of facts, or how words stand to each other in a sentence; an inquiry of this kind, which occupied many British philosphers of the recent past, goes by the name of the philosophy of language, or language analysis.

If we switch our attention to humanity, more specific questions naturally arise. What do human beings, as living things, have in common with other living things? What do they not have common? Or, given two people, what differentiates one from the other, making each one an individual? Or, are human activities, such as thinking and willing, radically different from the activities of animals or a computer solving an engineering problem? Is there some kind of life after death? Do we have a destiny? Why are some actions of ours called good, and others not? A list like this can go on indefinitely, but the point made here is that they are philosophical questions because they initiate a search for the deeper meaning of human life. They are questions all of us can and must ask at the risk of running foul of Socrates' time-honored dictum: "the unexamined life is not worth living."

Examples of experience abound, everyone of them giving us further entrée into reality. They can come from natural science, mathematics, psychology, anthropology; from our self-understanding as knowing and willing beings; from our inward consciousness of our selves, our emotions, our choices; from fears of loneliness, alienation, despair; from love, friendship, desire, joy; from laughter, sorrow; from social life, from privacy; from government, law; from history and religion; in short, from all those experiences whereby reality as a whole makes itself known to the human mind in the course of time.

Another helpful way of getting to understand what philosophy is is to look at the derivation of the word. The word "philosophy" is of Greek origin and signifies "love of wisdom" (*philia*, love; *sophia*, wisdom). Once again, wisdom stands for more than the kind of knowledge a pilot has who knows how to set a compass for direction or the sociologist who knows the right sampling device for making a survey. We do not call the pilot or the sociologist "wise" because each knows how to use the compass or the sampling device. Wisdom looks for more; it touches a level where separate things can be seen in unity, or disparate things in interrelatedness. Perhaps this is something like what Aristotle had in mind when he said that wisdom deals with "first causes and the principles of things."

The pursuit of truth is not the domain of any one person, as though any one person's mind were ample enough to embrace all; the pursuit of truth belongs to many, and stretches over long periods of human history. This continuing pursuit is often expressed in the phrase "perennial philosophy," which bespeaks the love of wisdom as it characterizes humanity's search in the course of time. Perennial philosophy does not refer to an unassailable body of truth handed on from generation to generation, for, even though there may be agreement on many things, philosophers do not agree on everything. Augustine, for example, holds to the immortality of the soul, Sartre does not; Aristotle says that cause and effect is an extra-mental relationship, Hume says it's mental; Leibniz claims proof for the existence of God, Nietzsche does not; Descartes asserts that knowledge begins with innate ideas, Locke flatly denies it; Aquinas maintains that man is social by nature, which Hobbes rejects; Kierkegaard insists on individuality as his primary concern, Marx insists on society; and thus it goes. As Hume observed, "There is nothing which is not the subject of debate, and in which men of learning are not of contrary opinions."

The difficulty in achieving certainty does not point to the impoverishment of philosophy; it points to the nature of reality whose very mystery precludes philosophers from abandoning their common search for meaning. Granted there are differences among them, philosophers are called philosophers because of their concern for investigating questions implied in their experience. Their concern is precisely with the problems of reality which, because of their significance, easily lead to disagreement: knowledge, morality, selfhood, cause and effect, language, art, law, happiness, good, love, virtue, determinism, freedom, and so on. This common search and common concern is what unites philosophers as philosophers, generating thereby a "unity of philosophical experience."

It follows from what has been said that beginning students, to get into the spirit of philosophy, do well to study philosophical problems in historical context; here they will observe philosophers at work and come to grips with the problems themselves in the historical setting which nurtured them; the history of philosophy will become for them what the laboratory is for students of science.

The historical span of philosophy in the west, which is the scope of this book, is about 2500 years, extending from the predecessors of Socrates down to our own day. This text covers the four main periods: ancient, medieval, modern, and contemporary. The first period, for the most part Greek, runs from the earliest Greek philosophers in the sixth century B.C. to the third century A.D.; here we shall see the Pre-Socratics, Socrates, Plato and Aristotle. The medieval period extends from the beginning of Christian philosophy around the fourth century down to the early part of the fifteenth century, with the coming of the Renaissance; in this period we shall meet St. Augustine, St. Anselm, St. Thomas Aquinas, Duns Scotus and Nicholas of Cusa. The modern period, also referred to as "classical" modern, begins in the early seventeenth century and goes to the middle of the nineteenth; the philosophers to be studied here are Descartes, Spinoza, Leibniz, Hobbes, Locke, Berkeley, Hume, Kant, Hegel and Mill. The contemporary period covers philosophers living today or in the recent past, from the middle of the nineteenth century, inasmuch as a great deal of contemporary thought has its origin in the second half of that century; here we shall consider Kierkegaard, Nietzsche, Marx, Bergson, James, Russell, Wittgenstein and Sartre.

It should be clear that, in a book dealing with two and a half milennia of western philosophy, not every philosopher can be discussed, nor every problem, lest it become an encyclopedia instead of a textbook. So some selection had to be made with all the perils of choice. The guiding principle has been to select philosphers who are representative, whose contributions are arguably major, and whose inclusion therefore would be more defensible than their exclusion. Selection hardly means that excluded philosophers are not important, nor their insights without merit; it simply means that the philosophers included serve, in the opinion of the author, as admirable historical profiles of the philosophical experience.

Contents

PART I: THE ANCIENT PERIOD   **1**
The Spirit of Greek Philosophy: Philosophy as Wonder

Introduction   1

Chapter 1. The Predecessors of Socrates   3

     Readings: Selected Fragments from the   11
         Pre-Socratics

Chapter 2. Socrates (469–399 B.C.)   25

     Readings: The Trial of Socrates (Plato's   28
         Apology)
         The Death of Socrates (from   49
         Phaedo)

Chapter 3. Plato (427–347 B.C.)   52

     Readings: Doctrine of Forms (General   58
         Statement, from *Parmenides*)
         Doctrine of Forms (Creation   60
         Myth, from *Timaeus*)
         Knowledge: Analogy of the Cave   63
         (from *The Republic*)
         Knowledge: The Divided Line   65
         (from *The Republic*)
         Virtue and the Highest Good   68
         (from *Laws*)
         The Philosopher-King (*Epistle   70
         VII*)

Chapter 4. Aristotle (384–322 B.C.)   73

     Readings: Toward a Definition of Wisdom   85
         (from *Metaphysics*)
         The Prime Mover: One and Eter-   89
         nal (from *Physics*)
         Thought, Contemplation, and the   94
         Life of God (from *Metaphysics*)

Happiness and Man's Good (from   97
Nicomachean Ethics)
Moral Virtue and the Mean   100
(from *Nicomachean Ethics*)
The End of Human Nature: Hap-   105
piness (from *Nicomachean Ethics*)
Wisdom and Virtue as the Basis   111
of Society (from *Politics*)
The Civil Society (from *Politics*)   112

PART II: THE MEDIEVAL PERIOD   **117**
The Spirit of Medieval Philosophy: Philosophy Meets Theology

Introduction   117

Chapter 5. St. Augustine (354–430)   121

Readings: Two Commandments of Love   128
(from *Commentary on St. John's Gospel*)
The Mystical Experience (from   129
Commentary on Psalm 41)
The Problem of Evil: 1 (from   131
Confessions)
The Problem of Evil: 2 (from   136
Enchiridion)
The Mystery of Time (from   138
Confessions)

Chapter 6. St. Anselm (1033–1109)   152

Readings: Faith Seeking Understanding   155
(from *Proslogion*)
The "Ontological Argument" for   156
the Existence of God (from *Proslogion*)

Chapter 7. St. Thomas Aquinas (1225–1274)   159

Readings: On the Existence of God (from   167
Summa theologiae)
The Problem of Evil (from   171
Summa theologiae)
On the Soul (from *Summa theologiae*) 175

The Unity of Man (from *Summa*   182
theologiae)

On Happiness (from *Summa con-*   187
tra Gentes)

On the Essence of Law (from   191
Summa theologiae)

On the Various Kinds of Law   196
(from *Summa theologiae*)

Chapter 8. Duns Scotus (1266–1308)   201

Readings: God as Creator and Conserver   205
(from *God and Creatures*)

Moral Goodness and Badness   208
(from *God and Creatures*)

The Indemonstrability of Immor-   213
tality (from the *Oxford Commentary*)

Chapter 9. Nicholas of Cusa (1401–1464)   218

Readings: The Maximum and the Minimum   222
Are the Same (from *Of Learned*
Ignorance)

How in the Infinite, Opposites   223
Are One (from *Of Learned Ignorance*)

Everything Is in Everything   225
(from *Of Learned Ignorance*)

PART III: THE MODERN PERIOD   **227**

The Spirit of Modern Philosophy: Philosophy and the Rise
of Modern Science

Introduction   227

Chapter 10. René Descartes (1596–1650)   233

Readings: *Discourse on Method*   239
Meditations on First Philosophy   251

Chapter 11. Baruch Spinoza (1632–1677)   270

Readings: Definitions and Axioms (from   275
Ethics)

Seven Propositions on Substance   276
(from *Ethics*)

A Summary Statement Concern-   277
ing God (from *Ethics*)
The Third Degree of Knowledge   283
and the Love of God (from *Ethics*)

Chapter 12. Gottfried Wilhelm Leibniz (1646–1716)   290

Readings: From *The Monadology*   295
Evil as Privation (from *Theodicy*)   303
The Analogy of the Boat (from   304
Theodicy)
No Better World Possible (from   305
Theodicy)

Chapter 13. Thomas Hobbes (1588–1679)   307

Readings: From *Leviathan, or the Matter,*   315
Form, and Power of a Commonwealth
Ecclesiastical and Civil

Chapter 14. John Locke (1632–1704)   338

Readings: From *Essay Concerning Human*   349
Understanding
From *The Second Treatise of*   379
Civil Government

Chapter 15. George Berkeley (1685–1753)   387

Readings: From *A Treatise Concerning the*   392
Principles of Human Knowledge
From *Three Dialogues Between*   404
Hylas and Philonous

Chapter 16. David Hume (1711–1776)   410

Readings: Impressions and Ideas (from *An*   415
Enquiry Concerning Human
Understanding)
Doubts Concerning the Under-   417
standing: The Cause-and-Effect
Relationship (from *An Enquiry*
Concerning Human Understanding)
The Advantages of Scepticism   426
(from *An Enquiry Concerning*

Human Understanding)
Dialogues Concerning Natural 430
Religion

Chapter 17. Immanuel Kant (1724–1804) 439

Readings: Introduction to the *Critique of* 444
Pure Reason
Transcendental Illusion 455
(from *Critique of Pure Reason*)
The Paralogism of Rational Psychol- 458
ogy (from *Critique of Pure Reason*)
The Three Regulative Ideas of 463
Pure Reason (from *Critique of Pure*
Reason)
The Categorical Imperative (from 467
Foundations of the Metaphysics
of Morals)
Postulates of Pure Practical Rea- 471
son (from *Critique of Practical Reason*)

Chapter 18. Georg Wilhelm Friedrich Hegel (1770–1831) 475

Readings: The Absolute as Process of 479
Self-Becoming (from *Phenomenology*
of Spirit)
The Introduction to 483
Phenomenology of Spirit: Consciousness
and the Dialectical Process
Time and the Self-Realization of 492
Spirit (from *Phenomenology of Spirit*)

Chapter 19. John Stuart Mill (1806–1873) 495

Readings: What Utilitarianism Is (from 502
Utilitarianism)
Of the Law of Universal Causation 507
(from *A System of Logic*)
Of Liberty and Necessity (from 512
A System of Logic)
Of the Logic of Practice, or Art; 518
Including Morality and Policy (from
A System of Logic)
On the Probable Futurity of the 519

Laboring Classes (from *Principles of Political Economy*)

Liberty (from *On Liberty*)   526

PART IV: THE CONTEMPORARY PERIOD   **535**

The Spirit of Contemporary Philosophy: The Ascendancy of the Person

Introduction   535

Chapter 20. Søren Kierkegaard (1813–1855)   539

Readings: The Search for Personal Meaning   544
(from *Journals*)
Abraham and "Breaking Through   548
the Universal" (from *Fear and
Trembling*)
The Subjective Truth, Inward-   552
ness: Truth Is Subjectivity (from
Concluding Unscientific Postscript)

Chapter 21. Friedrich Nietzsche (1844–1900)   563

Readings: The Death of God and the As-   569
cendancy of the Overman (from
Thus Spoke Zarathustra)
Fearlessness (from *The Gay   572
Science*)
Anti-Christ and Revaluation   575
(from *The Anti-Christ*)

Chapter 22. Karl Marx (1816–1883)   582

Readings: A Chapter in the Exploitation of   586
the Working Man (from *Das Kapital*)
On the Alienation of Man (from   592
*Economic and Philosophical
Manuscripts*)

Chapter 23. Henri Bergson (1859–1941)   599

Readings: From *Creative Evolution*   603
Open Morality and Dynamic Re-   611
ligion (from *The Two Sources of
Morality and Religion*)

Chapter 24. William James (1842–1910)   613

    Readings: The Meaning of Pragmatism,   617
          (from *What Is Pragmatism* ?)
          The Pragmatic Method Applied to   619
          the Problem of Substance, (from
          What Is Pragmatism?)
          The Pragmatic Method Applied to   620
          The Problem of Religion (from *What*
          Is Pragmatism?)
          The Will to Believe   622

Chapter 25. Bertrand Russell (1872–1970)   638

    Readings: Mathematics and Logic (from   643
          Introduction to Mathematical
          Philosophy)
          Man's Place in the Universe   651
          (from *An Outline of Philosophy*)
          The Value of Philosophy (from   654
          The Problems of Philosophy)

Chapter 26. Ludwig Wittgenstein (1889–1951)   660

    Readings: Preface to *Tractatus Logico-*   667
          Philosophicus
          Language as Picture (from   668
          Tractatus Logico-Philosophicus)
          Beyond the Limits of Language   674
          (from *Tractatus Logico-Philosophicus*)
          Language as Language-Games   677
          (from *Philosophical Investigations*)

Chapter 27. Jean-Paul Sartre (1905–1980)   683

    Readings: The Meaning of Existentialism   689
          (from *Existentialism and Humanism*)
          Reflections on Being and Noth-   694
          ingness (from *Being and Nothingness*)
          Reflections on Dialectical Reason   705
          (from *Critique of Dialectical Reason*)

Selected Bibliography   717
Glossary   729

Table of Problems: Readings

I. KNOWLEDGE

Plato, Doctrine of forms   58
    (*Parmenides*)
    Analogy of the cave   63
    (*Republic*)
    The divided line   65
    (*Republic*)
Aristotle, Towards a definition of wisdom   85
    (*Metaphysics*)
Descartes, *Discourse on Method*, Part II, Part IV   239
Spinoza, Third degree of knowledge and love of God   283
    (*Ethics*)
Locke, Origin of ideas, simple and complex ideas,   349
    sensation and reflection, knowledge, truth
    (*Essay concerning Human Understanding*)
Berkeley, First principles of knowledge, abstract   392
    ideas, sense knowledge, "to be is to be per-
    ceived," material substance
    (*A Treatise concerning the Principles of Human Knowledge*)
Hume, Impressions and ideas   415
    The advantages of scepticism   426
    (*An Enquiry concerning Human Understanding*)
Kant, Introduction to the *Critique of Pure Reason*   444
Kierkegaard, The subjective truth, inwardness: truth   552
    is subjectivity
    (*Concluding Unscientific Postscript*)
James, The meaning of pragmatism   617
    (*What Is Pragmatism?*)
    The Will to Believe   622
Russell, Mathematics and logic   643
    (*Introduction to Mathematical Philosophy*)
    The value of philosophy   654
    (*The Problems of Philosophy*)
Wittgenstein, Preface to *Tractatus*   667
    Logico-Philosophicus
    Language as picture   668

(*Tractatus Logico-Philosophicus*)
Language as language-games   667
(*Philosophical Investigations*)

II. METAPHYSICS

Thales, Testimonies   11
Pythagoras, Fragments and testimonies   12
Empedocles, Fragments   21
Anaxagoras, Fragments   22
Plato, Doctrine of forms (creation myth)   60
    (*Timaeus*)
St. Augustine, The mystery of time   138
    (*Confessions*)
St. Thomas Aquinas, On the soul   175
    (*Summa theologiae*)
Spinoza, Definitions and axioms   275
    (*Ethics*)
    Seven propositions on substance   276
    (*Ethics*)
Leibniz, *The Monadology*   295
    Evil as privation   303
    (*Theodicy*)
    The analogy of the boat   304
    (*Theodicy*)
Hume, The cause and effect relationship   417
    (*An Enquiry concerning Human*
    Understanding)
Kant, Transcendental illusion   455
    (*Critique of Pure Reason*)
    The paralogism of rational psychology   458
    (*Critique of Pure Reason*)
    The three regulative ideas of pure reason   463
    (*Critique of Pure Reason*)
Hegel, The introduction to *Phenomenology of Spirit*   483
    Time and the self-realization of Spirit   492
    (*Phenomenology of Spirit*)
Mill, Universal causation   507
    (*A System of Logic*)
Bergson, Creative evolution, duration, continuity of   603
    life, divergent tendencies
    (*Creative Evolution*)
James, The problem of substance   619
    (*What Is Pragmatism*)

III. RELIGION

Pythagoras, Testimonies   12
Aristotle, The prime mover: one and eternal   89
    (*Physics*)
    Thought, comtemplation and the life of God   94
    (*Metaphysics*)
St. Augustine, Two commandments of love   128
    (*Commentary on St. John's Gospel*)
    The mystical experience   129
    (*Commentary on Psalm 41*)
    The problem of evil: 1   131
    (*Confessions*)
    The problem of evil: 2   136
    (*Enchiridion*)
St. Anselm, Faith seeking understanding   155
    (*Proslogion*)
    The "ontological" argument   156
    (*Proslogion*)
St. Thomas Aquinas, On the existence of God   167
    (*Summa theologiae*)
    The problem of evil   171
    (*Summa theologiae*)
Duns Scotus, God as creator and conserver   205
    (*God and Creatures*)
Nicholas of Cusa, The maximum and the minimum   222
    are the same; how in the infinite, opposites are
    one; everything is in everything
    (*On Learned Ignorance*)
Descartes, *Meditations on First Philosophy*   251
Spinoza, A summary statement concerning God   277
    (*Ethics*)
Leibniz, No better world possible   305
    (*Theodicy*)
Berkeley, Matter and spirit, immaterialism, the   404
    existence of God
    (*Three Dialogues between Hylas and
    Philonous*)
Hume, *Dialogues concerning Natural Religion*   430
Hegel, The Absolute as process of self-becoming   479
    (*Phenomenology of Spirit*)
Nietzsche, Anti-Christ and revaluation   575
    (*The Anti-Christ*)
James, The problem of religion   620
    (*What Is Pragmatism?*)

IV. THE HUMAN BEING

Democritus, Fragments 23

Aristotle, Happiness and man's good 97
    (*Nicomachean Ethics*)

St. Thomas Aquinas, The unity of man 182
    (*Summa theologiae*)
    On happiness 187
    (*Summa contra Gentiles*)

Duns Scotus, The indemonstrability of 213
    immortality
    (*Oxford Commentary*)

Descartes, *Meditations of First Philosophy* 251

Mill, On the probable futurity of the laboring 519
    classes
    (*Principles of Political Economy*)

Kierkegaard, The search for personal meaning 544
    (*Journals*)

Nietzsche, The death of God and the ascendancy 569
    of the Overman
    (*Thus Spoke Zarathrustra*)
    Fearlessness 572
    (*The Gay Science*)

Marx, A chapter in the exploitation of the 586
    working man
    (*Kapital*)
    On the alienation of man 592
    (*Economic and Philosophical Manuscripts*)

Bergson, Philosophy and the life of the spirit 603
    (*Creative Evolution*)
    Open morality and dynamic religion 611
    (*The Two Sources of Morality and Religion*)

Russell, Man's place in the universe 651
    (*The Problems of Philosophy*)

Sartre, The meaning of existentialism 689
    (*Existentialism and Humanism*)
    Anguish 694
    (*Being and Nothingness*)
    Transcendence: value and suffering; freedom 694
    (*Being and Nothingness*)
    Towards a "critique of dialectical reason" 705
    (*Critique of Dialectical Reason*)

V. ETHICS, MORALITY AND POLITICAL PHILOSOPHY

Heraclitus, Fragments and testimonies   14
Plato, The trial of Socrates   28
  (*Apology*)
  The death of Socrates   49
  (*Phaedo*)
  Virtue and the highest good   68
  (*Laws*)
  The Philosopher-King   70
  (*Epistle VII*)
Aristotle, Moral virtue and the mean   100
  (*Nicomachean Ethics*)
  The end of human nature: happiness   105
  (*Nicomachean Ethics*)
  Wisdom and virtue as the basis of society   111
  (*Politics*)
  The civil society   112
  (*Politics*)
St. Thomas Aquinas, On the essence of law   191
  (*Summa theologiae*)
  On the various kinds of law   196
  (*Summa theologiae*)
Duns Scotus, Moral goodness and badness   208
  (*God and Creatures*)
Hobbes, The natural state of man, contract,   315
  law, liberty and commonwealth
  (*Leviathan*)
Locke, State of nature, civil society and   379
  government
  (*The Second Treatise of Civil Government*)
Kant, The categorical imperative   467
  (*Foundations of the Metaphysics of Morals*)
  Postulates of pure practical reason   471
  (*Critique of Practical Reason*)
Mill, What utilitarianism is   502
  (*Utilitarianism*)
  Of liberty and necessity   512
  (*A System of Logic*)
  Liberty   526
  (*On Liberty*)
Kierkegaard, Abraham and "breaking   552
  through the universal"
  (*Fear and Trembling*)

The Ancient Period

The Spirit of Greek Philosophy: Philosophy as Wonder

It is impossible to think of philosophy without considering the history, heritage, ancestry, or culture in which it germinated. We cannot, for example, think of any Renaissance figure without recalling the vibrant intellectual environment that gave him birth, or of today's space probes without recalling the technological heritage that makes them possible. This does not mean that there was always a hand-in-glove relationship between philosophy and the prevailing culture, because often it was the prevailing culture that philosophers opposed; nevertheless philosophers, like the rest of us, are children of their time.

The Greek world, where philosophy was born, included not only present-day Greece but extended east to the shores of Asia Minor (present-day Turkey) and the many islands in the Aegean, and west to Sicily and southern Italy; though not a political entity, it was united by race, language, custom, religious feeling, and tradition. In this Greek world, long before the first recognized philosopher appeared, a culture already existed: civic life existed in city-states like Athens, Sparta, Thebes, and Corinth; the rich literature of Homer and Hesiod prevailed, filled with myths, heroes, and legends; and religion suffused the Greeks' daily life, though it was fractioned into countless beliefs and rites proper to the gods and goddesses who lorded it over all. Subsequently, Greek culture was enriched with the poetry of Solon (c. 640–558 B.C.), as well as by the wise measures he took as a respected statesman. Some one hundred to two hundred years later, in its flowering as the dominant city-state, Athens saw the rise of its three great tragedians, Aeschylus, Sophocles, and Euripides, and two of its great historians, Herodotus and Thucydides. The genius of Greece created such a climate of poetry, drama, religion, music, science, polity, and even sport that the total Greek experience was unparalleled in the history of the West. Part of this experience was philosophy itself as it unfolded from its beginnings with Thales, through the golden age of Socrates, Plato, and Aristotle in the fifth and fourth centuries B.C. to the Stoics and Epicureans in the late fourth and early third centuries B.C.

If we ask what kinds of things the early philosophers thought about, we find the classic response in the opening pages of Aristotle's *Metaphysics:* "For it is owing to their wonder that men both now and at first began to philosophize; they wondered originally at the obvious difficulties, then advanced little by little and stated difficulties about greater matters, e.g. about the phenomena of the moon and those of the sun and of the stars, and about the genesis of the universe." Indeed, the first philosophers of Greece were awed by the world of nature, a world offering an endless variety of activity, of elements, of shapes, of movement, of bodily things both living and nonliving. Such a world inspired wonder — wonder both in the sense of admiration and in the sense of responding to an invitation to inquire why things are the way they are. This same spirit inspired the later philosophers too as they broadened the horizons of their predecessors, culminating in the achievements of Plato and Aristotle, who between them inaugurated two distinct, but complementary, traditions in the history of philosophy.

In a sense, Greek philosophy never died, for it continued to nourish generation after generation of thinkers. Of course, not every aspect of Greek philosophy produced its counterpart in subsequent thought, but allowing for the vagaries of history, its influence has been pervasive. For many Christian philosopher-theologians in the age that was its direct inheritor, Greek philosophy was the vehicle of reason (and, for some, providentially appointed) for conveying revealed truth, whether in claiming the existence of the very God who revealed, or in establishing the framework for temporal man's imaging the eternal, or in providing rational support for the immortality of the soul. Further indebtedness to Greek philosophy is seen in every subsequent inquiry, down to our own day, into the meaning of life, ethics, psychology, knowledge, death, destiny, cosmos, law, government, society, and happiness; indeed, two great Greek themes, the one and the many (unity in reality) and being and becoming (permanence in change), are so basic that they emerge in different guises throughout philosophy and can be used as guidelines in writing its history. Specific instances of influence aside, the priceless bequest of Greek philosophy to its heirs is its spirit of wonder in the face of reality. All else is derived from this spirit. To study this period is both a privilege and a necessity; it is its own reward.

1

The Predecessors of Socrates

Introduction

The philosophers preceding Socrates lived in the sixth and early fifth centuries B.C. and are collectively called the *pre-Socratics*. Their original writings suffered the fate of many works of antiquity and do not exist today, so that we do not have direct access to their thought. Nevertheless, through quotations and references to their work by later authors who either did have access to them or were in a position to pass on received information, some of their ideas have come down to us. By painstaking research, scholars have been able to reconstruct something of their background and to develop a picture of the main lines of their thought.

Philosophy began in that part of the Greek world known as Ionia, roughly corresponding to the western part of present-day Turkey and some nearby islands. Why philosophy originated in Ionia is a matter of conjecture, but surely some of the creative impulse that produced the Greek epics there was still to be found; and several of its principal cities, having developed as sea and land termini joining East and West, tended to become intellectual centers as well. Such a center was Miletus, which counted among its citizens Thales, Anaximander, and Anaximenes, the first three Greek philosophers who are presumed to have had a successive teacher–student relationship. Because of the region, they are referred to as *Ionians*; because of their citizenship, they are referred to as *Milesians*; and because of their primary concern with the natural world, or cosmos, they are often referred to as *cosmologists*.

The philosopher generally recognized as the first in Western philosophy was *Thales*, who was born in the last quarter of the seventh century and who flourished in Miletus in the early part of the sixth century. Though he apparently wrote nothing, he was acknowledged as a man of great wisdom, displaying an enormous range of knowledge as an astronomer, a mathematician, and a statesman. He was accorded the honor of being listed among the Seven Sages of Greece. In converting his theoretical knowledge into practice, he seemed to have little trouble: he gave ship pilots the means of charting their course by the stars; he made recommendations for the establishment of effective governing bodies; and once, when the soldiers of King Croesus could not cross a river running in front of them, he is said to have diverted the flow so that the river ran behind them. His practical sense took an economic turn too when, on one occasion, having predicted a large olive crop, he cornered the market on olive presses so that the growers had to rent them from him — a story to which Aristotle wryly adds that Thales demonstrated how easy it was for philosophers to become rich if they so wanted. But not even his renown, Plato writes, prevented a servant girl from laughing at him when he "was looking up to study the stars and tumbled down a well. She scoffed at him for being so eager to know what was happening in the sky that he could not see what lay at his feet."

From his observation of the all-pervading presence of water in the growth and nourishment of living things, and from his belief that the earth rests on water, Thales concluded that all things derive in some way from water. In terms of the one and the many previously mentioned, the many things of the natural world are held together as one, as a universe, because water is their underlying principle and the source of their unity. We must not be put off by the seeming naiveté of Thales; he clearly saw that, where there are many things, no unity is possible unless there is a basis for it, unless the many share it. In his view of water as the primal element, Thales discovered what, for him, was the substrate of unity in the cosmos and the basic reason why the cosmos was able to render itself shareable in the manifold of physical things.

He was making sure that reality as a whole did not rob the individual of its individuality. In fact, the relationship between the one and the many is reciprocal, and it is an enduring insight that the very uniqueness of the individual flows from its relationship to reality as a whole. Philosophers have to maintain a delicate balance: not to emphasize the one (reality as a whole) at the expense of the many (as individuals), or the many at the expense of the one. The reciprocal relationship is what supports both the individual and the whole.

Adding to this notion of cosmic unity the belief that all things are "full of gods," Thales was expressing the vitality, the life of the cosmos, which, as god filled, commands our wonder all the more and our reverence as well.

Faithful to the central thought of Thales, the other Milesians sought elsewhere for the unifying factor of the cosmos. *Anaximander*, relying perhaps on the notion that things are generated only by their opposites, believed that the common origin of all things was completely unlike that which was generated; if that which was generated was finite and bounded and many, then that which generated it was Infinite and Boundless and One. For *Anaximenes* the unifying substrate was air, from which, by its properties of condensation and rarefaction, the many were formed.

In his enthusiasm for geometry, Thales proved to be a herald of the love affair the Greeks had with mathematics. Wherever there is an intellectual ferment in the natural sciences, there is bound to be one in mathematics as well. This was true of Greece, where all the cultural ingredients were present for science and mathematics to grow. We can ask what there is about mathematics which makes for the incredible fascination it has over the human mind. Perhaps it is because mathematics extends the mind and leads it to unassailable conclusions; or perhaps it is because it produces order, organizing things under the umbrella of unity, thereby doing precisely what the mind naturally yearns to do. At any rate, mathematics is the favorite language of the sciences in its capacity to express their findings, to unify them, and to open up new avenues of discovery.

There was every reason then for *Pythagoras*, the sixth-century mathematician-philosopher who spent his early years on the island of Samos and his later years at Croton in southern Italy, in his inquiry into unity, to think that real things and their relationships are somehow expressible by number, if indeed they are not actual numbers themselves. There must be a profound analogy between the unity of numbers and the unity of the universe. Though there are many numbers, they are still one, for no number is conceivable without 1; further, every number other than 1 is generated by 1. So, without surrendering the difference between any number and all other numbers, or differences like odd and even, all numbers must be seen as belonging to the unity of their common origin in 1. And if many numbers are the expression of a basic harmonious unity, there is no reason why the many things of the universe cannot be expressed in the same way. That at least seemed to be Pythagoras's hope, and he received some encouragement from his interest in music when he discovered that the interval between notes on the musical scale can be expressed numerically, depending on the length of the string required to produce them; if physical length and tone are so easily expressed by number, perhaps the rest of the universe is too.

For an ardent thinker like Pythagoras, mathematics became the touchstone for a deeper vision of cosmic unity; for if the number 1 is found in the composition of every other number, and if all numbers share the unity of 1, then can one not envision that at the head of all reality stands the One, Unity, and that all things share it? It is the culmination of man's desire to rest in a transcendent peace. The possibility of sharing the One was, for Pythagoras, the mystical aspect of mathematics. There is a level of reality that man is drawn to, that he does not truly comprehend, yet is convinced that reaching it is his calling as a human being. This idea may not be found explicitly in the works of Pythagoras, but it is the only way in which our knowledge of his teaching and his life fits together. An anecdote informs us that Pythagoras believed in the transmigration of souls; that is, the soul does not cease to exist when the body dies but is reembodied in another: "And once, they saw him passing by when a puppy was being beaten, he pitied it, and spoke as follows: 'Stop! Cease your beating, because this is really the soul of a man who was my friend: I recognized it as I heard it cry aloud.' Another fragment from a later Pythagorean, in referring to the doctrines of Pythagoras, states, "The ancient theologians and seers also bear witness that because of certain punishments the soul is yoked to the body and buried in it as in a tomb." Release from the body and from the cycle of reincarnation indicates Pythagoras's belief in the immortality of the soul and the care that must be taken to ween oneself gradually from the body by a lifelong process of purification. To this end, he established a community of men and women. It was a secret society and apparently had a full program of study, dietary rules, prohibitions, and permissions. It was established mainly for the pursuit of holiness, which in turn meant the pursuit of purification whereby the soul was released from the body. Final perfection, then, comes when the soul is freed from the body and united, or reunited, with the One.

While Thales and Pythagoras were struggling with the notion of unity in their own way, *Heraclitus* was trying to do the same thing in yet another way. Again, about the philosopher himself very little is known for sure, but he can be situated at the turn of the sixth and fifth centuries at Ephesus, a seaport town just north of Miletus; he was probably a member of one of its more influential families. Whether he ever wrote a book is not known, but what has come down to us is a fairly generous collection of short, pithy statements, rather like aphorisms or epigrams, whose language is obscure but whose content is thought-provoking. Perhaps Heraclitus wanted to imitate the oracle at Delphi: "The lord whose oracle is at Delphi neither speaks nor conceals, but indicates." Heraclitus too never "said" anything; he only "indicated." Even among the ancients he was referred to as the "obscure one."

Among all the phenomena, or manifestations, of reality, the one that struck Heraclitus most forcefully was that of change. Nothing remains permanent or static; everything changes in a sea of change. In the same moment that we notice that a thing is, we also notice that it has become something else. The leaves change, animals change, humans change, the heavens change, and even if a thing appears unchanging, we suddenly realize that as everything else about it changes, so does the thing itself because its relationships change. As another philosopher would say many centuries later, there is "more" in becoming than in being. The image Heraclitus uses is "All things flow." That is, all things exist as though they are part of a stream, continually flowing, running, changing, always different; so much so that, as Plato records, Heraclitus maintained that it was "impossible to step into the same river twice."

Yet universal change does not mean disorder or chance togetherness like that of a heap of stones. No, the many changing things, or the "manifold" of change, despite their seeming randomness, are disposed in orderly fashion. The mind has to undergo a reengagement with reality; we are dealing with reality for sure, but a reality on the move, a literal "uni-verse" in which all things turn around as one. So, for Heraclitus, two main questions arise: what is the source of this unified motion, and what is the agency whereby movement is provided?

In answer to the first question Heraclitus says, "Listening not to me but to the Logos it is wise to agree that all things are one." This fragment, together with others, suggests that movement is not self-originated, but originates on a higher level, and that the originator also presides over this movement and ensures its unity. Movement means not only natural or physical activity, but human activity as well. In another fragment Heraclitus states that "It is necessary to follow the common; but although the Logos is common the many live as though they had a private understanding." There is a distinct moral dimension in Heraclitus's work, centering on the unity that human actions should have with the Logos. Human actions are as manifold as any others; they are in flux, and they change in a never-ending stream of action; thus there is a great risk of dispersion, of meaninglessness, unless they too share a higher focus of unity. To see this unity is a large part of the search for wisdom expressed by Heraclitus in the words "I sought out myself," a motif to become traditional in Greek philosophy.

The term *logos* has an extremely revealing and valuable history. Its basic meaning in Greek is word or discourse, but it takes on, according to the historical context, a host of other meanings as well such as law, reason, intelligence, and wisdom. As Greek philosophy, at a much later date, interacted with Hebrew and Christian thought, logos came to mean person inasmuch as the spoken word projects the person speaking. In the New Testament, John refers to Christ personified as the Word spoken by God. Obviously we cannot say precisely what Heraclitus means, but a good guess is that he is using a play on words: when you hear *my* logos (word, discourse, message), I trust you hear *the* Logos (orderer, law, reason).

In answer to the second question, the Greeks came to recognize four elements as basic: earth, air, fire and water, each a primitive contributor to the stuff of the world. But fire, life-giving in its warmth and long revered for its sacred character, took on a special power in the form of lightning as it accompanies the thunderbolt: it "steers the universe." Couple this saying with "The mixed drink separates if it is not stirred" and the image is that of the universe turning as it is constantly being struck by lightning, thus achieving unity in movement or unity in becoming. Whether fire, for Heraclitus, is somehow endowed with intelligence is hard to say, but that it effects the work of intelligence in producing unity is clear.

Heraclitus sums up his prophetic pronouncements by rebuking those who are indifferent to the transcendent vision, who fail to respond to the call of the highest wisdom. "Of the Logos, which is as I describe it, men always prove to be uncomprehending, both before they have heard it and when once they have heard it. For although all things happen according to this Logos men are like people of no experience, even when they experience such words and deeds as I explain, when I distinguish each thing according to its constitution and declare how it is; but the rest of men fail to notice what they do after they wake up just as they forget what they do when asleep."

If being and becoming are the two sides of reality's coin, and if Heraclitus chose becoming as the more promising side, it was not long before another philosopher, *Parmenides*, chose the other; so strongly did he come down on the side of being that he refused to admit that change takes place at all. Parmenides, a contemporary of Heraclitus, flourished in the first decade of the fifth century. He lived in Elea, a city on the southwestern coast of Italy, was active in political life, and in his early days was probably a Pythagorean. He made at least one trip to Athens, where he and his disciple Zeno met a budding young philosopher by the name of Socrates.

As a literary style well suited for expressing wonder, poetry can hardly be surpassed; Parmenides uses it to usher his listeners into the mystery of being. In a poem he tells of a vision in which he was swept upward in a carriage to the domain of light, where the "goddess of light" was to unfold for him the way of Truth as compared with the way of opinion. The way of opinion is the way human beings normally look at reality, but it is deceptive. Men are accustomed to see things in opposition to each other, such as light–dark or dense–rare, and then they proceed to put not-being opposite being, as though not-being were a real thing. The goddess enlightens Parmenides with the Truth, that *only* being is and it is impossible for it not to be: "Being has no coming-into-being and no destruction, for it is whole ... without motion, and without end. And it never Was, nor Will Be, because it Is now, a Whole all together, One, continuous; for what creation of it will you look for? How, whence could it have sprung? Nor shall I allow you to speak or think of it as springing from Not-Being; for it is neither expressible nor thinkable that What-Is-Not Is ... Thus it must Be absolutely, or not at all."

We can appreciate the difficulty Parmenides had. When we affirm *being* of a thing, there is no problem: it *is*, it has existence, it has being. But the moment we say a thing *changes* —a piece of wood burns, an acorn grows, a bird flies — we are saying that it *becomes* what it *is not.* "Is" turns into "is not," "being" into "not-being." In this analysis, not-being is equivalent to being, and for Parmenides a contradiction so blatant that the only remaining course was to deny that change ever really occurs. So the change-saturated world about us only *seems* to be; it is not real, and the statements we make based on it only *seem* to be true. What is based on seeming cannot be truth, only opinion.

Followers of Parmenides tried to draw out further implications of their master's teaching by means of examples calculated to demonstrate the absurdity of change. In a series of paradoxes for which he is famous, Zeno of Elea hoped to show that the idea of motion is self-contradictory. One such paradox concerns the runner trying to run the length of a stadium. He can never really get to the other end, because, before he reaches it, he must go half way first, and then halfway again, and so on *ad infinitum.* In another paradox, Achilles will never catch up with the tortoise because, by the time he gets to the point where the tortoise is, it has moved on to another point, and so on *ad infinitum.*

What Parmenides is saying is that being designates the real, and if we want the truth we have to rely on being that is unchanging, permanent. Heraclitus, on the other hand, is saying that becoming designates the real, and if we want the truth we have to rely on a thing's change or activity to reveal it to us. It is not as though these two philosophers have nothing in common, for both, one holding to being and the other to becoming, insist on the unity of the cosmos. But in their approach to reality they centralize the companion problems of being and becoming, and the one and the many, as the issues that emerge at all times whenever thinkers attempt to understand the real world.

Reaction to these problems was not long in coming; though the next generation of philosophers saw the profound truth in the positions of both Parmenides and Heraclitus, they also saw that there was something unforgiving in the extreme way in which they were presented. They realized that they had to say yes to the assertion that "what is, is" and yes to the assertion that "all things flow"; but they also realized that they had to say no to any assertion that denied the obviousness of change or permanence. The next generation, in the second half of the fifth century, included *Empedocles* of Acragas in Sicily, *Anaxagoras* of Clazomenae (just north of Miletus), *Leucippus* of Miletus, and a little later, *Democritus* of Abdera (in Thrace on the northern shore of the Aegean). What these four had in common was their search for a way to affirm the being of the physical cosmos (it always was, is, and will be the same) and not to betray their experience of change in the cosmos. So they all agreed on the idea of a cosmos composed of small particles, ultimate in nature, constantly in motion to allow for changing configurations without undergoing change themselves, and eternally existing so that they never come to be, but always are.

Empedocles, whose world view was widely influential and who seems to have had a respectable grasp of medicine, was the first philosopher to propound the classical four elements of earth, air, fire and water, which he referred to as the "roots of all"; the ultimate particles were each composed of these elements. But in their midst there were two great forces at work, Love and Strife; when Love prevailed there was harmony because the mixture of elements was properly balanced, but when Strife prevailed there was disharmony because the mixture was unbalanced. Empedocles apparently held that Love and Strife were physical forces, though their names suggest more.

Anaxagoras differed from Empedocles in two significant ways. First, the ultimate particles did not consist of earth, air, fire, and water, but of an indefinite variety; and since "in everything there is a portion of everything," the objects configured in the world differ because one kind of particle dominates all others. Second, the force whereby the particles moved had to be outside the particles and independent of them, and therefore completely unlike them. This force is Mind, or Nous, described in the famous fragment no. 12 as infinite, self-ruling, the finest, the purest, omniscient. Even if we cannot be sure that Anaxagoras took Mind to be spiritual and transcendent, by introducing it to account for motion as an unmoved mover, he already marks a revolutionary departure from the past.

But it fell to Leucippus and Democritus to follow the cosmology of ultimate particles to its extreme implications and, since it is often impossible to unravel the individual contributions of each, both are credited as the founders of philosophical *atomism* in its classical dress. Like Empedocles and Anaxagoras, they remained true to the Eleatic notion of unchanging being and called for unchanging ultimate particles; these particles, they maintained, were extended in space, unlimited in number, and, though perhaps mathematically divisible, were physically indivisible, for this reason they were called *atoms*, from *atomon*, that which cannot be cut or divided. Unlike Empedocles and

Anaxagoras, they arrived at a completely mechanistic explanation of motion and rejected any agency even vaguely suggestive of the noncorporeal, like Love and Strife, or Mind, invoked to cause motion in particles; there was no need to "begin" motion, it was always there. Democritus seems to have held that all movements and configurations of atoms are brought about not by chance but by a necessity natural to the atoms themselves. Apart from his cosmological views, Democritus believed that the conduct of life should be based on happiness, which, in turn, meant "well-being" or "cheerfulness," that is, the capacity to make balanced judgments with regard to choosing goods of the soul over goods of the body: "He who chooses the advantages of the soul chooses things more divine, but he who chooses those of the body, chooses things human."

We have seen in the pre-Socratic philosophers the first effort in the West to explore the real rationally, based on what was given by way of wonder through experience. It was perfectly natural that the first questions they pondered were those raised by the cosmos, the physical world, and that in the beginning little distinction was made between natural science and philosophy; but philosophy soon began to sort itself out by facing such problems as unity in plurality, and being and becoming. These were accompanied by corollary questions about the stuff of the universe, particles, atoms, basic elements, source of motion, and so on, but also by parallel questions such as the meaning of knowledge, wisdom, human behavior, and human destiny. In all, a profound and fertile start for the subsequent growth of philosophy.

Readings

Selected Fragments from the Pre-Socratics

(Note: Since no writing of the Pre-Socratics are extant, what we know of their teaching has come from references made to them by later writers. If the references are seen as direct quotations, they are called *fragments*; otherwise, they are called *testimonies* or simply *statements* about the philosopher in question. The fragments have been gathered together in a work accepted as the standard reference by Diels, whose numbering is followed, as shown. Sources in English as indicated.)

Thales
Testimonies

1. Thales is traditionally the first to have revealed the investigation of nature to the Greeks; he had many predecessors, as also Theophrastus thinks, but so far surpassed them as to blot out all who came be-

fore him. He is said to have left nothing in the form of writings except the so-called *Nautical star-guide*.

2. Yet they do not all agree as to the number and the nature of these principles. Thales, the founder of this type of philosophy, says the principle is water (for which reason he declared that the earth rests on water), getting the notion perhaps from seeing that the nutriment of all things is moist, and that heat itself is generated from the moist and kept alive by it (and that from which they come to be is a principle of all things). He got his notion from this fact, and from the fact that the seeds of all things have a moist nature, and that water is the origin of the nature of moist things.

3. For moist natural substances, since it is easily formed into each different thing, is accustomed to undergo very various changes: that part of it which is exhaled is made into air, and the finest part is kindled from air into aither, while when water is compacted and changes into slime it becomes earth. Therefore Thales declared that water, of the four elements, was the most active, as it were, as a cause.

4. Certain thinkers say that soul is intermingled in the whole universe, and it is perhaps for that reason Thales came to the opinion that all things are full of gods.

5. Some think he (Thales) was the first to study the heavenly bodies and to foretell eclipses of the sun and solstices, as Eudemus says in his history of astronomy; for which reason both Xenophanes and Herodotus express admiration; and both Heraclitus and Democritus bear witness for him.

6. Hieronymus says that he (Thales) actually measured the pyramids by their shadow, having observed the time when our own shadow is equal to our height.

7. Eudemus in the *History of geometry* refers this theorem to Thales; for the method by which they say demonstrated the distance of ships out at sea must, he says, have entailed the use of this theorem.

Pythagoras
Testimonies

1. Empedocles too bears witness to this, writing of him: 'And there was among them a man of rare knowledge, most skilled in all manner of wise works, a man who had won the utmost wealth of wisdom; for whensoever he strained with all his mind, he easily saw everything of all the things that are, in ten, yes, twenty lifetimes of men'.

2. Pythagoras wrote nothing ...

3. None the less the following became universally known; first, that he maintains that the soul is immortal; next, that it changes into other kinds of living things; also that events recur in certain cycles, and that nothing is ever absolutely new; and finally, that all living things should

be regarded as akin. Pythagoras seems to have been the first to bring these beliefs into Greece.

4. If one were to believe the Pythagoreans, with the result that the same individual things will recur, then I shall be talking to you again sitting as you are now, with this printer in my hand, and everything else will be just as it is now, and it is reasonable to suppose that the time then is the same as now.

5. Let the rules to be pondered be these: When you are going out to a temple, worship first, and on your way neither say nor do anything else connected with your daily life. . . . Sacrifice and worship without shoes on. . . . Follow the gods and restrain your tongue above all else. . . . Speak not of Pythagorean matters without light. . . . Disbelieve nothing strange about the gods or about religious beliefs. . . Be not possessed by irrepressible mirth. . . . Abstain from beans. . . . Abstain from living things.

6. So Pythagoras turned geometrical philosophy into a form of liberal education by seeking its first principles in a higher realm of reality. . . .

7. Life, he said, is like a festival; just as some come to the festival to compete, some to ply their trade, but the best people come as spectators, so in life the slavish men go hunting for fame or gain, the philosophers for the truth.

8. The Pythagoreans, according to Aristoxenus, practised the purification of the body by medicine, that of the soul by music.

9. Ten is the very nature of number. . . . And again, Pythagoras maintains, the power of the number ten lies in the number four, the tetrad. This is the reason: if one starts at the unit and adds the successive numbers up to four, one will make up the number ten. . . . If, that is, one takes the unit, adds two, then three and then four, one will make up the number ten. . . . And so the Pythagoreans used to invoke the tetrad as their most binding oath: 'Nay, by him that gave to our generation the tetractys, which contains the fount and root of eternal nature.

10. Contemporaneously with these philosophers and before them, the so-called Pythagoreans, who were the first to take up mathematics, not only advanced this study, but also having been brought up in it they thought its principles were the principles of all things. Since of these principles numbers are by nature the first, and in numbers they seemed to see many resemblances to the things that exist and come into being—more than in fire and earth and water (such and such a modification of numbers being justice, another being soul and reason, another being opportunity—and similarly almost all other things being numerically expressible); since, again, they saw that the modifications and the ratios of the musical scales were expressible in numbers;—

since, then, all other things seemed in their whole nature to be modelled on numbers, and numbers seemed to be the first things in the whole of nature, they supposed the elements of numbers to be the elements of all things, and the whole heaven to be a musical scale and a number. And all the properties of numbers and scales which they could show to agree with the attributes and parts and the whole arrangement of the heavens, they collected and fitted into their scheme; and if there was a gap anywhere, they readily made additions so as to make their whole theory coherent. E.g. as the number 10 is thought to be perfect and to comprise the whole nature of numbers, they say that the bodies which move through the heavens are ten, but as the visible bodies are only nine, to meet this they invent a tenth—the 'counter-earth'. We have discussed these matters more exactly elsewhere.

Heraclitus
Fragments

1. Of the Logos which is as I describe it men always prove to be uncomprehending, both before they have heard it and when once they have heard it. For although all things happen according to this Logos men are like people of no experience, even when they experience such words and deeds as I explain, when I distinguish each thing according to its constitution and declare how it is; but the rest of men fail to notice what they do after they wake up just as they forget what they do when asleep.

2. Therefore it is necessary to follow the common; but although the Logos is common the many live as though they had a private understanding.

8. That which is in opposition is in concert, and from things that differ comes the most beautiful harmony.

12. Upon those that step into the same rivers different and different waters flow. ... It scatters and ... gathers ... it comes together and flows away ... approaches and departs.

18. If one does not expect the unexpected one will not find it out, since it is not to be searched out, and difficult to compass.

19. Men who do not know how to listen or how to speak.

26. A man in the night kindles a light for himself when his vision is extinguished; living, he is in contact with the dead, when asleep, and with the sleeper, when awake.

27. There await men after they are dead things which they do not expect or imagine.

30. This ordered universe (cosmos), which is the same for all, was not created by any one of the gods or of mankind, but it was ever and is and shall be ever-living Fire, kindled in measure and quenched in measure.

36. For souls it is death to become water, for water it is death to become earth; from earth water comes-to-be, and from water, soul.

40. Much learning does not teach one to have intelligence. . . .

41. That which is wise is one; to understand the purpose which steers all things through all things.

47. Let us not conjecture at random about the greatest things.

49a. In the same river, we both step and do not step, we are and we are not.

50. Listening not to me but to the Logos it is wise to agree that all things are one.

51. They do not understand how that which differs with itself is in agreement: harmony consists of opposing tension, like that of the bow and the lyre.

60. The way up and the way down is one and the same.

64. The thunder-bolt (i.e. Fire) steers the universe.

67. God is day night, winter summer, war peace, satiety hunger (all the opposites, this is the meaning); he undergoes alteration in the way that fire, when it is mixed with spices, is named according to the scent of each of them.

73. We must not act and speak like men asleep.

90. There is an exchange: all things for Fire and Fire for all things, like goods for gold and gold for goods.

91. It is not possible to step twice into the same river.

93. The lord whose oracle is that at Delphi neither speaks nor conceals, but indicates.

101. I searched into myself.

102. To God, all things are beautiful, good and just; but men have assumed some things to be unjust, others just.

112. Moderation is the greatest virtue, and wisdom is to speak the truth and to act according to nature, paying heed (thereto).

116. All men have the capacity of knowing themselves and acting with moderation.

123. Nature likes to hide.

125. The 'mixed drink' (i.e. mixture of wine, grated cheese and barley-meal) also separates if it is not stirred.

Testimonies

1. According to Heraclitus we become intelligent by drawing in this divine reason (logos) through breathing, and forgetful when asleep, but we regain our senses when we wake up again. For in sleep, when the channels of perception are shut, our mind is sundered from its kinship with the surrounding, and breathing is the only point of attachment to be preserved, like a kind of root; being sundered, our mind casts off its former power of memory. But in the waking state it again peeps out

through the channels of perception as though through a kind of window, and meeting with the surrounding it puts on its power of reason. . . .

(From *The Presocratic Philosophers*, by G.S. Kirk and J.E. Raven. New York: Cambridge University Press, 1971. Copyrighted and reprinted by permission of Cambridge University Press.)

2. Coming to his particular tenets, we may state them as follows: fire is the element, all things are exchange for fire and come into being by rarefaction and condensation; but of this he gives no clear explanation. All things come into being by conflict of opposites, and the sum of things flows like a stream. Further, all that is is limited and forms one world. And it is alternately born from fire and again resolved into fire in fixed cycles to all eternity, and this is determined by destiny. Of the opposites that which tends to birth or creation is called war and strife, and that which tends to destruction by fire is called concord and peace.

Change he called a pathway up and down, and this determines the birth of the world. For fire by contracting turns into moisture, and this condensing turns into water; water again when congealed turns into earth. This process he calls the downward path. Then again earth is liquefied, and thus gives rise to water, and from water the rest of the series is derived. He reduces nearly everything to exhalation from the sea. This process is the upward path.

Exhalations arise from earth as well as from sea; those from sea are bright and pure, those from earth dark. Fire is fed by the bright exhalations, the moist element by the others.

He does not make clear the nature of the surrounding element. He says, however, that there are in it bowls with their concavities turned toward us, in which the bright exhalations collect and produce flames. These are the heavenly bodies.

The flame of the sun is the brightest and hottest; and other stars are further from the earth and for that reason give it less light and heat. The moon, which is nearer to the earth, traverses a region which is not pure. The sun, however, moves in a clear and untroubled region, and keeps a proportionate distance from us. That is why it gives us more heat and light. Eclipses of the sun and moon occur when the bowls are turned upwards; the monthly phases of the moon are due to the bowl turning round in its place little by little.

Day and night, months, seasons and years, rains and winds and other similar phenomena are accounted for by the various exhalations. Thus the bright exhalation, set aflame in the hollow orb of the sun, produces day, the opposite exhalation when it has got the mastery causes night; the increase of warmth due to the bright exhalation produces summer, whereas the preponderance of moisture due to the dark exhalation brings about winter. His explanations of other phenomena are in harmony with this.

He gives no account of the nature of the earth, nor even of the bowls. These, then, were his opinions.

(Reprinted by permission of the publishers and the Loeb Classical Library from *Lives of the Eminent Philosophers*, translated by R. D. Hicks, Cambridge, Mass.: Harvard University Press, 1925.)

Parmenides

1. The mares which carry me conveyed me as far as my desire reached, when the goddesses who were driving had set me on the famous highway which bears a man who has knowledge through all the cities. Along this way I was carried; for by this way the exceedingly intelligent mares bore me, drawing the chariot, and the maidens directed the way. The axle in the naves gave forth a pipe-like sound as it glowed (for it was driven round by the two whirling circles (*wheels*) at each end) whenever the maidens, daughters of the Sun, having left the Palace of Night, hastened their driving towards the light, having pushed back their veils from their heads with their hands.

There (*in the Palace of Night*) are the gates of the paths of Night and Day, and they are enclosed with a lintel above and a stone threshold below. The gates themselves are filled with great folding doors; and of these Justice, mighty to punish, has the interchangeable keys. The maidens, skilfully cajoling her with soft words, persuaded her to push back the bolted bar without delay from the gates; and these, flung open, revealed a wide gaping space, having swung their jambs, richly-wrought in bronze, reciprocally in their sockets. This way, then, straight through them went the maidens, driving chariot and mares along the carriage-road.

And the goddess received me kindly, and took my right hand in hers, and thus she spoke and addressed me:

'Young man, companion of immortal charioteers, who comest by the help of the steeds which bring thee to our dwelling: welcome! — since no evil fate has despatched thee on thy journey by this road (for truly it is far from the path trodden by mankind); no, it is divine command and Right. Thou shalt inquire into everything: both the motionless heart of well-rounded Truth, and also the opinions of mortals, in which there is no true reliability. But nevertheless thou shalt learn these things (*opinions*) also — how one should go through all the things-that-seem, without exception, and test them.

2. Come, I will tell you — and you must accept my word when you have heard it — the ways of inquiry which alone are to be thought: the one that IT IS, and it is not possible for IT NOT TO BE, is the way of credibility, for it follows Truth; the other, that IT IS NOT, and that

IT is bound NOT TO BE: this I tell you is a path that cannot be explored; for you could neither recognise that which is NOT, nor express it.

3. For it is the same thing to think and to be.

4. Observe nevertheless how things absent are securely present to the mind; for it will not sever Being from its connection with Being, whether it is scattered everywhere utterly throughout the universe, or whether it is collected together.

5. It is all the same to me from what point I begin, for I shall return again to this same point.

6. One should both say and think that Being Is; for To Be is possible, and Nothingness is not possible. This I command you to consider; for from the latter way of search first of all I debar you. But next I debar you from that way along which wander mortals knowing nothing, two-headed, for perplexity in their bosoms steers their intelligence astray, and they are carried along as deaf as they are blind, amazed, uncritical hordes, by whom To Be and Not To Be are regarded as the same and not the same, and (*for whom*) in everything there is a way of opposing stress.

7,8. For this (*view*) can never predominate, that That Which Is Not exists. You must debar your thought from this way of search, nor let ordinary experience in its variety force you along this way, (*namely, that of allowing*) the eye, sightless as it is, and the ear, full of sound, and the tongue, to rule; but (*you must*) judge by means of the Reason (*Logos*) the much-contested proof which is expounded by me.

There is only one other description of the way remaining, (*namely*), that (*What Is*) Is. To this way there are very many sign-posts: that Being has no coming-into-being and no destruction, for it is whole of limb, without motion, and without end. And it never Was, nor Will Be, because it Is now, a Whole all together, One, continuous; for what creation of it will you look for? How, whence (*could it have*) sprung? Nor shall I allow you to speak or think of it as springing from Not-Being; for it is neither expressible nor thinkable that What-Is-Not Is. Also, what necessity impelled it, if it did spring from Nothing, to be produced later or earlier? Thus it must Be absolutely, or not at all. Nor will the force of credibility ever admit that anything should come into being, beside Being itself, out of Not-Being. So far as that is concerned, Justice has never released (*Being*) in its fetters and set it free either to come into being or to perish, but holds it fast. The decision on these matters depends on the following: IT IS, or IT IS NOT. It is therefore decided — as is inevitable — (*that one must*) ignore the one way as unthinkable and inexpressible (for it is no true way) and take the other as the way of Being and Reality. How could Being perish? How could it come into being? If it came into being, it Is Not; and so too if it is about-to-be at some future time. Thus Coming-into-Being is quenched, and Destruction also into the unseen.

Nor is Being divisible, since it is all alike. Nor is there anything (*here or*) there which could prevent it from holding together, nor any lesser thing, but all is full of Being. Therefore it is altogether continuous; for Being is close to Being.

But it is motionless in the limits of mighty bonds, without beginning, without cease, since Becoming and Destruction have been driven very far away, and true conviction has rejected them. And remaining the same in the same place, it rests by itself and thus remains there fixed; for powerful Necessity holds it in the bonds of a Limit, which constrains it round about, because it is decreed by divine law that Being shall not be without boundary. For it is not lacking; but if it were (*spatially infinite*), it would be lacking everything.

To think is the same as the thought that It Is; for you will not find thinking without Being, in (*regard to*) which there is an expression. For nothing else either is or shall be except Being, since Fate has tied it down to be a whole and motionless; therefore all things that mortals have established, believing in their truth, are just a name: Becoming and Perishing, Being and Not-Being, and Change of position, and alteration of bright colour.

But since there is a (*spatial*) Limit, it is complete on every side, like the mass of a well-rounded sphere, equally balanced from its centre in every direction; for it is not bound to be at all either greater or less in this direction or that; nor is there Not-Being which could check it from reaching to the same point, nor is it possible for Being to be more in this direction, less in that, than Being, because it is an inviolate whole. For, in all directions equal to itself, it reaches its limits uniformly.

At this point I cease my reliable theory (*Logos*) and thought, concerning Truth; from here onwards you must learn the opinions of mortals, listening to the deceptive order of my words.

They have established (*the custom of*) naming two forms, one of which ought not to be (*mentioned*): that is where they have gone astray. They have distinguished them as opposite in form, and have marked them off from another by giving them different signs: on one side the flaming fire in the heavens, mild, very light (*in weight*), the same as itself in every direction, and not the same as the other. This (*other*) also is by itself and opposite: dark Night, a dense and heavy body. This world-order I describe to you with all its phenomena, in order that no intellect of mortal men may outstrip you.

9. But since all things are named Light and Night, and names have been given to each class of things according to the power of one or the other (*Light or Night*), everything is full equally of Light and invisible Night, as both are equal, because to neither of them belongs any share (of the other).

10. You shall know the nature of the heavens, and all the signs in the heavens, and the destructive works of the pure bright torch of the sun, and whence they came into being. And you shall learn of the wandering works of the round-faced moon, and its nature; and you shall know also the surrounding heaven, whence it sprang and how Necessity brought and constrained it to hold the limits of the stars.

11. (I will describe) how earth and sun and moon, and the heavens common to all, and the Milky Way in the heavens, and outermost Olympus, and the hot power of the stars, hastened to come into being.

12. For the narrower rings were filled with unmixed Fire, and those next to them with Night, but between (these) rushes the portion of Flame. And in the centre of these is the goddess who guides everything; for throughout she rules over cruel Birth and Mating, sending the female to mate with the male, and conversely again the male with the female.

13. First of all the gods she devised Love.

14. (*The moon*): Shining by night with a light not her own, wandering round the earth.

15. (*The moon*): Always gazing towards the rays of the sun.

15a. (*Earth*): Rooted in water.

16. For according to the mixture of much-wandering limbs which each man has, so is the mind which is associated with mankind: for it is the same thing which thinks, namely the constitution of the limbs in men, all and individually; for it is excess (of the Light or Night-element) which makes Thought.

17. On the right, boys, on the left, girls ... (*in the womb*).

18. When a woman and a man mix the seeds of Love together, the power (*of the seeds*) which shapes (*the embryo*) in the veins out of different blood can mould well-constituted bodies only if it preserves proportion. For if the powers war (*with each other*) when the seed is mixed, and do not make a unity in the body formed by the mixture, they will terribly harass the growing (*embryo*) through the twofold seed of the (*two*) sexes.

19. Thus, therefore, according to opinion, were these things created, and are now, and shall hereafter from henceforth grow and then come to an end. And from these things men have established a name as a distinguishing mark for each.

Testimonies

1. The same kind of argument holds good against Parmenides also, besides any that may apply specially to his view: the answer to him being that '*this* is not true' and '*that* does not follow'. His assumption that one is used in a single sense only is false, because it is used in several. His conclusion does not follow, because if we take only white things, and if 'white' has a single meaning, none the less what is white

will be many and not one. For what is white will not be one either in the sense that it is continuous or in the sense that it must be defined in only one way. 'Whiteness' will be different from 'what has whiteness'. Nor does this mean that there is anything that can exist separately, over and above what is white. For 'whiteness' and 'that which is white' differ in definition, not in the sense that they are things which can exist apart from each other. But Parmenides had not come in sight of this distinction.

Empedocles
Fragments

8. And I shall tell you another thing: there is no creation of substance in any one of mortal existences, nor any end in execrable death, but only mixing and exchange of what has been mixed; and the name 'substance' (*Phusis, 'nature'*) is applied to them by mankind.

11. Fools! — for they have no long-sighted thoughts, since they imagine that what previously did not exist comes into being, or that a thing dies and is utterly destroyed.

17. I shall tell of a double (*process*): at one time it increased so as to be a single One out of Many; at another time again it grew apart so as to be Many out of One. There is a double creation of mortals and a double decline: the union of all things causes the birth and destruction of the one (*race of mortals*), the other is reared as the elements grow apart, and then flies asunder. And these (*elements*) never cease their continuous exchange, sometimes uniting under the influence of Love, so that all become One, at other times again each moving apart through the hostile force of Hate. Thus in so far as they have the power to grow into One out of Many, and again, when the One grows apart and Many are formed, in this sense they come into being and have no stable life; but in so far as they never cease their continuous exchange, in this sense they remain always unmoved (*unaltered*) as they follow the cyclic process.

But come, listen to my discourse! For be assured, learning will increase your understanding. As I said before, revealing the aims of my discourse, I shall tell you of a double process. At one time it increased so as to be a single One out of Many; at another time it grew apart so as to be Many out of One — Fire and Water and Earth and the boundless height of Air, and also execrable Hate apart from these, of equal weight in all directions, and Love in their midst, their equal in length and breadth. Observe her with your mind, and do not sit with wondering eyes! She it is who is believed to be implanted in mortal limbs also; through her they think friendly thoughts and perform harmonious actions, calling her Joy and Aphrodite. No mortal man has perceived her as she moves in and out among them. But you must listen to the undeceitful progress of my argument.

All these (*Elements*) are equal and of the same age in their creation; but each presides over its own office, and each has its own character, and they prevail in turn in the course of Time. And besides these, nothing else comes into being, nor does anything cease. For if they had been perishing continuously, they would Be no more; and what could increase the Whole? And whence could it have come? In what direction could it perish, since nothing is empty of these things? No, but these things alone exist, and running through one another they become different things at different times, and are ever continuously the same.

Anaxagoras
Fragments

1. (*Opening sentences from his book 'On Natural Science'*): All Things were together, infinite in number and in smallness. For the Small also was infinite. And since all were together, nothing was distinguishable because of its smallness. For Air and Aether dominated all things, both of them being infinite. For these are the most important (*Elements*) in the total mixture, both in number and in size.

4. Conditions being thus, one must believe that there are many things of all sorts in all composite products, and the seeds of all Things, which contain all kinds of shapes and colours and pleasant savours. And men too were fitted together, and all other creatures which have life. And the men possessed both inhabited cities and artificial works just like ourselves, and they had sun and moon and the rest, just as we have, and the earth produced for them many and diverse things, of which they collected the most useful, and now use them for their dwellings. This I say concerning Separation, that it must have taken place not only with us, but elsewhere.

Before these things were separated off, all things were together, nor was any colour distinguishable, for the mixing of all Things prevented this, (*namely*) the mixing of moist and dry and hot and cold and bright and dark, and there was a great quantity of earth in the mixture, and seeds infinite in number, not at all like one another. For none of the other things either is like any other. And as this was so, one must believe that all Things were present in the Whole.

6. And since there are equal (*quantitative*) parts of Great and Small, so too similarly in everything there must be everything. It is not possible (*for them*) to exist apart, but all things contain a portion of everything. Since it is not possible for the Least to exist, it cannot be isolated, nor come into being by itself; but as it was in the beginning, so now, all things are together. In all things there are many things, and of the things separated off, there are equal numbers in (*the categories*) Great and Small.

12. Other things all contain a part of everything, but Mind is infinite and self-ruling, and is mixed with no Thing, but is alone by itself. If it were not by itself, but were mixed with anything else, it would have had a share of all Things, if it were mixed with anything; for in everything there is a portion of everything, as I have said before. And the things mixed (*with Mind*) would have prevented it, so that it could not rule over any Thing in the same way as it can being alone by itself. For it is the finest of all Things, and the purest, and has complete understanding of everything, and has the greatest power. All things which have life, both the greater and the less, are ruled by Mind. Mind took command of the universal revolution, so as to make (*things*) revolve at the outset. And at first things began to revolve from some small point, but now the revolution extends over a greater area, and will spread even further. And the things which were mixed together, and separated off, and divided, were all understood by Mind. And whatever they were going to be, and whatever things were then in existence that are not now, and all things that now exist and whatever shall exist — all were arranged by Mind, as also the revolution now followed by the stars, the sun and moon, and the Air and Aether which were separated off. It was this revolution which caused the separation off. And dense separates from rare, and hot from cold, and bright from dark, and dry from wet. There are many portions of many things. And nothing is absolutely separated off or divided the one from the other except Mind. Mind is all alike, both the greater and the less. But nothing else is like anything else, but each individual thing is and was most obviously that of which it contains the most.

(From *Ancilla to the Pre-Socratic Philosophers*. Trans. Kathleen Freeman, Oxford: Basil Blackwell, 1947. Reprinted by permission of Basil Blackwell.)

Democritus
Fragments

34. Man is a universe in little (*Microcosm*).

37. He who chooses the advantages of the soul chooses things more divine, but he who chooses those of the body, chooses things human.

191. Cheerfulness is created for men through moderation of enjoyment and harmoniousness of life. Things that are in excess or lacking are apt to change and cause great disturbance in the soul. Souls which are stirred by great divergences are neither stable nor cheerful. Therefore one must keep one's mind on what is attainable, and be content with what one has, paying little heed to things envied and admired, and not dwelling on them in one's mind. Rather must you consider the lives of those in distress, reflecting on their intense sufferings, in order that your own possessions and condition may seem great and enviable, and you may, by ceasing to desire more, cease to suffer in your soul.

For he who admires those who have, and who are called happy by other mortals, and who dwells on them in his mind every hour, is constantly compelled to undertake something new and to run the risk, through his desire, of doing something irretrievable among those things which the laws prohibit. Hence one must not seek the latter, but must be content with the former, comparing one's own life with that of those in worse cases, and must consider oneself fortunate, reflecting on their sufferings, in being so much better off than they. If you keep to this way of thinking, you will live more serenely, and will expel those not-negligible curses in life, envy, jealousy and spite.

Review Questions

1. How does philosophy begin in wonder?
2. Discuss the importance of the one and the many, and of being and becoming, for the early Greek philosophers.
3. Describe the efforts to achieve unity that underlay the thought of Thales, Pythagoras, Heraclitus and Parmenides.
4. What kind of opposition exists between being and not-being? Between being and becoming?

2

Socrates (469–399 B.C.)

Introduction

The three great Greek philosophers, Socrates, Plato, and Aristotle, appeared in a relatively short space of time in the fifth and fourth centuries, with Socrates enormously influencing the young Plato and Plato, in turn, enormously influencing the young Aristotle. Together they stand for the value of knowledge, the worth of virtue, and the unflagging pursuit of human meaning. Together they represent one of the most sustained efforts of the human mind to work its way into the mystery of reality, into the rich diversity of the real world and its overarching unity. Western philosophy has been in their enduring debt ever since.

Socrates, who died in 399 B.C., was a fifth-century person. He was the son of a sculptor and is said to have done some sculpting himself. He lived in Athens, leaving it only a few times on military expeditions. Though never a political candidate, he was very much involved in city affairs. It was as a thinker and teacher that he gained his reputation.

Though institutions of learning as they exist today were not part of the Greek world at that time, for a certain segment of society a kind of formal education could be gained from a group of teachers who traveled from place to place, taking payment for their services. They were known as sophists because their profession was to instruct in *sophia*, or wisdom. Earlier no opprobrium had been associated with this term which not infrequently was applied to a number of eminent learned men. As time went on, however, it came to be used pejoratively and even scornfully because sophists were looked upon not as purveyors of wisdom but as pretenders; not as seekers of the truth but as artists of persuasion. Hence the word "sophistry" became attached to an argument that on first hearing, sounds cogent but on analysis is seen to be fallacious.

Socrates can be thought of as belonging to this class of teacher, but inasmuch as he supported the highest ideals of education, he cannot be thought of as contributing to the disesteem into which the sophists fell.

He never took payment for teaching; he was acknowledged to be skillful in pedagogy; as a familiar figure in Athens, he was always to be found in earnest dialogue with others. Ironically, while he was thus garnering respect for himself, he was also suffering ridicule as an outspoken political critic and as a practitioner of sophistry; one of the charges brought against him was that he made "the weaker argument defeat the stronger." On the Greek stage the playwright Aristophanes satirized him in a comedy, *The Clouds*, in which he was lampooned as the Master of the Thinking Factory.

The portrait given by Plato, as well as by Xenophon, shows Socrates to have been a man thoroughly set against the pretensions of knowledge. Plato records that, far from pretending to know, he even prized his ignorance, for when he was informed by a friend that the oracle at Delphi had referred to him as the wisest man in Athens, Socrates, after diligently seeking to learn to how this could be true, finally decided that it was because he was aware of his ignorance, whereas others were not aware of theirs: "I am better off than he is, — for he knows nothing and thinks that he knows; I neither know nor think that I know." His encouragement of youth to think things through for themselves, his own search for the meaning of wisdom, his willingness and to die out of fidelity to his convictions are not characteristics of a person interested in argument for the sake of argument, but rather as a means of submitting life to an examination. This estimate of Socrates is supported by Xenophon, who writes, "For myself, I have described him as he was — so religious that he did nothing without counsel from the gods; so just that he did no injury, however small, to any man, but conferred the greatest benefit on all who dealt with him; so self-controlled that he never chose the pleasanter rather than the better course; so wise that he was unerring in his judgment of the better and the worse. . . . To me then he seemed to be all that a truly good and happy man must be."

Socrates was not handsome or imposing; he never wrote a recorded word. Yet he was an inspiration. That is, he was a seeker after truth in a personally attractive way, a consequence perhaps of his attitude that friendship is suited to the finding of truth. At any rate, love and wisdom were not far apart, but joined together in a truth–person context. The truth formed a link with the person: a deeper grasp of the truth meant a deeper grasp of the person, and a deeper grasp of the person meant a deeper grasp of the truth. The high regard Socrates had for his students as human beings and thinkers in their own right prompted him to draw out answers from them rather than to supply them — the so-called socratic method of teaching. His concern for ethical principles, his integrity vis–à–vis a state-imposed religion, his composure in the face of a final verdict from his judges, all bear out the authenticity of Phaedo's testimony: "Such was the end of our comrade, who was, we may fairly say, of those whom we knew in our time, the bravest and also the wisest and most upright man."

The main feature of Socrates's thought, and the one on which all other aspects of his philosophy depend, is that of *ethical wisdom* — the recognition of the fundamental importance of the ethical in the life of man and of doing good as the basic principle of human activity. Socrates gave the concepts of virtue and goodness insistent attention, first by acknowledging myriad good acts, such as acts of courage, piety, and justice, and then by trying to discover their inward unity — that is, their essence, nature, or definition. Aristotle praised Socrates as the first philosopher who, in "seeking the universal in these ethical matters, fixed thought for the first time on definitions." But clearly Socrates's focal point was the personal, for the notion he was always trying to clarify was that of what a virtuous person might be, or, put another way, what it was, in the last analysis, that could rightly be called wisdom.

Two considerations converge in Socrates's analysis of wisdom: that virtue is knowledge and that happiness resides in the possession of such knowledge. The first of these ideas seems contrary to our expectations, for we have ample experience that a person, with full knowledge, can do wrong. So, how is it, then, that virtue is knowledge? What Socrates has in mind is that knowledge, such as the knowledge of courage, piety, or justice, by its very nature flows immediately into active, practical life so that a person is morally compelled to become courageous, pious, or just — in short, to become virtuous; if he does not become virtuous, he does not really know — he is not really wise. Hence, in the *Phaedo*, Socrates says, "In fact, it is wisdom that makes possible courage and self-control and integrity or, in a word, true goodness."

With regard to the second consideration, Socrates is well aware that there is no such thing as a perfect definition of happiness, for happiness is a matter of continuing personal experience and is not easily open to definition. Yet happiness is the quest of all — a sense of satisfaction or fulfillment that occurs when our actions are right or good. This is certainly Socrates's meaning in one of Plato's minor dialogues called *Charmides*, in which Socrates and some of his friends are discussing the relationship between knowledge and happiness. Though it is clear that by acting according to knowledge "we shall act well and be happy," not just any kind of knowledge, for example, knowledge of medicine, or ship piloting, or winning battles, or shoemaking, or playing checkers — important as it may otherwise be — is destined to make us happy. No, it is the knowledge of good and evil that holds the key. And granted that the dialogue portends some uncertainties for the young Charmides, Socrates reassures him that wisdom is a great good:

"for wisdom and temperance I believe to be really a great good. And happy are you, Charmides, if you possess it . . . rest assured that the more wise and temperate you are, the happier you will be."

To what extent Socrates was committed to wisdom can be seen at the moment of greatest personal intensity: the moment of his death. He viewed death as a life event, pregnant with philosophical importance, for in death, as in a prism, life can be seen as the unity of happiness, goodness, truth, and all the other characteristics identified with humanity. Though this is true for everyone, it is especially true for Socrates, who, under the sentence of death, was able to convert his last days into a privileged stillpoint for contemplating the meaning of life and life's values. Without a doubt, the most important problem a philosopher has to face is the problem of death. Indeed, Socrates offered no more arresting description of philosophy than that philosophy is "practicing death."

The "practice of death" refers to what one does with his life, the way one lives, the ideals he holds, the convictions he has, the practice in which he externalizes what is internal: death is a life-directing reality. That is why, for those who have led a good life, a life of "holiness," the future holds no fears and death can be thought of only as a blessing. The Pythagorean element of purification is evidently at work in Socrates's thinking, for the soul must be cleansed of all attachments to the body, all those enticements of the bodily world which draw us away from the spiritual world at the risk of putting off, through another period of this life's restlessness, the time of enduring peace. The fulfillment of life is surely what Socrates sought, but such fulfillment, achievable here only inchoately, is achievable finally in the hereafter. Among the last words Socrates uttered before taking the poison cup were: "There is one way, then, in which a man can be free from all anxiety about the fate of his soul — if in life he has abandoned bodily pleasures and adornments, as foreign to his purpose and likely to do more harm than good, and has devoted himself to the pleasures of acquiring knowledge, and so by decking his soul not with a borrowed beauty but with its own — with self-control, and goodness, and courage, and liberality, and truth — has fitted himself to await his journey to the next world."

Readings

The Trial of Socrates (Plato's Apology)

How you, O Athenians, have been affected by my accusers, I cannot tell; but I know that they almost made me forget who I was—so persuasively did they speak; and yet they have hardly uttered a word of truth. But of the many falsehoods told by them, there was one which quite amazed me;—I mean when they said that you should be upon your guard and not allow yourselves to be deceived by the force of my eloquence. To say this, when they were certain to be detected as soon as I opened my lips and proved myself to be anything but a great speaker, did indeed appear to me most shameless—unless by the force of eloquence they mean the force of truth; for if such is their meaning, I admit that I am eloquent. But in how different a way from theirs! Well, as I was saying, they have scarcely spoken the truth at all; but from me you shall hear the whole truth: not, however, delivered after their manner in a set oration duly ornamented with words and phrases. No, by heaven! but I shall use the words and arguments which occur to me at the moment; for I am confident in the justice of my cause: at my time of life I ought not to be appearing before you, O men of Athens, in the character of a juvenile orator—let not one expect it of me. And I must beg of you to grant me a favour:—If I defend myself in my accustomed manner, and you hear me using the words which I have been in the habit of using in the agora, at the tables of the money-changers, or anywhere else, I would ask you not to be surprised, and not to interrupt me on this account. For I am more than seventy years of age, and appearing now for the first time in a court of law, I am quite a stranger to the language of the place; and therefore I would have you regard me as if I were really a stranger, whom you would excuse if he spoke in his native tongue, and after the fashion of his country:—Am I making an unfair request of you? Never mind the manner, which may or may not be good; but think only of the truth of my words, and give heed to that: let the speaker speak truly and the judge decide justly.

And first, I have to reply to the older charges and to my first accusers, and then I will go on to the later ones. For of old I have had many accusers, who have accused me falsely to you during many years; and I am more afraid of them than of Anytus and his associates, who are dangerous, too, in their own way. But far more dangerous are the others, who began when you were children, and took possession of your minds with their falsehoods, telling of one Socrates, a wise man, who speculated about the heaven above, and searched into the earth beneath, and made the worse appear the better cause. The disseminators of this tale are the accusers whom I dread; for their hearers are apt to fancy that such enquirers do not believe in the existence of the gods. And they are many, and their charges against me are of ancient date, and they were made by them in the days when you were more impressible than you are now—in childhood, or it may have been in youth—and the cause when heard went by default, for there was none to answer. And hardest of all, I do not know and cannot tell the names of my accusers; unless in the chance case of a Comic poet. All who from envy and malice have persuaded you—some of them having first convinced themselves—all this class of men are most difficult to deal with; for I cannot have them up here, and cross-examine them, and therefore I must simply fight with shadows in my own defence, and argue when there is no one who answers. I will ask you then to assume with me, as I was saying, that my opponents are of two kinds; one recent, the other ancient: and I hope that you will see the propriety of my answering the latter first, for these accusations you heard long before the others, and much oftener.

Well, then, I must make my defence, and endeavor to clear away in a short time, a slander which has lasted a long time. May I succeed, if to succeed be for my good and yours, or likely to avail me in my cause! The task is not an easy one; I quite understand the nature of it. And so leaving the event with God, in obedience to the law I will now make my defence.

I will begin at the beginning, and ask what is the accusation which has given rise to the slander of me, and in fact has encouraged Meletus to prefer this charge against me. Well, what do the slanderers say? They shall be my prosecutors, and I will sum up their words in an affidavit: 'Socrates is an evil-doer, and a curious person, who searches into things under the earth and in heaven, and he makes the worse appear the better cause; and he teaches the aforesaid doctrines to others.' Such is the nature of the accusation: it is just what you have yourselves seen in the comedy of Aristophanes, who has introduced a man whom he calls Socrates, going about and saying that he walks in air, and talking a deal of nonsense concerning matters of which I do not pretend to know either much or little—not that I mean to speak disparagingly of any one who is a student of natural philosophy. I should be very sorry if Meletus could bring so grave a charge against me. But the simple truth is, O Athenians, that I have nothing to do with physical speculations. Very many of those here present are witnesses to the truth of this, and to them I appeal. Speak then, you who have heard me, and tell your neighbours whether any of you have ever known me hold forth in few words or in many upon such matters. ...You hear their answer. And from what they say of this part of the charge you will be able to judge of the truth of the rest.

As little foundation is there for the report that I am a teacher, and take money; this accusation has no more truth in it than the other. Although, if a man were really able to instruct mankind, to receive money for giving instruction would, in my opinion, be an honour to him. There is Gorgias of Leontium, and Prodicus of Ceos, and Hippias of Elis, who go the round of the cities, and are able to persuade the young men to leave their own citizens by whom they might be taught for nothing, and come to them whom they not only pay, but are thankful if they may be allowed to pay them. There is at this time a Parian philosopher residing in Athens, of whom I have heard; and I came to hear of him in this way:—I came across a man who has spent a world of money on the Sophists, Callias, the son of Hipponicus, and knowing that he had sons, I asked him: 'Callias,' I said, 'if your two sons were foals or calves, there would be no difficulty in finding some one to put over them; we should hire a trainer of horses, or a farmer probably, who would improve and perfect them in their own proper virtue and excellence; but as they are human beings, whom are you thinking of placing over them? Is there any one who understands human and political virtue? You must have thought about the matter, for you have sons; is there any one?' 'There is,' he said. 'Who is he?' said I; 'and of what country? and what does he charge?' 'Evenus the Parian,' he replied; 'he is the man, and his charge is five minae.' Happy is Evenus, I said to myself, if he really has this wisdom, and teaches at such a moderate charge. Had I the same, I should have been very proud and conceited; but the truth is that I have no knowledge of the kind.

I dare say, Athenians, that some one among you will reply, 'Yes, Socrates, but what is the origin of these accusations which are brought against you; there must have been something strange which you have been doing? All these rumours and this talk about you would never have arisen if you had been like other men: tell us, then, what is the cause of them, for we should be sorry to judge hastily of you.' Now I regard this as a fair challenge, and I will endeavour to explain to you the reason why I am called wise and have such an evil fame. Please to attend then. And although some of you may think that I am joking, I declare that I will tell you the entire truth. Men of Athens, this reputation of mine has come of a certain sort of wisdom which I possess. If you ask me what kind of wisdom, I reply, wisdom such as may perhaps be attained by man, for to that extent I am inclined to believe that I am wise; whereas the persons of whom I was speaking have a superhuman wisdom, which I may fail to describe, because I have it not myself; and he who says that I have, speaks falsely, and is taking away my character. And here, O men of Athens, I must beg you not to interrupt me, even if I seem to say something extravagant. For the word which I will speak is not mine. I will refer you to a witness who is worthy of credit; that witness shall be the God of Delphi—he will tell you about my wisdom, if I have any, and of what sort it is. You must have known Chaerephon; he was early a friend of mine, and also a friend of yours, for he shared in the recent exile of the people, and returned with you. Well, Chaerephon, as you know, was very impetuous in all his doings, and he went to Delphi and boldly asked the oracle to tell him wheth er—as I was saying, I must beg you not to interrupt—he asked the oracle to tell him whether any one was wiser than I was, and the Pythian prophetess answered, that there was no man wiser. Chaerephon is dead himself; but his brother, who is in court, will confirm the truth of what I am saying.

Why do I mention this? Because I am going to explain to you why I have such an evil name. When I heard the answer, I said to myself, What can the god mean? and what is the interpretation of his riddle? for I know that I have no wisdom, small or great. What then can he mean when he says that I am the wisest of men? And yet he is a god, and cannot lie; that would be against his nature. After long consideration, I thought of a method of trying the question. I reflected that if I could only find a man wiser than myself, then I might go to the god with a refutation in my hand. I should say to him, 'Here is a man who is wiser than I am; but you said that I was the wisest.' Accordingly I went to one who had the reputation of wisdom, and observed him—his name I need not mention; he was a politician whom I selected for examination—and the result was as follows: When I began to talk with him, I could not help thinking that he was not really wise, although he was thought wise by many, and still wiser by himself; and thereupon I tried to explain to him that he thought himself wise, but was not really wise; and the consequence was that he hated me, and his enmity was shared by several who were present and heard me. So I left him, saying to myself, as I went away: Well, although I do not suppose that either of us knows anything really beautiful and good, I am better off than he is,—for he knows nothing, and thinks that he knows; I neither know nor think that I know. In this latter particular, then, I seem to have slightly the advantage of him. Then I went to another who had still higher pretensions to wisdom, and my conclusion was exactly the same. Whereupon I made another enemy of him, and of many others besides him.

Then I went to one man after another, being not unconscious of the enmity which I provoked, and I lamented and feared this: But necessity was laid upon me,—the word of God, I thought, ought to be considered first. And I said to myself, Go I must to all who appear to know, and find out the meaning of the oracle. And I swear to you, Athenians, by the dog I swear!—for I must tell you the truth—the result of my mission was just this: I found that the men most in repute were all but the most foolish; and that others less esteemed were really wiser and better. I will tell you the tale of my wanderings and of the 'Herculean' labours, as I may call them, which I endured only to find at last the oracle irrefutable. After the politicians, I went to the poets; tragic, dithyrambic, and all sorts. And there, I said to myself, you will be instantly detected; now you will find out that you are more ignorant than they are. Accordingly, I took them some of the most elaborate passages in their own writings, and asked what was the meaning of them—thinking that they would teach me something. Will you believe me? I am almost ashamed to confess the truth, but I must say that there is hardly a person present who would not have talked better about their poetry than they did themselves. Then I knew that not by wisdom do poets write poetry, but by a sort of genius and inspiration; they are like diviners or soothsayers who also say many fine things, but do not understand the meaning of them. The poets appeared to me to be much in the same case; and I further observed that upon the strength of their poetry they believed themselves to be the wisest of men in other things in which they were not wise. So I departed, conceiving myself to be superior to them for the same reason that I was superior to the politicians.

At last I went to the artisans, for I was conscious that I knew nothing at all, as I may say, and I was sure that they knew many fine things; and here I was not mistaken, for they did know many things of which I was ignorant, and in this they certainly were wiser than I was. But I observed that even the good artisans fell into the same error as the poets;—because they were good workmen they thought that they also knew all sorts of high matters, and this defect in them overshadowed their wisdom; and therefore I asked myself on behalf of the oracle, whether I would like to be as I was, neither having their knowledge nor their ignorance, or like them in both; and I made answer to myself and to the oracle that I was better off as I was.

This inquisition has led to my having many enemies of the worst and most dangerous kind, and has given occasion also to many calumnies. And I am called wise, for my hearers always imagine that I myself possess the wisdom which I find wanting in others: but the truth is, O men of Athens, that God only is wise; and by his answer he intends to show that the wisdom of men is worth little or nothing; he is not speaking of Socrates, he is only using my name by way of illustration, as if he said, He, O men, is the wisest, who, like Socrates, knows that his wisdom is in truth worth nothing. And so I go about the world, obedient to the god, and search and make enquiry into the wisdom of any one, whether citizen or stranger, who appears to be wise; and if he is not wise, then in vindication of the oracle I show him that he is not wise; and my occupation quite absorbs me, and I have no time to give either to any public matter of interest or to any concern of my own, but I am in utter poverty by reason of my devotion to the god.

There is another thing:—young men of the richer classes, who have not much to do, come about me of their own accord; they like to hear the pretenders examined, and they often imitate me, and proceed to examine others; there are plenty of persons, as they quickly discover, who think that they know something, but really know little or nothing;

and then those who are examined by them instead of being angry with themselves are angry with me: This confounded Socrates, they say; this villainous misleader of youth!—and then if somebody asks them, Why, what evil does he practice or teach? they do not know, and cannot tell; but in order that they may not appear to be at a loss, they repeat the ready-made charges which are used against all philosophers about teaching things up in the clouds and under the earth, and having no gods, and making the worse appear the better cause; for they do not like to confess that their pretence of knowledge has been detected— which is the truth; and as they are numerous and ambitious and ener- getic, and are drawn up in battle array and have persuasive tongues, they have filled your ears with their loud and inveterate calumnies. And this is the reason why my three accusers, Meletus and Anytus and Lycon, have set upon me; Meletus, who has a quarrel with me on be- half of the poets; Anytus, on behalf of the craftsmen and politicians; Lycon, on behalf of the rhetoricians: and as I said at the beginning, I cannot expect to get rid of such a mass of calumny all in a moment. And this, O men of Athens, is the truth and the whole truth; I have concealed nothing, I have dissembled nothing. And yet, I know that my plainness of speech makes them hate me, and what is their hatred but a proof that I am speaking the truth?—Hence has arisen the prejudice against me; and this is the reason of it, as you will find out either in this or in any future enquiry.

I have said enough in my defence against the first class of my accus- ers; I turn to the second class. They are headed by Meletus, that good man and true lover of his country, as he calls himself. Against these, too, I must try to make a defence:—Let their affidavit be read: it con- tains something of this kind: It says that Socrates is a doer of evil, who corrupts the youth; and who does not believe in the gods of the state, but has other new divinities of his own. Such is the charge; and now let us examine the particular counts. He says that I am a doer of evil, and corrupt the youth; but I say, O men of Athens that Meletus is a doer of evil, in that he pretends to be in earnest when he is only in jest, and is so eager to bring men to trial from a pretended zeal and interest about matters in which he really never had the smallest interest. And the truth of this I will endeavour to prove to you.

Come hither, Meletus, and let me ask a question of you. You think a great deal about the improvement of youth?

Yes, I do.

Tell the judges, then, who is their improver; for you must know, as you have taken the pains to discover their corrupter, and are citing and accusing me before them. Speak, then, and tell the judges who their improver is.—Observe, Meletus, that you are silent, and have nothing to say. But is not this rather disgraceful, and a very considerable proof of what I was saying, that you have no interest in the matter? Speak up, friend, and tell us who their improver is.

The laws.

But that, my good sir, is not my meaning. I want to know who the person is, who, in the first place, knows the laws.

The judges, Socrates, who are present in court.

What, do you mean to say, Meletus, that they are able to instruct and improve youth?

Certainly they are.

What, all of them, or some only and not others?

All of them.

By the goddess Here, that is good news! There are plenty of improvers, then. And what do you say of the audience,—do they improve them?

Yes, they do.

And the senators?

Yes, the senators improve them.

But perhaps the members of the assembly corrupt them?—or do they too improve them?

They improve them.

Then every Athenian improves and elevates them; all with the exception of myself; and I alone am their corrupter? Is that what you affirm?

That is what I stoutly affirm.

I am very unfortunate if you are right. But suppose I ask you a question: How about horses? Does one man do them harm and all the world good? Is not the exact opposite the truth? One man is able to do them good, or at least not many;—the trainer of horses, that is to say, does them good, and others who have to do with them rather injure them? Is not that true, Meletus, of horses, or of any other animals? Most assuredly it is; whether you and Anytus say yes or no. Happy indeed would be the condition of youth if they had one corrupter only, and all the rest of the world were their improvers. But you, Meletus, have sufficiently shown that you never had a thought about the young; your carelessness is seen in your not caring about the very things which you bring against me.

And now, Meletus, I will ask you another question—by Zeus I will: Which is better, to live among bad citizens, or among good ones? Answer, friend, I say; the question is one which may be easily answered. Do not the good do their neighbours good, and the bad do them evil?

Certainly.

And is there any one who would rather be injured than benefited by those who live with him? Answer, my good friend, the law requires you to answer—does any one like to be injured?

Certainly not.

And when you accuse me of corrupting and deteriorating the youth, do you allege that I corrupt them intentionally or unintentionally?

Intentionally, I say.

But you have just admitted that the good do their neighbours good, and evil do them evil. Now, is that a truth which your superior wisdom has recognized thus early in life, and am I, at my age, in such darkness and ignorance as not to know that if a man with whom I have to live is corrupted by me, I am very likely to be harmed by him; and yet I corrupt him, and intentionally, too—so you say, although neither I nor any other human being is ever likely to be convinced by you. But either I do not corrupt them, or I corrupt them unintentionally; and on either view of the case you lie. If my offence is unintentional, the law has no cognizance of unintentional offences: you ought to have taken me privately, and warned and admonished me; for if I had been better advised, I should have left off doing what I only did unintentionally—no doubt I should; but you would have nothing to say to me and refused to teach me. And now you bring me up in this court, which is a place not of instruction, but of punishment.

It will be very clear to you, Athenians, as I was saying, that Meletus has no care at all, great or small, about the matter. But still I should like to know, Meletus, in what I am affirmed to corrupt the young. I suppose you mean, as I infer from your indictment, that I teach them not to acknowledge the gods which the state acknowledges, but some other new divinities or spiritual agencies in their stead. These are the lessons by which I corrupt the youth, as you say.

Yes, that I say emphatically.

Then, by the gods, Meletus, of whom we are speaking, tell me and the court, in somewhat plainer terms, what you mean! for I do not as yet understand whether you affirm that I teach other men to acknowledge some gods, and therefore that I do believe in gods, and am not an entire atheist—this you do not lay to my charge,—but only you say that they are not the same gods which the city recognizes—the charge is that they are different gods. Or, do you mean that I am an atheist simply, and a teacher of atheism?

I mean the latter—that you are a complete atheist.

What an extraordinary statement! Why do you think so, Meletus? Do you mean that I do not believe in the godhead of the sun or moon, like other men?

I assure you, judges, that he does not: for he says that the sun is stone, and the moon earth.

Friend Meletus, you think that you are accusing Anaxagoras: and you have but a bad opinion of the judges, if you fancy them illiterate to such a degree as not to know that these doctrines are found in the books of Anaxagoras the Clazomenian, which are full of them. And so, forsooth, the youth are said to be taught them by Socrates, when there are not unfrequently exhibitions of them at the theatre (price of admission one drachma at the most); and they might pay their money, and laugh at Socrates if he pretends to father these extraordinary views. And so, Meletus, you really think that I do not believe in any god?

I swear by Zeus that you believe absolutely in none at all.

Nobody will believe you, Meletus, and I am pretty sure that you do not believe yourself. I cannot help thinking, men of Athens, that Meletus is reckless and impudent, and that he has written this indictment in a spirit of mere wantonness and youthful bravado. Has he not compounded a riddle, thinking to try me? He said to himself:—I shall see whether the wise Socrates will discover my facetious contracdiction, or whether I shall be able to deceive him and the rest of them. For he certainly does appear to me to contradict himself in the indictment as much as if he said that Socrates is guilty of not believing in the gods, and yet of believing in them—but this is not like a person who is in earnest.

I should like you, O men of Athens, to join me in examining what I conceive to be his inconsistency; and do you, Meletus, answer. And I must remind the audience of my request that they would not make a disturbance if I speak in my accustomed manner:

Did ever man, Meletus, believe in the existence of human things, and not of human beings? ... I wish, men of Athens, that he would answer, and not be always trying to get up an interruption. Did ever any man believe in horsemanship, and not in horses? or in flute-playing, and not in flute-players? No, my friend; I will answer to you and do the court, as you refuse to answer for yourself. There is no man who ever did. But now please to answer the next question: Can a man believe in spiritual and divine agencies, and not in spirits or demigods?

He cannot.

How lucky I am to have extracted that answer, by the assistance of the court! But then you swear in the indictment that I teach and believe in divine or spiritual agencies (new or old, no matter for that); at any rate, I believe in spiritual agencies,—so you say and swear in the affidavit; and yet if I believe in divine beings, how can I help believing in spirits or demigods;—must I not? To be sure I must; and therefore I may assume that your silence gives consent. Now what are spirits or demigods? are they not either gods or the sons of gods?

Certainly they are.

But this is what I call the facetious riddle invented by you: the demigods or spirits are gods, and you say first that I do not believe in gods, and then again that I do believe in gods; that is, if I believe in demigods. For if the demigods are the illegitimate sons of gods, whether by the nymphs or by any other mothers, of whom they are said to be the sons—what human being will ever believe that there are no gods if they are the sons of gods? You might as well affirm the existence of mules, and deny that of horses and asses. Such nonsense, Meletus, could only have been intended by you to make trial of me. You have put this into the indictment because you had nothing real of which to accuse me. But no one who has a particle of understanding will ever be convinced by you that the same men can believe in divine and super-human things, and yet not believe that there are gods and demigods and heroes.

I have said enough in answer to the charge of Meletus: any elaborate defence is unnecessary; but I know only too well how many are the en-mities which I have incurred, and this is what will be my destruction if I am destroyed;—not Meletus, nor yet Anytus, but the envy and de-traction of the world, which has been the death of many good men, and will probably be the death of many more; there is no danger of my be-ing the last of them.

Some one will say: And are you not ashamed, Socrates, of a course of life which is likely to bring you to an untimely end? To him I may fairly answer: There you are mistaken: a man who is good for anything ought not to calculate the change of living or dying; he ought only to consider whether in doing anything he is doing right or wrong—acting the part of a good man or of a bad. Whereas, upon you view, the heroes who fell at Troy were not good for much, and the son of Thetis above all, who altogether despised danger in comparison with disgrace; and when he was so eager to slay Hector, his goddess mother said to him, that if he avenged his companion Patroclus, and slew Hector, he would die himself—'Fate,' she said, in these or the like words, 'waits for you next after Hector;' he, receiving this warning, utterly despised danger and death, and instead of fearing them, feared rather to live in dis-honour, and not to avenge his friend. 'Let me die forthwith,' he replies, 'and be avenged of my enemy, rather than abide here by the beaked ships, a laughing-stock and a burden of the earth.' Had Achilles any thought of death and danger? For wherever a man's place is, whether the place which he has chosen or that in which he has been placed by a commander, there he ought to remain in the hour of danger; he should not think of death or of anything but of disgrace. And this, O men of Athens, is a true saying.

Strange, indeed, would be my conduct, O men of Athens, if I who, when I was ordered by the generals whom you chose to command me at Potidaea and Amphipolis and Delium, remained where they placed me, like any other man, facing death—if now, when, as I conceive and imagine, God orders me to fulfil the philosopher's mission of searching into myself and other men, I were to desert my post through fear of death, or any other fear; that would indeed be strange, and I might justly be arraigned in court for denying the existence of the gods, if I disobeyed the oracle because I was afraid of death, fancying that I was wise when I was not wise. For the fear of death is indeed the pretence of wisdom, and not real wisdom, being a pretence of knowing the unknown; and no one knows whether death, which men in their fear apprehend to be the greatest evil, may not be the greatest good. Is not this ignorance of a disgraceful sort, the ignorance which is the conceit that man knows what he does not know? And in this respect only I believe myself to differ from men in general, and may perhaps claim to be wiser than they are:—that whereas I know but little of the world below, I do not suppose that I know: but I do know that injustice and disobedience to a better, whether God or man, is evil and dishonourable, and I will never fear or avoid a possible good rather than a certain evil. And therefore if you let me go now, and are not convinced by Anytus, who said that since I had been prosecuted I must be put to death (or if not that I ought never to have been prosecuted at all); and that if I escape now, your sons will all be utterly ruined by listening to my words—if you say to me, Socrates, this time we will not mind Anytus, and you shall be let off, but upon one condition, that you are not to enquire and speculate in this way any more, and that if you are caught doing so again you shall die;—if this was the condition on which you let me go, I should reply: Men of Athens, I honour and love you; but I shall obey God rather than you, and while I have life and strength I shall never cease from the practice and teaching of philosophy, exhorting any one whom I meet and saying to him after my manner: You, my friend,—a citizen of the great and mighty and wise city of Athens,—are you not ashamed of hearing up the greatest amount of money and honour and reputation, and caring so little about wisdom and truth and the greatest improvement of the soul, which you never regard or heed at all? And if the person with whom I am arguing, says: Yes, but I do care; then I do not leave him or let him go at once; but I proceed to interrogate and examine and cross-examine him, and if I think that he has no virtue in him, but only says that he has, I reproach him with undervaluing the greater, and overvaluing the less. And I shall repeat the same words to every one whom I meet, young and old, citizen and alien, but especially to the citizens, inasmuch as they are my brethren. For know that this is the command of God; and I believe that no greater good has ever happened in the state than my service to the God. For I do nothing but go about persuading you all, old and young alike, not to take thought for your persons or your properties, but first and chiefly to care about the greatest improvement of the soul. I tell you that virtue is not given by money, but that from virtue comes money and every other good of man, public as well as private. This is my teaching, and if this is the doctrine which corrupts the youth, I am a mischievous person. But if any one says that this is not my teaching, he is speaking an untruth. Wherefore, O men of Athens, I say to you, do as Anytus bids or not as Anytus bids, and either acquit me or not; but whichever you do, understand that I shall never alter my ways, not even if I have to die many times.

Men of Athens, do not interrupt, but hear me; there was an understanding between us that you should hear me to the end: I have something more to say, at which you may be inclined to cry out; but I believe that to hear me will be good for you, and therefore I beg that you will not cry out. I would have you know, that if you kill such an one as I am, you will injure yourselves more than you will injure me. Nothing will injure me, not Meletus nor yet Anytus—they cannot, for a bad man is not permitted to injure a better than himself. I do not deny that Anytus may, perhaps, kill him, or drive him into exile, or deprive him of civil rights; and he may imagine, and others may imagine, that he is inflicting a great injury upon him: but there I do not agree. For the evil of doing as he is doing—the evil of unjustly taking away the life of another—is greater far.

And now, Athenians, I am not going to argue for my own sake, as you may think, but for yours, that you may not sin against the God by condemning me, who am his gift to you. For if you kill me you will not easily find a successor to me, who, if I may use such a ludicrous figure of speech, am a sort of gadfly, given to the state by God; and the state is a great and noble steed who is tardy in his motions owing to his very size, and requires to be stirred into life. I am that gadfly which God has attached to the state, and all day long and in all places am always fastening upon you, arousing and persuading and reproaching you. You will not easily find another like me, and therefore I would advise you to spare me. I dare say that you may feel out of temper (like a person who is suddenly awakened from sleep), and you think that you might easily strike me dead as Anytus advises, and then you would sleep on for the remainder of your lives, unless God in his care of you sent you another gadfly. When I say that I am given to you by God, the proof of my mission is this:—if I had been like other men, I should not have neglected all my own concerns or patiently seen the neglect of them during all these years, and have been doing yours, coming to you individually like a father or elder brother, exhorting you to regard virtue; such conduct, I say, would be unlike human nature. If I had gained anything, or if my exhortations had been paid, there would have been some sense in my doing so; but now, as you will perceive, not even the impudence of my accusers dares to say that I have ever exacted or sought pay of any one; of that they have no witness. And I have a sufficient witness to the truth of what I say—my poverty.

Some one may wonder why I go about in private giving advice and busying myself with the concerns of others, but do not venture to come forward in public and advise the state. I will tell you why. You have heard me speak at sundry times and in divers places of an oracle or sign which comes to me, and is the divinity which Meletus ridicules in the indictment. This sign, which is a kind of voice, first began to come to me when I was a child; it always forbids but never commands me to do anything which I am going to do. This is what deters me from being a politician. And rightly, as I think. For I am certain, O men of Athens, that if I had engaged in politics, I should have perished long ago, and done no good either to you or to myself. And do not be offended at my telling you the truth: for the truth is, that no man who goes to war with you or any other multitude, honestly striving against the many lawless and unrighteous deeds which are done in a state, will save his life; he who will fight for the right, if he would live even for a brief space, must have a private station and not a public one.

I can give you convincing evidence of what I say, not words only, but what you value far more—actions. Let me relate to you a passage of my own life which will prove to you that I should never have yielded to injustice from any fear of death, and that 'as I should have refused to yield' I must have died at once. I will tell you a tale of the courts, not very interesting perhaps, but nevertheless true. The only office of state which I ever held, O men of Athens, was that of senator: the tribe Antiochis, which is my tribe, had the presidency at the trial of the generals who had not taken up the bodies of the slain after the battle of Arginusae; and you proposed to try them in a body, contrary to law, as you all thought afterwards; but at the time I was the only one of the Prytanes who was opposed to the illegality, and I gave my vote against you; and when the orators threatened to impeach and arrest me, and you called and shouted, I made up my mind that I would run the risk, having law and justice with me, rather than take part in your injustice because I feared imprisonment and death. This happened in the days of the democracy. But when the oligarchy of the Thirty was in power, they sent for me and four others into the rotunda, and bade us bring Leon the Salaminian from Salamis, as they wanted to put him to death. This was a specimen of the sort of commands which they were always giving with the view of implicating as many as possible in their crimes; and then I showed, not in word only but in deed, that, if I may be allowed to use such an expression, I cared not a straw for death, and that my great and only care was lest I should do an unrighteous or unholy thing. For the strong arm of that oppressive power did not frighten me into doing wrong; and when we came out of the rotunda the other four went to Salamis and fetched Leon, but I went quietly home. For which I might have lost my life, had not the power of the Thirty shortly afterwards come to an end. And many will witness to my words.

Now do you really imagine that I could have survived all these years, if I had led a public life, supposing that like a good man I had always maintained the right and had made justice, as I ought, the first thing? No indeed, men of Athens, neither I nor any other man. But I have been always the same in all my actions, public as well as private, and never have I yielded any base compliance to those who are slanderously termed my disciples, or to any other. Not that I have any regular disciples. But if any one likes to come and hear me while I am pursuing my mission, whether he be young or old, he is not excluded. Nor do I converse only with those who pay; but any one, whether he be rich or poor, may ask and answer me and listen to my words; and whether he turns out to be a bad man or a good one, neither result can be justly imputed to me; for I never taught or professed to teach him anything. And if any one says that he has ever learned or heard anything from me in private which all the world has not heard, let me tell you that he is lying.

But I shall be asked, Why do people delight in continually conversing with you? I have told you already, Athenians, the whole truth about this matter: they like to hear the cross-examination of the pretenders to wisdom; there is amusement in it. Now this duty of cross-examining other men has been imposed upon me by God; and has been signified to me by oracles, visions, and in every way in which the will of divine power was ever intimated to any one. This is true, O Athenians; or, if not true, would be soon refuted. If I am or have been corrupting the youth, those of them who are now grown up and become sensible that I gave them bad advice in the days of their youth should come forward as accusers, and take their revenge; or if they do not like to come themselves, some of their relatives, fathers, brothers, or other kinsmen, should say what evil their families have suffered at my hands. Now is their time. Many of them I see in the court. There is Crito, who is of the same age and of the same deme with myself, and there is Critobulus his son, whom I also see. Then again there is Lysanias of Sphettus, who is the father of Aeschines—he is present; and also there is Antiphon of Cephisus, who is the father of Epigenes; and there are the brothers of several who have associated with me. There is Nicostratus the son of Theosdotides, and the brother of Theodotus (now Theodotus himself is dead, and therefore he, at any rate, will not seek to stop him); and there is Paralus the son of Demodocus, who had a brother Theages; and Adeimantus the son of Ariston, whose brother Plato is present; and Aeantodorus, who is the brother of Apollodorus, whom I also see. I might mention a great many others, some of whom Meletus should have produced as witnesses in the course of his speech; and let him still produce them, if he has forgotten—I will make way for him. And let him say, if he has any testimony of the sort which he can produce. Nay, Athenians, the very opposite is the truth. For all these are ready to witness on behalf of the corrupter, of the injurer of their kindred, as Meletus and Anytus call me; not the corrupted youth only—there might have been a motive for that—but their uncorrupted elder relatives. Why should they too support me with their testimony? Why, indeed, except for the sake of truth and justice, and because they know that I am speaking the truth, and that Meletus is a liar.

Well, Athenians, this and the like of this is all the defence which I have to offer. Yet a word more. Perhaps there may be some one who is offended at me, when he calls to mind how he himself on a similar, or even a less serious occasion, prayed and entreated the judges with many tears, and how he produced his children in court, which was a moving spectacle, together with a host of relations and friends; whereas I, who am probably in danger of my life, will do none of these things. The contrast may occur to his mind, and he may be set against me, and vote in anger because he is displeased at me on this account. Now if there be such a person among you,—mind, I do not say that there is,—to him I may fairly reply: My friend, I am a man, and like other men, a creature of flesh and blood, and not 'of wood or stone' as Homer says; and I have a family, yes, and sons, O Athenians, three in number, one almost a man, and two others who are still young; and yet I will not bring any of them hither in order to petition you for an acquittal. And why not? Not from any self-assertion or want of respect for you. Whether I am or am not afraid of death is another question, of which I will not now speak. But, having regard to public opinion, I feel that such conduct would be discreditable to myself, and to you, and to the whole state. One who has reached my years, and who has a name for wisdom, ought not to demean himself. Whether this opinion of me be deserved or not, at any rate the world has decided that Socrates is in some way superior to other men. And if those among you who are said to be superior in wisdom and courage, and any other virtue, demean themselves in this way, how shameful is their conduct! I have seen men of reputation, when they have been condemned, behaving in the strangest manner: they seemed to fancy that they were going to suffer something dreadful if they died, and that they could be immortal if you only allowed them to live; and I think that such are a dishonour to the state, and that any stranger coming in would have said of them that the most eminent men of Athens, to whom the Athenians themselves give honour and command, are no better than women. And I say that these things ought not to be done by those of us who have a reputation; and if they are done, you ought not to permit them; you ought rather to show that you are far more disposed to condemn the man who gets up a doleful scene and makes the city ridiculous, than him who holds his peace.

But, setting aside the question of public opinion, there seems to be something wrong in asking a favour of a judge, and thus procuring an acquittal, instead of informing and convincing him. For his duty is, not to make a present of justice, but to give judgment; and he has sworn that he will judge according to the laws, and not according to his own good pleasure; and we ought not to encourage you, nor should you allow yourself to be encouraged, in this habit of perjury—there can be no piety in that. Do not then require me to do what I consider dishonourable and impious and wrong, especially now, when I am being tried for impiety on the indictment of Meletus. For if, O men of Athens, by force of persuasion and entreaty I could overpower your oaths, then I should be teaching you to believe that there are no gods, and in defending should simply convict myself of the charge of not believing in them. But that is not so—far otherwise. For I do believe that there are gods, and in a sense higher than that in which any of my accusers believe in them. And to you and to God I commit my cause, to be determined by you as is best for you and me.

There are many reasons why I am not grieved, O men of Athens, at the vote of condemnation. I expected it, and am only surprised that the votes are so nearly equal; for I had thought that the majority against me would have been far larger; but now, had thirty votes gone over to the other side, I should have been acquitted. And I may say, I think, that I have escaped Meletus. I may say more; for without the assistance of Anytus and Lycon, any one may see that he would not have had a fifth part of the votes, as the law requires, in which case he would have incurred a fine of a thousand drachmae.

And so he proposes death as the penalty. And what shall I propose on my part, O men of Athens? Clearly that which is my due. And what is my due? What return shall be made to the man who has never had the wit to be idle during his whole life; but has been careless of what the many care for—wealth, and family interests, and military offices, and speaking in the assembly, and magistracies, and plots, and parties. Reflecting that I was really too honest a man to be a politician and live, I did not go where I could do no good to you or to myself; but where I could do the greatest good privately to every one of you, thither I went, and sought to persuade every man among you that he must look to himself, and seek virtue and wisdom before he looks to his private interests, and look to the state before he looks to the interests of the state; and that this should be the order which he observes in all his actions. What shall be done to such an one? Doubtless some good thing, O men of Athens, if he has his reward; and the good should be of a kind suitable to him. What would be a reward suitable to a poor man who is your benefactor, and who desires leisure that he may instruct you? There can be no reward so fitting as maintenance in the

Prytaneum, O men of Athens, a reward which he deserves far more than the citizen who has won the prize at Olympia in the horse or chariot race, whether the chariots were drawn by two horses or by many. For I am in want, and he has enough; and he only gives you the appearance of happiness, and I give you the reality. And if I am to estimate the penalty fairly, I should say that maintenance in the Prytaneum is the just return.

Perhaps you think that I am braving you in what I am saying now, as in what I said before about the tears and prayers. But this is not so. I speak rather because I am convinced that I never intentionally wronged any one, although I cannot convince you—the time has been too short; if there were a law at Athens, as there is in other cities, that a capital cause should not be decided in one day, then I believe that I should have convinced you. But I cannot in a moment refute great slanders; and, as I am convinced that I never wronged another, I will assuredly not wrong myself. I will not say of myself that I deserve any evil, or propose any penalty. Why should I? Because I am afraid of the penalty of death which Meletus proposes? When I do not know whether death is a good or an evil, why should I propose a penalty which would certainly be an evil? Shall I say imprisonment? And why should I live in prison, and be the slave of the magistrates of the year—of the Eleven? Or shall the penalty be a fine, and imprisonment until the fine is paid? There is the same objection. I should have to lie in prison, for money I have none, and cannot pay. And if I say exile (and this may possibly be the penalty which you will affix), I must indeed be blinded by the love of life, if I am so irrational as to expect that when you, who are my own citizens, cannot endure my discourses and words, and have found them so grievous and odious that you will have no more of them, others are likely to endure me. No indeed, men of Athens, that is not very likely. And what a life should I lead, at my age, wandering from city to city, ever changing my place of exile, and always being driven out! For I am quite sure that wherever I go, there, as here, the young men will flock to me; and if I drive them away, their elders will drive me out at their request; and if I let them come, their fathers and friends will drive me out for their sakes.

Some one will say: Yes, Socrates, but cannot you hold your tongue, and then you may go into a foreign city, and no one will interfere with you? Now I have great difficulty in making you understand my answer to this. For if I tell you that to do as you say would be a disobedience to the God, and therefore that I cannot hold my tongue, you will not believe that I am serious; and if I say again that daily to discourse about virtue, and of those other things about which you hear me examining myself and others, is the greatest good of man, and that the unexamined life is not worth living, you are still less likely to believe me.

Yet I say what is true, although a thing of which it is hard for me to persuade you. Also, I have never been accustomed to think that I deserve to suffer any harm. Had I money I might have estimated the offence at what I was able to pay, and not have been much the worse. But I have none, and therefore I must ask you to proportion the fine to my means. Well, perhaps I could afford a mina, and therefore I propose that penalty: Plato, Crito, Critobulus, and Apollodorus, my friends here, bid me say thirty minae, and they will be the sureties. Let thirty minae be the penalty; for which sum they will be ample security to you.

Not much time will be gained, O Athenians, in return for the evil name which you will get from the detractors of the city, who will say that you killed Socrates, a wise man; for they will call me wise, even although I am not wise, when they want to reproach you. If you had waited a little while, your desire would have been fulfilled in the course of nature. For I am far advanced in years, as you may perceive, and not far from death. I am speaking now not to all of you, but only to those who have condemned me to death. And I have another thing to say to them: You think that I was convicted because I had no words of the sort which would have procured my acquittal—I mean, if I had thought fit to leave nothing undone or unsaid. Not so; the deficiency which led to my conviction was not of words—certainly not. But I had not the boldness or impudence or inclination to address you as you would have liked me to do, weeping and wailing and lamenting, and saying and doing many things which you have been accustomed to hear from others, and which, as I maintain, are unworthy of me. I thought at the time that I ought not to do anything common or mean when in danger: nor do I now repent of the style of my defence; I would rather die having spoken after my manner, than speak in your manner and live. For neither in war nor yet at law ought I or any man to use every way of escaping death. Often in battle there can be no doubt that if a man will throw away his arms, and fall on his knees before his pursuers, he may escape death; and in other dangers there are other ways of escaping death, if a man is willing to say and do anything. The difficulty, my friends, is not to avoid death, but to avoid unrighteousness; for that runs faster than death. I am old and move slowly, and the slower runner has overtaken me, and my accusers are keen and quick, and the faster runner, who is unrighteousness, has overtaken them. And now I depart hence condemned by you to suffer the penalty of death,—they too go their ways condemned by the truth to suffer the penalty of villainy and wrong; and I must abide by my award—let them abide by theirs. I suppose that these things may be regarded as fated,—and I think that they are well.

And now, O men who have condemned me, I would fain prophesy to you; for I am about to die, and in the hour of death men are gifted with prophetic power. And I prophesy to you who are my murderers, that immediately after my departure punishment far heavier than you have inflicted on me will surely await you. Me you have killed because you wanted to escape the accuser, and not to give an account of your lives. But that will not be as you suppose: far otherwise. For I say that there will be more accusers of you than there are now; accusers whom hitherto I have restrained: and as they are younger they will be more inconsiderate with you, and you will be more offended at them. If you think that by killing men you can prevent some one from censuring your evil lives, you are mistaken; that is not a way of escape which is either possible or honourable; the easiest and the noblest way is not to be disabling others, but to be improving yourselves. This is the prophecy which I utter before my departure to the judges who have condemned me.

Friends, who would have acquitted me, I would like also to talk with you about the thing which has come to pass, while the magistrates are busy, and before I go to the place at which I must die. Stay then a little, for we may as well talk with one another while there is time. You are my friends, and I should like to show you the meaning of this event which has happened to me. O my judges—for you I may truly call judges—I should like to tell you of a wonderful circumstance. Hitherto the divine faculty of which the internal oracle is the source has constantly been in the habit of opposing me even about trifles, if I was going to make a slip or error in any matter; and now as you see there has come upon me that which may be thought, and is generally believed to be, the last and worst evil. But the oracle made no sign of opposition, either when I was leaving my house in the morning, or when I was on my way to the court, or while I was speaking, at anything which I was going to say; and yet I have often been stopped in the middle of a speech, but now in nothing I either said or did touching the matter in hand has the oracle opposed me. What do I take to be the explanation of this silence? I will tell you. It is an intimation that what has happened to me is a good, and that those of us who think that death is an evil are in error. For the customary sign would surely have opposed me had I been going to evil and not to good.

Let us reflect in another way, and we shall see that there is great reason to hope that death is a good; for one of two things—either death is a state of nothingness and utter unconsciousness, or, as men say, there is a change and migration of the soul from this world to another. Now if you suppose that there is no consciousness, but a sleep like the sleep of him who is undisturbed even by dreams, death will be an unspeakable gain. For if a person were to select the night in which his sleep was undisturbed even by dreams, and were to compare with this the other days and nights of his life, and then were to tell us how many days and nights he had passed in the course of his life better and more pleasantly than this one, I think that any man, I will not say a private man, but even the great king will not find many such days or nights, when compared with the others. Now if death be of such a nature, I say that to die is gain; for eternity is then only a single night. But if death is the journey to another place, and there, as men say, all the dead abide, what good, O my friends and judges, can be greater than this? If indeed when the pilgrim arrives in the world below, he is delivered from the professors of justice in this world, and finds the true judges who are said to give judgment there, Minos and Rhadamanthus and Aeacus and Triptolemus, and other sons of God who were righteous in their own life, that pilgrimage will be worth making. What would not a man give if he might converse with Orpheus and Musaeus and Hesiod and Homer? Nay, if this be true, let me die again and again. I myself, too, shall have a wonderful interest in there meeting and conversing with Palamedes, and Ajax the son of Telamon, and any other ancient hero who has suffered death through an unjust judgment; and there will be no small pleasure, as I think, in comparing my own sufferings with theirs. Above all, I shall then be able to continue my search into true and false knowledge; as in this world, so also in the next; and I shall find out who is wise, and who pretends to be wise, and is not. What would not a man give, O judges, to be able to examine the leader of the great Trojan expedition; or Odysseus or Sisyphus, or numberless others, men and women too! What infinite delight would there be in conversing with them and asking them questions! In another world they do not put a man to death for asking questions: assuredly not. For besides being happier than we are, they will be immortal, if what is said is true.

Wherefore, O judges, be of good cheer about death, and know of a certainty, that no evil can happen to a good man, either in life or after death. He and his are not neglected by the gods; nor has my own approaching end happened by mere chance. But I see clearly that the time had arrived when it was better for me to die and be released from trouble; wherefore the oracle gave no sign. For which reason, also, I am not angry with my condemners, or with my accusers; they have done me no harm, although they did not mean to do me any good; and for this I may gently blame them.

Still I have a favour to ask of them. When my sons are grown up, I would ask you, O my friends, to punish them; and I would have you trouble them, as I have troubled you, if they seem to care about riches, or anything, more than about virtue; or if they pretend to be something when they are really nothing,—then reprove them, as I have reproved you, for not caring about that for which they ought to care, and thinking that they are something when they are really nothing. And if you do this, both I and my sons will have received justice at your hands.

The hour of departure has arrived, and we go our ways—I to die, and you to live. Which is better God only knows.

The Death of Socrates (from *Plato's Phaedo*)

We will do our best, said Crito: And in what way shall we bury you?

In any way that you like; but you must get hold of me, and take care that I do not run away from you. Then he turned to us, and added with a smile:—I cannot make Crito believe that I am the same Socrates who have been talking and conducting the argument; he fancies that I am the other Socrates whom he will soon see, a dead body—and he asks, How shall he bury me? And though I have spoken many words in the endeavour to show that when I have drunk the poison I shall leave you and go to the joys of the blessed,—these words of mine, with which I was comforting you and myself, have had, as I perceive, no effect upon Crito. And therefore I want you to be surety for me to him now, as at the trial he was surety to the judges for me: but let the promise be of another sort; for he was surety for me to the judges that I would remain, and you must be my surety to him that I shall not remain, but go away and depart; and then he will suffer less at my death, and not be grieved when he sees my body being burned or buried. I would not have him sorrow at my hard lot, or say at the burial, Thus we lay out Socrates, or, Thus we follow him to the grave or bury him; for false words are not only evil in themselves, but they infect the soul with evil. Be of good cheer then, my dear Crito, and say that you are burying my body only, and do with that whatever is usual, and what you think best.

When he had spoken these words, he arose and went into a chamber to bathe; Crito followed him and told us to wait. So we remained behind, talking and thinking of the subject of discourse, and also of the greatness of our sorrow; he was like a father of whom we were being bereaved, and we were about to pass the rest of our lives as orphans. When he had taken the bath his children were brought to him—(he had two young sons and an elder one); and the women of his family also came, and he talked to them and gave them a few directions in the presence of Crito; then he dismissed them and returned to us.

Now the hour of sunset was near, for a good deal of time had passed while he was within. When he came out, he sat down with us again after his bath, but not much was said. Soon the jailer, who was the servant of the Eleven, entered and stood by him, saying:—To you, Socrates, whom I know to be the noblest and gentlest and best of all who ever came to this place, I will not impute the angry feelings of other men, who rage and swear at me, when, in obedience to the authorities, I bid them drink the poison—indeed, I am sure that you will not be angry with me; for others, as you are aware, and not I, are to blame. And so fare you well, and try to bear lightly what must needs be—you know my errand. Then bursting into tears he turned away and went out.

Socrates looked at him and said: I return your good wishes, and will do as you bid. Then turning to us, he said, How charming the man is: since I have been in prison he has always been coming to see me, and at times he would talk to me, and was as good to me as could be, and now see how generously he sorrows on my account. We must do as he says, Crito; and therefore let the cup be brought, if the poison is prepared: if not, let the attendant prepare some.

Yet, said Crito, the sun is still upon the hill-tops, and I know that many a one has taken the draught late, and after the announcement has been made to him, he has eaten and drunk, and enjoyed the society of his beloved; do not hurry—there is time enough.

Socrates said: Yes, Crito, and they of whom you speak are right in so acting, for they think that they will be gainers by the delay; but I am right in not following their example, for I do not think that I should gain anything by drinking the poison a little later; I should only be ridiculous in my own eyes for sparing and saving a life which is already forfeit. Please then to do as I say, and not to refuse me.

Crito made a sign to the servant, who was standing by; and he went out, and having been absent for some time, returned with the jailer carrying the cup of poison. Socrates said: You, my good friend, who are experienced in these matters, shall give me directions how I am to proceed. The man answered: You have only to walk about until your legs are heavy, and then to lie down, and the poison will act. At the same time he handed the cup to Socrates, who in the easiest and gentlest manner, without the least fear or change of colour or feature, looking at the man with all his eyes, Echecrates, as his manner was, took the cup and said: What do you say about making a libation out of this cup to any god? May I, or not? The man answered: We only prepare, Socrates, just so much as we deem enough. I understand, he said: but I may and must ask the gods to prosper my journey from this to the other world—even so—and so be it according to my prayer. Then raising the cup to his lips, quite readily and cheerfully he drank off the poison. And hitherto most of us had been able to control our sorrow; but now when we saw him drinking, and saw too that he had finished the draught, we could no longer forbear, and in spite of myself my own tears were flowing fast; so that I covered my face and wept, not for him, but at the thought of my own calamity in having to part from such a friend. Nor was I the first; for Crito, when he found himself unable to restrain his tears, had got up, and I followed; and at that moment, Apollodorus, who had been weeping all the time, broke out in a loud and passionate cry which made cowards of us all. Socrates alone retained his calmness: What is this strange outcry? he said. I sent away the women mainly in order that they might not misbehave in this way, for I have been told that a man should die in peace. Be quiet then, and have patience. When we heard his words we were ashamed, and refrained our tears; and he walked about until, as he said, his legs began to fail, and then he lay on his back, according to the directions, and the man who gave him the poison now and then looked at his feet and legs; and after a while he pressed his foot hard, and asked him if he could feel; and he said, No; and then his leg, and so upwards and upwards, and showed us that he was cold and stiff. And he felt them himself, and said: When the poison reaches the heart, that will be the end. He was beginning to grow cold about the groin, when he uncovered his face, for he had covered himself up, and said—they were his last words—he said: Crito, I owe a cock to Asclepius; will you remember to pay the debt? The debt shall be paid, said Crito; is there anything else? There was no answer to this question; but in a minute or two a movement was heard, and the attendants uncovered him; his eyes were set, and Crito closed his eyes and mouth.

Such was the end, Echecrates, of our friend; concerning whom I may truly say, that of all the men of his time whom I have known, he was the wisest and justest and best.

Review Questions

1. In what way does Socrates identify wisdom with virtue?
2. What does Socrates mean by his stunning description of philosophy as "practicing death"?
3. What possibility of immortality do you find in Socratic thought?
4. What constitutes a good person for Socrates?
5. Centuries later, Kierkegaard will refer to Socrates as a "tragic hero." Do you consider this an apt characterization?
6. How does Socrates justify his defiance of authority?

Plato (427–347 B.C.)

Introduction

The second of the great trinity of Greek philosophers was born in Athens in 428/27 B.C.; according to an ancient account, he was later called Plato because of his broad forehead. He came from a family that was, by all reports, educated, aristocratic, and politically influential. It was no doubt assumed that he would enter political life, but his disaffection from the ineptness and injustice of Athenian "democracy," especially on the execution of Socrates, turned him to the pursuit of philosophy with the cherished hope that someday philosophy and politics would combine to bring about a happier life: "the human race will not see better days" until philosophers become politicians or politicians become philosophers.

For the next ten or eleven years after the death of Socrates, Plato traveled throughout Greece, going as far as southern Italy and Sicily to various centers of intellectual activity. During this time he began some lifelong friendships, intensified a philosophic cast of mind, and wrote his early works, which were known, because of their central figure, as the "Socratic dialogues," such as the *Apology, Gorgias, Meno,* and *Crito.* These and several other works were done before Plato's most significant work was even begun — the founding of the Academy.

When Plato was about forty years of age, and after this period of travel, reflection, and writing, he founded a school just outside Athens which became known as the Academy. It was a quiet retreat where teachers and students could be together daily, where, despite a rigorous intellectual discipline and a fairly formal administrative structure, respect and friendship flourished. It was a place, in Plato's eyes, that provided an opportunity for the pursuit of pure, disinterested knowledge, particularly scientific knowledge with mathematics at its core, so that students devoted to the truth could become true public servants. The students came from all over Greece; they came to share the adventure of learning, to experience growth toward wisdom, and to receive a spark of life from the revered founder of the Academy. Given the

Academy's influence and its status as the forerunner of the modern university, it is not surprising that, for some historians, its founding was one of the outstanding intellectual events in the history of the West.

Plato and the Academy were to become inseparable until his death in 347 B.C.; except for the time when he returned to Sicily, his life was spent there, and daily his voice was heard within its walls. He seems to have lectured without notes, yet his words were precise. He focused on dialectic as the primary educational method; it was the method of question and answer, with every attempt made to satisfy the rigors of reason and clarity uniquely achievable in the form of a dialogue; in this form, Plato's works were delivered to the public. Among the dialogues of Plato's middle life were the *Phaedo, Symposium,* and *Republic*; later, the *Parmenides, Timaeus,* and lastly the *Laws.*

We can be sure, because it pervades his writings, that one of the ongoing dialogues Plato conducted with his students related to the even then traditional question of being and becoming — the search for the permanent element in things subject, as they all are, to change; this was a continuation of the Socratic search for the *essence* of things. Once we realize that, for Plato, the pressing question was how to escape the ever-changing world of Heraclitus, we also realize why he leaned toward the permanent, and why he emphasized being rather than becoming. It is all too obvious, Plato held, that changing things are not as important as permanent things and therefore occupy a lower rank in the hierarchy of the real; they are not "really real." Things-as-becoming can never have the same value as things-as-being. So Plato's search for the permanent, for essences, is also a search for the higher and nobler. The oak is a tree, the maple is a tree, the spruce is a tree; yet the individual oak, maple, and spruce change, but not the *meaning of tree.* Further, if individual trees perish, where do we find the essence of tree that does not perish? Surely there must be a place where the tree exists in all its perfection — the ideal tree, the essential tree. Plato, of course, does not mean a physical tree, since that, as an individual, would be subject to the same problem he is trying to solve. What he means is that the tree stripped of all its changing features — akin to the idea we have in our minds — must exist somewhere, unchanging, in a permanent, perfect *world of ideas.* And what is said of tree can be said of anything else: dog, man, wisdom, virtue.

The distinction between changing and lower on one hand, and unchanging and higher on the other, is borne out in the famous allegory of the cave, a parable in which Plato summarizes a number of his main doctrines. He asks us to imagine a subterranean cave, lightless except for a fire that casts its light over a low mid-wall to the end-wall of the cave. When figures and shapes of all sorts are moved along the mid-wall, their shadows are reflected on the end-wall, as though it were a screen. Further, imagine a group of men situated between the end-wall and the mid-wall who have, since childhood, been chained like prisoners so that they continually face the end-wall. The only things they ever see, then, are shadows — their own and those of the objects moved along the mid-wall behind them, and the only sounds they ever hear are the cave's echoes of real sounds.

If one of these men is suddenly freed and walks around to see the whole affair in the light of the fire, he is jolted into the awareness that the real is utterly different from what he had taken to be real — the difference between truth and illusion. If he then struggles to the mouth of the cave and sees the sun in all its brightness, he marvels at beholding light itself and all other things in that light. He then reaches the highest point in his understanding that there are things more real than the things he previously knew, and that the difference between opinion and true knowledge is forever fixed. Thus the distinction made by Parmenides receives ardent support from Plato, that is, the more our grasp of things tends toward the unchanging, the more rightly it has to be called *knowledge*, and true knowledge is knowledge of the eternal and higher world. Imprisoned in the world of opinion, men have become too blind to see and too deaf to hear the logos of the higher world whose truth would set them free.

The blazing light of that vision does not remain on a speculative level. On realizing that the Light — eternal, permanent, and in unchanging — can be nothing less than the Idea of Good, which, as the highest of all Forms, is the cause of all things "right and beautiful," the beholder is drawn to translate the dynamism of that vision into a life of practical goodness for others, a life of ethical and political wisdom.

To acquire a fuller picture of the relationship between the changing and the unchanging, it is necessary to underscore Plato's view that although the two worlds are opposites, they are nonetheless correlatives. Essence is indeed found in changing things, but in a vague and imperfect way; better, as it is found in this world, it is a pointer to the world beyond, where it is found in its perfect form. Yet the relationship involves more than mere pointing; there is an inner bond between the two worlds. Essence in the unchanging world is immanent in the changing one, so that the changing world shares the unchanging world, participates in it. The changing world exists in time, and in the beautiful phrase of the *Timaeus*, "time is the moving image of eternity." Put differently, essence has two dimensions, one found in the unchanging world of the perfect and the other in the changing world of the imperfect; but the only explanation for the imperfect is that it shares the perfect in a limited way. The doctrine of *participation*, as it is sometimes called, eventually became a favorite of later Christian philosophers, who employed it to show how the created world is one with the uncreated world.

Because of the continuity of this world with the higher world, Plato was consistent in concluding that knowledge does not come to us anew, as though with an absolute beginning, but is somehow always possessed by us. Following Socrates, he takes learning to be a *process of recalling*. Learning occurs not because a teacher conveys new ideas to the student, but because the teacher supplies the conditions necessary to draw forth from the student the knowledge he already possesses. This concept is exemplified in an episode in which Socrates invites a slave boy, therefore untaught, to join a group of friends in order to ask him a series of questions about mathematics. Though the boy is given none of the answers, Socrates successfully draws him out. Socrates infers that the answers already rest within the boy, unrecognized because they are latent but recognized when they are summoned forth under the proper conditions. Plato's final view is that the boy, like all of us, must have been endowed with knowledge in a previous state and transported it, forgotten, into this one. The knowledge we had as we *preexisted* in the world of ideas, with its pure intelligibility, becomes obscured in this world of physical things; that is why, like the prisoners in the cave, we have to make a renewed effort to see reality in the eternal light.

Plato's emphasis on the eternal world vis-à-vis the changing world discloses, very early in the history of philosophy, one of the fundamental problems in epistemology: the ontological status of what we know. The question is whether or not ideas refer to objects outside the mind; do they refer to real existences? If so, to what do they actually refer? We have already seen Plato's response to this question: inasmuch as the individual material thing changes while its meaning does not — the tree perishes but not the idea of it — there must be some real thing "out there" that answers to our idea of it. Sometimes this position is referred to as *realism*, and since there are no hard and fast rules governing the use of the terms *realism* and *idealism*, we have to readjust our understanding of them according to the contexts in which they are used. Believing as he does that there *are* in reality things answering precisely to our ideas of them, Plato's epistemological stance is one of extreme realism. Ideas for Plato are universal, essential, formal, and detached from matter; therefore, corresponding to these characteristics is the existence of the world of universals, essences, forms, immaterial things; otherwise, ideas would be devoid of meaning.

If, however, a philosopher begins with the opposite belief, that because only individual things exist, our knowledge is only individual, then common knowledge is impossible. This extreme position coincides with the philosophical outlook of the pre-Socratic atomists, for whom, since atoms are the only real things, knowledge had to be equally "a-tomic" to be called real. For Democritus, for example, there could be no genuine distinction between thought and sensation; in fragment 125, the senses say to the intellect: "Miserable Mind, you get your evidence from us, and do you try to overthrow us? The overthrow will be your downfall."

Two widely divergent views then, are as follows: there are, or are not, real things outside the mind called essences, forms, Ideas, or universals that correspond to the concepts in our minds. Is there any other option? Looking ahead to Plato's student and friend, Aristotle thought so. He argued against his master's doctrine on the real existence of Ideas, pointing out the contradiction he said it implied: a universal could never be a substance, for then you could never call it a "this," which is the designation used of existing things. Still, for Aristotle, universal knowledge is real knowledge even though there are no universals as such existing outside the mind. For him only *individual* things exist, yet it is possible for me to have knowledge of an individual *in common* with other individual things, and this commonality is in fact rooted in their existence. In Aristotle's view, therefore, when I say "Socrates is a man" and "Plato is a man," I mean that they are both *really* men; humanity is *realized* in each. To deny this common, or universal, feature would be to deny what I mean. Ideas, in their formal, essential, general, or universal aspects, have real content, but not in the extreme sense spoken of by Plato. Likewise, abstractions like justice and honesty have objective content because they refer to individual acts that have a moral character in common.

The history of philosophy shows the reemergence of this same issue, although in various forms: in the Middle Ages in the controversy between realism and nominalism, in the context of seventeenth-century rationalism and empiricism, and in the recent problem of what makes scientific knowledge possible.

Plato's insistence on the superiority of permanence, unchange, the formal, the essential, the intellectualist comes down with special force on another problem, that of the relationship between soul and body. It is clear that the body of man is subject to change and impermanence, so if there is a part of man not subject to change and impermanence, it must be the part that knows the unchanging and permanent; whatever knows the permanent must itself be permanent in some way; whatever knows essences must itself somehow be an essence. In man, this is the soul. Strictly speaking, then, for Plato the soul is not a "part" of man; it is the *whole* man; by nature *man is soul* only. The relationship of soul to body is not, as it would be for Aristotle, two principles metaphysically united to form one being or two vectors constituting one force; it is more like the relationship of a captain to his ship or a rider to his horse — two separate beings maintaining their distinction even while cooperating with each other. This is what is meant by *Platonic dualism*, and as a dualistic approach to man it draws with it, as the history of philosophy shows, a host of problems touching on the meaning of experience that were not directly addressed by Plato. But very much in keeping with the ethical side of his patrimony, from Pythagoras to Socrates, Plato saw man's task as freeing himself from the body. This can be done only by riveting our attention on the eternal world of Forms and acting according to its summonses. This is a duty particularly incumbent on the philosopher, the lover of wisdom, who understands the role of purification, of overcoming the weight of the body, of seeing man's eternal goal in the separation of soul from body, and in the return to the higher world in which he preexisted; in this sense, the philosopher lives day by day with his mind's eye on death, and "makes dying a profession."

The phrase *Platonic dualism*, however, refers not only to the distinction between soul and body but also to the distinction between permanent and passing, unchanging and changing, higher and lower, being and becoming, knowledge and opinion, real and not as real. This overall dualism is part of the heritage of most religious traditions because the notions of higher and lower are a fundamental reading of reality. In the West, it is woven, along with other elements from the East, into the fabric of the Christian world view and, in its extreme form, displays the remarkable trait of reappearing in particular projects of Christian piety under the rubric of matter as evil and spirit as good.

The perfection of the permanent and unchanging has special relevance for Plato in the practical realms of ethics and politics too. Here Plato, along with Socrates, tries to find what is common to all types of human action and thereby to unveil the pure form of each virtue as a guide to doing good. Inasmuch as knowledge in the highest degree is knowledge of what *is* in the highest degree — the essences in the world of Ideas — then perfect knowledge of the Good should beget actions that are good; if it does not, our knowledge is not yet perfect: perfect knowledge means perfect virtue. But in this, our embodied life, such knowledge and such virtue, are not possible. Imperfection enters in because of the body and all its trappings. What the philosopher, indeed, what everyone has to do is to work at getting beyond the trappings and then to perceive the perfect by a steady, contemplative effort. In this sense, a higher degree of knowledge means a higher degree of virtue, and the rightful name of knowledge-virtue is *wisdom*.

Wisdom, however, is not a matter just for the individual; it is a matter for the entire state, which, in turn, should be governed by the highest principles. The state should somehow be the incarnation of justice, so much so that if any citizen were incapable of understanding the meaning of justice for himself, he would come to understand it by see-ing it "writ large" in the state. The shape of the state, entrusted to its rulers, is modeled after the eternal Forms; it is, therefore, as perfect as it can be in the world of human affairs, a Utopia, an Idea-1 state based on the Ideas. Plato's perception of such a state is minutely detailed; he specifies, for example, the exact number of citizens, the stratification of classes, the treatment of slaves, marriage, childrearing, and other precise features bearing on his overall purpose of showing that the state is a natural society intended for the good of man. The state exists for its citizens, not the other way around.

The proper education of potential rulers is of special concern and importance; it is to be given in particular areas and over a long period of time to allow for the candidate's development. In Plato's own words, "those who have survived the tests and approved themselves altogether the best in every task and form of knowledge must be brought at last to the goal. We shall require them to turn upward the vision of their souls and fix their gaze on that which sheds light on all, and when they have thus beheld the good itself they shall use it as a pattern for the right ordering of the state and the citizens and themselves throughout the remainder of their lives, each in his turn, devoting the greater part of their time to the study of philosophy." Much is at stake; humanity itself is at stake: "Unless either philosophers become kings in our states or those whom we call our kings and rulers take to the pursuit of phi-losophy seriously and adequately, and there is a conjunction of these two things, political power and philosophical intelligence . . . there can be no cessation of troubles for our states, nor, I fancy, for the human race either."

Readings

Doctrine of Forms (General Statement, from *Parmenides*)

Socrates, he said, your eagerness for discussion is admirable. And now tell me. Have you yourself drawn this distinction you speak of and separated apart on the one side forms themselves and on the other the things that share in them? Do you believe that there is such a thing as likeness itself apart from the likeness that we possess, and so on with unity and plurality and all the terms in Zeno's argument that you have just been listening to?

Certainly I do, said Socrates.

And also in cases like these, asked Parmenides, is there, for example, a form of rightness or of beauty or of goodness, and of all such things?

Yes.

And again, a form of man, apart from ourselves and all other men like us—a form of man as something by itself? Or a form of fire or of water?

I have often been puzzled about those things, Parmenides, whether one should say that the same thing is true in their case or not.

Are you also puzzled, Socrates, about cases that might be thought absurd, such as hair or mud or dirt or any other trivial and undignified objects? Are you doubtful whether or not to assert that each of these has a separate form distinct from things like those we handle?

Not at all, said Socrates. In these cases, the things are just the things we see; it would surely be too absurd to suppose that they have a form. All the same, I have sometimes been troubled by a doubt whether what is true in one case may not be true in all. Then, when I have reached that point, I am driven to retreat, for fear of tumbling into a bottomless pit of nonsense. Anyhow, I get back to the things which we were just now speaking of as having forms, and occupy my time with thinking about them.

That, replied Parmenides, is because you are still young, Socrates, and philosophy has not yet taken hold of you so firmly as I believe it will someday. You will not despise any of these objects then, but at present your youth makes you still pay attention to what the world will think. However that may be, tell me this. You say you hold that there exist certain forms, of which these other things come to partake and so to be called after their names; by coming to partake of likeness or largeness or beauty or justice, they become like or large or beautiful or just?

Certainly, said Socrates.

Then each thing that partakes receives as its share either the form as a whole or a part of it? Or can there be any other way of partaking besides this?

No, how could there be?

Do you hold, then, that the form as a whole, a single thing, is in each of the many, or how?

Why should it not be in each, Parmenides?

If so, a form which is one and the same will be at the same time, as a whole, in a number of things which are separate, and consequently will be separate from itself.

No, it would not, replied Socrates, if it were like one and the same day, which is in many places at the same time and nevertheless is not separate from itself. Suppose any given form is in them all at the same time as one and the same thing in that way.

I like the way you make out that one and the same thing is in many places at once, Socrates. You might as well spread a sail over a number of people and then say that the one sail as a whole was over them all. Don't you think that is a fair analogy?

Perhaps it is.

Then would the sail as a whole be over each man, or only a part over one, another part over another?

Only a part.

In that case, Socrates, the forms themselves must be divisible into parts, and the things which have a share in them will have a part for their share. Only a part of any given form, and no longer the whole of it, will be in each thing.

Evidently, on that showing.

Are you, then, prepared to assert that we shall find the single form actually being divided? Will it still be one?

Certainly not.

No, for consider this. Suppose it is largeness itself that you are going to divide into parts, and that each of the many large things is to be large by virtue of a part of largeness which is smaller than largeness itself. Will not that seem unreasonable?

It will indeed.

And again, if it is equality that a thing receives some small part of, will that part, which is less than equality itself, make its possessor equal to something else?

No, that is impossible.

Well, take smallness. Is one of us to have a portion of smallness, and is smallness to be larger than that portion, which is a part of it? On this supposition again smallness itself will be larger, and anything to which the portion taken is added will be smaller, and not larger, than it was before.

That cannot be so.

Well then, Socrates, how are the other things going to partake of your forms, if they can partake of them neither in part nor as wholes?

Really, said Socrates, it seems no easy matter to determine in any way.

Doctrine of Forms (Creation Myth, from *Timaeus*)

CRITIAS: Let me proceed to explain to you, Socrates, the order in which we have arranged our entertainment. Our intention is that Timaeus, who is the most of an astronomer among us, and has made the nature of the universe his special study, should speak first, beginning with the generation of the world and going down to the creation of man; next, I am to receive the men whom he has created, and of whom some will have profited by the excellent education which you have given them; and then, in accordance with the tale of Solon, and equally with his law, we will bring them into court and make them citizens, as if they were those very Athenians whom the sacred Egyptian record has recovered from oblivion, and thenceforward we will speak of them as Athenians and fellow citizens.

SOCRATES: I see that I shall receive in my turn a perfect and splendid feast of reason. And now, Timaeus, you, I suppose, should speak next, after duly calling upon the gods.

TIMAEUS: All men, Socrates, who have any degree of right feeling at the beginning of every enterprise, whether small or great, always call upon God. And we, too, who are going to discourse of the nature of the universe, how created or how existing without creation, if we be not altogether out of our wits, must invoke the aid of gods and goddesses and pray that our words may be above all acceptable to them and in consequence to ourselves. Let this, then, be our invocation of the gods, to which I add an exhortation of myself to speak in such manner as will be most intelligible to you, and will most accord with my own intent.

First then, in my judgment, we must make a distinction and ask, what is that which always is and has no becoming, and what is that which is always becoming and never is? That which is apprehended by intelligence and reason is always in the same state, but that which is conceived by opinion with the help of sensation and without reason is always in a process of becoming and perishing and never really is. Now everything that becomes or is created must of necessity be created by some cause, for without a cause nothing can be created. The work of the creator, whenever he looks to the unchangeable and fashions the form and nature of his work after an unchangeable pattern, must necessarily be made fair and perfect, but when he looks to the created only and uses a created pattern, it is not fair or perfect. Was the heaven then or the world, whether called by this or by any other more appropriate name—assuming the name, I am asking a question which has to be asked at the beginning of an inquiry about anything—was the world, I say, always in existence and without beginning, or created, and had it a beginning? Created, I reply, being visible and tangible and having a body, and therefore sensible, and all sensible things are apprehended by opinion and sense, and are in a process of creation and created. Now that which is created must, as we affirm, of necessity be created by a cause. But the father and maker of all this universe is past finding out, and even if we found him, to tell of him to all men would be impossible. This question, however, we must ask about the world. Which of the patterns had the artificer in view when he made it—the pattern of the unchangeable or of that which is created? If the world be indeed fair and the artificer good, it is manifest that he must have looked to that which is eternal, but if what cannot be said without blasphemy is true, then to the created pattern. Everyone will see that he must have looked to the eternal, for the world is the fairest of creations and he is the best of causes. And having been created in this way, the world has been framed in the likeness of that which is apprehended by reason and mind and is unchangeable, and must therefore of necessity, if this is admitted, be a copy of something. Now it is all-important that the beginning of everything should be according to nature. and in speaking of the copy and the original we may assume that words are akin to the matter which they describe; when they relate to the lasting and permanent and intelligible, they ought to be lasting and unalterable, and, as far as their nature allows, irrefutable and invincible—nothing less. But when they express only the copy or likeness and not the eternal things themselves, they need only be likely and analogous to the former words. As being is to becoming, so is truth to belief. If then, Socrates, amidst the many opinions about the gods and the generation of the universe, we are not able to give notions which are altogether and in every respect exact and consistent with one another, do not be surprised. Enough if we adduce probabilities as likely as any others, for we must remember that I who am the speaker and you who are the judges are only mortal men, and we ought to accept the tale which is probable and inquire no further.

SOCRATES: Excellent, Timaeus, and we will do precisely as you bid us. The prelude is charming and is already accepted by us—may we beg of you to proceed to the strain?

TIMAEUS: Let me tell you then why the creator made this world of generation. He was good, and the good can never have any jealousy of anything. And being free from jealousy, he desired that all things should be as like himself as they could be. This is in the truest sense the origin of creation and of the world, as we shall do well in believing on the testimony of wise men. God desired that all things should be good and nothing bad, so far as this was attainable. Wherefore also finding the whole visible sphere not at rest, but moving in an irregular and disorderly fashion, out of disorder he brought order, considering that this was in every way better than the other. Now the deeds of the best could never be or have been other than the fairest, and the creator, reflecting on the things which are by nature visible, found that no unintelligent creature taken as a whole could ever be fairer than the intelligent taken as a whole, and again that intelligence could not be present in anything which was devoid of soul. For which reason, when he was framing the universe, he put intelligence in soul, and soul in body, that he might be the creator of a work which was by nature fairest and best. On this wise, using the language of probability, we may say that the world came into being—a living creature truly endowed with soul and intelligence by the providence of God.

When the father and creator saw the creature which he had made moving and living, the created image of the eternal gods, he rejoiced, and in his joy determined to make the copy still more like the original, and as this was an eternal living being, he sought to make the universe eternal, so far as might be. Now the nature of the ideal being was everlasting, but to bestow this attribute in its fullness upon a creature was impossible. Wherefore he resolved to have a moving image of eternity, and when he set in order the heaven, he made this image eternal but moving according to number, while eternity itself rests in unity, and this image we call time. For there were no days and nights and months and years before the heaven was created, but when he constructed the heaven he created them also. They are all parts of time, and the past and future are created species of time, which we unconsciously but wrongly transfer to eternal being, for we say that it 'was,' or 'is,' or 'will be,' but the truth is that 'is' alone is properly attributed to it, and that 'was' and 'will be' are only to be spoken of becoming in time, for they are motions, but that which is immovably the same forever cannot become older or younger by time, nor can it be said that it came into being in the past, or has come into being now, or will come into being in the future, nor is it subject at all to any of those states which affect moving and sensible things and of which generation is the cause. These are the forms of time, which imitates eternity and revolves according to a law of number. Moreover, when we say that what has become is become and what becomes is becoming, and that what will become is about to become and that the nonexistent is nonexistent—all these are inaccurate modes of expression. But perhaps this whole subject will be more suitably discussed on some other occasion.

Knowledge: Analogy of the Cave (from *The Republic*, Book VII)

Next, said I, compare our nature in respect of education and its lack to such an experience as this. Picture men dwelling in a sort of subterranean cavern with a long entrance open to the light on its entire width. Conceive them as having their legs and necks fettered from childhood, so that they remain in the same spot, able to look forward only, and prevented by the fetters from turning their heads. Picture further the light from a fire burning higher up and at a distance behind them, and between the fire and the prisoners and above them a road along which a low wall has been built, as the exhibitors of puppet shows have partitions before the men themselves, above which they show the puppets.

All that I see, he said.

See also, then, men carrying past the wall implements of all kinds that rise above the wall, and human images and shapes of animals as well, wrought in stone and wood and every material, some of these bearers presumably speaking and others silent.

A strange image you speak of, he said, and strange prisoners.

Like to us, I said. For, to begin with, tell me do you think that these men would have seen anything of themselves or of one another except the shadows cast from the fire on the wall of the cave that fronted them?

How could they, he said, if they were compelled to hold their heads unmoved through life?

And again, would not the same be true of the objects carried past them?

Surely.

If then they were able to talk to one another, do you not think that they would suppose that in naming the things that they saw they were naming the passing objects?

Necessarily.

And if their prison had an echo from the wall opposite them, when one of the passers-by uttered a sound, do you think that they would suppose anything else than the passing shadow to be the speaker?

By Zeus, I do not, said he.

Then in every way such prisoners would deem reality to be nothing else than the shadows of the artificial objects.

Quite inevitably, he said.

Consider, then, what would be the manner of the release and healing from these bonds and this folly if in the course of nature something of this sort should happen to them. When one was freed from his fetters and compelled to stand up suddenly and turn his head around and walk and to lift up his eyes to the light, and in doing all this felt pain and, because of the dazzle and glitter of the light, was unable to discern the objects whose shadows he formerly saw, what do you suppose would be his answer if someone told him that what he had seen before was all a cheat and an illusion, but that now, being nearer to reality and turned toward more real things, he saw more truly? And if also one should point out to him each of the passing objects and constrain him by questions to say what it is, do you not think that he would be at a loss and that he would regard what he formerly saw as more real than the things now pointed out to him?

Far more real, he said.

And if he were compelled to look at the light itself, would not that pain his eyes, and would he not turn away and flee to those things which he is able to discern and regard them as in very deed more clear and exact than the objects pointed out?

It is so, he said.

And if, said I, someone should drag him thence by force up the ascent which is rough and steep, and not let him go before he had drawn him out into the light of the sun, do you not think that he would find it painful to be so haled along, and would chafe at it, and when he came out into the light, that his eyes would be filled with its beams so that he would not be able to see even one of the things that we call real?

Why, no, not immediately, he said.

Then there would be need of habituation, I take it, to enable him to see the things higher up. And at first he would most easily discern the shadows and, after that, the likenesses or reflections in water of men and other things, and later, the things themselves, and from these he would go on to contemplate the appearances in the heavens and heaven itself, more easily by night, looking at the light of the stars and the moon, than by day the sun and the sun's light.

Of course.

And so, finally, I suppose, he would be able to look upon the sun itself and see its true nature, not by reflections in water or phantasms of it in an alien setting, but in and by itself in its own place.

Necessarily, he said.

This image then, dear Glaucon, we must apply as a whole to all that has been said, likening the region revealed through sight to the habitation of the prison, and the light of the fire in it to the power of the sun. And if you assume that the ascent and the contemplation of the things above is the soul's ascension to the intelligible region, you will not miss my surmise, since that is what you desire to hear. But Gods knows whether it is true. But, at any rate, my dream as it appears to me is that in the region of the known the last thing to be seen and hardly seen is the idea of good, and that when seen it must needs point us to the conclusion that this is indeed the cause for all things of all that is right and beautiful, giving birth in the visible world to light, and the author of light and itself in the intelligible world being the authentic source of truth and reason, and that anyone who is to act wisely in private or public must have caught sight of this.

I concur, he said, so far as I am able.

Come then, I said, and join me in this further thought, and do not be surprised that those who have attained to this height are not willing to occupy themselves with the affairs of men, but their souls ever feel the upward urge and the yearning for that sojourn above. For this, I take it, is likely if in this point too the likeness of our image holds.

Knowledge: The Divided Line (from The Republic, Book VI)

Apply this comparison to the soul also in this way. When it is firmly fixed on the domain where truth and reality shine resplendent it apprehends and knows them and appears to possess reason, but when it inclines to that region which is mingled with darkness, the world of becoming and passing away, it opines only and its edge is blunted, and it shifts its opinions hither and thither, and again seems as if it lacked reason. . . . You surely apprehend the two types, the visible and the intelligible.

I do.

Represent them then, as it were, by a line divided into two unequal sections and cut each section again in the same ratio—the section, that is, of the visible and that of the intelligible order—and then as an expression of the ratio of their comparative clearness and obscurity you will have, as one of the sections of the visible world, images. By images I mean, first, shadows, and then reflections in water and on surfaces of dense, smooth, and bright texture, and everything of that kind, if you apprehend.

I do.

As the second section assume that of which this is a likeness or an image, that is, the animals about us and all plants and the whole class of objects made by man.

I so assume it, he said.

Would you be willing to say, said I, that the division in respect of reality and truth or the opposite is expressed by the proportion—as is the opinable to the knowable so is the likeness to that of which it is a likeness?

I certainly would.

Consider then again the way in which we are to make the division of the intelligible section.

In what way?

By the distinction that there is one section of it which the soul is compelled to investigate by treating as images the things imitated in the former division, and by means of assumptions from which it proceeds not up to a first principle but down to a conclusion, while there is another section in which it advances from its assumption to a beginning or principle that transcends assumption, and in which it makes no use of the images employed by the other section, relying on ideas only and progressing systematically through ideas.

I don't fully understand what you mean by this, he said.

Well, I will try again, said I, for you will better understand after this preamble. For I think you are aware that students of geometry and reckoning and such subjects first postulate the odd and the even and the various figures and three kinds of angles and other things akin to these in each branch of science, regard them as known, and, treating them as absolute assumptions, do not deign to render any further account of them to themselves or others, taking it for granted that they are obvious to everybody. They take their start from these, and pursuing the inquiry from this point on consistently, conclude with that for the investigation of which they set out.

Certainly, he said, I know that.

And do you not also know that they further make use of the visible forms and talk about them, though they are not thinking of them but of those things of which they are a likeness, pursuing their inquiry for the sake of the square as such and the diagonal as such, and not for the sake of the image of it which they draw? And so in all cases. The very things which they mold and draw, which have shadows and images of themselves in water, these things they treat in their turn as only images, but what they really seek is to get sight of those realities which can be seen only by the mind.

True, he said.

This then is the class that I described as intelligible, it is true, but with the reservation first that the soul is compelled to employ assumptions in the investigation of it, not proceeding to a first principle because of its inability to extricate itself from and rise above its assumptions, and second, that it uses as images or likenesses the very objects that are themselves copied and adumbrated by the class below them, and that in comparison with these latter are esteemed as clear and held in honor.

I understand, said he, that you are speaking of what falls under geometry and the kindred arts.

Understand then, said I, that by the other section of the intelligible I mean that which the reason itself lays hold of by the power of dialectic, treating its assumptions not as absolute beginnings but literally as hypotheses, underpinnings, footings, and springboards so to speak, to enable it to rise to that which requires no assumption and is the starting point of all, and after attaining to that again taking hold of the first dependencies from it, so to proceed downward to the conclusion, making no use whatever of any object of sense but only of pure ideas moving on through ideas to ideas and ending with ideas.

I understand, he said, not fully, for it is no slight task that you appear to have in mind, but I do understand that you mean to distinguish the aspect of reality and the intelligible, which is contemplated by the power of dialectic, as something truer and more exact than the object of the so-called arts and sciences whose assumptions are arbitrary starting points. And though it is true that those who contemplate them are compelled to use their understanding and not their senses, yet because they do not go back to the beginning in the study of them but start from assumptions you do not think they possess true intelligence about them although the things themselves are intelligibles when apprehended in conjunction with a first principle. And I think you call the mental habit of geometers and their like mind or understanding and not reason because you regard understanding as something intermediate between opinion and reason.

Your interpretation is quite sufficient, I said. And now, answering to these four sections, assume these four affections occurring in the soul—intellection or reason for the highest, understanding for the second, belief for the third, and for the last, picture thinking or conjecture—and arrange them in a proportion, considering that they participate in clearness and precision in the same degree as their objects partake of truth and reality.

I understand, he said. I concur and arrange them as you bid.

(From *Plato: The Republic*, translated by Paul Shorey, Loeb Classical Library. Cambridge MA: Harvard University Press, 1953.)

Virtue and the Highest Good (from *Laws,* Book IV)

ATHENIAN: My friends!—this is what I would say to them—God, who, as the old saw has it, holds in his hands beginning, end, and middle of all that is, moves through the cycle of nature, straight to his end, and ever at his side walks right, the justicer of them that forsake God's law. He that would be happy follows close in her train with lowly and chastened mien, but whoso is lifted up with vanity—with pride of riches or rank or foolish conceit of youthful comeliness—and all on fire within with wantonness, as one that needs neither governor nor guide, but is fitted rather to be himself a guide to others—such a one is left alone, forsaken of God. In his abandonment he takes to him others like himself, and works general confusion by his frantic career. Now to some he seems to be some great one, but after no long while he makes no stinted amend to right by the sheer ruin of himself, his house, and his state. Now since these things are so, what must the man of judgment do or purpose, and what forbear?

CLINIAS: So much is plain; every man must purpose to be of the company who follow after the god.

ATHENIAN: What line of conduct, then, is dear to God and a following of him? There is but one, and it is summed up in one ancient rule, the rule that 'like'—when it is a thing of due measure—'loves its like.' For things that have no measure can be loved neither by one another nor by those that have. Now it is God who is, for you and me, of a truth the 'measure of all things,' much more truly than, as they say, 'man.' So he who would be loved by such a being must himself become such to the utmost of his might, and so, by this argument, he that is temperate among us is loved by God, for he is like God, whereas he that is not temperate is unlike God and at variance with him; so also it is with the unjust, and the same rule holds in all else. Now from this rule, I would have you note, follows another—of all rules, to my mind, the grandest and truest, which is this. For the good man 'tis most glorious and good and profitable to happiness of life, aye, and most excellently fit, to do sacrifice and be ever in communion with heaven through prayer and offerings and all manner of worship, but for the evil, entirely the contrary. For the evil man is impure of soul, where the other is pure, and from the polluted neither good men nor God may ever rightly accept a gift; thus all this toil taken with heaven is but labor thrown away for the impious, though ever seasonable in the pious.

Here, then, is the target at which we have to aim, but what shall we call the shafts which make straight for it, and the engine from which they are fired? Well, first, I say, the mark of godliness will be truly hit if the gods of the lower world are held in honor next to the Olympians, and the patron deities of the state, the even, the second best, and the left hand being consecrated to them, their superior counterparts to the powers which have just been named. After these gods a man of judgment will do worship to spirits, and after them to heroes, and I would give the next place to each man's images of his household gods, worshiped as the law directs.

And now we come to honor to be shown to parents while they are yet in life. Here religion demands the due discharge of this earliest and heaviest debt, the most sacred of all our obligations. It bids a man count all he has and owns at the service of those who gave him birth and breeding, to minister to their needs to his utmost ability, first with his substance, then with his body, and then with his mind, in repayment of a loan of care and painful labor made so long ago on the security of his youth, and now to be made good to his elders in their age and sore necessity. Moreover, all his life through, a man should observe particular reverence of tongue toward his parents, for light and winged speech brings heavy doom; right has her appointed messenger, Nemesis, to keep watch over the matter. So one should yield to them when they feel anger, and discharge it, in word or deed, and understand that 'tis but natural in a father who thinks himself wronged by his son to be moved to uncommon anger. But when parents are once no more, the most modest burial is the best. A man should not exceed the customary pomps, nor yet come short of those wherewith his forefathers were wont to entomb their own sires; he should keep also to the same rule in paying the decent annual rites of tendance to the departed. Above all, he should honor the deceased at all times by keeping the memory of them green, while he expends on them what is proportionate to the means fortune permits him. If we act thus and frame our lives to this model, we shall, one and all, always reap the due reward from heaven and the higher powers, and our days, for the main of life, will be passed with bright hopes. As regards duties to children and kinsmen, friends and fellow citizens, as well as works of pious service to strangers, and our relations with them all, by discharge whereof, as the law enjoins, a man should adorn and illustrate his life—in all this the actual recital of the laws will, with heaven's consent, ensure our society bliss and well-being, in part by persuasion, and in part by enforced and legal correction of characters not amenable to persuasion.

(From *Laws*. Trans. A.E. Taylor. London: J.M. Dent & Sons Ltd. Publishers, 1934. Reprinted by permission of J.M. Dent.)

The Philosopher-King (Epistle VII)

Next, it seems, we must try to discover and point out what it is that is now badly managed in our cities, and that prevents them from being so governed, and what is the smallest change that would bring a state to this manner of government, preferably a change in one thing, if not, then in two, and, failing that, the fewest possible in number and the slightest in potency.

By all means, he said.

There is one change, then, said I, which I think that we can show would bring about the desired transformation. It is not a slight or an easy thing but it is possible.

What is that? said he.

I am on the very verge, said I, of what we likened to the greatest wave of paradox. But say it I will, even if, to keep the figure, it is likely to wash us away on billows of laughter and scorn. Listen.

I am all attention, he said.

Unless, said I, either philosophers become kings in our states or those whom we now call our kings and rulers take to the pursuit of philosophy seriously and adequately, and there is a conjunction of these two things, political power and philosophical intelligence, while the motley horde of the natures who at present pursue either apart from the other are compulsorily excluded, there can be no cessation of troubles, dear Glaucon, for our states, nor, I fancy, for the human race either. Nor, until this happens, will this constitution which we have been expounding in theory ever be put into practice within the limits of possibility and see the light of the sun. But this is the thing that has made me so long shrink from speaking out, because I saw that it would be a very paradoxical saying. For it is not easy to see that there is no other way of happiness either for private or public life.

Now as I considered these matters, as well as the sort of men who were active in politics, and the laws and the customs, the more I examined them and the more I advanced in years, the harder it appeared to me to administer the government correctly. For one thing, nothing could be done without friends and loyal companions, and such men were not easy to find ready at hand, since our city was no longer administered according to the standards and practices of our fathers. Neither could such men be created afresh with any facility. Furthermore the written law and the customs were being corrupted at an astounding rate. The result was that I, who had at first been full of eagerness for a public career, as I gazed upon the whirlpool of public life and saw the incessant movement of shifting currents, at last felt dizzy, and, while I did not cease to consider means of improving this particular situation and indeed of reforming the whole constitution, yet, in regard to action, I kept waiting for favorable moments, and finally saw clearly in regard to all states now existing that without exception their system of government is bad. Their constitutions are almost beyond redemption except through some miraculous plan accompanied by good luck. Hence I was forced to say in praise of the correct philosophy that it affords a vantage point from which we can discern in all cases what is just for communities and for individuals, and that accordingly the human race will not see better days until either the stock of those who rightly and genuinely follow philosophy acquire political authority, or else the class who have political control be led by some dispensation of providence to become real philosophers.

This conviction I held when I reached Italy and Sicily on my first visit. Upon my arrival, moreover, I found myself utterly at odds with the sort of life that is there termed a happy one, a life taken up with Italian and Syracusan banquets, an existence that consists in filling oneself up twice a day, never sleeping alone at night, and indulging in all the practices attendant on that way of living. In such an environment no man under heaven, brought up in self-indulgence, could ever grow to be wise. So marvelous a temperament as that is not in nature. That a man should grow up sober-minded would also be quite out of the question, and one might make the same statement about the other qualities that go to make up excellence of character. Neither can a city be free from unrest under any laws, be those laws what they may, while its citizens think fit to spend everything on excesses, meanwhile making it a rule, however, to avoid all industry except such as is devoted to banquets and drinking bouts and painstaking attention to the gratification of lust. It is inevitable that in such cities there should be an unending succession of governments—tyranny, oligarchy, democracy—one after another, while the very name of just and equal government is anathema to those in control.

Now holding this conviction in addition to the former, I traveled on to Syracuse. Perhaps it was chance, but certainly it looks as if a higher power was at that time contriving to lay a foundation for the recent events in which Dion and the city of Syracuse were concerned, for more too, I fear, unless you now follow the advice I am giving you the second time. But what can I mean when I say that my visit to Syracuse at that time was the beginning of everything? In my intercourse at that time with the young Dion, as I set before him in theory my ideals for mankind and advised him to make them effective in practice, I seem to have been unaware that I was in a way contriving, all unknown to myself, a future downfall of tyranny. At any rate Dion, who was very quick of apprehension and especially so in regard to my instruction on this occasion, responded to it more keenly and more enthusiastically than any other young man I ever met, and resolved to live for the remainder of his life differently from most of the Greeks in Italy and Sicily, holding virtue dearer than pleasure or than luxury.

(From *Thirteen Epistles of Plato*, trans. by L. A. Post. Oxford: Oxford University Press, 1925. Reprinted by Permission of Oxford University Press.)

Review Questions

1. What are Plato's reasons for holding that a world of ideas, separate from this world, exists?
2. Explain the difference between truth and illusion in Plato's epistemology.
3. Why do both Plato and Socrates describe learning as a process of recollection?
4. Explain what is meant by Platonic dualism. How does this concept apply to human nature?
5. What is the meaning of creation for Plato? Of participation?
6. What is the role of civil society for Plato?

4

Aristotle (384–322 B.C.)

Introduction

Aristotle was born in Stagira, a town that lay between Thrace and Macedonia, in 384 B.C. He was the son of a physician, and because his father was a friend of the king of Macedonia, he lived at the royal court and shared its cultural life and social status. He acquired an interest in the art of medicine and dissection from his father, who no doubt laid down a firm basis for his son's scientific bent and lifelong sense of careful observation. Orphaned as a boy, and now growing into young manhood, Aristotle went to Athens at the age of seventeen to enroll at the Academy, where his guardians knew he would get the best education available in Greece.

Though we have no detailed reports on the relationship between teacher and student, we know Aristotle respected and admired Plato, with whom he lived for twenty years, until the time of Plato's death. His experience at the Academy was an exercise in friendship as well as in learning, for Plato was, to him, not only a revered philosopher but also a friend. In his writings, Aristotle's regard for Plato is shown at every turn, even while he is criticizing his master's views. In a famous passage, in which he feels obliged to reject the doctrine of Ideas, he acknowledges that it was introduced by friends of his, yet "it would perhaps be thought to be better, indeed to be our duty, for the sake of maintaining the truth even to destroy what touches us closely, especially as we are philosophers or lovers of wisdom; for, while both are dear, piety requires us to honour truth above our friends."

After Plato's death, Aristotle left Athens for Assos, a town on the northern coast of present-day Turkey, probably having been invited there by Hermias, a former fellow student at the Academy; he had risen from the status of slave to king and was still committed to the ideal of politician-philosopher. From the island of Lesbos, where he had gone after Assos, Aristotle was requested by King Philip of Macedon to become the tutor of his thirteen-year-old son, Alexander, later known as Alexander the Great. Aristotle stayed at the court for eight years, until Alexander became the ruler of Macedonia after the assassination of his father in 336. During these years, Aristotle's interest in biology was heightened; he spent endless hours in the collection and study of marine life while at the seacoast, and to the flora and fauna of Macedonia.

He returned to Athens in 335–34 to begin the most productive period of his life. He established a school, just to the northeast of Athens, at a place with buildings and gardens called the *Lyceum*, after the god Apollo, one of whose titles was Lyceus. The spot was mentioned by Plato as the favorite haunt of Socrates. At the Lyceum the pattern of the Academy was duplicated — a close community, friendly, intent on learning, given to much dialogue particularly while strolling along the garden path, the *peripatos*, whence the followers of Aristotle were called *Peripatetics*. Aristotle amassed an invaluable collection of manuscripts for the school's library, which became the exemplar for subsequent great libraries of the West, especially that of Alexandria. Many of Aristotle's writings, done before the founding of the Lyceum, have been lost, but most of his extant writings were completed there. His numerous writings include treatises on logic (*Categories, Prior and Posterior Analytics*), physical treatises (*Physics, On the Heavens, On the Soul*), the *Metaphysics*, moral and political treatises (*Nicomachean Ethics, Politics*), and the *Rhetoric* and *Poetics*.

When Alexander the Great died in 323 a strong anti-Macedonian feeling arose in Athens, and because he was known to have had long-standing Macedonian ties, Aristotle, fearing a false charge of "impiety," left Athens so that, in his words, the Athenians would not "sin twice against philosophy." He went to Chalcis, his mother's native city, where he died in 322.

In his thought, Aristotle was agile, well balanced, and unprejudiced; his first approach was to let things speak for themselves. We saw earlier the danger of labeling any philosopher as a rationalist or an empiricist. For the former, the process of knowing moves from the mind to things, as though, by examining the mind, we know what things are; for the latter, the process of knowing moves from things to the mind; the mind, that is, knows only what things tell it. Philosophers often emphasize one direction over the other. In this sense, Plato favored the rationalist, spiritualist, mathematical, universal side, whereas Aristotle favored the empirical, experiential, individual side. His scientific bent would not allow him to depart from the evidence: we learn what human beings are by observing what they do; we learn rhetoric by hearing persuasive people speak; we learn the habits of animals by watching them in action; we learn the rules of correct thinking by studying ourselves thinking correctly.

Perhaps as good an example as any of Aristotle's systematic, thorough work is his treatises on logic, known collectively as the *Organon*, which are traditionally grouped together and presented first in the body of his works. Granted that there are many truths we know directly, such as things we know by experience (e.g., the stove is hot, I want to sit down) or by intuition (e.g., the whole is greater than any of its parts; whatever is wrong ought not be done), there are many other truths we know indirectly, among which are those we arrive at by argumentation, that is, by *reasoning*, the process whereby we go from what we know to what we do not know. To reason correctly is a prime requisite for a thinker, and the study of correct thinking, generally called *logic* today but called *analytic* by Aristotle, is an indispensable tool for making headway in any branch of knowledge. The purpose of logic is to investigate the *form* reasoning takes when we pass from "certain things being stated" (called *premises*) to "something other than what is stated" (called a *conclusion*), which follows of necessity. Logic, then, deals with *words* and *propositions* with which reasoning, in the form of a *syllogism*, is expressed; to these factors Aristotle gives detailed consideration.

Basically, a word (or term) is a symbol: "Spoken words are the symbols of mental experience and written words are the symbols of spoken words." There are two major divisions of terms, among many made by Aristotle: a division into univocal and equivocal, and into universal and particular. A term is *univocal* if it is used in several sentences with the same meaning. In the sentences "Man is an animal" and "An ox is an animal," the word *animal* is used with the same meaning. In the sentences "The riverside is a bank" and "The savings institution is a bank," the word *bank* is used in different senses and is therefore *equivocal*. A term is *universal* when it refers to all the members of a class, as in "all men" or, negatively, "no man." But a term is *particular* when it does not refer to all members of a class, as in "some men," which indicates its less than universal usage. It should be clear that the precise meaning of the term comes from the way it is actually used in a sentence.

Terms are used in propositions, which are sentences affirming or denying one thing or another. Propositions, like terms, are universal or particular: universal if the predicate refers to all the members of a class, as in "All men are wise"; particular if it refers only to some, as in "Some men are wise." They are affirmative if they affirm the predicate of the subject, negative if they deny it. Two propositions having the same subject and predicate can differ from each other in a number of ways; the difference is called *opposition*. The principal kind of opposition is called *contradiction*, wherein the difference is so strong that the two propositions cannot be both true and false at the same time: "All men are wise" and "Some men are not wise" cannot both be true or false together.

The syllogism is the heart of Aristotelian logic, and "it belongs to the philosopher, i.e. to him who is studying the nature of all substance, to inquire also into the principles of syllogism." The syllogism helps the philosopher extend his knowledge because it makes explicit what was implicit in the premises. If premises are given as true, then the conclusion necessarily follows as true; for example, if "All Athenians are Greek" and "Some philosophers are Athenians," then it is necessarily true that "Some philosophers are Greek." There are three terms in the premises, which yield only two in the conclusion, because one term (Athenians) is the "middle" term against which the others are measured and is excluded in the conclusion. The kind of reasoning expressed in the syllogism is known as *deductive* reasoning, inasmuch as it moves from the general to the particular (or less general).

There is a second kind of reasoning, called *inductive*, to which Aristotle did not give the same thorough examination as he gave to deductive reasoning; broadly speaking, induction moves from the particular to the universal: "Induction is a passage from individuals to universals." How this movement takes place depends, it seems, upon the context in which the particular–universal relationship arises: a different configuration, or status, of particulars gives rise to a different kind of particular–universal relationship. For example, you can simply enumerate every case and then collect them in a universal statement by saying "All." Or, on seeing one three–sided plane figure called a *triangle*, you can state that "All triangles are three-sided" because you have grasped the nature of the triangle and expressed it in its definition. When Aristotle avers that there is no induction without sense perception, he perhaps comes close to the modern notion that induction is the approach of the natural sciences in that generalizations are based on positive observation, because somehow the universal "is elicited from the several groups of singulars." If you drop zinc into acid, a chemical reaction takes place, and this happens a second and a third time, you have no doubt that it will happen again and always; that is, you have scientific certitude.

Aristotle's works on logic represent a tremendous effort to analyze how the human mind proceeds in doing logical thinking; it is all the more astonishing when we realize that he had no predecessors in logic. Indeed, he was aware of breaking new ground; whereas in other areas of knowledge one builds on previous contributions, in this case there were none: "Of this inquiry, on the other hand, it was not the case that part of the work had been thoroughly done before, while part had not. Nothing existed at all." Once the work was begun, however, and the foundation laid, Aristotle would have been the first to applaud the complements to his logic provided by the later Greek Stoics, by the logicians of the Middle Ages, and by modern logicians using symbolic logic. The very last sentence of his logical treatises captures both his confidence and his humility: if after inspecting the work and finding it satisfactory, he says, "there must remain for all of you, or for our students, the task of extending us your pardon for the shortcomings of the inquiry, and for the discoveries thereof your warm thanks."

If logic is the instrument for philosophical thinking, what the philosopher thinks about is the main concern, and for Aristotle, at the very center of his thought is the question of *being*. The word *metaphysics*, traditionally used to designate the philosophy of being, was not supplied by Aristotle but probably by his later disciples, although, according to a widely held story, despite its unreliability, it was supplied by an ancient cataloguer, thought to be Andronicus of Rhodes in the first century B.C., who, in assembling the works of Aristotle, placed an untitled work after the *Physics* and simply called it the "Work After the Physics" (in Greek, *meta-ta-physica*), or *Metaphysics*. In any case, metaphysics is the science which goes "beyond physics" because it goes beyond what is given in sense experience; it reaches to what is highest, separated from matter, divine, whence Aristotle is prompted to call this kind of inquiry "wisdom," or "first philosophy," or even "theology." Aristotle further defines metaphysics as the study that "investigates being as being and the attributes which belong to this in virtue of its own nature." The object of metaphysics, then, is *being as being* or *being as such*. These phrases seem rather awkward at first, but what they mean is that among all the characteristics of a thing, there is one without which none of the others would be possible: its existence. It would be a strange commentary indeed if all the other characteristics of a thing were inquired into, but not this one.

Metaphysics then raises questions like these: Why do things exist, rather than not exist? What is there about the nature of being that allows it to change? Are things caused? What does causality mean? Why are there many things? Or are they really one? Do things have to be? If so, why? Why are some things independent, others not? Is there a being so necessary that without it nothing else would be? Questions like these are the staple of traditional metaphysics, and they are so basic that they form the philosopher's primary orientation, often leading to an entirely new world view, as in the case of Spinoza, Hegel, Bergson, and Whitehead. There is a strong human need for unity, a natural tendency to look for patterns drawing things together. The scientist looks for laws governing discrete phenomena. The economist searches for the causes controlling the ebb and flow of economic well-being. The conductor tries to orchestrate disparate sounds into harmony. The reasonable person wants his actions to express a coherent life. The metaphysician, too, faced with the dizzying plurality of things in reality, is eager to find out why we call them by a common name, *being*.

The analysis of being seems doomed to frustration because it involves, at the very outset, the investigation of truth and the difficulties

attached thereto; in Aristotle's words: "The investigation of the truth
is in one way hard, in another easy. An indication of this is found in
the fact that no one is able to attain the truth adequately, while, on the
other hand, we do not collectively fail. ... Therefore, since the truth
seems to be like the proverbial door, which no one can fail to hit, in
this respect it must be easy, but the fact that we can have a whole
truth and not the particular part we aim at shows the difficulty of it."

At stake here is the fundamental question, what does our knowledge
refer to, to be called *truth*? There is no doubt that, for Aristotle, truth
is the name we give to the relationship between our intellect and what
the intellect considers, between knowing and what is known, between
knowledge and reality. In Aristotelian terms, we do not know a truth
unless we know its cause; and what a thing *is*, its very *being*, is the
cause of our knowing it, that is, the cause of truth: "as each thing is in
respect of being, so it is in respect of truth." This statement underscores Aristotle's doctrine that whatever is, is knowable, and therefore
"the soul is in a way all things" — not that the soul knows everything,
but that the soul, in knowing "being," knows "Being."

Immediately following our knowledge of being comes our knowledge
of not-being: when we know that a thing is, we also know that it cannot
not be. What Aristotle said in logic, that contradictory propositions
cannot both be true and cannot both be false, is said here with regard
to being itself: there is no intermediary, no middle ground, between being and nonbeing; is and is not, being and nonbeing, be-ing and not being are mutually exclusive; in this respect, Aristotle certainly agrees
with Parmenides. When Aristotle writes, "To say of what is that it is
not, or of what is not that it is, is false," he is stating what, for him,
is the most basic truth of metaphysics, for without it no other truth
would be possible, no judgment would stand because affirmation and
negation would have the same meaning. In later centuries this principle would be referred to as the *principle of contradiction*, or better,
the *principle of noncontradiction*.

In early Greek philosophy, we should recall, Parmenides was so overwhelmed by the nature of being (permanence, stability) that anything
hinting at nonbeing was under suspicion. Heraclitus, on the other
hand, saw a universe on the move and tried to avoid any notion of reality that would make it static; in that sense, being was under suspicion.
These two positions represent historical extremes in reaction to a phenomenon as immediate to us as it was to them, the *phenomenon of
change*.

After Plato's effort to resolve reality into the changing and the
changeless, Aristotle took his turn, in facing the problem of change. He
never thought that change was something to get around, as though it
were unreal or stood in the way of knowing reality. Rather, it was the

high road for getting to the heart of things. Every change, however slight, reveals some facet of the way a thing *is*, for a thing must *be* such as to allow the change to take place. In the broadest terms, a thing ready to undergo a change is not yet what it will become: the marble, ready to become a statue, is still a chunk; the boy, ready to become a man, is still a boy; the arrow, ready to hit the target, is still in the bow; the unknowing intellect, ready to know, is still unknowing. What the thing becomes, it is not now; it would be a contradiction to state that a thing is what it will become, for then it would both be and not be at the same time. The marble cannot be both a chunk and a statute at the same time; nor the boy both a boy and a man; nor the arrow both in the target and in the bow; nor the intellect both unknowing and knowing.

Yet no change would occur *in the thing* unless the thing was of such a nature as to permit it; in other words, there must be some factors or principles within the thing to allow for the change. Although the principles involved vary according to the kind of change involved, in general they can be referred to as the *principle of actuality* and the *principle of potentiality*, or the *actual principle* and the *potential principle*, or simply, *act* and *potency*. They are the counterparts of each other in such a way that act imparts to potency all the concrete determinations found in a given being; act "perfects" potency. As applied to physical things, Aristotle calls these principles *form* (act) and *matter* (potency), whence his teaching on this subject is called the *hylomorphic* doctrine, from the Greek words *hyle* (matter) and *morphe* (form). Matter, with no innate determination, has its actuality in a being precisely because it is determined by form, as the actualizing principle, to be this individual: "by matter I mean that which, not being a 'this' actually, is potentially a 'this.'"

Another aspect of being whose existence is confirmed in the phenomenon of change is that of *substance*. Substance is the factor that continues to exist in a changing thing while other factors like shape, color, movement, and health cease to exist. It has therefore a permanence, a relatively independent existence, and a primary claim on the meaning of being. This claim is another fundamental concept in the history of philosophy. For Plato, as an example, the changing nature of this world required the unchanging nature of the world of ideas as the true substance of the real. St. Thomas saw in substance the primary reality that, if destroyed, would destroy all reality as well. The notion of independence of substance, renewed in modern times by Descartes, was brought to its apex by Spinoza, for whom substance is that which *is* in itself and *conceived* through itself, and is therefore applicable only to all of reality taken as a whole. In later times, substance suffered a setback in the attack on metaphysics, first advanced by Locke and Berkeley, and then propounded by Hume, who set the pace for the empirical tradition, in which substance is either passed over or denied entirely as outside our experience.

But for Aristotle, substance is knowable in and through *accidents*, or *qualities*, such as shape, color, movement, and health, which do not exist on their own but *in* that which is shaped, colored, moving, healthy—namely, substance. The word *substance* has had a varied career, but as used here it is of later Latin coinage and means literally "that which stands under," that is, under the changing factors, under the accidents. So, relative to substance, accidents are knowable inasmuch as they exist in something else; and substance, relative to accidents, is knowable inasmuch as it exists on its own and is therefore the prime reason for designating a thing as an individual entity. As Aristotle writes: "'white' is accidental to man, because though he is white, whiteness is not his essence. But if *all* statements are accidental, there will be nothing primary about which they are made. . . . There must be something which denotes substance." It is this fact that separates the ingrained empiricist from the metaphysician: the empiricist holds that shape, color, movement, and health are knowable in themselves and do not lead to any further conclusion; the metaphysician, beginning with these qualities, insists that they are knowable indeed, but *as existing in something else*, called substance.

Substance of a special kind exists in *living* things, in which the principles of form and matter are called *soul* and *body*. The living thing is an organism, that is, a body organized to live, but its life does not come about because it is a body — there are many things made of matter that are not alive. Since, however, the body is living, its life must come about because of another principle, called *soul*, which enlivens it: "the soul is the . . . actuality of a natural body having life potentially within it. The body so described is a body which is organized." Whence Aristotle refers to living things as *besouled*, or *animate* (*anima*, Latin for soul; therefore *animal*).

In applying this principle to man, we can see not only how original was Aristotle's view on the nature of man but also how radically different it was from Plato's and from the tradition behind him. For Aristotle, soul and body are not separate entities in man, but correlative constituents of *one* being; man is neither body alone nor soul alone, but a single substance composed of both. The unity of man is a matter of experience and common sense, which is "why we can wholly dismiss as unnecessary the question of whether the soul and body are one." Aristotle's view, that man is a unitary being composed of body and soul, and Plato's view, that man is spirit only, embody the profound difference between two opposing traditions on the definition of man for centuries to come. This difference generates far-reaching consequences in the way we understand the deliverances of the senses, our inward experience, knowledge, the approach we take toward mental health or psychosomatic medicine, and our attitude toward pain, suffering, and the social ills of this world. The problem of body and soul is another classical problem in the history of philosophy.

Let us return once more to the phenomenon of change, for change involves other considerations with regard to being. If we see a marble statue, in our mind is the vision of the chunk from which it came, and we ask who made it. Or if we see the stones at Stonehenge, large and mysteriously arranged, we ask how this arrangement came about. Or, in this age of environmental concerns, we ask what causes acid rain. These questions arise naturally because they seem to follow the natural expectation that something traditionally called *causality* is at work.

It takes a great effort to dampen that expectation, but it has been done. Parmenides, we will recall, led the way for those who would not countenance the reality of change because it would have meant a coming-to-be from not-being, which was, they maintained, impossible. The problem here, as Aristotle avers, is very difficult, but it is not solved by either wishing it away or giving up. As he sees it, it was by failing to make the proper qualification that "these thinkers gave the matter up . . . thus doing away with all becoming." Aristotle himself solves the problem by going about it another way; he does not begin a priori, but from the *experienced* fact that change *does* occur. He does not say that because change is unthinkable, it does not take place; rather, change does take place, therefore it can. In terms we have previously discussed, whatever changes had the potentiality (potency) within itself to become what it was not; therefore, potency must be a constitutive factor within it. Aristotle does not disagree in absolute terms with those who deny change but rather in qualified terms: "We ourselves are in agreement with them in holding that nothing can be said without qualification to come from what is not. But nevertheless we maintain that a thing may 'come to be from what is not' — that is, in a qualified sense."

It follows that whatever comes to be cannot be now and therefore must be brought about: it is the "bluing" of the red litmus paper that, as the coming-to-be in question, must be brought about. It is brought about by that which is called *cause* in reference to the coming-to-be called *effect*. Any coming-to-be requires a cause; one of the meanings of cause, Aristotle states, is that "from which the change or the resting from change first begins . . . in general the maker [is] a cause of the thing made and the change-producing of the changing." So the connection between cause and effect is inherent in the very nature of being; it is a necessary connection that, for Aristotle, is at the center of metaphysics. Centuries later, David Hume would prove right in holding that the undoing of the principle of causality entails the undoing of metaphysics, which was precisely the consequence of his insistence on a chronological or temporal conjunction between cause and effect rather than a necessary conjunction between them. Aristotle's view, in contrast to Hume's, is that chronology is simply a calendar and of itself supplies no explanation for the change taking place. However, once we establish the causal order, the chronology makes sense.

Aristotle calls for four different kinds, of causes, inasmuch as there are four different kinds of connection between cause and effect: material, formal, efficient, and final. The material cause is the matter from which a thing comes into being; the formal cause is the determining factor; the efficient cause is that which, by its activity, brings about a change; the final cause is the purpose, or end, "for the sake of which a thing is." A simple example will illustrate: the marble is the material cause of the statue; the formal cause is the shape the marble takes; the efficient cause is the sculptor who works the marble; and the final cause is the production of a work of art. The main point here is not to enumerate the kinds of causes but to underline the fact that there can be different kinds depending on the kind of influence exerted on the coming-to-be in question.

Using the principle of causality, Aristotle is able to analyze the unity of the cosmos. It is obvious that things are not thrown together in a haphazard heap in which nothing has any relationship to anything else. An unmistakable unity is there to begin with, an orderly movement of things that accounts for their being called a *world* or a *cosmos*. The arguments Aristotle offers in the *Metaphysics* and the *Physics* complement each other regarding his well-known doctrine on the origin of motion. Given that all physical things of our experience move, no one of them can move itself; movement requires that a thing *be moved* by another. But this process of being moved by another cannot go on *ad infinitum*, so there must be a mover by whose influence all motion takes place. This is the *Prime Mover*, whose first attribute must be to move everything without itself being moved; therefore, an *unmoved* mover. But there are other attributes with which such a being must be endowed, attributes including life, activity, thought, goodness, and eternity. Book Twelve of the *Metaphysics* is the culmination of Aristotle's reflection on the kind of being the Prime Mover must be, and Chapter Seven contains the following passage: "The first mover, then, exists of necessity; and it is in this sense a first principle. ... And life also belongs to God; for the actuality of thought is life, and God is that actuality; and God's self-dependent actuality is life most good and eternal. We say therefore that God is a living being, eternal, most good, so that life and duration continuous and eternal belong to God; for this *is* God."

We are left with the question of whether or not there is a relationship between the divine being and the human being. To answer this question is the purpose of the *Nicomachean Ethics*, in which Aristotle, already disposed to think in terms of ultimates, proposes to seek an ultimate function for man: "Have the carpenter, then, and the tanner certain functions or activities,and has man none? Is he born without a function? ... What then can this be?" Aristotle focuses on human activity in its two aspects, the activity itself and the good at which it aims; he announces his project in the opening lines of the *Ethics*: "Every art and every inquiry, and similarly every action and pursuit, is thought to aim at some good; and for this reason the good has rightly been declared to be that at which all things aim."

The human activity involved is not any activity a human being is capable of, but that which is human activity at its highest point, whose proper name is virtue, and precisely moral virtue. Moral virtue, though not easy to define, focuses on the concrete actions a person performs and the measured sense he has regarding them: "to feel them at the right times, with reference to the right objects, towards the right people, with the right motive, and in the right way." A good action thus exhibits due proportion, neither excessive nor defective, but midway between them; this is Aristotle's doctrine of the *mean*. A virtuous action is one that lies between the extremes of too much and too little, excess or defect, both of which are vices; so, for example, in regard to the feeling of confidence, courage is the mean between the excess of rashness and the defect of cowardice; in regard to the feeling of shame, modesty is the mean between bashfulness and shamelessness.

Not every virtue, however, is a mean, and so not every action is to be measured in this way; but every action is to be measured — measured in its rightness by prudence or, in a larger sense, by "practical wisdom," the wisdom whose field is moral practice. Practical wisdom is the sense of governance we have in directing our free and voluntary choices to ends befitting us as human beings; it is, in Aristotle's words, "a true and reasoned state of capacity to act with regard to the things that are good or bad for men."

Good is the aim of every action but, given the fact that goods can be ordered in relation to one another, there must be a highest good to which practical wisdom directs us. And if the possession of any good is what makes us happy to some extent, the possession of the highest good is the highest happiness, the ultimate goal of all our actions. At this point there are some unclear elements in Aristotle's presentation, but this much is clear: happiness, which is the possession of the good, is ultimately an act of contemplating, or of beholding, the good; but to contemplate the good is to enter into union with it; so, if contemplating God means entering into union with the life of God, this is the highest activity of man and his ultimate happiness. The conclusion of the *Ethics* is one with the *Metaphysics*, in which the "divine element" in man coincides with the "possession" of God by an act of thought, called *contemplation*, which is the "most pleasant and best" we can perform. This is perhaps best said by Aristotle in the last lines of one of his earlier ethical works, the *Eudemian Ethics*: "What choice, then, or possession of the natural goods — whether bodily goods, wealth, friends, or other things — will most produce the contemplation of God, that choice or possession is best; this is the noblest standard, but any that through deficiency or excess hinders one from the contemplation and service of God is bad; this man possesses in his soul, and this is the best standard for the soul."

As we have seen, the golden age of Socrates, Plato, and Aristotle did not occur suddenly but was introduced by generations of earlier philosophers. Likewise, as we move toward the Christian era, we do not arrive there suddenly, but with a tapering off through several centuries of post-Aristotelian philosophers. Among these were the Epicureans and Stoics. The former are named after Epicurus, who taught a thoroughgoing atomism, inherited from Democritus, in which all things are composed of ultimate, indivisible particles of matter whose continual rearrangement accounts for change and the variety of things. The Stoics, whose founder was Zeno of Cition, are named after the *stoa*, or porch, where he taught. For the Stoics, the end of life was virtue, and the main purpose of virtue was to control oneself so as to be undisturbed by the troubles of life. Both groups, unconcerned about goods and possessions, heeded the injunction of Epicurus that "Vain is the word of the philosopher which does not heal some suffering in man" and sought to allay the fear of death by insisting that after death there is no life and that, as a consequence, there is no need to fear the punishment of the gods for the wrongs we do or for the fate we endure. Since man is composed of matter only, when the atoms break up, man no longer exists; fear of the afterlife is therefore groundless, and one may put one's mind at ease.

Well after the time of Epicurus and Zeno, we find another philosopher, Plotinus, who, though he lived in the third century of the Christian era, revived the great themes of Plato in a philosophic outlook often referred to as *Neoplatonism*. Inspired by Plato's overarching doctrines of the superiority of the eternal to the temporal, the world of Ideas as the world of pure being, the nature of man's participation in the Ideal world, and man's purification and return to the eternal, Plotinus constructed a pyramid of reality in which the very being of the One overflows, or emanates, into the formation of every other being, particularly into those with intelligence. And if this is the route whereby man comes from God, it is also the route he takes back. This is a mysticism of the highest order in which all distinctions are transcended and the soul recognizes that it is one with the One. Plotinus in his own right, but even more Plato through him, had a profound influence on the early Christian thinkers, the Fathers of the Church.

Readings

Toward a Definition of Wisdom (from *Metaphysics,* Book I)

1. All men by nature desire to know. An indication of this is the delight we take in our senses; for even apart from their usefulness they are loved for themselves; and above all others the sense of sight. For not only with a view to action, but even when we are not going to do anything, we prefer seeing (one might say) to everything else. The reason is that this, most of all the senses, makes us know and brings to light many differences between things.

By nature animals are born with the faculty of sensation, and from sensation memory is produced in some of them, though not in others. And therefore the former are more intelligent and apt at learning than those which cannot remember; those which are incapable of hearing sounds are intelligent though they cannot be taught, e.g. the bee, and any other race of animals that may be like it; and those which besides memory have this sense of hearing can be taught.

The animals other than man live by appearances and memories, and have but little of connected experience; but the human race lives also by art and reasonings. Now from memory experience is produced in men; for the several memories of the same thing produce finally the capacity for a single experience. And experience seems pretty much like science and art, but really science and art come to men through experience; for 'experience made art', as Polus says, 'but inexperience luck'. Now art arises when from many notions gained by experience one universal judgement about a class of objects is produced. For to have a judgement that when Callias was ill of this disease this did him good, and similarly in the case of Socrates and in many individual cases, is a matter of experience; but to judge that it has done good to all persons of a certain constitution, marked off in one class, when they were ill of this disease, e.g. to phlegmatic or bilious people when burning with fever—this is a matter of art.

With a view to action experience seems in no respect inferior to art, and men of experience succeed even better than those who have theory without experience. (The reason is that experience is knowledge of individuals, art of universals, and actions and productions are all concerned with the individual; for the physician does not cure man, except in an incidental way, but Callias or Socrates or some other called by some such individual name, who happens to be a man. If, then, a man has the theory without the experience, and recognizes the universal but does not know the individual included in this, he will often fail to cure; for it is the individual that is to be cured.) But yet we think that knowledge and understanding belong to art rather than to experience, and we suppose artists to be wiser than men of experience (which implies that Wisdom depends in all cases rather on knowledge); and this because the former know the cause, but the latter do not. For men of experience know that the thing is so, but do not know why, while the others know the 'why' and the cause. Hence we think also that the master-workers in each craft are more honourable and know in a truer sense and are wiser than the manual workers, because they know the causes of the things that are done (we think the manual workers are like certain lifeless things which act indeed, but act without knowing what they do, as fire burns—but while the lifeless things perform each of their functions by a natural tendency, the labourers perform them through habit); thus we view them as being wiser not in virtue of being able to act, but of having the theory for themselves and knowing the causes. And in general it is a sign of the man who knows and of the man who does not know, that the former can teach, and therefore we think art more truly knowledge than experience is; for artists can teach, and men of mere experience cannot.

Again, we do not regard any of the senses as Wisdom; yet surely these give the most authoritative knowledge of particulars. But they do not tell us the 'why' of anything—e.g. why fire is hot; they only say that it is hot.

At first he who invented any art whatever that went beyond the common perceptions of man was naturally admired by men, not only because there was something useful in the inventions, but because he was thought wise and superior to the rest. But as more arts were invented, and some were directed to the necessities of life, others to recreation, the inventors of the latter were naturally always regarded as wiser than the inventors of the former, because their branches of knowledge did not aim at utility. Hence when all such inventions were already established, the sciences which do not aim at giving pleasure or at the necessities of life were discovered, and first in the places where men first began to have leisure. This is why the mathematical arts were founded in Egypt; for there the priestly caste was allowed to be at leisure.

We have said in the Ethics what the difference is between art and science and the other kindred faculties; but the point of our present discussion is this, that all men suppose what is called Wisdom to deal with the first causes and the principles of things; so that, as has been said before, the man of experience is thought to be wiser than the possessors of any sense-perception whatever, the artist wiser than the men of experience, the master-worker than the mechanic, and the theoretical kinds of knowledge to be more of the nature of Wisdom than the productive. Clearly then Wisdom is knowledge about certain principles and causes.

2. Since we are seeking this knowledge, we must inquire of what kind are the causes and the principles, the knowledge of which is Wisdom. If one were to take the notions we have about the wise man, this might perhaps make the answer more evident. We suppose first, then, that the wise man knows all things, as far as possible, although he has not knowledge of each of them in detail; secondly, that he who can learn things that are difficult, and not easy for man to know, is wise (sense-perception is common to all, and therefore easy and no mark of Wisdom); again, that he who is more exact and more capable of teaching the causes is wiser, in every branch of knowledge; and that of the sciences, also, that which is desirable on its own account and for the sake of knowing it is more of the nature of Wisdom than that which is desirable on account of its results, and the superior science is more of the nature of Wisdom than the ancillary; for the wise man must not be ordered but must order, and he must not obey another, but the less wise must obey him.

Such and so many are the notions, then, which we have about Wisdom and the wise. Now of these characteristics that of knowing all things must belong to him who has in the highest degree universal knowledge; for he knows in a sense all the instances that fall under the universal. And these things, the most universal, are on the whole the hardest for men to know; for they are farthest from the senses. And the most exact of the sciences are those which deal most with first principles; for those which involve fewer principles are more exact than those which involve additional principles, e.g. arithmetic than geometry. But the science which investigates causes is also instructive, in a higher degree, for the people who instruct us are those who tell the causes of each thing. And understanding and knowledge pursued for their own sake are found most in the knowledge of that which is most knowable (for he who chooses to know for the sake of knowing will choose most readily that which is most truly knowledge, and such is the knowledge of that which is most knowable); and the first principles and the causes are most knowable; for by reason of these, and from these, all other things come to be known, and not these by means of the things subordinate to them. And the science which knows to what end each thing must be done is the most authoritative of the sciences, and more authoritative than any ancillary science; and this end is the good of that thing, and in general the supreme good in the whole of nature. Judged by all the tests we have mentioned, then, the name in question falls to the same science; this must be a science that investigates the first principles and causes; for the good, i.e. the end, is one of the causes.

That it is not a science of production is clear even from the history of the earliest philosophers. For it is owing to their wonder that men both now begin and at first began to philosophize; they wondered originally at the obvious difficulties, then advanced little by little and stated difficulties about the greater matters, e.g. about the phenomena of the moon and those of the sun and of the stars, and about the genesis of the universe. And a man who is puzzled and wonders thinks himself ignorant (whence even the lover of myth is in a sense a lover of Wisdom, for the myth is composed of wonders); therefore since they philosophized in order to escape from ignorance, evidently they were pursuing science in order to know, and not for any utilitarian end. ...

Hence also the possession of it might be justly regarded as beyond human power; for in many ways human nature is in bondage, so that according to Simonides 'God alone can have this privilege', and it is unfitting that man should not be content to seek the knowledge that is suited to him.. . .

For the most divine science is also most honourable; and this science alone must be, in two ways, most divine. For the science which it would be most meet for God to have is a divine science, and so is any science that deals with divine objects; and this science alone has both these qualities; for (1) God is thought to be among the causes of all things and to be a first principle, and (2) such a science either God alone can have, or God above all others. All the sciences, indeed, are more necessary than this, but none is better.

Yet the acquisition of it must in a sense end in something which is the opposite of our original inquiries. For all men begin, as we said, by wondering that things are as they are, as they do about self-moving marionettes, or about the solstices or the incommensurability of the diagonal of a square with the side; for it seems wonderful to all who have not yet seen the reason, that there is a thing which cannot be measured even by the smallest unit. But we must end in the contrary and, according to the proverb, the better state, as is the case in these instances too when men learn the cause; for there is nothing which would surprise a geometer so much as if the diagonal turned out to be commensurable.

We have stated, then, what is the nature of the science we are searching for, and what is the mark which our search and our whole investigation must reach.

(From *The Works* of Aristotle Translated into English, ed. W.D. Ross. Trans. by W.D. Ross. Oxford: Oxford University Press, 1924. Reprinted by permission of Oxford University Press.)

The Prime Mover: One and Eternal (from *Physics,* Books I and VIII)

1. Everything that is in motion must be moved by something. For if it has not the source of its motion in itself it is evident that it is moved by something other than itself, for there must be something else that moves it. If on the other hand it has the source of its motion in itself, let AB be taken to represent that which is in motion essentially of itself and not in virtue of the fact that something belonging to it is in motion. Now in the first place to assume that AB, because it is in motion as a whole and is not moved by anything external to itself, is therefore moved by itself—this is just as if, supposing that JK is moving KL and is also itself in motion, we were to deny that JL is moved by anything on the ground that it is not evident which is the part that is moving it and which the part that is moved. In the second place that which is in motion without being moved by anything does not necessarily cease from its motion because something else is at rest, but a thing must be moved by something if the fact of something else having ceased from its motion causes it to be at rest. Thus, if this is accepted, everything that is in motion must be moved by something. For AB, which has been taken to represent that which is in motion, must be divisible, since everything that is in motion is divisible. Let it be divided, then, at C. Now if CB is not in motion, then AB will not be in motion: for if it is, it is clear that AC would be in motion while BC is at rest, and thus AB cannot be in motion essentially and primarily. But ex hypothesi AB is in motion essentially and primarily. Therefore if CB is not in motion AB will be at rest. But we have agreed that that which is at rest if something else is not in motion must be moved by something. Consequently, everything that is in motion must be moved by something: for that which is in motion will always be divisible, and if a part of it is not in motion the whole must be at rest.

Since everything that is in motion must be moved by something, let us take the case in which a thing is in locomotion and is moved by something that is itself in motion, and that again is moved by something else that is in motion, and that by something else, and so on continually: then the series cannot go on to infinity, but there must be some first movent. For let us suppose that this is not so and take the series to be infinite. Let A then be moved by B, B by C, C by D, and so on, each member of the series being moved by that which comes next to it. Then since ex hypothesi the movent while causing motion is also itself in motion, and the motion of the moved and the motion of the movent must proceed simultaneously (for the movent is causing motion and the moved is being moved simultaneously) it is evident that the respective motions of A, B, C, and each of the other moved movents are simultaneous. Let us take the motion of each separately and let E be the motion of A, F of B, and G and H respectively the motions of C and D: for though they are all moved severally one by another, yet we may still take the motion of each as numerically one, since every motion is from something to something and is not infinite in respect of its extreme points. By a motion that is numerically one I mean a motion that proceeds from something numerically one and the same to something numerically one and the same in a period of time numerically one and the same: for a motion may be the same generically, specifically, or numerically: it is generically the same if it belongs to the same category, e.g. substance or quality: it is specifically the same if it proceeds from something specifically the same to something specifically the same, e.g. from white to black or from good to bad, which is not of a kind specifically distinct: it is numerically the same if it proceeds from something numerically one to something numerically one in the same period of time, e.g. from a particular white to a particular black, or from a particular place to a particular place, in a particular period of time: for if the period of time were not one and the same, the motion would no longer be numerically one though it would still be specifically one. We have dealt with this question above. Now let us further take the time in which A has completed its motion, and let it be represented by J. Then since the motion of A is finite the time will also be finite. But since the movents and the things moved are infinite, the motion EFGH, i.e. the motion that is composed of all the individual motions, must be infinite. For the motions of A, B, and the others may be equal, or the motions of the others may be greater: but assuming what is conceivable, we find that whether they are equal or some are greater, in both cases the whole motion is infinite. And since the motion of A and that of each of the others are simultaneous, the whole motion must occupy the same time as the motion of A: but the time occupied by the motion of A is finite: consequently the motion will be infinite in a finite time, which is impossible.

It might be thought that what we set out to prove has thus been shown, but our argument so far does not prove it, because it does not yet prove that anything impossible results from the contrary supposition: for in a finite time there may be an infinite motion, though not of one thing, but of many: and in the case that we are considering this is so: for each thing accomplishes its own motion, and there is no impossibility in many things being in motion simultaneously. But if (as we see to be universally the case) that which primarily is moved locally and corporeally must be either in contact with or continuous with that which moves it, the things moved and the movents must be continuous or in contact with one another, so that together they all form a single unity: whether this unity is finite or infinite makes no difference to our present argument; for in any case since the things in motion are infinite in number the whole motion will be infinite, if, as is theoretically possible, each motion is either equal to or greater than that which follows it in the series: for we shall take as actual that which is theoretically possible. If, then, A, B, C, D form an infinite magnitude that passes through the motion EFGH in the finite time J, this involves the conclusion that an infinite motion is passed through in a finite time: and whether the magnitude in question is finite or infinite this is in either case impossible. Therefore the series must come to an end, and there must be a first movent and a first moved: for the fact that this impossibility results only from the assumption of a particular case is immaterial, since the case assumed is theoretically possible, and the assumption of a theoretically possible case ought not to give rise to any impossible result. . . .

6. Since there must always be motion without intermission, there must necessarily be something, one thing or it may be a plurality, that first imparts motion, and this first movent must be unmoved. Now the question whether each of the things that are unmoved but impart motion is eternal is irrelevant to our present argument: but the following considerations will make it clear that there must necessarily be some such thing, which, while it has the capacity of moving something else, is itself unmoved and exempt from all change, which can affect it neither in an unqualified nor in an accidental sense. Let us suppose, if any one likes, that in the case of certain things it is possible for them at different times to be and not to be, without any process of becoming and perishing (in fact it would seem to be necessary, if a thing that has not parts at one time is and at another time is not, that any such thing should without undergoing any process of change at one time be and at another time not be). And let us further suppose it possible that some principles that are unmoved but capable of imparting motion at one time are and at another time are not. Even so, this cannot be true of *all* such principles, since there must clearly be something that *causes* things that move themselves at one time to be and at another not to be. For, since nothing that has not parts can be in motion, that which moves itself must as a whole have magnitude, though nothing that we have said makes this necessarily true of every movent. So the fact that some things become and others perish, and that this is so continuously, cannot be caused by any one of those things that, though they are unmoved, do not always exist: nor again can it be caused by any of those which move certain particular things, while others move other things. The eternity and continuity of the process cannot be caused either by any one of them singly or by the sum of them, because this causal relation must be eternal and necessary, whereas the sum of these movents is infinite and they do not all exist together. It is clear, then, that though there may be countless instances of the per-

ishing of some principles that are unmoved but impart motion, and though many things that move themselves perish and are succeeded by others that come into being, and though one thing that is unmoved moves one thing while another moves another, nevertheless there is something that comprehends them all, and that as something apart from each one of them, and this it is that is the cause of the fact that some things are and others are not and of the continuous process of change: and this causes the motion of the other movents, while they are the causes of the motion of other things. Motion, then, being eternal, the first movent, if there is but one, will be eternal also: if there are more than one, there will be a plurality of such eternal movents. We ought, however, to suppose that there is one rather than many, and a finite rather than an infinite number. When the consequences of either assumption are the same, we should always assume that things are finite rather than infinite in number, since in things constituted by nature that which is finite and that which is better ought, if possible, to be present rather than the reverse: and here it is sufficient to assume only one movent, the first of unmoved things, which being eternal will be the principle of motion to everything else.

The following argument also makes it evident that the first movent must be something that is one and eternal. We have shown that there must always be motion. That being so, motion must also be continuous, because what is always is continuous, whereas what is merely in succession is not continuous. But further, if motion is continuous, it is one: and it is one only if the movent and the moved that constitute it are each of them one, since in the event of a thing's being moved now by one thing and now by another the whole motion will not be continuous but successive.

Moreover a conviction that there is a first unmoved something may be reached not only from the foregoing arguments, but also by considering again the principles operative in movents. Now it is evident that among existing things there are some that are sometimes in motion and sometimes at rest. This fact has served above to make it clear that it is not true either that all things are in motion or that all things are at rest or that some things are always at rest and the remainder always in motion: on this matter proof is supplied by things that fluctuate between the two and have the capacity of being sometimes in motion and sometimes at rest. The existence of things of this kind is clear to all: but we wish to explain also the nature of each of the other two kinds and show that there are some things that are always unmoved and some things that are always in motion. In the course of our argument directed to this end we established the fact that everything that is in motion is moved by something, and that the movent is either unmoved or in motion, and that, if it is in motion, it is moved either by itself or by something else and so on throughout the series: and so we proceeded to the position that the first principle that directly causes things that are in motion to be moved is that which moves itself, and the first principle of the whole series is the unmoved. Further it is evident from actual observation that there are things that have the characteristic of moving themselves, e.g. the animal kingdom and the whole class of living things. This being so, then, the view was suggested that perhaps it may be possible for motion to come to be in a thing without having been in existence at all before, because we see this actually occurring in animals: they are unmoved at one time and then again they are in motion, as it seems. We must grasp the fact, therefore, that animals move themselves only with one kind of motion, and that this is not strictly originated by them. The cause of it is not derived from the animal itself: it is connected with other natural motions in animals, which they do not experience through their own instrumentality, e.g. increase, decrease, and respiration: these are experienced by every animal while it is at rest and not in motion in respect of the motion set up by its own agency: here the motion is caused by the atmosphere and by many things that enter into the animal: thus in some cases the cause is nourishment: when it is being digested animals sleep, and when it is being distributed through the system they awake and move themselves, the first principle of this motion being thus originally derived from outside. Therefore animals are not always in continuous motion by their own agency: it is something else that moves them, itself being in motion and changing as it comes into relation with each several thing that moves itself. (Moreover in all these self-moving things the first movent and cause of their self-motion is itself moved by itself, though in an accidental sense: that is to say, the body changes its place, so that that which is in the body changes its place also and is a self-movent through its exercise of leverage.) Hence we may confidently conclude that if a thing belongs to the class of unmoved movents that are also themselves moved accidentally, it is impossible that it should cause continuous motion. So the necessity that there should be motion continuously requires that there should be a first movent that is unmoved even accidentally, if, as we have said, there is to be in the world of things an unceasing and undying motion, and the world is to remain permanently self-contained and within the same limits: for if the first principle is permanent, the universe must also be permanent, since it is continuous with the first principle. (We must distinguish, however, between accidental motion of a thing by itself and such motion by something else, the former being confined to perishable things, whereas the latter belongs also to certain first principles of heavenly bodies, of all those, that is to say, that experience more than one locomotion.)

And further, if there is always something of this nature, a movent that is itself unmoved and eternal, then that which is first moved by it must be eternal. Indeed this is clear also from the consideration that there would otherwise be no becoming and perishing and no change of any kind in other things, which require something that is in motion to move them: for the motion imparted by the unmoved will always be imparted in the same way and be one and the same, since the unmoved does not itself change in relation to that which is moved by it. But that which is moved by something that, though it is in motion, is moved directly by the unmoved stands in varying relations to the things that it moves, so that the motion that it causes will not be always the same: by reason of the fact that it occupies contrary positions or assumes contrary forms at different times it will produce contrary motions in each several thing that it moves and will cause it to be at one time at rest and at another time in motion.

The foregoing argument, then, has served to clear up the point about which we raised a difficulty at the outset—why is it that instead of all things being either in motion or at rest, or some things being always in motion and the remainder always at rest, there are things that are sometimes in motion and sometimes not? The cause of this is now plain: it is because, while some things are moved by an eternal unmoved movent and are therefore always in motion, other things are moved by a movent that is in motion and changing, so that they too must change. But the unmoved movent, as has been said, since it remains permanently simple and unvarying and in the same state, will cause motion that is one and simple.

(From *The Works of Aristotle Translated into English*, ed. W.D. Ross. Trans. by R.P. Hardie and R.K. Gaye. Oxford: Oxford University Press, 1930. Reprinted by permission of Oxford University Press.)

Thought, Contemplation, and the Life of God (from *Metaphysics,* Book XII)

7. Since (1) this is a possible account of the matter, and (2) if it were not true, the world would have proceeded out of night and 'all things together' and out of non-being, these difficulties may be taken as solved. There is, then, something which is always moved with an unceasing motion, which is motion in a circle; and this is plain not in theory only but in fact. Therefore the first heaven must be eternal. There is therefore also something which moves it. And since that which is moved and moves is intermediate, there is something which moves without being moved, being eternal, substance, and actuality. And the object of desire and the object of thought move in this way; they move without being moved. The primary objects of desire and of thought are the same. For the apparent good is the object of appetite, and the real good is the primary object of rational wish. But desire is consequent on

opinion rather than opinion on desire; for the thinking is the start-ing-point. And thought is moved by the object of thought, and one of the two columns of opposites is in itself the object of thought; and in this, substance is first, and in substance, that which is simple and ex-ists actually. (The one and the simple are not the same; for 'one' means a measure, but 'simple' means that the thing itself has a certain na-ture.) But the beautiful, also, and that which is in itself desirable are in the same column; and the first in any class is always best, or analo-gous to the best.

That a final cause may exist among unchangeable entities is shown by the distinction of its meanings. For the final cause is (a) some being for whose good an action is done, and (b) something at which the ac-tion aims; and of these the latter exists among unchangeable entities though the former does not. The final cause, then, produces motion as being loved, but all other things move by being moved.

Now if something is moved it is capable of being otherwise than as it is. Therefore if its actuality is the primary form of spatial motion, then in so far as it is subject to change, in *this* respect it is capable of being otherwise—in place, even if not in substance. But since there is something which moves while itself unmoved, existing actually, this can in no way be otherwise than as it is. For motion in space is the first of the kinds of change, and motion in a circle the first kind of spatial motion; and this the first mover *produces*. The first mover, then, exists of necessity; and in so far as it exists by necessity, its mode of being is good, and it is in this sense a first principle. For the necessary has all these senses—that which is necessary perforce because it is contrary to the natural impulse, that without which the good is impossible, and that which cannot be otherwise but can exist only in a single way.

On such a principle, then, depend the heavens and the world of na-ture. And it is a life such as the best which we enjoy, and enjoy for but a short time (for it is ever in this state, which we cannot be), since its actuality is also pleasure. (And for this reason are waking, perception, and thinking most pleasant, and hopes and memories are so on account of these.) And thinking in itself deals with that which is best in itself, and that which is thinking in the fullest sense with that which is best in the fullest sense. And thought thinks on itself because it shares the nature of the object of thought; for it becomes an object of thought in coming into contact with and thinking its objects, so that thought and object of thought are the same. For that which is *capable* of receiving the object of thought, i.e. the essence, is thought. But it is *active* when it *possesses* this object. Therefore the possession rather than the recep-tivity is the divine element which thought seems to contain, and the act of contemplation is what is most pleasant and best. If, then, God is always in that good state in which we sometimes are, this compels our wonder; and if in a better this compels it yet more. And God *is* in a better state. And life also belongs to God; for the actuality of thought is life, and God is that actuality; and God's self-dependent actuality is life most good and eternal. We say therefore that God is a living being, eternal, most good, so that life and duration continuous and eternal belong to God; for this *is* God.

Those who suppose, as the Pythagoreans and Speusippus do, that supreme beauty and goodness are not present in the beginning, because the beginnings both of plants and of animals are causes, but beauty and completeness are in the *effects* of these, are wrong in their opinion. For the seed comes from other individuals which are prior and complete, and the first thing is not seed but the complete being; e.g. we must say that before the seed there is a man—not the man produced from the seed, but another from whom the seed comes.

It is clear then from what has been said that there is a substance which is eternal and unmovable and separate from sensible things. It has been shown also that this substance cannot have any magnitude, but is without parts and indivisible (for it produces movement through infinite time, but nothing finite has infinite power; and, while every magnitude is either infinite or finite, it cannot, for the above reason, have finite magnitude, and it cannot have infinite magnitude because there is no infinite magnitude at all). But it has also been shown that it is impassive and unalterable; for all the other changes are posterior to change of place.

9. The nature of the divine thought involves certain problems; for while thought is held to be the most divine of things observed by us, the question how it must be situated in order to have that character involves difficulties. For if it thinks of nothing, what is there here of dignity? It is just like one who sleeps. And if it thinks, but this depends on something else, then (since that which is its substance is not the act of thinking, but a potency) it cannot be the best substance; for it is through thinking that its value belongs to it. Further, whether its substance is the faculty of thought or the act of thinking, what does it think of? Either of itself or of something else; and if of something else, either of the same thing always or of something different. Does it matter, then, or not, whether it thinks of the good or of any chance thing? Are there not some things about which it is incredible that it should think? Evidently, then, it thinks of that which is most divine and precious, and it does not change; for change would be change for the worse, and this would be already a movement. First, then, if 'thought' is not the act of thinking but a potency, it would be reasonable to suppose that the continuity of its thinking is wearisome to it. Secondly, there would evidently be something else more precious than thought, viz. that which is thought of. For both thinking and the act of thought

will belong even to one who thinks of the worst thing in the world, so that if this ought to be avoided (and it ought, for there are even some things which it is better not to see than to see), the act of thinking cannot be the best of things. Therefore it must be of itself that the divine thought thinks (since it is the most excellent of things), and its thinking is a thinking on thinking.

But evidently knowledge and perception and opinion and understanding have always something else as their object, and themselves only by the way. Further, if thinking and being thought of are different, in respect of which does goodness belong to thought? For to be an act of thinking and to *be* an object of thought are not the same thing. We answer that in some cases the knowledge is the object. In the productive sciences it is the substance or essence of the object, matter omitted, and in the theoretical sciences the definition or the act of thinking is the object. Since, then, thought and the object of thought are not different in the case of things that have not matter, the divine thought and its object will be the same, i.e. the thinking will be one with the object of its thought.

A further question is left—whether the object of the divine thought is composite; for if it were, thought would change in passing from part to part of the whole. We answer that everything which has not matter is indivisible—as human thought, or rather the thought of composite beings, is in a certain period of time (for it does not possess the good at this moment or at that, but its best, being something *different* from it, is attained only in a whole period of time), so throughout eternity is the thought which has *itself* for its object.

(From *The Works of Aristotle Translated into English*, ed. W.D. Ross. Trans. by W.D. Ross. Oxford: Oxford University Press, 1924. Reprinted by permission of Oxford University Press.)

Happiness and Man's Good (from *Nicomachean Ethics*, Book I)

1. Every art and every inquiry, and similarly every action and pursuit, is thought to aim at some good; and for this reason the good has rightly been declared to be that at which all things aim. But a certain difference is found among ends; some are activities, others are products apart from the activities that produce them. Where there are ends apart from the actions, it is the nature of the products to be better than the activities. Now, as there are many actions, arts, and sciences, their ends also are many; the end of the medical art is health, that of shipbuilding a vessel, that of strategy victory, that of economics wealth. But where such arts fall under a single capacity—as bridle-making and the other arts concerned with the equipment of horses

fall under the art of riding, and this and every military action under strategy, in the same way other arts fall under yet others—in all of these the ends of the master arts are to be preferred to all the subordinate ends; for it is for the sake of the former that the latter are pursued. It makes no difference whether the activities themselves are the ends of the actions, or something else apart from the activities, as in the case of the sciences just mentioned.

2. If, then, there is some end of the things we do, which we desire for its own sake (everything else being desired for the sake of this), and if we do not choose everything for the sake of something else (for at that rate the process would go on to infinity, so that our desire would be empty and vain), clearly this must be the good and the chief good. Will not the knowledge of it, then, have a great influence on life? Shall we not, like archers who have a mark to aim at, be more likely to hit upon what is right? If so, we must try, in outline at least to determine what it is, and of which of the sciences or capacities it is the object. It would seem to belong to the most authoritative art and that which is most truly the master art. And politics appears to be of this nature; for it is this that ordains which of the sciences should be studied in a state, and which each class of citizens should learn and up to what point they should learn them; and we see even the most highly esteemed of capacities to fall under this, e.g. strategy, economics, rhetoric; now, since politics uses the rest of the sciences, and since, again, it legislates as to what we are to do and what we are to abstain from, the end of this science must include those of the others, so that this end must be the good for man. For even if the end is the same for a single man and for a state, that of the state seems at all events something greater and more complete whether to attain or to preserve; though it is worth while to attain the end merely for one man, it is finer and more godlike to attain it for a nation or for city-states. These, then, are the ends at which our inquiry aims, since it is political science, in one sense of that term.

7. Let us again return to the good we are seeking, and ask what it can be. It seems different in different actions and arts; it is different in medicine, in strategy, and in the other arts likewise. What then is the good of each? Surely that for whose sake everything else is done. In medicine this is health, in strategy victory, in architecture a house, in any other sphere something else, and in every action and pursuit the end; for it is for the sake of this that all men do whatever else they do. Therefore, if there is an end for all that we do, this will be the good achievable by action, and if there are more than one, these will be the goods achievable by action.

So the argument has by a different course reached the same point; but we must try to state this even more clearly. Since there are evidently more than one end, and we choose some of these (e.g. wealth, flutes, and in general instruments) for the sake of something else, clearly not all ends are final ends; but the chief good is evidently something final. Therefore, if there is only one final end, this will be what we are seeking, and if there are more than one, the most final of these will be what we are seeking. Now we call that which is in itself worthy of pursuit more final than that which is worthy of pursuit for the sake of something else, and that which is never desirable for the sake of something else more final than the things that are desirable both in themselves and for the sake of that other thing, and therefore we call final without qualification that which is always desirable in itself and never for the sake of something else.

Now such a thing happiness, above all else, is held to be; for this we choose always for itself and never for the sake of something else, but honour, pleasure, reason, and every virtue we choose indeed for themselves (for if nothing resulted from them we should still choose each of them), but we choose them also for the sake of happiness, judging that by means of them we shall be happy. Happiness, on the other hand, no one chooses for the sake of these, nor, in general, for anything other than itself.

From the point of view of self-sufficiency the same result seems to follow; for the final good is thought to be self-sufficient. Now by self-sufficient we do not mean that which is sufficient for a man by himself, for one who lives a solitary life, but also for parents, children, wife, and in general for his friends and fellow citizens, since man is born for citizenship. But some limit must be set to this; for if we extend our requirement to ancestors and descendants and friends' friends we are in for an infinite series. Let us examine this question, however, on another occasion; the self-sufficient we now define as that which when isolated makes life desirable and lacking in nothing; and such we think happiness to be; and further we think it most desirable of all things, without being counted as one good thing among others—if it were so counted it would clearly be made more desirable by the addition of even the least of goods; for that which is added becomes an excess of goods, and of goods the greater is always more desirable. Happiness, then, is something final and self-sufficient, and is the end of action.

Presumably, however, to say that happiness is the chief good seems a platitude, and a clearer account of what it is is still desired. This might perhaps be given, if we could first ascertain the function of man. For just as for a flute-player, a sculptor, or any artist, and, in general, for all things that have a function or activity, the good and the 'well' is thought to reside in the function, so would it seem to be for man, if he has a function. Have the carpenter, then, and the tanner certain functions or activities, and has man none? Is he born without a function? Or as eye, hand, foot, and in general each of the parts evidently has a function, may one lay it down that man similarly has a function apart from all these? What then can this be? Life seems to be common even to plants, but we are seeking what is peculiar to man. Let us exclude, therefore, the life of nutrition and growth. Next there would be a life of perception, but *it* also seems to be common even to the horse, the ox, and every animal. There remains, then, an active life of the element that has a rational principle; of this, one part has such a principle in the sense of being obedient to one, the other in the sense of possessing one and exercising thought. And, as 'life of the rational element' also has two meanings, we must state that life in the sense of activity is what we mean; for this seems to be the more proper sense of the term. Now if the function of man is an activity of soul which follows or implies a rational principle, and if we say 'a so-and-so' and 'a good so-and-so' have a function which is the same in kind, e.g. a lyre-player and a good lyre-player, and so without qualification in all cases, eminence in respect of goodness being added to the name of the function (for the function of a lyre-player is to play the lyre, and that of a good lyre-player is to do so well): if this is the case, [and we state the function of man to be a certain kind of life, and this to be an activity or actions of the soul implying a rational principle, and the function of a good man to be the good and noble performance of these, and if any action is well performed when it is performed in accordance with the appropriate excellence: if this is the case,] human good turns out to be activity of soul in accordance with virtue, and if there are more than one virtue, in accordance with the best and most complete.

But we must add 'in a complete life'. For one swallow does not make a summer, nor does one day; and so too one day, or a short time, does not make a man blessed and happy.

Moral Virtue and the Mean (from *Nicomachean Ethics*, Book II)

6. We must, however, not only describe virtue as a state of character, but also say what sort of state it is. We may remark, then, that every virtue or excellence both brings into good condition the thing of which it is the excellence and makes the work of that thing be done well; e.g. the excellence of the eye makes both the eye and its work good; for it is by the excellence of the eye that we see well. Similarly the excellence of the horse makes a horse both good in itself and good at running and at carrying its rider and at awaiting the attack of the enemy. Therefore, if this is true in every case, the virtue of man also will be the state of character which makes a man good and which makes him do his own work well.

How this is to happen we have stated already, but it will be made plain also by the following consideration of the specific nature of virtue. In everything that is continuous and divisible it is possible to take more, less, or an equal amount, and that either in terms of the thing itself or relatively to us; and the equal is an intermediate between excess and defect. By the intermediate in the object I mean that which is equidistant from each of the extremes, which is one and the same for all men; by the intermediate relatively to us that which is neither too much nor too little—and this is not one, nor the same for all. For instance, if ten is many and two is few, six is the intermediate, taken in terms of the object; for it exceeds and is exceeded by an equal amount; this is intermediate according to arithmetical proportion. But the intermediate relatively to us is not to be taken so; if ten pounds are too much for a particular person to eat and two too little, it does not follow that the trainer will order six pounds; for this also is perhaps too much for the person who is to take it, or too little—too little for Milo, too much for the beginner in athletic exercises. The same is true of running and wrestling. Thus a master of any art avoids excess and defect, but seeks the intermediate and chooses this—the intermediate not in the object but relatively to us.

If it is thus, then, that every art does its work well—by looking to the intermediate and judging its works by this standard (so that we often say of good works of art that it is not possible either to take away or to add anything, implying that excess and defect destroy the goodness of works of art, while the mean preserves it; and good artists, as we say, look to this in their work), and if, further, virtue is more exact and better than any art, as nature also is, then virtue must have the quality of aiming at the intermediate. I mean moral virtue; for it is this that is concerned with passions and actions, and in these there is excess, defect, and the intermediate. For instance, both fear and confidence and appetite and anger and pity and in general pleasure and pain may be felt both too much and too little, and in both cases not well; but to feel them at the right times, with reference to the right objects, towards the right people, with the right motive, and in the right way, is what is both intermediate and best, and this is characteristic of virtue. Similarly with regard to actions also there is excess, defect, and the intermediate. Now virtue is concerned with passions and actions, in which excess is a form of failure, and so is defect, while the intermediate is praised and is a form of success; and being praised and being successful are both characteristics of virtue. Therefore virtue is a kind of mean, since, as we have seen, it aims at what is intermediate.

Again, it is possible to fail in many ways (for evil belongs to the class of the unlimited, as the Pythagoreans conjectured, and good to that of the limited), while to succeed is possible only in one way (for which reason also one is easy and the other difficult—to miss the mark easy, to hit it difficult); for these reasons also, then, excess and defect are characteristic of vice, and the mean of virtue;

For men are good in but one way, but bad in many.

Virtue, then, is a state of character concerned with choice, lying in a mean, i.e. the mean relative to us, this being determined by a rational principle, and by that principle by which the man of practical wisdom would determine it. Now it is a mean between two vices, that which depends on excess and that which depends on defect; and again it is a mean because the vices respectively fall short of or exceed what is right in both passions and actions, while virtue both finds and chooses that which is intermediate. Hence in respect of its substance and the definition which states its essence virtue is a mean, with regard to what is best and right an extreme.

But not every action nor every passion admits of a mean; for some have names that already imply badness, e.g. spite, shamelessness, envy, and in the case of actions adultery, theft, murder; for all of these and suchlike things imply by their names that they are themselves bad, and not the excesses or deficiencies of them. It is not possible, then, ever to be right with regard to them; one must always be wrong. Nor does goodness or badness with regard to such things depend on committing adultery with the right woman, at the right time, and in the right way, but simply to do any of them is to go wrong. It would be equally absurd, then, to expect that in unjust, cowardly, and voluptuous action there should be a mean, an excess, and a deficiency; for at that rate there would be a mean of excess and of deficiency, an excess of excess, and a deficiency of deficiency. But as there is no excess and deficiency of temperance and courage because what is intermediate is in a sense an extreme, so too of the actions we have mentioned there is no mean nor any excess and deficiency, but however they are done they are wrong; for in general there is neither a mean of excess and deficiency, nor excess and deficiency of a mean.

7. We must, however, not only make this general statement, but also apply it to the individual facts. For among statements about conduct those which are general apply more widely, but those which are particular are more genuine, since conduct has to do with individual cases, and our statements must harmonize with the facts in these cases. We may take these cases from our table. With regard to feelings of fear and confidence courage is the mean; of the people who exceed, he who exceeds in fearlessness has no name (many of the states have no name), while the man who exceeds in confidence is rash, and he who exceeds in fear and falls short in confidence is a coward. With regard

to pleasures and pains—not all of them, and not so much with regard to the pains—the mean is temperance, the excess self-indulgence. Persons deficient with regard to the pleasures are not often found; hence such persons also have received no name. But let us call them 'insensible'.

With regard to giving and taking of money the mean is liberality, the excess and the defect prodigality and meanness. In these actions people exceed and fall short in contrary ways; the prodigal exceeds in spending and falls short in taking, while the mean man exceeds in taking and falls short in spending. (At present we are giving a mere outline or summary, and are satisfied with this; later these states will be more exactly determined.) With regard to money there are also other dispositions—a mean, magnificence (for the magnificent man differs from the liberal man; the former deals with large sums, the latter with small ones), an excess, tastelessness and vulgarity, and a deficiency, niggardliness; these differ from the states opposed to liberality, and the mode of their difference will be stated later.

With regard to honour and dishonour the mean is proper pride, the excess is known as a sort of 'empty vanity', and the deficiency is undue humility; and as we said liberality was related to magnificence, differing from it by dealing with small sums, so there is a state similarly related to proper pride, being concerned with small honours while that is concerned with great. For it is possible to desire honour as one ought, and more than one ought, and less, and the man who exceeds in his desires is called ambitious, the man who falls short unambitious, while the intermediate person has no name. The dispositions also are nameless, except that that of the ambitious man is called ambition. Hence the people who are at the extremes lay claim to the middle place; and we ourselves sometimes call the intermediate person ambitious and sometimes unambitious, and sometimes praise the ambitious man and sometimes the unambitious. The reason of our doing this will be stated in what follows; but now let us speak of the remaining states according to the method which has been indicated.

With regard to anger also there is an excess, a deficiency, and a mean. Although they can scarcely be said to have names, yet since we call the intermediate person good-tempered let us call the mean good temper; of the persons at the extremes let the one who exceeds be called irascible, and his vice irascibility, and the man who falls short an inirascible sort of person, and the deficiency inirascibility.

There are also three other means, which have a certain likeness to one another, but differ from one another: for they are all concerned with intercourse in words and actions, but differ in that one is concerned with truth in this sphere, the other two with pleasantness; and of this one kind is exhibited in giving amusement, the other in all the circumstances of life. We must therefore speak of these too, that we may the better see that in all things the mean is praiseworthy, and the extremes neither praiseworthy nor right, but worthy of blame. Now most of these states also have no names, but we must try, as in the other cases, to invent names ourselves so that we may be clear and easy to follow. With regard to truth, then, the intermediate is a truthful sort of person and the mean may be called truthfulness, while the pretence which exaggerates is boastfulness and the person characterized by it a boaster, and that which understates is mock modesty and the person characterized by it mock-modest. With regard to pleasantness in the giving of amusement the intermediate person is ready-witted and the disposition ready wit, the excess is buffoonery and the person characterized by it a buffoon, while the man who falls short is a sort of boor and his state is boorishness. With regard to the remaining kind of pleasantness, that which is exhibited in life in general, the man who is pleasant in the right way is friendly and the mean is friendliness, while the man who exceeds is an obsequious person if he has no end in view, a flatterer if he is aiming at his own advantage, and the man who falls short and is unpleasant in all circumstances is a quarrelsome and surly sort of person.

There are also means in the passions and concerned with the passions; since shame is not a virtue, and yet praise is extended to the modest man. For even in these matters one man is said to be intermediate, and another to exceed, as for instance the bashful man who is ashamed of everything; while he who falls short or is not ashamed of anything at all is shameless, and the intermediate person is modest. Righteous indignation is a mean between envy and spite, and these states are concerned with the pain and pleasures that are felt at the fortunes of our neighbours; the man who is characterized by righteous indignation is pained at undeserved good fortune, the envious man, going beyond him, is pained at all good fortune, and the spiteful man falls so far short of being pained that he even rejoices. But these states there will be an opportunity of describing elsewhere; with regard to justice, since it has not one simple meaning, we shall, after describing the other states, distinguish its two kinds and say how each of them is a mean; and similarly we shall treat also of the rational virtues.

9. That mortal virtue is a mean, then, and in what sense it is so, and that it is a mean between two vices, the one involving excess, the other deficiency, and that it is such because its character is to aim at what is intermediate in passions and in actions, has been sufficiently stated. Hence also it is no easy task to be good. For in everything it is no easy task to find the middle, e.g. to find the middle of a circle is not for every one but for him who knows; so, too, any one can get angry—that is easy—or give or spend money; but to do this to the right person, to

the right extent, at the right time, with the right motive, and in the right way, *that* is not for every one, nor is it easy; wherefore goodness is both rare and laudable and noble.

Hence he who aims at the intermediate must first depart from what is the more contrary to it, as Calypso advises—

Hold the ship out beyond that surf and spray.

For of the extremes one is more erroneous, one less so; therefore, since to hit the mean is hard in the extreme, we must as a second best, as people say, take the least of the evils; and this will be done best in the way we describe.

But we must consider the things towards which we ourselves also are easily carried away; for some of us tend to one thing, some to another; and this will be recognizable from the pleasure and the pain we feel. We must drag ourselves away to the contrary extreme; for we shall get into the intermediate state by drawing well away from error, as people do in straightening sticks that are bent.

Now in everything the pleasant or pleasure is most to be guarded against; for we do not judge it impartially. We ought, then, to feel towards pleasure as the elders of the people felt towards Helen, and in all circumstances repeat their saying; for if we dismiss pleasure thus we are less likely to go astray. It is by doing this, then, (to sum the matter up) that we shall best be able to hit the mean.

But this is no doubt difficult, and especially in individual cases; for it is not easy to determine both how and with whom and on what provocation and how long one should be angry; for we too sometimes praise those who fall short and call them good-tempered, but sometimes we praise those who get angry and call them manly. The man, however, who deviates little from goodness is not blamed, whether he do so in the direction of the more or of the less, but only the man who deviates more widely; for *he* does not fail to be noticed. But up to what point and to what extent a man must deviate before he becomes blameworthy it is not easy to determine by reasoning, any more than anything else that is perceived by the senses; such things depend on particular facts, and the decision rests with perception. So much, then, is plain, that the intermediate state is in all things to be praised, but that we must incline sometimes towards the excess, sometimes towards the deficiency; for so shall we most easily hit the mean and what is right.

The End of Human Nature: Happiness (from *Nicomachean Ethics*, Book X)

6. Now that we have spoken of the virtues, the forms of friendship, and the varieties of pleasure, what remains is to discuss in outline the

nature of happiness, since this is what we state the end of human nature to be. Our discussion will be the more concise if we first sum up what we have said already. We said, then, that it is not a disposition; for if it were it might belong to some one who was asleep throughout his life, living the life of a plant, or, again, to some one who was suffering the greatest misfortunes. If these implications are unacceptable, and we must rather class happiness as an activity, as we have said before, and if some activities are necessary, and desirable for the sake of something else, while others are so in themselves, evidently happiness must be placed among those desirable in themselves, not among those desirable for the sake of something else; for happiness does not lack anything, but is self-sufficient. Now those activities are desirable in themselves from which nothing is sought beyond the activity. And of this nature virtuous actions are thought to be; for to do noble and good deeds is a thing desirable for its own sake.

Pleasant amusements also are thought to be of this nature; we choose them not for the sake of other things; for we are injured rather than benefited by them, since we are led to neglect our bodies and our property. But most of the people who are deemed happy take refuge in such pastimes, which is the reason why those who are ready-witted at them are highly esteemed at the courts of tyrants; they make themselves pleasant companions in the tyrants' favourite pursuits, and that is the sort of man they want. Now these things are thought to be of the nature of happiness because people in despotic positions spend their leisure in them, but perhaps such people prove nothing; for virtue and reason, from which good activities flow, do not depend on despotic position; nor, if these people, who have never tasted pure and generous pleasure, take refuge in the bodily pleasures, should these for that reason be thought more desirable; for boys, too, think the things that are valued among themselves are the best. It is to be expected, then, that, as different things seem valuable to boys and to men, so they should to bad men and to good. Now, as we have often maintained, those things are both valuable and pleasant which are such to the good man; and to each man the activity in accordance with his own disposition is most desirable, and, therefore, to the good man that which is in accordance with virtue. Happiness, therefore, does not lie in amusement; it would, indeed, be strange if the end were amusement, and one were to take trouble and suffer hardship all one's life in order to amuse oneself. For, in a word, everything that we choose we choose for the sake of something else—except happiness, which is an end. Now to exert oneself and work for the sake of amusement seems silly and utterly childish. But to amuse oneself in order that one may exert oneself, as Anacharsis puts it, seems right; for amusement is a sort of relaxation, and we need relaxation because we cannot work continuously. Relaxation, then, is not an end; for it is taken for the sake of activity.

The happy life is thought to be virtuous; now a virtuous life requires exertion, and does not consist in amusement. And we say that serious things are better than laughable things and those connected with amusement, and that the activity of the better of any two things—whether it be two elements of our being or two men—is the more serious; but the activity of the better is *ipso facto* superior and more of the nature of happiness. And any chance person—even a slave—can enjoy the bodily pleasures no less than the best man; but no one assigns to a slave a share in happiness—unless he assigns to him also a share in human life. For happiness does not lie in such occupations, but, as we have said before, in virtuous activities.

7. If happiness is activity in accordance with virtue, it is reasonable that it should be in accordance with the highest virtue; and this will be that of the best thing in us. Whether it be reason or something else that is this element which is thought to be our natural ruler and guide and to take thought of things noble and divine, whether it be itself also divine or only the most divine element in us, the activity of this in accordance with its proper virtue will be perfect happiness. That this activity is contemplative we have already said.

Now this would seem to be in agreement both with what we said before and with the truth. For, firstly, this activity is the best (since not only is reason the best thing in us, but the objects of reason are the best of knowable objects); and, secondly, it is the most continuous, since we can contemplate truth more continuously than we can *do* anything. And we think happiness has pleasure mingled with it, but the activity of philosophic wisdom is admittedly the pleasantest of virtuous activities; at all events the pursuit of it is thought to offer pleasures marvellous for their purity and their enduringness, and it is to be expected that those who know will pass their time more pleasantly than those who inquire. And the self-sufficiency that is spoken of must belong most to the contemplative activity. For while a philosopher, as well as a just man or one possessing any other virtue, needs the necessaries of life, when they are sufficiently equipped with things of that sort the just man needs people towards whom and with whom he shall act justly, and the temperate man, the brave man, and each of the others is in the same case, but the philosopher, even when by himself, can contemplate truth, and the better the wiser he is; he can perhaps do so better if he has fellow-workers, but still he is the most self-sufficient. And this activity alone would seem to be loved for its own sake; for nothing arises from it apart from the contemplating, while from practical activities we gain more or less apart from the action. And happiness is thought to depend on leisure; for we are busy that we may have leisure, and make war that we may live in peace. Now the activity of the practical virtues is exhibited in political or military affairs, but the actions concerned with these seem to be unleisurely. Warlike actions are completely so (for no one chooses to be at war, or provokes war, for the sake of being at war; any one would seem absolutely murderous if he were to make enemies of his friends in order to bring about battle and slaughter); but the action of the statesman is also unleisurely, and—apart from the political action itself—aims at despotic power and honours, or at all events happiness, for him and his fellow citizens—a happiness different from political action, and evidently sought as being different. So if among virtuous actions political and military actions are distinguished by nobility and greatness, and these are unleisurely and aim at an end and are not desirable for their own sake, but the activity of reason, which is contemplative, seems both to be superior in serious worth and to aim at no end beyond itself, and to have its pleasure proper to itself (and this augments the activity), and the self-sufficiency, leisureliness, unweariedness (so far as this is possible for man), and all the other attributes ascribed to the supremely happy man are evidently those connected with this activity, it follows that this will be the complete happiness of man, if it be allowed a complete term of life (for none of the attributes of happiness is _in_complete).

But such a life would be too high for man; for it is not in so far as he is man that he will live so, but in so far as something divine is present in him; and by so much as this is superior to our composite nature is its activity superior to that which is the exercise of the other kind of virtue. If reason is divine, then, in comparison with man, the life according to it is divine in comparison with human life. But we must not follow those who advise us, being men, to think of human things, and, being mortal, of mortal things, but must, so far as we can, make ourselves immortal, and strain every nerve to live in accordance with the best thing in us; for even if it be small in bulk, much more does it in power and worth surpass everything. This would seem, too, to be each man himself, since it is the authoritative and better part of him. It would be strange, then, if he were to choose not the life of his self but that of something else. And what we said before will apply now; that which is proper to each thing is by nature best and most pleasant for each thing; for man, therefore, the life according to reason is best and pleasantest, since reason more than anything else _is_ man. This life therefore is also the happiest.

8. But in a secondary degree the life in accordance with the other kind of virtue is happy; for the activities in accordance with this befit our human estate. Just and brave acts, and other virtuous acts, we do in relation to each other, observing our respective duties with regard to contracts and services and all manner of actions and with regard to passions; and all of these seem to be typically human. Some of them

seem even to arise from the body, and virtue of character to be in many ways bound up with the passions. Practical wisdom, too, is linked to virtue of character, and this to practical wisdom, since the principles of practical wisdom are in accordance with the moral virtues and rightness in morals is in accordance with practical wisdom. Being connected with the passions also, the moral virtues must belong to our composite nature; and the virtues of our composite nature are human; so, therefore, are the life and the happiness which correspond to these. The excellence of the reason is a thing apart; we must be content to say this much about it, for to describe it precisely is a task greater than our purpose requires. It would seem, however, also to need external equipment but little, or less than moral virtue does. Grant that both need the necessaries, and do so equally, even if the statesman's work is the more concerned with the body and things of that sort; for there will be little difference there; but in what they need for the exercise of their activities there will be much difference. The liberal man will need money for the doing of his liberal deeds, and the just man too will need it for the returning of services (for wishes are hard to discern, and even people who are not just pretend to wish to act justly); and the brave man will need power if he is to accomplish any of the acts that correspond to his virtue, and the temperate man will need opportunity; for how else is either he or any of the others to be recognized? It is debated, too, whether the will or the deed is more essential to virtue, which is assumed to involve both; it is surely clear that its perfection involves both; but for deeds many things are needed, and more, the greater and nobler the deeds are. But the man who is contemplating the truth needs no such thing, at least with a view to the exercise of his activity; indeed they are, one may say, even hindrances, at all events to his contemplation; but in so far as he is a man and lives with a number of people, he chooses to do virtuous acts; he will therefore need such aids to living a human life.

But that perfect happiness is a contemplative activity will appear from the following consideration as well. We assume the gods to be above all other beings blessed and happy; but what sort of actions must we assign to them? Acts of justice? Will not the gods seem absurd if they make contracts and return deposits, and so on? Acts of a brave man, then, confronting dangers and running risks because it is noble to do so? Or liberal acts? To whom will they give? It will be strange if they are really to have money or anything of the kind. And what would their temperate acts be? Is not such praise tasteless, since they have no bad appetites? If we were to run through them all, the circumstances of action would be found trivial and unworthy of gods. Still, every one supposes that they *live* and therefore that they are active; we cannot suppose them to sleep like Endymion. Now if you take

away from a living being action, and still more production, what is left
but contemplation? Therefore the activity of God, which surpasses all
others in blessedness, must be contemplative; and of human activities,
therefore, that which is most akin to this must be most of the nature
of happiness.

This is indicated, too, by the fact that the other animals have no
share in happiness, being completely deprived of such activity. For
while the whole life of the gods is blessed, and that of men too in so
far as some likeness of such activity belongs to them, none of the other
animals is happy, since they in no way share in contemplation. Happiness extends, then, just so far as contemplation does, and those to
whom contemplation more fully belongs are more truly happy, not as
a mere concomitant but in virtue of the contemplation; for this is in itself precious. Happiness, therefore, must be some form of contemplation.

But, being a man, one will also need external prosperity; for our nature is not self-sufficient for the purpose of contemplation, but our
body also must be healthy and must have food and other attention.
Still, we must not think that the man who is to be happy will need
many things or great things, merely because he cannot be supremely
happy without external goods; for self-sufficiency and action do not involve excess, and we can do noble acts without ruling earth and sea; for
even with moderate advantages one can act virtuously (this is manifest
enough; for private persons are thought to do worthy acts no less than
despots—indeed even more); and it is enough that we should have so
much as that; for the life of the man who is active in accordance with
virtue will be happy. Solon, too, was perhaps sketching well the happy
man when he described him as moderately furnished with externals
but as having done (as Solon thought) the noblest acts, and lived tem-
perately; for one can with but moderate possessions do what one ought.
Anaxagoras also seems to have supposed the happy man not to be rich
nor a despot, when he said that he would not be surprised if the happy
man were to seem to most people a strange person; for they judge by
externals, since these are all they perceive. The opinions of the wise
seem, then, to harmonize with our arguments. But while even such
things carry some conviction, the truth in practical matters is discerned from the facts of life; for these are the decisive factor. We must
therefore survey what we have already said, bringing it to the test of
the facts of life, and if it harmonizes with the facts we must accept it,
but if it clashes with them we must suppose it to be mere theory. Now
he who exercises his reason and cultivates it seems to be both in the
best state of mind and most dear to the gods. For if the gods have any
care for human affairs, as they are thought to have, it would be reasonable both that they should delight in that which was best and most

akin to them (i.e. reason) and that they should reward those who love and honour this most, as caring for the things that are dear to them and acting both rightly and nobly. And that all these attributes belong most of all to the philosopher is manifest. He, therefore, is the dearest to the gods. And he who is that will presumably be also the happiest; so that in this way too the philosopher will more than any other be happy.

(From *The Works of Aristotle Translated into English*, ed. W.D. Ross. Trans. W.D. Ross. Oxford: Oxford University Press, 1915. Reprinted by permission of Oxford University Press.)

Wisdom and Virtue as the Basis of Society (from *Politics*, Book VII)

1. He who would duly inquire about the best form of a state ought first to determine which is the most eligible life; while this remains uncertain the best form of the state must also be uncertain; for, in the natural order of things, those may be expected to lead the best life who are governed in the best manner of which their circumstances admit. We ought therefore to ascertain, first of all, which is the most generally eligible life, and then whether the same life is or is not best for the state and for individuals.

Assuming that enough has been already said in discussions outside the school concerning the best life, we will now only repeat what is contained in them. Certainly no one will dispute the propriety of that partition of goods which separates them into three classes, viz. external goods, goods of the body, and goods of the soul, or deny that the happy man must have all three. For no one would maintain that he is happy who has not in him a particle of courage or temperance or justice or prudence, who is afraid of every insect which flutters past him, and will commit any crime, however great, in order to gratify his lust of meat or drink, who will sacrifice his dearest friend for the sake of half-a-farthing, and is as feeble and false in mind as a child or a madman. These propositions are almost universally acknowledged as soon as they are uttered, but men differ about the degree or relative superiority of this or that good. Some think that a very moderate amount of virtue is enough, but set no limit to their desires of wealth, property, power, reputation, and the like. To whom we reply by an appeal to facts, which easily prove that mankind do not acquire or preserve virtue by the help of external goods, but external goods by the help of virtue, and that happiness, whether consisting in pleasure or virtue, or both, is more often found with those who are most highly cultivated in their mind and in their character, and have only a moderate share of external goods, than among those who possess external goods to a useless extent but are deficient in higher qualities; and this is not only matter of experience, but, if reflected upon, will easily appear to be in accordance with reason. For, whereas external goods have a limit, like any other instrument, and all things useful are of such a nature that where there is too much of them they must either do harm, or at any rate be of no use, to their possessors, every good of the soul, the greater it is, is also of greater use, if the epithet useful as well as noble is appropriate to such subjects. No proof is required to show that the best state of one thing in relation to another corresponds in degree of excellence to the interval between the natures of which we say that these very states are states: so that, if the soul is more noble than our possessions or our bodies, both absolutely and in relation to us, it must be admitted that the best state of either has a similar ratio to the other. Again, it is for the sake of the soul that goods external and goods of the body are eligible at all, and all wise men ought to choose them for the sake of the soul, and not the soul for the sake of them.

Let us acknowledge then that each one has just so much of happiness as he has of virtue and wisdom, and of virtuous and wise action. God is a witness to us of this truth, for he is happy and blessed, not by reason of any external good, but in himself and by reason of his own nature. And herein of necessity lies the difference between good fortune and happiness; for external goods come of themselves, and chance is the author of them, but no one is just or temperate by or through chance. In like manner, and by a similar train of argument, the happy state may be shown to be that which is best and which acts rightly; and rightly it cannot act without doing right actions, and neither individual nor state can do right actions without virtue and wisdom. Thus the courage, justice, and wisdom of a state have the same form and nature as the qualities which give the individual who possesses them the name of just, wise, or temperate.

Thus much may suffice by way of preface: for I could not avoid touching upon these questions, neither could I go through all the arguments affecting them; these are the business of another science.

Let us assume then that the best life, both for individuals and states, is the life of virtue, when virtue has external goods enough for the performance of good actions. If there are any who controvert our assertion, we will in this treatise pass them over, and consider their objections hereafter.

The Civil Society (from *Politics,* Book I)

1. Every state is a community of some kind, and every community is established with a view to some good; for mankind always act in order to obtain that which they think good. But, if all communities aim

at some good, the state or political community, which is the highest of all, and which embraces all the rest, aims at good in a greater degree than any other, and at the highest good.

Some people think that the qualifications of a statesman, king, householder, and master are the same, and that they differ, not in kind, but only in the number of their subjects. For example, the ruler over a few is called a master; over more, the manager of a household; over a still larger number, a statesman or king, as if there were no difference between a great household and a small state. The distinction which is made between the king and the statesman is as follows: When the government is personal, the ruler is a king; when, according to the rules of the political science, the citizens rule and are ruled in turn, then he is called a statesman.

But all this is a mistake; for governments differ in kind, as will be evident to any one who considers the matter according to the method which has hitherto guided us. As in other departments of science, so in politics, the compound should always be resolved into the simple elements or least parts of the whole. We must therefore look at the elements of which the state is composed, in order that we may see in what the different kinds of rule differ from one another, and whether any scientific result can be attained about each one of them.

2. He who thus considers things in their first growth and origin, whether a state or anything else, will obtain the clearest view of them. In the first place there must be a union of those who cannot exist without each other; namely, of male and female, that the race may continue (and this is a union which is formed, not of deliberate purpose, but because, in common with other animals and with plants, mankind have a natural desire to leave behind them an image of themselves), and of natural ruler and subject, that both may be preserved. For that which can foresee by the exercise of mind is by nature intended to be lord and master, and that which can with its body give effect to such foresight is a subject, and by nature a slave; hence master and slave have the same interest. Now nature has distinguished between the female and the slave. For she is not niggardly, like the smith who fashions the Delphian knife for many uses; she makes each thing for a single use, and every instrument is best made when intended for one and not for many uses. But among barbarians no distinction is made between women and slaves, because there is no natural ruler among them: they are a community of slaves, male and female. Wherefore the poets say—

'It is meet that Hellenes should rule over barbarians';

as if they thought that the barbarian and the slave were by nature one.

Out of these two relationships between man and woman, master and slave, the first thing to arise is the family, and Hesiod is right when he says—

'First house and wife and an ox for the plough',

for the ox is the poor man's slave. The family is the association established by nature for the supply of men's everyday wants, and the members of it are called by Charondas 'companions of the cupboard', and by Epimenides the Cretan, 'companions of the manger.' But when several families are united, and the association aims at something more than the supply of daily needs, the first society to be formed is the village. And the most natural form of the village appears to be that of a colony from the family, composed of the children and grandchildren, who are said to be suckled with the same milk'. And this is the reason why Hellenic states were originally governed by kings; because the Hellenes were under royal rule before they came together, as the barbarians still are. Every family is ruled by the eldest, and therefore in the colonies of the family the kingly form of government prevailed because they were of the same blood. As Homer says:

'Each one gives law to his children and to his wives.'

For they lived dispersedly, as was the manner in ancient times. Wherefore men say that the Gods have a king, because they themselves either are or were in ancient times under the rule of a king. For they imagine, not only the forms of the Gods, but their ways of life to be like their own.

When several villages are united in a single complete community, large enough to be nearly or quite self-sufficing, the state comes into existence, originating in the bare needs of life, and continuing in existence for the sake of a good life. And therefore, if the earlier forms of society are natural, so is the state, for it is the end of them, and the nature of a thing is its end. For what each thing is when fully developed, we call its nature, whether we are speaking of a man, a horse, or a family. Besides, the final cause and end of a thing is the best, and to be self-sufficing is the end and the best.

Hence it is evident that the state is a creation of nature, and that man is by nature a political animal. And he who by nature and not by mere accident is without a state, is either a bad man or above humanity; he is like the

'Tribeless, lawless, hearthless one,'

whom Homer denounces—the natural outcast is forthwith a lover of war; he may be compared to an isolated piece at draughts.

Now, that man is more of a political animal than bees or any other gregarious animals is evident. Nature, as we often say, makes nothing in vain, and man is the only animal whom she has endowed with the gift of speech. And whereas mere voice is but an indication of pleasure or pain, and is therefore found in other animals (for their nature attains to the perception of pleasure and pain and the intimation of them to one another, and no further), the power of speech is intended to set forth the expedient and inexpedient, and therefore likewise the just and the unjust. And it is a characteristic of man that he alone has any sense of good and evil, of just and unjust, and the like, and the association of living beings who have this sense makes a family and a state.

Further, the state is by nature clearly prior to the family and to the individual, since the whole is of necessity prior to the part; for example, if the whole body be destroyed, there will be no foot or hand, except in an equivocal sense, as we might speak of a stone hand; for when destroyed the hand will be no better than that. But things are defined by their working and power; and we ought not to say that they are the same when they no longer have their proper quality, but only that they have the same name. The proof that the state is a creation of nature and prior to the individual is that the individual, when isolated, is not self-sufficing; and therefore he is like a part in relation to the whole. But he who is unable to live in society, or who has no need because he is sufficient for himself, must be either a beast or a god: he is no part of a state. A social instinct is implanted in all men by nature, and yet he who first founded the state was the greatest of benefactors. For man, when perfected, is the best of animals, but, when separated from law and justice, he is the worst of all; since armed injustice is the more dangerous, and he is equipped at birth with arms, meant to be used by intelligence and virtue, which he may use for the worst ends. Wherefore, if he have not virtue, he is the most unholy and the most savage of animals, and the most full of lust and gluttony. But justice is the bond of men in states, for the administration of justice, which is the determination of what is just, is the principle of order in political society.

(Trans. B. Jowett)

Review Questions

1. Compare rationalism and empiricism, using Plato and Aristotle as points of departure.
2. What, for Aristotle, is the role of logic?

3. What does Aristotle mean by defining metaphysics as the science of *being as such*?
4. Is there, for Aristotle, a contradiction between being and nonbeing?
5. In Aristotle's analysis, what is there in being that allow change, or becoming, to take place?
6. What does Aristotle mean by *cause*?
7. How does Aristotle come to the conclusion that living things have a soul or are "besouled"?
8. Outline Aristotle's argument for a Prime Mover.
9. What need does Aristotle see for a governed society?

PART II

The Medieval Period

The Spirit of Medieval Philosophy: Philosophy Meets Theology

Earlier we saw that the major divisions of the history of philosophy are usually given as ancient, medieval, modern, and contemporary, knowing that dates cannot be assigned as the absolute beginning or end of cultural eras. The Greek period, for example, extends well into the Christian era, and the Christian era was well underway before it could be identified as a culture. Locating periods in time for the purpose of discussion varies according to the goal of the historian, but it is reasonable to designate the medieval period as beginning with St. Augustine in the fourth century A.D. Augustine was one of many Christian writers who were known as *Fathers of the Church*, a term which, in its usually accepted meaning, refers to all Christian writers of the early Church. In Latin the word for father is *pater*, the root from which the words used in referring to this early period are derived: *patrology, patristics, patristic age*. The earlier Church Fathers of the second and third centuries had as their main concern the defense of the fledgling Church and are therefore called *apologists*, from *apology*, the customary word for a defense tract. If they wrote in Greek, like Justin Martyr and Irenaeus, they are called *Greek apologists*; if in Latin, like Tertullian and Lactantius, *Latin apologists*. The later Fathers, like Augustine, Basil the Great, Gregory of Nyssa, John Damascene, and Gregory the Great, were intellectual believers who tried to incorporate insights from various areas of knowledge, especially philosophy, into the texture of belief in order to develop an explanation of faith that would satisfy the demands of human reason.

Christianity as a religion did not become widespread until several centuries after its founding, having had to go underground in many places in the Roman Empire to save itself. But as it gradually became accepted, it became identified with the life of the people, so that during the Middle Ages there were no clear boundaries among religion,

117

culture, and society; they evolved as one. The term *Christian Middle Ages* is the label that many historians use in referring to this period, although no one can say that it is *the* definitive Christian period. Yet, allowing for the substantial contributions of thinkers representing the Jewish and Islamic faiths, the period in Europe is identifiable as Christian. Belief in Christ, membership in the Church, the supremacy of the pope, the use of the sacraments, and acceptance of the Bible were all part of daily life. Architecture, painting, sculpture, music, education, and a host of other human activities were fashioned into expressions of belief. It was an age of faith.

If, as we saw earlier, experience invites reflection, then reflection on the experience of faith is precisely in order because faith is the fundamental experience of reality that a believer has. Because of the nature of faith, analysis can proceed in several different directions depending on what is stressed. For example, if stress is placed on the rational, that is, if an attempt is made to satisfy primarily the demands of the intellect while bracketing what theologians call *revealed data*, the analysis emphasizes the philosophical aspects of faith. This approach tends to make the act of faith a sort of conclusion to a logical process and to negate the suprarational character of faith. If, on the other hand, stress is placed on revealed data, that is, if an attempt is made to establish these data as revealed while bracketing the demands of the intellect, the analysis favors the nonrational aspects of faith. This approach tends to separate the act of faith from any kind of rational content thus making the act of faith totally suprarational. During the Middle Ages, for the main line of Christian thinkers who avoided tipping the scales to either extreme, faith was explicated in the context of a theology that tried to blend philosophical insights with the scholarly exegesis of revealed data.

The imperative of faith to explain itself is announced in the phrase "faith seeking to be understood" or "faith seeking understanding" (*fides quaerens intellectum*), which, as a constant medieval theme, underlines the effort required in formulating its truths; it employs ideas from any discipline if they help to probe its meaning or to show that, whatever personal commitment to the suprarational it entails, faith is nonetheless reasonable.

Described in this way, medieval philosophy worked within theology to focus on questions that dealt with God and humans: God's existence; what He must be like in His inner life and what this means for people; what an individual's relationship to God is; man's destiny; the goal of human behavior; and countless other questions that show historically how Christian thought either developed ideas inherited from Greek thinkers or discovered radically new ones unfathomed in a Greek context. For example, though Aristotle wrote some insightful and beautiful pages on God and His inner life, it was the Christian thinkers, using what they learned from the Scriptures, who delineated a new understanding of the relationship between the divine and the human as one of love. Not only is God the Transcendent, the Creator, the Almighty, the Immense, but He is also Love. In saying "God is love," St. John is saying that God's very transcendence, power, and presence are, as far as man is concerned, *for the sake of man.* The world is not God's plaything; it is His cherished creation coming forth freely from His measureless abundance. The sacred character of creation, the meaning of personhood, the completion of one's mortal life here by immortal life hereafter, and the feeling that man could finally defeat evil, are all indications of a new opening for human understanding as the Greek tradition passed into the Christian.

CHAPTER 5

St. Augustine (354–430)

Introduction

St. Augustine is the Christian thinker *par excellence*; he combines the intellectual and personal forces previously described to create a profound commitment to religious life, and he typifies the anxiety endured by one who is torn between the appeal of God's revelation and fidelity to his own intellect, and between his longing to lead a quiet life and the call to the busyness of a bishop's office. Having found himself in so many different situations, and having generated respect as a man of learning, he was obliged to address a wide variety of contemporary problems both practical and academic; but because his theology is personal and open-ended, it never fails to shed light on the problems of any given time; he is always contemporaneous — a theologian for all seasons. Intellectuals in the West respect and admire him.

The son of a Christian mother and a pagan father, Aurelius Augustinus was a Roman, born in 354 in North Africa in the small town of Thagaste, the present-day Souk-Ahras in Algeria. The area, known as Numidia, was a province of the Roman Empire and thoroughly Latin in culture; it contained the city of Carthage, held to be the greatest city of the West after Rome. Augustine's birth and education made him a true heir of Latin antiquity. His early formal education was completed at Carthage; it was a literary education emphasizing the art of rhetoric, with some attention paid to philosophy. Rhetoric, the art of speaking and writing persuasively according to rigorous rules of presentation, was a highly prized talent, and Augustine's commitment to it contributed to his persuasiveness in years to come. Philosophy was part of his education but was not particularly exciting, except for one work, Cicero's *Hortensius*, which inspired him to a love of the discipline that never abated.

Following the not unusual practice of the time, Augustine lived for years with a woman who was not his legal wife; they had a son, Adeodatus ("God-given"), who died a young man. At the age of twenty, after his father died, Augustine turned to teaching to support his family. In 383 he went to Rome, where he became a professor of rhetoric, and in the same year he received an appointment as the public orator of Milan. Just outside Milan, at Cassiciacum, he established a retreat for himself and some friends where he could devote himself to reflection, study, and writing.

Until then, Augustine had never considered himself a Christian. He deemed Christianity a religion for simple folk, for the uneducated and unlettered. He, whose Latin usage was exquisitely classical, was put off by the Bible because he found it primitive in style and contradictory; the basic problem for him was that conversion meant full acceptance of the Christian life, and this he was not prepared to do. However, whether it was the example of his mother, later to be honored as a saint, or the influence of St. Ambrose, the bishop of Milan whose sermons Augustine attended for the sheer force of his rhetoric, or the attractiveness of the Christian saints whose lives he had read is not clear, nevertheless, like many other famous figures whose future life crystallized in a single moment, Augustine experienced an instant of explosive clarity in which he knew, without doubt, that he was called to become a Christian.

In a poignant description in the *Confessions*, Augustine recounts how, having long been absorbed in the things of the spirit but unwilling to take a decisive step, he heard a child's voice admonishing him to "take and read." He put his hands on the New Testament he had been reading and, in his own words, "I snatched it up, opened it and in silence read the passage upon which my eyes first fell: 'Not in rioting and drunkenness, not in chambering and impurities, not in contention and envy, but put ye on the Lord Jesus Christ and make not provision for the flesh in its concupiscences.' I had no wish to read further, and no need. For in that instant, with the very ending of the sentence, it was as though a light of utter confidence shone in all my heart, and all the darkness of uncertainty vanished away." Augustine, with his son and some friends, was baptized the following year by St. Ambrose.

After his conversion, Augustine's life was never the same. If he had delayed conversion because it involved the full acceptance of the Christian life, full acceptance was now upon him. What he wanted, first and foremost, was to think out the God–man relationship, and this could be done only in solitude. As an echo of Socrates's injunction to "know thyself," Augustine knew that the experience of God had to come from within; to ignore the self is to ignore God who dwells there: "Too late have I loved You, O Beauty ever ancient and ever new. Too late have I loved You! For behold You were within me, and I without ... You were with me, but I was not with You." So, a short while after his baptism, Augustine prepared to leave Milan for his native Thagaste, where he would resume his quiet way of life. But his retreat was not to last, for, one day when he was visiting the church in nearby Hippo, the most important city after Carthage, the people cried out for him to become their priest. Augustine finally yielded to their insistence, became a priest, and then later the bishop of Hippo; yet, even after giving up his contemplative life for the active ministry, he still cherished the ideal of a peaceful, contemplative life and tried, insofar as he could, to follow it while busily engaged in ecclesiastical affairs.

Augustine's influence spread far and wide. His advice was sought from all quarters and from all sorts of petitioners. He preached and wrote incessantly; he traveled considerably. His sermons were eagerly attended, his books and letters anxiously awaited. He once wrote a letter to the great biblical scholar St. Jerome, and because the messenger allowed it to be copied, its contents were known to everyone long before Jerome himself received it! What can be said of an active contemplative who wrote 113 books, 218 letters, and 500 sermons? Uneven at times, unclear at times, ambiguous at times, it is true; but in so vast an undertaking, even Augustine knew that failings were to be expected. Thus, toward the end of his life, he felt compelled to review all his works in his *Retractions* and to publish his final comments. Augustine's most famous work is his *Confessions*, perhaps the first autobiography of its kind. To this must be added his work *On the Trinity*, and his last great work, *The City of God*, in which he used the sack of Rome by the Visigoths in 410 to demonstrate the passing nature of temporal power in contrast to another power that does not pass.

Though much of Augustine's thought grew from within, and in the undisturbed peace of solitude, much of it was forged in a climate of controversy, in which he emerged as the protector of orthodoxy against those theologies that, in his eyes, would distort the true Christian message. Two such theologies, which had become the centers of distinctly religious movements, stood out. The first of these was founded by a third-century Persian named Mani, who proclaimed himself an Apostle of Jesus Christ and the Paraclete (Holy Spirit) as well; thus *Manicheism* presented itself as the perfect form of Christianity. It made pretentious promises for a spiritual life without surrendering one's own reason, thus making it attractive to the young Augustine. One of its basic doctrines was that of extreme dualism between matter and spirit, to the extent that matter was considered evil and spirit good. But as Augustine came to see, this view of matter can go in two directions: either the Christian must avoid every contact with matter — which can lead to a life of severe asceticism—or the Christian can do anything at all regarding matter, since it would make no difference to his or her spiritual life — which can lead to a life of dissolute behavior. Mainly because he was led by what he thought was the exemplary life of its practitioners, Augustine was enthusiastic about Manicheism at first, but as time went on he came to realize the fantasy it really was and began to polemicize against it.

The second theology that Augustine challenged presented a much more intricate problem, for it had to do with man's relationship with God vis-à-vis the need for grace. The monk Pelagius had for some time maintained that the divine gift of grace was not necessary for human salvation and that man possessed within himself all the ingredients required; if grace meant anything, it meant simply a sign of adoption by God. Perhaps Pelagius arrived at this conclusion in order to underscore what man must do for himself to advance spiritually. At any rate, Augustine, whose dramatic conversion must be recalled, reacted against this notion, for it seemed to belittle, if not remove entirely, God's role in salvation, making salvation a completely human event to the exclusion of God's saving action. In one form or another, now original sin, now predestination, now free will, the polemic against Pelagianism was to continue until Augustine's death. Without trying to write finis to the delicate questions interwoven in this polemic, it shows Augustine's unequivocal contention that man's "ascending" to God can be accomplished only with God's "condescending" to man.

God and man. God and myself. That was all Augustine wanted to know. He was not demeaning other kinds of knowledge, but his purpose was to go directly to that ultimate knowledge by which all other knowledge stands or falls, and without which no other knowledge has any importance. Knowledge without bearing on either God or man is not worthy of the name because it has no personal significance and, to that extent, is "depersonalized." When Augustine uses the word *science* he means knowledge dealing with the practical, the many and, in general, the knowledge of temporal things; such knowledge is necessary, for without it the virtues needed for right living cannot be obtained. *Wisdom*, on the other hand, tends to draw the many to unity. It is concerned with the contemplation of eternal and immutable truth. All truth, for Augustine, has a personal dimension, and once the characteristics of eternity and immutability are touched, truth must be seen as Truth, and the ultimate Truth is Person-alized in the God who is Truth. Hence, the search for truth is, in essence, the search for the Person to whom we can relate as persons, to whom we can commit ourselves, confident that in reality He commits Himself to us first.

With this orientation, Augustine took the inward path to discover that the existence of God is confirmed by the very nature of truth. The inward path discloses ascending levels of knowledge, and at the highest level, that of reason, truth is beheld as immutable and eternal. It is not so much the content of a truth, such as seven and three are ten, that is its prime characteristic, but its very incorruptibility: that seven and three are ten is *incorruptibly* true, and incorruptibility cannot emanate from what is mutable and temporal, only from what is immutable and eternal.

The discovery of God in ourselves sets forth the kind of linkage we have with Him. When called upon for a definition of man, rather than offering one like "rational animal," Augustine offers "image of God," a description carried down through the Middle Ages. Man is like God, yes; and this likeness is already a badge of honor; but man's crowning glory resides in his being God's *image* — a unique likeness because it is produced by the original as an expression of itself. Two things can have a likeness to each other without having any further relationship; two samples of handwriting can be like each other, but the relationship stops there. Image adds to the notion of likeness the fact of a resemblance to the original, made by the original, much like the image in a mirror. As the image of God, man bears a profound resemblance to the original. He is brought into being by God the Creator; all his perfections are participations of the uncreated and unlimited perfection of God the Exemplar; his growth in freedom is a growth unto God, who is infinitely free. Further, in His inmost being, God is triune, which, to use classical Christian terminology, means a trinity of persons in one nature. Whatever else this may signify for Augustine, the ruling idea is that plurality-unity pervades all reality because at the head of it there is a Trinity of Persons acting within One Nature; and by an extension of the very activity "generating" the Trinity, all other things are also generated. Everything, then, bears an impression of the Trinity, but it is man, God's image, in whom the clearest resemblance is to be found. At man's inmost point, at that point of the soul where the unity of man is concentrated, there are three recognizable vectors into which this unity is resolved: mind, knowledge, and love. Though they are separate from one another, they are still one with each other, for the mind in knowing knows itself, and in knowing itself loves itself: "When the mind knows and loves itself, there is a trinity of mind, love and knowledge ... wonderfully, these three are inseparable from each other yet, while each is a single thing unto itself, they are all one when considered relatively to each other."

In addition to the image-of-God relationship, there is still another dimension of human nature: the societal dimension. Of course, man is aware of what society is, and his experience of living in society demonstrates both its need and appropriateness. It is this very life in society that is revealed as having a transcendent richness, for inasmuch as God is the supreme unity and yet triune, He is the perfect exemplar of society as unity, a community of Three Persons sharing a common life. As the image of God, man must translate this divine unity-in-society into a human reality by working toward a society unified by love. Even though we are all individual units, we are encompassed by the larger unity of human society, and we are drawn to see in each person the "neighbor" of the Gospel: "You ask, 'who is my neighbor?' Why, every person is your neighbor!"

It should be clear by now that Augustine's philosophy is a philosophy of love. For him, love is a principle of unity, of completion, of meaning. The myriad aspects of reality would lapse into incomprehensible fragmentation unless some way were found to hold them all together. Beyond the sources of unity supplied by mechanics and mathematics, so significantly essayed by the Greek philosophers, for Augustine, in keeping with his personalist outlook, the only successful way is the way of love. We know from our experience that love draws us into unity with the one we love; and we know that love draws all other things into it, thus becoming the center of a new world. So it is with the bond between God and man, a bond of love that gives humanity its meaning. It cannot be otherwise; man, by his very being, is drawn to God; or, in Augustine's phrase, borrowing from the physics of the ancient world in which objects tend to move toward the places assigned them by nature and, once there remaining at rest, man *gravitates* towards Him: "A body, by its weight, is borne to its proper place . . . but my love is my weight, and I am borne to wherever I should be borne" — a sentiment that is reechoed in Augustine's writings and encapsulated in his most often quoted saying, "My heart is restless until it rest in Thee, My God."

Yet our relationship with God is not given all at once; it is subject to growth, as is true of all organic things. Our relationship is a gradual growing unto God, a growth by degrees. To outline this growth, spiritual writers talk of "steps" or "stages" in the approach to God; Augustine does the same, but the number of stages makes no difference — sometimes he speaks of three, sometimes four or five or seven. In his book *On Nature and Grace* he presents a scale of four degrees based on charity; in *The Magnitude of the Soul* he discusses seven stages in the ascent of the soul to the contemplation of God. The number of stages towards fulfillment is not important, but the idea of growth is. Using the generally accepted threefold division of one's journey to God into the purgative, illuminative, and unitive ways, Augustine sees, in the first place, that we must free ourselves from the hold the world has on us. Love of the world connotes the sway that material and sensual things have over the mind and will; it includes the obvious gross vices, as well as the more subtler and less tangible. Augustine continually speaks of fleeing from the world, which does not mean condemnation, for the world is a good creature of God; it means, rather, a detachment from the world whereby we view created goods as means to the end, and not as ends in themselves. In the illuminative way, the soul quickens in its response to God; we take up more consciously the life of virtue and pursue cleanness of heart, moved by the light of God's truth in us. This stage is marked by an abiding awareness of God's presence in the life of the soul, an awareness Augustine calls "sensing God"; the more one senses God, the more one lives in His presence, becoming like Him, abounding in charity. The final stage Augustine conceives to be the most intimate union we have with God, brought about by contemplative knowledge, at once intuitive and experiential, wherein God is perceived as *the* transcendent reality and the soul is correspondingly flooded with love. In its fullest meaning, this stage is the happiness of the blessed in heaven, but on earth it can be experienced from time to time as a mystical experience, a perception of Something Unchangeable, filling the beholder with indescribable joy.

But the fulfillment of our humanity is hardly accomplished without our cooperation, a lifelong reaching out for those things that nourish our humanity and a rejection of those destructive of it. Therefore, the key to this growth is *freedom*, the personal dimension of the human being that is at the same time its grandeur and its misery. Whatever theological controversy Augustine's discussion of freedom occasioned in later centuries, he was never satisfied with a determinism of any kind because, by destroying man's power of self-definition, it made genuine growth impossible; personal control would be surrendered to the impersonal forces of the world. As William James put it centuries later, if freedom is denied, then necessity and impossibility between them rule the destinies of the world.

That I am free is obvious to Augustine: "I hold nothing so firmly or surely as that I have a will by which I am moved to the enjoyment of things: what could I possibly call mine if the will, by which I choose or refuse, is not mine." The freedom Augustine speaks of is not only the possibility of free choice but the deeper question of how free choice is used — what is freedom for? Real freedom is the freedom to make choices befitting our humanity, in acts of charity, honesty, justice, respect, trust, acceptance, and so on; so used, freedom is the engine for the enlargement of our humanity. But if freedom is used to make choices unbecoming our humanity, such as acts of injustice, hatred, distrust, meanness, and unconcern, then it is not real freedom at all but its perversion; it is inhuman, it is wrong, it is sin. In a word, human nature is destined for the good; and this destiny is achieved only with man's free participation, for freedom is the glory of human nature.

It is precisely at this point that a huge problem looms for Augustine: the problem of evil. Evil creates an impasse for free will and a roadblock in the path to God. The problem was a long-standing one for Augustine, going back to his pre-Christian days when he was a Manichean. Though evil is a problem for all mankind, it is a special one for Augustine, who, having committed himself to Christianity, also committed himself to the God who is good and who acts out of love. He clearly poses the problem when he writes: "If the activity of the will in turning away from God is without doubt a sin, can we say that God is the cause of sin?" In a larger framework, the problem is as follows: God is good, and whatever is created by Him is good; but there is evil in the world — natural disasters, physical defects, accidental destruction, suffering, sin. How, in a world created by the good God, can there be evil? In facing the challenge of this once and forever problem, the Bishop of Hippo assumed the role of God's protector. He could not allow evil in the world to be charged against God as though it were the result of impotence, lack of compassion, or malevolence on His part. In trying to solve the problem radically, Augustine's view can be called metaphysical in that evil attaches to the very nature of the created being. Once we understand that God is the only perfect being, and not lacking in any good, it follows that any being less than God is not fully perfect and in some respect is lacking in good; imperfection is rooted in its very being. Imperfection, in the form of privation, defectiveness, or lack, is called evil and can be found only in that which is — only, therefore, in what is good. You cannot speak of God as the cause of that which is not, or the cause of the absence of good; therefore, you cannot speak of God as the author of evil, any more than you can speak of an artist, having painted his flowers yellow, as the cause of their not being red.

It is not difficult to see how Augustine concluded that moral evil in a human act is essentially a privation of what that act ought to be. Somehow the finite nature of the will explains why it is able to initiate a "defective" movement": "A wicked will is the cause of all evils." Or as Augustine put it in *The City of God,* "No one ought to wonder whether an evil will has an 'efficient' cause, — rather its cause is not 'efficient' but 'deficient' because an evil will is not an 'effect' but a 'defect.' " True freedom, then, does not lie in the choice between good and evil; it lies only in the choice of the good. Freedom is found in the practice of virtue, in the pursuit of justice, in the doing of God's will; only the good are free. As expressed in Augustine's simple formula, "The law of freedom is the law of love."

With Augustine the problem of evil is not solved. However, his reflections on the nature of evil have become a permanent fixture in Western Christian thought because of the effort he made to show that God's bidding for the world will be done and that nothing, not even evil, can overcome the goodness that suffuses His creation.

Readings

Two Commandments of Love (from Commentary on St. John's Gospel)

How then can we take these two things our Lord told the paralytic to do as standing for those two precepts of charity? 'Pick up your bed, he says, and walk' (John 5:8). Now brothers, let us run over those two precepts together. After all, you ought to know them backwards; it is not enough just to recall them when you are reminded of them, they should never be out of your thoughts. You should be thinking about them absolutely all the time, that God is to be loved, and your neighbour; God 'with your whole heart and your whole soul, and your whole mind, and your neighbour as yourself'. These are the two things to be thought about and meditated on, these are the things to be kept in mind, these are the things to be done, the things to be carried out, every minute of the day. Loving God comes first in the issue of the order, but loving your neighbour comes first in carrying it out. He who gave you these two commandments of love would not of course put your neighbour first, God second; no, God first, your neighbour second. But *you* cannot yet see God, it is by loving your neighbour that you will first deserve to see him; it is only by loving your neighbour that you can polish up your eyes to see God with, as St. John says quite plainly; 'If you do not love the brother you see, how will you be able to love the God you do not see?' (1 John 4:20). Look you are told, 'Love God'. If you say to me 'Show him to me, if I am to love him', what can I reply except what John himself says, 'No one has ever seen God' (John 1:18)? But in case you should jump to the conclusion that seeing God is therefore no concern of yours at all, he also says 'God is love, and he who remains in love, remains in God' (1 John 4:16). So love your neighbour; then look inside yourself at what you love him with; and there, as far as you can, you will see God. So begin by loving your neighbour. 'Break your bread to the hungry, and bring the needy man without a roof over his head into your house; if you see him naked, clothe him, and do not despise the domestics of your seed' (Isa. 58:7). And what will you yourself get out of doing these things? 'Then will your light burst forth like the dawn.' Your light is your God, and he is like the dawn for you, because he will come to you after the night of this world. In himself he neither rises nor sets, he stays the same always. But for you on your return to him he will rise, just as for you on your separation from him he set. So 'Pick up your bed' seems to me to be saying 'Love your neighbour.'

The Mystical Experience (from *Commentary on Psalm* 41)

Every day then I hear, 'Where is your God?' Every day I feed on my tears; day and night therefore I am led to ponder on what I have heard, 'Where is your God?' I myself have also looked for my God, in order if possible to see something, not just believe it. I can see easily enough what my God has made, I cannot see my God himself who made them. . . .

So I look for my God then in visible bodily things, and I do not find him; I look for his substance in myself, as though he were something like me, and I do not find him here either; I begin to perceive that my God is something above the soul. Therefore, in order to find him, 'These things did I ponder, and I poured out my soul above myself.' . . . As for me, as long as I do not see him, as long as I am put off, I eat my tears day and night. But I have pondered over my search for my God, and longing to look at the invisible things of God understood through the things he has made, I have poured out my soul above it-self. Now there is nothing left for me to reach except my God. Above my soul there is the house of my God. That is where he lives, where he can see me from, where he created me from, where he directs and advises me from, where he cheers me on and calls me from, where he guides me from, where he leads me from, where he brings me through to at last.

You see, the fact is that he who has such an exalted and exclusive house, also has a tent here on earth. His tent on earth is his Church still on its foreign travels from home. But this is where he must be looked for, because in the tent is to be found the road which leads to the house. After all, when I poured out my soul above myself to reach my God, why precisely did I do it? 'Because I will proceed in the place of the wonderful tent as far as the house of my God'. . . . There are already many things to wonder at in this tent. . . . There are the virtues in the soul that obeys God to marvel at, but I am still walking in the place of the tent. I pass even these things by, and marvellous though the tent is, I am struck with amazement when I come through to the house of my God. He speaks about this house in another psalm, where he is worried by the very hard question why it is that the bad on this earth very often have a good time, and the good a bad time, and he says 'I undertook to know this, there is toil before me until I en-ter the sanctuary of God, and gain understanding in the last things' (Ps. 72:16). For that is where the fountain of understanding is, in the sanctuary of God, in his house. There this man gained understanding in the last things, and solved his problem about the prosperity of the wicked and the toils of the just. . . . He came to know it in the sanctu-ary of God. By climbing up the tent, he came to the house of God.

While he is wondering at the members of the tent, he is led up to the house of God by following a sort of sweetness, an inward something or other, a hidden delight, as though the strains of some melodious in-strument were issuing from the house of God. . . . And it is from these eternal, everlasting festivities that the ears of our minds catch a some-thing, a sweet melodious echo,—but only if the world is not making a din. The man who walks in this tent, and turns over in his mind the wonderful things God has done for the redemption of the faithful, is struck and bewitched by the sounds of that festival in heaven, drawn by them like the stag to the fountain of waters.

But as long as we are in the body, brothers, we are travelling abroad from God (2 Cor. 5:6); and the corruptible body weighs down the soul, and this earthly dwelling presses on the mind that thinks many things (Wisd. 9:15). And so even if, by walking in desire, we manage somehow or other to dispel the clouds and to reach up to those sounds at times, and succeed by straining our ears in catching something from that house of God; yet under the burden of our weakness we fall back again to the humdrum things we are used to. And just as up there we found something to rejoice about, so here there is no lack of something to groan about. . . . So he takes another look at himself on his return, as it were, from those heights, and he says to himself, on finding himself in this sad world and comparing it to those things he went in to see and came out again after seeing, he says, 'Why are you sad, my soul, and why do you trouble me?' Here we are, having just been cheered by a sort of inward sweetness, here we are having just succeeded with the topmost point of the mind in catching a glimpse, sudden and momentary though it was, of an unchangeable something; why do you still trouble me, why are you still sad? You haven't any doubts now about your God; you are not any more without a reply to those who say, 'Where is your God?' I have now actually experienced the Absolute, that unchangeable something, why do you still trouble me? 'Hope in God.' And suppose his soul silently answers him Why indeed do I trouble you, except because I am not yet there where that sweet something is, where I was snatched away to only for a passing glimpse? Can I yet drink of that fountain with nothing to be afraid of? Am I yet quite safe from my lusts, as though they had been tamed and broken? Isn't my enemy the devil still watching out for me? Do you expect me not to trouble you while I am still set in the world, still traipsing abroad from the house of my God?—But 'hope in God', is still his reply to his anxious soul. . . .

(Trans. by E. Hill in *St. Augustine* by Henri Marrow. New York: Harper Torchbooks; 1957, and reprinted here by permission.)

The Problem of Evil: 1 (from *Confessions*)

III

But though I said and firmly held that the Lord God was incorruptible and unalterable and in no way changeable, the true God who made not only our souls but our bodies also, and not only our souls and bodies but all things whatsoever, as yet I did not see, clear and unravelled, what was the cause of Evil. Whatever that cause might be, I saw that no explanation would do which would force me to believe the immutable God mutable; for if I did that I should have been the very thing I was trying to find [namely a cause of evil]. From now it was with no anxiety that I sought it, for I was sure that what the Manichees said was not true. With all my heart I rejected them, because I saw that while they inquired as to the source of evil, they were full of evil themselves, in that they preferred rather to hold that Your substance suffered evil than that their own substance committed it.

So I set myself to examine an idea I had heard—namely that our free-will is the cause of our doing evil, and Your just judgment the cause of our suffering evil. I could not clearly discern this. I endeavoured to draw the eye of my mind from the pit, but I was again plunged into it; and as often as I tried, so often was I plunged back. But it raised me a little towards Your light that I now was as much aware that I had a will as that I had a life. And when I willed to do or not do anything, I was quite certain that it was myself and no other who willed, and I came to see that the cause of my sin lay there.

But what I did unwillingly, it still seemed to me that I rather suffered than did, and I judged it to be not my fault but my punishment: though as I held You most just, I was quite ready to admit that I was being justly punished.

But I asked further: "Who made me? Was it not my God, who is not only Good but Goodness itself? What root reason is there for my willing evil and failing to will good, which would make it just for me to be punished? Who was it that set and ingrafted in me this root of bitterness, since I was wholly made by my most loving God? If the devil is the author, where does the devil come from? And if by his own perverse will he was turned from a good angel into a devil, what was the origin in him of the perverse will by which he became a devil, since by the all-good Creator he was made wholly angel?" By such thoughts I was cast down again and almost stifled; yet I was not brought down so far as the hell of that error where no man confesses unto you, the error which holds rather that You suffer evil than that man does it.

IV

I now tried to discover other truths, as I had already come to realise that incorruptible is better than corruptible, so that You must be incorruptible, whatever might be Your nature. For no soul ever has been able to conceive or ever will be able to conceive anything better than You, the supreme and perfect Good. Therefore since the incorruptible is unquestionably to be held greater than the corruptible—and I so held it—I could now draw the conclusion that unless You were incor-

ruptible there was something better than my God. But seeing the superiority of the incorruptible, I should have looked for You in that truth
and have learned from it where evil is—that is learned the origin of the
corruption by which Your substance cannot be violated. For there is no
way in which corruption can affect our God, whether by His will or by
necessity or by accident: for He is God, and what He wills is good, and
Himself is Goodness; whereas to be corrupted is not good. Nor are You
against Your will constrained to anything, for Your will is not greater
than Your power. It would be greater, only if You were greater than
Yourself: for God's will and God's power are alike God Himself. And
what unlooked for accident can befall You, since You know all things?
No nature exists save because You know it. Why indeed should I multiply reasons to show that the substance which is God is not corruptible, since if it were, it would not be God?

V

I sought for the origin of evil, but I sought in an evil manner, and
failed to see the evil that there was in my manner of enquiry. I ranged
before the eyes of my mind the whole creation, both what we are able
to see—earth and sea and air and stars and trees and mortal creatures;
and what we cannot see—like the firmament of the Heaven above, and
all its angels and spiritual powers: though even these I imagined as if
they were bodies disposed each in its own place. And I made one great
mass of God's Creation, distinguished according to the kinds of bodies
in it, whether they really were bodies, or only such bodies as I imagined spirits to be. I made it huge, not as huge as it is, which I had no
means of knowing, but as huge as might be necessary, though in every
direction finite. And I saw You, Lord, in every part containing and
penetrating it, Yourself altogether infinite: as if Your Being were a sea,
infinite and immeasurable everywhere, though still only a sea: and
within it there were some mighty but not infinite sponge, and that
sponge filled in every part with the immeasurable sea. Thus I conceived Your Creation as finite, and filled utterly by Yourself, and You
were Infinite. And I said: "Here is God, and here is what God has created; and God is good, mightily and incomparably better than all these;
but of His goodness He created them good: and see how He contains
and fills them.
  "Where then is evil, and what is its source, and how has it crept into
the Creation? What is its root, what is its seed? Can it be that it is
wholly without being? But why should we fear and be on guard against
what is not? Or if our fear of it is groundless, then our very fear is itself an evil thing. For by it the heart is driven and tormented for no
cause; and that evil is all the worse, if there is nothing to fear yet we

do fear. Thus either there is evil which we fear, or the fact that we fear is evil.

"Whence then is evil, since God who is good made all things good? It was the greater and supreme Good who made these lesser goods, but Creator and Creation are alike good. Whence then comes evil? Was there perhaps some evil matter of which He made this creation, matter which He formed and ordered, while yet leaving in it some element which He did not convert into good? But why? Could He who was omnipotent be unable to change matter wholly so that no evil might remain in it? Indeed why did He choose to make anything of it and not rather by the same omnipotence cause it wholly not to be? Could it possibly have existed against His will? And if it had so existed from eternity, why did He allow it so long to continue through the infinite spaces of time past, and then after so long a while choose to make something of it? If He did suddenly decide to act, surely the Omnipotent should rather have caused it to cease to be, that He Himself, the true and supreme and infinite Good, alone should be. Or, since it was not good that He who was good should frame and create something not good, could He not have taken away and reduced to nothing that matter which was evil, and provided good matter of which to create all things? For He would not be omnipotent if He could not create something good without the aid of matter which He had not created."

Such thoughts I revolved in my unhappy heart, which was further burdened and gnawed at by the fear that I should die without having found the truth. But at least the faith of Your Christ, Our Lord and Saviour, taught by the Catholic Church, stood firm in my heart, though on many points I was still uncertain and swerving from the norm of doctrine. Yet my mind did not forsake it, but drank of it more deeply with every day that passed.

XII

And it became clear to me that corruptible things are good: if they were supremely good they could not be corrupted, but also if they were not good at all they could not be corrupted: if they were supremely good they would be incorruptible, if they were in no way good there would be nothing in them that might corrupt. For corruption damages; and unless it diminished goodness, it would not damage. Thus either corruption does no damage, which is impossible or—and this is the certain proof of it—all things that are corrupted are deprived of some goodness. But if they were deprived of all goodness, they would be totally without being. For if they might still be and yet could no longer be corrupted, they would be better than in their first state, because they would abide henceforth incorruptibly. What could be more monstrous than to say that things could be made better by losing all their goodness? If they were deprived of all goodness, they would be altogether nothing: therefore as long as they are, they are good. Thus whatsoever things are, are good; and that evil whose origin I sought is not a substance, because if it were a substance it would be good. For either it would be an incorruptible substance, that is to say, the highest goodness; or it would be a corruptible substance, which would not be corruptible unless it were good. Thus I saw and clearly realized that You have made all things good, and that there are no substances not made by You. And because all the things You have made are not equal, they have a goodness [over and above] as a totality: because they are good individually, and they are very good altogether, for our God has made all things very good.

XIII

To You, then, evil utterly is not—and not only to You, but to Your whole creation likewise, evil is not: because there is nothing over and above Your creation that could break in or derange the order that You imposed upon it. But in certain of its parts there are some things which we call evil because they do not harmonize with other things; yet these same things do harmonize with still others and thus are good; and in themselves they are good. All these things which do not harmonize with one another, do suit well with that lower part of creation which we call the earth, which has its cloudy and windy sky in some way apt to it. God forbid that I should say: "I wish that these things were not"; because even if I saw only them, though I should want better things, yet even for them alone I should praise You: for that You are to be praised, things of earth show—*dragons, and all deeps, fire, hail, snow, ice, and stormy winds, which fulfil Thy word; mountains and all hills, fruitful trees and all cedars; beasts and all cattle, serpents and feathered fowl; kings of the earth and all people, princes and all judges of the earth; young men and maidens, old men and young, praise Thy name.* And since from the heavens, O our God, *all Thy angels praise Thee in the high places, and all Thy hosts, sun and moon, all the stars and lights, the heavens of heavens, and the waters that are above the heavens, praise thy name*—I no longer desired better, because I had thought upon them all and with clearer judgment I realized that while certain higher things are better than lower things, yet all things together are better than the higher alone.

The Problem of Evil: 2 (from *Enchiridion*)

12. All of nature, therefore, is good, since the Creator of all nature is supremely good. But nature is not supremely and immutably good as is the Creator of it. Thus the good in created things can be diminished and augmented. For good to be diminished is evil; still, however much it is diminished, something must remain of its original nature as long as it exists at all. For no matter what kind or however insignificant a thing may be, the good which is its "nature" cannot be destroyed without the thing itself being destroyed. There is good reason, therefore, to praise an uncorrupted thing, and if it were indeed an incorruptible thing which could not be destroyed, it would doubtless be all the more worthy of praise. When, however, a thing is corrupted, its corruption is an evil because it is, by just so much, a privation of the good. Where there is no privation of the good, there is no evil. Where there is evil, there is a corresponding diminution of the good. As long, then, as a thing is being corrupted, there is good in it of which it is being deprived; and in this process, if something of its being remains that cannot be further corrupted, this will then be an incorruptible entity [*natura incorruptibilis*], and to this great good it will have come through the process of corruption. But even if the corruption is not arrested, it still does not cease having some good of which it cannot be further deprived. If, however, the corruption comes to be total and entire, there is no good left either, because it is no longer an entity at all. Wherefore corruption cannot consume the good without also consuming the thing itself. Every actual entity [*natura*] is therefore good; a greater good if it cannot be corrupted, a lesser good if it can be. Yet only the foolish and unknowing can deny that it is still good even when corrupted. Whenever a thing is consumed by corruption, not even the corruption remains, for it is nothing in itself, having no subsistent being in which to exist.

13. From this it follows that there is nothing to be called evil if there is nothing good. A good that wholly lacks an evil aspect is entirely good. Where there is some evil in a thing, its good is defective or defectible. Thus there can be no evil where there is no good. This leads us to a surprising conclusion: that, since every being, in so far as it is a being, is good, if we then say that a defective thing is bad, it would seem to mean that we are saying that what is evil is good, that only what is good is ever evil and that there is no evil apart from something good. This is because every actual entity is good [*omnis natura bonum est.*] Nothing evil exists *in itself*, but only as an evil aspect of some actual entity. Therefore, there can be nothing evil except something good. Absurd as this sounds, nevertheless the logical connections of the argument compel us to it as inevitable. At the same time, we must take warning lest we incur the prophetic judgment which reads: "Woe to

those who call evil good and good evil: who call darkness light and light darkness; who call the bitter sweet and the sweet bitter." Moreover the Lord himself saith: "An evil man brings forth evil out of the evil treasure of his heart." What, then, is an evil man but an evil entity [*natura mala*], since man is an entity? Now, if a man is something good because he is an entity, what, then, is a bad man except an evil good? When, however, we distinguish between these two concepts, we find that the bad man is not bad because he is a man, nor is he good because he is wicked. Rather, he is a good entity in so far as he is a man, evil in so far as he is wicked. Therefore, if anyone says that simply to be a man is evil, or that to be a wicked man is good, he rightly falls under the prophetic judgment: "Woe to him who calls evil good and good evil." For this amounts to finding fault with God's work, because man is an entity of God's creation. It also means that we are praising the defects in this particular man *because* he is a wicked person. Thus, every entity, even if it is a defective one, in so far as it is an entity, is good. In so far as it is defective, it is evil.

14. Actually, then, in these two contraries we call evil and good, the rule of the logicians fails to apply. No weather is both dark and bright at the same time; no food or drink is both sweet and sour at the same time; no body is, at the same time and place, both white and black, nor deformed and well-formed at the same time. This principle is found to apply in almost all disjunctions: two contraries cannot coexist in a single thing. Nevertheless, while no one maintains that good and evil are not contraries, they can not only coexist, but the evil cannot exist at all without the good, or in a thing that is not a good. On the other hand, the good can exist without evil. For a man or an angel could exist and yet not be wicked, whereas there cannot be wickedness except in a man or an angel. It is good to be a man, good to be an angel; but evil to be wicked. These two contraries are thus coexistent, so that if there were no good in what is evil, then the evil simply could not be, since it can have no mode in which to exist, nor any source from which corruption springs, unless it be something corruptible. Unless this something is good, it cannot be corrupted, because corruption is nothing more than the deprivation of the good. Evils, therefore, have their source in the good, and unless they are parasitic on something good, they are not anything at all. There is no other source whence an evil thing can come to be. If this is the case, then, in so far as a thing is an entity, it is unquestionably good. If it is an incorruptible entity, it is a great good. But even if it is a corruptible entity, it still has no mode of existence except as an aspect of something that is good. Only by corrupting something good can corruption inflict injury.

15. But when we say that evil has its source in the good, do not suppose that this denies our Lord's judgment: "A good tree cannot bear

evil fruit." This cannot be, even as the Truth himself declareth: "Men do not gather grapes from thorns," since thorns cannot bear grapes. Nevertheless, from good soil we can see both vines and thorns spring up. Likewise, just as a bad tree does not grow good fruit, so also an evil will does not produce good deeds. From a human nature, which is good in itself, there can spring forth either a good or an evil will. There was no other place from whence evil could have arisen in the first place except from the nature—good in itself—of an angel or a man. This is what our Lord himself most clearly shows in the passage about the trees and the fruits, for he said: "Make the tree good and the fruits will be good, or make the tree bad and its fruits will be bad." This is warning enough that bad fruit cannot grow on a good tree nor good fruit on a bad one. Yet from that same earth to which he was referring, both sorts of trees can grow.

(Reprinted from *Augustine: Confessions and Enchiridion,* translated and edited by Albert C. Outler (Volume VII: The Library of Christian Classics). First published MCMLV, Great Britain: SCM Press, Ltd., London and USA: The Westminster Press, Philadelphia. Reprinted by permission.)

The Mystery of Time (from *Confessions,* Book Eleven)

X

Surely those are still in their ancient error who say to us: "What was God doing before He made heaven and earth?" If, they say, He was at rest and doing nothing, why did He not continue to do nothing for ever after as for ever before? If it was a new movement and a new will in God to create something. He had never created before, how could that be a true eternity in which a will should arise which did not exist before? For the will of God is not a creature: it is prior to every creature, since nothing would be created unless the will of the Creator first so willed. The will of God belongs to the very substance of God. Now if something arose in the substance of God which was not there before, that substance could not rightly be called eternal; but if God's will that creatures should be is from eternity, why are creatures not from eternity?

XI

Those who speak thus do not yet understand You, O Wisdom of God, Light of minds: they do not yet understand how the things are made that are made by You and in You. They strive for the savour of eternity, but their mind is still tossing about in the past and future movements of things, and is still vain.

Who shall lay hold upon their mind and hold it still, that it may stand a little while, and a little while glimpse the splendour of eternity which stands for ever: and compare it with time whose moments never stand, and see that it is not comparable. Then indeed it would see that a long time is long only from the multitude of movements that pass away in succession, because they cannot co-exist: that in eternity nothing passes but all is present, whereas time cannot be present all at once. It would see that all the past is thrust out by the future, and all the future follows upon the past, and past and future alike are wholly created and upheld in their passage by that which is always present? Who shall lay hold upon the mind of man, that it may stand and see that time with its past and future must be determined by eternity, which stands and does not pass, which has in itself no past or future. Could my hand have the strength [so to lay hold upon the mind of man] or could my mouth by its speaking accomplish so great a thing?

XII

I come now to answer the man who says: "What was God doing before He made Heaven and earth?" I do not give the jesting answer—said to have been given by one who sought to evade the force of the question—"He was getting Hell ready for people who pry too deep." To poke fun at a questioner is not to see the answer. My reply will be different. I would much rather say "I don't know," when I don't, than hold one up to ridicule who had asked a profound question, and win applause for a worthless answer.

But, O my God, I say that You are the Creator of all creation, and if by the phrase heaven and earth we mean all creation, then I make bold to reply: Before God made heaven and earth, He did not make anything. For if He had made something, what would it have been but a creature? And I wish I knew all that it would be profitable for me to know, as well as I know that no creature was made before any creature was made.

XIII

But a lighter mind, adrift among images of time and its passing, might wonder that You, O God almighty and all-creating and all-conserving, Maker of heaven and earth, should have abstained from so vast a work for the countless ages that passed before You actually wrought it. Such a mind should awaken and realize how ill-grounded is his wonder.

How could countless ages pass when You, the Author and Creator of all ages, had not yet made them? What time could there be that You had not created? or how could ages pass, if they never were?

Thus, since You are the Maker of all times, if there actually was any time before You made heaven and earth, how can it be said that You were not at work? If there was time, You made it, for time could not pass before You made time. On the other hand, if before heaven and earth were made there was no time, then what is meant by the question "What were You doing *then*?" If there was not any time, there was not any "then".

It is not in time that You are before all time: otherwise You would not be before all time. You are before all the past by the eminence of Your ever-present eternity: and You dominate all the future in as much as it is still to be: and once it has come it will be past: *but Thou art always the self-same, and Thy years shall not fail.* Your years neither go nor come: but our years come and go, that all may come. Your years abide all in one act of abiding: for they abide and the years that go are not thrust out by those that come, for none pass: whereas our years shall not all be, till all are no more. Your years are as a single day; and Your day comes not daily but is today, a today which does not yield place to any tomorrow or follow upon any yesterday. In You today is eternity: thus it is that You begot one co-eternal with Yourself to whom you said: *Today have I begotten Thee.* You are the Maker of all time, and before all time You are, nor was there ever a time when there was no time!

XIV

At no time then had You not made anything, for time itself You made. And no time is co-eternal with You, for You stand changeless; whereas if time stood changeless, it would not be time. What then is time? Is there any short and easy answer to that? Who can put the answer into words or even see in it his mind? Yet what commoner or more familiar word do we use in speech than time? Obviously when we use it, we know what we mean, just as when we hear another use it, we know what he means.

What then is time? If no one asks me, I know; if I want to explain it to a questioner, I do not know. But at any rate this much I dare affirm I know: that if nothing passed there would be no past time; if nothing were approaching, there would be no future time; if nothing were, there would be no present time.

But the two times, past and future, how can they *be*, since the past is no more and the future is not yet? On the other hand, if the present were always present and never flowed away into the past, it would not be time at all, but eternity. But if the present is only time, because it flows away into the past, how can we say that it *is*? For it is, only because it will cease to be. Thus we can affirm that time *is* only in that it tends towards not-being.

XV

Yet we speak of a long time or a short time, applying these phrases only to past or future. Thus for example we call a hundred years ago a long time past, and a hundred years hence a long time ahead, and ten days ago a short time past, ten days hence a short time ahead. But in what sense can that which does not exist be long or short? The past no longer is, the future is not yet. Does this mean that we must not say: "It is long," but of the past "It was long," of the future "It will be long?"

O, my Lord, my Light, here too man is surely mocked by your truth! If we say the past was long, was it long when it was already past or while it was still present? It could be long only while it was in existence to *be* long. But the past no longer exists; it cannot be long, because it is not at all.

Thus we must not say that the past was long: for we shall find nothing in it capable of being long, since, precisely because it is past, it is not at all. Let us say then that a particular time was long while it was present, because in so far as it was present, it was long. For it had not yet passed away and so become non-existent; therefore it still was something, and therefore capable of being long: though once it passed away, it ceased to be long by ceasing to be.

Let us consider, then, O human soul, whether present time can be long: for it has been given you to feel and measure time's spaces. What will you answer me?

Are the present hundred years a long time? But first see whether a hundred years *can* be present. If it is the first year of the hundred, then that year is present, but the other ninety-nine are still in the future, and so as yet are not: if we are in the second year, then one year is past, one year is present, the rest future. Thus whichever year of our hundred-year period we choose as present, those before it have passed away, those after it are still to come. Thus a hundred years cannot be present.

But now let us see if the chosen year is itself present. If we are in the first month, the others are still to come, if in the second, the first has passed away and the rest are not yet. Thus a year is not wholly present while it runs, and if the whole of it is not present, then the year is not present. For a year is twelve months, and the month that happens to be running its course is the only one present, the others either are no longer or as yet are not. Even the current month is not present, but only one day of it: if that day is the first, the rest are still to come; if the last, the rest are passed away; if somewhere between, it has days past on one side and days still to come on the other.

Thus the present, which we have found to be the only time capable of being long, is cut down to the space of scarcely one day. But if we examine this one day, even it is not wholly present. A day is composed of twenty-four hours—day-hours, night-hours: the first hour finds the rest still to come, the last hour finds the rest passed away, any hour between has hours passed before it, hours to come after it. And that one hour is made of fleeing moments: so much of the hour as has fled away is past, what still remains is future. If we conceive of some point of time which cannot be divided into even the minutest parts of moments, that is the only point that can be called present: and that point flees at such lightning speed from being future to being past, that it has no extent of duration at all. For if it were so extended, it would be divisible into past and future: the present has no length.

Where, then, is there a time that can be called long? Is it the future? But we cannot say of the future "It is long" because as yet it is not at all and therefore is not long. We say "It will be long." But when will it be long? While it is still in the future, it will not be long, because it does not yet exist and so cannot be long. Suppose we say, then, that it is to be long only when, coming out of the future [which is not yet], it begins to be and is now present—and thus something, and thus capable of being long. But the present cries aloud, as we have just heard, that it cannot have length.

XVI

Yet, Lord, we are aware of periods of time; we compare one period with another and say that some are longer, some shorter. We measure how much one is longer than another and say that it is double, or triple, or single, or simply that one is as long as the other. But it is time actually passing that we measure by our awareness; who can measure times past which are now no more or times to come which are not yet, unless you are prepared to say that that which does not exist can be measured? Thus while time is passing, it can be perceived and measured; but when it has passed it cannot, for it is not.

XVII

I am seeking, Father, not saying: O, my God, aid me and direct me.

Perhaps it might be said that there are not three times, past, present and future, as we learnt in boyhood and have taught boys: but only present, because the other two do not exist. Or perhaps that these two do exist, but that time comes forth from some secret place when from future it becomes present, and departs into some secret place when from present it becomes past. For where have those who prophesied the future seen the future, if it does not yet exist? What does not exist cannot be seen. And those who describe the past could not describe it truly if they did not mentally see it: and if the past were totally without existence it would be totally impossible to see it. Hence both past and future must exist.

XVIII

Suffer me, Lord, to push my inquiry further; O my Hope, let not my purpose go awry.

If the future and the past exist, I want to know where they are. And if I cannot yet know this, at least I do know that wherever they are, they are there not as future or past, but present. If wherever they are they are future, then in that place they are not yet; if past, then they are there no more. Thus wherever they are and whatever they are, they *are* only as present. When we relate the past truly, it is not the things themselves that are brought forth from our memory—for these have passed away: but words conceived from the images of the things: for the things stamped their prints upon the mind as they passed through it by way of the senses. Thus for example my boyhood, which no longer exists, is in time past, which no longer exists; but the likeness of my boyhood, when I recall it and talk of it, I look upon in time present, because it is still present in my memory.

Whether the case is similar with prophecies of things to come—namely that images of things which are not yet are seen in advance as now existent—I confess, O my God, that I do not know. But this I do know, that we ordinarily consider our future actions in advance, and that this consideration is present, but the action we are thinking of does not yet exist, because it is future; when we have actually set about it and have begun to do what we planned, then that action will exist, because then it will not be future but present.

Whatever may be the mode of this mysterious foreseeing of things to come, unless the thing is it cannot be seen. But what now is, is not future but present. Therefore when we speak of seeing the future obviously what is seen is not the things which are not yet because they are still to come, but their causes or perhaps the signs that foretell them, for these causes and signs do exist here and now. Thus to those who see them now, they are not future but present, and from them things to come are conceived by the mind and foretold. These concepts already exist, and those who foretell are gazing upon them, present within themselves.

Let me take one example from a vast number of such things.

I am looking at the horizon at dawn: I foretell that the sun is about to rise. What I am looking at is present, what I foretell is future—not the sun, of course, for it now is, but its rising which is not yet. But unless I could imagine the actual rising in my mind, as now when I speak of it, I could not possibly foretell it. But the dawn which I see in the sky is not the sunrise, although it precedes the sunrise; nor is the dawn the image of the sunrise that is in my mind. But both—the dawn and the image of the sunrise—are present and seen by me, so that the sunrise which is future can be told in advance. Thus the future is not yet; and if it is not yet, it is not; and if it is not, then it is totally impossible to see it. But it can be foretold from things present which now exist and are seen.

XIX

But You, O Ruler of Your creation, how is it that You can show souls things that are to come? For such things You have told Your prophets. In what manner do You show the future to man, for whom nothing future yet is? Or do You show only present signs of things to come? For what does not exist obviously cannot be shown. The means You use is altogether beyond my gaze; my eyes have not the strength; of myself I shall never be able to see so deep, but in You I shall be able, when you grant it, O lovely Light of the eyes of my spirit.

XX

At any rate it is now quite clear that neither future nor past actually exists. Nor is it right to say there are three times, past, present and future. Perhaps it would be more correct to say: there are three times, a present of things past, a present of things present, a present of things future. For these three exist in the mind, and I find them nowhere else: the present of things past is memory, the present of things present is sight, the present of things future is expectation. If we are allowed to speak thus, I see and admit that there are three times, that three times truly are.

By all means continue to say that there are three times, past, present and future; for, though it is incorrect, custom allows it. By all means say it. I do not mind, I neither argue nor object: provided that you understand what you are saying and do not think future or past now exists. There are few things that we phrase properly; most things we phrase badly: but what we are trying to say is understood.

XXI

I said a little while ago that we measure time in its passing, so that we are able to say that this period of time is to that as two to one, or that this is of the same duration as that, and can measure and describe any other proportions of time's parts.

Thus, as I said, we measure time in its passing. If you ask me how I know this, my answer is that I know it because we measure time, and we cannot measure what does not exist, and past and future do not exist. But how do we measure time present, since it has no extent? It is measured while it is passing; once it has passed, it cannot be measured, for then nothing exists to measure.

But where does time come from, and by what way does it pass, and where does it go, while we are measuring it? Where is it from?—obviously from the future. By what way does it pass?—by the present. Where does it go?—into the past. In other words it passes from that which does not yet exist, by way of that which lacks extension, into that which is no longer.

But how are we measuring time unless in terms of some kind of duration? We cannot say single or double or triple or equal or proportioned in any other way, save of the duration of periods of time. But in what duration do we measure time while it is actually passing? In the future, from which it comes? But what does not yet exist cannot be measured. In the present, then, by which it passes? But that which has no space cannot be measured. In the past, to which it passes? But what no longer exists cannot be measured.

XXII

My mind burns to solve this complicated enigma. O Lord my God, O good Father, for Christ's sake I beseech Thee, do not shut off these obscure familiar problems from my longing, do not shut them off and leave them impenetrable but let them shine clear for me in the light of Thy mercy, O Lord. Yet whom shall I question about them? And to whom more fruitfully than to Thee shall I confess my ignorance: for Thou art not displeased at the zeal with which I am on fire for Thy Scriptures. Grant me what I love: for it is by Your gift that I love. Grant me this gift, Father, *who dost know how to give good gifts to Thy children*. Grant it because I have *studied that I might know and it is a labour in my sight* until Thou shalt open it to me. For Christ's sake I beseech Thee, in the name of Him who is the Holy of Holies, that no one prevent me. *I have believed, therefore* have I spoken. This my hope; for this do I live, *that I may see the delight of the Lord. Behold Thou hast made my days old, and they pass away*: but how I know not.

We are forever talking of time and of times. "How long did he speak," "How long did it take him to do that," "For how long a time did I fail to see this," "This syllable is double the length of that." So we speak and so we hear others speak, and others understand us, and we them. They are the plainest and commonest of words, yet again they are profoundly obscure and their meaning still to be discovered.

XXIII

I once heard a learned man say that time is simply the movement of the sun and moon and stars. I did not agree. For why should not time rather be the movement of all bodies? Supposing the lights of heaven were to cease and the potter's wheel moved on, would there not be time by which we could measure its rotations and say that these were at equal intervals, or some slower, some quicker, some taking longer, some shorter? And if we spoke thus, should we not ourselves be speaking in time: would there not be in our words some syllables long, some short—because some would sound for a longer time, some for a shorter?

O God, grant unto men to see by some small example the elements in common between small things and great. There are stars and the lights of heaven *to be for signs and for seasons and for days and years.* This is evident; but just as I would not affirm that one turn of that little wooden wheel is a day, neither should my philosopher say that it is no time at all.

What I am trying to come at is the force and nature of time, by which we measure the movement of bodies and say for example that this movement is twice as long as that. A day means not only the length of time that the sum is above the earth—so that we distinguish day from night—but the time of the sun's whole circuit from east to east—as we say that so many days have passed, so many days being used to include their nights, for the nights are not reckoned separately. Thus, since a day is constituted by the movement of the sun and its completed circle from east to east, I wish to know whether a day is that movement itself, or simply the time the movement takes, or both.

If the movement of the sun through one complete circuit were the day, then it would be a day even if the sun sped through its course in a space of time equal to an hour. If the time the sun now takes to complete its circuit is the day, then it would not be a day if between one sunrise and the next there were only the space of an hour: the sun would have to go round twenty-four times to make one day. But if to constitute a day there is needed both the movement of the sun through one circuit and the time the sun now takes, then you would not have a day if the sun completed its whole circuit in an hour, nor again if the sun stood still and as much time passed as the sun normally takes to complete its journey from one morning to the next.

But I shall not at the moment pursue the question of what it is that we call a day. I shall continue to seek what time is, by which we measure the sun's journey: so that we should say that it had gone round in half its accustomed time, if it went round in a space of time equivalent to twelve hours. And comparing its normal time with this twelve-hour time, we should say that the latter was single, the former double; yet the sun would in the one case have made its journey from east to east in the shorter time, in the other in the longer [so that time is something independent of the sun's movement].

Let no one tell me that the movement of the heavenly bodies is time: when at the prayer of a man the sun stood still that he might complete his victory in battle, the sun stood still but time moved on. The battle was continued for the necessary length of time and was finished.

Therefore I see time as in some way extended. But do I see it? Or do I only seem to see it? Thou wilt show me, O Light, O Truth.

XXIV

Would You have me agree with one who said that time is the movement of a body? You would not: for I learn that no body moves save in time: You have said it. But I do not learn that the movement of the body is time: You have not said it. For when a body is in motion, it is by time that I measure how long it is in motion from the beginning of its movement till it ceases to move. And if I did not see when the movement began, and if it moved on without my seeing when it ceased, I should be able to measure only from the moment I began to look until the moment I stopped looking. If I look for a long time, all I can say is that the time is long, but not how long it is, because when we say how long a time, we say it by comparison: as for example: this is as long as that, or this is twice that, and such like. But if we could note the point of space from which a body in motion comes or the point to which it goes, or could distinguish its parts if it is moving on its axis, we should be able to say how much time has elapsed for the movement of the body, or its part, from one place to another.

Thus since the movement of a body is not the same as our measurement of how long the movement takes, who can fail to see which of these is more deserving of the name of time? A body moves at different speeds, and sometimes stands still; but time enables us to measure not only its motion but its rest as well; and we say "It was at rest for the same length of time as it was in motion," or "It was at rest twice or thrice as long as it was in motion" or any other proportion, whether precisely measured or roughly estimated.

Therefore time is not the movement of a body.

XXV

I confess to You, Lord, that I still do not know what time is. And again I confess to You, Lord, that I know that I am uttering these things in time: I have been talking of time for a long time, and this long time would not be a long time unless time had passed. But how do I know this, since I do not know what time is? Or perhaps I do know, but simply do not know how to express what I know. Alas for me, I do not even know what I do not know! See me, O my God, I stand before You and I do not lie: as my speech is, so is my heart. *For Thou lightest my lamp, O Lord; O my God, enlighten my darkness.*

XXVI

Does not my soul speak truly to You when I say that I can measure time? For so it is, O Lord my God, I measure it and I do not know what it is that I am measuring. I measure the movement of a body, using time to measure it by. Do I not then measure time itself? Could I measure the movement of a body—its duration and how long it takes to move from place to place—if I could not measure the time in which it moves?

But if so, what do I use to measure time with? Do we measure a longer time by a shorter one, as we measure a beam in terms of cubits? Thus we say that the duration of a long syllable is measured by the space of a short syllable and is said to be double. Thus we measure the length of poems by the lengths of the lines, and the lengths of the lines by the lengths of the feet, and the lengths of the feet by the lengths of the syllables, and the lengths of long syllables by the lengths of short. We do not measure poems by pages, for that would be to measure space not time; we measure by the way the voice moves in uttering the poem, and we say: "It is a long poem, for it consists of so many lines; the lines are long for they are composed of so many feet; the feet are long for they include so many syllables; this syllable is long for it is the double of a short syllable."

But not by all this do we arrive at an exact measure of time. It may well happen that a shorter line may take longer if it is recited slowly than a longer line hurried through. And the same is true of a poem or a foot or a syllable.

Thus it seems to me that time is certainly extendedness—but I do not know what it is extendedness of: probably of the mind itself. Tell me, O my God, what am I measuring, when I say either, with no aim at precision, that one period is longer than the other, or, precisely, that one is double the other? That I measure time, I know. But I do not measure the future, for it is not yet; nor the present, for it is not extended in space; nor the past, which no longer exists. So what do I measure? Is it time in passage but not past? So I have already said.

XXVII

Persevere, O my soul, fix all the power of your gaze. *God is our help-er. He made us, and not we ourselves.* Fix your gaze where truth is whitening toward the dawn.

Consider the example of a bodily voice. It begins to sound, it sounds and goes on sounding, then it ceases: and now there is silence, the sound has passed, the sound no longer is. It was future before it began to sound, and so could not be measured, for as yet it did not exist; and now it cannot be measured because now it exists no longer. Only while sounding could it be measured for then it was, and so was measurable. But even then it was not standing still; it was moving, and moving out of existence. Did this make it more measurable? Only in the sense that by its passing it was spread over a certain space of time which made it measurable: for the present occupies no space.

At any rate, let us grant that it could be measured. And now again imagine a voice. It begins to sound and goes on sounding continuously without anything to break its even flow. Let us measure it, while it is sounding. For when it has ceased to sound, it will be past and will no longer be measurable. Let us measure it then and say how long it is. But it is still sounding and can be measured only from its beginning when it began to sound to its end, when it ceased. For what we measure is the interval between some starting point and some conclusion. This means that a sound which is not yet over cannot be measured so that we may say how long or short it is, nor can it be said either to be equal to some other sound or single or double or any other proportion in relation to it. But when it *is* over, it will no longer be. Then how will it be possible to measure it? Yet we do measure time—not that which is not yet, nor that which is no longer, nor that which has no duration, nor that which lacks beginning and end. Thus it seems that we measure neither time future nor time past nor time present nor time passing: and yet we measure time.

Deus creator omnium: This line is composed of eight syllables, short and long alternately: the four short syllables, the first, third, fifth, seventh are single in relation to the four long syllables, the second, fourth, sixth, eighth. Each long syllable has double the time of each short syllable. I pronounce them and I say that it is so, and so it is, as is quite obvious to the ear. As my ear distinguishes I measure a long syllable by a short and I perceive that it contains it twice. But since I hear a syllable only when the one before it has ceased—the one before being short and the one following long—how am I to keep hold of the short syllable, and how shall I see it against the long one to measure it and find that the long one is twice its length—given that the long syllable does not begin to sound until the short one has ceased? And again can

I measure the long one while it is present, since I cannot measure it until it is completed? And its completion is its passing out of existence.

What then is it that I measure? Where is the short syllable by which I measure? Where is the long syllable which I measure? Both have sounded, have fled away, have gone into the past, are now no more: yet I do measure, and I affirm with confidence, in so far as a practised sense can be trusted, that one is single, the other double, in the length of time it occupies. And I could not do this unless they had both passed away and ended. Thus it is not the syllables themselves that I measure, for they are now no more, but something which remains engraved in my memory.

It is in you, O my mind, that I measure time. Do not bring against me, do not bring against yourself the disorderly throng of your impressions. In you, I say, I measure time. What I measure is the impress produced in you by things as they pass and abiding in you when they have passed: and it is present. I do not measure the things themselves whose passage produced the impress; it is the impress that I measure when I measure time. Thus either that is what time is, or I am not measuring time at all.

But when we measure silences, and say that some particular silence lasted as long as some particular phrase, do we not stretch our mind to measure the phrase as though it were actually sounded, so as to be able to form a judgment of the relation between the space of the silence and that space of time? For without voice or lips we can go through poems and verses and speeches in our minds, and we can allow for the time it takes for their movement, one part in relation to another, exactly as if we were reciting them aloud. If a man decides to utter a longish sound and settles in his mind how long the sound is to be, he goes through that space of time in silence, entrusts it to his memory, then begins to utter the sound, and it sounds until it reaches the length he had fixed for it. Or rather I should say [not that it sounds but] that it has sounded and will sound: for as much of it as has been uttered at a given moment has obviously sounded, and what remains will sound: and so he completes the sound: at every moment his attention, which is present, causes the future to make its way into the past, the future diminishing and the past growing, until the future is exhausted and everything is past.

XXVIII

But how is the future diminished or exhausted, since the future does not yet exist: or how does the past grow, since it no longer is? Only because, in the mind which does all this, there are three acts. For the mind expects, attends and remembers: what it expects passes, by way of what it attends to, into what it remembers. Would anyone deny that the future is as yet not existent? But in the mind there is already an expectation of the future. Would anyone deny that the past no longer exists? Yet still there is in the mind a memory of the past. Would anyone deny that the present time lacks extension, since it is but a point that passes on? Yet the attention endures, and by it that which is to be passes on its way to being no more. Thus it is not the future that is long, for the future does not exist: a long future is merely a long expectation of the future; nor is the past long since the past does not exist: a long past is merely a long memory of the past.

Suppose that I am about to recite a psalm that I know. Before I begin, my expectation is directed to the whole of it; but when I have begun, so much of it as I pluck off and drop away into the past becomes matter for my memory; and the whole energy of the action is divided between my memory, in regard to what I have said, and my expectation, in regard to what I am still to say. But there is a present act of attention, by which what was future passes on its way to becoming past. The further I go in my recitation, the more my expectation is diminished and my memory lengthened, until the whole of my expectation is used up when the action is completed and has passed wholly into my memory. And what is true of the whole psalm, is true for each part of the whole, and for each syllable: and likewise for any longer action, of which the canticle may be only a part: indeed it is the same for the whole life of man, of which all a man's actions are parts: and likewise for the whole history of the human race, of which all the lives of all men are parts.

(From *The Confessions of St. Augustine*. Trans. F. J. Sheed. Used with permission of Sheed & Ward, 115 E. Armour Blvd., Kansas City, Mo. 64141-0281.)

Review Questions

1. Discuss St. Augustine as typical of the medieval theologian in working insights from philosophy into theology.
2. Is it true that St. Augustine took a narrow view of knowledge because all he wanted to know was God and himself?
3. Why is the concept of the unchangeability of truth so important to St. Augustine?
4. What dimension does St. Augustine add to our understanding of human nature by describing man as God's image?
5. What does Augustine mean by the *ascent to God*?
6. In Augustine's view, what relation is there between freedom and sin?
7. Explain how Augustine attempts to reconcile evil in the world with the goodness of God.
8. For Augustine, what is time and how does it relate to eternity?

CHAPTER 6

St. Anselm (1033–1109)

Introduction

What rhetoric was for St. Augustine, dialectics was for St. Anselm. Both of these activities deal with words. Rhetoric's strength comes from style — the moving, personal, emotional, telling use of words; dialectics' strength comes from the argument itself — the unadorned, unimpassioned, public, suprapersonal use of reasoning, to the extent that, if the argument is rejected, reason itself is rejected.

How the centerpiece of education changed from rhetoric in the time of Augustine to dialectics in the time of Anselm is an engaging story. From the early Middle Ages down to the mid-eleventh century, education, limited as in classical times to the few, was inherited from the Greek and Roman civilizations. Some time after the radical innovations in education wrought by Plato, his colleague Isocrates, and Aristotle, rhetoric became the goal of the educated man. This goal was handed down to Roman civilization and reached its high point in Cicero in the first century B.C. After struggling for its life in its formative years, the Church became more and more independent and self-assured; in the matter of learning, Christian writers came to rely on Christian literature alone and to look upon non-Christian literature as pagan and therefore unfit for Christian consumption. There were adumbrations of this attitude even in St. Augustine and St. Jerome; in a well-known anecdote, Jerome tells of a vision he had in which he was turned out at the Judgment with the words, "You are a Ciceronian, not a Christian; for where your treasure is, there is your heart also." Historically symbolic was the year 529 A.D., for in that year the Emperor Justinian, a Christian, closed Plato's Academy, which had survived as an educational center for nine hundred years; in the same year the first abbey was founded by St. Benedict at Monte Cassino, presaging the remarkable role Benedictine monastic schools were to have in the future.

For a variety of reasons, intellectual activity was subdued in the seventh and eight centuries, a situation that Charlemagne set about to remedy in the ninth century when education became more available through cathedral and monastic schools and the good offices of the village priest. The program of studies was both an inheritance and a bequest, for it drew upon the so-called seven liberal arts from Greek and Roman antiquity and, in the later Middle Ages, became consecrated as the *trivium* (grammar, logic, and rhetoric) and *quadrivium* (arithmetic, geometry, astronomy, and music). The Carolingian renaissance saw a revival of interest in classical authors, which meant a revival of interest in rhetoric, not as a formal goal but, together with grammar, as a basis for a literary education, while logic temporarily marked time. But as the eleventh century neared, the century of Anselm, logic or dialectics burgeoned. In the service of the Christian faith, dialectics was seen to have countless applications, from the rational grasp of the existence of God to the meaning of the Eucharist. This approach made such bold inroads as to make a number of theologians apprehensive, fearful that the mysteries of faith would be negated by rationalizing them.

St. Anselm was one of those who felt called upon to explore faith by means of dialectics. This decision disturbed his teacher Lanfranc, who reproached him with writing theological treatises without even quoting Holy Scripture. Contention, however, was the furthest thing from Anselm's mind, bent, as he was, on leading the life of a monk. He is one of those personalities who, like his master Augustine six centuries before him, "instantaneously win our affection before they have won our admiration." He was born of a noble family in Aosta, Italy, in 1033 but repudiated the kind of life expected of him to pursue a monastic life of learning. As a young man he made his way to Bec, in Normandy, where a recently established Benedictine abbey was achieving fame and respect under its abbott, Lanfranc. Anselm lived the life of a monk — prayed, taught, wrote, and worked — for thirty-three years, the last fifteen of which he served as abbott, attracting, by his example, monks from all over Europe. In 1078 he was called to England to become archbishop of Canterbury, a post that, through many a stormy and violent episode, he held until his death in 1109.

As with Augustine, Anselm's consuming interest was theology, yet he hoped to satisfy the demands of his intellect in trying to *understand* the truths he already held by faith, whence the title of one of his main works, *Proslogion*, bears the subtitle, actually the original title, of *Faith Seeking Understanding*; we have already seen this as one of the characteristics of the Middle Ages. "I desire," he writes, "to understand, if only a little, the truth of Yours which my heart already believes and loves. Indeed I do not seek to understand that I may believe; no, I believe so that I may understand."

Such was Anselm's mind in pondering the problem of God's existence. Philosophically, Anselm is the originator of a mode of arguing to the existence of God called the *ontological argument,* a name, for better or worse, attached to it since the time of Kant. Two of Anselm's works, the *Monologion* (a soliloquy) and the *Proslogion* (a discourse), were responses to the request he had received from some of his monks for a meditation on the meaning of faith; both of these works deal with God and His attributes. In the *Monologion* he argues the existence of God from several data of experience, showing how these data are inexplicable without God as their cause. These arguments are not original with Anselm and are therefore not the ones for which he is remembered. But the ontological argument in the *Proslogion* follows an entirely different route because, though it is presented as an argument, it is actually an explication of what is immediately evident and therefore takes on the shape of an intuition. This approach explains both its beguiling attractiveness and its total rejection by many subsequent philosophers. The brevity of the argument is matched only by the incredibly large number of commentaries written on it down through the centuries.

The argument of the Proslogion runs as follows: there is a thought in our minds of a being so great that no other being greater than it can be thought of; but it would be impossible for this being not to exist outside our minds, for the simple reason that to exist outside our minds is greater than to exist inside our minds only; therefore such a being, called God, exists. In Anselm's own words: "We believe that You are something than which no greater can be conceived. But can it be that such a nature does not exist, since 'the fool said in his heart, there is no God'? For sure, even this fool, when he hears the very thing I am saying 'something than which nothing greater can be conceived' understands what he hears; and what he understands is in his intellect, even though he does not understand that it exists. For it is one case for a thing to be in the understanding, it is another to understand a thing to be. ... Even the fool is convinced that there exists at least in the intellect that than which nothing greater can be conceived. ... And certainly that than which nothing greater can be conceived cannot exist in the mind only. If it exists only in the mind, it can also be conceived of in reality, which is greater. This would be a clear contradiction: if 'that than which nothing greater can be conceived' exists only in the mind, the very same 'that than which nothing greater can be conceived' is also that than which a greater can be conceived. Therefore, there exists without doubt a being than which nothing greater can be conceived, both in the mind and in reality."

A monk named Gaunilo seems to have spoken on behalf of all those who would like to have cautioned Anselm to stop because something did not quite add up. What Gaunilo said, in effect, was that if you can affirm the existence of God from the concept of God, you can affirm the existence of anything from its concept. And then Gaunilo proceeded to make a famous case for the concept of an island, in a sense a "lost island," which is a place of "inestimable wealth of all manner of riches and delicacies"; this island, following Anselm's logic, really exists. The point here is that the nonexistence of a thing does not mean that I cannot have an idea of it; so, in having an idea of an island, I cannot tell whether it exists or not. But Anselm, who charmingly declares that he would love to give back to the distraught monk "his lost island, not to be lost again," responds to the objection by averring that the concept of God is unique because it is greater than anything else we can think of; this is not so of the concept of the island, nor of any other concept but God. So the argument still stands.

If Anselm had lived in the seventeenth century, his argument would have been referred to as *rationalistic*; that is, the argument does not begin with experience, which would have anchored it in reality; rather, it begins with the idea, or concept, of the all-perfect being, and in the idea of the all-perfect being the idea of existence is necessarily included. The argument therefore does not appeal to those who think that it short-circuits experience, which is why it is rejected by Thomas Aquinas and others in the Thomistic-Aristotelian tradition, as well as by the whole range of empirically bound philosophers such as Locke, Hume, and Kant. It does, however, appeal to Bonaventure and others of the Augustinian tradition in the Middle Ages, as well as to Descartes, Leibniz, Spinoza, and Hegel, all of whom recognize in it a claim validated by its directness. At any rate, it is clear that the ontological argument never lets go, for it always has its adherents. So it can never be thought of as part of a philosopher's dream world; it cannot be dismissed out of hand. It remains as a challenge, as a sticking point for philosophers who ask whether God exists.

Readings

Faith Seeking Understanding (from Proslogion)

After I had published, at the pressing entreaties of several of my brethren, a certain short tract [the *Monologion*] as an example of meditation on the meaning of faith from the point of view of one seeking, through silent reasoning within himself, things he knows not—reflecting that this was made up of a a connected chain of many arguments, I began to wonder if perhaps it might be possible to find one single argument that for its proof required no other save itself, and that by itself would suffice to prove that God really exists, that He is the supreme good needing no other and is He whom all things have need of for their being and well-being, and also to prove whatever we believe about the Divine Being. But as often and as diligently as I turned my thoughts to this, sometimes it seemed to me that I had almost reached what I was seeking, sometimes it eluded my acutest thinking completely, so that finally, in desperation, I was about to give up what I was looking for as something impossible to find. However, when I had decided to put aside this idea altogether, lest by uselessly occupying my mind it might prevent other ideas with which I could make some progress, then, in spite of my unwillingness and my resistance to it, it began to force itself upon me more and more pressingly. So it was that one day when I was quite worn out with resisting its importunacy, there came to me, in the very conflict of my thoughts, what I had despaired of finding, so that I eagerly grasped the notion which in my distraction I had been rejecting.

Judging, then, that what had given me such joy to discover would afford pleasure, if it were written down, to anyone who might read it, I have written the following short tract dealing with this question as well as several others, from the point of view of one trying to raise his mind to contemplate God and seeking to understand what he believes. In my opinion, neither this tract nor the other I mentioned before deserves to be called a book or to carry its author's name, and yet I did not think they should be sent forth without some title (by which, so to speak, they might invite those into whose hands they should come, to read them); so I have given to each its title, the first being called *An Example of Meditation on the Meaning of Faith*, and the sequel *Faith in Quest of Understanding*.

However, as both of them, under these titles, had already been copied out by several readers, a number of people (above all the reverend Archbishop of Lyons, Hugh, apostolic delegate to Gaul, who commanded me by his apostolic authority) have urged me to put my name to them. For the sake of greater convenience I have named the first book *Monologion*, that is, a soliloquy; and the other *Proslogion*, that is, an allocution.

The "Ontological Argument" for the Existence of God (from *Proslogion*)

Chapter II

That God Truly Exists

Well then, Lord, You who give understanding to faith, grant me that I may understand, as much as You see fit, that You exist as we believe You to exist, and that You are what we believe You to be. Now we believe that You are something than which nothing greater can be thought. Or can it be that a thing of such a nature does not exist, since 'the Fool has said in his heart, there is no God' [Ps. xiii, I, lii. I]? But surely, when this same Fool hears what I am speaking about, namely, 'something-than-which-nothing-greater-can-be-thought', he understands what he hears, and what he understands is in his mind, even if he does not understand that it actually exists. For it is one thing for an object to exist in the mind, and another thing to understand that an object actually exists. Thus, when a painter plans beforehand what he is going to execute, he has [the picture] in his mind, but he does not yet think that it actually exists because he has not yet executed it. However, when he has actually painted it, then he both has it in his mind and understands that it exists because he has now made it. Even the Fool, then, is forced to agree that something-than-which-nothing-greater-can-be-thought exists in the mind, since he understands this when he hears it, and whatever is understood is in the mind. And surely that-than-which-a-greater-cannot-be-thought cannot exist in the mind alone. For if it exists solely in the mind even, it can be thought to exist in reality also, which is greater. If then that-than-which-a-greater-*cannot*-be-thought exists in the mind alone, this same that-than-which-a-greater-cannot-be-thought is that-than-which-a-greater-*can*-be-thought. But this is obviously impossible. Therefore there is absolutely no doubt that something-than-which-a-greater-cannot-be-thought exists both in the mind and in reality.

Chapter III

That God Cannot Be Thought Not to Exist

And certainly this being so truly exists that it cannot be even thought not to exist. For something can be thought to exist that cannot be thought not to exist, and this is greater than that which can be thought not to exist. Hence, if that-than-which-a-greater-cannot-be-thought can be thought not to exist, then that-than-which-a-greater-cannot-be-thought is not the same as that-than-which-a-greater-cannot-be-thought, which is absurd. Something-than-which-a-greater-cannot-be-thought exists so truly then, that it cannot be even thought not to exist.

And You, Lord our God, are this being. You exist so truly, Lord my God, that You cannot even be thought not to exist. And this is as it should be, for if some intelligence could think of something better than You, the creature would be above its creator and would judge its creator—and that is completely absurd. In fact, everything else there is, except You alone, can be thought of as not existing. You alone, then, of all things most truly exist and therefore of all things possess existence to the highest degree; for anything else does not exist as truly, and so possesses existence to a lesser degree. Why then did 'the Fool say in his heart, there is no God' [Ps. xiii. I, lii. I] when it is so evident to any rational mind that You of all things exist to the highest degree? Why indeed, unless because he was stupid and a fool?

Chapter IV

How 'the Fool Said in His Heart' What Cannot Be Thought

How indeed has he 'said in his heart' what he could not think; or how could he not think what he 'said in his heart', since to 'say in one's heart' and to 'think' are the same? But if he really (indeed, since he really) both thought because he 'said in his heart' and did not 'say in his heart' because he could not think, there is not only one sense in which something is 'said in one's heart' or thought. For in one sense a thing is thought when the word signifying it is thought; in another sense when the very object which the thing is understood. In the first sense, then, God can be thought not to exist, but not at all in the second sense. No one, indeed, understanding what God is can think that God does not exist, even though he may say these words in his heart either without any [objective] signification or with some peculiar signification. For God is that-than-which-nothing-greater-can-be-thought. Whoever really understands this understands clearly that this same being so exists that not even in thought can it not exist. Thus whoever understands that God exists in such a way cannot think of Him as not existing.

I give thanks, good Lord, I give thanks to You, since what I believed before through Your free gift I now so understand through Your illumination, that if I did not want to *believe* that You existed, I should nevertheless be unable not to *understand* it.

(From *St. Anselm's Proslogian.* Trans. M. J. Charlesworth. Oxford: Oxford University Press, 1965. Reprinted by permission of Oxford University Press.)

Review Questions

1. Describe the relationship between Christian and non-Christian thought at the time of St. Anselm that made the introduction of dialectics suspect to orthodox theology.
2. What is the meaning of *faith seeking understanding*?
3. To argue from the idea of God to the existence of God is called the *ontological argument*; discuss its validity.

St. Thomas Aquinas (1225 – 1274)

Introduction

The intellectual rebirth of the eleventh century continued unabated for several hundred years, bringing new life to dormant areas of knowledge and to an increasing number of students who desired to learn. It was an age of great excitement in which art, architecture, music, and literature, as well as philosophy and theology, were eagerly pursued. In the realms of philosophy and theology, those who gave a distinctive coloring to the times were people like Peter Abelard, John of Salisbury, St. Bernard of Clairvaux, Roger Bacon, William of Auvergne, Alexander Hales, Albert the Great, St. Bonaventure, and St. Thomas Aquinas. The works of the Arabian philosophers Avicenna and Averroes, and the Jewish theologian Moses Maimonides, were so impressive that the Christian West would not have been the same without them. Many of the scholastic centers established in the ninth and tenth centuries, during the following three or four hundred years, developed into university centers that, together with a number of newly founded universities, transformed the educational landscape of Western Europe. In cities like Salerno, Bologna, Paris, Oxford, Cambridge, Padua, Naples, Salamanca, Prague, Vienna, Heidelberg, and Cologne, thousands of students and their masters came together to pursue learning under the title of *universitas*.

Philosophically, history took a dramatic turn with the rediscovery of the works of Aristotle. Except for some of his logical works, translated by Boethius, the writings of the Stagirite were all but unknown in the West; even during the patristic age, Aristotle was seldom more than a name. Of the Greek philosophers, it was Plato who was known to the early Christian thinkers; they saw in his philosophy a heralding of the Christian message. But now, principally as a result of the expansion of Islamic culture westward through North Africa into Spain and Portugal, Aristotle's writings was made available to the West through the texts and commentaries of the Arabian philosophers already mentioned. A new and refreshing breeze therefore blew among the early thirteenth century scholars, owing largely to the good sense of Albert the Great and Thomas Aquinas, who recognized the stature of Aristotle and had his works translated into Latin. Many theologians felt that theology could be articulated anew with the help of Aristotle; for St. Thomas, Aristotle was "the Philosopher." However, there were other theologians who felt that, since Aristotle represented only the "natural" mind at work, his philosophy could never be helpful to theology and might even be inimical to it. These opposing attitudes hardened until the anti-Aristotelian faction succeeded in having a final ecclesiastical condemnation issued in 1277 against a mixed bag of propositions, authentically Aristotelian or presumed to be so, which included a number held by the now deceased Thomas Aquinas, though he was not mentioned by name. Despite this reversal, the philosophy of Aristotle and Thomas continued to gain adherence, but damage was certainly done to the acceptance of a synthesis that St. Thomas had tried to create.

St. Thomas was immersed in this academic ferment. He was a university student and professor; he wrote his works mainly for use in the university; an academic quality permeates his writings. Inasmuch as he was the complete academic, his personality never, or very seldom, spoke through his writings; he was content to let the argument speak for itself. Though he was academically rigorous, we know from his biographers that there was a warmth and an emotional side to the Angelic Doctor; we know this too from the hymns and poetry he composed.

It follows that the life of St. Thomas was basically uneventful, and the main points are simply told. He was born in 1224 or 1225 in the small town of Aquino, near Naples, and was educated as a youngster by the Benedictines at the monastery of Monte Cassino. Later he became a student at the newly founded University of Naples. He subsequently entered the Dominican Order, the center of a swirling controversy, and six or seven years later was ordained a priest. From 1245 to 1252 he carried on his studies at the universities of Paris and Cologne, and finally received his license to teach at Paris in 1256. He taught at various places including Paris, Rome, and Naples. In 1274 he died as a result of an accident while en route to the Council of Lyons, to which he had been invited.

As with all great personages, there are stories or legends that reveal his character. While he was studying under Albert in Cologne, he colleagues called him "the dumb ox," apparently in reference to both his size and his reserved personality, whereupon Albert is supposed to have proclaimed that in spite of his name, his bellowing would be heard throughout the world. Another story tells of his dining at a banquet with King St. Louis IX of France when he became so abstracted that, with a sudden outburst, he slammed his fist on the table, exclaiming, "I have it! At last I can beat the Manicheans!" The king quickly summoned a scribe to take down Thomas's thoughts. Finally, several months before he died, Thomas was often wrapped in contemplation; he stopped writing and confided to his companion of many years that, because of the illuminating visions vouchsafed him, everything he had written seemed like straw.

St. Thomas is often presented as a great synthesizer, which indeed he was. But even though he had committed the entire Bible to memory and was able to dictate to six or seven secretaries at one time, it would be unfair to think of him as a kind of pretechnological computer. His reputation as a synthesizer is based instead on his coherent view of reality, in which he weaves together truths from reason and revelation so that the completed tapestry is woven with ideas inherited from his predecessors, a fresh understanding of Aristotle, the believing acceptance of the Bible, and his own insights. Every philosopher has a view of reality, assumed if not stated, in which the parts and the whole are so related as to become mutually self-defining, and in St. Thomas's view the principal relationship is between God and man, so that whatever we know about God is a humanizing truth for man, and whatever we know about man enlarges our knowledge of God.

Thus, the architectonic of Aquinas's work is bold and clear, but its working out is complex. Three main clusters of problems indicate the nature of his thought: epistemology and its correlation with the unity of man, the mystery of existence, and the perfectibility of man.

With regard to the first, man is an intelligent being, his highest power is his intellect, and it is this that separates him from all other material beings. There is, consequently, a tendency to define man *only* in terms of the intellect, a tendency with an ample tradition down to St. Thomas's day and far beyond. We have seen this in the early Greek philosophers, particularly Plato, as well as in the early Christian writers who were inclined to identify man as spirit, for spirit has greater nobility than matter. If this is true, it follows that the body is merely an accompaniment to the soul; it is, depending on one's outlook, an instrument, an ally, a close friend, a burden, or a tomb, but in no case does it constitute *one being* with soul. This "spiritualistic" view of man is held by its partisans to be corroborated by the intellect's mode of knowing things in their *general* or *universal* character: it knows *man, tree, animal*. This must be a higher kind of knowledge because the *idea* of man, tree, or animal does not change, whereas the individual man, tree, or animal does. So the intellect must be in *direct contact* with these objects and has no essential need of the body to know them. Further, matter is inimical to this mode of knowing and, whatever its real nature, is inferior to spirit; this is why, in the Platonic tradition, the *really real* world is the world of ideas, which man, as spirit, somehow shares.

For St. Thomas, sharing Aristotle's radical position, there is too much here contrary to experience. Of course, man knows material things in a universal way, but he also knows them in particular; of course, he knows them in a general way, but he also knows them as individuals; of course, he knows them in a nonsensible way, but he also knows them in a sensible way. The same person, the one person, possesses both kinds of knowledge, one consciousness attaching to different aspects of reality. The human being is aware of its own unity, so that, although there is a distinction between body and soul, there is no separation of them in the being of man. As St. Thomas writes in the beginning of his treatise on man, "Since, then, sensation is an operation of man, but not proper to the soul, it is clear that man is not only a soul, but something composed of soul and body."

In more detail, man has the privilege of self-knowledge and can testify to his own experience of unity. Man is *aware* that it is he, the same person, who understands, and wills, and loves, and hates, and desires; the same being who wakes up as went to sleep, the same being whose hand was burned on the stove who performs an act of charity. There is a chain of unity running from sense knowledge to the highest functions of the intellect. If anyone, then, as Aquinas puts it, denies that the intellect is one with the body, "he must explain how it is that this action of understanding is the action of this particular man; for each one is conscious that it is he himself who understands." Whatever man is, he is one. His very being is living; his very existence is to-be-living-with-this-kind-of-life.

Acknowledging the fact of man's unity, the question can be changed from "Is man one?" to "Why is man one?" What St. Thomas is really looking for is the *radical reason* for life in this living, material thing called man. Man cannot be what he is without matter, but that fact does not make matter the radical reason for life. Matter cannot be the radical reason for life because then everything endowed with matter would be alive, which is contrary to fact. Nor can it be that a thing is alive because of the way matter is disposed or arranged in patterns of functional unity because, as previously noted, that does not account for the unity of existence of the total living being. So, if there is a living unity among the material components of man's being, it must be because of some factor beyond them. How all the physical activities taking place in the body are integrated into a unitary life is one of the mysteries of life, but that they are so integrated is beyond doubt, especially in man, in the center of whose consciousness unity is unimpeachable.

If man possesses life, but does not possess it because of a material principle, he must possess it because of a principle that is not material, or immaterial, called *soul.* The words *besouled* and *animate* (from *anima,* the Latin word for soul) refer to the living thing composed of matter and that which enlivens it. Since the meaning of *immaterial* is not given to us directly, St. Thomas approaches it indirectly by way of negation; this is his favorite way of saying something valid in the absence of direct, experiential knowledge. What he is saying is that the soul *is* without matter in its makeup. Man therefore is not body alone, nor soul alone, nor any combination of these in which body and soul are thought of as two independent beings functioning together, like rider and horse, or pilot and ship, to use the appropriate Platonic images. They are metaphysically related to each other, forming one being in which the soul enlivens the body.

In addition to immateriality, or simplicity, there is a further characteristic of the soul designated by the word *spirituality.* Strictly speaking, *simplicity* means, for St. Thomas, without matter, and, of itself, does not necessarily mean the ability to function independently of matter; spirituality adds to the notion of simplicity the notion of independence of matter. A thing may be independent of another, but not in every respect; or dependent on another, but not in every respect. A painter, for example, is independent of (or dependent on) his brush, but not in every respect. A builder is independent of (or dependent on) his ladder, but not in every respect. So the human soul can be independent of (or dependent on) matter, though not in every respect. But can it be shown that the soul is actually *independent* of matter in *any* respect? St. Thomas holds that the soul does function in some respects independently of matter; therefore, the soul *is* in some respects independent of matter, that is, spiritual.

St. Thomas holds to the independence of the soul on many counts, but in the context of epistemology he maintains that it can be shown in at least two ways. The first is based on *universal knowledge,* which, as we have seen, is a constant theme in the history of philosophy. In reality, only individual things exist, such as this tree, this dog, this man; however, we not only know *this* tree in its individuality, we know "tree" in general; we know what a tree is in all cases. Further, this tree is this tree for any number of reasons, one of them being the matter of which it is composed. If the act of knowing were composed of matter, it would be limited in the same way to this one and only tree, and knowledge of tree in general would be impossible; but since our knowledge of tree is universal as well, the intellect cannot be material: whatever acts without matter must *be* without matter.

The act of *reflection* is another indication of the intellect's independence of matter. Reflection here does not mean "thinking inwardly," or quiet meditation, but the "bending back" of a thing on itself, its re-flection. Take the action of touch, proper to the hand. The hand can touch itself if the fingertips touch the palm, but the whole hand cannot touch the whole hand, that is, the whole hand cannot bend back on the whole hand. The reason is that the hand is composed of matter; one part can touch another part, but the whole cannot touch itself. Likewise, the eye cannot see itself; it cannot bend back on itself because it is blocked by the very matter of which it is made. But the act of knowing is entirely different, for the act of knowing _knows itself_: we, as knowers, know that we know. The intellect, then, knows itself in the act of knowing, — a perfect example of re-flection, of bending back. This act of the intellect must, therefore, be independent of matter.

So here, for St. Thomas, is a clear instance of dependence– independence. In knowing, the soul (intellect) depends on the body for access to material things, that is, for sense knowledge: nothing is in the intellect unless it is first in the sense. But it does not follow that the intellect is dependent on matter for every one of its activities, as in the instances of universal knowledge and reflection just discussed.

The second cluster of problems St. Thomas faced was that concerning the mystery of existence. Any feature that determines a thing to be what it actually is is called a _perfection_, and the highest of all perfections is _existence_. At one and the same time, a thing is this _individual_ kind of thing, and is this individual _kind_ of thing, and _is_ this individual kind of thing; in a sequence measured by understanding and not by time, it cannot be called _this_, or this _kind_, unless it first _is_. Now any one of these aspects is a mystery, — a cause for wonder. That a thing is a tree, and not a dog, is cause for wonder; that it is _this_ tree, and not that, is cause for wonder; but that a tree _is_ in the first place is cause for the highest wonder. Existence is the perfection, the determination, that makes a thing real: to _be_ is to be _real_. That is why things of our imagination remain fantasies, and though they have some relation to existence, they are not real because they do not exist; so, the flying horse, the golden mountain, the lost island can somehow be conceptualized, inasmuch as their components are real, but they themselves are not real.

The mystery of existence, like all mysteries, is only partially open to reason, for although much of it is penetrable by reason, much more remains impenetrable. Existence is a question whose answer generates other questions; one question answered leaves many others unanswered. Perhaps that is why Democritus forbade his students to ask where his atoms came from. But St. Thomas, in a far different tradition, was compelled to ask such a question. How do things come to exist? The things St. Thomas is asking about are things that _do not have to be_: the tree, which came into existence anew, is cut down and ceases to be; a human being, who before did not exist, now comes into existence. If they do not have to be, and yet they are, there must be an explanation of why they are, why they came to be. So, either-or: either all these things cause themselves to be, or they are caused to be by an uncaused being. But it is impossible for anything to cause itself to be, for then it would have to be and not be at the same time. Since one side of a contradiction has to stand, it follows that an uncaused being exists. This is a simple statement of the well-know "five ways" of St. Thomas to demonstrate the existence of God, all of which begin from a different starting point but coalesce into the argument from causality.

St. Thomas holds that an infinite series cannot be invoked to explain why any given thing exists when it does not have to. If A requires cause B, which in turn requires cause C, which in turn requires cause D, and so on, even if the number of causes were infinite, the entire series, taken together, would still be insufficient to explain why A exists in the first place, for each cause in the series would itself be caused; insufficiency added to insufficiency can never add up to sufficiency. The cause has to be *totally* different from what it is called upon to explain, and therefore an *uncaused* cause whose very existence is necessary.

To those who would hold that an infinite series is not impossible and therefore does not require a *first* cause, St. Thomas would answer that the force of the argument is *existential*, not numerical. A thing that does not have to be (sometimes called *contingent*), and yet is, means that its very *is-ness* is caused here and now by the being that has to be (sometimes called *necessary*), just as the sound-ing of the trumpet requires a trumpeter: be-ing points to Be-ing, exist-ence points to Existence. This is basically why St. Thomas could not accept the ontological argument as he knew it from St. Anselm: the idea of the all-perfect is not based on existence, that is, on extra-mental reality; it begins in the mind and must stay there.

It is obvious, as we turn to perfectibility as the third main characteristic of Thomas's thought, that man bears a special relationship to God: he depends on Him for his existence; he is the highest visible creation; he has a natural tendency toward Him, a tendency whose satisfaction is man's ultimate fulfillment and completion of his humanity: "Man has a natural tendency to be completed in goodness." Nevertheless the human being is subject to the growth pattern of all living things, but as befitting an intelligent and free nature. The "unfinished" dimension of the human being is a typical Christian stance in which "finishing" is the growth of one's humanity toward fulfillment in God.

But with Aquinas there is an emphasis on those ingredients of growth that answer the question, why do we call a person good? We do not call a person good because he or she is a good doctor, carpenter, musician, or gas station attendant, for we know full well that a person can be a good doctor, carpenter, musician, or gas station attendant and still be a bad person; by the same token, a person can be a bad doctor, carpenter, musician, or gas station attendant and still be a good person. As Thomas says, "moral acts and human acts are the same," that is, they are human not only because thy are done freely but also because they shape humanity to its end — they make a person human; in a sense, by them a person creates himself as a person.

Yet, with the full array of possibilities before us, how can we know which actions are right, and therefore good, and which ones we ought to do? Are they the ones that would give us the most pleasure? Not necessarily. Are they the ones that would be most useful? Not necessarily. The ones that most people would do? Not necessarily. The ones most satisfying to us emotionally? Not necessarily. Standing squarely on his rigorous intellectualism, St. Thomas holds that the moral quality of an action is grasped by our _reason_, that is, by our _understanding_ of the action in its full context, which prompts us to say, "this is right, and to be done." Sometimes the moral quality of an action can be grasped directly; at other times, because of many complexities, we may have to reflect on it, research it, consult on it before we _see_ it. And though we realize that there is an aspect of morality that is universal, or general, because of a human nature common to all human beings, we also realize that there is a subjective aspect as well, because any action is done in concrete, specific circumstances by an individual. St. Thomas comments approvingly on Aristotle when he writes: "Disquisitions on general morality are not entirely trustworthy, and the ground becomes more uncertain when one wishes to descend to individual cases in detail. The factors are infinitely variable, and cannot be settled either by art or precedent. Judgment should be left to the people concerned. Each must set himself to act according to the immediate situation and the circumstances involved. The decision may be unerring in the concrete, despite the uneasy debate in the abstract. Nevertheless, the moralist can provide some help and direction in such cases." Conscience is precisely what reason says or dictates; to reject it is to reject the voice of God: "To disparage the dictate of reason is equivalent to contemning the command of God."

In terms of law, then, God's eternal plan is participated in by man in and through reason, a process referred to by St. Thomas as the _natural law_. It underscores the fact that every human action is done for an end (is _teleological_) and that the ultimate end is God's ultimate purpose for rational creation. Consequently, the moral man is the one who does the _right_ thing, the one who respects the law within him summoning him to act in accordance with his humanity. This is the sense of _justice_ (_jus_ meaning right or law), a sense not founded on duty for duty's sake but on love — the principle of life in every human action. In this way, the human being who in this life experiences love in so many fleeting instances perceives his gradual movement toward God as the All-Good whom he is called to love in the final stage of his unfolding.

Readings

On the Existence of God (from *Summa theologiae,* Part I)

Question II

First Article

Whether the Existence of God Is Self-Evident?

We proceed thus to the First Article:—

Objection 1. It seems that the existence of God is self-evident. For those things are said to be self-evident to us the knowledge of which exists naturally in us, as we can see in regard to first principles. But as Damascene says, *the knowledge of God is naturally implanted in all.* Therefore the existence of God is self-evident.

Obj. 2. Further, those things are said to be self-evident which are known as soon as the terms are known, which the Philosopher says is true of the first principles of demonstration. Thus, when the nature of a whole and of a part is known, it is at once recognized that every whole is greater than its part. But as soon as the signification of the name God is understood, it is at once seen that God exists. For by this name is signified that thing than which nothing greater can be conceived. But that which exists actually and mentally is greater than that which exists only mentally. Therefore, since as soon as the name *God* is understood it exists mentally, it also follows that it exists actually. Therefore the proposition *God exists* is self-evident.

Obj. 3. Further, the existence of truth is self-evident. For whoever denies the existence of truth grants that truth does not exist: and, if truth does not exist, then the proposition *Truth does not exist* is true: and if there is anything true, there must be truth. But God is truth itself: *I am the way, the truth, and the life* (Jo. xiv. 6). Therefore *God exists* is self-evident.

On the contrary, No one can mentally admit the opposite of what is self-evident, as the Philosopher states concerning the first principles of demonstration. But the opposite of the proposition *God is* can be mentally admitted: *The fool said in his heart, There is no God* (Ps. lii. I). Therefore, that God exists is not self-evident.

I answer that, A thing can be self-evident in either of two ways: on the one hand, self-evident in itself, though not to us; on the other, self-evident in itself, and to us. A proposition is self-evident because the predicate is included in the essence of the subject: *e.g., Man is an animal,* for animal is contained in the essence of man. If, therefore, the essence of the predicate and subject be known to all, the proposition will be self-evident to all; as is clear with regard to the first principles of demonstration, the terms of which are certain common notions that no one is ignorant of, such as being and non-being, whole and part, and the like. If, however, there are some to whom the essence of the predicate and subject is unknown, the proposition will be self-evident in itself, but not to those who do not know the meaning of the predicate and subject of the proposition. Therefore, it happens, as Boethius says, that there are some notions of the mind which are common and self-evident only to the learned, as that incorporeal substances are not in space. Therefore I say that this proposition, *God exists,* of itself is self-evident, for the predicate is the same as the subject, because God is His own existence as will be hereafter shown. Now because we do not know the essence of God, the proposition is not self-evident to us, but needs to be demonstrated by things that are more known to us, though less known in their nature—namely, by His effects.

Reply Obj. 1. To know that God exists in a general and confused way is implanted in us by nature, inasmuch as God is man's beatitude. For man naturally desires happiness, and what is naturally desired by man is naturally known by him. This, however, is not to know absolutely that God exists; just as to know that someone is approaching is not the same as to know that Peter is approaching, even though it is Peter who is approaching; for there are many who imagine that man's perfect good, which is happiness, consists in riches, and others in pleasures, and others in something else.

Reply Obj. 2. Perhaps not everyone who hears this name God understands it to signify something than which nothing greater can be thought, seeing that some have believed God to be a body. Yet, granted that everyone understands that by this name *God* is signified something than which nothing greater can be thought, nevertheless, it does not therefore follow that he understands that what the name signifies exists actually, but only that it exists mentally. Nor can it be argued that it actually exists, unless it be admitted that there actually exists something than which nothing greater can be thought; and this precisely is not admitted by those who hold that God does not exist.

Reply Obj. 3. The existence of truth in general is self-evident, but the existence of a Primal Truth is not self-evident to us.

Third Article

Whether God Exists?

We proceed thus to the Third Article:—

Objection 1. It seems that God does not exist; because if one of two contraries be infinite, the other would be altogether destroyed. But the name God means that He is infinite goodness. If, therefore, God existed, there would be no evil discoverable; but there is evil in the world. Therefore God does not exist.

Obj. 2. Further, it is superfluous to suppose that what can be accounted for by a few principles has been produced by many. But it seems that everything we see in the world can be accounted for by other principles, supposing God did not exist. For all natural things can be reduced to one principle, which is nature; and all voluntary things can be reduced to one principle, which is human reason, or will. Therefore there is no need to suppose God's existence.

On the contrary, It is said in the person of God: *I am Who am* (*Exod.* iii. 14).

I answer that, The existence of God can be proved in five ways.

The first and more manifest way is the argument from motion. It is certain, and evident to our senses, that in the world some things are in motion. Now whatever is moved is moved by another, for nothing can be moved except it is in potentiality to that towards which it is moved; whereas a thing moves inasmuch as it is in act. For motion is nothing else than the reduction of something from potentiality to actuality. But nothing can be reduced from potentiality to actuality, except by something in a state of actuality. Thus that which is actually hot, as fire, makes wood, which is potentially hot, to be actually hot, and thereby moves and changes it. Now it is not possible that the same thing should be at once in actuality and potentiality in the same respect, but only in different respects. For what is actually hot cannot simultaneously be potentially hot; but it is simultaneously potentially cold. It is therefore impossible that in the same respect and in the same way a thing should be both mover and moved, *i.e.,* that it should move itself. Therefore, whatever moved must be moved by another. If that by which it is moved be itself moved, then this also must needs be moved by another, and that by another again. But this cannot go on to infinity, because then there would be no first mover, and, consequently, no other mover, seeing that subsequent movers move only inasmuch as they are moved by the first mover; as the staff moves only because it is moved by the hand. Therefore it is necessary to arrive at a first mover, moved by no other; and this everyone understands to be God.

The second way is from the nature of efficient cause. In the world of sensible things we find there is an order of efficient causes. There is no case known (neither is it, indeed, possible) in which a thing is found to be the efficient cause of itself; for so it would be prior to itself, which is impossible. Now in efficient causes it is not possible to go on to infinity, because in all efficient causes following in order, the first is the cause of the intermediate cause, and the intermediate is the cause of the ultimate cause, whether the intermediate cause be several, or one only. Now to take away the cause is to take away the effect. Therefore, if there be no first cause among efficient causes, there will be no ultimate, nor any intermediate, cause. But if in efficient causes it is possible to go on to infinity, there will be no first efficient cause, neither will there be an ultimate effect, nor any intermediate efficient causes; all of which is plainly false. Therefore it is necessary to admit a first efficient cause, to which everyone gives the name of God.

The third way is taken from possibility and necessity, and runs thus. We find in nature things that are possible to be and not to be, since they are found to be generated, and to be corrupted, and consequently, it is possible for them to be and not to be. But it is impossible for these always to exist, for that which can not-be at some time is not. Therefore, if everything can not-be, then at one time there was nothing in existence. Now if this were true, even now there would be nothing in existence, because that which does not exist begins to exist only through something already existing. Therefore, if at one time nothing was in existence, it would have been impossible for anything to have begun to exist; and thus even now nothing would be in existence— which is absurd. Therefore, not all beings are merely possible, but there must exist something the existence of which is necessary. But every necessary thing either has its necessity caused by another, or not. Now it is impossible to go on to infinity in necessary things which have their necessity caused by another, as has been already proved in regard to efficient causes. Therefore we cannot but admit the existence of some being having of itself its own necessity, and not receiving it from another, but rather causing in others their necessity. This all men speak of as God.

The fourth way is taken from the gradation to be found in things. Among beings there are some more and some less good, true, noble, and the like. But *more* and *less* are predicated of different things according as they resemble in their different ways something which is the maximum, as a thing is said to be hotter according as it more nearly resembles that which is hottest; so that there is something which is truest, something best, something noblest, and, consequently, something which is most being, for those things that are greatest in truth are greatest in being, as it is written in *Metaph.* ii. Now the maximum in any genus is the cause of all in that genus, as fire, which is the maximum of heat, is the cause of all hot things, as is said in the same book.

Therefore there must also be something which is to all beings the cause of their being, goodness, and every other perfection; and this we call God.

The fifth way is taken from the governance of the world. We see that things which lack knowledge, such as natural bodies, act for an end, and this is evident from their acting always, or nearly always, in the same way, so as to obtain the best result. Hence it is plain that they achieve their end, not fortuitously, but designedly. Now whatever lacks knowledge cannot move towards an end, unless it be directed by some being endowed with knowledge and intelligence; as the arrow is directed by the archer. Therefore some intelligent being exists by whom all natural things are directed to their end; and this being we call God.

Reply Obj. 1. As Augustine says: *Since God is the highest good, He would not allow any evil to exist in His works, unless His omnipotence and goodness were such as to bring good even out of evil.* This is part of the infinite goodness of God, that He should allow evil to exist, and out of it produce good.

Reply Obj. 2. Since nature works for a determinate end under the direction of a higher agent, whatever is done by nature must be traced back to God as to its first cause. So likewise whatever is done voluntarily must be traced back to some higher cause other than human reason and will, since these can change and fail; for all things that are changeable and capable of defect must be traced back to an immovable and self-necessary first principle, as has been shown.

The Problem of Evil (from *Summa theologiae*, Part I)

Question XLVIII

First Article

Whether Evil Is a Nature?

We proceed thus to the First Article:—

Objection 1. It would seem that evil is a nature. For every genus is a nature. But evil is a genus, for the Philosopher says that *good and evil are not in a genus, but are genera of other things.* Therefore evil is a nature.

Obj. 2. Further, every difference which constitutes a species is a nature. But evil is a difference constituting a species in the field of morals; for a bad habit differs in species from a good habit, as does liberality from illiberality. Therefore evil signifies a nature.

Obj. 3. Further, each extreme of two contraries is a nature. But evil and good are not opposed as privation and habit, but as contraries, as the Philosopher shows by the fact that between good and evil there is an intermediate position, and from evil there can be a return to good. Therefore evil signifies a nature.

Obj. 4. Further, what is not, acts not. But evil acts, for it corrupts good. Therefore evil is a being and a nature.

Obj. 5. Further, nothing belongs to the perfection of the universe except what is a being and a nature. But evil belongs to the perfection of the universe of things, for Augustine says *that the admirable beauty of the universe is made up of all things. In which even what is called evil, well ordered and in its place, makes better known the greatness of the good.* Therefore evil is a nature.

On the contrary, Dionysius says that *Evil is neither a being nor a good.*

I answer that, One opposite is known through the other, as darkness is known through light. Hence, what evil is must be known from the nature of good. Now, we have said above that good is everything that is appetible; and thus, since every nature desires its own being and its own perfection, it must be said also that the being and the perfection of any nature is good. Hence it is impossible that evil signifies any being, or any form or nature. Therefore, by the name *evil* there must be signified some absence of good. And this is what is meant by saying that *evil is neither a being nor a good.* For since being, as such, is good, the absence of being involves the absence of good.

Reply Obj. 1. Aristotle speaks there according to the opinion of the Pythagoreans, who thought that evil was a kind of nature, and therefore they asserted the existence of good and evil as genera. For Aristotle, especially in his logical works, was in the habit of bringing forward examples that in his time were probable in the opinion of some philosophers. Or, it may be said that, as the Philosopher says, *the first kind of contrariety is habit and privation*, being verified in all contraries; for one contrary is always imperfect in relation to another, as black in relation to white, and bitter in relation to sweet. And in this way good and evil are said to be genera, not absolutely, but in regard to contraries; because, just as every form has the nature of good, so every privation, as such, has the nature of evil.

Reply Obj. 2. Good and evil are not constitutive differences except in moral matters, which receive their species from the end, which is the object of the will, the source of all morality. And because good has the nature of an end, for this reason good and evil are specific differences in moral matters—the good in itself, but evil as the absence of the due end. Yet neither does the absence of the due end by itself constitute a species in moral matters, except as the absence is joined to an undue end; just as we do not find the privation of the substantial form in natural things; unless it is joined to another form. Thus, therefore, the evil which is a constitutive difference in morals is a certain good joined to the privation of another good; just as the end proposed by the intemperate man is not the privation of the good of reason, but the delight of sense against the order of reason. Hence evil is not as such a constitutive difference, but by reason of the good that is annexed.

Reply Obj. 3. The answer to this objection appears from the above. For the Philosopher there speaks of good and evil in morality. Now in that respect, between good and evil there is something intermediate; as good is considered something rightly ordered, and evil a thing not only out of right order, but also injurious to another. Hence the Philosopher says that a *prodigal man is foolish, but not evil.* And from this evil in morality, there may be a return to good, but not from any sort of evil; for from blindness there is no return to sight, although blindness is an evil.

Reply Obj. 4. A thing is said to act in a threefold sense. In one way, *formally*, as when we say that whiteness makes white; and in that sense evil considered even as a privation is said to corrupt good, for it is itself a corruption or privation of good. In another sense, a thing is said to act *effectively*, as when a painter makes a wall white. Thirdly, it is said in the sense of the *final cause*, as the end is said to effect by moving the efficient cause. But in these last two ways evil does not effect anything of itself, that is, as a privation, but by virtue of the good annexed to it. For every action comes from some form; and everything which is desired as an end is a perfection. Therefore, as Dionysius says, evil does not act, nor is it desired, except by virtue of some good joined to it: while of itself it is nothing definite, and outside the scope of our will and intention.

Reply Obj. 5. As was said above, the parts of the universe are ordered to each other, according as one acts on the other, and according as one is the end and exemplar of the other. But, as was said above, this can happen to evil only as joined to some good. Hence evil neither belongs to the perfection of the universe, nor comes under the order of the universe, except accidentally, that is, by reason of some good joined to it.

Third Article

Whether Evil Is In Good as in Its Subject?

We proceed thus to the Third Article:—

Objection I. It would seem that evil is not in good as its subject. For good is something that exists. But Dionysius says that *evil does not exist, nor is it in that which exists.* Therefore, evil is not in good as its subject.

Obj. 2. Further, evil is not a being, whereas good is a being. But non-being does not require being as its subject. Therefore, neither does evil require good as its subject.

Obj. 3. Further, one contrary is not the subject of another. But good and evil are contraries. Therefore, evil is not in good as in its subject.

Obj. 4. Further, the subject of whiteness is called white. Therefore, also, the subject of evil is evil. If, therefore, evil is in good as in its subject, it follows that good is evil, against what is said (*Isa.* v. 20): *Woe to you who call evil good, and good evil!*

On the contrary, Augustine says that evil exists only in good.

I answer that, As was said above, evil indicates the absence of good. But not every absence of good is evil. For absence of good can be taken in a privative and in a negative sense. Absence of good, taken negatively, is not evil; otherwise, it would follow that what does not exist is evil, and also that every thing would be evil because of not having the good belonging to something else. For instance, a man would be evil because he did not have the swiftness of the roe, or the strength of a lion. But the absence of good, taken in a privative sense, is an evil; as, for instance, the privation of sight is called blindness.

Now, the subject of privation and of form is one and the same—viz., being in potentiality, whether it be being in potentiality absolutely, as primary matter, which is the subject of the substantial form and of the privation of the opposite form; or whether it be being in potentiality relatively, and actuality absolutely, as in the case of a transparent body, which is the subject both of darkness and light. It is, however, manifest that the form which makes a thing actual is a perfection and a good. Hence, every actual being is a good; and likewise every potential being, as such, is a good, as having a relation to good. For as it has being in potentiality, so it has goodness in potentiality. Therefore, the subject of evil is good.

Reply Obj. I. Dionysius means that evil is not in existing things as a part, or as a natural property of any existing thing.

Reply Obj. 2. *Non-being,* understood negatively, does not require a subject; but privation is negation in a subject, as the Philosopher says, and such a *non-being* is an evil.

Reply Obj. 3. Evil is not in the good opposed to it as in its subject, but in some other good, for the subject of blindness is not *sight,* but *the animal.* Yet it appears, as Augustine says, that the rule of dialectic here fails, the rule, namely, which says that contraries cannot exist together. But this is to be taken according to the universal meaning of good and evil, but not in reference to any particular good and evil. For white and black, sweet and bitter, and like contraries, are considered as contraries only in a special sense, because they exist in some determinate genera; whereas good enters into every genus. Hence one good can coexist with the privation of another good.

Reply Obj. 4. The prophet invokes woe to those who say that good as such is evil. But this does not follow from what is said above, as is clear from the explanation given.

On the Soul (from *Summa theologiae,* Part I)

Question LXXV

On Man Who Is Composed of a Spiritual and a Corporeal Substance: And First, Concerning What Belongs to the Essence of the Soul *(In Seven Articles)*

First Article

Whether the Soul is a Body?

We proceed thus to the First Article:—

Objection I. It would seem that the soul is a body. For the soul is the mover of the body. Nor does it move unless moved. First, because apparently nothing can move unless it is itself moved, since nothing gives what it has not. For instance, what is not hot does not give heat. Secondly, because if there be anything that moves and is itself not moved, it must be the cause of eternal and uniform movement, as we find proved *Physics* viii. Now this does not appear to be the case in the movement of an animal, which is caused by the soul. Therefore the soul is a moved mover. But every moved mover is a body. Therefore the soul is a body.

Obj. 2. Further, all knowledge is caused by means of a likeness. But the can be no likeness of a body to an incorporeal thing. If, therefore, the soul were not a body, it could not have knowledge of corporeal things.

Obj. 3. Further, between the mover and the moved there must be contact. But contact is only between bodies. Since, therefore, the soul moves the body, it seems that the soul must be a body.

On the contrary, Augustine says that the soul is *simple in comparison with the body, inasmuch as it does not occupy space by any bulk.*

I answer that, To seek the nature of the soul, we must premise that the soul is defined as the first principle of life in those things in our world which live; for we call living things *animate,* and those things which have no life, *inanimate.* Now life is shown principally by two activities, knowledge and movement. The philosophers of old, not being able to rise above their imagination, supposed that the principle of these actions was something corporeal; for they asserted that only bodies were real things, and that what is not corporeal is nothing. Hence they maintained that the soul is some sort of body. This opinion can be proved in many ways to be false; but we shall make use of only one proof, which shows quite universally and certainly that the soul is not a body.

It is manifest that not every principle of vital action is a soul, for then the eye would be a soul, as it is a principle of vision; and the same might be applied to the other instruments of the soul. But it is the first principle of life which we call the soul. Now, though a body may be a principle of life, as the heart is a principle of life in an animal, yet no body can be the first principle of life. For it is clear that to be a principle of life, or to be a living thing, does not belong to a body as a body, since, if that were the case, every body would be a living thing, or a principle of life. Therefore a body is competent to be a living thing, or even a principle of life, as such a body. Now that it is actually such a body it owes to some principle which is called its act. Therefore the soul, which is the first principle of life, is not a body, but the act of a body; just as heat, which is the principle of calefaction, is not a body, but anact of a body.

Reply Obj. I. Since everything which is moved must be moved by something else, a process which cannot be prolonged indefinitely, we must allow that not every mover is moved. For, since to be moved is to pass from potentiality to actuality, the mover gives what it has to the thing moved, inasmuch as it causes it to be in act. But, as is shown in Physics viii., there is a mover which is altogether immovable, and which is not moved either essentially or accidentally; and such a mover can cause an eternally uniform movement. There is, however, another kind of mover, which, though not moved essentially, is moved accidentally; and for this reason it does not cause a uniform movement. Such a mover is the soul. There is, again, another mover, which is moved essentially—namely, the body. And because the philosophers of old believed that nothing existed but bodies, they maintained that every mover is moved, and that the soul is moved essentially, and is a body.

Reply Obj. 2. It is not necessary that the likeness of the thing known be actually in the nature of the knower. But given a being which knows potentially, and afterwards knows actually, the likeness of the thing known must be in the nature of the knower, not actually, but only potentially; and thus color is not actually in the pupil of the eye, but only potentially. Hence it is necessary, not that the likeness of corporeal things be actually in the nature of the soul, but that there be a potentiality in the soul for such a likeness. But the ancient naturalists did not know how to distinguish between actuality and potentiality; and so they held that the soul must be a body in order to have knowledge of a body, and that it must be composed of the principles of which all bodies are formed.

Reply Obj. 3. There are two kinds of contact, that of *quantity*, and that of *power*. By the former a body can be touched only by a body; by the latter a body can be touched by an incorporeal reality, which moves that body.

Second Article

Whether the Human Soul Is Something Subsistent?

We proceed thus to the Second Article:—

Objection I. It would seem that the human soul is not something subsistent. For that which subsists is said to be *this particular thing*. Now *this particular thing* is said not of the soul, but of that which is composed of soul and body. Therefore the soul is not something subsistent.

Obj. 2. Further, everything subsistent operates. But the soul does not operate, for, as the Philosopher says, *to say that the soul feels or understand is like saying that the soul weaves or builds*. Therefore the soul is not subsistent.

Obj. 3. Further, if the soul were something subsistent, it would have some operation apart from the body. But it has no operation apart from the body, not even that of understanding; for the act of understanding does not take place without a phantasm, which cannot exist apart from the body. Therefore the human soul is not something subsistent.

On the contrary, Augustine says: *Whoever understands that the nature of the mind is that of a substance and not that of a body, will see that those who maintain the corporeal nature of the mind are led astray because they associate with the mind those things without which they are unable to think of any nature*—i.e., imaginary pictures of corporeal things. Therefore the nature of the human mind is not only incorporeal, but it is also a substance, that is, something subsistent.

I answer that, It must necessarily be allowed that the principle of intellectual operation, which we call the soul of man, is a principle both incorporeal and subsistent. For it is clear that by means of the intellect man can know all corporeal things. Now whatever knows certain things cannot have any of them in its own nature, because that which is in it naturally would impede the knowledge of anything else. Thus we observe that a sick man's tongue, being unbalanced by a feverish and bitter humor, is insensible to anything sweet, and everything seems bitter to it. Therefore, if the intellectual principle contained within itself the nature of any body, it would be unable to know all bodies. Now every body has its own determinate nature. Therefore it is impossible for the intellectual principle to be a body. It is also impossible for it to understand by means of a bodily organ, since the determinate nature of that organ would likewise impede knowledge of all bodies; as when a certain determinate color is not only in the pupil of the eye, but also in a glass vase, the liquid in the vase seems to be of that same color.

Therefore the intellectual principle, which we call the mind or the intellect, has essentially an operation in which the body does not share. Now only that which subsists in itself can have an operation in itself. For nothing can operate but what is actual, and so a thing operates according as it is; for which reason we do not say that heat imparts heat, but that what is hot gives heat. We must conclude, therefore, that the human soul, which is called intellect or mind, is something incorporeal and subsistent.

Reply Obj. 1. *This particular thing* can be taken in two senses. Firstly, for anything subsistent; secondly, for that which subsists and is complete in a specific nature. The former sense excludes the inherence of an accident or of a material form; the latter excludes also the imperfection of the part, so that a hand can be called *this particular thing* in the first sense, but not in the second. Therefore, since the human soul is a part of human nature, it can be called *this particular thing* in the first sense, as being something subsbut not in the second, for in this sense the composite of body and soul is said to be *this particular thing*.

Reply Obj. 2. Aristotle wrote those words as expressing, not his own opinion, but the opinion of those who said that to understand is to be moved, as is clear from the context. Or we may reply that to operate through itself belongs to what exists through itself. But for a thing to exist through itself, it suffices sometimes that it be not inherent, as an accident or a material form; even though it be part of something. Nevertheless, that is rightly said to subsist through itself which is neither inherent in the above sense, nor part of anything else. In this sense, the eye or the hand cannot be said to subsist through itself; nor can it for that reason be said to operate through itself. Hence the operation of the parts is through each part attributed to the whole. For we say that man sees with the eye, and feels with the hand, and not in the same sense as when we say that what is hot gives heat by its heat; for heat, strictly speaking, does not give heat. We may therefore say that the soul understands just as the eye sees; but it is more correct to say that man understands through the soul.

Reply Obj. 3. The body is necessary for the action of the intellect, not as its organ of action, but on the part of the object; for the phantasm is to the intellect what color is to the sight. Neither does such a dependence on the body prove the intellect to be non-subsistent, or otherwise it would follow that an animal is non-subsistent simply because it requires external sensibles for sensation.

Third Article

Whether the Souls of Brute Animals Are Subsistent?

We proceed thus to the Third Article:—

Objection 1. It would seem that the souls of brute animals are subsistent. For man is of the same genus as other animals, and, as we have shown, the soul of man is subsistent. Therefore the souls of other animals are subsistent.

Obj. 2. Further, the relation of the sensitive power to sensible objects is like the relation of the intellectual power to intelligible objects. But the intellect, without the body, apprehends intelligible objects. Therefore the sensitive power, without the body, perceives sensible objects. Therefore, since the souls of brute animals are sensitive, they are subsistent, for the same reason that the human soul, which is intellectual, is subsistent.

Obj. 3. Further, the soul of brute animals moves the body. But the body is not a mover, but is moved. Therefore the soul of brute animals has an operation apart from the body.

On the contrary, Is what is written in the book *De Ecclesiasticis Dogmatibus: Man alone we believe to have a subsistent soul; whereas the souls of animals are not subsistent.*

I answer that, The early philosophers made no distinction between sense and intellect, and referred both to a corporeal principle, as has been said. Plato, however, drew a distinction between intellect and sense, but he referred both to an incorporeal principle, maintaining that sensing, like understanding, belongs to the soul as such. From this it follows that even the souls of brute animals are subsistent. But Aristotle held that, of the operations of the soul, understanding alone is performed without a corporeal organ. On the other hand, sensation and the attendant operations of the sensitive soul are evidently accompanied with change in the body; and thus, in the act of vision, the pupil of the eye is affected by the likeness of color. So with the other senses. Hence it is clear that the sensitive soul has no *per se* operation of its own, and that every operation of the sensitive soul belongs to the composite. Therefore we conclude that as the souls of brute animals have no *per se* operations they are not subsistent. For the operation of anything follows the mode of its being.

Reply Obj. 1. Although man is of the same *genus* as other animals, he is of a different *species*. Now, specific difference is derived from the difference of form; nor does every difference of form necessarily imply a diversity of *genus*.

Reply Obj. 2. The relation of the sensitive power to the sensible object is in one way the same as that of the intellectual power to the intelligible object, in so far as each is in potentiality to its object. But in another way their relations differ, inasmuch as the impression of the sensible on the sense is accompanied with change in the body; so that when the intensity of the sensible is excessive, the sense is corrupted. This is a thing that never occurs in the case of the intellect. For an intellect that understands the highest of intelligible objects is more able afterwards to understand those that are lower.—If, however, in the process of intellectual operation the body is weary, this result is accidental, inasmuch as the intellect requires the operation of the sensitive powers in the production of the phantasms.

Reply Obj. 3. A motive power is of two kinds. One, the appetitive power, which commands motion. The operation of this power in the sensitive soul is not without the body; for anger, joy and passions of a like nature are accompanied by some change in the body. The other motive power is that which executes motion in adapting the members for obeying the appetite; and the act of this power does not consist in moving, but in being moved. Whence it is clear that to move is not an act of the sensitive soul without the body.

Sixth Article

Whether the Human Soul Is Corruptible?

We proceed thus to the Sixth Article:—

Objection 1. It would seem that the human soul is corruptible. For those things that have a like beginning and process seemingly have a like end. But the beginning, by generation, of men is like that of animals, for they are made from the earth. And the process of life is alike in both; because *all things breathe alike, and man hath nothing more than the beast,* as it is written (*Eccles.* iii. 19). Therefore, as the same text concludes, *the death of man and beast is one, and the condition of both is equal.* But the souls of brute animals are corruptible. Therefore the human soul too is corruptible.

Obj. 2. Further, whatever is out of nothing can return to nothingness, because the end should correspond to the beginning. But as it is written (*Wis.* ii. 2), *We are born of nothing*; and this is true, not only of the body, but also of the soul. Therefore, as is concluded in the same passage, *After this we shall be as if we had not been,* even as to our soul.

Obj. 3. Further, nothing is without its own proper operation. But the operation proper to the soul, which is to understand through a phantasm, cannot be without the body. For the soul understands nothing without a phantasm, and *there is no phantasm without the body,* as the Philosopher says. Therefore the soul cannot survive the dissolution of the body.

On the contrary, Dionysius says that human souls owe to divine goodness that they are *intellectual,* and that they have an *incorruptible substantial life.*

I answer that, We must assert that the intellectual principle which we call the human soul is incorruptible. For a thing may be corrupted in two ways—in itself and accidentally. Now it is impossible for any subsistent being to be generated or corrupted accidentally, that is, by the generation or corruption of something else. For generation and corruption belong to a thing in the same way that being belongs to it, which is acquired by generation and lost by corruption. Therefore, whatever has being in itself cannot be generated or corrupted except in itself; while things which do not subsist, such as accidents and material forms, acquire being or lose it through the generation or corruption of composites. Now it was shown above that the souls of brutes are not self-subsistent, whereas the human soul is, so that the souls of brutes are corrupted, when their bodies are corrupted, while the human soul could not be corrupted unless it were corrupted in itself. This is impossible, not only as regards the human soul, but also as regards anything subsistent that is a form alone. For it is clear that what belongs to a thing by virtue of the thing itself is inseparable from it. But being belongs to a form, which is an act, by virtue of itself. And thus, matter acquires actual being according as it acquires form; while it is corrupted so far as the form is separated from it. But it is impossible for a form to be separated from itself; and therefore it is impossible for a subsistent form to cease to exist.

Granted even that the soul were composed of matter and form, as some pretend, we should nevertheless have to maintain that it is incorruptible. For corruption is found only where there is contrariety, since generation and corruption are from contraries and into contraries. Therefore the heavenly bodies, since they have no matter subject to contrariety, are incorruptible. Now there can be no contrariety in the intellectual soul; for it is a receiving subject according to the manner of its being, and those things which it receives are without contrariety. Thus, the notions even of contraries are not themselves contrary, since contraries belong to the same science. Therefore it is impossible for the intellectual soul to be corruptible.

Moreover we may take a sign of this from the fact that everything naturally aspires to being after its own manner. Now, in things that have knowledge, desire ensues upon knowledge. The senses indeed do not know being, except under the conditions of *here* and *now*, whereas the intellect apprehends being absolutely, and for all time; so that everything that has an intellect naturally desires always to exist. But a natural desire cannot be in vain. Therefore every intellectual substance is incorruptible.

Reply Obj. 1. Solomon reasons thus in the person of the foolish, as expressed in the words of *Wis.* ii. Therefore the saying that man and animals have a like beginning in generation is true of the body; for all animals alike are made of earth. But it is not true of the soul. For while the souls of brutes are produced by some power of the body, the human soul is produced by God. To signify this, it is written of other animals: *Let the earth bring forth the living soul* (*Gen.* i. 24); while of man it is written (*Gen.* ii. 7) that *He breathed into his face the breath of life.* And so in the last chapter of *Ecclesiastes* (xii. 7) it is concluded: *The dust returns into its earth from whence it was; and the spirit returns to God Who gave it.* Again, the process of life is alike as to the body, concerning which it is written (*Eccles.* iii. 19): *All things breathe alike,* and (*Wis.* ii. 2), *The breath in our nostrils is smoke.* But the process is not alike in the case of the soul, for man has understanding whereas animals do not. Hence it is false to say: *Man has nothing more than beasts.* Thus death comes to both alike as to the body, but not as to the soul.

Reply Obj. 2. As a thing can be created, not by reason of a passive potentiality, but only by reason of the active potentiality of the Creator, Who can produce something out of nothing, so when we say that a thing can be reduced to nothing, we do not imply in the creature a potentiality to non-being, but in the Creator the power of ceasing to sustain being. But a thing is said to be corruptible because there is in it a potentiality to non-being.

Reply Obj. 3. To understand through a phantasm is the proper operation of the soul by virtue of its union with the body. After separation from the body, it will have another mode of understanding, similar to other substances separated from bodies, as will appear later on.

The Unity of Man (from *Summa theologiae*, Part I)

Question LXXVI

First Article

Whether the Intellectual Principle Is United to The Body as Its Form?

We proceed thus to the First Article:—

Objection I. It seems that the intellectual principle is not united to the body as its form. For the Philosopher says that the *intellect is separate*, and that it is not the act of any body. Therefore it is not united to the body as its form.

Obj. 2. Further, every form is determined according to the nature of the matter of which it is the form; otherwise no proportion would be required between matter and form. Therefore if the intellect were united to the body as its form, since every body has a determinate nature, it would follow that the intellect has a determinate nature; and thus, it would not be capable of knowing all things, as is clear from what has been said. This is contrary to the nature of the intellect. Therefore the intellect is not united to the body as its form.

Obj. 3. Further, whatever receptive power is an act of a body, receives a form materially and individually; for what is received must be received according to the condition of the receiver. But the form of the thing understood is not received into the intellect materially and individually, but rather immaterially and universally. Otherwise, the intellect would not be capable of knowing immaterial and universal objects, but only individuals, like the senses. Therefore the intellect is not united to the body as its form.

Obj. 4. Further, power and action have the same subject, for the same subject is what can, and does, act. But intellectual action is not the action of a body, as appears from the above. Therefore neither is the intellectual power a power of the body. But a virtue or a power cannot be more abstract or more simple than the essence from which the virtue or power is derived. Therefore, neither is the substance of the intellect the form of a body.

Obj. 5. Further, whatever has being in itself is not united to the body a its form, because a form is that *by which* a thing exists; which means that the very being of a form does not belong to the form by itself. But the intellectual principle has being in itself and is subsistent, as was said above. Therefore it is not united to the body as its form.

Obj. 6. Further, whatever exists in a thing by reason of its nature exists in it always. But to be united to matter belongs to the form by reason of its nature, because form is the act of matter, not by any accidental quality, but by its own essence; or otherwise matter and form would not make a thing substantially one, but only accidentally one. Therefore, a form cannot be without its own proper matter. But the intellectual principle, since it is incorruptible, as was shown above, remains separate from the body, after the dissolution of the body. Therefore the intellectual principle is not united to the body as its form.

On the contrary, According to the Philosopher in *Metaph.* viii., difference is derived from the form. But the difference which constitutes man is *rational*, which is said of man because of his intellectual principle. Therefore the intellectual principle is the form of man.

I answer that, We must assert that the intellect which is the principle of intellectual operation is the form of the human body. For that whereby primarily anything acts is a form of the thing to which the act is attributed. For instance, that whereby a body is primarily healed is health, and that whereby the soul knows primarily is knowledge; hence health is a form of the body, and knowledge is a form of the soul. The reason for this is that nothing acts except so far as it is in act; and so, a thing acts by that whereby it is in act. Now it is clear that the first thing by which the body lives is the soul. And as life appears through various operations in different degrees of living things, that whereby we primarily perform each of all these vital actions is the soul. For the soul is the primary principle of our nourishment, sensation, and local movement; and likewise of our understanding. Therefore this principle by which primarily we understand, whether it be called the intellect or the intellectual soul, is the form of the body. This is the demonstration used by Aristotle.

But if anyone say that the intellectual soul is not the form of the body, he must explain how it is that this action of understanding is the action of this particular man; for each one is conscious that it is he himself who understands. Now an action may be attributed to anyone in three ways, as is clear from the Philosopher. For a thing is said to move or act, either by virtue of its whole self, for instance, as a physician heals; or by virtue of a part, as a man sees by his eye; or through an accidental quality, as when we say that something that is white builds, because it is accidental to the builder to be white. So when we say that Socrates or Plato understands, it is clear that this is not attributed to him accidentally, since it is ascribed to him as man, which is predicated of him essentially. We must therefore say either that Socrates understands by virtue of his whole self, as Plato maintained, holding that man is an intellectual soul; or that the intellect is a part of Socrates. The first cannot stand, as was shown above, because it is one and the same man who is conscious both that he understands and that he senses. But one cannot sense without a body, and therefore the body must be some part of man. It follows therefore that the intellect by which Socrates understands is a part of Socrates, so that it is in some way united to the body of Socrates.

As to this union, the Commentator held that it is through the intelligible species, as having a double subject, namely, the possible intellect and the phantasms which are in the corporeal organs. Thus, through the intelligible species, the possible intellect *is linked* to the body of this or that particular man. But this link or union does not sufficiently explain the fact that the act of the intellect is the act of Socrates. This can be clearly seen from comparison with the sensitive power, from which Aristotle proceeds to consider things relating to the intellect. For the relation of phantasms to the intellect is like the relation of colors to the sense of sight, as he says *De Anima iii*. Therefore, just as the species of colors are in the sight, so the species of phantasms are in the possible intellect. Now it is clear that because the colors, the likenesses of which are in the sight, are on a wall, the action of seeing is not attributed to the wall; for we do not say that the wall sees, but rather that it is seen. Therefore, from the fact that the species of phantasms are in the possible intellect, it does not follow that Socrates, in whom are the phantasms, understands, but that he or his phantasms are understood.

Some, however, have tried to maintain that the intellect is united to the body as its mover, and hence that the intellect and body form one thing in such a way that the act of the intellect could be attributed to the whole. This is, however, absurd for many reasons. First, because the intellect does not move the body except through the appetite, whose movement presupposes the operation of the intellect. The reason therefore why Socrates understands is not because he is moved by his intellect, but rather, contrariwise, he is moved by his intellect because he understands.—Secondly, because, since Socrates is an individual in a nature of one essence composed of matter and form, if the intellect be not the form, it follows that it must be outside the essence, and then the intellect is to the whole Socrates as a motor to the thing moved. But to understand is an action that remains in the agent, and does not pass into something else, as does the action of heating. Therefore the action of understanding cannot be attributed to Socrates for the reason that he is moved by his intellect.—Thirdly, because the action of a mover is never attributed to the thing moved, except as to an instrument, just as the action of a carpenter is attributed to a saw. Therefore, if understanding is attributed to Socrates as the action of his mover, it follows that it is attributed to him as to an instrument. This is contrary to the teaching of the Philosopher, who holds that understanding is not possible through a corporeal instrument.—Fourthly, because, although the action of a part be attributed to the whole, as the action of the eye is attributed to a man, yet it is never attributed to another part, except perhaps accidentally; for we do not say that the hand sees because the eye sees. Therefore, if the intellect and Socrates are united in the above manner, the action of the intellect cannot be attributed to Socrates. If, however, Socrates be a whole composed of a union of the intellect with whatever else belongs to Socrates, but with the supposition that the intellect is united to the other parts of Socrates only as a mover, it follows that Socrates is not one absolutely, and consequently neither a being absolutely, for a thing is a being according as it is one.

There remains, therefore, no other explanation than that given by Aristotle—namely, that this particular man understands because the intellectual principle is his form. Thus from the very operation of the intellect it is made clear that the intellectual principle is united to the body as its form.

The same can be clearly shown from the nature of the human species. For the nature of each thing is shown by its operation. Now the proper operation of man as man is to understand, for it is in this that he surpasses all animals. Whence Aristotle concludes that the ultimate happiness of man must consist in this operation as properly belonging to him. Man must therefore derive his species from that which is the principle of this operation. But the species of each thing is derived from its form. It follows therefore that the intellectual principle is the proper form of man.

But we must observe that the nobler a form is, the more it rises above corporeal matter, the less it is subject to matter, and the more it excels matter by its power and its operation. Hence we find that the form of a mixed body has an operation not caused by its elemental qualities. And the higher we advance in the nobility of forms, the more we find that the power of the form excels the elementary matter; as the vegetative soul excels the form of the metal, and the sensitive soul excels the vegetative soul. Now the human soul is the highest and noblest of forms. Therefore, in its power it excels corporeal matter by the fact that it has an operation and a power in which corporeal matter has no share whatever. This power is called the intellect.

It is well to remark, furthermore, that if anyone held that the soul is composed of matter and form, it would follow that in no way could the soul be the form of the body. For since form is an act, and matter is being only in potentiality, that which is composed of matter and form cannot in its entirety be the form of another. But if it is a form by virtue of some part of itself, then that part which is the form we call the soul, and that of which it is the form we call the *primary animate*, as was said above.

Reply Obj. 1. As the Philosopher says, the highest natural form (namely, the human soul) to which the consideration of the natural philosopher is directed is indeed separate, but it exists in matter. He proves this from the fact *that man and the sun generate man from matter*. It is separate according to its intellectual power, because an intellectual power is not the power of a corporeal organ, as the power of seeing is the act of the eye; for understanding is an act which cannot be performed by a corporeal organ, as can the act of seeing. But it exists in matter in so far as the soul itself, to which this power belongs, is the form of the body, and the term of human generation. And so the Philosopher says that the *intellect is separate*, because it is not the power of a corporeal organ.

From this it is clear how to answer the Second and Third objections. For in order that man may be able to understand all things by means of his intellect, and that his intellect may understand all things immaterial and universal, it is sufficient that the intellectual power be not the act of the body.

Reply Obj. 4. The human soul, by reason of its perfection, is not a form immersed in matter, or entirely embraced by matter. Therefore there is nothing to prevent some power of the soul from not being the act of the body, although the soul is essentially the form of the body.

Reply Obj. 5. The soul communicates that being in which it subsists to the corporeal matter, out of which and the intellectual soul there results one being; so that the being of the whole composite is also the being of the soul. This is not the case with other non-subsistent forms. For this reason the human soul retains its own being after the dissolution of the body; whereas it is not so with other forms.

Reply Obj. 6. To be united to the body belongs to the soul by reason of itself, just as it belongs to a light body by reason of itself to be raised up. And just as a light body remains light, when removed from its proper place, retaining meanwhile an aptitude and an inclination for its proper place, so the human soul retains its proper being when separated from the body, having an aptitude and a natural inclination to be united to the body.

On Happiness (from *Summa contra Gentes*, IV)

Chapter XXXVII

That Man's Ultimate Happiness Consists in Contemplating God

Accordingly, if man's ultimate happiness does not consist in external things, which are called goods of fortune; nor in goods of the body; nor in goods of the soul, as regards the sensitive part; nor as regards the intellectual part, in terms of the life of moral virtue; nor in terms of the intellectual virtues which are concerned with action, namely, art and prudence:—it remains for us to conclude that man's ultimate happiness consists in the contemplation of truth.

For this operation alone is proper to man, and it is in it that none of the other animals communicates.

Again. This is not directed to anything further as to its end, since the contemplation of the truth is sought for its own sake.

Again. By this operation man is united to beings above him, by becoming like them; because of all human actions this alone is both in God and in the separate substances. Also, by this operation man comes into contact with those higher beings, through knowing them in any way whatever.

Besides, man is more self-sufficing for this operation, seeing that he stands in little need of the help of external things in order to perform it.

Further. All other human operations seem to be ordered to this as to their end. For perfect contemplation requires that the body should be disencumbered, and to this effect are directed all the products of art that are necessary for life. Moreover, it requires freedom from the disturbance caused by the passions, which is achieved by means of the moral virtues and of prudence; and freedom from external disturbance, to which the whole governance of the civil life is directed. So that, if we consider the matter rightly, we shall see that all human occupations appear to serve those who contemplate the truth.

Now, it is not possible that man's ultimate happiness consist in contemplation based on the understanding of first principles; for this is most imperfect, as being most universal, containing potentially the knowledge of things. Moreover, it is the beginning and not the end of human inquiry, and comes to us from nature, and not through the pursuit of the truth. Nor does it consist in contemplation based on the sciences that have the lowest things for their object, since happiness must consist in an operation of the intellect in relation to the most noble intelligible objects. It follows then that man's ultimate happiness consists in wisdom, based on the consideration of divine things.

It is therefore evident also by way of induction that man's ultimate happiness consists solely in the contemplation of God, which conclusion was proved above by arguments.

Chapter XLVIII

That Man's Ultimate Happiness Is Not In This Life

Seeing, then, that man's ultimate happiness does not consist in that knowledge of God whereby He is known by all or many in a vague kind of opinion, nor again in that knowledge of God whereby He is known in the speculative sciences through demonstration, nor in that knowledge whereby He is known through faith, as we have proved above; and seeing that it is not possible in this life to arrive at a higher knowledge of God in His essence, or at least so that we understand other separate substances, and thus know God through that which is nearest to Him, so to say, as we have proved; and since we must place our ultimate happiness in some kind of knowledge of God, as we have shown:—it is impossible for man's happiness to be in this life.

Again. Man's last end is the term of his natural appetite, so that when he has obtained it, he desires nothing more; because if he still has a movement towards something, he has not yet reached an end wherein to be at rest. Now this cannot happen in this life, since the more man understands, the more is the desire to understand increased in him (for this is natural to man), unless perhaps there be someone who understands all things. Now in this life this never did nor can happen to anyone that was a mere man, seeing that in this life we are unable to know separate substances which in themselves are most intelligible, as we have proved. Therefore man's ultimate happiness cannot possibly be in this life.

Besides. Whatever is in motion towards an end has a natural desire to be established and at rest therein. Hence a body does not move away from the place towards which it has a natural movement, except by a violent movement which is contrary to that appetite. Now happiness is the last end which man naturally desires. Therefore it is his natural desire to be established in happiness. Consequently, unless together with happiness he acquires a state of immobility, he is not yet happy, since his natural desire is not yet at rest. When, therefore, a man acquires happiness, he also acquires stability and rest; so that all agree in conceiving stability as a necessary condition of happiness. Hence the Philosopher says: *We do not look upon the happy man as a kind of chameleon.* Now in this life there is no sure stability, since, however happy a man may be, sickness and misfortune may come upon him, so that he is hindered in the operation, whatever it be, in which happiness consists. Therefore man's ultimate happiness cannot be in this life.

Moreover. It would seem unfitting and unreasonable for a thing to take a long time in becoming, and to have but a short time in being; for it would follow that for a longer duration of time nature would be deprived of its end. Hence we see that animals which live but a short time are perfected in a short time. But if happiness consists in a perfect operation according to perfect virtue, whether intellectual or moral, it cannot possibly come to man except after a long time. This is most evident in speculative matters, wherein man's ultimate happiness consists, as we have proved; for hardly is man able to arrive at perfection in the speculations of science, even though he reach the last stage of life, and then, in the majority of cases, but a short space of life remains to him. Therefore man's ultimate happiness cannot be in this life.

Further. All admit that happiness is a perfect good, or else it would not bring rest to the appetite. Now perfect good is that which is wholly free from any admixture of evil; just as that which is perfectly white is that which is entirely free from any admixture of black. But man cannot be wholly free from evils in this state of life, and not only from evils of the body, such as hunger, thirst, heat, cold and the like, but also from evils of the soul. For there is no one who at times is not disturbed by inordinate passions; who sometimes does not go beyond the mean, wherein virtue consists, either in excess or in deficiency; who is not deceived in some thing or another; or who at least is not ignorant of what he would wish to know, or does not feel doubtful about an opinion of which he would like to be certain. Therefore no man is happy in this life.

Again. Man naturally shuns death, and is sad about it, not only shunning it at the moment when he feels its presence, but also when he thinks about it. But man, in this life, cannot obtain not to die. Therefore it is not possible for man to be happy in this life.

Besides. Ultimate happiness consists, not in a habit, but in an operation, since habits are for the sake of actions. But in this life it is impossible to perform any action continuously. Therefore man cannot be entirely happy in this life.

Further. The more a thing is desired and loved, the more does its loss bring sorrow and pain. Now happiness is most desired and loved. Therefore its loss brings the greatest sorrow. But if there be ultimate happiness in this life, it will certainly be lost, at least by death. Nor is it certain that it will last till death, since it is possible for every man in this life to encounter sickness, whereby he is wholly hindered from the operation of virtue, *e.g.*, madness and the like, which hinder the use of reason. Such happiness therefore always has sorrow naturally connected with it, and consequently it will not be perfect happiness.

But someone might say that, since happiness is a good of the intellectual nature, perfect and true happiness is for those in whom the intellectual nature is perfect, namely, in separate substances, and that in man it is imperfect, and by a kind of participation. For man can arrive at a full understanding of the truth only by a sort of movement of inquiry; and he fails entirely to understand things that are by nature most intelligible, as we have proved. Therefore neither is happiness, in its perfect nature, possible to man; but he has a certain participation of it, even in this life. This seems to have been Aristotle's opinion about happiness. Hence, inquiring whether misfortunes destroy happiness, he shows that happiness seems especially to consist in deeds of virtue, which seem to be most stable in this life, and concludes that those who in this life attain to this perfection are happy as *men*, as though not attaining to happiness absolutely, but in a human way.

We must now show that this explanation does not remove the foregoing arguments. For although man is below the separate substances according to the order of nature, he is above irrational creatures, and so he attains his ultimate end in a more perfect way than they. Now these attain their last end so perfectly that they seek nothing further. Thus a heavy body rests when it is in its own proper place, and when an animal enjoys sensible pleasure, its natural desire is at rest. Much more, therefore, when man has obtained his last end, must his natural desire be at rest. But this cannot happen in this life. Therefore in this life man does not obtain happiness considered as his proper end, as we have proved. Therefore he must obtain it after this life.

Again. Natural desire cannot be empty, since *nature does nothing in vain.* But nature's desire would be empty if it could never be fulfilled. Therefore man's natural desire can be fulfilled. But not in this life, as we have shown. Therefore it must be fulfilled after this life. Therefore man's ultimate happiness is after this life.

Besides. As long as a thing is in motion towards perfection, it has not reached its last end. Now in the knowledge of truth all men are always in motion and tending towards perfection; because those who follow make discoveries in addition to those made by their predecessors, as is also stated in *Metaph.* ii. Therefore in the knowledge of truth man is not situated as though he had arrived at his last end. Since, then, as Aristotle himself shows, man's ultimate happiness in this life consists apparently in speculation, whereby he seeks the knowledge of truth, we cannot possibly allow that man obtains his last end in this life.

Moreover. Whatever is in potentiality tends to become actual, so that as long as it is not wholly actual, it has not reached its last end. Now our intellect is in potentiality to the knowledge of all the forms of things, and it becomes actual when it knows any one of them. Consequently, it will not be wholly actual, nor in possession of its last end, except when it knows all things, at least all these material things. But man cannot obtain this through the speculative sciences, by which we know truth in this life. Therefore man's ultimate happiness cannot be in this life.

For these and like reasons, Alexander and Averroes held that man's ultimate happiness does not consist in that human knowledge obtained through the speculative sciences, but in that which results from a union with a separate substance, which union they deemed possible to man in this life. But as Aristotle realized that man has no knowledge in this life other than that which he obtains through the speculative sciences, he maintained that man attains to a happiness which is not perfect, but a human one.

Hence it becomes sufficiently clear how these great minds suffered from being so straitened on every side. We, however, shall be freed from these straits if we hold, in accordance with the foregoing arguments, that man is able to reach perfect happiness after this life, since man has an immortal soul; and that in that state his soul will understand in the same way as separate substances understand, as we proved in the Second Book.

Therefore man's ultimate happiness will consist in that knowledge of God which the human mind possesses after this life, a knowledge similar to that by which separate substances know him. Hence our Lord promises us a *reward ... in heaven* (*Matt.* v. 12) and states (*Matt.* xxii. 30) that the saints *shall be as the angels*, who always see God in heaven (*Matt.* xviii. 10).

On the Essence of Law (from *Summa theologiae*, Part I-II)

Question XC

First Article

Whether law Is Something Pertaining To Reason?

We proceed thus to the First Article:—

Objection I. It would seem that law is not something pertaining to reason. For the Apostle says (*Rom.* vii. 23): *I see another law in my members*, etc. But nothing pertaining to reason is in the members, since the reason does not make use of a bodily organ. Therefore law is not something pertaining to reason.

Obj. 2. Further, in the reason there is nothing else but power, habit and act. But law is not the power itself of reason. In like manner, neither is it a habit of reason, because the habits of reason are the intellectual virtues, of which we have spoken above. Nor again is it an act of reason, because then law would cease when the act of reason ceases, for instance, while we are asleep. Therefore law is nothing pertaining to reason.

Obj. 3. Further, the law moves those who are subject to it to act rightly. But it belongs properly to the will to move to act, as is evident from what has been said above. Therefore law pertains, not to the reason, but to the will, according to the words of the Jurist: *Whatsoever pleaseth the sovereign has the force of law.*

On the contrary, It belongs to the law to command and to forbid. But it belongs to reason to command, as was stated above. Therefore law is something pertaining to reason.

I answer that, Law is a rule and measure of acts, whereby man is induced to act or is restrained from acting; for lex [*law*] is derived from ligare [*to bind*], because it binds one to act. Now the rule and measure of human acts is the reason, which is the first principle of human acts, as is evident from what has been stated above. For it belongs to the reason to direct to the end, which is the first principle in all matters of action, according to the Philosopher. Now that which is the principle in any genus is the rule and measure of that genus: for instance, unity in the genus of numbers, and the first movement in the genus of movements. Consequently, it follows that law is something pertaining to reason.

Reply Obj. I. Since law is a kind of rule and measure, it may be in something in two ways. First, as in that which measures and rules; and since this is proper to reason, it follows that, in this way, law is in the reason alone.— Secondly, as in that which is measured and ruled. In this way, law is in all those things that are inclined to something because of some law; so that any inclination arising from a law may be called a law, not essentially, but by participation as it were. And thus the inclination of the members to concupiscence is called *the law of the members*.

Reply Obj. 2. Just as, in external acts, we may consider the work and the work done, for instance, the work of building and the house built, so in the acts of reason, we may consider the act itself of reason, *i.e.*, to understand and to reason, and something produced by this act. With regard to the speculative reason, this is first of all the definition; secondly, the proposition; thirdly, the syllogism or argument. And since the practical reason also makes use of the syllogism in operable matters, as we have stated above and as the philosopher teaches, hence we find in the practical reason something that holds the same position in regard to operations as, in the speculative reason, the proposition holds in regard to conclusions. Such universal propositions of the practical reason that are directed to operations have the nature of law. And these propositions are sometimes under our actual consideration, while sometimes they are retained in the reason by means of a habit.

Reply Obj. 3. Reason has its power of moving from the will, as was stated above; for it is due to the fact that one wills the end, that the reason issues its commands as regards things ordained to the end. But in order that the volition of what is commanded may have the nature of law, it needs to be in accord with some rule of reason. And in this sense is to be understood the saying that the will of the sovereign has the force of law; or otherwise the sovereign's will would savor of lawlessness rather than of law.

Second Article

Whether Law Is Always Directed To The Common Good?

We proceed thus to the Second Article:—

Objection I. It would seem that law is not always directed to the common good as to its end. For it belongs to law to command and to forbid. Butcommands are directed to certain individual goods. Therefore the end of law is not always the common good.

Obj. 2. Further, law directs man in his actions. But human actions are concerned with particular matters. Therefore law is directed to some particular good.

Obj. 3. Further, Isidore says: *If law is based on reason, whatever is based on reason will be a law.* But reason is the foundation not only of what is ordained to the common good, but also of that which is directed to private good. Therefore law is not directed only to the good of all, but also to the private good of an individual.

On the contrary, Isidore says that *laws are enacted for no private profit, but for the common benefit of the citizens.*

I answer that, As we have stated above, law belongs to that which is a principle of human acts, because it is their rule and measure. Now as reason is a principle of human acts, so in reason itself there is something which is the principle in respect of all the rest. Hence to this principle chiefly and mainly law must needs be referred. Now the first principle in practical matters, which are the object of the practical reason, is the last end: and the last end of human life is happiness or beatitude, as we have stated above. Consequently, law must needs concern itself mainly with the order that is in beatitude. Moreover, since every part is ordained to the whole as the imperfect to the perfect, and since one man is a part of the perfect community, law must needs concern itself properly with the order directed to universal happiness. Therefore the Philosopher, in the above definition of legal matters, mentions both happiness and the body politic, since he says that we call those legal matters *just which are adapted to produce and preserve happiness and its parts for the body politic.* For the state is a perfect community, as he says in *Politics* i.

Now, in every genus, that which belongs to it chiefly is the principle of the others, and the others belong to that genus according to some order towards that thing. Thus fire, which is chief among hot things, is the cause of heat in mixed bodies, and these are said to be hot in so far as they have a share of fire. Consequently, since law is chiefly ordained to the common good, any other precept in regard to some individual work must needs be devoid of the nature of a law, save in so far as it regards the common good. Therefore every law is ordained to the common good.

Reply Obj. I. A command denotes the application of a law to matters regulated by law. Now the order to the common good, at which law aims, is applicable to particular ends. And in this way commands are given even concerning particular matters.

Reply Obj. 2. Actions are indeed concerned with particular matters, but those particular matters are referable to the common good, not as to a common genus or species, but as to a common final cause, according as the common good is said to be the common end.

Reply Obj. 3. Just as nothing stands firm with regard to the speculative reason except that which is traced back to the first indemonstrable principles, so nothing stands firm with regard to the practical reason, unless it be directed to the last end which is the common good. Now whatever stands to reason in this sense has the nature of a law.

Third Article

Whether The Reason Of Any Man Is Competent To Make Laws?

We proceed thus to the Third Article:—

Objection I. It would seem that the reason of any man is competent to make laws. For the Apostle says (*Rom.* ii. 14) that *when the Gentiles, who have not the law, do by nature those things that are of the law, . . . they are a law to themselves.* Now he says this of all in general. Therefore anyone can make a law for himself.

Obj. 2. Further, as the Philosopher says, *the intention of the lawgiver is to lead men to virtue.* But every man can lead another to virtue. Therefore the reason of any man is competent to make laws.

Obj. 3. Further, just as the sovereign of a state governs the state, so every father of a family governs his household. But the sovereign of a state can make laws for the state. Therefore every father of a family can make laws for his household.

On the contrary, Isidore says, and the *Decretals* repeat: *A law is an ordinance of the people, whereby something is sanctioned by the Elders together with the Commonalty.* Therefore not everyone can make laws.

I answer that, A law, properly speaking, regards first and foremost the order to the common good. Now to order anything to the common good belongs either to the whole people, or to someone who is the vicegerent of the whole people. Hence the making of a law belongs either to the whole people or to a public personage who has care of the whole people; for in all other matters the directing of anything to the end concerns him to whom the end belongs.

Reply Obj. I. As was stated above, a law is in a person not only as in one that rules, but also, by participation, as in one that is ruled. In the latter way, each one is a law to himself, in so far as he shares the direction that he receives from one who rules him. Hence the same text goes on: *Who show the work of the law written in their hearts (Rom.* ii. 15).

Reply Obj. 2. A private person cannot lead another to virtue efficaciously; for he can only advise, and if his advice be not taken, it has no coercive power, such as the law should have, in order to prove an efficacious inducement to virtue, as the Philosopher says. But this coercive power is vested in the whole people or in some public personage, to whom it belongs to inflict penalties, as we shall state further on. Therefore the framing of laws belongs to him alone.

Reply Obj. 3. As one man is a part of the household, so a household is a part of the state; and the state is a perfect community, according to Politics i. Therefore, just as the good of one man is not the last end, but is ordained to the common good, so too the good of one household-is ordained to the good of a single state, which is a perfect community. Consequently, he that governs a family can indeed make certain commands or ordinances, but not such as to have properly the nature of law.

Fourth Article

Whether Promulgation Is Essential to Law?

We proceed thus to the Fourth Article:—

Objection 1. It would seem that promulgation is not essential to law. For the natural law, above all, has the character of law. But the natural law needs no promulgation. Therefore it is not essential to law that it be promulgated.

Obj. 2. Further, it belongs properly to law to bind one to do or not to do something. But the obligation of fulfilling a law touches not only those in whose presence it is promulgated, but also others. Therefore promulgation is not essential to law.

Obj. 3. Further, the binding force of law extends even to the future, *since laws are binding in matters of the future,* as the jurists say. But promulgation concerns those who are present. Therefore it is not essential to law.

On the contrary, It is laid down in the *Decretals* that *laws are established when they are promulgated.*

I answer that, As was stated above, a law is imposed on others as a rule and measure. Now a rule or measure is imposed by being applied to those who are to be ruled and measured by it. Therefore, in order that a law obtain the binding force which is proper to a law, it must needs be applied to the men who have to be ruled by it. But such application is made by its being made known to them by promulgation. Therefore promulgation is necessary for law to obtain its force.

Thus, from the four preceding articles, the definition of law may be gathered. Law is nothing else than an ordinance of reason for the common good, promulgated by him who has the care of the community.

Reply Obj. 1. The natural law is promulgated by the very fact that God instilled it into man's mind so as to be known by him naturally.

Reply Obj. 2. Those who are not present when a law is promulgated are bound to observe the law, in so far as it is made known or can be made known to them by others, after it has been promulgated.

Reply Obj. 3. The promulgation that takes place in the present extends to future time by reason of the durability of written characters, by which means it is continually promulgated. Hence Isidore says that lex [law] is derived from legere [to read] because it is written.

On the Various Kinds of Law (from *Summa theologiae,* Part I-II)

Question XCI

First Article

Whether There Is an Eternal Law?
We proceed thus to the First Article:—

Objection 1. It would seem that there is no eternal law. For every law is imposed on someone. But there was not someone from eternity on whom a law could be imposed, since God alone was from eternity. Therefore no law is eternal.

Obj. 2. Further, promulgation is essential to law. But promulgation could not be from eternity, because there was no one to whom it could be promulgated from eternity. Therefore no law can be eternal.

Obj. 3. Further, law implies order to an end. But nothing ordained to an end is eternal, for the last end alone is eternal. Therefore no law is eternal.

On the contrary, Augustine says: *That Law which is the Supreme Reason cannot be understood to be otherwise than unchangeable and eternal.*

I answer that, As we have stated above, law is nothing else but a dictate of practical reason emanating from the ruler who governs a perfect community. Now it is evident, granted that the world is ruled by divine providence, as was stated in the First Part, that the whole community of the universe is governed by the divine reason. Therefore the very notion of the government of things in God, the ruler of the universe, has the nature of a law. And since the divine reason's conception of things is not subject to time, but is eternal, according to *Prov.* viii. 23, therefore it is that this kind of law must be called eternal.

Reply Obj. 1. Those things that do not exist in themselves exist in God, inasmuch as they are known and preordained by Him, according to *Rom.* iv. 17: *Who calls those things that are not, as those that are.* Accordingly, the eternal concept of the divine law bears the character of an eternal law in so far as it is ordained by God to the government of things foreknown by Him.

Reply Obj. 2. Promulgation is made by word of mouth or in writing, and in both ways the eternal law is promulgated, because both the divine Word and the writing of the Book of Life are eternal. But the promulgation cannot be from eternity on the part of the creature that hears or reads.

Reply Obj. 3. Law implies order to the end actively, namely, in so far as it directs certain things to the end; but not passively,—that is to say, the law itself is not ordained to the end, except accidentally, in a governor whose end is extrinsic to him, and to which end his law must needs be ordained. But the end of the divine government is God Himself, and His law is not something other than Himself. Therefore the eternal law is not ordained to another end.

Second Article

Whether There Is In Us a Natural Law?

We proceed thus to the Second Article:

Objection 1. It would seem that there is no natural law in us. For man is governed sufficiently by the eternal law, since Augustine says that *the eternal law is that by which it is right that all things should be most orderly.* But nature does not abound in superfluities as neither does she fail in necessaries. Therefore man has no natural law.

Obj. 2. Further, by the law man is directed, in his acts, to the end, as was stated above. But the directing of human acts to their end is not

a function of nature, as is the case in irrational creatures, which act for
an end solely by their natural appetite; whereas man acts for an end
by his reason and will. Therefore man has no natural law.

Obj. 3. Further, the more a man is free, the less is he under the law.
But man is freer than all the animals because of his free choice, with
which he is endowed in distinction from all other animals. Since, therefore, other animals are not subject to a natural law, neither is man subject to a natural law.

On the contrary, the Gloss on *Rom.* ii. 14 (*When the Gentiles, who
have not the law, do by nature those things that are of the law*) comments as follows: *Although they have no written law, yet they have
the natural law, whereby each one knows, and is conscious of, what
is good and what is evil.*

I answer that, As we have stated above, law, being a rule and measure, can be in a person in two ways: in one way, as in him that rules
and measures; in another way, as in that which is ruled and measured,
since a thing is ruled and measured in so far as it partakes of the rule
or measure. Therefore, since all things subject to divine providence are
ruled and measured by the eternal law, as was stated above, it is evident that all things partake in some way in the eternal law, in so far
as, namely, from its being imprinted on them, they derive their respective inclinations to their proper acts and ends. Now among all others,
the rational creature is subject to divine providence in a more excellent
way, in so far as it itself partakes of a share of providence, by being
provident both for itself and for others. Therefore it has a share of the
eternal reason, whereby it has a natural inclination to its proper act
and end; and this participation of the eternal law in the rational creature is called the natural law. Hence the Psalmist, after saying (*Ps.* iv.
6): *Offer up the sacrifice of justice,* as though someone asked what the
works of justice are, adds: *Many say, Who showeth us good things?* in
answer to which question he says: *The light of Thy countenance, O
Lord, is signed upon us.* He thus implies that the light of natural reason, whereby we discern what is good and what is evil, which is the
function of the natural law, is nothing else than an imprint on us of the
divine light. It is therefore evident that the natural law is nothing else
than the rational creature's participation of the eternal law.

Reply Obj. 1. This argument would hold if the natural law were
something different from the eternal law; whereas it is nothing but a
participation thereof, as we have stated above.

Reply Obj. 2. Every act of reason and will in us is based on that
which is according to nature, as was stated above. For every act of reasoning is based on principles that are known naturally, and every act
of appetite in respect of the means is derived from the natural appetite
in respect of the last end. Accordingly, the first direction of our acts
to their end must needs be through the natural law.

Reply Obj. 3. Even irrational animals partake in their own way of the eternal reason, just as the rational creature does. But because the rational creature partakes thereof in an intellectual and rational manner, therefore the participation of the eternal law in the rational creature is properly called a law, since a law is something pertaining to reason, as was stated above. Irrational creatures, however, do not partake thereof in a rational manner, and therefore there is no participation of the eternal law in them, except by way of likeness.

Third Article

Whether There Is a Human Law?

We proceed thus to the Third Article:—

Objection 1. It would seem that there is not a human law. For the natural law is a participation of the eternal law, as was stated above. Now through the eternal law *all things are most orderly*, as Augustine states. Therefore the natural law suffices for the ordering of all human affairs. Consequently there is no need for a human law.

Obj. 2. Further, law has the character of a measure, as was stated above. But human reason is not a measure of things, but vice versa, as is stated in Metaph. x. Therefore no law can emanate from the human reason.

Obj. 3. Further, a measure should be most certain, as is stated in *Metaph.* x. But the dictates of the human reason in matters of conduct are uncertain, according to *Wis.* ix. 14: *The thoughts of mortal men are fearful, and our counsels uncertain.* Therefore no law can emanate from the human reason.

On the contrary, Augustine distinguishes two kinds of law, the one eternal, the other temporal, which he calls human.

I answer that, As we have stated above, a law is a dictate of the practica reason. Now it is to be observed that the same procedure takes place in the practical and in the speculative reason, for each proceeds from principles to conclusions, as was stated above. Accordingly, we conclude that, just as in the speculative reason, from naturally known indemonstrable principles we draw the conclusions of the various sciences, the knowledge of which is not imparted to us by nature, but acquired by the efforts of reason, so too it is that from the precepts of the natural law, as from common and indemonstrable principles, the human reason needs to proceed to the more particular determination of certain matters. These particular determinations, devised by human reason, are called human laws, provided that the other essential conditions of law be observed, as was stated above. Therefore Tully says in his *Rhetoric* that *justice has its source in nature; thence certain things came into custom by reason of their utility; afterwards these things which emanated from nature, and were approved by custom, were sanctioned by fear and reverence for the law.*

Reply Obj. 1. The human reason cannot have a full participation of the dictate of the divine reason, but according to its own mode, and imperfectly. Consequently, just as on the part of the speculative reason, by a natural participation of divine wisdom, there is in us the knowledge of certain common principles, but not a proper knowledge of each single truth, such as that contained in the divine wisdom, so, too, on the part of the practical reason, man has a natural participation of the eternal law, according to certain common principles, but not as regards the particular determinations of individual cases, which are, however, contained in the eternal law. Hence the need for human reason to proceed further to sanction them by law.

Reply Obj. 2. Human reason is not of itself, the rule of things. But the principles impressed on it by nature are the general rules and measures of all things relating to human conduct, of which the natural reason is the rule and measure, although it is not the measure of things that are from nature.

Reply Obj. 3. The practical reason is concerned with operable matters, which are singular and contingent, but not with necessary things, with which the speculative reason is concerned. Therefore human laws cannot have that inerrancy that belongs to the demonstrated conclusions of the sciences. Nor is it necessary for every measure to be altogether unerring and certain, but according as it is possible in its own particular genus.

(From *Basic Writings of St. Thomas Aquinas*, ed. Anton Pegis. New York: Macmillan Publishing Company, 1945. Reprinted by permission of the estate of Anton C. Pegis.)

Review Questions

1. Show the importance of the rediscovery of Aristotle for Western thought.
2. How does the epistemology of St. Thomas lead to the conclusion, contrary to Plato's view, that body and soul form one being in man?
3. In what way is Thomas's philosophy existential?
4. What is St. Thomas' position on the norm for judging right from wrong?
5. How does St. Thomas demonstrate the existence of god?
6. Discuss St. Thomas' view on the presence of evil in the world.
7. What is St. Thomas' view on happiness and how a person achieves it?
8. Discuss the meaning of eternal law and natural law in St. Thomas.

8

Duns Scotus (1266–1308)

Introduction

The intellectual life of theology, which began in earnest in the early thirteenth century, continued unabated into the early fourteenth; it was expressed in academic centers throughout Europe in a busy program of study, lectures, public defense of theses, and public disputations that involved masters and students alike in the ongoing excitement of divine science. As one would expect, besides the theological factiousness that sometimes arose, there were legitimate preferences and traditions in theology that one might have embraced as a more fitting articulation of a faith that all theologians held in common. Such traditions were coming to be recognized in the theological undertakings of the Dominicans and Franciscans, young religious orders that within a dozen years of each other established chairs of theology at the University of Paris, the most prestigious school of theology in Christendom. Toward the end of the century, the Dominicans counted Albert the Great and Thomas Aquinas among their most respected theologians, and the Franciscans did the same with Alexander of Hales and Bonaventure. It is perhaps unhistorical to talk of different types of theology clashing with each other in the early thirteenth century, although the rediscovered Aristotle had to compete successfully against a series of prohibitions laid down by churchmen fearful of the faith's being contaminated by a naturalistic philosophy. St. Augustine, however, was the patrimony of all the theologians of the time, and with the advent of Aristotle the philosophical makeup of a thinker like Aquinas was that of an Augustinian Aristotelianism. But among the theologians of the next generation, no doubt feeling the impact of the famous prohibitions of 1277 purporting to safeguard the faith by condemning certain theses of "Aristotelianism," was Duns Scotus, whose philosophical makeup was that of an Aristotelian Augustinianism, thus restoring the great latin Father to pride of place without losing the benefit of the Stagirite's mighty contributions.

Though he died young and left most of his writings unfinished, Duns Scotus exercised a profound influence for several centuries during which, because of the precise distinctions he made, he was known as the Subtle Doctor. It was this very propensity for making distinctions and his lack of literary grace that disenchanted the literary humanists of the Renaissance, who mocked him and the "Duns-men" as hair splitters and sophists, thus causing the word *dunce* to enter pejoratively into present-day language. Yet this same Duns Scotus was hailed by the American philosopher C.S. Peirce as one of the profoundest metaphysicians who ever lived and was spoken of as reality's "rarest veinèd unraveller" by the poet Gerard Manley Hopkins out of gratitude for deepening his insight into the inwardness of being, called *inscape* by the poet.

Not much is known for sure of Scotus's early years, but scholars now agree that he was born around 1266 in Scotland, bearing the family or place name of Duns. He was ordained a priest in Northampton as a member of the Order of Friars Minor, the Franciscans, in 1291. He was sent to the Franciscan house of studies at Oxford, where he undertook the thirteen-year preparation for the mastership in theology, devoting considerable effort to his lectures, which eventuated in his major work, the *Opus oxoniense,* or *The Oxford Commentary.* Because of his acknowledged ability, he completed his mastership requirement by teaching for a year at the University of Paris in 1302. But inasmuch as he sided with Pope Boniface VIII in a feud that developed with King Philip the Fair over taxation of church property, Scotus had to leave France; when the feud subsided, he returned to Paris. In 1307 he became professor of theology at Cologne, where he died the following year. In addition to *The Oxford Commentary,* Scotus's other more important writings are the *Opus parisiense (Reportata parisiensia)* or *The Paris Commentary; Quaestiones quodlibetales,* translated as *God and Creatures, the Quodlibetal Questions;* and *De primo principio,* translated as *A Treatise on God as First Principle.*

As one who studies the science of God, the theologian must be prepared to give his reasons for saying that God exists, and his reasons have to fall into one of two categories: either we *know* that God exists or we *hold* that God exists on nonrational grounds. Scotus definitely belongs to the first category, and though his proof is complicated in itself, it has historical complications as well. He rejects any form of argumentation that can be called physical, such as Aristotle's argument for the Prime Mover, because it cannot go beyond the physical things with which it begins. Yet the existence of God "is demonstrable by a demonstration of fact from creatures." What seems to be at the heart of Scotus's proof is a historical problem stemming from Avicenna, a well-known Arabian commentator on Aristotle, who saw an unequivocal necessity in all that God does, so that even a creaturely thing thought to be contingent is in some way necessary; this struck Scotus as patently denying God's freedom, so he wanted to avoid it at all costs. He therefore shifted the emphasis from the fact of a contingent thing's existence to the fact of its being _possible_, it being true, of course, that a conclusion of a thing's possibility can be made from its actuality: whatever is actual is possible, though whatever is possible is not therefore actual. Now Scotus felt on safer ground because he was able to show that God both exists and is free at the same time; if there are possibles, it is only because a being necessarily exists that can freely produce them as possible, and so he argues: something is possible; since its possibility does not come from within itself, it must come from something else as its cause; but an infinite series of causes to account for possibility is impossible; therefore, something necessarily and actually exists that freely causes possibles, and is itself uncaused. The series Scotus has in mind is such that the "posterior" is immediately and always dependent on the "prior," one that is "essentially ordered"; this is opposed to an "accidentally ordered" series such as the one exemplified in the child's being fathered by the father being fathered by the father and so on, in which immediate dependence is not always required, and the series could therefore theoretically be infinite.

It soon becomes clear that Scotus is working from a concept of metaphysics different from that of Thomas Aquinas, for example. This concept, perhaps oversimplified, is that essence is prior to existence. The first thing the intellect knows, and therefore the primary "intelligible," is not that a thing _is_, but _what_ it is, so that "being" refers first and foremost to "essence." In other words, existence is a "modality" of essence, and not the other way around. One cannot speak of essence without speaking of some corresponding degree of existence, and when a thing actually exists, it is because God has willed to "complete" the existential capabilities of that essence in its individual determination. It is not as though existence must be added to essence, as in the metaphysics of Aquinas, for it is already present in the texture of essence, simply awaiting a further determination on God's part.

The indeterminateness of essence can be garnered from the fact that the response to the question "what?" when asked of Socrates is exactly the same as when asked of Peter, Paul, Mary, James, and so on; that response is "man"; man can be predicated of one or many, it is both singular and universal. What makes the singular referent an individual is the _thisness_ (_haecceitas_ in latin) it possesses, which makes it unique and unshared by anything else. So, for example, there must be something in Socrates that makes him Socrates and no one else; his color, his shape, his size, and so on are only external signs of his individuality. The thisness of Socrates is the very "form," Scotus says, that functions as the determining element previously discussed. The form is not really distinct from the being it is the form of, even though the mind sometimes thinks that way; thus a "formal distinction" is different from a "real distinction" in that the latter signifies that several things are distinct entities.

We are now in a better position to understand Scotus's view on the relationship of creatures to God. By a special act, God produces an individually existing thing separate from Himself: "Now what is primarily the term of a creative act as such is formally an individual or a 'this.' " Yet, every created thing, before it is created, is "creatable," which means that somehow it is present in the very being of God and pertains to the very essence of God. But not everything that pertains to the very essence of God is for that reason creatable, for creatibility itself is a matter of divine option; otherwise Scotus would, he felt, fall into the trap, as Avicenna did, of putting God under necessity and creatures under fatalism. God's designations, then, are possibles; they are essences that, in God and by God, have a direct reference to existence subject to a further and ultimate determination (form) as this or that individual created thing. Existence, then, is not a determination that comes from without, as already indicated; it comes from within the texture of essence. This is the heart of the difference between Scotus's and Thomas's existentialism.

Another feature of Scotist metaphysics — that being can be predicated "univocally" of God and creatures — enters at this point. Recall the huge problem faced by St. Thomas and in fact by any philosopher who is concerned with the relationship between God and creatures: if you call a creature a being and then call God a being, are you therefore saying they are the same, as when you say that Socrates is a man and Paul is a man? If being means exactly the same, then it is *univocal*; if there is no similarity of meaning, it is *equivocal*. If the first were true, God and creatures are one; if the second, there is no way of talking about God at all. So Thomas developed the third way of *analogy*, a way allowing being to be said of God in a radically different way from the way it is said of creatures, and yet with some similarity. Thomas could do this because his metaphysics of existence allows an analogy between the way God is proportioned to His existence and the way creatures are proportioned to their existence. But Scotus's metaphysics of essence would not permit this interpretation of analogy, for he insisted that being expresses a commonness between God and creatures; being is univocal, at least in one sense of the word: "It is clear that 'being' has a primacy of commonness in regard to the primary intelligibles, that is, to the quidditative concepts of the genera, species, individuals, and all their essential parts, and to the Uncreated Being."

But being, for Scotus, is not a genus or a class, like "man" or "animal"; it transcends them; it is a "transcendental", like "wise" and "good." So the difference between God and creatures, of whom being is truly said, is in the way the transcendental applies, that is, either as infinite or finite: "Whatever [predicates] are common to God and creatures are of such kind [ie, transcendental], pertaining as they do to being in its indifference to what is infinite and finite. For in so far as they pertain to God they are infinite, whereas in so far as they belong to creatures they are finite."

In Scotus's creaturely world, as with theologians generally, it is the creature man, endowed with the special grace of intellect and will, who can relate to God knowingly and lovingly. If one asks which is the higher faculty, he will find, according to Scotus, that it is the will, for it is by the will, a "rational will" to be sure, that man achieves what he exists for — the love of God. We saw how much Scotus wants to protect the freedom of God against all necessity, so that His will is the pervasive force of creation, and the highest expression of His will toward man is His love. In return, the highest expression of man's free will is in loving God. In a sense, the love of God for man and the love of man for God is a mutual union of freedoms. Man's actions, then, are considered good if they are done in accordance with the love of God; the love of God becomes the norm of morality, which is acknowledged by man in the right use of his reason.

The completion of man's love for God is attained in life beyond death. As a Christian theologian, Scotus believes that man is immortal, but, hard as he tries to say that immortality can be proved by reason, he rejects all rational arguments that purport to prove it; the most these arguments show is that immortality is probable. He considers all the arguments he finds in Aristotle, Aquinas, and even Augustine, and yet his summary opinion is: "It can be stated that although there are probable reasons for this second proposition [i.e., that the intellective soul is immortal] these are not demonstrative, nor for that matter are they even necessary reasons." Nevertheless, immortality is a certainty, and we can readily understand how this fact creates for Scotus a further opportunity to rejoice in the certainty of faith as a gift of God.

Readings

God as Creator and Conserver (from *God and Creatures*)

Question Twelve, Article I

Is the Real Relation of the Creature to God as Creator and as Conserver the Same?

12.5 [Affirmative answer and its proof] As for the first, the relation of a creature to God as creator and conserver can be said to be the same.

Proof: For something that is the same both conceptually and in reality there is but one essential dependence of the same type upon something conceptually and really the same. But the existence [*existentia*] of a permanent or enduring creature is absolutely the same in creation and conservation, and the supporting term, namely, the divine volition, is absolutely identical both conceptually and in reality; and the relationship not only to the creator but also to the conserver is the same sort of essential dependence. Therefore [there is but one relation of the creature to God as creator and conserver].

12.6 Proof of the major: If there were several absolutely essential dependence-relations between extremes absolutely identical, they would be like the dependence of the creature on God as efficient and as final cause. But these two types of dependence seem to be of different kinds, for if they were of the same nature they would be incompatible in the same subject under the same aspect. If something depends upon another in such a way that the latter's support is adequate, it will not depend upon it with a second dependence-relationship of the same kind. Otherwise it would be completely supported in each of these dependencies without the other and would depend and not depend upon such—and this, when the term provides complete and full support in each case of dependency.

12.7 The minor has three parts:

Proof of the first part, viz., that the existence of something that is permanent or endures is the same in creation and conservation: The difference between the permanent and the successive consists in this, that what is successive as long as it continues always has a new or different being [*esse*] for each successive part. The permanent on the contrary always has the same being. Neither does it change partially, for otherwise it would be successive. Neither does it change totally, for otherwise for each different moment it would have a totally different being, which is absurd.

12.8 Proof of the second part of the minor, viz., that it is the same divine volition that supports the dependence-relation of the thing both as created and as conserved: The divine volition remains the same in regard to anything that is able to be willed. Now this volition represents the proximate intrinsic term for anything extrinsic.

12.9 The third part of the minor, viz., that both relations are relationships of essential dependence, is clear as regards creation. As for conservation, the proof is this: A thing depends essentially in existing [*in essendo*] on that from which it has being [*esse*]. Such is the conservation of the conserving cause according to the words of Augustine: "For the power of the creator, omnipotent and supporting all, is the cause by which every creature subsists. If such power should cease to rule what has been created, all would cease to be and nature would vanish. It is not like the case of a builder of houses. When he has completed the construction, he leaves, and after he has ceased working and has gone away, his work still stands. But the world could not stand, not even for a wink of the eye, if God withdrew his ruling hand."

12.10 [Objections and their solutions] Here one might object that the ground for the creature's relation to God as creator is not its existence taken in an absolute or unqualified sense, but rather the creation itself considered passively. Similarly the ground for the creature's relation to God as conserver is not its existence taken absolutely but rather the conservation itself considered passively. This is proved from the Philosopher, who says that relations of the second type are based upon activity and passivity. Now even though a creature's existence considered absolutely be the same afterwards as it was at the first moment, it is no more obvious that creation and conservation considered passively are the same than are the relationships we are investigating.

12.11 To this it can be said that the Philosopher does not think that acting [*actio*] and being acted upon [*passio*] are the proximate foundations for relations of the second type, for a relation does not remain if its foundations is gone. Relations of the second type, however, do remain even though the action and being acted upon do not. For example, one remains a father even though his begetting is not an ongoing act. What he says about the second-type relations being founded on the active and passive must not be understood to mean that action and passion are the proximate grounds or foundation proper, but rather that they represent an intervening disposition between the relation and its proper foundation. Now it is the active and passive potencies themselves that can be called the immediate grounds for acting and being acted upon. And although the intervention of action and being acted upon are required, they are not needed to ground the relation, but are a kind of prerequisite, as it were, if the relationship is to be based upon such a ground [as the potencies].

12.12 In our particular case, however, there seems no need to admit that the fundamental reason for the creature's relationship to God as creating and conserving is that it is being acted upon or affected. For properly speaking, the capacity of being acted upon [*passio*] occurs only when the patient receives some form from the agent, for according to the Philosopher in the *Metaphysics*: "The active potency is the principle of transmuting another qua other." Therefore the passive potency is the principle of being changed or transmuted by another. Such a change only occurs when a patient receives something from an agent. But in conservation and creation this does not occur, but the whole is created and the whole conserved completely by the creator and the conserver, and it is not just a part of it as is the case when a patient receives a form from the agent.

12.13 But here there is an objection based on Augustine's words: "Air is not made bright by the sun, but it becomes bright." Otherwise, when the sun sets, the air would remain bright. Now it seems that every creature depends on God for its being in the way the air depends upon the sun for its illumination, which was the point of his analogy of being illumined by the sun. Therefore no creature is made into a being [*facta in esse*], but it continually comes to be [*fit in esse*], and as a consequence the being [*esse*] of a creature is in a continual state of becoming.

12.14 I reply: The Philosopher says that some things [like the day or a game] are in a state of becoming [*in fieri*] and do not have complete being [like a substance], but are in succession. By contrast, some [like man or a house] are said to be in fact [*in facto esse*], when they have their being complete and do not depend for their being on something extrinsic. Now a creature, however, is at all times equally dependent upon God for its being, for it always has the same being from him through the same divine volition. In this sense one could say that the production of a divine person is always *in fieri*, for such a person could never have being if he were not actually receiving it from his producer, and nevertheless the being of the person is most permanent. In similar fashion, although the being of a creature is permanent, nevertheless as regards God it is always in a quasi state of becoming, that is to say, it is always actually depending on the cause which gives it being and it is never in *facto esse*, i.e., it is never actual [*in actu*] apart from and independent of everything else. However, it is not *in fieri* in the sense that it is different from moment to moment, and in contrast to this, it is in *facto esse*, i.e., it has being complete and needs nothing in addition.

Moral Goodness and Badness (from *God and Creatures*)

Question Eighteen, Article 1

The Source of Moral Goodness or Badness

18.8 [Description of moral goodness] The moral goodness of an act consists in its having all that the agent's right reason declares must pertain to the act or the agent in acting.

18.9 [Clarification] This description is explained as follows: Just as the primary goodness of a being, called "essential" and consisting in the integrity or perfection of the being itself, implies positively that there is no imperfection so that all lack or diminution of perfection is excluded, so the being's secondary goodness, which is something over and above, or "accidental," consists in its being perfectly suited to or in complete harmony with something else—something which ought to have it or which it ought to have. And this two-way suitability is commonly connected. As an example of the first, health is said to be good for man because it suits him. [As an example of the second,] food is called good because it has an appropriate taste. Augustine gives examples of both. "Health without pain or fatigue is good," he says. This refers to the first type of suitability, since health is good for man because it suits him. Then Augustine adds: "Good is the face of a man with regular features, a cheerful expression, and glowing color." This is an instance of the second, because here the face is called good for having what is appropriate to it.

There is this difference between the two. What suits someone is said to be good for him, that is, for him it is a good or a perfection, but we do not speak of it as being accidentally or denominatively good in itself. That to which something is appropriate, on the other hand, is called good denominatively because it has what is suited to it. In the first case, the form takes its name from the subject in which it is. As the soul is called "human," so something is called "good for man" because it is a human good. In the second case, the subject gets its designation from the form. Thus we say a man is good because of some good he has.

Now an act is by nature apt to be in agreement with its agent as well as to have something suited to itself. On both counts then it can be called "good" with a goodness that is accidental. This is true in general of a natural act as well, so that this goodness, which consists in having what is appropriate to it, is not only an accidental, but also a natural, goodness.

18.10 Furthermore, some agents without intellect and will neither judge nor can judge what is appropriate to their acts. In such a case, what is suitable is determined by natural causes alone and they incline the agent to act. Or if in addition there be the judgment of some mind and the movement of some will, it would be that of God alone as universal director and mover of the whole of nature. Now the goodness in the act of an agent without intellect and will is merely natural.

18.11 Over and above this general judgment [of God] about the suitability of the action (which concerns agents alike that act with or without knowledge), a general judgment is involved in the case of agents endowed with an intrinsic knowledge of their actions. Those with sense knowledge alone somehow apprehend the suitability of the object of their action. But whether or not they judge the action appropriate, the goodness of the action does not transcend the natural. Others act by virtue of intellectual knowledge, which alone is able to pass judgment, properly speaking, upon the appropriateness of the action. Such agents are suited by nature to have an intrinsic rule of rectitude for their actions. Only they can have an act whose goodness is moral.

18.12 But for this it is not enough that the agent have the ability to adjudicate the appropriateness of his acts. He must actually pass judgment upon the act and carry it out in accord with that judgment. If one is in error and still acts in accord with the correct judgment of another, he is not acting rightly, for by his own knowledge he was meant to regulate his actions and in this case he is not acting in accord with it but against it, and hence he does not act rightly. Similarly,such an agent elicits the sort of act as lies in his power. Now he has in his power the sort of act he deliberately elicits, for the power of free choice consists either formally or concomitantly in knowledge and election. And so it appears clear how the moral goodness of the act lies in its suitability judged according to the agent's right reason.

18.13 [Explanation of all that right reason demands of the act] We explain the added qualification [in 18.8], "all that must pertain to the act," in this way: Every judgment begins with something certain. Now the first judgment about the appropriateness cannot presuppose some knowledge determined by another intellect; otherwise it would not be first. Hence it presupposes something certain but judged by this intellect, namely: the nature of the agent and the power by which he acts together with the essential notion of the act. If these three notions are given, no other knowledge is needed to judge whether or not this particular act is suited to this agent and this faculty. For instance, if one knows what man is, what his intellectual powers are, and what an act of understanding is, then it is clear to him that it befits man to understand with his intellect. Knowing what it means to attain knowledge, it would also be clear to him what it is not appropriate for his mind to reach. Similarly, it is evident from the notions of the nature, the potency, and the act why understanding does not befit the brute, or rather why it is not compatible with his nature. For this first judgment, based precisely on the nature of the agent, the operative power and the act, reveals not something just ill-matched, i.e., some unbecoming or disorderly connection, but a simple inconsistency, i.e., the absolute impossibility of any such union.

18.14 What is more, from these three notions one can conclude what object is appropriate to a given act of a certain agent. Take the act of eating, for example. Food capable of restoring what man has lost would be its appropriate object, whereas a stone or something nourishing for animals but not for man would not be.

This delimitation introduced by the object first brings the act under the generic heading of moral. Not that the nature of its object determines its moral species; rather it opens it to further moral determination, for when an act has an appropriate object, it is capable of further moral specification in view of the circumstances in which it is performed. That is why an act is said to receive its generic goodness from its object, for just as genus is potential with respect to differences, so the goodness derived from its object first puts it into the generic class of moral acts. Only goodness of nature is presupposed. And once it has generic goodness, the way is open to all the additional moral specifications.

18.15 The procedure for determining specific goodness, called "goodness from circumstances," is as follows: The first goodness comes, it seems, from the circumstances of the end, for given the nature of the agent, of the action, of the object, one immediately concludes that such an action ought to be performed by this agent for such an end, and that it ought to be chosen and wanted for the sake of such an end. This circumstance is not precisely characteristic of the act as actually performed or not, but rather of the act as willed and related to this end by an act of the will. Indeed, the decision to do something for a worthy purpose is no less good when the external act that ensues fails to achieve that end than when it succeeds.

The next circumstance seems to be the manner in which the action is performed. How it ought to be performed we infer from all or from some of the aforementioned considerations.

Next come our conclusions regarding the appropriate time. For a given action done for such a purpose and in such a manner is not always befitting such an agent; it is appropriate only when the act can be directed to or can attain such an end.

Last of all is the circumstance of place. Indeed there are many acts with complete moral goodness in which place plays no part.

18.16 It is clear then how many conditions right reason sets down, for according to the description given above [in 18.8], to be perfectly good, an act must be faultless on all counts. Hence Dionysius declares: "Good requires that everything about the act be right, whereas evil stems from any single defect." "Everything," he explains, includes all the circumstances.

18.17 Objection: Circumstances are relations whereas good is a quality, according to the *Ethics*; virtue is also a quality, according to the *Categories*.

I answer: According to the *Physics*: "All virtue and malice are relative." That acts be good or virtuous, therefore, implies one or several relations. But like "healthy" or "beautiful," "good" or "virtuous" are spoken of, and predicated, as qualities, and this commonly happens with the fourth type of quality.

18.18 [The source of moral badness] In view of the second part of the citation [in 18.16] from Dionysius we ought to look into the source of moral badness in an act.

Badness can be opposed to goodness in an act either privatively or as its contrary. Man is said to be bad in this second sense if he has some vice, for though this implies a privation of a perfection that should be there, a vice is certainly a positive habit. In the other sense, man is said to be bad privately if he lacks the goodness he ought to have, even if he does not have the contrary vice or vicious habit.

18.19 We find this distinction in Boethius where he explains the first characteristic of quality: "They say justice is not contrary to injustice, for they think injustice is a privation and not a contrary state." And he adds in refutation: "Many habits are expressed in privative terms such as 'illiberality' and 'imprudence.' These would never be contrasted with virtues, which are habits, if they themselves were not habits."

18.20 Reason also justifies this distinction. For it can happen that an act is performed under circumstances that are not all they should be [to make the act morally good], yet neither are they so improper that they ought not to be there, for instance, when an action is neither directed to an appropriate end nor to an inappropriate one. In such a case the act is bad only privatively, not contrarily as it would be if it were performed for some unlawful purpose. And from many similar acts, a corresponding habit would arise, namely, one whose "badness" is privative rather than a positive contrary. For example, to give alms, not for a good end such as the love of God or to help one's neighbor, but not for a bad end either such as out of vainglory or to hurt someone, is an act of this sort that is privatively, not contrarily, bad.

It is to such privative "badness" that Dionysius refers when he states that the absence of any one of the required circumstances suffices to render the act bad. But for it to be bad contrarily there must be some positive circumstance present that involves some deformity.

18.21 Briefly, then, just as moral goodness is integral suitability, so moral badness is unsuitability. Privative badness is a lack of suitability, i.e., the absence of what ought to be there, whereas badness as the contrary of goodness is unsuitability as a contrary state, i.e., as some condition that is incompatible with suitability.

18.22 [Corollary] From what has been said this corollary follows: The same fundamental act can have a manifold moral goodness. It is not just that it is correct in all its circumstances (something which invests the act not with many goodnesses but with one integral goodness), but it can also have at the same time all that is needed for two distinct virtues, and thus be directed to several ends according to different dictates of perfect prudence. For example, I go to church to fulfill an obligation in justice, because of obedience or some vow. And I also go out of charity or love of God, to pray or to worship him. And I also go out of fraternal charity to edify my neighbor. In short the more morally good motives there are, the better the act is. This is true whether the goodness in question be moral goodness alone or that additional goodness we call meritorious.

18.23 In like fashion, badness multiplies if one and the same act violates several dictates of reason.

(From *John, God and Creatures: The Quodlibetal Questions.* Trans. Felix Alluntis and Allan B. Wolter. © 1975 by Princeton University Press. Reprinted by permission of Princeton University Press.)

The Indemonstrability of Immortality (from the *Oxford Commentary*)

[*Second Proposition: The intellective soul is immortal*]. The method of dealing with the second proposition, Viz. that the intellective soul is immortal, is the same as that used with the first. The testimony of those philosophers who held this is adduced first.

[*Arguments for immortality*: Arg. I]. Aristotle, in *De anima*, BK. II, says that the "intellect differs from the rest as what is eternal differs from what is perishable". And if someone objects that it is something different and apart only in so far as its operations are concerned, the proposed conclusion still follows, for according to Aristotle in *De anima*, BK. I, if it can be set apart by reason of its operations it can also exist apart.

[Arg. IV]. Also, he says in his work *De generatione animalium*: "It remains for the intellect alone to enter from the outside". Hence, the intellect does not receive existence by way of generation but rather from an extrinsic cause; consequently, it cannot cease to exist by perishing. Neither can any inferior cause corrupt the soul since its existence does not come under the power of any such cause, for it owes its existence directly to a higher cause.

[*Arguments against immortality*: Arg. I]. The Philosopher, however, seems to take the opposite view, for at the end of Metaphysics, BK. VII, he expresses the opinion that the only parts which could be separated from the whole are the elements, i.e. the material parts, for in this sense he understands elements here. In addition to these elements it is necessary to assume the existence of some form in the whole which is the totality of that which exists. This form could not exist in separation from the material part once the whole no longer exists. Hence, if he grants that the intellective soul is the form of man, as is evident from the proof of the preceding proposition, he does not admit that it exists in separation from matter, once the whole no longer exists.

[Arg. II]. Likewise, it seems to be one of his principles that what begins to exist ceases to exist. Hence, in his work *De caelo et mundo*, against Plato, he seems to consider it impossible that anything could have come into existence and still be eternal and imperishable. And in the Physics he says: "Whatever has a beginning has an end".

[*Scotus's Opinion*]. It can be stated that although there are probable reasons for this second proposition, these are not demonstrative, nor for that matter are they even necessary reasons.

[*Reply to the arguments for immortality*]. The testimonies of the philosophers—the first way used to prove the proposition—can be solved in two ways. First of all, it is doubtful what the Philosopher really held on this point, for he speaks differently in different places and has different principles, from some of which one thing seems to follow whereas from others the very opposite can be inferred. Wherefore, it is probable that he was always doubtful about this conclusion and at one time seems to be drawn to one side and at other times to the other depending on whether the subject matter he was treating at the moment was more in accord with the one or with the other.

Another answer, and one more in accord with facts, is that not all the statements by the philosophers were established by proofs both necessary and evident to natural reason. Frequently, what they gave was nothing more than rather persuasive probable arguments or what was commonly held by earlier philosophers. For this reason, the Philosopher in *De caelo et mundo*, BK. II, in the chapter on the two difficult questions, says: "We must now attempt to state the probable solution, for we regard the zeal of one whose thirst after philosophy leads him to accept even slight indications where it is very difficult to see one's way, as a proof rather of modesty than of over-confidence". Hence, in those matters where they could find nothing better without contradicting the principles of philosophy, "slight indications" frequently had to suffice for the philosophers. As he says in the same chapter: "Accounts of other stars are given by the Egyptians and Babylonians ... from whom many of our beliefs about particular stars are derived". Therefore, the philosophers agreed to things sometimes because of probable persuasive reasons, at other times because they had asserted as principles, propositions which were not necessary truths. And this reply would suffice for all the testimonies cited above; even if they clearly asserted the proposed conclusion, they still do not establish it. Nevertheless, these arguments can be answered in order as follows.

[*To I*]. To the first: Aristotle understands this separation to mean nothing more than that the intellect does not use the body in performing its operation, and for this reason it is incorruptible as to function. This is to be understood in the sense that it is unlike an organic power which perishes precisely because the organ decays. This type of decay pertains exclusively to an organic faculty. For according to the Philosopher in *De anima*, BK. I, if an old man were given the eye of a young man, he would indeed see as well as the youth. Hence, the faculty of vision grows weak or decays only from the standpoint of its organ and not in so far as its operation directly is concerned. From the fact that the intellect, however, is incapable of decay in the sense that it has no organ by which it could perish, it does not follow that the intellect is imperishable as to function in an unqualified sense, for then it would indeed follow that it is also imperishable in being as the argument maintains. What does follow is this. So far as its ability to operate alone is concerned, the intellect is incapable of dissolution in the same sense that an organic power is corruptible. Absolutely speaking, however, the intellect is assumed to be perishable according to the Philosopher's statement in *De anima*, BK. III, that the intellect perishes in us once the interior sense perishes. And this is just what one would have to maintain if he assumed the soul to be a principle which has an operation proper to the composite as a whole. The composite, however, is perishable. Consequently, its operative principle is also perishable. That the soul is the operative principle of the whole composite and that its operation is also that of the whole is just what Aristotle seems to say in *De anima*, BK. I.

[To IV]. As for the other, it is very doubtful what Aristotle held in regard to the origin of the intellective soul. For if he assumed that God does not immediately produce anything new, but merely moves the heaven with an eternal movement and this only as a remote agent, then by what separate agent did Aristotle assume the soul was produced from without? If you say it was by one of the Intelligences, then we encounter a double difficulty; one, because an Intelligence cannot create a substance (as I prove in BK. IV, dist. i); the other, because such a being cannot immediately produce anything new any more than God could, for according to the Philosopher's principles regarding the immutability of the agent it follows that the action of such a being is eternal. Neither do we see any way in which Aristotle could claim that the intellective soul is the effect of some natural agent without violating his principles, because he seems to assume the soul to be imperishable in *Metaphysics*, BK. XII. And no form that is the effect of a natural agent is imperishable in an unqualified sense.

But it can be said that he assumed the soul received existence immediately from God and that this existence was something new. For it would follow readily enough from his principles that it would have received existence, since Aristotle assumed no eternal bodiless pre-existence; neither did he hold that the soul existed previously in some other body; nor does it seem possible according to reason that a soul which presupposes no material principle could have received its existence from anyone other than God.

To the contrary: If this explanation were true, Aristotle would have admitted creation. —I reply that this does not follow, for he did not assume a production of the intellective soul distinct from the production of the composite, just as he did not assume one production for fire and another for the fire form. What he posited was the animation of the organic body and this incidentally involved the production of its soul. Now we admit two types of production, one from the soul's non-existence to existence and this we call creation, the other is the passage of the body from an inanimate to an animate state and this is the production of a living body by a change in the proper sense of the word. If anyone, therefore, were to assume merely the second type of production he would not thereby postulate a creation. And this was the case with Aristotle.

But even if you avoid asserting a creation according to Aristotle, how is it possible to save the idea that something new is produced by an agent that is immutable? —I reply that the only way is to explain what is new in terms of something in the patient or recipient of the action. According to Aristotle, if a new effect depended solely upon the active cause, some variation in the efficient cause itself would be required. But a new effect that depends upon both the recipient and the agent can be accounted for in terms of something new in the recipient alone and not in the agent. And thus we could say that in the present instance God by a natural necessity changed an organic body into a living substance just as soon as the body was capable of receiving life. And natural causes will determine just when the latter becomes ready to receive it, and hence at this moment God produces this new change so that it comes to life.

But why must this new entity be attributed to God as to its [immediate] efficient cause? —I reply that the reason is this. Just as God, the first agent, is continually operating by some action on a patient which remains constantly in the same condition according to Aristotle, so likewise if something is capable of receiving some new form which cannot be caused by any secondary cause, God must be its immediate cause; and yet for all that something new comes into existence. For it is necessary to postulate some active potency that corresponds to every passive potency. Now if there is no such created cause corresponding to the new passive potency, then its immediate corresponding cause will be divine.

(From the *Oxford Commentary*. Trans. of *Opus oxoniense* by Allan B. Wolter. London: Thomas Nelson and Sons Ltd., 1962. Reprinted by permission of Thomas Nelson.)

Review Questions

1. What does Scotus mean by the statement that "essence is existence"?
2. Discuss Scotus' emphasis on individuality.

3. How, in Scotus' view, can a predicate apply to God and creatures in common without God and creatures being the same?
4. Discuss Scotus' proof for the existence of God based on possibles.
5. How does Scotus' view on the making of moral judgments compare with that of St. Thomas?
6. Why does Scotus hold that immortality is not provable by reason?

9

Nicholas of Cusa
(1401–1464)

Introduction

We cannot expect a period of intense activity, such as the thirteenth century was in theology and philosophy, to continue unabated. As enthusiasm and excitement wane, so do originality and creativity, and thus the way is paved for authority to become the sole basis for one's opinions. We have seen, for example, the influential role that the philosophy of Aristotle played in the thirteenth century and how some theologians, experiencing difficulty with his work, effectively censured it. Yet Aristotle held on, and so highly regarded did his authority later become in particular quarters that studies in science, cosmology, logic, poetics, and metaphysics became in effect studies in Aristotle, much to the chagrin of experimentalists like Galileo, who chided the "Aristotelians" for looking into the books of Aristotle more than they looked into the book of nature. The creative use of Aristotle, as witnessed in St. Thomas, was gone.

Though the fourteenth century was intellectually rich in many other ways — as being, for example, the first century of the glorious Italian Renaissance — it was the end of the philosophy–theology adventure of the Middle Ages. The names of John Duns Scotus and William of Ockham loom large in the early decades of the century, but for the most part there was so much party politics involved in the ongoing opposition between the Franciscans and the Dominicans that intellectual energy seemed to be devoted more to the development of loyalty than to the enrichment of theology.

Before considering the modern age, it would be rewarding to catch the spirit of a fifteenth-century figure who was neither Franciscan nor Dominican, but a "secular" priest, Nicholas of Cusa. He was not an academic but an active ecclesiastic, a bishop, a cardinal of the Church, and a kind of mystic on horseback.

Nicholas was born in 1401 in the small German village of Cusa on the Moselle River and left home at a very early age, destined to make his mark as an ecclesiastic. Through a benefactor he was educated with the Brothers of the Common Life at Deventer in the Lowlands, where high value was placed on piety and humility, as can be seen in the *Imitation of Christ*, whose author was also nurtured at Deventer. He studied law at Padua and theology at Cologne, and from that point on received a succession of ecclesiastical appointments. The Church in the fifteenth century was experiencing turbulent times, and in the major crises Cusa played a role in trying to establish harmony among the conflicting parties. In dispute as to the highest authority in the Church, Council or Pope, Cusa was on the side of conciliar authority at the Council of Basel, only to find himself later on the papal side. To heal the long-standing rift between the Latin and Greek churches, Cusa labored to develop a reunion formula agreeable to both; he traveled many miles and many months to carry out the work of reform in the Church, for which there was pressing need. How he could be so active and yet find time to write is a secret that few people have discovered. He died in 1464.

Like other great thinkers of the Middle Ages, Cusa was mainly concerned with the ventilation of theology with new insights, particularly from philosophy, as stated in his best-known work, *On Learned Ignorance*. From the start, Cusa's philosophy was God centered: How can we talk about God? What is the relationship between God and man? Is there a final completion of man in God? These are the kinds of questions for which Cusa had to rethink metaphysics and epistemology.

It is a problem to know how to talk of God when we have nothing to which to compare Him. The power of reason can take us just so far, because it deals with categories, oppositions, and contradictions, all of which have meaning only in the limited world. Discursive reasoning does not give up its prerogatives easily, but until it recognizes that it cannot move us beyond the finite, and admits that it is ignorant the moment it strikes a wall it cannot scale, it will never give us an understanding of God. However, the moment it does admit its ignorance, it has already become enlightened, hence the term *learned ignorance* that Cusa applies to this state of mind.

At this point, Cusa invokes a special illumination from on high, a light that removes stumbling blocks from his path toward an understanding of the divine: all opposites, all contradictions, are dissolved in Him who is the *coincidence of opposites*. The notion of opposites as reconciled in the divine is not a particularly new doctrine, but Cusa uses it in an original way: as a foundation for thinking about the infinity of God and how it relates to the created world. The basic meaning of opposition is that one thing is not another because of some difference between them; therefore, they are set, or posited, against one other (op-posit). However, opposition, or even contradiction, holds only when speaking of finite beings, which is the domain of discursive reasoning and the logic proper to it. When speaking of God, the infinite, opposition has no meaning because there is no other to compare Him to; all the perfections found in opposite things in the finite realm — the very perfections that makes them different — are found in God.

In this sense, God is at once the *maximum* and the *minimum*. The maximum is the "most" of anything: the highest perfection, the greatest degree of power; the minimum is the "least" of anything: the barest perfection, the lowest degree of power. So Cusa, in probing for a new kind of logic to deal with the infinite, concludes that in God the maximum and the minimum are identified, as expressed in their definitions, which turn out to be identical in each case: "that which cannot be less than it is." In any event, Cusa's use of the maximum and minimum stresses the metaphysical importance he attaches to the coincidence of opposites as a testimony to the incomprehensible transcendence of God and to the inclusion therein of finite things: "maximum and minimum ... have here an absolutely transcendent value embracing all things in their absolute simplicity."

We have seen before, as in Pythagoras, and shall see again, as in Descartes, the supple use of mathematics to illuminate metaphysical problems. Nicholas of Cusa was not proficient in mathematics, but he was in tune with its rhythm and, in a series of ingenious examples, shows how it is helpful in understanding God as the coincidence of opposites. Let us take one example to demonstrate his purpose. Every line you can draw is a finite line, and every circle is a finite circle. But if the line is tangent to the circle at A, the angle at any chosen point between the line and the circle will get smaller and smaller as the circle gets larger and larger; as it approaches infinity, the circle will touch the line and coincide with it. This coincidence will, of course, never take place as long as you are dealing with the finite, but according to Cusa, it helps us to understand how in the infinite all opposition dissolves.

Cusa, like every other philosopher immersed in reflections on God, is fully aware that ultimately inquiry into God is inquiry into the world, and that what he has been saying of God as the maximum, as the coincidence of opposites, has to be looked at a second time from the side of creatures. Of course, Cusa holds that God is the creator and has an independent existence; all other things are creatures and have an existence dependent on Him. Unity in reality, based upon this God–creature relationship, calls for a oneness between Creator and created that does not obliterate their separateness. In putting this relationship into focus, Cusa amalgamated the Neoplatonic notion of the world as an outpouring of God's substance, the traditional Christian notion of the world's creation by a distinct act of the Creator's will, and his own notion of God as universal. All things preexist as ideas in God, and their existence as things "outside" God add nothing to their nature. The universe, all things taken together, is then a contracted form of the maximum and is to be looked upon as the *concrete universal* or the *relatively infinite*: "the universe is only a restricted form of the maximum. It is restricted or concrete, because it holds all its being from the Absolute; and because it is a maximum, it reproduces the Absolute Maximum in the greatest possible way. ... It is infinitely contracted to the relatively infinite."

An interesting corollary to the notion of the world as infinite is that the earth is not, for Cusa, the center of the universe. Note that this conclusion, though it anticipates by a century the revolutionary doctrine of Copernicus, was not based on empirical evidence but on philosophical reasons. If the world is even relatively infinite, then in no way can it have a center: "Just as the earth is not the centre of the world, so the circumference of the world is not the sphere of the fixed stars, despite the fact that by comparison the earth seems nearer the centre and heaven nearer the circumference." Therein lies the difference, and it is a vast one, between Copernicus and Cusa: for Copernicus the sun replaces the earth as the center of the universe; for Cusa there is no center.

To develop another phase of his breathtaking sweep of unity, Cusa enlarges on a phrase from Anaxagoras: "everything is in everything." God is in all things, all things are in God. God is in all things because the universe is a contracted maximum, "so it follows that all is in all, and each in each ... each creature receives all, so that in any creature all creatures are found in a relative way." Cusa does not mean that one thing is "actually" contained in another, but rather "virtually." Having recourse to his line-circle example as the basis of metaphor, Cusa means that, just as the line virtually contains the circle, so does any individual thing of the universe contain the universe within itself: virtually, though not actually. In a remarkable foreshadowing of Spinoza and Leibniz, Cusa writes: "all things are what they are, because they could not be otherwise nor better."

Cusa subscribes to the theme of man as the image of God, a constant theme, as we have seen, in the Middle Ages, but he refracts it through the prism of his own terminology. Human nature contains within itself such a combination of perfections that it is midway between superior and inferior, and "embracing within itself all things, has very reasonably been dubbed by the ancients the microcosm or world in miniature." But man's realization of his true image comes only after the satisfaction of what is highest in him, namely, his intellect. Once again, it is not important to know how many degrees of knowledge there are in Cusa's view, which varies, but only that knowledge rises from sensory knowledge through discursive reasoning to the intellect — a graduation discussed earlier. At its highest point the intellect's grasp — called *intuition, contemplation, vision* — is of the unity of all things in God without employing the use of reason, logic, or words; it is the mystical union of oneself with God, the mystical return of the finite to the infinite. The cycle of return is made actual by the interposing of Christ in our lives, and since He was raised to the maximum as the God-man, all humanity is raised to the maximum in Him: "he is the first beginning of their setting forth and the last end of their return."

Cusa was a member of no school of theologians or philosophers, nor did he generate a following of any kind. He was a solitary thinker, standing head and shoulders above his contemporaries, and except for several isolated instances, as in the accolade given him by Giordano Bruno, he remained to be discovered by later generations. His rediscovery encouraged the philosopher Karl Jaspers to write, "Living in time, he is timeless in spirit, one of those who, clad in the raiment of their day and nation, meet as equals over the millennia to discuss the destiny of man."

Readings

The Maximum and the Minimum Are the Same (from *Of Learned Ignorance,* Book I)

There can be nothing greater in existence than the simple, absolute maximum; and since it is greater than our powers of comprehension—for it is infinite truth—our knowledge of it can never mean that we comprehend it. It is above all that we can conceive, for its nature excludes degrees of 'more' and 'less'. All the things, in fact, that we apprehend by our senses, reason or intellect are so different from one another that there is no precise equality between them. The maximum equality, therefore, in which there is no diversity or difference from any other, is completely beyond our understanding; and for that reason the absolute maximum is in act most perfect, since it is in act all that it can be. Being all that it can be, it is, for one and the same reason, as great as it can be and as small as it can be. By definition the minimum is that which cannot be less than it is; and since that is also true of the maximum, it is evident that the minimum is identified with the maximum.

This becomes clearer when you restrict your considerations to the maximum and the minimum of quantity. The maximum quantity is infinitely great, whilst the minimum is infinitely small. Now, if mentally you lay aside the notions of greatness and smallness, you are left with the maximum and the minimum without quantity, and it becomes clear that the maximum and the minimum are one and the same; in fact, the minimum is as much a superlative as the maximum. The maximum and the minimum, then, are equally predicable of absolute quantity, since in it they are identified.

Distinctions, therefore, are only found to exist among things which are susceptible of 'more' and 'less'; and they exist among these in different ways; in no way do they exist in the absolute maximum, for it is above any form of affirmation and negation. Existence and non-existence can be equally predicated of all that which is conceived to exist; and non-existence cannot to any greater degree than existence be affirmed of all that is conceived not to exist. But the absolute maximum, in consequence, is all things and, whilst being all, it is none of them; in other words, it is at once the maximum and minimum of being. There is, in fact, no difference between these two affirmations: 'God, who is the absolute maximum itself, is light'; and 'God is light at its highest, therefore He is light at its lowest'. It could not be otherwise; for the absolute maximum would not be the realization of all possible perfection, if it were not infinite and if it were not the end to which all things are ordained, whilst it stands subordinate to none. With God's help, we shall explain this in the pages that follow.

This is far and away beyond our understanding, which is fundamentally unable by any rational process to reconcile contradictories. We proceed to truth through the things made known to us by nature; and, as this process falls very far short of the infinite power of the maximum, we are unable to link together by means of it contradictories which are infinitely distant from one another. We know that the absolute maximum is infinite, that it is all things since it is one with the minimum; but this knowledge is away and above any understanding we could reach by discursive reasoning. In this book the terms maximum and minimum are not restricted to quantity of mass or of force; they have here an absolutely transcendent value embracing all things in their absolute simplicity.

How in the Infinite, Opposites Are One (from *Of Learned Ignorance,* Book I)

If there were an infinite line, I maintain that it would be at once a straight line, a triangle, a circle, a sphere; similarly, if there were an infinite sphere, it would at once be a circle, a triangle and a line; and it would be likewise with the infinite triangle and infinite circle.

In the first place, it is evident that the infinite line would be a straight line. The diameter of a circle is a straight line; the circumference is a curved line and longer than the diameter. Now, if the curve of the circumference becomes less curved as the circle expands, the circumference of the absolutely greatest possible circle will be the smallest possible curve; it will be, therefore, absolutely straight. The maximum and the minimum are, therefore, so identified that we most clearly perceive that in the infinite there is the absolute maximum of straightness with the absolute minimum of curve. A study of the figure here given will dispel all possible doubt on this point. We see that the arc C–D of the larger circle is less curved than the arc E–F of the smaller circle, and that E-F is itself less curved than the arc G–H of a still smaller circle; the straight line A–B will, therefore, be the arc of the greatest possible circle.

In this our first point is proved, for we have shown that the simply infinite line is, of necessity, perfectly straight, and that in such a line straightness and curve are not mutually exclusive but are one and the same thing.

Everything Is in Everything (from *Of Learned Ignorance*, Book II)

From a keen study of what has already been said we come to understand easily enough, perhaps even more fully than Anaxagoras himself, the depth of the truth he expressed in the words 'everything is everything'. For from the First Book we learned that God is in all things in such a way that all things are in him; in the previous chapter we discovered that God is in all things by the medium, as it were, of the universe; so it follows that all is in all, and each in each. As if by nature's order it was that the most perfect—the universe—came into being before all things, so that anything might be in anything. In fact, in every creature the universe is the creature; consequently each creature receives all, so that in any creature all creatures are found in a relative way. Since all creatures are finite, no creature could be all things in act; but all things are contracted in order to form each creature. If, then, all things are in all, it is clear that all is prior to the individual; and all here does not signify plurality, for prior to the individual there is no plurality. For that reason all without plurality has preceded the individual in the order of nature with the consequence that in any actual individual there is not more than one: all without plurality is that one.

Only by way of contraction is the universe in things; in fact it is restricted by each actually existing thing to be actually what each thing is. Everything actually existing is in God, for He is the act of all. Act means perfection and the realization of what was possible. Since the universe restricted is in each actually existing individual, then evidently God, Who is in the universe, is in every individual and every individual actually existing is, like the universe, immediately in God. To say that 'everything is in everything' is the same as saying that God, by the intermediary of the universe, is in all things and that the universe, by the intermediary of all things, is in God. How God is without any diversity in all, since everything is everything, and how all is in God, because all is in all, are truths of a very high order which are clearly understood by keen minds. The universe is in each individual in such a way that each individual is in it, with the result that in each individual the universe is by contraction what the particular individual is; and every individual in the universe is the universe, though the universe is in each individual in a different way and each thing is in the universe in a different way.

Here is an example: The infinite line is clearly a line, a triangle, a circle and a sphere; but a finite line receives its existence from the infinite line, and the infinite line is all that the finite line is. All, therefore, that is identified with the infinite line—line, triangle and the others— is also found identified with the finite line. Every figure in the finite line is the line itself; but that does not mean that the triangle or circle or sphere is actually present in it. That everything is in everything does not imply actual presence, for the actual unity of the thing would be destroyed by such a plurality; but the triangle in the line is the line, the circle in the line is the line, and so on. To note that a line can only actually exist in a body—a point to be proved elsewhere—helps you to see this more clearly. No one doubts that in a body with length, breadth and depth all the figures are virtually contained. So in an actual line all the figures are actually the line itself, and in a triangle all are the triangle and so on. In a stone all is stone, in the vegetative soul all is soul, in life all is life, in a sense all is that sense, in sight all is sight, in hearing all is hearing, in the imagination all is imagination, in reason all is reason, in the understanding all is understanding, in God all is God. From that you see how the unity of things or the universe exists in plurality and conversely how plurality exists in unity.

You will also see on closer study how each individual in actual existence is at peace, for all in the individual is the individual and the individual in God is God; and there appears the wonderful unity of things, the admirable equality and the most remarkable connection, by which all is in all. In this we see the one source of the connection and diversity of things. An individual could not be actually all things, for it would be God, and therefore all things would be actualized in it in the way in which they can exist as individual natures. Nor can any two things be absolutely equal, as we proved above when we saw that all things were made in varying degrees of being—like the being which could not possess all at once the perfection of incorruptibility and was made to exist without corruption in temporal succession. Consequently, all things are what they are, because they could not be otherwise nor better.

(From *Of Learned Ignorance*. Trans. G. Heron. London: Routledge & Kegan Paul PLC., 1954. Reprinted by permission of Routledge & Kegan Paul.)

Review Questions

1. Discuss the notion of *learned ignorance* in Cusa's philosophy.
2. For Cusa, in what sense are opposites reconciled, or made one, in God?
3. Cusa holds that, without losing their creaturehood, created things are still one with God. Explain.

PART III

The Modern Period

The Spirit of Modern Philosophy: Philosophy and the Rise of Science

The seventeenth century marked a turning point in the intellectual history of Europe in which the turmoils and agonies of previous times began to achieve a recognizable direction and a clear identity; it deserves to be called the beginning of a new age. It was one of those rare centuries that bristled with fresh ideas, new paths, and rich possibilities, and with a spirit uplifted by the opening up of unexpected horizons in human self-understanding. All areas of intellectual activity were ventilated by its creative breath: literature, art, theology, political science; philosophy and science alone boasted of such geniuses as Galileo, Descartes, Spinoza, Leibniz, Pascal, Bacon, Locke, Harvey, Huyghens, Kepler, and Newton. Indeed, Alfred North Whitehead proclaimed the seventeenth-century formulation of the laws of gravity and the three laws of motion the "greatest single intellectual success which mankind has achieved."

The period covering the two and a half centuries or so prior to the seventeenth saw the Middle Ages come to an end. It was a theocentric age for most of Europe, an age of common faith, religious practice, Church, and a society shaped by them that lasted for hundreds of years. But a unified Christianity was not destined to last, and long before the Reformation took place, there were many forces at work wearing unity away. For a whole range of reasons, the Church was looked upon as having abandoned the simplicity of its founder, of having lost the sense of the sacred in its mission and its ministers, and of having, in the name of God, abused its power in public and private life. The more internal reform was delayed, the more dissatisfaction grew and the more the forces at work coalesced. Among them was the ongoing struggle between Church and state, each trying to define and enlarge its sphere of jurisdiction against the other. The struggle was epitomized in the quarrel between Pope Boniface VIII and King Philip IV (the Fair) of France, for when the Pope laid claim to supremacy in France as part of his universal dominion, the king took violent measures against him and finally had him clapped in jail.

Similarly, the unity between theology and philosophy that had prevailed in the high Middle Ages was beginning to dissolve. The general rubric of "faith seeking understanding," indicative of the willingness of theology to use other areas of knowledge in its service, had been mainly true of philosophy; we have already seen, for example, the role played by the two great Greek traditions, Platonic and Aristotelian, in transferring insights from philosophy to theology. But this relationship, which had proven so fruitful, was now becoming suspect, and theology and philosophy were under pressure to assert their independence. This is clearly seen in the powerful figure of William of Ockham, a Franciscan monk who studied and taught at Oxford in the early fourteenth century; his teaching that the transcendence of God places Him so much beyond rational grasp as to make Him unknowable except by faith began to weaken metaphysics as the foundation of philosophy, a view destined to hold for centuries. Ockham's political views were just as divisive and aligned him with the swelling antipapal sentiment; he was compelled to flee to the protection of Emperor Ludwig IV of Bavaria, to whom, as legend has it, he said, "O Emperor, defend me with your sword, and I will defend you with my pen."

The forces that tended to erode the medieval world continued into the Renaissance that followed — broadly speaking, from the late fourteenth century to the middle of the sixteenth. Church and state were still at odds with each other, the state still trying to organize itself into a center of life for its citizens and the Church still trying to maintain its internal unity against powerful centrifugal forces. The situation of each cannot better be personified than in two notable figures, Niccolo Machiavelli (1469–1527) and Martin Luther (1483–1546). Machiavelli, after many years as a civil servant in Florence, came to the conclusion that, no Christian order being possible, the hope for an orderly existence rests with the state, and that the order and unity of the state can be defended against enemies within and without only by a strong monarch who displays absolute rule. His "prince" had to be both a lion and a fox, endowed with cunning and power, dedicated to the belief that when the safety of the country is at stake, "no consideration of what is just or unjust, merciful or cruel, praiseworthy or shameful, must intervene." Though not as influential in Italy as in other parts of Europe, Machiavelli's work is the first effort of its kind in modern political theory.

The collective energy of all the reformers before him, crying for renovation of the Church, finally exploded in Luther, an Augustinian monk, with such power that it sent shock waves throughout Europe that are still felt today. As a brilliant professor and theologian—a new St. Paul, they called him — he was an Ockhamist regarding God's total Otherness and His absolute will, and emphasized the powerlessness of human reason compared to faith. In his intensely religious soul there were so many pressures growing from his sense of creatureliness and unworthiness that he despaired of his own salvation unless he rejected the pretensions of reason, so-called good works, ecclesiastical authority, the fearfulness of sin, and his own will; he had only to believe firmly in the Lord Jesus. Despite his enigmatic traits, he was the right person at the right time to release the pent-up frustration of the people with Church and authority, thus bringing to a definitive end the unity of medieval religion and inaugurating a new age of religion in Europe.

There were so many cross-currents during the age of Machiavelli and Luther that the intellectual history of the time is not a straight line; it resembles less the neat track of an arrow in flight than the surface of a boiling cauldron whose ingredients keep pushing to the top. It was the time when learned books were being written in the vernacular; Machiavelli wrote in Italian, Luther in German. The advent of movable type and the printing press made books far more available than manuscripts ever were. Art and architecture peaked in artists like da Vinci, Raphael, Titian, and Michelangelo. It was an age in which the Counter-Reformation was initiated by Pope Paul III shortly before Luther died. And it was an age, with the Copernican revolutionary doctrine of a heliocentric universe, in which modern science began in earnest.

In regard to our immediate concern, the dominant position of theology as "queen of the sciences" slowly receded, accompanied by the separation of philosophy from theology; this allowed a greater effort to explain things to the satisfaction of reason without first invoking divine causality for the successful workings of nature. In terms of finding new grounds for certitude, it meant that the individual was free to follow his own intellectual direction. In some cases, this resulted in *classical humanism*, a renewed interest in the pre-Christian classics, both Greek and Latin. In other cases, it resulted in the hope of discovering the meaning of man on his own terms, a kind of philosophical humanism: now that reason had been separated from revelation, the proper study of mankind was man. Although there was, however short-lived, a revival in Platonic studies, particularly in the Florentine Academy of Marsilio Ficino, who tried to show the compatibility of Platonic ideals with Christianity, the fortunes of philosophy during the Renaissance were the fortunes of Aristotelianism tied, as it was, to the great theological systems of the late thirteenth and early fourteenth centuries. Aristotelianism was beginning to fall out of favor as its philosophy or its science came to be viewed as confining, dogmatic, or simply wrong.

This turn of events could only terminate, in some instances, in a feeling of despair of finding any real certitude, especially the kind required for the conduct of life. Such was the attitude of the eminent essayist Michel de Montaigne (1533–92), who found any system building offensive and, to that extent, was antischolastic if not antirational. If his motto was "I don't know," reminiscent of the scepticism of later Greek philosophy, it was because philosophy had no sure response to the important questions of life. Is the soul immortal? This is a not unimportant question for one who is concerned about the values of life. Some philosophers, Montaigne said, persuasively demonstrate that the soul is immortal; others that it is not, or that we have none to worry about. Philosophy thus cancels itself out and offers no solutions for human perplexities. Better turn to nature, or revelation, or history, or social conventions, not because there is absolute truth in them but because as "truths of fact" they offer the best chance for equanimity.

Though Francis Bacon (1561–1626) agreed with the antischolastic stand of Montaigne, he did not agree with his view that the human mind is incapable of certitude. In this Bacon represents the new spirit straining for recognition, the spirit of science, the spirit of experiment, the spirit of induction, which would provide, in his view, the opportunity to achieve certitude that the human mind had never enjoyed before. Though not a scientist himself, but a civil servant for years, Bacon had a high regard for the experimental method as the way to know the world, and believed that knowing the world is the precondition for improving it. His project for the Great Instauration, or Renewal, was human control of the universe for the betterment of man. Since "not much can be known in nature by the way which is now in use," the way has to be cleared up first. The obstacles in the way, he wrote in *Novum Organum*, are the false opinions and errors, called *idols*, accumulated from the past. Of the four groups of idols — of the tribe, the cave, the marketplace, and the theater — it is the last that is devoted to philosophy. Here Bacon sweepingly rejects all past philosophies because they systematically departed from the real world to create unreal worlds of their own: "These I call Idols of the Theater; because in my judgment all the received systems are but so many stage-plays, representing worlds of their own creation after an unreal and scenic fashion." Even the so-called empirical school of philosophy is to be rejected because of the "narrowness" of its experiments and its hurry to draw conclusions far more sweeping than those warranted by its findings. Bacon sees the fruitfulness of the scientific method in carefully monitored experimentation and in directing its conclusions to the advancement of man.

The man who best exemplifies, after Bacon's paradigm, the passing of the old world view and the advent of the new is Galileo Galilei (1564–1642), the scientist who mocked the Aristotelians while he wrested secrets from nature using the new method of experimentation and reflection. In him the medieval world view, mainly because of its religious entwinements, battled with the new scientific spirit in one of the most dramatic moments in intellectual history. Though a professor at the University of Padua, Galileo pitied the academics who had eyes only for books and not for the real world, and were therefore unfit for the investigation of nature. For centuries the Aristotelian world picture had put the earth at the center of the universe, with the planets and the sun revolving around it. The earth, and not the sun, was the center for two reasons: the sun could be "observed" turning about the earth, and the earth was where man dwelled. For the Christian believer, there was an additional reason for holding the same view: Sacred Scripture gave countless examples of the "fact" that the sun moves and not the earth, and Sacred Scripture, as God's word, cannot be wrong. Some time before Galileo, the Polish monk-astronomer Copernicus began to theorize that something was amiss with the received system because it did not square with his observations and mathematical calculations. However, the mere switch of the sun's position with that of the earth would generally set the universe aright. This view came to be supported by other astronomers, like Johannes Kepler, but it was Galileo who was able, with the aid of the newly invented telescope, to strengthen the conviction that Copernicus was right.

Because of this tension between religion and science, Church authorities, fearful of yet another shock to ecclesiastical stability and the truth of faith, and concerned about the ordinary person's belief, put Copernicus' book *On Revolutions* on the Index of Prohibited Books in 1616, and in 1633 tried and condemned Galileo. Kneeling before the eminent cardinals and inquisitors, the seventy-year-old Galileo had to recant his "errors" that the sun is the center of the world and does not move, and that the earth is not the center of the world and that it moves. A sympathetic story has it that as the old man got up, he shook his head and said, "Still, it moves!" The dismay this event caused in the intellectual world cannot be calculated, but as an indication, Descartes pulled back his book *Traité du monde* because it accepted the Copernican view; it was published only after he died.

It is clear, then, that the new picture of the planetary system was more than just another event in the history of astronomy; it was, in actuality, a *revolution*. It was a revolution in our understanding of nature, for a cosmology two thousand years old was not to be overturned lightly. It was a revolution in the role of authority, for now the authority of neither Aristotle nor the Bible could be offered in evidence. It was, overall, a revolution in man's understanding of himself, for man could not achieve a radically new view of nature, of authority, and of the Bible without envisioning a whole new tissue of relationships in which he identified himself.

Such was the intellectual atmosphere at the beginning of the new age. In the ensuing chapters, the seventeenth-century philosophers Descartes, Spinoza, Leibniz on the continent, and Locke and Hobbes in England will be presented as the immediate heirs of this experience, and the problems they focus on derive directly from it. Later, Berkeley, Hume, and Kant still deal with questions originating in the early seventeenth century but give special attention to the question of human knowledge. Finally, Hegel and Mill represent the last phase of modern philosophy before an entirely new direction occurs leading to the contemporary period.

CHAPTER 10

René Descartes (1596–1650)

Introduction

Skepticism of the kind personified by Montaigne was completely unacceptable to Descartes because it was a skepticism of the intellect. Considering it intolerable for the highest human faculty to be unsure of itself, his ardent desire was to discover a path to certitude, certitude no one could question, in short, an "unshakable certitude," a *quid inconcussum*. His response had to emerge from the new scientific spirit, and it fell to him to employ the method of mathematics as the key to certitude and the weapon against skepticism.

René Descartes was born in 1596 near Tours in France and died in 1650. He was educated at the Jesuit College of La Flèche, which had long enjoyed a reputation for excellence in mathematics. For several years he saw military service in Germany and other places in central Europe; he lived in Paris for a few years, but requiring a quieter life, he went in 1628 to Holland, where he expected to find more leisure and a freer intellectual atmosphere. In 1649 he went to Sweden at the invitation of Queen Christina, who wanted to be tutored in the new philosophy by the great man himself. He was there for only a few months during the winter, which proved so uncongenial to his health that he succumbed to tuberculosis early in 1650. His major works in philosophy include *Discourse on Method* (1637), *Meditations on First Philosophy* (1641), *Principles of Philosophy* (1644), and *The Passions of the Soul* (1649); published posthumously were *Rules for the Direction of the Mind* and *Traité du monde*, which, as previously noted, was written fairly early but withheld when Galileo was condemned.

The education of Descartes in mathematics was no accident, for interest in mathematics was the mark of the times. It dominated the seventeenth century to such an extent that any intellectual, whatever his concerns, was enormously interested in mathematics as well. As we saw in discussing Pythagoras, mathematics has a fascination all its own. It is the language of the sciences and, in many cases, controls their progress; it is a powerfully unifying force; and, above all, it is *certain*, for one step does not follow another without being inevitable. Small wonder that, for Descartes and for many like him, mathematics was the paradigm for all knowledge.

As he pondered the question of certitude, the young Descartes saw that if mathematics is certain, all other areas of knowledge can be seen as certain too if they can be shown to be mathematical in some way; to show them to be mathematical is the primary objective of his method. In the second part of the *Discourse on Method*, Descartes recounts an incident from his early years. While he was in Germany on military service and musing during a winter night in a "stove-heated room" on the problem of the unity of the sciences, it suddenly occurred to him that harmony among disparate things is always the achievement of one agent: diverse parts of the universe harmonized by one divine law; the grace of a building wrought by one workman; the beauty of a city laid out by one master designer. In a variation on the last example, a master designer, instead of razing all the old buildings, razes only some; the others he saves by putting them in "brackets," later to reincorporate them into the new plan if they are seen to fit. Such, at any rate, was Descartes' hope, and the attempt to mathematicize all knowledge is appropriately called *universal mathematics*.

Mathematics is deductive; that is, from a prior truth, other truths are drawn out or deduced; what is enfolded is unfolded; what is implicit is made explicit. But the process must have a beginning, which is variously called *quantity* or *extension*, the characteristic that allows things to be thought of as spatial. The concept of quantity does not require one to know what a thing is composed of as long as it has dimensionality. And so begins the interplay of plane figures, lines, solids, and numbers, which leads to the beguiling array of relationships known as mathematics.

Descartes' plan, despite its inherent difficulties, had the appearance of simplicity and the spark to make it attractive to those who longed to replace the old scholasticism. If quantity is the initial truth of mathematics, and from it all other mathematical truths are deduced, all that has to be done is to discover what is parallel to quantity in other sciences and from it to deduce the body of truths proper to those sciences. The deductive method, for Descartes, is valid not only for mathematics but also for medicine, ethics, philosophy, and all other areas of knowledge.

To proceed in an orderly fashion, Descartes devised four rules to be followed as part of his *method*: (1) to accept nothing as true that is not known to be true, and to use in making a judgment only what is presented to the mind so clearly and distinctly that it cannot be doubted; (2) to divide each problem into its essential parts; (3) to begin with those things that are easiest to know and proceed to the more complex; (4) to make sure that nothing is omitted. In the first rule, we see that "clear and distinct" characteristics are required by Descartes for making a true judgment; they are invoked by him at every turn in working out his basic philosophy. Further, he distinguishes three classes of ideas: adventitious, invented (factitious), and clear and distinct; it is the last class that is the most important for Descartes from an epistemological point of view, for it is their very clarity and distinctness that make these ideas undoubtable and therefore the basis for certitude. And if he was asked, "How do clear and distinct ideas get into our minds?", Descartes, to avoid a further series of questions that could go on indefinitely and therefore supply no answer, responded that they do not "get" there, they "are" there — they are *innate*. Questions about the existence and nature of innate ideas have caused a great deal of controversy, but without doubt such ideas were attractive to a mathematical-deductive mind. Following a line, then, that seems to express Descartes' view, innate ideas are not to be thought of as fully formed objects in the mind waiting for recognition; rather, they are produced by the natural tendency of the mind to think in a given way when the occasion occurs. This belief is somewhat reminiscent of Socrates' view of learning as a drawing out of what is already in the mind.

One of these ideas serves as the basis of a judgment that, as true, is destined to become the initial principle in Descartes' philosophy. To discover what that idea-judgment is constitutes part of the Cartesian method and is referred to as the *method of doubt*, therefore, *methodic doubt*: the process of calling into question any judgment or proposition, regardless of how true it may seem to be, in order to get to one that cannot be doubted or that, perhaps, in the very act of being doubted, is affirmed. This does not mean that all other judgments, like old buildings, are permanently rejected; rather, they are temporarily stored to be reconsidered later. We can call into doubt, for example, judgments based on sensations because they sometimes appear contradictory or because, as far as we know, they may be caused by an evil demon; in short, "I could feign that I had no body, that there was no world, nor any place in which I might be."

But, Descartes continues, "I could not feign that I was not," and so the proposition *I think, therefore I am* (*cogito ergo sum*) is beyond doubt, or is affirmed while doubting, and is therefore true and certain. For Descartes, then, this truth is known immediately, that is, without any other medium or means; it is an idea directly grasped, an *intuition* of the self as a thinking being. Even though the famous phrase looks like an abbreviated syllogism — as though from the fact that I think, I conclude that I exist — Descartes meant it to be taken as one intuition but with two moments: the first moment is of the self as *thinking*, the second moment is of the self as *being*. For Descartes, I *know* this; it is true, it is unshakable, it is the *quid inconcussum.*

With such a starting point, Descartes could safely proceed to the explication of the major truths of his philosophical system: the nature of man, the existence of God, and the existence of the external world.

That man exists, there is no doubt, as we have seen in the statement *I think, therefore I am*. Yet in the clarity and distinctness of this truth there is *nothing but* thought, that is, I am a *thinking* being, and my nature is the nature of my thinking. The nature of man is spirit, and only spirit. To anticipate a bit — since we do not yet know whether the external world exists — what Descartes is saying is that the idea of thought does not contain within itself the idea of matter, so that matter, or body, cannot be part of the definition of man and does not belong to his nature. We will shortly discuss the huge problem of the mind–body relationship in Descartes and the meaning of Cartesian dualism as it follows from the understanding of man as thought only.

The second truth, the existence of God, is made possible by the presence in our minds of the idea of an all-perfect being, and there are two approaches to this idea. The first is in line with traditional approaches: the idea of an all-perfect being, inasmuch as it is all-perfect, cannot be of our making because we are imperfect beings; therefore, it must be caused in us by a being that is all-perfect. The second approach, however, though reminiscent of the ontological argument of St. Anselm, is thoroughly Cartesian. The idea of the all-perfect being possesses in itself the idea of every perfection possible: the idea of being supreme, eternal, infinite, all-knowing, all-good, and so on. More than that, the idea of the all-perfect *necessarily* contains within itself the idea of existence; therefore, the all-perfect exists. The all-perfect, God, does not have a mental, or idea-1, existence only, but an existence *outside* the mind; God really exists. There is no argument against the fact that a triangle necessarily implies three interior angles equalling 180 degrees, so there is no argument against the fact that the *existence* of God is necessarily implied in the idea of God. When some persons opposed this view with the objection that from the idea of a golden mountain you cannot infer its existence, Descartes responded, "of course not," because the idea of its existence is not necessarily implied in the idea of the golden mountain. The *only* idea in which the idea of existence is necessarily implied is the idea of the all-perfect.

By the end of the seventeenth century, the ontological argument had gained many adherents, including Spinoza and Leibniz; but other philosophers, not possessing the Cartesian mind, maintained that the only way to conclude that God exists is to *begin* with the *existence* of something you can experience; otherwise, if your route begins *in the mind*, it stays there.

The third major truth, the existence of the external world, also begins with clear and distinct ideas. Descartes announces his project economically with the words, "There now remains only the inquiry as to whether material things exist," and he proceeds by examining the ideas of them insofar as they "are in my thought, and to determine which of them are distinct and which confused." Upon examination, then, we discern the idea of matter in its pure, geometrical form, namely, *quantity*, or *extension* "in length, breadth and depth"; it is clear and distinct, but the idea of existence is not necessarily included in it, unlike the second deduction, in which the idea of existence is necessarily included in the idea of the all-perfect. Along with our awareness of the idea of extension, we are aware of ideas of *sensation*, that is, of "ideas received by way of the senses." They come to us at various times, often uncontrolled and even unwanted, yet they exist. They therefore do not come from the mind itself, and the only possible conclusion is that they come from another substance called *body*, with which the mind experiences some kind of union, and in virtue of which it becomes related epistemologically to all other bodies. There is then an *external world*, a world outside mind, that is different in substance from mind.

A critic of Descartes could anticipate a sense of triumph in objecting that sensations offer no guarantee whatsoever of the existence of bodily things because we cannot rule out the possibility that sensations deceive us into making a false conclusion. But Descartes then played his trump card, asking, how can you possibly speak of deception where God is involved? If I am deceived regarding my sensations, then God is thereby charged with deceiving me! But God is all-truthful and would not, could not, deceive me or allow me to be deceived; therefore, the conclusion that bodily things exist is both certain and true.

Philosophers can and do lean in one direction or another in considering the problem of knowledge, and in a sense one's epistemological orientation is the key to one's philosophical makeup. The question is, how does the mind get to know in the first place? Historically, this question has two answers: the mind is already endowed with something like innate ideas, or the mind starts out as a blank and somehow acquires knowledge. In classical modern philosophy these opposing views were taken up by Descartes and his younger English contemporary, John Locke. For Descartes, as we have seen, ideas are innate, already present in the mind, so that the question of how they get there in the first place is superfluous: when mind is given, so are innate ideas. This position was required of Descartes in view of his basic philosophy of man, namely, that man is mind only, and in the consequent separation of mind and body, sensation becomes the activity of body only; so the question of how sensation could lead to intellectual knowledge becomes problematical. But Locke's view was that we have no innate ideas, for it is obvious, from our experience, that we come to know things for the first time as we sense them; so the mind, to begin with, is a clear slate, a *tabula rasa*, a tablet on which nothing has yet been written; writing appears as sensation takes place; nothing is in the intellect unless it is first in the sense — a belief that has been accepted by a host of philosophers from Aristotle on down.

Descartes must have felt that there was something untidy about his epistemology, perhaps because he sensed that somehow he was flying in the face of experience; this would explain why he required body and mind to be in the closest relationship without essentially being united, as in the Aristotelian doctrine. Locke, on the other hand, felt that he was indeed relying on experience, and that is why he looked to sensation as the origin of all knowledge; but in this view he went so far as to hold that, for all we know, it might be possible, in God's power, for matter to be endowed with the ability to think. What Descartes held was that knowledge originated in the intellect itself, without the partnership of sense. What Locke held was that the origin of knowledge was in the sense, to the possible exclusion of intellect as partner, a position taken to its logical extreme in the next century by David Hume.

We now have a better vantage point from which to explain some other aspects of the mind–body relationship. It is clear that Descartes' real world admits two substances, body (quantity, extension, matter) and mind (spirit, thought); his position is often referred to as *Cartesian dualism*. His toughest problem is the relationship of mind to body, for having determined that man is by nature mind, the question becomes: how closely is mind related to body without forming one being? The traditional Aristotelian view is that man is *one* being composed of two principles, body and soul; body and soul are dual principles of one being. In the living organism they are not separated, for the soul is the life-giving principle to the body and is, therefore, one with it. This view Descartes eschewed and, while speaking in the context of mind and body, avoided the use of the word *soul* because it denoted an essential ordering to the body. Nevertheless, while not speaking of them as forming one being, Descartes spoke of body and mind as intimately related, as two independent substances acting together, close but separate.

What then is the *living* body for Descartes? Having come thus far, there is only one possible answer: the body is an aggregate of physical parts operating on physical principles; it is a *machine* or an automaton. But it is a machine so exquisite, so finely honed to its task, that only God could fashion it. The body is not really a living thing; it has no need of a soul; it is not enlivened. And if a living thing has no need of a soul, then its activities are similar to those of any material thing: *all* material things operate on the basis of physical principles only. So, in a broader sense, movement in the universe is not all due to the activity of spirit, as held centuries before, but to matter's own inherent powers, and it was on this fact, as Descartes saw it, that he based his hopes for man's control of the universe for man's benefit.

Descartes' influence was vast; it dominated philosophical thought in continental Europe for the next century and a half. He satisfied himself and all those in tune with his rationalist approach that he had found a way to combat skepticism compatible with the mathematical model, and he compelled subsequent philosophers to rethink basic problems such as knowledge and certitude, mind and body, experience and deduction. That is why the metaphysical problems he dealt with — man, God, world — keep coming back in modern philosophy. Some interesting conclusions, however, were reached by a number of philosophers who were won over by the attractiveness of Descartes' method but could not follow him all the way; they moved on to extreme positions already latent in the Cartesian scheme. Bishop Berkeley, as we shall see, had to part company with Descartes on his way of getting to the material world, and concluded that the only reality is spirit and that sensations were nothing more than "states of mind." At the other extreme, La Mettrie maintained that Descartes never convincingly demonstrated the need for spirit and concluded that man is only a machine.

Descartes was the first of three outstanding seventeenth-century philosophers on the continent usually referred to as *rationalists*. This name is applied because it signifies a tendency, in the matter of knowledge, to move from the mind outward to things, a tendency often found in the mathematical mind. In the following pages, we will consider the other two rationalists, Spinoza and Leibniz.

Readings

Discourse on Method

PART II

I was then in Germany, to which country I had been attracted by the wars which are not yet at an end. And as I was returning from the coronation of the Emperor to join the army, the setting in of winter detained me in a quarter where, since I found no society to divert me, while fortunately I had also no cares or passions to trouble me, I remained the whole day shut up alone in a stove-heated room, where I had complete leisure to occupy myself with my own thoughts. One of the first of the considerations that occurred to me was that there is very often less perfection in works composed of several portions, and carried out by the hands of various masters, than in those on which one individual alone has worked. Thus we see that buildings planned and carried out by one architect alone are usually more beautiful and better proportioned than those which many have tried to put in order and improve, making use of old walls which were built with other ends in view. In the same way also, those ancient cities which, originally mere villages, have become in the process of time great towns, are usually badly constructed in comparison with those which are regularly laid out on a plain by a surveyor who is free to follow his own ideas. Even though, considering their buildings each one apart, there is often as much or more display of skill in the one case than in the other, the former have large buildings and small buildings indiscriminately placed together, thus rendering the streets crooked and irregular, so that it might be said that it was chance rather than the will of men guided by reason that led to such an arrangement. And if we consider that this happens despite the fact that from all time there have been certain officials who have had the special duty of looking after the buildings of private individuals in order that they may be public ornaments, we shall understand how difficult it is to bring about much that is satisfactory in operating only upon the works of others. Thus I imagined that those people who were once half-savage, and who have become civilized only by slow degrees, merely forming their laws as the disagreeable necessities of their crimes and quarrels constrained them, could not succeed in establishing so good a system of government as those who, from the time they first came together as communities, carried into effect the constitution laid down by some prudent legislator. Thus it is quite certain that the constitution of the true Religion whose ordinances are of God alone is incomparably better regulated than any other. And, to come down to human affairs, I believe that if Sparta was very flourishing in former times, this was not because of the excellence of each and every one of its laws, seeing that many were very strange and even contrary to good morals, but because, being drawn up by one individual, they all tended towards the same end. And similarly I thought that the sciences found in books—in those at least whose reasonings are only probable and which have no demonstrations, composed as they are of the gradually accumulated opinions of many different individuals—do not approach so near to the truth as the simple reasoning which a man of common sense can quite naturally carry out respecting the things which come immediately before him. Again I thought that since we have all been children before being men, and since it has for long fallen to us to be governed by our appetites and by our teachers (who often enough contradicted one another, and none of whom perhaps counselled us always for the best), it is almost impossible that our judgments should be so excellent or solid as they should have been had we had complete use of our reason since our birth, and had we been guided by its means alone.

It is true that we do not find that all the houses in a town are rased to the ground for the sole reason that the town is to be rebuilt in another fashion, with streets made more beautiful; but at the same time we see that many people cause their own houses to be knocked down in order to rebuild them, and that sometimes they are forced so to do where there is danger of the houses falling of themselves, and when the foundations are not secure. From such examples I argued to myself that there was no plausibility in the claim of any private individual to reform a state by altering everything, and by overturning it throughout, in order to set it right again. Nor is it likewise probable that the whole body of the Sciences, or the order of teaching established by the Schools should be reformed. But as regards all the opinions which up to this time I had embraced, I thought I could not do better than endeavour once for all to sweep them completely away, so that they might later on be replaced, either by others which were better, or by the same, when I had made them conform to the uniformity of a rational scheme. And I firmly believed that by this means I should succeed in directing my life much better than if I had only built on old foundations, and relied on principles of which I allowed myself to be in youth persuaded without having inquired into their truth. For although in so doing I recognised various difficulties, these were at the same time not unsurmountable, nor comparable to those which are found in reformation of the most insignificant kind in matters which concern the public. In the case of great bodies it is too difficult a task to raise them again when they are once thrown down, or even to keep them in their places when once thoroughly shaken; and their fall cannot be otherwise than very violent. Then as to any imperfections that they may possess (and the very diversity that is found between them is sufficient to tell us that these in many cases exist) custom has doubtless greatly mitigated them, while it has also helped us to avoid, or insensibly corrected a number against which mere foresight would have found it difficult to guard. And finally the imperfections are almost always more supportable than would be the process of removing them, just as the great roads which wind about amongst the mountains become, because of being frequented, little by little so well-beaten and easy that it is much better to follow them than to try to go more directly by climbing over rocks and descending to the foot of precipices.

This is the reason why I cannot in any way approve of those turbulent and unrestful spirits who, being called neither by birth nor fortune to the management of public affairs, never fail to have always in their minds some new reforms. And if I thought that in this treatise there was contained the smallest justification for this folly, I should be very sorry to allow it to be published. My design has never extended beyond trying to reform my own opinion and to build on a foundation which is entirely my own. If my work has given me a certain satisfaction, so that I here present to you a draft of it, I do not so do because I wish to advise anybody to imitate it. Those to whom God has been most beneficent in the bestowal of His graces will perhaps form designs which are more elevated; but I fear much that this particular one will seem too venturesome for many. The simple resolve to strip oneself of all opinions and beliefs formerly received is not to be regarded as an example that each man should follow, and the world may be said to be mainly composed of two classes of minds neither of which could prudently adopt it. There are those who, believing themselves to be cleverer than they are, cannot restrain themselves from being precipitate in judgment and have not sufficient patience to arrange their thoughts in proper order; hence, once a man of this description had taken the liberty of doubting the principles he formerly accepted, and had deviated from the beaten track, he would never be able to maintain the path which must be followed to reach the appointed end more quickly, and he would hence remain wandering astray all through his life. Secondly, there are those who having reason or modesty enough to judge that they are less capable of distinguishing truth from falsehood than some others from whom instruction might be obtained, are right in contenting themselves with following the opinions of these others rather than in searching better ones for themselves.

For myself I should doubtless have been of these last if I had never had more than a single master, or had I never known the diversities which have from all time existed between the opinions of men of the greatest learning. But I had been taught, even in my College days, that there is nothing imaginable so strange or so little credible that it has not been maintained by one philosopher or other, and I further recognised in the course of my travels that all those whose sentiments are very contrary to ours are yet not necessarily barbarians or savages, but may be possessed of reason in as great or even a greater degree than ourselves. I also considered how very different the self-same man, identical in mind and spirit, may become, according as he is brought up from childhood amongst the French or Germans, or has passed his whole life amongst Chinese or cannibals. I likewise noticed how even in the fashions of one's clothing the same thing that pleased us ten years ago, and which will perhaps please us once again before ten years are passed, seems at the present time extravagant and ridiculous. I thus concluded that it is much more custom and example that persuade us than any certain knowledge, and yet in spite of this the voice of the majority does not afford a proof of any value in truths a little difficult to discover, because such truths are much more likely to have been discovered by one man than by a nation. I could not, however, put my finger on a single person whose opinions seemed preferable to those of others, and I found that I was, so to speak, constrained myself to undertake the direction of my procedure.

But like one who walks alone and in the twilight I resolved to go so slowly, and to use so much circumspection in all things, that if my advance was but very small, at least I guarded myself well from falling. I did not wish to set about the final rejection of any single opinion which might formerly have crept into my beliefs without having been introduced there by means of Reason, until I had first of all employed sufficient time in planning out the task which I had undertaken, and in seeking the true Method of arriving at a knowledge of all the things of which my mind was capable.

Among the different branches of Philosophy, I had in my younger days to a certain extent studied Logic; and in those of Mathematics, Geometrical Analysis and Algebra—three arts or sciences which seemed as though they ought to contribute something to the design I had in view. But in examining them I observed in respect to Logic that the syllogisms and the greater part of the other teaching served better in explaining to others those things that one knows (or like the art of Lully, in enabling one to speak without judgment of those things of which one is ignorant) than in learning what is new. And although in reality Logic contains many precepts which are very true and very good, there are at the same time mingled with them so many others which are hurtful or superfluous, that it is almost as difficult to separate the two as to draw a Diana or a Minerva out of a block of marble which is not yet roughly hewn. And as to the Analysis of the ancients and the Algebra of the moderns, besides the fact that they embrace only matters the most abstract, such as appear to have no actual use, the former is always so restricted to the consideration of symbols that it cannot exercise the Understanding without greatly fatiguing the Imagination; and in the latter one is so subjected to certain rules and formulas that the result is the construction of an art which is confused and obscure, and which embarrasses the mind, instead of a science which contributes to its cultivation. This made me feel that some other Method must be found, which, comprising the advantages of the three, is yet exempt from their faults. And as a multiplicity of laws often furnishes excuses for evil-doing, and as a State is hence much better ruled when, having but very few laws, these are most strictly observed; so, instead of the great number of precepts of which Logic is composed, I believed that I should find the four which I shall state quite sufficient, provided that I adhered to a firm and constant resolve never on any single occasion to fail in their observance.

The first of these was to accept nothing as true which I did not clearly recognise to be so: that is to say, carefully to avoid precipitation and prejudice in judgments, and to accept in them nothing more than what was presented to my mind so clearly and distinctly that I could have no occasion to doubt it.

The second was to divide up each of the difficulties which I examined into as many parts as possible, and as seemed requisite in order that it might be resolved in the best manner possible.

The third was to carry on my reflections in due order, commencing with objects that were the most simple and easy to understand, in order to rise little by little, or by degrees, to knowledge of the most complex, assuming an order, even if a fictitious one, among those which do not follow a natural sequence relatively to one another.

The last was in all cases to make enumerations so complete and reviews so general that I should be certain of having omitted nothing.

Those long chains of reasoning, simple and easy as they are, of which geometricians make use in order to arrive at the most difficult demonstrations, had caused me to imagine that all those things which fall under the cognizance of man might very likely be mutually related in the same fashion; and that, provided only that we abstain from receiving anything as true which is not so, and always retain the order which is necessary in order to deduce the one conclusion from the other, there can be nothing so remote that we cannot reach to it, nor so recondite that we cannot discover it. And I had not much trouble in discovering which objects it was necessary to begin with, for I already knew that it was with the most simple and those most easy to apprehend. Considering also that of all those who have hitherto sought for the truth in the Sciences, it has been the mathematicians alone who have been able to succeed in making any demonstrations, that is to say producing reasons which are evident and certain, I did not doubt that it had been by means of a similar kind that they carried on their investigations. I did not at the same time hope for any practical result in so doing, except that my mind would become accustomed to the nourishment of truth and would not content itself with false reasoning. But for all that I had no intention of trying to master all those particular sciences that receive in common the name of Mathematics; but observing that, although their objects are different, they do not fail to agree in this, that they take nothing under consideration but the various relationships or proportions which are present in these objects, I thought that it would be better if I only examined these proportions in their general aspect, and without viewing them otherwise than in the objects which would serve most to facilitate a knowledge of them. Not that I should in any way restrict them to these objects, for I might later on all the more easily apply them to all other objects to which they were applicable. Then, having carefully noted that in order to comprehend the proportions I should sometimes require to consider each one in particular, and sometimes merely keep them in mind, or take them in groups, I thought that, in order the better to consider them in detail, I should picture them in the form of lines, because I could find no method more simple nor more capable of being distinctly represented to my imagination and senses. I considered, however, that in order to keep them in my memory or to embrace several at once, it would be essential that I should explain them by means of certain formulas, the shorter the better. And for this purpose it was requisite that I should borrow all that is best in Geometrical Analysis and Algebra, and correct the errors of the one by the other.

As a matter of fact, I can venture to say that the exact observation of the few precepts which I had chosen gave me so much facility in sifting out all the questions embraced in these two sciences, that in the two or three months which I employed in examining them—commencing with the most simple and general, and making each truth that I discovered a rule for helping me to find others—not only did I arrive at the solution of many questions which I had hitherto regarded as most difficult, but, towards the end, it seemed to me that I was able to determine in the case of those of which I was still ignorant, by what means, and in how far, it was possible to solve them. In this I might perhaps appear to you to be very vain if you did not remember that having but one truth to discover in respect to each matter, whoever succeeds in finding it knows in its regard as much as can be known. It is the same as with a child, for instance, who has been instructed in Arithmetic and has made an addition according to the rule prescribed; he may be sure of having found as regards the sum of figures given to him all that the human mind can know. For, in conclusion, the Method which teaches us to follow the true order and enumerate exactly every term in the matter under investigation contains everything which gives certainty to the rules of Arithmetic.

But what pleased me most in this Method was that I was certain by its means of exercising my reason in all things, if not perfectly, at least as well as was in my power. And besides this, I felt in making use of it that my mind gradually accustomed itself to conceive of its objects more accurately and distinctly; and not having restricted this Method to any particular matter, I promised myself to apply it as usefully to the difficulties of other sciences as I had done to those of Algebra. Not that on this account I dared undertake to examine just at once all those that might present themselves; for that would itself have been contrary to the order which the Method prescribes. But having noticed that the knowledge of these difficulties must be dependent on principles derived from Philosophy in which I yet found nothing to be certain, I thought that it was requisite above all to try to establish certainty in it. I considered also that since this endeavour is the most important in all the world, and that in which precipitation and prejudice were most to be feared, I should not try to grapple with it till I had attained to a much riper age than that of three and twenty, which was the age I had reached. I thought, too, that I should first of all employ much time in preparing myself for the work by eradicating from my mind all the wrong opinions which I had up to this time accepted, and accumulating a variety of experiences fitted later on to afford matter for my reasonings, and by ever exercising myself in the Method which I had prescribed, in order more and more to fortify myself in the power of using it.

PART IV

I do not know that I ought to tell you of the first meditations there made by me, for they are so metaphysical and so unusual that they may perhaps not be acceptable to everyone. And yet at the same time, in order that one may judge whether the foundations which I have laid are sufficiently secure, I find myself constrained in some measure to refer to them. For a long time I had remarked that it is sometimes requisite in common life to follow opinions which one knows to be most uncertain, exactly as though they were indisputable, as has been said above. But because in this case I wished to give myself entirely to the search after Truth, I thought that it was necessary for me to take an apparently opposite course, and to reject as absolutely false everything as to which I could imagine the least ground of doubt, in order to see if afterwards there remained anything in my belief that was entirely certain. Thus, because our senses sometimes deceive us, I wished to suppose that nothing is just as they cause us to imagine it to be; and because there are men who deceive themselves in their reasoning and fall into paralogisms, even concerning the simplest matters of geometry, and judging that I was as subject to error as was any other, I rejected as false all the reasons formerly accepted by me as demonstrations. And since all the same thoughts and conceptions which we have while awake may also come to us in sleep, without any of them being at that time true, I resolved to assume that everything that ever entered into my mind was no more true than the illusions of my dreams. But immediately afterwards I noticed that whilst I thus wished to think all things false, it was absolutely essential that the 'I' who thought this should be somewhat, and remarking that this truth '*I think, therefore I am*' was so certain and so assured that all the most extravagant suppositions brought forward by the sceptics were incapable of shaking it, I came to the conclusion that I could receive it without scruple as the first principle of the Philosophy for which I was seeking.

And then, examining attentively that which I was, I saw that I could conceive that I had no body, and that there was no world nor place where I might be; but yet that I could not for all that conceive that I was not. On the contrary, I saw from the very fact that I thought of doubting the truth of other things, it very evidently and certainly followed that I was; on the other hand if I had only ceased from thinking, even if all the rest of what I had ever imagined had really existed, I should have no reason for thinking that I had existed. From that I knew that I was a substance the whole essence or nature of which is to think, and that for its existence there is no need of any place, nor does it depend on any material thing; so that this 'me,' that is to say, the soul by which I am what I am, is entirely distinct from body, and is even more easy to know than is the latter; and even if body were not, the soul would not cease to be what it is.

After this I considered generally what in a proposition is requisite in order to be true and certain; for since I had just discovered one which I knew to be such, I thought that I ought also to know in what this certainty consisted. And having remarked that there was nothing at all in the statement 'I think, therefore I am' which assures me of having thereby made a true assertion, excepting that I see very clearly that to think it is necessary to be, I came to the conclusion that I might assume, as a general rule, that the things which we conceive very clearly and distinctly are all true—remembering, however, that there is some difficulty in ascertaining which are those that we distinctly conceive.

Following upon this, and reflecting on the fact that I doubted, and that consequently my existence was not quite perfect (for I saw clearly that it was a greater perfection to know than to doubt), I resolved to inquire whence I had learnt to think of anything more perfect than I myself was; and I recognised very clearly that this conception must proceed from some nature which was really more perfect. As to the thoughts which I had of many other things outside of me, like the heavens, the earth, light, heat, and a thousand others, I had not so much difficulty in knowing whence they came, because, remarking nothing in them which seemed to render them superior to me, I could believe that, if they were true, they were dependencies upon my nature, in so far as it possessed some perfection; and if they were not true, that I held them from nought, that is to say, that they were in me because I had something lacking in my nature. But this could not apply to the idea of a Being more perfect than my own, for to hold it from nought would be manifestly impossible; and because it is no less contradictory to say of the more perfect that it is what results from and depends on the less perfect, than to say that there is something which proceeds from nothing, it was equally impossible that I should hold it from myself. In this way it could but follow that it had been placed in me by a Nature which was really more perfect than mine could be, and which even had within itself all the perfections of which I could form any idea—that is to say, to put it in a word, which was God. To which I added that since I knew some perfections which I did not possess, I was not the only being in existence (I shall here use freely, if you will allow, the terms of the School); but that there was necessarily some other more perfect Being on which I depended, or from which I acquired all that I had. For if I had existed alone and independent of any others, so that I should have had from myself all that perfection of being in which I participated to however small an extent, I should have been able for the same reason to have had all the remainder which I knew that I lacked; and thus I myself should have been infinite, eternal, immutable, omniscient, all-powerful, and, finally, I should have all the perfections which I could discern in God. For, in pursuance of the reasonings which I have just carried on, in order to know the nature of God as far as my nature is capable of knowing it, I had only to consider in reference to all these things of which I found some idea in myself, whether it was a perfection to possess them or not. And I was assured that none of those which indicated some imperfection were in Him, but that all else was present; and I saw that doubt, inconstancy, sadness, and such things, could not be in Him considering that I myself should have been glad to be without them. In addition to this, I had ideas of many things which are sensible and corporeal, for, although I might suppose that I was dreaming, and that all that I saw or imagined was false, I could not at the same time deny that the ideas were really in my thoughts. But because I had already recognised very clearly in myself that the nature of the intelligence is distinct from that of the body, and observing that all composition gives evidence of dependency, and that dependency is manifestly an imperfection, I came to the conclusion that it could not be a perfection in God to be composed of these two natures, and that consequently He was not so composed. I judged, however, that if there were any bodies in the world, or even any intelligences or other natures which were not wholly perfect, their existence must depend on His power in such a way that they could not subsist without Him for a single moment.

After that I desired to seek for other truths, and having put before myself the object of the geometricians, which I conceived to be a continuous body, or a space indefinitely extended in length, breadth, height or depth, which was divisible into various parts, and which might have various figures and sizes, and might be moved or transposed in all sorts of ways (for all this the geometricians suppose to be in the object of their contemplation), I went through some of their simplest demonstrations, and having noticed that this great certainty which everyone attributes to these demonstrations is founded solely on the fact that they are conceived of with clearness, in accordance with the rule which I have just laid down, I also noticed that there was nothing at all in them to assure me of the existence of their object. For, to take an example, I saw very well that if we suppose a triangle to be given, the three angles must certainly be equal to two right angles; but for all that I saw no reason to be assured that there was any such triangle in existence, while on the contrary, on reverting to the examination of the idea which I had of a Perfect Being, I found that in this case existence was implied in it in the same manner in which the equality of its three angles to two right angles is implied in the idea of a triangle; or in the idea of a sphere, that all the points on its surface are equidistant from its centre, or even more evidently still. Consequently it is at least as certain that God, who is a Being so perfect, is, or exists, as any demonstration of geometry can possibly be.

What causes many, however, to persuade themselves that there is difficulty in knowing this truth, and even in knowing the nature of their soul, is the fact that they never raise their minds above the things of sense, or that they are so accustomed to consider nothing excepting by imagining it, which is a mode of thought specially adapted to material objects, that all that is not capable of being imagined appears to them not to be intelligible at all. This is manifest enough from the fact that even the philosophers in the Schools hold it as a maxim that there is nothing in the understanding which has not first of all been in the senses, in which there is certainly no doubt that the ideas of God and of the soul have never been. And it seems to me that those who desire to make use of their imagination in order to understand these ideas, act in the same way as if, to hear sounds or smell odours, they should wish to make use of their eyes: excepting that there is indeed this difference, that the sense of sight does not give us less assurance of the truth of its objects, than do those of scent or of hearing, while neither our imagination nor our senses can ever assure us of anything, if our understanding does not intervene.

If there are finally any persons who are not sufficiently persuaded of the existence of God and of their soul by the reasons which I have brought forward, I wish that they should know that all other things of which they perhaps think themselves more assured (such as possessing a body, and that there are stars and an earth and so on) are less certain. For, although we have a moral assurance of these things which is such that it seems that it would be extravagant in us to doubt them, at the same time no one, unless he is devoid of reason, can deny, when a metaphysical certainty is in question, that there is sufficient cause for our not having complete assurance, by observing the fact that when asleep we may similarly imagine that we have another body, and that we see other stars and another earth, without there being anything of the kind. For how do we know that the thoughts that come in dreams are more false than those that we have when we are awake, seeing that often enough the former are not less lively and vivid than the latter? And though the wisest minds may study the matter as much as they will, I do not believe that they will be able to give any sufficient reason for removing this doubt, unless they presuppose the existence of God. For to begin with, that which I have just taken as a rule, that is to say, that all the things that we very clearly and very distinctly conceive of are true, is certain only because God is or exists, and that He is a Perfect Being, and that all that is in us issues from Him. From this it follows that our ideas or notions, which to the extent of their being clear or distinct are ideas of real things issuing from God, cannot but to that extent be true. So that though we often enough have ideas which have an element of falsity, this can only be the case in regard to those which have in them somewhat that is confused or obscure, because in so far as they have this character they participate in negation—that is, they exist in us as confused only because we are not quite perfect. And it is evident that there is no less repugnance in the idea that error or imperfection, inasmuch as it is imperfection, proceeds from God, than there is in the idea of truth or perfection proceeding from nought. But if we did not know that all that is in us of reality and truth proceeds from a perfect and infinite Being, however clear and distinct were our ideas, we should not have any reason to assure ourselves that they had the perfection of being true.

But after the knowledge of God and of the soul has thus rendered us certain of this rule, it is very easy to understand that the dreams which we imagine in our sleep should not make us in any way doubt the truth of the thoughts which we have when awake. For even if in sleep we had some very distinct idea such as a geometrician might have who discovered some new demonstration, the fact of being asleep would not militate against its truth. And as to the most ordinary error in our dreams, which consists in their representing to us various objects in the same way as do our external senses, it does not matter that this should give us occasion to suspect the truth of such ideas, because we may be likewise often enough deceived in them without our sleeping at all, just as when those who have the jaundice see everything as yellow, or when stars or other bodies which are very remote appear much smaller than they really are. For, finally, whether we are awake or asleep, we should never allow ourselves to be persuaded excepting by the evidence of our Reason. And it must be remarked that I speak of our Reason and not of our imagination nor of our senses; just as though we see the sun very clearly, we should not for that reason judge that it is of the size of which it appears to be; likewise we could quite well distinctly imagine the head of a lion on the body of a goat, without necessarily concluding that a chimera exists. For Reason does not insist that whatever we see or imagine thus is a truth, but it tells us clearly that all our ideas or notions must have some foundation of truth. For otherwise it could not be possible that God, who is all perfection and truth, should have placed them within us. And because our reasonings are never so evident nor so complete during sleep as during wakefulness, although sometimes our imaginations are then just as lively and acute, or even more so, Reason tells us that since our thoughts cannot possibly be all true, because we are not altogether perfect, that which they have of truth must infallibly be met with in our waking experience rather than in that of our dreams.

Meditations on First Philosophy

MEDITATION V

Of the Essence of Material Things, and, Again, of God, that He Exists

Many other matters respecting the attributes of God and my own nature or mind remain for consideration; but I shall possibly on another occasion resume the investigation of these. Now (after first noting what must be done or avoided, in order to arrive at a knowledge of the truth) my principal task is to endeavour to emerge from the state of doubt into which I have these last days fallen, and to see whether nothing certain can be known regarding material things.

But before examining whether any such objects as I conceive exist outside of me, I must consider the ideas of them in so far as they are in my thought, and see which of them are distinct and which confused.

In the first place, I am able distinctly to imagine that quantity which philosophers commonly call continuous, or the extension in length, breadth, or depth, that is in this quantity, or rather in the object to which it is attributed. Further, I can number in it many different parts, and attribute to each of its parts many sorts of size, figure, situation and local movement, and, finally, I can assign to each of these movements all degrees of duration.

And not only do I know these things with distinctness when I consider them in general, but, likewise [however little I apply my attention to the matter], I discover an infinitude of particulars respecting numbers, figures, movements, and other such things, whose truth is so manifest, and so well accords with my nature, that when I begin to discover them, it seems to me that I learn nothing new, or recollect what I formerly knew—that is to say, that I for the first time perceive things which were already present to my mind, although I had not as yet applied my mind to them.

And what I here find to be most important is that I discover in myself an infinitude of ideas of certain things which cannot be esteemed as pure negations, although they may possibly have no existence outside of my thought, and which are not framed by me, although it is within my power either to think or not to think them, but which possess natures which are true and immutable. For example, when I imagine a triangle, although there may nowhere in the world be such a figure outside my thought, or ever have been, there is nevertheless in this figure a certain determinate nature, form, or essence, which is immutable and eternal, which I have not invented, and which in no wise depends on my mind, as appears from the fact that diverse properties of that triangle can be demonstrated, viz. that its three angles are equal to two right angles, that the greatest side is subtended by the greatest angle, and the like, which now, whether I wish it or do not wish it, I recognise very clearly as pertaining to it, although I never thought of the matter at all when I imagined a triangle for the first time, and which therefore cannot be said to have been invented by me.

Nor does the objection hold good that possibly this idea of a triangle has reached my mind through the medium of my senses, since I have sometimes seen bodies triangular in shape; because I can form in my mind an infinitude of other figures regarding which we cannot have the least conception of their ever having been objects of sense, and I can nevertheless demonstrate various properties pertaining to their nature as well as to that of the triangle, and these must certainly all be true since I conceive them clearly. Hence they are something, and not pure negation; for it is perfectly clear that all that is true is something, and I have already fully demonstrated that all that I know clearly is true. And even although I had not demonstrated this, the nature of my mind is such that I could not prevent myself from holding them to be true so long as I conceive them clearly; and I recollect that even when I was still strongly attached to the objects of sense, I counted as the most certain those truths which I conceived clearly as regards figures, numbers, and the other matters which pertain to arithmetic and geometry, and, in general, to pure and abstract mathematics.

But now, if just because I can draw the idea of something from my thought, it follows that all which I know clearly and distinctly as pertaining to this object does really belong to it, may I not derive from this an argument demonstrating the existence of God? It is certain that I no less find the idea of God, that is to say, the idea of a supremely perfect Being, in me, than that of any figure or number whatever it is; and I do not know any less clearly and distinctly that an [actual and] eternal existence pertains to this nature than I know that all that which I am able to demonstrate of some figure or number truly pertains to the nature of this figure or number, and therefore, although all that I concluded in the preceding Meditations were found to be false, the existence of God would pass with me as at least as certain as I have ever held the truths of mathematics (which concern only numbers and figures) to be.

This indeed is not at first manifest, since it would seem to present some appearance of being a sophism. For being accustomed in all other things to make a distinction between existence and essence, I easily persuade myself that the existence can be separated from the essence of God, and that we can thus conceive God as not actually existing. But, nevertheless, when I think of it with more attention, I clearly see that existence can no more be separated from the essence of God than can its having its three angles equal to two right angles be separated from the essence of a [rectilinear] triangle, or the idea of a mountain from the idea of a valley; and so there is not any less repugnance to our conceiving a God (that is, a Being supremely perfect) to whom existence is lacking (that is to say, to whom a certain perfection is lacking), than to conceive of a mountain which has no valley.

But although I cannot really conceive of a God without existence any more than a mountain without a valley, still from the fact that I conceive of a mountain with a valley, it does not follow that there is such a mountain in the world; similarly although I conceive of God as possessing existence, it would seem that it does not follow that there is a God which exists; for my thought does not impose any necessity upon things, and just as I may imagine a winged horse, although no horse with wings exists, so I could perhaps attribute existence to God, although no God existed.

But a sophism is concealed in this objection; for from the fact that I cannot conceive a mountain without a valley, it does not follow that there is any mountain or any valley in existence, but only that the mountain and the valley, whether they exist or do not exist, cannot in any way be separated one from the other. While from the fact that I cannot conceive God without existence, it follows that existence is inseparable from Him, and hence that He really exists; not that my thought can bring this to pass, or impose any necessity on things, but, on the contrary, because the necessity which lies in the thing itself, i.e. the necessity of the existence of God determines me to think in this way. For it is not within my power to think of God without existence (that is of a supremely perfect Being devoid of a supreme perfection) though it is in my power to imagine a horse either with wings or without wings.

And we must not here object that it is in truth necessary for me to assert that God exists after having presupposed that He possesses every sort of perfection, since existence is one of these, but that as a matter of fact my original supposition was not necessary, just as it is not necessary to consider that all quadrilateral figures can be inscribed in the circle; for supposing I thought this, I should be constrained to admit that the rhombus might be inscribed in the circle since it is a quadrilateral figure, which, however, is manifestly false. [We must not, I say, make any such allegations because] although it is not necessary that I should at any time entertain the notion of God, nevertheless whenever it happens that I think of a first and a sovereign Being, and, so to speak, derive the idea of Him from the storehouse of my mind, it is necessary that I should attribute to Him every sort of perfection, although I do not get so far as to enumerate them all, or to apply my mind to each one in particular. And this necessity suffices to make me conclude (after having recognised that existence is a perfection) that this first and sovereign Being really exists; just as though it is not necessary for me ever to imagine any triangle, yet, whenever I wish to consider a rectilinear figure composed only of three angles, it is absolutely essential that I should attribute to it all those properties which serve to bring about the conclusion that its three angles are not greater than two right angles, even although I may not then be considering this point in particular. But when I consider which figures are capable of being inscribed in the circle, it is in no wise necessary that I should think that all quadrilateral figures are of this number; on the contrary, I cannot even pretend that this is the case, so long as I do not desire to accept anything which I cannot conceive clearly and distinctly. And in consequence there is a great difference between the false suppositions such as this, and the true ideas born within me, the first and principal of which is that of God. For really I discern in many ways that this idea is not something factitious, and depending solely on my thought, but that it is the image of a true and immutable nature; first of all, because I cannot conceive anything but God himself to whose essence existence [necessarily] pertains; in the second place because it is not possible for me to conceive two or more Gods in this same position; and, granted that there is one such God who now exists, I see clearly that it is necessary that He should have existed from all eternity, and that He must exist eternally; and finally, because I know an infinitude of other properties in God, none of which I can either diminish or change.

For the rest, whatever proof or argument I avail myself of, we must always return to the point that it is only those things which we conceive clearly and distinctly that have the power of persuading me entirely. And although amongst the matters which I conceive of in this way, some indeed are manifestly obvious to all, while others only manifest themselves to those who consider them closely and examine them attentively; still, after they have once been discovered, the latter are not esteemed as any less certain than the former. For example, in the case of every right-angled triangle, although it does not so manifestly appear that the square of the base is equal to the squares of the two other sides as that this base is opposite to the greatest angle; still, when this has once been apprehended, we are just as certain of its truth as of the truth of the other. And as regards God, if my mind were not pre-occupied with prejudices, and if my thought did not find itself on all hands diverted by the continual pressure of sensible things, there would be nothing which I could know more immediately and more easily than Him. For is there anything more manifest than that there is a God, that is to say, a Supreme Being, to whose essence alone existence pertains?

And although for a firm grasp of this truth I have need of a strenuous application of mind, at present I not only feel myself to be as assured of it as of all that I hold as most certain, but I also remark that the certainty of all other things depends on it so absolutely, that without this knowledge it is impossible ever to know anything perfectly.

For although I am of such a nature that as long as I understand anything very clearly and distinctly, I am naturally impelled to believe it to be true, yet because I am also of such a nature that I cannot have my mind constantly fixed on the same object in order to perceive it clearly, and as I often recollect having formed a past judgment without at the same time properly recollecting the reasons that led me to make it, it may happen meanwhile that other reasons present themselves to me, which would easily cause me to change my opinion, if I were ignorant of the facts of the existence of God, and thus I should have no true and certain knowledge, but only vague and vacillating opinions. Thus, for example, when I consider the nature of a [rectilinear] triangle, I who have some little knowledge of the principles of geometry recognise quite clearly that the three angles are equal to two right angles, and it is not possible for me not to believe this so long as I apply my mind to its demonstration; but so soon as I abstain from attending to the proof, although I still recollect having clearly comprehended it, it may easily occur that I come to doubt its truth, if I am ignorant of there being a God. For I can persuade myself of having been so constituted by nature that I can easily deceive myself even in those matters which I believe myself to apprehend with the greatest evidence and certainty, especially when I recollect that I have frequently judged matters to be true and certain which other reasons have afterwards impelled me to judge to be altogether false.

But after I have recognised that there is a God—because at the same time I have also recognised that all things depend upon Him, and that He is not a deceiver, and from that have inferred that what I perceive clearly and distinctly cannot fail to be true—although I no longer pay attention to the reasons for which I have judged this to be true, provided that I recollect having clearly and distinctly perceived it no contrary reason can be brought forward which could ever cause me to doubt of its truth; and thus I have a true and certain knowledge of it. And this same knowledge extends likewise to all other things which I recollect having formerly demonstrated, such as the truths of geometry and the like; for what can be alleged against them to cause me to place them in doubt? Will it be said that my nature is such as to cause me to be frequently deceived? But I already know that I cannot be deceived in the judgment whose grounds I know clearly. Will it be said that I formerly held many things to be true and certain which I have afterwards recognised to be false? But I had not had any clear and distinct knowledge of these things, and not as yet knowing the rule whereby I assure myself of the truth, I had been impelled to give my assent from reasons which I have since recognised to be less strong than I had at the time imagined them to be. What further objection can then be raised? That possibly I am dreaming (an objection I myself made a little while ago), or that all the thoughts which I now have are no more true than the phantasies of my dreams? But even though I slept the case would be the same, for all that is clearly present to my mind is absolutely true.

And so I very clearly recognise that the certainty and truth of all knowledge depends alone on the knowledge of the true God, in so much that, before I knew Him, I could not have a perfect knowledge of any other thing. And now that I know Him I have the means of acquiring a perfect knowledge of an infinitude of things, not only of those which relate to God Himself and other intellectual matters, but also of those which pertain to corporeal nature in so far as it is the object of pure mathematics [which have no concern with whether it exists or not].

MEDITATION VI

Of the Existence of Material Things, and of the Real Distinction Between the Soul and Body of Man

Nothing further now remains but to inquire whether material things exist. And certainly I at least know that these may exist in so far as they are considered as the objects of pure mathematics, since in this aspect I perceive them clearly and distinctly. For there is no doubt that God possesses the power to produce everything that I am capable of perceiving with distinctness, and I have never deemed that anything was impossible for Him, unless I found a contradiction in attempting to conceive it clearly. Further, the faculty of imagination which I possess, and of which, experience tells me, I make use when I apply myself to the consideration of material things, is capable of persuading me of their existence; for when I attentively consider what imagination is, I find that it is nothing but a certain application of the faculty of knowledge to the body which is immediately present to it, and which therefore exists.

And to render this quite clear, I remark in the first place the difference that exists between the imagination and pure intellection [or conception]. For example, when I imagine a triangle, I do not conceive it only as a figure comprehended by three lines, but I also apprehend these three lines as present by the power and inward vision of my mind, and this is what I call imagining. But if I desire to think of a chiliagon, I certainly conceive truly that it is a figure composed of a thousand sides, just as easily as I conceive of a triangle that it is a figure of three sides only; but I cannot in any way imagine the thousand sides of a chiliagon [as I do the three sides of a triangle], nor do I, so to speak, regard them as present [with the eyes of my mind]. And although in accordance with the habit I have formed of always employing the aid of my imagination when I think of corporeal things, it may happen that in imagining a chiliagon I confusedly represent to myself some figure, yet it is very evident that this figure is not a chiliagon, since it in no way differs from that which I represent to myself when I think of a myriagon or any other many-sided figure; nor does it serve my purpose in discovering the properties which go to form the distinction between a chiliagon and other polygons. But if the question turns upon a pentagon, it is quite true that I can conceive its figure as well as that of a chiliagon without the help of my imagination; but I can also imagine it by applying the attention of my mind to each of its five sides, and at the same time to the space which they enclose. And thus I clearly recognise that I have need of a particular effort of mind in order to effect the act of imagination, such as I do not require in order to understand, and this particular effort of mind clearly manifests the difference which exists, between imagination and pure intellection.

I remark besides that this power of imagination which is in one, inasmuch as it differs from the power of understanding, is in no wise a necessary element in my nature, or in [my essence, that is to say, in] the essence of my mind; for although I did not possess it I should doubtless ever remain the same as I now am, from which it appears that we might conclude that it depends on something which differs from me. And I easily conceive that if some body exists with which my mind is conjoined and united in such a way that it can apply itself to consider it when it pleases, it may be that by this means it can imagine corporeal objects; so that this mode of thinking differs from pure intellection only inasmuch as mind in its intellectual activity in some manner turns on itself, and considers some of the ideas which it possesses in itself; while in imagining it turns towards the body, and there beholds in it

something conformable to the idea which it has either conceived of itself or perceived by the senses. I easily understand, I say, that the
imagination could be thus constituted if it is true that body exists; and
because I can discover no other convenient mode of explaining it, I
conjecture with probability that body does exist; but this is only with
probability, and although I examine all things with care, I nevertheless
do not find that from this distinct idea of corporeal nature, which I
have in my imagination, I can derive any argument from which there
will necessarily be deduced the existence of body.

But I am in the habit of imagining many other things besides this
corporeal nature which is the object of pure mathematics, to wit, the
colours, sounds, scents, pain, and other such things, although less distinctly. And inasmuch as I perceive these things much better through
the senses, by the medium of which, and by the memory, they seem to
have reached my imagination, I believe that, in order to examine them
more conveniently, it is right that I should at the same time investigate
the nature of sense perception, and that I should see if from the ideas
which I apprehend by this mode of thought, which I call feeling, I cannot derive some certain proof of the existence of corporeal objects.

And first of all I shall recall to my memory those matters which I
hitherto held to be true, as having perceived them through the senses,
and the foundations on which my belief has rested; in the next place
I shall examine the reasons which have since obliged me to place them
in doubt; in the last place I shall consider which of them I must now
believe.

First of all, then, I perceived that I had a head, hands, feet, and all
other members of which this body—which I considered as a part, or
possibly even as the whole, of myself—is composed. Further I was sensible that this body was placed amidst many others, from which it was
capable of being affected in many different ways, beneficial and hurtful, and I remarked that a certain feeling of pleasure accompanied
those that were beneficial, and pain those which were harmful. And in
addition to this pleasure and pain, I also experienced hunger, thirst,
and other similar appetites, as also certain corporeal inclinations towards joy, sadness, anger, and other similar passions. And outside myself, in addition to extension, figure, and motions of bodies, I remarked
in them hardness, heat, and all other tactile qualities, and, further,
light and colour, and scents and sounds, the variety of which gave me
the means of distinguishing the sky, the earth, the sea, and generally
all the other bodies, one from the other. And certainly, considering the
ideas of all these qualities which presented themselves to my mind,
and which alone I perceived properly or immediately, it was not without reason that I believed myself to perceive objects quite different
from my thought, to wit, bodies from which those ideas proceeded; for

I found by experience that these ideas presented themselves to me without my consent being requisite, so that I could not perceive any object, however desirous I might be, unless it were present to the organs of sense; and it was not in my power not to perceive it, when it was present. And because the ideas which I received through the senses were much more lively, more clear, and even, in their own way, more distinct than any of those which I could of myself frame in meditation, or than those I found impressed on my memory, it appeared as though they could not have proceeded from my mind, so that they must necessarily have been produced in me by some other things. And having no knowledge of those objects excepting the knowledge which the ideas themselves gave me, nothing was more likely to occur to my mind than that the objects were similar to the ideas which were caused. And because I likewise remembered that I had formerly made use of my senses rather than my reason, and recognised that the ideas which I formed of myself were not so distinct as those which I perceived through the senses, and that they were most frequently even composed of portions of these last, I persuaded myself easily that I had no idea in my mind which had not formerly come to me through the senses. Nor was it without some reason that I believed that this body (which by a certain special right I call my own) belonged to me more properly and more strictly than any other; for in fact I could never be separated from it as from other bodies; I experienced in it and on account of it all my appetites and affections, and finally I was touched by the feeling of pain and the titillation of pleasure in its parts, and not in the parts of other bodies which were separated from it. But when I inquired, why, from some, I know not what, painful sensation, there follows sadness of mind, and from the pleasurable sensation there arises joy, or why this mysterious pinching of the stomach which I call hunger causes me to desire to eat, and dryness of throat causes a desire to drink, and so on, I could give no reason excepting that nature taught me so; for there is certainly no affinity (that I at least can understand) between the craving of the stomach and the desire to eat, any more than between the perception of whatever causes pain and the thought of sadness which arises from this perception. And in the same way it appeared to me that I had learned from nature all the other judgments which I formed regarding the objects of my senses, since I remarked that these judgments were formed in me before I had the leisure to weigh and consider any reasons which might oblige me to make them.

But afterwards many experiences little by little destroyed all the faith which I had rested in my senses; for I from time to time observed that those towers which from afar appeared to me to be round, more closely observed seemed square, and that colossal statues raised on the summit of these towers, appeared as quite tiny statues when viewed from the bottom; and so in an infinitude of other cases I found error in judgments founded on the external senses. And not only in those founded on the external senses, but even in those founded on the internal as well; for is there anything more intimate or more internal than pain? And yet I have learned from some persons whose arms or legs have been cut off, that they sometimes seemed to feel pain in the part which had been amputated, which made me think that I could not be quite certain that it was a certain member which pained me, even although I felt pain in it. And to those grounds of doubt I have lately added two others, which are very general; the first is that I never have believed myself to feel anything in waking moments which I cannot also sometimes believe myself to feel when I sleep, and as I do not think that these things which I seem to feel in sleep, proceed from objects outside of me, I do not see any reason why I should have this belief regarding objects which I seem to perceive while awake. The other was that being still ignorant, or rather supposing myself to be ignorant, of the author of my being, I saw nothing to prevent me from having been so constituted by nature that I might be deceived even in matters which seemed to me to be most certain. And as to the grounds on which I was formerly persuaded of the truth of sensible objects, I had not much trouble in replying to them. For since nature seemed to cause me to lean towards many things from which reason repelled me, I did not believe that I should trust much to the teachings of nature. And although the ideas which I receive by the senses do not depend on my will, I did not think that one should for that reason conclude that they proceeded from things different from myself, since possibly some faculty might be discovered in me—though hitherto unknown to me—which produced them.

But now that I begin to know myself better, and to discover more clearly the author of my being, I do not in truth think that I should rashly admit all the matters which the senses seem to teach us, but, on the other hand, I do not think that I should doubt them all universally.

And first of all, because I know that all things which I apprehend clearly and distinctly can be created by God as I apprehend them, it suffices that I am able to apprehend one thing apart from another clearly and distinctly in order to be certain that the one is different from the other, since they may be made to exist in separation at least by the omnipotence of God; and it does not signify by what power this separation is made in order to compel me to judge them to be different: and, therefore, just because I know certainly that I exist, and that meanwhile I do not remark that any other thing necessarily pertains to my nature or essence, excepting that I am a thinking thing, I rightly conclude that my essence consists solely in the fact that I am a thinking thing [or a substance whose whole essence or nature is to think].

And although possibly (or rather certainly, as I shall say in a moment) I possess a body with which I am very intimately conjoined, yet because, on the one side, I have a clear and distinct idea of myself inasmuch as I am only a thinking and unextended thing, and as, on the other, I possess a distinct idea of body, inasmuch as it is only an extended and unthinking thing, it is certain that this I [that is to say, my soul by which I am what I am], is entirely and absolutely distinct from my body, and can exist without it.

I further find in myself faculties employing modes of thinking peculiar to themselves, to wit, the faculties of imagination and feeling, without which I can easily conceive myself clearly and distinctly as a complete being; while, on the other hand, they cannot be so conceived apart from me, that is without an intelligent substance in which they reside, for [in the notion we have of these faculties, or, to use the language of the Schools] in their formal concept, some kind of intellection is comprised, from which I infer that they are distinct from me as its modes are from a thing. I observe also in me some other faculties such as that of change of position, the assumption of different figures and such like, which cannot be conceived, any more than can the preceding, apart from some substance to which they are attached, and consequently cannot exist without it; but it is very clear that these faculties, if it be true that they exist, must be attached to some corporeal or extended substance, and not to an intelligent substance, since in the clear and distinct conception of these there is some sort of extension found to be present, but no intellection at all. There is certainly further in me a certain passive faculty of perception, that is, of receiving and recognising the ideas of sensible things, but this would be useless to me [and I could in no way avail myself of it], if there were not either in me or in some other thing another active faculty capable of forming and producing these ideas. But this active faculty cannot exist in me [inasmuch as I am a thing that thinks] seeing that it does not presuppose thought, and also that those ideas are often produced in me without my contributing in any way to the same, and often even against my will; it is thus necessarily the case that the faculty resides in some substance different from me in which all the reality which is objectively in the ideas that are produced by this faculty is formally or eminently contained, as I remarked before. And this substance is either a body, that is, a corporeal nature in which there is contained formally [and really] all that which is objectively [and by representation] in those ideas, or it is God Himself, or some other creature more noble than body in which that same is contained eminently. But, since God is no deceiver, it is very manifest that He does not communicate to me these ideas immediately and by Himself, nor yet by the intervention of some creature in which their reality is not formally, but only eminently, contained. For since He has given me no faculty to recognise that this is the case, but, on the other hand, a very great inclination to believe [that they are sent to me or] that they are conveyed to me by corporeal objects, I do not see how He could be defended from the accusation of deceit if these ideas were produced by causes other than corporeal objects. Hence we must allow that corporeal things exist. However, they are perhaps not exactly what we perceive by the senses, since this comprehension by the senses is in many instances very obscure and confused; but we must at least admit that all things which I conceive in them clearly and distinctly, that is to say, all things which, speaking generally, are comprehended in the object of pure mathematics, are truly to be recognised as external objects.

As to other things, however, which are either particular only, as, for example, that the sun is of such and such a figure, etc., or which are less clearly and distinctly conceived, such as light, sound, pain and the like, it is certain that although they are very dubious and uncertain, yet on the sole ground that God is not a deceiver, and that consequently He has not permitted any falsity to exist in my opinion which He has not likewise given me the faculty of correcting, I may assuredly hope to conclude that I have within me the means of arriving at the truth even here. And first of all there is no doubt that in all things which nature teaches me there is some truth contained; for by nature, considered in general, I now understand no other thing than either God Himself or else the order and disposition which God has established in created things; and by my nature in particular I understand no other thing than the complexus of all the things which God has given me.

But there is nothing which this nature teaches me more expressly [nor more sensibly] than that I have a body which is adversely affected when I feel pain, which has need of food or drink when I experience the feelings of hunger and thirst, and so on; nor can I doubt there being some truth in all this.

Nature also teaches me by these sensations of pain, hunger, thirst, etc., that I am not only lodged in my body as a pilot in a vessel, but that I am very closely united to it, and so to speak so intermingled with it that I seem to compose with it one whole. For if that were not the case, when my body is hurt, I, who am merely a thinking thing, should not feel pain, for I should perceive this wound by the understanding only, just as the sailor perceives by sight when something is damaged in his vessel; and when my body has need of drink or food, I should clearly understand the fact without being warned of it by confused feelings of hunger and thirst. For all these sensations of hunger, thirst, pain, etc. are in truth none other than certain confused modes of thought which are produced by the union and apparent intermingling of mind and body.

Moreover, nature teaches me that many other bodies exist around mine, of which some are to be avoided, and others sought after. And certainly from the fact that I am sensible of different sorts of colours, sounds, scents, tastes, heat, hardness, etc., I very easily conclude that there are in the bodies from which all these diverse sense-perceptions proceed certain variations which answer to them, although possibly these are not really at all similar to them. And also from the fact that amongst these different sense-perceptions some are very agreeable to me and others disagreeable, it is quite certain that my body (or rather myself in my entirety, inasmuch as I am formed of body and soul) may receive different impressions agreeable and disagreeable from the other bodies which surround it.

But there are many other things which nature seems to have taught me, but which at the same time I have never really received from her, but which have been brought about in my mind by a certain habit which I have of forming inconsiderate judgments on things; and thus it may easily happen that these judgments contain some error. Take, for example, the opinion which I hold that all space in which there is nothing that affects [or makes an impression on] my senses is void; that in a body which is warm there is something entirely similar to the idea of heat which is in me; that in a white or green body there is the same whiteness or greenness that I perceive; that in a bitter or sweet body there is the same taste, and so on in other instances; that the stars, the towers, and all other distant bodies are of the same figure and size as they appear from far off to our eyes, etc. But in order that in this there should be nothing which I do not conceive distinctly, I should define exactly what I really understand when I say that I am taught somewhat by nature. For here I take nature in a more limited signification than when I term it the sum of all the things given me by God, since in this sum many things are comprehended which only pertain to mind (and to these I do not refer in speaking of nature) such as the notion which I have of the fact that what has once been done cannot ever be undone and an infinitude of such things which I know by the light of nature [without the help of the body]; and seeing that it comprehends many other matters besides which only pertain to body, and are no longer here contained under the name of nature, such as the quality of weight which it possesses and the like, with which I also do not deal; for in talking of nature I only treat of those things given by God to me as a being composed of mind and body. But the nature here described truly teaches me to flee from things which cause the sensation of pain, and seek after the things which communicate to me the sentiment of pleasure and so forth; but I do not see that beyond this it teaches me that from those diverse sense-perceptions we should ever form any conclusion regarding things outside of us, without having [carefully and maturely] mentally examined them before-hand. For it seems to me that it is mind alone, and not mind and body in conjunction, that is requisite to a knowledge of the truth in regard to such things. Thus, although a star makes no larger an impression on my eye than the flame of a little candle there is yet in me no real or positive propensity impelling me to believe that it is not greater than that flame; but I have judged it to be so from my earliest years, with-out any rational foundation. And although in approaching fire I feel heat, and in approaching it a little too near I even feel pain, there is at the same time no reason in this which could persuade me that there is in the fire something resembling this heat any more than there is in it something resembling the pain; all that I have any reason to believe from this is, that there is something in it, whatever it may be, which excites in me these sensations of heat or of pain. So also, although there are spaces in which I find nothing which excites my senses, I must not from that conclude that these spaces contain no body; for I see in this, as in other similar things, that I have been in the habit of perverting the order of nature, because these perceptions of sense hav-ing been placed within me by nature merely for the purpose of signify-ing to my mind what things are beneficial or hurtful to the composite whole of which it forms a part, and being up to that point sufficiently clear and distinct, I yet avail myself of them as though they were abso-lute rules by which I might immediately determine the essence of the bodies which are outside me, as to which, in fact, they can teach me nothing but what is most obscure and confused.

But I have already sufficiently considered how, notwithstanding the supreme goodness of God, falsity enters into the judgments I make. Only here a new difficulty is presented—one respecting those things the pursuit or avoidance of which is taught me by nature, and also re-specting the internal sensations which I possess, and in which I seem to have sometimes detected error [and thus to be directly deceived by my own nature]. To take an example, the agreeable taste of some food in which poison has been intermingled may induce me to partake of the poison, and thus deceive me. It is true, at the same time, that in this case nature may be excused, for it only induces me to desire food in which I find a pleasant taste, and not to desire the poison which is unknown to it; and thus I can infer nothing from this fact, except that my nature is not omniscient, at which there is certainly no reason to be astonished, since man, being finite in nature, can only have knowl-edge the perfectness of which is limited.

But we not unfrequently deceive ourselves even in those things to which we are directly impelled by nature, as happens with those who when they are sick desire to drink or eat things hurtful to them. It will perhaps be said here that the cause of their deceptiveness is that their nature is corrupt, but that does not remove the difficulty, because a sick man is none the less truly God's creature than he who is in health; and it is therefore as repugnant to God's goodness for the one to have a deceitful nature as it is for the other. And as a clock composed of wheels and counter-weights no less exactly observes the laws of nature when it is badly made, and does not show the time properly, than when it entirely satisfies the wishes of its maker, and as, if I consider the body of a man as being a sort of machine so built up and composed of nerves, muscles, veins, blood and skin, that though there were no mind in it at all, it would not cease to have the same motions as at present, exception being made of those movements which are due to the direction of the will, and in consequence depend upon the mind [as opposed to those which operate by the disposition of its organs], I easily recognise that it would be as natural to this body, supposing it to be, for example, dropsical, to suffer the parchedness of the throat which usually signifies to the mind the feeling of thirst, and to be disposed by this parched feeling to move the nerves and other parts in the way requisite for drinking, and thus to augment its malady and do harm to itself, as it is natural to it, when it has no indisposition, to be impelled to drink for its good by a similar cause. And although, considering the use to which the clock has been destined by its maker, I may say that it deflects from the order of its nature when it does not indicate the hours correctly; and as, in the same way, considering the machine of the human body as having been formed by God in order to have in itself all the movements usually manifested there, I have reason for thinking that it does not follow the order of nature when, if the throat is dry, drinking does harm to the conservation of health, nevertheless I recognise at the same time that this last mode of explaining nature is very different from the other. For this is but a purely verbal characterisation depending entirely on my thought, which compares a sick man and a badly constructed clock with the idea which I have of a healthy man and a well made clock, and it is hence extrinsic to the things to which it is applied; but according to the other interpretation of the term nature I understand something which is truly found in things and which is therefore not without some truth.

But certainly although in regard to the dropsical body it is only so to speak to apply an extrinsic term when we say that its nature is corrupted, inasmuch as apart from the need to drink, the throat is parched; yet in regard to the composite whole, that is to say, to the mind or soul united to this body, it is not a purely verbal predicate, but a real error of nature, for it to have thirst when drinking would be hurtful to it. And thus it still remains to inquire how the goodness of God does not prevent the nature of man so regarded from being fallacious.

In order to begin this examination, then, I here say, in the first place, that there is a great difference between mind and body, inasmuch as body is by nature always divisible, and the mind is entirely indivisible. For, as a matter of fact, when I consider the mind, that is to say, myself inasmuch as I am only a thinking thing, I cannot distinguish in myself any parts, but apprehend myself to be clearly one and entire; and although the whole mind seems to be united to the whole body, yet if a foot, or an arm, or some other part, is separated from my body, I am aware that nothing has been taken away from my mind. And the faculties of willing, feeling, conceiving, etc. cannot be properly speaking said to be its parts, for it is one and the same mind which employs itself in willing and in feeling and understanding. But it is quite otherwise with corporeal or extended objects, for there is not one of these imaginable by me which my mind cannot easily divide into parts, and which consequently I do not recognise as being divisible; this would be sufficient to teach me that the mind or soul of man is entirely different from the body, if I had not already learned it from other sources.

I further notice that the mind does not receive the impressions from all parts of the body immediately, but only from the brain, or perhaps even from one of its smallest parts, to wit, from that in which the common sense is said to reside, which, whenever it is disposed in the same particular way, conveys the same thing to the mind, although meanwhile the other portions of the body may be differently disposed, as is testified by innumerable experiments which it is unnecessary here to recount.

I notice, also, that the nature of body is such that none of its parts can be moved by another part a little way off which cannot also be moved in the same way by each one of the parts which are between the two, although this more remote part does not act at all. As, for example, in the cord ABCD [which is in tension] if we pull the last part D, the first part A will not be moved in any way differently from what would be the case if one of the intervening parts B or C were pulled, and the last part D were to remain unmoved. And in the same way, when I feel pain in my foot, my knowledge of physics teaches me that this sensation is communicated by means of nerves dispersed through the foot, which, being extended like cords from there to the brain, when they are contracted in the foot, at the same time contract the inmost portions of the brain which is their extremity and place of origin, and then excite a certain movement which nature has established in order to cause the mind to be affected by a sensation of pain represented as existing in the foot. But because these nerves must pass through the tibia, the thigh, the loins, the back and the neck, in order to reach from the leg to the brain, it may happen that although their extremities which are in the foot are not affected, but only certain ones of their intervening parts [which pass by the loins or the neck], this action will excite the same movement in the brain that might have been excited there by a hurt received in the foot, in consequence of which the mind will necessarily feel in the foot the same pain as if it had received a hurt. And the same holds good of all the other perceptions of our senses.

I notice finally that since each of the movements which are in the portion of the brain by which the mind is immediately affected brings about one particular sensation only, we cannot under the circumstances imagine anything more likely than that this movement, amongst all the sensations which it is capable of impressing on it, causes mind to be affected by that one which is best fitted and most generally useful for the conservation of the human body when it is in health. But experience makes us aware that all the feelings with which nature inspires us are such as I have just spoken of; and there is therefore nothing in them which does not give testimony to the power and goodness of the God [who has produced them]. Thus, for example, when the nerves which are in the feet are violently or more than usually moved, their movement, passing through the medulla of the spine to the inmost parts of the brain, gives a sign to the mind which makes it feel somewhat, to wit, pain, as though in the foot, by which the mind is excited to do its utmost to remove the cause of the evil as dangerous and hurtful to the foot. It is true that God could have constituted the nature of man in such a way that this same movement in the brain would have conveyed something quite different to the mind; for example, it might have produced consciousness of itself either in so far as it is in the brain, or as it is in the foot, or as it is in some other place between the foot and the brain, or it might finally have produced consciousness of anything else whatsoever; but none of all this would have contributed so well to the conservation of the body. Similarly, when we desire to drink, a certain dryness of the throat is produced which moves its nerves, and by their means the internal portions of the brain; and this movement causes in the mind the sensation of thirst, because in this case there is nothing more useful to us than to become aware that we have need to drink for the conservation of our health; and the same holds good in other instances.

From this it is quite clear that, notwithstanding the supreme goodness of God, the nature of man, inasmuch as it is composed of mind and body, cannot be otherwise than sometimes a source of deception. For if there is any cause which excites, not in the foot but in some part of the nerves which are extended between the foot and the brain, or even in the brain itself, the same movement which usually is produced when the foot is detrimentally affected, pain will be experienced as though it were in the foot, and the sense will thus naturally be deceived; for since the same movement in the brain is capable of causing but one sensation in the mind, and this sensation is much more frequently excited by a cause which hurts the foot than by another existing in some other quarter, it is reasonable that it should convey to the mind pain in the foot rather than in any other part of the body. And although the parchedness of the throat does not always proceed, as it usually does, from the fact that drinking is necessary for the health of the body, but sometimes comes from quite a different cause, as is the case with dropsical patients, it is yet much better that it should mislead on this occasion than if, on the other hand, it were always to deceive us when the body is in good health; and so on in similar cases.

And certainly this consideration is of great service to me, not only in enabling me to recognise all the errors to which my nature is subject, but also in enabling me to avoid them or to correct them more easily. For knowing that all my senses more frequently indicate to me truth than falsehood respecting the things which concern that which is beneficial to the body, and being able almost always to avail myself of many of them in order to examine one particular thing, and, besides that, being able to make use of my memory in order to connect the present with the past, and of my understanding which already has discovered all the causes of my errors, I ought no longer to fear that falsity may be found in matters every day presented to me by my senses. And I ought to set aside all the doubts of these past days as hyperbolical and ridiculous, particularly that very common uncertainty respecting sleep, which I could not distinguish from the waking state; for at present I find a very notable difference between the two, inasmuch as our memory can never connect our dreams one with the other, or with the whole course of our lives, as it unites events which happen to us while we are awake. And, as a matter of fact, if someone, while I was awake, quite suddenly appeared to me and disappeared as fast as do the images which I see in sleep, so that I could not know from whence the form came nor whither it went, it would not be without reason that I should deem it a spectre or a phantom formed by my brain [and similar to those which I form in sleep], rather than a real man. But when I perceive things as to which I know distinctly both the place from which they proceed, and that in which they are, and the time at which they appeared to me; and when, without any interruption, I can connect the perceptions which I have of them with the whole course of my life, I am perfectly assured that these perceptions occur while I am waking and not during sleep. And I ought in no wise to doubt the truth of such matters, if, after having called up all my senses, my memory, and my understanding, to examine them, nothing is brought to evidence by any one of them which is repugnant to what is set forth by the others. For because God is in no wise a deceiver, it follows that I am not deceived in this. But because the exigencies of action often oblige us to make up our minds before having leisure to examine matters carefully, we must confess that the life of man is very frequently subject to error in respect to individual objects, and we must in the end acknowledge the infirmity of our nature.

(From *The Philosophical Works of Descartes,* trans. by E. S. Haldane and G. R. T. Ross. New York: Dover Publications, Inc., 1911.)

Review Questions

1. Describe the philosophical skepticism of the seventeenth century to which Descartes reacted.
2. Discuss the role of *cogito ergo sum* (I think, therefore I am) in the philosophy of Descartes.
3. What is the meaning of deduction? What is its role in mathematics?
4. Is there any difference between *deduction* and *rationalism*?
5. Explain Descartes' philosophical method.
6. What is the meaning of *universal mathematics*? Compare Descartes with Pythagoras.
7. Explain how Descartes arrives at the conclusion that man consists of spirit only. How does this generate the mind–body problem?
8. Discuss the following: the mind–body problem as originated in modern times by Descartes stemmed from his failure to be consistently faithful to experience.
9. Compare the ontological argument of Descartes with that of St. Anselm.
10. What do you think of Descartes' demonstration of the existence of the external world?
11. In what way can Cartesian philosophy by considered as paving the way for a mechanistic interpretation of the world?

11

Baruch Spinoza (1632–1677)

Introduction

The seventeenth century is the only century in which a book entitled *Ethics, Demonstrated in a Geometrical Manner* could have been written. It was a tribute by Baruch (Benedict) Spinoza to the mathematical method, to the demand for rigorous fidelity to clear and distinct ideas, and to the certitude attending the deductive method. Spinoza (1632–77) was of Jewish-Portuguese ancestry; his family emigrated to Amsterdam so that they could practice their faith freely. The young Spinoza was an intense student, a linguist, a scholar of Jewish sacred writings and of the Kabbala, an amalgam of Jewish and neo-Platonic writings. As he began to develop his own thought, he became less able to accept the orthodox Judaism of his family and was at length excommunicated from the synagogue at the age of twenty-four. He earned his livelihood as a lens maker, which was, in a sense, the practical aspect of his theoretical knowledge of optics. Though he led a retired life, he was the center of active philosophical discussion; he enjoyed a wide reputation in intellectual circles, not because of the publication of his works, which for the most part appeared posthumously, but because of privately circulated papers. He was even offered a professorship in philosophy at the University of Heidelberg but rejected it, feeling that he could better maintain his intellectual freedom unattached to academe.

The title of Spinoza's major work is a declaration of his main interest: the conduct of human life. What, he asked, can we finally count on as happiness for man, as blessedness, as salvation? To achieve this objective, Spinoza had to develop an entire metaphysics that embraced all reality; only then could reality's constituents, like human conduct, be meaningfully considered. If a part is not seen in its totality, it is not seen at all. Spinoza's effort to see totality first has been likened to seeing reality as a pyramid from the top down rather than from the base up. His philosophical vision is of all reality as a whole, as one; if *one* reality is given, only *one* substance is given, which Spinoza variously calls *substance, nature,* or *God*. If there is only one substance, everything is one with substance, or one with nature, or one with God. Spinoza's system is *monistic*, and because there is a complete identification of reality with God, his metaphysics has often been called *pantheistic monism*. Further, striking a chord reminiscent of Greek philosophy, Spinoza held that, because whatever is, *is*, there is a necessity pervading reality and things are necessarily what they are.

Spinoza's notion of God goes completely against the traditional doctrine, in which God is transcendent, personal, and infinitely free; He is the Creator who chooses to create *freely*, not out of necessity. Of all reality, God is the only necessary being; all other beings, though they truly are, are beings whose existence is not necessary. Bearing in mind that one's theist is someone else's atheist, it is not surprising that Spinoza was an atheist to many of his contemporaries; in comparison to the romantic writers of the following century, he was a man who was drunk with God.

Let us follow the course Spinoza takes to make his system cohere. In the *Ethics*, which looks like a manual of mathematics, with definitions, axioms, theorems, and Q.E.D.'s, the definition of substance is given as "that which is in itself, and is conceived through itself . . . that of which a conception can be formed independently of any other conception." As we analyze this definition, a number of concepts emerge. Typical of the rationalist cast of mind, the movement is from idea to things, and the *conception* of reality is what reality *is*. There is a perfect correspondence between the logical order (within the mind) and the ontological order (outside the mind). Further, what can the definition of substance refer to, except reality taken as a whole? It cannot refer to any part of reality, for any part, by its nature, cannot be conceived of except in reference to the whole; therefore, it cannot be "conceived through itself." Again, substance has to be *infinite*, for anything less than infinite would mean that it could not be "formed independently of any other conception."

Spinoza's use of the word *substance* differs greatly, therefore, from the traditional use where it is generally correlative with *accident*. An accident is a quality like white, square, or smiling; it is clear that these qualities do not exist on their own, for *something* has to be white, or square, or smiling (except the smile of the Cheshire cat!). The something that is white, or square, or smiling is called *substance*, and, in a relative sense, it exists on its own: the accidents exist in and through the substance, but the substance does not exist in and through the accidents. Spinoza, then, in his use of the word *substance*, intensified the meaning of independence and made it apply uniquely to reality taken as a whole.

Even though Spinoza considers everything as one with substance, we still have to ask, how does he understand individual things *as* tions of substance; this requires some explanation. Substance is infinite and possesses an infinite number of constituents called *attributes*. An attribute is defined as that which the intellect perceives as constituting the essence of substance. That is, attributes are not conceivable in and through anything other than themselves; therefore, we can only perceive them as constituting the essence of substance. However, only two such attributes are known to us: *extension* and *thought*. Extension (body, matter, quantity) refers to all extended things taken together as one, and thought (mind, understanding, spirit) refers to all minds taken together as one. Now, all particular things of our experience — this person, this pencil, this act, this mental activity — come under either the attribute of thought or the attribute of extension. They are called by Spinoza *modes*: A mode is a modification of Substance, or that which exists in and is conceived through something other than itself. This scheme of substance-attribute-mode is Spinoza's response to a problem as old as philosophy itself: how is reality as one related to reality as many? Regarding an individual pencil, a full statement of Spinoza's view would be as follows: this pencil is a mode-of-substance-under-the-attribute-of-body; that is, all individuals (particulars) are one-with-substance without losing their own individuality (particularity).

Spinoza's reaction to Cartesian dualism can be appreciated at this juncture. For Descartes, "John" is identifiable as a man because mind and body are *two* substances joined so that they may act together. For Spinoza, however, "John" is identifiable as a man because mind and body are two attributes of *one* substance; these two attributes do not have to brought together, as in Descartes' view, because they are already together. Without trying to discuss the merits of either scheme, it is quite clear that Descartes' solution to the mind–body problem was unsatisfactory to Spinoza because there was no way, once their unity was disturbed, to reunite them. Spinoza's scheme ensures that there is no separation to start with.

All philosophers, in one way or another, hold to a hierarchy of knowledge; that is, there are degrees of knowledge, one of higher value than another. Spinoza speaks of three types of knowledge, the first of which is knowledge that is *confused and inadequate*, inasmuch as it pertains to ideas of sensation; *scientific* knowledge is knowledge that is adequate and clear, manifesting some consistency and logical relationship among ideas. The third degree is the one Spinoza has been pursuing all along, namely, *intuitive* knowledge — the intuition of things as they are in the whole of reality, the vision of things in nature; it is the grasp of unity, or the intellectual contemplation of the real as one with God. Intellectual contemplation of God is, we will recall, the

individual? His answer is that individuals exist as modes or modifica-
final stage of man's ascent to God in the Western tradition and is the
chief characteristic of man's happiness, inchoate here but complete
hereafter. It signifies the utmost clarity in our understanding of who
God is and our relationship with Him. Because we see Him as He is,
we love Him as He is, as the all-good and loving God who created us
by a free act of His loving creation. But for Spinoza, intellectual contemplation is the seeing of things in their eternal *necessity*. Things are
what they are because they have to be that way; in God all things are
necessary. Pleasure and pain, good and evil, take on a new appearance
once necessity is grasped. Evil, for example, is evil only from man's
viewpoint, not God's; when seen from God's viewpoint, evil is understood to be natural and part of nature's necessity. Human freedom,
which, for Spinoza, is philosophy's ultimate goal, is not the prerogative
of spontaneous choice but the highest intellectual grasp of necessity,
the intuition of the eternal God. It is the third kind of knowledge, from
which arises, necessarily, the intellectual love of God. Freedom, happiness, blessedness, and salvation are synonyms and consist in "the constant and eternal love towards God, or is God's love towards men." The
one who understands this is the wise man, described by Spinoza as the
person who is conscious of himself, of God, and of things, and, guided
by eternal necessity, always possesses true acquiescence of his spirit.
Such an understanding is found in very few people but, indeed, "all
things excellent are as difficult as they are rare."

The fact that, for Spinoza, every single thing must be thought of in
concert with others has special relevance for his philosophy of community. Insofar as human beings associate with one another naturally, the
consideration of society is found in the *Ethics*; but his ideas on the political shaping of society are found in the political works,
Theologico-Political Treatise and *A Political Treatise*.

All things act according to the powers assigned them by nature, and
inasmuch as this principle applies to men in a unique way, men lead
their lives by *power*, even to the extent that they achieve, sometimes
by force and cunning, what they can for themselves: "By the right and
ordinance of nature, I merely mean those natural laws wherewith we
conceive every individual to be conditioned by nature, so as to live and
act in a given way . . . the rights of an individual extend to the utmost
limits of his power as it has been conditioned. Now it is the sovereign
law and right of nature that each individual should endeavor to preserve itself as it is, without regard to anything but itself." The phrase
used here, *natural law*, has nothing to do with the traditional scholastic use of the phrase, in which it is defined as moral law; for Spinoza
it is simply a statement of fact regarding the place man occupies in na-

ture's pyramid. Left to themselves, in the state of nature, human beings would be a sorry lot indeed, for "men are naturally enemies."

These raw characteristics of man's nature are compensated for by *reason*. Human life is to be a life of reason, for by it man is able to hold his emotions, especially anger and hatred, in control, and it is precisely this which is made possible by human beings living together with each other: "to man there is nothing more useful than man — nothing." Everyone wants to live without fear, putting at a distance enmity, hatred, anger, and deceit: "when all is said, they will find that men can provide for their wants much more easily by mutual help, and that only by unifying their forces can they escape from the dangers that on every side beset them." So man, by the use of his reason, is able to achieve a higher view of his relationship to other men and to understand that his nature demands society; man is social by nature.

But unless there is some sort of agreement to live together, there will be no living together at all: "men must necessarily come to an agreement to live together as securely and well as possible." This agreement, or *compact*, makes it possible to give man's social nature an organized, specific shape called the *state*; men, by this general compact, yield to the ruling or sovereign power those individual rights that will enable the state to flourish within the sphere of reason. Thus, the good that redounds to man by ceding these rights for the common weal far surpasses what he could lay claim to alone. The laws of the sovereign, directed as they are to the common good, must be obeyed by all, and so firm is Spinoza on this point that he identifies sin with disobedience: "Sin, then, is nothing else but disobedience, which is therefore punished by the right of the State only." Peace, freedom, religious tolerance, justice, harmony, and security all follow a government founded on reason. And of all the various types of civil states, the one having the best promise of reasonableness is *democracy*, defined as "a society which wields all its power as a whole." Further, democracy is, of all forms of government, "the most natural, and the most consonant with individual liberty."

During his lifetime, though he had acquired a reputation for rigorous and innovative thinking, Spinoza was roundly criticized and condemned by both philosophers and theologians. A century or so later, he was rediscovered and reevaluated principally by the German romantics, who saw in his writings a kinship with their own feeling of a closeness with nature. Even so great a writer as Goethe said that his chief concern, in accordance with the teachings of Spinoza, was to gain eternity for his spirit.

Readings

Definitions and Axioms (from *Ethics,* Part I)

Definitions

I

By that which is *self-caused,* I mean that of which the essence involves existence, or that of which the nature is only conceivable as existent.

II. A thing is called *finite after its kind,* when it can be limited by another thing of the same nature; for instance, a body is called finite because we always conceive another greater body. So, also, a thought is limited by another thought, but a body is not limited by thought, nor a thought by body.

III. By *substance,* I mean that which is in itself, and is conceived through itself: in other words, that of which a conception can be formed independently of any other conception.

IV. By *attribute,* I mean that which the intellect perceives as constituting the essence of substance.

V. By *mode,* I mean the modifications of substance, or that which exists in, and is conceived through, something other than itself.

VI. By *God,* I mean a being absolutely infinite—that is, a substance consisting in infinite attributes, of which each expresses eternal and infinite essentiality.

Explanation.—I say absolutely infinite, not infinite after its kind: for, of a thing infinite only after its kind, infinite attributes may be denied; but that which is absolutely infinite, contains in its essence whatever expresses reality, and involves no negation.

VII. That thing is called free, which exists solely by the necessity of its own nature, and of which the action is determined by itself alone. On the other hand, that thing is necessary, or rather constrained, which is determined by something external to itself to a fixed and definite method of existence or action.

VIII. By *eternity,* I mean existence itself, in so far as it is conceived necessarily to follow solely from the definition of that which is eternal.

Explanation.—Existence of this kind is conceived as an eternal truth, like the essence of a thing, and, therefore, cannot be explained by means of continuance or time, though continuance may be conceived without a beginning or end.

Axioms

I. Everything which exists, exists either in itself or in something else.

II. That which cannot be conceived through anything else must be conceived through itself.

III. From a given definite cause an effect necessarily follows; and, on the other hand, if no definite cause be granted, it is impossible that an effect can follow.

IV. The knowledge of an effect depends on and involves the knowledge of a cause.

V. Things which have nothing in common cannot be understood, the one by means of the other; the conception of one does not involve the conception of the other.

VI. A true idea must correspond with its ideate or object.

VII. If a thing can be conceived as non-existing, its essence does not involve existence.

Seven Propositions on Substance (from *Ethics,* Part I)

Propositions

PROP. I. *Substance is by nature prior to its modifications.*

Proof.—This is clear from Deff. iii. and v.

PROP. II. *Two substances, whose attributes are different, have nothing in common.*

Proof.—Also evident from Def. iii. For each must exist in itself, and be conceived through itself; in other words, the conception of one does not imply the conception of the other.

PROP. III. *Things which have nothing in common cannot be one the cause of the other.*

Proof.—If they have nothing in common, it follows that one cannot be apprehended by means of the other (Ax. v.), and, therefore, one cannot be the cause of the other (Ax. iv.). *Q.E.D.*

PROP. IV. *Two or more distinct things are distinguished one from the other, either by the difference of the attributes of the substances, or by the difference of their modifications.*

Proof.—Everything which exists, exists either in itself or in something else (Ax. i.),—that is (by Deff. iii. and v.), nothing is granted in addition to the understanding, except substance and its modifications. Nothing is, therefore, given besides the understanding, by which several things may be distinguished one from the other, except the substances, or, in other words (see Ax. iv.), their attributes and modifications. *Q.E.D.*

PROP. V. *There cannot exist in the universe two or more substances having the same nature or attribute.*

Proof.—If several distinct substances be granted, they must be distinguished one from the other, either by the difference of their attributes, or by the difference of their modifications (Prop. iv.). If only by the difference of their attributes, it will be granted that there cannot be more than one with an identical attribute. If by the difference of their modifications—as substance is naturally prior to its modifications (Prop. i.),—it follows that setting the modifications aside, and considering substance in itself, that is truly, (Deff. iii. and vi.), there cannot be conceived one substance different from another,—that is (by Prop. iv.), there cannot be granted several substances, but one substance only. *Q.E.D.*

PROP. VI. *One substance cannot be produced by another substance.*

Proof.—It is impossible that there should be in the universe two substances with an identical attribute, i.e. which have anything common to them both (Prop. ii.), and, therefore (Prop. iii.), one cannot be the cause of another, neither can one be produced by the other. *Q.E.D.*

Corollary.—Hence it follows that a substance cannot be produced by anything external to itself. For in the universe nothing is granted, save substances and their modifications (as appears from Ax. i. and Deff. iii. and v.). Now (by the last Prop.) substance cannot be produced by another substance, therefore it cannot be produced by anything external to itself. *Q.E.D.* This is shown still more readily by the absurdity of the contradictory. For, if substance be produced by an external cause, the knowledge of it would depend on the knowledge of its cause (Ax. iv.), and (by Def. iii.) it would itself not be substance.

PROP. VII. *Existence belongs to the nature of substance.*

Proof.—Substance cannot be produced by anything external (Corollary, Prop. vi.), it must, therefore, be its own cause—that is, its essence necessarily involves existence, or existence belongs to its nature.

A Summary Statement Concerning God (from *Ethics,* Part I, Appendix)

... In the foregoing I have explained the nature and properties of God. I have shown that he necessarily exists, that he is one: that he is, and acts solely by the necessity of his own nature; that he is the free cause of all things, and how he is so; that all things are in God, and so depend on him, that without him they could neither exist nor be conceived; lastly, that all things are predetermined by God, not through his free will or absolute fiat, but from the very nature of God or infinite power. I have further, where occasion offered, taken care to remove the prejudices, which might impede the comprehension of my demonstrations. Yet there still remain misconceptions not a few, which might and may prove very grave hindrances to the understanding of the concatenation of things, as I have explained it above. I have therefore thought it worth while to bring these misconceptions before the bar of reason.

All such opinions spring from the notion commonly entertained, that all things in nature act as men themselves act, namely, with an end in view. It is accepted as certain, that God himself directs all things to a definite goal (for it is said that God made all things for man, and man that he might worship him). I will, therefore, consider this opinion, asking first, why it obtains general credence, and why all men are naturally so prone to adopt it? Secondly, I will point out its falsity; and, lastly, I will show how it has given rise to prejudices about good and bad, right and wrong, praise and blame, order and confusion, beauty and ugliness, and the like. However, this is not the place to deduce these misconceptions from the nature of the human mind: it will be sufficient here, if I assume as a starting point, what ought to be universally admitted, namely, that all men are born ignorant of the causes of things, that all have the desire to seek for what is useful to them, and that they are conscious of such desire. Herefrom it follows, first, that men think themselves free inasmuch as they are conscious of their volitions and desires, and never even dream, in their ignorance, of the causes which have disposed them so to wish and desire. Secondly, that men do all things for an end, namely, for that which is useful to them, and which they seek. Thus it comes to pass that they only look for a knowledge of the final causes of events, and when these are learned, they are content, as having no cause for further doubt. If they cannot learn such causes from external sources, they are compelled to turn to considering themselves, and reflecting what end would have induced them personally to bring about the given event, and thus they necessarily judge other natures by their own. Further, as they find in themselves and outside themselves many means which assist them not a little in their search for what is useful, for instance, eyes for seeing, teeth for chewing, herbs and animals for yielding food, the sun for giving light, the sea for breeding fish, &c., they come to look on the whole of nature as a means for obtaining such conveniences. Now as they are aware, that they found these conveniences and did not make them, they think they have cause for believing, that some other being has made them for their use. As they look upon things as means, they cannot believe them to be self-created; but, judging from the means which they are accustomed to prepare for themselves, they are bound to believe in some ruler or rulers of the universe endowed with human freedom, who have arranged and adapted everything for human use. They are bound to estimate the nature of such rulers (having no information on the subject) in accordance with their own nature, and therefore they assert that the gods ordained everything for the use of man, in order to bind man to themselves and obtain from him the highest honour. Hence also it follows, that everyone thought out for himself, according to his abilities, a different way of worshipping God, so that God might love him more than his fellows, and direct the whole course of nature for the satisfaction of his blind cupidity and insatiable avarice. Thus the prejudice developed into superstition, and took deep root in the human mind; and for this reason everyone strove most zealously to understand and explain the final causes of things; but in their endeavour to show that nature does nothing in vain, i.e., nothing which is useless to man, they only seem to have demonstrated that nature, the gods, and men are all mad together. Consider, I pray you, the result: among the many helps of nature they were bound to find some hindrances, such as storms, earthquakes, diseases, &c.: so they declared that such things happen, because the gods are angry at some wrong done them by men, or at some fault committed in their worship. Experience day by day protested and showed by infinite examples, that good and evil fortunes fall to the lot of pious and impious alike; still they would not abandon their inveterate prejudice, for it was more easy for them to class such contradictions among other unknown things of whose use they were ignorant, and thus to retain their actual and innate condition of ignorance, than to destroy the whole fabric of their reasoning and start afresh. They therefore laid down as an axiom, that God's judgments far transcend human understanding. Such a doctrine might well have sufficed to conceal the truth from the human race for all eternity, if mathematics had not furnished another standard of verity in considering solely the essence and properties of figures without regard to their final causes. There are other reasons (which I need not mention here) besides mathematics, which might have caused men's minds to be directed to these general prejudices, and have led them to the knowledge of the truth.

I have now sufficiently explained my first point. There is no need to show at length, that nature has no particular goal in view, and that final causes are mere human figments. This, I think, is already evident enough, both from the causes and foundations on which I have shown such prejudice to be based, and also from Prop. xvi., and the Corollary of Prop. xxxii., and, in fact, all those propositions in which I have shown, that everything in nature proceeds from a sort of necessity, and with the utmost perfection. However, I will add a few remarks, in order to overthrow this doctrine of a final cause utterly. That which is really a cause it considers as an effect, and vice versa: it makes that which is by nature first to be last, and that which is highest and most perfect to be most imperfect. Passing over the questions of cause and priority as self-evident, it is plain from Props. xxi., xxii., xxiii. that that effect is most perfect which is produced immediately by God; the effect which requires for its production several intermediate causes is, in that respect, more imperfect. But if those things which were made immediately by God were made to enable him to attain his end, then the things which come after, for the sake of which the first were made, are necessarily the most excellent of all.

Further, this doctrine does away with the perfection of God: for, if God acts for an object, he necessarily desires something which he lacks. Certainly, theologians and metaphysicians draw a distinction between the object of want and the object of assimilation; still they confess that God made all things for the sake of himself, not for the sake of creation. They are unable to point to anything prior to creation, except God himself, as an object for which God should act, and are therefore driven to admit (as they clearly must), that God lacked those things for whose attainment he created means, and further that he desired them.

We must not omit to notice that the followers of this doctrine, anxious to display their talent in assigning final causes, have imported a new method of argument in proof of their theory—namely, a reduction, not to the impossible, but to ignorance; thus showing that they have no other method of exhibiting their doctrine. For example, if a stone falls from a roof on to someone's head, and kills him, they will demonstrate by their new method, that the stone fell in order to kill the man; for, if it had not by God's will fallen with that object, how could so many circumstances (and there are often many concurrent circumstances) have all happened together by chance? Perhaps you will answer that the event is due to the facts that the wind was blowing, and the man was walking that way. "But why," they will insist, "was the wind blowing, and why was the man at that very time walking that way?" If you again answer, that the wind had then sprung up because the sea had begun to be agitated the day before, the weather being previously calm, and that the man had been invited by a friend, they will again insist: "But why was the sea agitated, and why was the man invited at that time?" So they will pursue their questions from cause to cause, till at last you take refuge in the will of God—in other words, the sanctuary of ignorance. So, again, when they survey the frame of the human body, they are amazed; and being ignorant of the causes of so great a work of art, conclude that it has been fashioned, not mechanically, but by divine and supernatural skill, and has been so put together that one part shall not hurt another.

Hence anyone who seeks for the true causes of miracles, and strives to understand natural phenomena as an intelligent being, and not to gaze at them like a fool, is set down and denounced as an impious heretic by those, whom the masses adore as the interpreters of nature and the gods. Such persons know that, with the removal of ignorance, the wonder which forms their only available means for proving and preserving their authority would vanish also. But I now quit this subject, and pass on to my third point.

After men persuaded themselves, that everything which is created is created for their sake, they were bound to consider as the chief quality in everything that which is most useful to themselves, and to account those things the best of all which have the most beneficial effect on mankind. Further, they were bound to form abstract notions for the explanation of the nature of things, such as *goodness, badness, order, confusion, warmth, cold, beauty, deformity,* and so on; and from the belief that they are free agents arose the further notions *praise* and *blame, sin* and *merit.*

I will speak of these latter hereafter, when I treat of human nature; the former I will briefly explain here.

Everything which conduces to health and the worship of God they have called *good,* everything which hinders these objects they have styled *bad;* and inasmuch as those who do not understand the nature of things do not verify phenomena in any way, but merely imagine them after a fashion, and mistake their imagination for understanding, such persons firmly believe that there is an *order* in things, being really ignorant both of things and their own nature. When phenomena are of such a kind, that the impression they make on our senses requires little effort of imagination, and can consequently be easily remembered, we say that they are *well-ordered;* if the contrary, that they are *ill-ordered* or *confused.* Further, as things which are easily imagined are more pleasing to us, men prefer order to confusion—as though there were any order in nature, except in relation to our imagination—and say that God has created all things in order; thus, without knowing it, attributing imagination to God, unless, indeed, they would have it that God foresaw human imagination, and arranged everything, so that it should be most easily imagined. If this be their theory, they would not, perhaps, be daunted by the fact that we find an infinite number of phenomena, far surpassing our imagination, and very many others which confound its weakness. But enough has been said on this subject. The other abstract notions are nothing but modes of imagining, in which the imagination is differently affected, though they are considered by the ignorant as the chief attributes of things, inasmuch as they believe that everything was created for the sake of themselves; and, according as they are affected by it, style it good or bad, healthy or rotten and corrupt. For instance, if the motion which objects we see communicate to our nerves be conducive to health, the objects causing it are styled *beautiful;* if a contrary motion be excited, they are styled *ugly.*

Things which are perceived through our sense of smell are styled fragrant or fetid; if through our taste, sweet or bitter, full-flavoured or insipid; if through our touch, hard or soft, rough or smooth, &c.

Whatsoever affects our ears is said to give rise to noise, sound, or harmony. In this last case, there are men lunatic enough to believe, that even God himself takes pleasure in harmony; and philosophers are not lacking who have persuaded themselves, that the motion of the heavenly bodies gives rise to harmony—all of which instances sufficiently show that everyone judges of things according to the state of his brain, or rather mistakes for things the forms of his imagination. We need no longer wonder that there have arisen all the controversies we have witnessed, and finally scepticism: for, although human bodies in many respects agree, yet in very many others they differ; so that what seems good to one seems bad to another; what seems well ordered to one seems confused to another; what is pleasing to one displeases another, and so on. I need not further enumerate, because this is not the place to treat the subject at length, and also because the fact is sufficiently well known. It is commonly said: "So many men, so many minds; everyone is wise in his own way; brains differ as completely as palates." All of which proverbs show, that men judge of things according to their mental disposition, and rather imagine than understand: for, if they understood phenomena, they would, as mathematics attest, be convinced, if not attracted, by what I have urged.

We have now perceived, that all the explanations commonly given of nature are mere modes of imagining, and do not indicate the true nature of anything, but only the constitution of the imagination; and, although they have names, as though they were entities, existing externally to the imagination, I call them entities imaginary rather than real; and, therefore, all arguments against us drawn from such abstractions are easily rebutted.

Many argue in this way. If all things follow from a necessity of the absolutely perfect nature of God, why are there so many imperfections in nature? such, for instance, as things corrupt to the point of putridity, loathsome deformity, confusion, evil, sin, &c. But these reasoners are, as I have said, easily confuted, for the perfection of things is to be reckoned only from their own nature and power; things are not more or less perfect, according as they delight or offend human senses, or according as they are serviceable or repugnant to mankind. To those who ask why God did not so create all men, that they should be governed only by reason, I give no answer but this: because matter was not lacking to him for the creation of every degree of perfection from highest to lowest; or, more strictly, because the laws of his nature are so vast, as to suffice for the production of everything conceivable by an infinite intelligence, as I have shown in Prop. xvi.

Such are the misconceptions I have undertaken to note; if there are any more of the same sort, everyone may easily dissipate them for himself with the aid of a little reflection.

The Third Degree of Knowledge and the Love of God (from *Ethics,* Part V)

... From all that has been said above it is clear, that we, in many cases, perceive and form our general notions:—(1.) From particular things represented to our intellect fragmentarily, confusedly, and without order through our senses (II. xxix. Coroll.); I have settled to call such perceptions by the name of knowledge from the mere suggestions of experience. (2.) From symbols, e.g., from the fact of having read or heard certain words we remember things and form certain ideas concerning them, similar to those through which we imagine things (II. xviii. note). I shall call both these ways of regarding things *knowledge of the first kind, opinion,* or *imagination.* (3.) From the fact that we have notions common to all men, and adequate ideas of the properties of things (II. xxxviii. Coroll., xxxix. and Coroll. and xl.); this I call *reason* and *knowledge of the second kind.* Besides these two kinds of knowledge, there is, as I will hereafter show, a third kind of knowledge, which we will call intuition. This kind of knowledge proceeds from an adequate idea of the absolute essence of certain attributes of God to the adequate knowledge of the essence of things.

PROP. XXV. *The highest endeavour of the mind, and the highest virtue is to understand things by the third kind of knowledge.*

Proof.—The third kind of knowledge proceeds from an adequate idea of certain attributes of God to an adequate knowledge of the essence of things (see its definition II. xl. note ii.); and, in proportion as we understand things more in this way, we better understand God (by the last Prop.); therefore (IV. xxviii.) the highest virtue of the mind, that is (IV. Def. viii.) the power, or nature, or (III. vii.) highest endeavour of the mind, is to understand things by the third kind of knowledge. *Q.E.D.*

PROP. XXVI. *In proportion as the mind is more capable of understanding things by the third kind of knowledge, it desires more to understand things by that kind.*

Proof.—This is evident. For, in so far as we conceive the mind to be capable of conceiving things by this kind of knowledge, we, to that extent, conceive it as determined thus to conceive things; and consequently (Def. of the Emotions, i.), the mind desires so to do, in proportion as it is more capable thereof. *Q.E.D.*

PROP. XXVII. *From this third kind of knowledge arises the highest possible mental acquiescence.*

Proof.—The highest virtue of the mind is to know God (IV. xxviii.), or to understand things by the third kind of knowledge (V. xxv.), and this virtue is greater in proportion as the mind knows things more by the said kind of knowledge (V. xxiv.): consequently, he who knows things by this kind of knowledge passes to the summit of human perfection, and is therefore (Def. of the Emotions, ii.) affected by the highest pleasure, such pleasure being accompanied by the idea of himself and his own virtue; thus (Def. of the Emotions, xxv.), from this kind of knowledge arises the highest possible acquiescence. *Q.E.D.*

PROP. XXVIII. *The endeavour or desire to know things by the third kind of knowledge cannot arise from the first, but from the second kind of knowledge.*

Proof.—This proposition is self-evident. For whatsoever we understand clearly and distinctly, we understand either through itself, or through that which is conceived through itself; that is, ideas which are clear and distinct in us, or which are referred to the third kind of knowledge (II. xl. note ii.) cannot follow from ideas that are fragmentary and confused, and are referred to knowledge of the first kind, but must follow from adequate ideas, or ideas of the second and third kind of knowledge; therefore (Def. of the Emotions, i.), the desire of knowing things by the third kind of knowledge cannot arise from the first, but from the second kind. *Q.E.D.*

PROP. XXIX. *Whatsoever the mind understands under the form of eternity, it does not understand by virtue of conceiving the present actual existence of the body, but by virtue of conceiving the essence of the body under the form of eternity.*

Proof.—In so far as the mind conceives the present existence of its body, it to that extent conceives duration which can be determined by time, and to that extent only has it the power of conceiving things in relation to time (V. xxi. II. xxvi.). But eternity cannot be explained in terms of duration (I. Def. viii. and explanation). Therefore to this extent the mind has not the power of conceiving things under the form of eternity, but it possesses such power, because it is of the nature of reason to conceive things under the form of eternity (II. xliv. Coroll. ii.), and also because it is of the nature of the mind to conceive the essence of the body under the form of eternity (V. xxiii.), for besides these two there is nothing which belongs to the essence of mind (II. xiii.). Therefore this power of conceiving things under the form of eternity only belongs to the mind in virtue of the mind's conceiving the essence of the body under the form of eternity. *Q.E.D.*

Note.—Things are conceived by us as actual in two ways; either as existing in relation to a given time and place, or as contained in God and following from the necessity of the divine nature. Whatsoever we conceive in this second way as true or real, we conceive under the form of eternity, and their ideas involve the eternal and infinite essence of God, as we showed in II. xlv. and note, which see.

PROP. XXX. _Our mind, in so far as it knows itself and the body under the form of eternity, has to that extent necessarily a knowledge of god, and knows that it is in God, and is conceived through God._

Proof.—Eternity is the very essence of God, in so far as this involves necessary existence (I. Def. viii.). Therefore to conceive things under the form of eternity, is to conceive things in so far as they are conceived through the essence of God as real entities, or in so far as they involve existence through the essence of God; wherefore our mind, in so far as it conceives itself and the body under the form of eternity, has to that extent necessarily a knowledge of God, and knows, &c. _Q.E.D._

PROP. XXXI. _The third kind of knowledge depends on the mind, as its formal cause, in so far as the mind itself is eternal._

Proof.—The mind does not conceive anything under the form of eternity, except in so far as it conceives its own body under the form of eternity (V. xxix.); that is, except in so far as it is eternal (V. xxi. xxiii.); therefore (by the last Prop.), in so far as it is eternal, it possesses the knowledge of God, which knowledge is necessarily adequate (II. xlvi.); hence the mind, in so far as it is eternal, is capable of knowing everything which can follow from this given knowledge of God (II. xl.), in other words, of knowing things by the third kind of knowledge (see Def. in II. xl. note ii.), whereof accordingly the mind (III. Def. i.), in so far as it is eternal, is the adequate or formal cause of such knowledge. _Q.E.D._

Note.—In proportion, therefore, as a man is more potent in this kind of knowledge, he will be more completely conscious of himself and of God; in other words, he will be more perfect and blessed, as will appear more clearly in the sequel. But we must here observe that, although we are already certain that the mind is eternal, in so far as it conceives things under the form of eternity, yet, in order that what we wish to show may be more readily explained and better understood, we will consider the mind itself, as though it had just begun to exist and to understand things under the form of eternity, as indeed we have done hitherto; this we may do without any danger of error, so long as we are careful not to draw any conclusion, unless our premisses are plain.

PROP. XXXII. _Whatsoever we understand by the third kind of knowledge, we take delight in and our delight is accompanied by the idea of God as cause._

Proof.—From this kind of knowledge arises the highest possible mental acquiescence, that is (Def. of the Emotions, xxv.), pleasure, and this acquiescence is accompanied by the idea of the mind itself (V. xxvii.), and consequently (V. xxx.) the idea also of God as cause. _Q.E.D._

Corollary.—From the third kind of knowledge necessarily arises the intellectual love of God. From this kind of knowledge arises pleasure accompanied by the idea of God as cause, that is (Def. of the Emotions, vi.), the love of God; not in so far as we imagine him as present (V. xxix.), but in so far as we understand him to be eternal; this is what I call the intellectual love of God.

PROP. XXXIII. *The intellectual love of God, which arises from the third kind of knowledge, is eternal.*

Proof.—The third kind of knowledge is eternal (V. xxxi. I. Ax. iii.); therefore (by the same Axiom) the love which arises therefrom is also necessarily eternal. *Q.E.D.*

Note.—Although this love towards God has (by the foregoing Prop.) no beginning, it yet possesses all the perfections of love, just as though it had arisen as we feigned in the Coroll. of the last Prop. Nor is there here any difference, except that the mind possesses as eternal those same perfections which we feigned to accrue to it, and they are accompanied by the idea of God as eternal cause. If pleasure consists in the transition to a greater perfection, assuredly blessedness must consist in the mind being endowed with perfection itself.

PROP. XXXVI. *The intellectual love of the mind towards God is that very love of God whereby God loves himself, not in so far as he is infinite, but in so far as he can be explained through the essence of the human mind regarded under the form of eternity; in other words, the intellectual love of the mind towards God is part of the infinite love wherewith God loves himself.*

Proof.—This love of the mind must be referred to the activities of the mind (V. xxxii. Coroll. and III. iii.); it is itself, indeed, an activity whereby the mind regards itself accompanied by the idea of God as cause (V. xxxii. and Coroll.); that is (I. xxv. Coroll. and II. xi. Coroll.), an activity whereby God, in so far as he can be explained through the human mind, regards himself accompanied by the idea of himself; therefore (by the last Prop.), this love of the mind is part of the infinite love wherewith God loves himself. *Q.E.D.*

Corollary.—Hence it follows that God, in so far as he loves himself, loves man, and, consequently, that the love of god towards men, and the intellectual love of the mind towards God are identical.

Note.—From what has been said we clearly understand, wherein our salvation, or blessedness, or freedom, consists: namely, in the constant and eternal love towards God, or in God's love towards men. This love or blessedness is, in the Bible, called Glory, and not undeservedly. For whether this love be referred to God or to the mind, it may rightly be called acquiescence of spirit, which (Def. of the Emotions, xxv. xxx.) is not really distinguished from glory. In so far as it is referred to God, it is (V. xxxv.) pleasure, if we may still use that term, accompanied by the idea of itself, and, in so far as it is referred to the mind, it is the same (V. xxvii.).

Again, since the essence of our mind consists solely in knowledge, whereof the beginning and the foundation is God (I. xv. and II. xlvii. note), it becomes clear to us, in what manner and way our mind, as to its essence and existence, follows from the divine nature and constantly depends on God. I have thought it worth while here to call attention to this, in order to show by this example how the knowledge of particular things, which I have called intuitive or of the third kind (II. xl. note ii.), is potent, and more powerful than the universal knowledge, which I have styled knowledge of the second kind. For, although in Part I. I showed in general terms, that all things (and consequently, also, the human mind) depend as to their essence and existence on God, yet that demonstration, though legitimate and placed beyond the chances of doubt, does not affect our mind so much, as when the same conclusion is derived from the actual essence of some particular thing, which we say depends on God.

PROP. XLI. *Even if we did not know that our mind is eternal, we should still consider as of primary importance piety and religion, and generally all things which, in Part IV., we showed to be attributable to courage and highmindedness.*

Proof.—The first and only foundation of virtue, or the rule of right living is (IV. xxii. Coroll. and xxiv.) seeking one's own true interest. Now, while we determined what reason prescribes as useful, we took no account of the mind's eternity, which has only become known to us in this Fifth Part. Although we were ignorant at that time that the mind is eternal, we nevertheless stated that the qualities attributable to courage and high-mindedness are of primary importance. Therefore, even if we were still ignorant of this doctrine, we should yet put the aforesaid precepts of reason in the first place. *Q.E.D.*

Note.—The general belief of the multitude seems to be different. Most people seem to believe that they are free, in so far as they may obey their lusts, and that they cede their rights, in so far as they are bound to live according to the commandments of the divine law. They therefore believe that piety, religion, and, generally, all things attributable to firmness of mind, are burdens, which, after death, they hope to lay aside, and to receive the reward for their bondage, that is, for their piety and religion; it is not only by this hope, but also, and chiefly, by the fear of being horribly punished after death, that they are induced to live according to the divine commandments, so far as their feeble and infirm spirit will carry them.

If men had not this hope and this fear, but believed that the mind perishes with the body, and that no hope of prolonged life remains for the wretches who are broken down with the burden of piety, they would return to their own inclinations, controlling everything in accordance with their lusts, and desiring to obey fortune rather than themselves. Such a course appears to me not less absurd than if a man, because he does not believe that he can by wholesome food sustain his body for ever, should wish to cram himself with poisons and deadly fare; or if, because he sees that the mind is not eternal or immortal, he should prefer to be out of his mind altogether, and to live without the use of reason; these ideas are so absurd as to be scarcely worth refuting.

PROP. XLII. *Blessedness is not the reward of virtue, but virtue itself; neither do we rejoice therein, because we control our lusts, but, contrariwise, because we rejoice therein, we are able to control our lusts.*

Proof.—Blessedness consists in love towards God (V. xxxvi. and note), which love springs from the third kind of knowledge (V. xxxii. Coroll.); therefore this love (III. iii. lix.) must be referred to the mind, in so far as the latter is active; therefore (IV. Def. viii.) it is virtue itself. This was our first point. Again, in proportion as the mind rejoices more in this divine love or blessedness, so does it the more understand (V. xxxii.); that is (V. iii. Coroll.), so much the more power has it over the emotions, and (V. xxxviii.) so much the less is it subject to those emotions which are evil; therefore, in proportion as the mind rejoices in this divine love or blessedness, so has it the power of controlling lusts. And, since human power in controlling the emotions consists solely in the understanding, it follows that no one rejoices in blessedness, because he has controlled his lusts, but, contrariwise, his power of controlling his lusts arises from this blessedness itself. *Q.E.D.*

Note.—I have thus completed all I wished to set forth touching the mind's power over the emotions and the mind's freedom. Whence it appears, how potent is the wise man, and how much he surpasses the ignorant man, who is driven only by his lusts. For the ignorant man is not only distracted in various ways by external causes without ever gaining the true acquiescence of his spirit, but moreover lives, as it were unwitting of himself, and of God, and of things, and as soon as he ceases to suffer, ceases also to be.

Whereas the wise man, in so far as he is regarded as such, is scarcely at all disturbed in spirit, but, being conscious of himself, and of God, and of things, by a certain eternal necessity, never ceases to be, but always possesses true acquiescence of his spirit.

If the way which I have pointed out as leading to this result seems exceedingly hard, it may nevertheless be discovered. Needs must it be hard, since it is so seldom found. How would it be possible, if salvation were ready to our hand, and could without great labour be found, that it should be by almost all men neglected? But all things excellent are as difficult as they are rare.

Review Questions

1. Spinoza's view of reality has been described as looking from the top of a pyramid down. Is this a suitable description?
2. Explain why Spinoza rejects any kind of pluralism, such as Cartesian dualism, in favor of monism. Does his monism lead to pantheism?
3. Spinoza admits differences in the universe; how does he do this and yet hold to absolute unity?
4. What is the meaning of *necessity* in Spinoza's thought?
5. For Spinoza, how do necessity and freedom relate to each other?
6. How does Spinoza equate the highest degree of knowledge with blessedness?
7. Why is there, in Spinoza's view, a need for human beings to establish a civil society?
8. How does Spinoza's view of substance compare with Aristotle's?

12

Gottfried Wilhelm Leibniz (1646–1716)

Introduction

The third continental rationalist philosopher is Gottfried Wilhelm Leibniz. He was born in Leipzig in 1646 and entered the university there at age fifteen. As a student he was an avid reader, delving into the works of philosophers like Aristotle, the Schoolmen, and Descartes, as well as those of scientists like Kepler and Galileo. Later he took up studies in mathematics and law, and was awarded a doctorate of laws at age twenty-one. For some time he served on diplomatic missions, and his travels in that capacity gave him the opportunity to meet many of the great persons of the day. On one such occasion he met Spinoza, eager to learn at first hand something of his curious doctrines, but Spinoza's drastic departure from the God of tradition made Leibniz a permanent critic of his philosophy. He looked upon Spinoza's "atheism" as a logical outcome of Cartesianism, to which he had maintained a long-standing opposition because of its interpretation of the physical world. An inventive mathematician, he discovered the calculus, or perhaps, due to several chronological ambiguities, he should be thought of as codiscovering it with the celebrated Sir Isaac Newton; he invented the first calculating machine. He had a profound devotion to science, and to advance its cause he founded an academy of sciences in Berlin that became highly esteemed. In another direction entirely, he expended a great effort in trying to bring about a reunion of the Christian churches — an ecumenist far ahead of his time. Time, however, was not kind to Leibniz in his declining years; his public service diminished, his influence waned, and when he died in 1716 he was generally a forgotten man — his death not even acknowledged by the academy he established.

If there is any one theme that serves as a key to Leibniz's philosophy, it is the theme of harmony — of *universal harmony* in which the world is seen as a harmoniously functioning whole because it is an ordered system founded by God. The image of the clock is a favorite with Leibniz, as with other authors of the same period, who marveled at the ingenuity of the clockmaker in being able to assemble the gears and springs and countless other moving parts to tell the precise time. The universe is "God's clock," and its wonderful functioning, in all its cunning detail, causes us to wonder at the ingenuity of the One who made it. Carrying this imagery still further, Leibniz refers to universal ordering as *preestablished harmony* because, in the very first moment of establishing the universe, God built an order into it that works itself out in the course of time. With particular reference to Cartesian dualism, Leibniz felt that Descartes' solution to the mind–body problem was unsatisfactory, so he suggested that the two substances might be thought of as two clocks, a soul clock and a body clock, and when a body event took place, a corresponding soul event took place at the same moment, not because the body event caused the soul event but because both events were caused simultaneously by God. On the religious level, Leibniz's interest in ecumenism was an attempt at ecclesiastical harmony, and his *Theodicy* was a mighty effort to reconcile evil in the world with God's goodness. All of these ideas were foreshadowed in the young Leibniz's essay *The Art of Combining Things*, in which he held that, given the consistent ordering of things, the universe lends itself to discovery by deductive reasoning.

It is to this question of harmony that Leibniz's most popularly known work, *The Monadology*, is addressed. By now we have come to appreciate the perennial nature of the problem of the one and the many, the problem of reconciling plurality and unity. To develop a solution, Leibniz devised an entirely new scheme, a scheme based on the existence of substances that he calls *monads* (from the Greek *monos*, meaning one). Anything of our experience is an aggregate, or is composed, but if we divide anything composed, the components themselves, being physical, will always have the characteristics of being composed. Since endless division is theoretically, if not physically possible, we must conclude that an aggregate is ultimately composed of *indivisible* things that, in consequence, have no parts, no extension, no figure; they are "simple" substances, called *monads*, and because they lie beyond the physical, they are *metaphysical*. They are not like atoms in the classical sense because the classical atom was the ultimate *physical* thing, not metaphysical.

In order to bring an infinite number of monads together in an overarching unity, Leibniz concludes, as did Spinoza, that the whole universe is in every part, and every part is in the whole universe, or, in terms of monads, the whole universe is in every monad, and every monad is in the whole universe. Leibniz ingeniously models his explanation of unity on the activity of knowledge. He holds that every monad is a *perceiving* entity, that is, is endowed with *perception*, however rudimentary, whereby the universe is registered, or mirrored, within it. Further, monads themselves are *windowless*, which means that they are not open to influence by other monads, which might cause them to have this perception, but are open only to God, who, as the supreme cause and orderer, brings the relationship among monads into perfect harmony. In understanding what Leibniz is after, it is helpful to recall Aristotle's dictum that the mind is one with what it knows. When the mind knows the tree, on the *level of knowledge*, the tree and the mind become one; the mind is one-with-the-tree, and the tree is one-with-the-mind. Likewise, for Leibniz, in every perception the perceiver and the object perceived become one, and inasmuch as any one monad is open to all others, the monad is one-with-the-universe and the universe is one-with-the-monad. The universe, therefore, and the part are one-with-each-other: plurality and unity — the many and the one — are expressions of a continuous whole.

With his system of monads Leibniz feels he has safeguarded God's supreme causality, ascertained the inner core of pre-established harmony, and maintained the individuality of things along with the unity of the universe.

That God exists, for Leibniz, is as incontestable as the air we breathe. He finds convincing the arguments offered by various philosophers of the past, such as the ontological argument of St. Anselm and Descartes, the argument from eternal truths of St. Augustine, and the arguments from causality developed by the Schoolmen. With regard to the last, however, Leibniz adds his own terminological refinement by using the phrase *sufficient reason*. The *principle of sufficient reason* means, in this context, that any contingent being, from the mere fact that it does not have to be, and yet is, must have a sufficient reason for its existence, which, however, is not found in the contingent being itself; therefore, the sufficient reason for its existence must be found in a being whose existence is necessary (that is, sufficient reason unto itself), which must be, which cannot not be — namely, God.

It was not so much the existence of God that puzzled Leibniz but another problem: granted that God is all perfect and all good, how is it possible for evil to exist in a world that the good God has made? Leibniz did not shirk this problem, but tried to face it head on with one of his lengthier works, *Theodicy*, whose subtitle is *Essays on the Goodness of God, the Freedom of Man and the Origin of Evil*. In the preface Leibniz refers to "the great question of the Free and the Necessary . . . in the production and origin of Evil" as one of the "great labyrinths where our reason very often goes astray." Every human being is touched by the problem; every human being can draw up a sad catalog of sufferings, and every human being must respond in some way. And every philosopher as well, from Socrates to Sartre, who claims a sensitivity to the moral climate of the universe, has had to search for some answer to evil in the pattern of the real.

As an ardent advocate of harmony in the universe, Leibniz could never have opted for a two-God system, as devised in some religions, wherein the God of Good presides over good in the world and the God of Evil over evil, the two locked in enduring combat. For Leibniz, this would be skirting the problem; common sense and philosophical consistency require him to aver that there is but one problem—which turns, however, on an internal polarity between God and evil. Out of fidelity to one's own intellect, the demand for a coherent view of the universe includes the existence of God, who, among His other attributes, is good; on the other hand, out of fidelity to one's own experience, the ravages of evil cannot be denied. So Leibniz's precise problem is to *reconcile* the goodness of God with the presence of evil in the world.

In one sense, for Leibniz, evil has to be present in anything that is not perfect; only God is perfect; therefore, anything less than God has to be limited, and insofar as it is limited, imperfect, or evil: "where shall we find the source of evil? ... there is an *original imperfection in the creature* before sin, because the creature is limited in its essence." To this kind of evil Leibniz assigns the term *metaphysical evil*. It is found in the very nature of created being and is therefore to be found in any world God might choose to create. But even though this given world is imperfect, it is the *best possible* world God could have created, for anything less than the best would be an insult to His goodness: "Now this supreme wisdom, united to a goodness that is no less infinite, cannot but have chosen the best." Leibniz did not feel that God's omnipotence was being compromised at all by saying that this is the best possible world, for a "better" world would be a contradiction. The caricature of Leibniz's position written by Voltaire in his *Candide*, witty as it is, hardly does justice to the huge problem the philosopher is trying to face.

In order to produce a world containing the greatest amount of good, God creates one in which there will be, and God knows there will be, evil. In that sense, God permits the evil so that He can produce the good; He does not cause or choose the evil. In an analogy, Leibniz observes that the downstream motion of a river carries the boats along with it, but the more heavily laden ones proceed more slowly; so, the river is the cause of the motion, not the retardation. Just so, "God is the cause of perfection in the nature and the actions of the creature, but the limitation of the receptivity of the creature is the cause of the defects there are in its action." Leibniz aligns himself with "the Platonists, St. Augustine and the Schoolmen" who say that God is not the cause of the "formal element" of evil, defined as "privation," or lack of perfection; God is not the cause of a being's lack of perfection, because such lack belongs to its very nature; but inasmuch as He is the cause of the being, He is only the cause of the good.

Physical evil consists in sufferings, sorrows, and miseries, which are brought about by man's evil will or by the "monstrosities of nature." Once again, the larger framework must be invoked, for small disorders are to be expected for the sake of the great order, and Leibniz quotes approvingly the adage of St. Bernard, "It belongs to the great order that there should be some small disorders." Upheavals of nature, whether eruptions, conflagration, or floods, are indeed evil; but considering the vast time scale involved and the fact that this earth is to be cultivated by man, even these evils redound to greater good.

Moral evil is sin, that is, an imperfection in the human act; it lacks the moral perfection that should be present in such an act. Once again, Leibniz links this concept to the basic notion of metaphysical evil in that God does not will such evil to take place, but He does will the goodness of the created *free* nature, knowing that it will sometimes lapse; but even this is permitted, not willed, for the production of greater good in the world. In creating man as free, God has to allow that freedom to stand.

Whether or not Leibniz was successful in solving the problem of evil, his effort is an outstanding example of the philosopher bending his genius to a condition that "perplexes almost all the human race."

We saw that Leibniz was convinced of the supreme orderliness of the universe, and this, in turn, was the primary requisite for a mind steeped in mathematics looking for a mathematical opening to new discoveries in that universe. Like Descartes, who had high expectations for his universal mathematics, Leibniz tried to develop a new logic that would go beyond the traditional forms. This new logic, called *universal characteristic*, would include only a few principles, and these would be *symbolized* in such a way as to make the logic a supple instrument for discovering new truths in any area of knowledge such as physics, mathematics, medicine, or theology, or for inventing new machines of all descriptions that would be useful in practical life: "Once the characteristic numbers are established for most concepts, mankind will possess a new instrument which will enhance the capabilities of the mind to a far greater extent than optical instruments strengthen the eyes, and will supersede the microscope and telescope to the same extent that reason is superior to eyesight." When he was only twenty-five years old, he had already created an imposing number of successful machines made possible by the use of symbolic logic: an arithmetic machine, a "living geometer," optical tubes, an instrument for locating ships, and a submarine.

Though much of Leibniz's philosophy met with a sympathetic response, support from his contemporaries for his new logic was never forthcoming. The events of later centuries proved that he was indeed far ahead of his time, for much work in this area was done by mathematicians and logicians like Boole, Whitehead, and Russell; still later, in our time, the insights of Leibniz have come to fruition in the dazzling versatility of computer technology.

Descartes, Spinoza, and Leibniz were the three outstanding figures in seventeenth century philosophy in continental Europe, and though they espoused different philosophies, they shared many common interests: the quest for certitude in knowledge; metaphysical questions concerning God, man, and the world; and the problem of unity and plurality. But the reason they are often referred to as *rationalists* is, as we have seen, their confidence in the method of deduction and their high expectations from the analysis of ideas. Their counterparts in Britain, though, felt that with such emphasis being placed on the deductive method, there was a danger of losing the empirical, an ardent champion of which was Francis Bacon. However, it was John Locke more than anyone else who staked out the claim for the empirical in the context of an even-tempered philosophy. But before we learn how he did this, we should first see Thomas Hobbes at work, for Hobbes himself was enthusiastic about the prospects of the deductive method.

Readings

From The Monadology

1. The monad of which we shall here speak is merely a simple substance, which enters into composites; simple, that is to say, without parts.

2. And there must be simple substances, since there are composites; for the composite is only a collection or aggregatum of simple substances.

3. Now where there are no parts, neither extension, nor figure, nor divisibility is possible. And these monads are the true atoms of nature, and, in a word, the elements of all things.

4. Their dissolution also is not at all to be feared, and there is no conceivable way in which a simple substance can perish naturally.

5. For the same reason there is no conceivable way in which a simple substance can begin naturally, since it cannot be formed by composition.

6. Thus it may be said that the monads can only begin or end all at once, that is to say, they can only begin by creation and end by annihilation; whereas that which is composite begins or ends by parts.

7. There is also no way of explaining how a monad can be altered or changed in its inner being by any other creature, for nothing can be transposed within it, nor can there be conceived in it any internal movement which can be excited, directed, augmented or diminished within it, as can be done in composites, where there is change among the parts. The monads have no windows through which anything can enter or depart. The accidents cannot detach themselves nor go about outside of substances, as did formerly the sensible species of the Schoolmen. Thus neither substance nor accident can enter a monad from outside.

8. Nevertheless, the monads must have some qualities, otherwise they would not even be entities. And if simple substances did not differ at all in their qualities there would be no way of perceiving any change in things, since what is in the compound can only come from the simple ingredients, and the monads, if they had no qualities, would be indistinguishable from one another, seeing also they do not differ in quantity. Consequently, a plenum being supposed, each place would always receive, in any motion, only the equivalent of what it had had before, and one state of things would be indistinguishable from another.

9. It is necessary, indeed, that each monad be different from every other. For there are never in nature two beings which are exactly alike and in which it is not possible to find an internal difference, or one founded upon an intrinsic quality (*dénomination*).

10. I take it also for granted that every created being, and consequently the created monad also, is subject to change, and even that this change is continuous in each.

11. It follows from what has just been said, that the natural changes of the monads proceed from an *internal principle*, since an external cause could not influence their inner being.

12. But, besides the principle of change, there must be an individuating *detail of changes*, which forms, so to speak, the specification and variety of the simple substances.

13. This detail must involve a multitude in the unity or in that which is simple. For since every natural change takes place by degrees, something changes and something remains; and consequently, there must be in the simple substance a plurality of affections and of relations, although it has no parts.

14. The passing state, which involves and represents a multitude in unity or in the simple substance, is nothing else than what is called *perception*, which must be distinguished from apperception or consciousness, as will appear in what follows. . . .

15. The action of the internal principle which causes the change or the passage from one perception to another, may be called *appetition;* it is true that desire cannot always completely attain to the whole perception to which it tends, but it always attains something of it and reaches new perceptions.

16. We experience in ourselves a multiplicity in a simple substance, when we find that the most trifling thought of which we are conscious involves a variety in the object. Thus all those who admit that the soul is a simple substance ought to admit this multiplicity in the monad. . . .

18. The name of *entelechies* might be given to all simple substances or created monads, for they have within themselves a certain perfection. . . .

19. If we choose to give the name *soul* to everything that has *perceptions* and *desires* in the general sense which I have just explained, all simple substances or created monads may be called souls, but as feeling is something more than a simple perception, I am willing that the general name of monads or entelechies shall suffice for those simple substances which have only perception, and that those substances only shall be called *souls* whose perception is more distinct and is accompanied by memory. . . .

29. But the knowledge of necessary and eternal truths is what distinguishes us from mere animals and furnishes us with *reason* and the sciences, raising us to a knowledge of ourselves and of God. This is what we call the rational soul or *spirit* in us.

30. It is also by the knowledge of necessary truths, and by their abstractions, that we rise to *acts of reflection*, which make us think of that which calls itself *"I"*, and to observe that this or that is within *us:* and it is thus that, in thinking of ourselves, we think of being, of substance, simple or composite, of the immaterial and of God himself, conceiving that what is limited in us is in him without limits. And these reflective acts furnish the principal objects of our reasonings.

31. Our reasonings are founded on *two great principles, that of contradiction,* in virtue of which we judge that to be *false* which involves contradiction, and that *true,* which is opposed or contradictory to the false.

32. And *that of sufficient reason,* in virtue of which we hold that no fact can be real or existent, no statement true, unless there be a sufficient reason why it is so and not otherwise, although most often these reasons cannot be known to us.

33. There are also two kinds of *truths,* those of *reasoning* and those of *fact.* Truths of reasoning are necessary and their opposite is impossible, and those of *fact* are contingent and their opposite is possible. When a truth is necessary its reason can be found by analysis, resolving it into more simple ideas and truths until we reach those which are primitive.

34. It is thus that mathematicians by analysis reduce speculative *theorems* and practical *canons* to *definitions, axioms* and *postulates.*

35. And there are finally simple ideas, definitions of which cannot be given; there are also axioms and postulates, in a word, *primary principles*, which cannot be proved, and indeed need no proof; and these are *identical propositions*, whose opposite involves an express contradiction.

36. But there must also be a *sufficient reason* for *contingent truths*, or those of *fact*,—that is, for the sequence of things diffused through the universe of created objects—where the resolution into particular reasons might run into a detail without limits, on account of the immense variety of the things in nature and the division of bodies *ad infinitum*. There is an infinity of figures and of movements, present and past, which enter into the efficient cause of my present writing, and there is an infinity of slight inclinations and dispositions, past and present, of my soul, which enter into the final cause.

37. And as all this *detail* only involves other contingents, anterior or more detailed, each one of which needs a like analysis for its explanation, we make no advance: and the sufficient or final reason must be outside of the sequence or *series* of this detail of contingencies, however infinite it may be.

38. And thus it is that the final reason of things must be found in a necessary substance, in which the detail of changes exists only eminently, as in their source; and this is what we call God.

39. Now this substance, being a sufficient reason of all this detail, which also is linked together throughout, *there is but one God, and this God is sufficient.*

40. We may also conclude that this supreme substance, which is unique, universal and necessary, having nothing outside of itself which is independent of it, and being a pure consequence of possible being, must be incapable of limitations and must contain as much of reality as is possible.

41. Whence it follows that God is absolutely perfect, *perfection* being only the magnitude of positive reality taken in its strictest meaning, setting aside the limits or bounds in things which have them. And where there are no limits, that is, in God, perfection is absolutely infinite.

42. It follows also that the creatures have their perfections from the influence of God, but that their imperfections arise from their own nature, incapable of existing without limits. For it is by this that they are distinguished from God.

43. It is also true that in God is the source not only of existences but also of essences, so far as they are real, or of that which is real in the possible. This is because the understanding of God is the region of

eternal truths, or of the ideas on which they depend, and because, without him, there would be nothing real in the possibilities, and not only nothing existing but also nothing possible.

44. For, if there is a reality in essences or possibilities or indeed in the eternal truths, this reality must be founded in something existing and actual, and consequently in the existence of the necessary being, in whom essence involves existence, or with whom it is sufficient to be possible in order to be actual.

45. Hence God alone (or the necessary being) has this prerogative, that he must exist if he is possible. And since nothing can hinder the possibility of that which possesses no limitations, no negation, and, consequently, no contradiction, this alone is sufficient to establish the existence of God *a priori*. We have also proved it by the reality of the eternal truths. But we have a little while ago [§§ 36–39] proved it also *a posteriori*, since contingent beings exist, which can only have their final or sufficient reason in a necessary being who has the reason of his existence in himself.

46. Yet we must not imagine, as some do, that the eternal truths, being dependent upon God, are arbitrary and depend upon his will, as Descartes seems to have held, and afterwards M. Poiret. This is true only of contingent truths, the principle of which is *fitness* or the choice of the *best*, whereas necessary truths depend solely on his understanding and are its internal object.

47. Thus God alone is the primitive unity or the original simple substance; of which all created or derived monads are the products, and are generated, so to speak, by continual fulgurations of the Divinity, from moment to moment, limited by the receptivity of the creature, to whom limitation is essential. . . .

51. But in simple substances the influence of one monad upon another is purely *ideal* and it can have its effect only through the intervention of God, inasmuch as in the ideas of God a monad may demand with reason that God in regulating the others from the commencement of things, have regard to it. For since a created monad can have no physical influence upon the inner being of another, it is only in this way that one can be dependent upon another. . . .

53. Now, as there is an infinity of possible universes in the ideas of God, and as only one of them can exist, there must be a sufficient reason for the choice of God, which determines him to select one rather than another.

54. And this reason can only be found in the *fitness*, or in the degrees of perfection, which these worlds contain, each possible world having a right to claim existence according to the measure of perfection which it possesses.

55. And this is the cause of the existence of the Best; namely, that his wisdom makes it known to God, his goodness makes him choose it, and his power makes him produce it.

56. Now this *connection*, or this adaptation, of all created things to each and of each to all, brings it about that each simple substance has relations which express all the others, and that, consequently, it is a perpetual living mirror of the universe. . . .

60. Besides, we can see, in what I have just said, the *a priori* reasons why things could not be otherwise than they are. Because God, in regulating all, has had regard to each part, and particularly to each monad, whose nature being representative, nothing can limit it to representing only a part of things; although it may be true that this representation is but confused as regards the detail of the whole universe, and can be distinct only in the case of a small part of things, that is to say, in the case of those which are nearest or greatest in relation to each of the monads; otherwise each monad would be a divinity. It is not as regards the object but only as regards the modification of the knowledge of the object, that monads are limited. They all tend confusedly toward the infinite, toward the whole; but they are limited and differentiated by the degrees of their distinct perceptions.

61. And composite substances are analogous in this respect with simple substances. For since the world is a *plenum*, rendering all matter connected, and since in a plenum every motion has some effect on distant bodies in proportion to their distance, so that each body is affected not only by those in contact with it, and feels in some way all that happens to them, but also by their means is affected by those which are in contact with the former, with which it itself is in immediate contact, it follows that this intercommunication extends to any distance whatever. And consequently, each body feels all that happens in the universe, so that he who sees all, might read in each that which happens everywhere, and even that which has been or shall be, discovering in the present that which is removed in time as well as in space. . . .

62. Thus, although each created monad represents the entire universe, it represents more distinctly the body which is particularly attached to it, and of which it forms the entelechy; and as this body expresses the whole universe through the connection of all matter in a plenum, the soul also represents the whole universe in representing this body, which belongs to it in a particular way.

63. The body belonging to a monad, which is its entelechy or soul, constitutes together with the entelechy what may be called a *living being*, and together with the soul what may be called an *animal*. . . .

64. Thus each organic body of a living being is a kind of divine machine or natural automaton, which infinitely surpasses all artificial automata. Because a machine which is made by man's art is not a ma-

chine in each one of its parts; for example, the teeth of a brass wheel have parts or fragments which to us are no longer artificial and have nothing in themselves to show the special use to which the wheel was intended in the machine. But nature's machines, that is, living bodies, are machines even in their smallest parts *ad infinitum*. Herein lies the difference between nature and art, that is, between the divine art and ours. . . .

66. Whence we see that there is a world of creatures, of living beings, of animals, of entelechies, of souls, in the smallest particle of matter.

67. Each portion of matter may be conceived of as a garden full of plants, and as a pond full of fishes. But each branch of the plant, each member of the animal, each drop of its humors is also such a garden or such a pond. . . .

69. Therefore there is nothing fallow, nothing sterile, nothing dead in the universe, no chaos, no confusion except in appearance; somewhat as a pond would appear from a distance, in which we might see the confused movement and swarming, so to speak, of the fishes in the pond, without discerning the fish themselves.

70. We see thus that each living body has a ruling entelechy, which in the animal is the soul; but the members of this living body are full of other living beings, plants, animals, each of which has also its entelechy or governing soul.

71. But it must not be imagined, as has been done by some people who have misunderstood my thought, that each soul has a mass or portion of matter belonging to it or attached to it forever, and that consequently it possesses other inferior living beings, destined to its service forever. For all bodies are, like rivers, in a perpetual flux, and parts are entering into them and departing from them continually.

72. Thus the soul changes its body only gradually and by degrees, so that it is never deprived of all its organs at once. There is often a metamorphosis in animals, but never metempsychosis nor transmigration of souls. There are also no entirely *separate* souls, nor *genii* without bodies. God alone is wholly without body. . . .

78. These principles have given me the means of explaining naturally the union or rather the conformity of the soul and the organic body. The soul follows its own peculiar laws and the body also follows its own laws, and they agree in virtue of the *pre-established harmony* between all substances, since they are all representations of one and the same universe.

79. Souls act according to the laws of final causes, by appetitions, ends and means. Bodies act in accordance with the laws of efficient causes or of motion. And the two realms, that of efficient causes and that of final causes, are in harmony with each other. . . .

83. Among other differences which exist between ordinary souls and minds *(esprits)*, some of which I have already mentioned, there is also,

this, that souls in general are the living mirrors or images of the universe of creatures, but minds or spirits are in addition images of the Divinity itself, or of the author of nature, able to know the system of the universe and to imitate something of it by architectonic samples, each mind being like a little divinity in its own department.

84. Hence it is that spirits are capable of entering into a sort of society with God, and that he is, in relation to them, not only what an inventor is to his machine (as God is in relation to the other creatures), but also what a prince is to his subjects, and even a father to his children.

85. Whence it is easy to conclude that the assembly of all spirits *(esprits)* must compose the City of God, that is, the most perfect state which is possible, under the most perfect of monarchs.

86. This City of God, this truly universal monarchy, is a moral world within the natural world, and the highest and most divine of the works of God; it is in this that the glory of God truly consists, for he would have none if his greatness and goodness were not known and admired by spirits. It is, too, in relation to this divine city that he properly has goodness; whereas his wisdom and his power are everywhere manifest.

87. As we have above established a perfect harmony between two natural kingdoms, the one of efficient, the other of final causes, we should also notice here another harmony between the physical kingdom of nature and the moral kingdom of grace; that is, between God considered as the architect of the mechanism of the universe and God considered as monarch of the divine city of spirits.

88. This harmony makes things progress toward grace by natural means. This globe, for example, must be destroyed and repaired by natural means, at such times as the government of spirits may demand it, for the punishment of some and the reward of others.

89. It may be said, farther, that God as architect satisfies in every respect God as legislator, and that therefore sins, by the order of nature and perforce even of the mechanical structure of things, must carry their punishment with them; and that in the same way, good actions will obtain their rewards by mechanical ways through their relations to bodies, although this cannot and ought not always happen immediately.

90. Finally, under this perfect government, there will be no good action unrewarded, no bad action unpunished; and everything must result in the well-being of the good, that is, of those who are not disaffected in this great State, who, after having done their duty, trust in providence, and who love and imitate, as is meet, the author of all good, finding pleasure in the contemplation of his perfections, according to the nature of truly *pure love*, which takes pleasure in the happiness of the beloved. This is what causes wise and virtuous persons to

work for all which seems in harmony with the divine will, presumptive or antecedent, and nevertheless to content themselves with that which God in reality brings to pass by his secret, consequent and decisive will, recognizing that if we could sufficiently understand the order of the universe, we should find that it surpasses all the wishes of the wisest, and that it is impossible to render it better than it is, not only for all in general, but also for ourselves in particular, if we are attached, as we should be, to the author of all, not only as to the architect and efficient cause of our being, but also as to our master and final cause, who ought to be the whole aim of our will, and who, alone, can make our happiness.

(Trans. by Robert Latta as revised in P. P. Weiner.)

Evil as Privation (from Theodicy, #20)

But it is necessary also to meet the more speculative and metaphysical difficulties which have been mentioned, and which concern the cause of evil. The question is asked first of all, whence does evil come? *Si Deus est, unde malum? Si non est, unde bonum?* The ancients attributed the cause of evil to *matter*, which they believed uncreate and independent of God: but we, who derive all being from God, where shall we find the source of evil? The answer is, that it must be sought in the ideal nature of the creature, in so far as this nature is contained in the eternal verities which are in the understanding of God, independently of his will. For we must consider that there is *an original imperfection in the creature* before sin, because the creature is limited in its essence; whence ensues that it cannot know all, and that it can deceive itself and commit other errors. Plato said in *Timaeus* that the world originated in Understanding united to Necessity. Others have united God and Nature. This can be given a reasonable meaning. God will be the Understanding; and the Necessity, that is, the essential nature of things, will be the object of the understanding, in so far as this object consists in the eternal verities. But this object is inward and abides in the divine understanding. And therein is found not only the primitive form of good, but also the origin of evil: the Region of the Eternal Verities must be substituted for matter when we are concerned with seeking out the source of things.

This region is the ideal cause of evil (as it were) as well as of good: but, properly speaking, the formal character of evil has no *efficient* cause, for it consists in privation, as we shall see, namely, in that which the efficient cause does not bring about. That is why the Schoolmen are wont to call the cause of evil *deficient*.

The Analogy of the Boat (from *Theodicy*, #30-1)

Let us suppose that the current of one and the same river carried along with it various boats, which differ among themselves only in the cargo, some being laden with wood, others with stone, and some more, the others less. That being so, it will come about that the boats most heavily laden will go more slowly than the others, provided it be assumed that the wind or the oar, or some other similar means, assist them not at all. It is not, properly speaking, weight which is the cause of this retardation, since the boats are going down and not upwards; but it is the same cause which also increases the weight in bodies that have greater density, which are, that is to say, less porous and more charged with matter that is proper to them: for the matter which passes through the pores, not receiving the same movement, must not be taken into account. It is therefore matter itself which originally is inclined to slowness or privation of speed; not indeed of itself to lessen this speed, having once received it, since that would be action, but to moderate by its receptivity the effect of the impression when it is to receive it. Consequently, since more matter is moved by the same force of the current when the boat is more laden, it is necessary that it go more slowly; and experiments on the impact of bodies, as well as reason, show that twice as much force must be employed to give equal speed to a body of the same matter but of twice the size. But that indeed would not be necessary if the matter were absolutely indifferent to repose and to movement, and if it had not this natural inertia whereof we have just spoken to give it a kind of repugnance to being moved. Let us now compare the force which the current exercises on boats, and communicates to them, with the action of God, who produces and conserves whatever is positive in creatures, and gives them perfection, being and force: let us compare, I say, the inertia of matter with the natural imperfection of creatures, and the slowness of the laden boat with the defects to be found in the qualities and the action of the creature; and we shall find that there is nothing so just as this comparison. The current is the cause of the boat's movement but not of its retardation; God is the cause of perfection in the nature and the actions of the creature, but the limitation of the receptivity of the creature is the cause of the defects there are in its action. Thus the Platonists, St. Augustine and the Schoolmen were right to say that God is the cause of the material element of evil which lies in the positive, and not of the formal element, which lies in privation. Even so one may say that the current is the cause of the material element of the retardation, but not of the formal; that is, it is the cause of the boat's speed without being the cause of the limits to this speed. And God is no more the cause of sin than the river's current is the cause of the retardation of the boat.

There is, then, a wholly similar relation between such and such an action of God, and such and such a passion or reception of the creature, which in the ordinary course of things is perfected only in proportion to its 'receptivity', such is the term used. And when it is said that the creature depends upon God in so far as it exists and in so far as it acts, and even that conservation is a continual creation, this is true in that God gives ever to the creature and produces continually all that in it is positive, good and perfect, every perfect gift coming from the Father of lights. The imperfections, on the other hand, and the defects in operations spring from the original limitation that the creature could not but receive with the first beginning of its being, through the ideal reasons which restrict it. For God could not give the creature all without making of it a God; therefore there must needs be different degrees in the perfection of things, and limitations also of every kind.

No Better World Possible (from *Theodicy*, #193-5)

Up to now I have shown that the Will of God is not independent of the rules of Wisdom, although indeed it is a matter for surprise that one should have been constrained to argue about it, and to do battle for a truth so great and so well established. But it is hardly less surprising that there should be people who believe that God only half observes these rules, and does not choose the best, although his wisdom causes him to recognize it; and, in a word, that there should be writers who hold that God could have done better. . . .

Yet philosophers and theologians dare to support dogmatically such a belief; and I have many times wondered that gifted and pious persons should have been capable of setting bounds to the goodness and the perfection of God. For to assert that he knows what is best, that he can do it and that he does it not, is to avow that it rested with his will only to make the world better than it is; but that is what one calls lacking goodness. It is acting against that axiom already quoted: *Minus bonum habet rationem mali.* If some adduce experience to prove that God could have done better, they set themselves up as ridiculous critics of his works. To such will be given the answer given to all those who criticize God's course of action, and who from this same assumption, that is, the alleged defects of the world, would infer that there is an evil God, or at least a God neutral between good and evil. And if we hold the same opinion . . . we shall, I say, receive this answer: You have known the world only since the day before yesterday, you see scarce farther than your nose, and you carp at the world. Wait until you know more of the world and consider therein especially the parts which present a complete whole (as do organic bodies); and you will find there a contrivance and a beauty transcending all imagination. Let us thence draw conclusions as to the wisdom and the goodness of the author of things, even in things that we know not. We find in the universe some things which are not pleasing to us; but let us be aware that it is not made for us alone. It is nevertheless made for us if we are wise: it will serve us if we use it for our service; we shall be happy in it if we wish to be.

Someone will say that it is impossible to produce the best, because there is no perfect creature, and that it is always possible to produce one which would be more perfect. I answer that what can be said of a creature or of a particular substance, which can always be surpassed by another, is not to be applied to the universe, which, since it must extend through all future eternity, is an infinity. Moreover, there is an infinite number of creatures in the smallest particle of matter, because of the actual division of the *continuum* to infinity. And infinity, that is to say, the accumulation of an infinite number of substances, is, properly speaking, not a whole any more than the infinite number itself, whereof one cannot say whether it is even or uneven. That is just what serves to confute those who make of the world a God, or who think of God as the Soul of the world; for the world or the universe cannot be regarded as an animal or as a substance.

(From Leibniz: *Theodicy*, ed. and trans. by C. Huggard. London: Routledge & Kegan Paul, 1951. Reprinted by permission of Routledge & Kagen Paul.)

Review Questions

1. Why did Leibniz reject Spinoza's conception of God?
2. Discuss the notion of *harmony* as the key to Leibniz's philosophy.
3. What were the basic reasons for Leibniz's development of the system of monadology?
4. Compare Leibniz's view of substance with that of Spinoza.
5. How does Leibniz defend God from the charge of being the author of evil?

13

Thomas Hobbes (1588–1679)

Introduction

On the whole, seventeenth-century European philosophy was uncongenial to the medieval scholastic tradition. As a reaction on the continent, as we have seen, philosophy took the form of rationalism, but in Britain, philosophy, uncongenial to both rationalism and scholasticism, was beginning to move in the direction of empiricism. Although Francis Bacon's *Novum Organum* was a frontal attack on Aristotelianism and a tour-de-force for the experimental method, it did not mean the collapse of the deductive method in England. Thomas Hobbes, sympathetic to continental thought as a result of several visits to France and Italy, chose to base his system of politics on the deductive method, taking as his inspiration the geometry of Euclid and the experiments of Galileo; from these he produced the unique political treatise for which he is best known, the *Leviathan*.

Thomas Hobbes was born in 1588 near Malmesbury, the son of an obscure and unlearned vicar. After his father died, his education was provided for by a well-to-do uncle who had him tutored in Greek and Latin at age six and well schooled until age fourteen, when he entered the University of Oxford. His education there was based on the scholastic tradition, which was strong in logic; and though he referred to himself as a good disputant in logic, he developed an aversion to scholasticism, especially in the form of Aristotelian philosophy, for which he later coined the pejorative term *Aristotelity*. His real enjoyment in learning came from reading the classics and poring over maps of all kinds, of the stars and the earth, "maps celestial and terrestrial," as he called them.

After he took his bachelor of arts degree, his appointment as tutor to the son of William Cavendish, the first Earl of Devonshire, inaugurated a lifelong relationship with three generations of the Cavendish family as tutor, scholar and friend; when the first earl and his son died within two years of each other, and after a short absence, Hobbes was invited to assume the same role for the third Earl of Devonshire. From the beginning of this warm patronage, a wider world opened up for Hobbes, enabling him to meet prominent people, use the rich family library, and travel abroad. Among the people Hobbes met in the household was Francis Bacon, who was then Lord Chancellor and later Baron Verulam; they held many cherished conversations and collaborated in translating some of Bacon's essays into Latin. Though Hobbes never mentioned any debt to Bacon, he could hardly have escaped being influenced by the older man's passion against Aristotle, his enthusiasm for the new science, and his insistence that philosophy's value lay in serving practical human needs. All along, Hobbes continued his devotion to Greek literature by translating, and publishing in 1628, Thucydides' *History of the Peloponnesian Wars*, which he considered an expression not only of his classical humanism but also of his budding interest in politics, with a bias in favor of governance by one person over a democracy, whose weakness, he held, Thucydides portrayed in the decline of democratic Athens.

Hobbes might well have thought that Thucydides' *History* would serve as a beacon for his fellow Englishmen, who were in a state of political turmoil, with years of civil war between the supporters of the monarchy and those who opposed it, between the royalists and the parliamentarians. The violence produced by both sides, exemplified in the eventual beheading of King Charles I in 1649, brought Hobbes to the conclusion that civil war was among the greatest evils that could befall mankind. Thus, without surrendering his love of the classics, he was drawn bit by bit to political philosophy and devoted his middle years to developing a paradigm for political stability.

Though his trips abroad were occasioned by tutorship, at least one was not, for Hobbes' political views, especially those espoused in his first philosophical work, *The Elements of Law*, were beginning to gain some recognition, and because they were taken to be supportive of the king, when the parliamentarians got into power, he thought it best for his health to leave England; he did so in 1641, referring to himself later on as the "first of all that fled." His intellectual life abroad was no less fashioned and nourished than at home, and though his intellectual experiences and excitements can be considered on their own, they all evolved together in the direction of the political philosophy culminating in *Leviathan*, published in 1651. In a sense, the origin of this work goes back to one of his earlier trips to the continent when he happened upon Euclid's book *The Elements of Geometry*; in it he read a proposition that he felt could not have been arrived at by demonstration, but as he read further he saw how Euclid actually did demonstrate a complex conclusion by proceeding step by step, from very simple mathematical propositions, and, in the charming words of his contemporary biographer, "by G—, said he ... *this is impossible!*" It was not as though Hobbes never knew anything before about the deductive method, but as so often happens, the realization of it came suddenly, and the path became clear to him for deducing the principles of politics from the initial starting point of human behavior, which would be evident to all.

A subsequent visit to the continent brought him into contact with Mersenne, who had formed a highly esteemed circle of intellectuals in Paris whose goal was to stay abreast of the latest thought in science and philosophy. Thus Hobbes met Descartes and learned firsthand of his attempt to mathematicize philosophy. A number of years later, when Descartes was about to publish his *Meditations*, he invited Hobbes to publish his "Objections" appended to it. On the same trip, in 1634, he met Galileo in Florence and, in addition to acknowledging the brilliance of Galileo's discoveries, became fascinated with his idea of motion, which was directly opposite to Aristotle's in that the natural state of things was conceived of as motion, not rest. Hobbes was also impressed with Galileo's method in science, the method of resolution and composition, of analysis and synthesis, which he himself would later employ.

In the eleven-year period following his flight from London, Hobbes was engaged as tutor to the Prince of Wales, later Charles II. But most of all, he was committed to completing his *Leviathan*, which he considered would become the final statement of his political thought, hoping that it would be acclaimed as the theoretical basis for government as well as a careful enunciation of practical statecraft. By now Hobbes' views were being met with inimical responses from all quarters; by various factions he was called an atheist, materialist, anti-Catholic, anti-Puritan, heretic, antiroyalist, and antiparliamentarian. And his new book was seized upon by opposing political groups as favoring their side. Hobbes did, as a matter of fact, submit a manuscript copy to his student, the future king, and as a countermeasure, he did reconcile himself with the Council of State in London. He was finally allowed to return to England in 1651.

From then on, Hobbes led a retired, yet hardly inactive, life. He regained the favor of the restored King Charles II and was even given a pension by him. As far as his political writings were concerned, although he wrote several books on politics, he refrained from having them published during his lifetime. He continued writing on mathematical and philosophical topics, was involved in several ongoing nonpolitical controversies, and, having been denied membership in the newly formed Royal Society, returned to his ancient love by translating the *Odyssey* and the *Iliad*. He died in 1679.

Anyone breaking new ground faces enormous difficulties in establishing the uniqueness of his position while trying to relate it to cognate ideas of the past. This is certainly true of Hobbes, who, though not always prompt to acknowledge the influence of past philosophers, did actually produce, in the view of some commentators, the masterpiece of political philosophy written in English and one of the most comprehensive systems of political philosophy in the classical modern period. In recent years there has been a renewed interest in his work, and even though there has never been a completely settled interpretation of his philosophy, contemporary studies have reevaluated his analysis of language and have compelled a second look at notions like morality, the role of God in his system, his immersion in scriptural concerns, the charge of atheism, and whether his theory of society was actually an early apology for a bourgeois society. There are further questions pertaining to nominalism and skepticism, and to what extent these are operative principles of his philosophy. Yet none of these questions prevents a presentation of the main line of his doctrine that all can agree with, as it is given in the *Leviathan* and extended on some points in his other works.

Hobbes begins by laying down strict parameters: the scope of philosophy is limited to the corporeal world. Body is his interest, and he means by it what Descartes and other philosopher-scientists of the seventeenth century meant by it — quantity, extension, tridimensionality, space-occupying. And inasmuch as *substance* is another word for *body*, any discourse touching on God or anything else as *incorporeal substance* is contradictory: "And according to this acceptation of the word, Substance and Body, signify the same thing; and therefore Substance incorporeal are words, which when they are joined together, destroy one another, as if a man should say, an Incorporeal Body." One reason for Hobbes' insistence on this idea springs from his view that the notions of God, infinite, eternal, incorporeal, and so on, are incomprehensible and therefore are not the object of reason, but of faith. We may know *that* God is, but not *what* He is; so, even if we grant the existence of these notions, they are beyond rationality, though not beyond actuality.

But another reason for Hobbes' insistence on the corporeal is the deductive certitude with which reality as mechanical can be treated. That is why the chief property of body for Hobbes is *motion*, the discovery of which so excited him in his visit to Galileo, and which paved the way for a mechanistic philosophy of the universe, Cartesian in approach, and amenable to the making of a system in which only motion is understandable. The cause-and-effect relationship, or the knowledge of *consequences*, holds throughout, supplying Hobbes with the intellectual instrument for understanding the unity already present in the universe, or the unity he wants to introduce, whence is derived Hobbes' definition of philosophy: "The Knowledge acquired by Reasoning, from the Manner of the Generation of any thing, to the Properties; or from the Properties, to some possible Way of Generation of the same; to the end be able to produce, as far as matter, and human force permit, such Effects, as human life requires." Note that a constitutive part — and as far as politics is concerned, the most important part — of philosophy is its orientation to the practical good of mankind. Philosophy is divided into two main parts, one pertaining to natural bodies and their consequences and the other to political bodies and their consequences; it is on this second part that Hobbes brings his philosophical method to bear.

Hobbes really wanted his system to be a *system*. It is debatable whether his system actually does or does not hold together, but logical consistency has to be seen as yielding to his desire for the end to be achieved. That is why he wanted everything to be held together by some kind of necessity, and the necessity he focused on was the necessity of matter in motion, from which other truths of his system could be *deduced*: "From seeing life is but a motion of Limbs, the beginning whereof is some principal part within; why may we not say, that all *Automata* (Engines that move themselves by springs and wheels as doth a watch) have an artificial life? For what is the Heart, but a *Spring*; and the *Nerves*, but so many *Wheels,* giving motion to the whole Body . . .?" And if man is made this way by the art of nature, man can, in turn, by his nature-imitating art, create society as an *artificial animal*: "For by Art is created that great *Leviathan* called a *Common-wealth*, or *State* (in Latin, *Civitas*) which is but an Artificial Man," in which sovereign, subjects, magistrates, rewards, punishment, business and so on are all likened to parts of the natural body. With this in mind, Hobbes proceeds to create a state of affairs that would be the best human art could devise for man's "commodious living." But deduction, indispensable as it is for system building, relies on prior knowledge to begin with, and for Hobbes this comes from experiencing what men actually do, by observing their actual conduct — a matter evident to all. From man's actual conduct, Hobbes would "resolve" where it comes from and "compose" where it ought to go.

What, then, is man really like? Basically, man is distrustful of his fellowman. If anyone doubts this, Hobbes avers, let him confirm it by his own experience: "Let him therefore consider with himself, when taking a journey, he arms himself, and seeks to go well accompanied; when going to sleep, he locks his doors; when even in his house he locks his chest; and this when he knows there be Laws, and public Officers, armed to revenge all injuries shall be done him; what opinion has he of his fellow subjects, when he rides armed; of his fellow Citizens when he locks his doors; and of his children, and servants, when he locks his chests. Does he not there as much accuse mankind by his actions, as I do by my words?"

With this experience, Hobbes probes a little deeper to uncover what man is originally, or primitively, or, to use his words, what man is *by nature*. Thus, Hobbes concludes that there is a *natural state of man*, a "state of nature" that is not to be taken as a historical fact, yet not as a mere abstraction either, for it is that condition to which man would be reduced were it not for the civilizing effects of organized society. The state of nature is not a pretty one, and it is tellingly described in a famous paragraph: "In such condition, there is no place for Industry; because the fruit thereof is uncertain; and consequently no Culture of the Earth; no Navigation, nor use of the commodities that may be imported by Sea; no commodious Building; no Instruments of moving, and removing such things as require much force; no Knowledge of the face of the Earth; no account of Time; no Arts; no Letters; no Society; and which is worst of all, continual fear, and danger of violent death; And the life of man, solitary, poor, nasty, brutish, and short." For Hobbes, the natural state of man is nothing short of a state of war. Regarding the use of the phrase "state of nature," Hobbes is the first writer to use it in this way; with a far different meaning, in a theological context, it is as old as Christianity, in which it signifies the natural state of man before the advent of divine grace, which raises the "natural" state of man to a "supernatural" one, although the natural never really existed.

But man can emerge from this sorry state that "mere Nature" has placed him in by attending to other aspects of his nature, namely, his passions and his reason. Among man's passions, the most fundamental one — the one that moves him to action — is *self-preservation*, or, as Hobbes also puts it, the *fear of death*, especially violent death, which he abhorred during the English civil wars. That is why he designates the *liberty* man has to preserve his life as the lodestar of his political theory and calls it *the* "Right of Nature"; on it all other rights and laws depend, and from it they can be deduced. In a word, the fear of death "inclines" man to its opposite, *peace*; peace is the only antidote to war. If man's passion for self-preservation inclines him to peace, it is *reason* that "discovers" the way. Reason, for Hobbes, though endowed with many functions, is a guide to conduct and is the ultimate arbiter of the morality of man's actions. From the way he uses the word *reason* and the phrase "right reason" — reminiscent of St. Thomas' use of it — we can reasonably ask, despite his thumping of Aristotle and the Schoolmen, whether he is not actually in their tradition in this matter. Reason, then, becomes Hobbes' vehicle for deducing the moral-political structure of the institution whose sole purpose is to ensure peace, namely, the *Common-wealth.* In the title of his masterpiece, Hobbes calls the Commonwealth the *Leviathan*, a reference to the biblical sea giant that rules as "king over all the children of pride."

Hobbes then proceeds by reason to deduce the *laws of nature*, that is, the rules by which man advances the cause of peace and protects himself against the destruction of his life. There are nineteen such laws and, though they are general, they implicitly contain all the particularities that comprise the bulk of Hobbes's work. Of the nineteen, which he sets forth in the fourteenth and fifteenth chapters of *Leviathan*, the first three are the operative heart of his doctrine.

The *first* law, the fundamental law of nature, is: "That every man ought to endeavour Peace, as far as he has hope of obtaining it; and when he cannot obtain it, that he may seek and use all helps and advantages of War." The purpose of this effort is "to seek Peace, and follow it."

To endeavor peace is the purpose of the *second* law: "That a man be willing, when others are so too, as far forth as for peace and defense of himself he shall think it necessary, to lay down this right to all things; and be contented with so much liberty against other men, as he would allow other men against himself." In the state of nature, men, acting individually, have the right to "all things" as would preserve their lives, and it is this right that becomes the object of concern if man is going to seek peace, not as an individual, but collectively with others; a mutual agreement among men would allow the enlargement of life for all. Such a mutual agreement is called by Hobbes a *Contract*, that is, a mutual transfer of rights by which all parties hope to achieve some higher good, and insofar as a contract may not involve the immediate delivery of what is contracted for but does involve the trust of another for future delivery, it is called a *pact*, or *covenant.*

This gives rise to the *third* law: "That men perform their Covenants made." Here is the entire matter of mutual trust, the violation of which causes injustice and injury and the undoing of the contract trustfully made.

Following the internal logic of the Laws of Nature — to ensure the endeavor toward peace, the reasonable laying down of rights, and the making and keeping of contracts — brings Hobbes to the only possible conclusion: that some kind of Common Power must be established to make the agreement of men "constant and lasting," and "thereby to secure them in such sort, as that by their own authority, and by the fruits of the Earth, they may nourish themselves and live contentedly." The common power envisioned by Hobbes is "one Man or an Assembly of men," called *Sovereign*, upon whom men can confer their power and strength, and who would act in any way whatsoever to guarantee the peace and safety of his subjects. Hobbes takes pains to point out that no one is giving up his person, which is inalienable, but that individuals contract with each other to give up their right of self-governance to the Sovereign so that all, united together, are themselves the author of the actions taken by the Sovereign. "This done, the Multitude so united in one Person, is called a *Commonwealth*." And thus is the "artificial man," which Hobbes set out to create, created.

Hobbes elaborates in detail the rights of the Sovereign, such as his power of appointing public ministers, controlling trade, meting out punishment, governing religious matters, and supervising education, to indicate that the Sovereign's power is *absolute* and that his subjects have the obligation to obey. Yet, to use current phraseology, the Sovereign is authoritarian but not totalitarian, for subjects have rights that are nontransferrable, or inalienable, such as integrity of life and limb, use of food and medicine necessary to maintain life and health, freedom from self-incrimination, buying and selling, and choice of residence; these and other similar rights the Sovereign must respect and in no way contravene.

Unity is the key to the commonwealth; the full title of Hobbes' work, *Leviathan, or the Matter, Form, and Power of a Common-wealth Ecclesiastical and Civil,* informs us that he is not writing of *two* commonwealths, one ecclesiastical and one civil, but of *one* commonwealth in which both ecclesiastical and civil governance are to be found. That this is the case is shown by the care he takes in explaining that what we know about God *naturally* (that is, through the natural dictates of right reason) is not at variance with what we know about God *prophetically* (that is, knowing the laws He gave through His chosen people). It is only reasonable for Hobbes to conclude that the prophetical is subsumed in the natural, because the natural is *eo ipso* prior, and this subsumption in no way destroys the features of the prophetical. The vast canvassing of Sacred Scripture that occupies almost half of the *Leviathan* is a painstaking, and clearly devotional, analysis of God's word in which Hobbes tries ingeniously to show that the Kingdom of God as described in the Bible is nothing less than the very commonwealth he discovered in the nature of man. So, the subsumption of the ecclesiastical into the civil has the authority of God's word to support it. Because the civil predominates, and because we know God's rule through the dictates of reason, the commonwealth is valid for "infidel" Sovereigns with non-Christian subjects, as it is for Christian Sovereigns with Christian subjects.

Motivated by the notion that philosophy is worthy of the name only when it deals with the benefit of mankind, perhaps Hobbes was all too conscious of making a truly original contribution to political philosophy. Certainly with the notions of the state of nature, the social contract, and the structure of the commonwealth, he felt that his vision of a new era of political stability was logical and unimpeachable, and therefore ought to enlist the support of the universities. On the one hand, he wrote in a tradition they were comfortable with, for to the extent that Socrates, Plato, and Aristotle held for a state that would best suit its citizens, Hobbes was in full agreement. On the other hand, ideals are far from making a state work, and Hobbes knew he was going beyond these philosophers in founding a *practical* political philosophy. He differed from them on a major theoretical point as well, for the great Greek thinkers maintained that man was social by nature, whereas Hobbes maintained that man was individual and even asocial by nature, so that if a society is formed, it is for the sake of the individual anxious to preserve himself in peace and security — in the view of some commentators, a kind of political hedonism. Yet, given the time in which he lived, Hobbes sought a genuine balance between society and the individual; this is reflected in his attempt to steer a middle course between the king and the people by denying that the king had direct authority by divine right to rule over a society that awaited him, as opposed to a Sovereign established by the several wills of all those who authorized his power, the momentous idea being that the people were able to empower the Sovereign. Hobbes thought of his doctrine as being universal, and if it is true that the universal can be achieved only through the particular, the particular set of circumstances prompting his mind and heart to work for universal peace was the English civil war, and so he concludes his treatise on the commonwealth of peace by reminding his readers, ruefully and hopefully, that it was "occasioned by the disorders of the present time."

Readings

From Leviathan, or the Matter, Form, and Power of a Commonwealth Ecclesiastical and Civil

Chapter XIII

Of the Natural Condition of Mankind as Concerning Their Felicity, and Misery

Nature hath made men so equal, in the faculties of the body and mind; as that, though there be found one man sometimes manifestly stronger is body or of quicker mind than another, yet when all is reckoned together, the difference between man and man is not so considerable, as that one man can thereupon claim to himself any benefit, to which another may not pretend as well as he. For as to the strength of body, the weakest has strength enough to kill the strongest, either by secret machination or by confederacy with others that are in the same danger with himself.

And as to the faculties of the mind—setting aside the arts grounded upon words, and especially that skill of proceeding upon general and infallible rules, called science; which very few have, and but in few things; as being not a native faculty, born with us; nor attained, as prudence, while we look after somewhat else—I find yet a greater equality amongst men, than that of strength. For prudence is but experience which equal time equally bestows on all men, in those things they equally apply themselves unto. That which may perhaps make such equality incredible, is but a vain conceit of one's own wisdom, which almost all men think they have in a greater degree than the vulgar; that is, than all men but themselves, and a few others, whom by fame, or for concurring with themselves, they approve. For such is the nature of men, that howsoever they may acknowledge many others to be more witty, or more eloquent, or more learned, yet they will hardly believe there be many so wise as themselves; for they see their own wit at hand, and other men's at a distance. But this proveth rather that men are in that point equal, than unequal. For there is not ordinarily a greater sign of the equal distribution of anything, than that every man is contented with his share.

From this equality of ability, ariseth equality of hope in the attaining of our ends. And therefore if any two men desire the same thing, which nevertheless they cannot both enjoy, they become enemies; and in the way to their end, which is principally their own conservation, and sometimes their delectation only, endeavor to destroy, or subdue one another. And from hence it comes to pass that where an invader hath no more to fear than another man's single power; if one plant, sow, build, or possess a convenient seat, others may probably be expected to come prepared with forces united, to disposses and deprive him, not only of the fruit of his labor, but also of his life or liberty. And the invader again is in the like danger of another.

And from this difference of one another, there is no way for any man to secure himself so reasonable as anticipation; that is, by force or wiles to master the persons of all men he can, so long, till he see no other power great enough to endanger him: and this is no more than his own conservation requireth, and is generally allowed. Also because there be some, that taking pleasure in contemplating their own power in the acts of conquest, which they pursue farther than their security requires; if others, that otherwise would be glad to be at ease within modest bounds, should not by invasion increase their power, they would not be able long time, by standing only on their defense, to subsist. And by consequence, such augmentation of dominion over men being necessary to a man's conservation, it ought to be allowed him.

Again, men have no pleasure, but on the contrary a great deal of grief, in keeping company, where there is no power able to overawe them all. For every man looketh that his companion should value him at the same rate he sets upon himself; and upon all signs of contempt, or undervaluing, naturally endeavors, as far as he dares (which amongst them that have no common power to keep them in quiet, is far enough to make them destroy each other), to extort a greater value from his contemners by damage, and from others by the example.

So that in the nature of man, we find three principal causes of quarrel. First, competition; second, difference; thirdly, glory.

The first maketh men invade for gain; the second, for safety; and the third, for reputation. The first use violence to make themselves masters of other men's persons, wives, children, and cattle; the second, to defend them; the third, for trifles, as a word, a smile, a different opinion, and any other sign of undervalue, either direct in their persons, or by reflection in their kindred, their friends, their nation, their profession, or their name.

Hereby it is manifest that during the time men live without a common power to keep them all in awe, they are in that condition which is called war; and such a war as is of every man against every man. For war consisteth not in battle only, or the act of fighting, but in a tract of time wherein the will to contend by battle is sufficiently known, and therefore the notion of time is to be considered in the nature of war, as it is in the nature of weather. For as the nature of foul weather lieth not in a shower or two of rain, but in an inclination thereto of many days together; so the nature of war consisteth not in actual fighting, but in the known disposition thereto, during all the time there is no assurance to the contrary. All other time is peace.

Whatsoever therefore is consequent to a time of war, where every man is enemy to every man; the same is consequent to the time, wherein men live without other security than what their own strength and their own invention shall furnish them withal. In such condition there is no place for industry, because the fruit thereof is uncertain: and consequently no culture of the earth; no navigation, nor use of the commodities that may be imported by sea; no commodious building; no instruments of moving, and removing, such things as require much force; no knowledge of the face of the earth; no account of time; no arts; no letters; no society; and which is worst of all, continual fear, and danger of violent death; and the life of man, solitary, poor, nasty, brutish, and short.

It may seem strange to some man that has not well weighed these things, that nature should thus dissociate, and render men apt to invade and destroy one another; and he may therefore, not trusting to this inference, made from the passions, desire perhaps to have the same confirmed by experience. Let him therefore consider with himself, when taking a journey, he arms himself and seeks to go well accompanied; when going to sleep, he locks his doors; when even in his house he locks his chests; and this when he knows there be laws, and public officers, armed, to revenge all injuries shall be done him: what opinion he has of his fellow-subjects, when he rides armed; of his fellow-citizens, when he locks his doors; and of his children, and servants, when he locks his chests. Does he not there as much accuse mankind by his actions, as I do by my words? But neither of us accuse man's nature in it. The desires, and other passions of man, are in themselves no sin. No more are the actions that proceed from those passions, till they know a law that forbids them: which till laws be made they cannot know; nor can any law be made, till they have agreed upon the person that shall make it.

It may peradventure be thought, there was never such a time nor condition of war as this; and I believe it was never generally so, over all the world: but there are many places where they live so now. For the savage people in many places of America, except the government of small families, the concord whereof dependeth on natural lust, have no government at all; and live at this day in that brutish manner, as I said before. Howsoever, it may be perceived what manner of life there would be, where there were no common power to fear; by the manner of life which men that have formerly lived under a peaceful government, use to degenerate into in a civil war.

But though there had never been any time wherein particular men were in a condition of war one against another; yet in all times, kings, and persons of sovereign authority, because of their independency, are in continual jealousies, and in the state and posture of gladiators; having their weapons pointing, and their eyes fixed on one another; that is, their forts, garrisons, and guns upon the frontiers of their kingdoms; and continual spies upon their neighbors; which is a posture of war. But because they uphold thereby the industry of their subjects, there does not follow from it that misery which accompanies the liberty of particular men.

To this war of every man against every man, this also is consequent: *that nothing can be unjust.* The notions of right and wrong, justice an injustice, have there no place. Where there is no common power, there is no law; where no law, no injustice. Force and fraud are in war the two cardinal virtues. Justice and injustice are none of the faculties neither of the body nor mind. If they were, they might be in a man that were alone in the world, as well as his senses and passions. They are qualities that relate to men in society, not in solitude. It is consequent also to the same condition, that there be no propriety, no dominion, no *mine* and *thine* distinct; but only that to be every man's, that he can get; and for so long as he can keep it. And thus much for the ill condition which man by mere nature is actually placed in; though with a possibility to come out of it, consisting partly in the passions, partly in his reason.

The passions that incline men to peace are fear of death, desire of such things as are necessary to commodious living, and a hope by their industry to obtain them. And reason suggesteth convenient articles of peace, upon which men may be drawn to agreement. These articles are they which otherwise are called the Laws of Nature whereof I shall speak more particularly in the two following chapters.

Chapter XIV

Of the First and Second Natural Laws, and of Contracts

The right of nature, which writers commonly call *jus naturale*, is the liberty each man hath to use his own power, as he will himself, for the preservation of his own nature; that is to say, of his own life; and consequently, of doing anything, which in his own judgment and reason, he shall conceive to be the aptest means thereunto.

By *liberty*, is understood, according to the proper signification of the word, the absence of external impediments: which impediments, may oft take away part of a man's power to do what he would; but cannot hinder him from using the power left him, according as his judgment and reason shall dictate to him.

A *law of nature, lex naturalis*, is a precept or general rule, found out by reason, by which a man is forbidden to do that which is destructive of his life, or taketh away the means of preserving the same; and to omit that by which he thinketh it may be best preserved. For though they that speak of this subject use to confound *jus* and *lex, right* and *law*; yet they ought to be distinguished: because *right* consisteth in liberty to do or to forbear, whereas *law* determineth and bindeth to one of them; so that law, and right differ as much as obligation and liberty; which in one and the same matter are inconsistent.

And because the condition of man, as hath been declared in the precedent chapter, is a condition of war of everyone against everyone; in which case everyone is governed by his own reason, and there is nothing he can make use of that may not be a help unto him in preserving his life against his enemies: it followeth, that in such a condition every man has a right to everything; even to one another's body. And therefore, as long as this natural right of every man to everything endureth, there can be no security to any man, how strong or wise soever he be, of living out the time which nature ordinarily alloweth men to live. And consequently it is a precept, or general rule of reason, *that every man ought to endeavor peace, as far as he has hope of obtaining it; and when he cannot obtain it, that he may seek and use all helps and advantages of war.* The first branch of which rule containeth the first and fundamental law of nature; which is, *to seek peace and follow it.* The second, the sum of the right of nature; which is, *by all means we can, to defend ourselves.*

From this fundamental law of nature, by which men are commanded to endeavor peace, is derived this second law: *that a man be willing, when others are so too, as far forth as for peace and defense of himself he shall think it necessary, to lay down this right to all things; and be contented with so much liberty against other men, as he would allow other men against himself.* For as long as every man holdeth this right, of doing anything he liketh, so long are all men in the condition of war. But if other men will not lay down their right, as well as he, then there is no reason for anyone to divest himself of his: for that were to expose himself to prey, which no man is bound to, rather than to dispose himself to peace. This is that law of the Gospel: *whatsoever you require that others should do to you, that do ye to them.* And that law of all men, *quod tibi fieri non vis, alteri ne feceris.*

To *lay down* a man's *right* to anything, is to *divest* himself of the *liberty,* of hindering another of the benefit of his own right to the same. For he that renounceth or passeth away his right, giveth not to any other man a right which he had not before; because there is nothing to which every man had not right by nature: but only standeth out of his way, that he may enjoy his own original right, without hindrance from him, not without hindrance from another. So that the effect which redoundeth to one man, by another man's defect of right, is but so much diminution of impediments to the use of his own right original.

Right is laid aside, either by simply renouncing it, or by transferring it to another. By *simply renouncing,* when he cares not to whom the benefit thereof redoundeth. By *transferring,* when he intendeth the benefit thereof to some certain person or persons. And when a man hath in either manner abandoned or granted away his right; then is he said to be *obliged,* or bound, not to hinder those to whom such right is granted or abandoned, from the benefit of it; and that he *ought,* and it is his *duty,* not to make void that voluntary act of his own; and that such hindrance is *injustice,* and *injury,* as being *sine jure;* the right being before renounced, or transferred. So that injury, or injustice, in the controversies of the world, is somewhat like to that, which in the disputations of scholars is called *absurdity.* For as it is there called an absurdity to contradict what one maintained in the beginning; so in the world, it is called injustice, and injury, voluntarily to undo that which from the beginning he had voluntarily done. The way by which a man either simply renounceth, or transferreth his right, is a declaration, or signification, by some voluntary and sufficient sign or signs, that he doth so renounce or transfer, or hath so renounced or transferred the same, to him that accepteth it. And these signs are either words only, or actions only, or, as it happeneth most often, both words and actions. And the same are the bonds, by which men are bound and obliged— bonds that have their strength, not from their own nature, for nothing is more easily broken than a man's word, but from fear of some evil consequence upon the rupture.

Whensoever a man transferreth his right, or renounceth it; it is either in consideration of some right reciprocally transferred to himself, or for some other good he hopeth for thereby. For it is a voluntary act; and of the voluntary acts of every man, the object is some *good to himself*. And therefor there be some rights which no man can be understood by any words, or other signs, to have abandoned or transferred. As first a man cannot lay down the right of resisting them that assault him by force, to take away his life; because he cannot be understood to aim thereby, at any good to himself. The same may be said of wounds, and chains, and imprisonment: both because there is no benefit consequent to such patience, as there is to the patience of suffering another to be wounded or imprisoned; as also because a man cannot tell, when he seeth men proceed against him by violence, whether they intend his death or not. And lastly the motive, an end for which this renouncing and transferring of right is introduced, is nothing else but the security of a man's person, in his life, and in the means of so preserving life as not to be weary of it. And therefore if a man by words, or other signs, seem to despoil himself of the end for which those signs were intended, he is not to be understood as if he meant it, or that it was his will, but that he was ignorant of how such words and actions were to be interpreted.

The mutual transferring of right, is that which men call *contract*.

There is difference between transferring of right to the thing, and transferring, or tradition—that is delivery—of the thing itself. For the thing may be delivered together with the translation of the right, as in buying and selling with ready money, or exchange of goods, or lands; and it may be delivered sometime after.

Again, one of the contractors may deliver the thing contracted for on his part, and leave the other to perform his part at some determinate time after, and in the meantime be trusted; and then the contract on his part is called *pact*, or *covenant*: or both parts may contract now to perform hereafter; in which cases, he that is to perform in time to come, being trusted, his performance is called *keeping of promise*, or faith; and the failing of performance, if it be voluntary, *violation of faith*.

Chapter XV

Of Other Laws of Nature

From that law of nature by which we are obliged to transfer to another such rights as, being retained, hinder the peace of mankind, there followeth a third; which is this, *that men perform their covenants made*: without which, covenants are in vain, and but empty words; and the right of all men to all things remaining, we are still in the condition of war.

And in this law of nature, consisteth the fountain and original of *justice*. For where no covenant hath preceded, there hath no right been transferred, and every man has right to everything; and consequently, no action can be unjust. But when a covenant is made, then to break it is *unjust* and the definition of *injustice* is no other than *the not performance of covenant*. And whatsoever is not unjust, is *just*.

But because covenants of mutual trust, where there is a fear of not performance on either part, as hath been said in the former chapter, are invalid; though the original of justice be the making of covenants; yet injustice actually there can be none, till the cause of such fear be taken away; which while men are in the natural condition of war, cannot be done. Therefore before the names of just and unjust can have place, there must be some coercive power, to compel men equally to the performance of their covenants, by the terror of some punishment greater than the benefit they expect by the breach of their covenant; and to make good that propriety which by mutual contract men acquire, in recompense of the universal right they abandon: and such power there is none before the erection of a commonwealth. And this is also to be gathered out of the ordinary definition of justice in the Schools; for they say, that *justice is the constant will of giving to every man his own*. And therefore where there is no own, that is no propriety, there is no injustice; and where is no coercive power erected, that is, where there is no commonwealth, there is no propriety; all men having right to all things: therefore where there is no commonwealth, there nothing is unjust. So that the nature of justice consisteth in keeping of valid covenants; but the validity of covenants begins not but with the constitution of a civil power sufficient to compel men to keep them, and then it is also that propriety begins. ...

Chapter XVII

Of the Causes, Generations, and Definition of a Commonwealth

The final cause, end, or design of men who naturally love liberty and dominion over others, in the introduction of that restraint upon them-selves in which we see them live in commonwealths, is the foresight of their own preservation, and of a more contented life thereby;

that is to say, of getting themselves out from that miserable condition of war, which is necessarily consequent, as hath been shown in Chapter XIII, to the natural passions of men, when there is no visible power to keep them in awe, and tie them by fear of punishment to the performance of their covenants and observation of those laws of nature set down in the fourteenth and fifteenth chapters.

For the laws of nature, as justice, equity, modesty, mercy, and, in sum, *doing to others as we would be done to,* of themselves, without the terror of some power to cause them to be observed, are contrary to our natural passions, that carry us to partiality, pride, revenge, and the like. And covenants, without the sword, are but words, and of no strength to secure a man at all. Therefore notwithstanding the laws of nature, which everyone hath then kept, when he has the will to keep them when he can do it safely; if there be no power erected, or not great enough for our security, every man will, and may, lawfully rely on his own strength and art, for caution against all other men. And in all places where men have lived by small families, to rob and spoil one another has been a trade, and so far from being reputed against the law of nature, that the greater spoils they gained, the greater was their honor; and men observed no other laws therein but the laws of honor; that is, to abstain from cruelty, leaving to men their lives, and instruments of husbandry. And as small families did then; so now do cities and kingdoms, which are but greater families, for their own security enlarge their dominions, upon all pretenses of danger and fear of invasion, or assistance that may be given to invaders, and endeavor as much as they can to subdue or weaken their neighbors, by open force and secret arts, for want of other caution, justly; and are remembered for it in after ages with honor.

Nor is it the joining together of a small number of men, that gives them this security; because in small numbers, small additions on the one side or the other make the advantage of strength so great, as is sufficient to carry the victory, and therefore gives encouragement to an invasion. The multitude sufficient to confide in for our security, is not determined by any certain number, but by comparison with the enemy we fear; and is then sufficient, when the odds of the enemy is not of so visible and conspicuous moment, to determine the event of war, as to move him to attempt.

And be there never so great a multitude, yet if their actions be directed according to their particular judgments and particular appetites, they can expect thereby no defense nor protection, neither against a common enemy nor against the injuries of one another. For being distracted in opinions concerning the best use and application of their strength, they do not help but hinder one another; and reduce their strength by mutual opposition to nothing: whereby they are easily, not only subdued by a very few that agree together; but also when there is no common enemy, they make war upon each other, for their particular interests. For if we could suppose a great multitude of men to consent in the observation of justice, and other laws of nature, without a common power to keep them all in awe, we might as well suppose all mankind to do the same; and then there neither would be, nor need to be any civil government or commonwealth at all, because there would be peace without subjection.

Nor is it enough for the security, which men desire should last all the time of their life, that they be governed and directed by one judgment for a limited time, as in one battle or one war. For though they obtain a victory by their unanimous endeavor against a foreign enemy; yet afterwards, when either they have no common enemy, or he that by one part is held for an enemy, is by another part held for a friend, they must needs by the difference of their interests dissolve, and fall again into a war amongst themselves. . . .

The only way to erect such a common power, as may be able to defend them from the invasion of foreigners and the injuries of one another, and thereby to secure them in such sort as that, by their own industry, and by the fruits of the earth, they may nourish themselves and live contentedly; is, to confer all their power and strength upon one man, or upon one assembly of men, that may reduce all their wills, by plurality of voices, unto one will: which is as much as to say, to appoint one man, or assembly of men, to bear their person; and everyone to own and acknowledge himself to be author of whatsoever he that so beareth their person, shall act or cause to be acted in those things which concern the common peace and safety; and therein to submit their wills, everyone to his will, and their judgments, to his judgment. This is more than consent, or concord; it is a real unity of them all, in one and the same person, made by covenant of every man with every man, in such manner as if every man should say to every man, *"I authorize and give up my right of governing myself to this man, or to this assembly of men, on this condition, that thou give up thy right to him, and authorize all his actions in like manner."* This done, the multitude so united in one person is called a commonwealth, in Latin *civitas.* This is the generation of that great LEVIATHAN, *or rather, to speak more reverently, of that mortal god, to which we owe under the immortal God,* our peace and defense. For by this authority, given him by every particular man in the commonwealth, he hath the use of so much power and strength conferred on him, that by terror thereof he is enabled to perform the wills of them all, to peace at home and mutual aid against their enemies abroad. And in him consisteth the essence of the commonwealth; which, to define it, is *one person, of whose acts a great multitude, by mutual covenants one with another, have made themselves every one the author, to the end he may use the strength and means of them all, as he shall think expedient, for their peace and common defense.*

And he that carrieth this person, is called *sovereign*, and said to have sovereign power; and everyone besides, his *subject*.

The attaining to this sovereign power is by two ways. One, by natural force; as when a man maketh his children to submit themselves and their children to his government, as being able to destroy them if they refuse; or by war subdueth his enemies to his will, giving them their lives on that condition. The other, is when men agree amongst themselves to submit to some man, or assembly of men, voluntarily, on confidence to be protected by him against all others. This latter, may be called a political commonwealth, or commonwealth by *institution*; and the former, a commonwealth by *acquisition*. And first, I shall speak of a commonwealth by institution.

Chapter XVIII

Of The Rights of Sovereigns by Institution

A Commonwealth is said to be *instituted*, when a multitude of men do agree and covenant, everyone with everyone, that to whatsoever man, or assembly of men, shall be given by the major part the right to present the person of them all, that is to say, to be their *representative*; everyone, as well he that voted for it as he that voted against it, shall authorize all the actions and judgments of that man, or assembly of men, in the same manner as if they were his own, to the end to live peaceably amongst themselves and be protected against other men.

From this institution of a commonwealth are derived all the *rights* and *faculties* of him, or them, on whom sovereign power is conferred by the consent of the people assembled.

First, because they covenant, it is to be understood they are not obliged by former covenant to anything repugnant hereunto. And consequently they that have already instituted a commonwealth, being thereby bound by covenant to own the actions and judgments of one, cannot lawfully make a new covenant amongst themselves, to be obedient to any other, in anything whatsoever, without his permission. And therefore, they that are subject to a monarch, cannot without his leave cast off monarchy, and return to the confusion of a disunited multitude; nor transfer their person from him that beareth it, to another man, or other assembly of men: for they are bound, every man to every man, to own, and be reputed author of all, that he that already is their sovereign shall do and judge fit to be done; so that any one man dissenting, all the rest should break their covenant made to that man, which is injustice: and they have also every man given the sovereignty to him that beareth their person; and therefore if they depose him, they take from him that which is his own, and so again it is injustice. . . .

Secondly, because the right of bearing the person of them all, is given to him they make sovereign, by covenant only of one to another, and not of him to any of them; there can happen no breach of covenant on the part of the sovereign; and consequently none of his subjects, by any pretense of forfeiture, can be freed from his subjection. That he which is made sovereign maketh no covenant with his subjects beforehand, is manifest; because either he must make it with the whole multitude, as one party to the covenant, or he must make a several covenant with every man. With the whole, as one party, it is impossible, because as yet they are not one person: and if he make so many several covenants as there be men, those covenants after he hath the sovereignty are void; because what act soever can be pretended by any one of them for breach thereof, is the act both of himself and of all the rest, because done in the person, and by the right of every one of them in particular.

Thirdly, because the major part hath by consenting voices declared a sovereign, he that dissented must now consent with the rest; that is, be contented to avow all the actions he shall do, or else justly be destroyed by the rest. For if he voluntarily entered into the congregation of them that were assembled, he sufficiently declared thereby his will, and therefore tacitly covenanted to stand to what the major part should ordain; and therefore if he refuse to stand thereto, or make protestation against any of their decrees, he does contrary to his covenant, and therefore unjustly. And whether he be of the congregation or not, and whether his consent be asked or not, he must either submit to their decrees, or be left in the condition of war he was in before; wherein he might without injustice be destroyed by any man whatsoever.

Fourthly, because every subject is by this institution author of all the actions and judgments of the sovereign instituted; it follows that whatsoever he doth, it can be no injury to any of his subjects, nor ought he to be by any of them accused of injustice. For he that doth anything by authority from another, doth therein no injury to him by whose authority he acteth: but by this institution of a commonwealth, every particular man is author of all the sovereign doth: and consequently he that complaineth of injury from his sovereign, complaineth of that whereof he himself is author; and therefore ought not to accuse any man but himself; no nor himself of injury, because to do injury to one's self, is impossible. It is true that they that have sovereign power may commit iniquity, but not injustice, or injury, in the proper signification.

Fifthly, and consequently to that which was said last, no man that hath sovereign power can justly be put to death, or otherwise in any manner by his subjects punished. For seeing every subject is author of the actions of his sovereign, he punisheth another for the actions committed by himself.

And because the end of this institution, is the peace and defense of them all, and whosoever has right to the end has right to the means; it belongeth of right, to whatsoever man or assembly that hath the sovereignty, to be judge both of the means of peace and defense, and also of the hindrances and disturbances of the same; and to do whatsoever he shall think necessary to be done, both beforehand, for the preserving of peace and security, by prevention of discord at home and hostility from abroad, and, when peace and security are lost, for the recovery of the same. And therefore,

Sixthly, it is annexed to the sovereignty, to be judge of what opinions and doctrines are averse, and what conducing to peace; and consequently, on what occasions, how far, and what men are to be trusted withal, in speaking to multitudes of people; and who shall examine the doctrines of all books before they be published. ...

Seventhly, is annexed to the sovereignty, the whole power of prescribing the rules, whereby every man may know what goods he may enjoy, and what actions he may do, without being molested by any of his fellow-subjects; and this is it men call *propriety*. For before constitution of sovereign power, as hath already been shown, all men had right to all things; which necessarily causeth war: and therefore this propriety, being necessary to peace, and depending on sovereign power, is the act of that power, in order to the public peace. ...

Eighthly, is annexed to the sovereignty, the right of judicature; that is to say, of hearing and deciding all controversies which may arise concerning law, either civil or natural, or concerning fact. For without the decision of controversies, there is no protection of one subject against the injuries of another. ...

Ninthly, is annexed to the sovereignty, the right of making war and peace with other nations and commonwealths; that is to say, of judging when it is for the public good, and how great forces are to be assembled, armed, and paid for that end; and to levy money upon the subjects, to defray the expenses thereof. ...

Tenthly, is annexed to the sovereignty, the choosing of all counsellors, ministers, magistrates, and offices, both in peace and war. For seeing the sovereign is charged with the end, which is the common peace and defense, he is understood to have power to use such means as he shall think most fit for his discharge.

Eleventhly, to the sovereign is committed the power of rewarding with riches, or honor, and of punishing with corporal or pecuniary punishment, or with ignominy, every subject according to the law he hath formerly made; or if there be no law made, according as he shall judge most to conduce to the encouraging of men to serve the commonwealth, or deterring of them from doing disservice to the same.

Lastly, considering what value men are naturally apt to set upon themselves, what respect they look for from others, and how little they value other men; from whence continually arise amongst them, emulation, quarrels, factions, and at last war, to the destroying of one another and diminution of their strength against a common enemy: it is necessary that there be laws of honor, and a public rate of the worth of such men as have deserved or are able to deserve well of the commonwealth; and that there be force in the hands of some or other, to put those laws in execution. . . .

These are the rights which make the essence of sovereignty, and which are the marks whereby a man may discern in what man, or assembly of men, the sovereign power is placed and resideth. For these are incommunicable and inseparable. . . .

This great authority being indivisible, and inseparably annexed to the sovereignty, there is little ground for the opinion of them that say of sovereign kings, though they be *singulis majores*, of greater power than every one of their subjects, yet they be *universis minores*, of less power than them all together. For if by 'all together' they mean not the collective body as one person, then 'all together' and 'every one' signify the same, and the speech is absurd. But if by 'all together' they understand them as one person, which person the sovereign bears, then the power of all together is the same with the sovereign's power, and so again the speech is absurd: which absurdity they see well enough when the sovereignty is in an assembly of the people, but in a monarch they see it not; and yet the power of sovereignty is the same in whomsoever it be placed.

Chapter XIX

Of The Several Kinds of Commonwealth by Institution, And of Succession to the Sovereign Power

The difference of commonwealths consisteth in the difference of the sovereign, or the person representative of all and every one of the multitude. And because the sovereignty is either in one man, or in an assembly of more than one; and into that assembly either every man hath right to enter, or not everyone, but certain men distinguished from the rest; it is manifest, there can be but three kinds of commonwealth. For the representative must needs be one man, or more; and if more, then it is the assembly of all, or but of a part. When the representative is one man, then is the commonwealth a *monarchy*; when an assembly of all that will come together, then it is a *democracy*, or popular commonwealth; when an assembly of a part only, then it is called an *aristocracy*. Other kind of commonwealth there can be none; for either one, or more, or all, must have the sovereign power, which I have shown to be indivisible, entire. . . .

Chapter XXI

Of The Liberty of Subjects

Liberty, or freedom, signifieth, properly, the absence of opposition: by opposition, I mean external impediments of motion; and may be applied no less to irrational and inanimate creatures, than to rational. For whatsoever is so tied, or environed, as it cannot move but within a certain space, which space is determined by the opposition of some external body, we say it hath not liberty to go further. And so of all living creatures, whilst they are imprisoned or restrained, with walls or chains, and of the water whilst it is kept in by banks or vessels, that otherwise would spread itself into a larger space, we use to say, they are not at liberty to move in such manner, as without those external impediments they would. But when the impediment of motion is in the constitution of the thing itself, we use not to say it wants the liberty, but the power to move; as when a stone lieth still, or a man is fastened to his bed by sickness.

And according to this proper and generally received meaning of the word, *a 'freeman' is he that in those things which by his strength and wit he is able to do, is not hindered to do what he has a will to.* But when the words 'free' and 'liberty' are applied to anything but bodies, they are abused; for that which is not subject to motion is not subject to impediment: and therefore, when it is said, for example, the way is free, no liberty of the way is signified, but of those that walk in it without stop. And when we say a gift is free, there is not meant any liberty of the gift, but of the giver, that was not bound by any law or covenant to give it. So when we 'speak freely,' it is not the liberty of voice or pronunciation, but of the man, whom no law hath obliged to speak otherwise than he did. Lastly, from the use of the word *free-will*, no liberty can be inferred of the will, desire, or inclination, but the liberty of the man; which consisteth in this, that he finds no stop, in doing what he has the will, desire, or inclination to do.

Fear and liberty are consistent; as when a man throweth his goods into the sea for *fear* the ship should sink, he doth it nevertheless very willingly, and may refuse to do it if he will; it is therefore the action of one that was *free*: so a man sometimes pays his debt, only for fear of imprisonment, which because nobody hindered him from detaining, was the action of a man at *liberty*. And generally all actions which men do in commonwealths, for fear of the law, are actions which the doers had liberty to omit.

Liberty and necessity are consistent: as in the water, that hath not only *liberty*, but a *necessity* of descending by the channel; so likewise in the actions which men voluntarily do: which, because they proceed from their will, proceed from *liberty*; and yet, because every act of man's will, and every desire, and inclination proceedeth from some cause, and that from another cause, in a continual chain, whose first link is in the hand of God the first of all causes, proceed from *necessity*. So that to him that could see the connection of those causes, the necessity of all men's voluntary actions, would appear manifest. And therefore God, that seeth and disposeth all things, seeth also that the liberty of man in doing what he will, is accompanied with the necessity of doing that which God will, and no more nor less. For though men may do many things which God does not command, nor is therefore author of them; yet they can have no passion nor appetite to anything of which appetite God's will is not the cause. And did not His will assure the *necessity* of man's will, and consequently of all that on man's will dependeth, the *liberty* of men would be a contradiction, and impediment to the omnipotence and liberty of God. And this shall suffice, as to the matter in hand, of that natural liberty, which only is properly called liberty.

But as men, for the attaining of peace and conservation of themselves thereby, have made an artificial man, which we call a commonwealth; so also have they made artificial chains, called *civil laws*, which they themselves, by mutual covenants, have fastened, at one end, to the lips of that man or assembly to whom they have given the sovereign power, and at the other end to their own ears. These bonds, in their own nature but weak, may nevertheless be made to hold, by the danger, though not by the difficulty, of breaking them.

In relation to these bonds only it is, that I am to speak now of the *liberty of subjects*. For seeing there is no commonwealth in the world wherein there be rules enough set down, for the regulating of all the actions and words of men; as being a thing impossible: it followeth necessarily that in all kinds of actions by the laws pretermitted, men have the liberty of doing what their own reasons shall suggest, for the most profitable to themselves. For if we take liberty in the proper sense for corporal liberty; that is to say, freedom from chains and prison; it were very absurd for men to clamor as they do, for the liberty they so manifestly enjoy. Again, if we take liberty for an exemption from laws, it is no less absurd for men to demand as they do, that liberty by which all other men may be masters of their lives. And yet, as absurd as it is, this is it they demand; not knowing that the laws are of no power to protect them, without a sword in the hands of a man, or men, to cause those laws to be put in execution. The liberty of a subject lieth therefore only in those things which in regulating their actions, the sovereign hath pretermitted: such as is the liberty to buy, and sell, and otherwise contract with one another; to choose their own abode, their own diet, their own trade of life, and institute their children as they themselves think fit; and the like.

Nevertheless we are not to understand that by such liberty, the sovereign power of life and death is either abolished or limited. For it has been already shown that nothing the sovereign representative can do to a subject, on what pretense soever, can properly be called injustice, or injury; because every subject is author of every act the sovereign doth; so that he never wanteth right to anything, otherwise than as he himself is the subject of God, and bound thereby to observe the laws of nature. . . .

The liberty whereof there is so frequent and honorable mention in the histories and philosophy of the ancient Greeks and Romans, and in the writings and discourse of those that from them have received all their learning in the politics, is not the liberty of particular men, but the liberty of the commonwealth; which is the same with that which every man then should have, if there were no civil laws nor commonwealth at all. And the effects of it also be the same. For as amongst masterless men, there is perpetual war of every man against his neighbor; no inheritance, to transmit to the son, nor to expect from the father; no propriety of goods or lands; no security; but a full and absolute liberty in every particular man: so in states, and commonwealths not dependent on one another, every commonwealth, not every man, has an absolute liberty, to do what it shall judge—that is to say, what that man, or assembly that representeth it, shall judge—most conducting to their benefit. But withal, they live in the condition of a perpetual war, and upon the confines of battle, with their frontiers armed, and cannons planted against their neighbors round about. The Athenians and Romans were free; that is, free commonwealths: not that any particular men had the liberty to resist their own representative, but that their representative had the liberty to resist or invade other people. There is written on the turrets of the city of Lucca in great characters at this day, the word *libertas*; yet no man can thence infer that a particular man has more liberty or immunity from the service of the commonwealth there than in Constantinople. Whether a commonwealth be monarchical or popular, the freedom is still the same. . . .

To come now to the particulars of the true liberty of a subject—that is to say, what are the things which, though commanded by the sovereign, he may nevertheless without injustice refuse to do,—we are to consider, what rights we pass away when we make a commonwealth; or, which is all one, what liberty we deny ourselves by owning all the actions, without exception, of the man, or assembly, we make our sovereign. For in the act of our *submission* consisteth both our *obligation* and our *liberty*; which must therefore be inferred by arguments taken from thence: there being no obligation on any man which ariseth not from some act of his own; for all men equally are by nature free. And because such arguments must either be drawn from the express words, "I authorize all his actions," or from the intention of him that submitteth himself to his power, which intention is to be understood by the end for which he so submitteth; the obligation, and liberty of the subject, is to be derived either from those words or others equivalent, or else from the end of the institution of sovereignty, namely, the peace of the subjects within themselves and their defense against a common enemy.

First therefore, seeing sovereignty by institution is by covenant of everyone to everyone; and sovereignty by acquisition, by covenants of the vanquished to the victor, or child to the parent; it is manifest that every subject has liberty in all those things, the right whereof cannot by covenant be transferred. I have shewn before, in the fourteenth chapter, that covenants not to defend a man's own body are void. Therefore:

If the sovereign command a man, though justly condemned, to kill, wound, or maim himself; or not to resist those that assault him; or to abstain from the use of food, air, medicine, or any other thing, without which he cannot live; yet hath that man the liberty to disobey.

If a man be interrogated by the sovereign, or his authority, concerning a crime done by himself, he is not bound, without assurance of pardon, to confess it; because no man, as I have shown in the same chapter, can be obliged by covenant to accuse himself.

Again, the consent of a subject to sovereign power is contained in these words, "I authorize, or take upon me, all his actions"; in which there is no restriction at all of his own former natural liberty: for by allowing him to kill me, I am not bound to kill myself when he commands me. It is one thing to say, "Kill me, or my fellow, if you please"; another thing to say, "I will kill myself, or my fellow." It followeth therefore, that:

No man is bound by the words themselves, either to kill himself or any other man; and consequently, that the obligation a man may sometimes have, upon the command of the sovereign to execute any dangerous or dishonorable office, dependeth not on the words of our submission, but on the intention, which is to be understood by the end thereof. When therefore our refusal to obey, frustrates the end for which the sovereignty was ordained, then there is no liberty to refuse; otherwise there is.

Upon this ground, a man that is commanded as a soldier to fight against the enemy, though his sovereign have right enough to punish his refusal with death, may nevertheless in many cases refuse, without injustice; as when he substituteth a sufficient soldier in his place: for in this case he deserteth not the service of the commonwealth. And there is allowance to be made for natural timorousness; not only to women, of whom no such dangerous duty is expected, but also to men of feminine courage. When armies fight, there is on one side, or both, a running away; yet when they do it not out of treachery, but fear, they are not esteemed to do it unjustly, but dishonorably. For the same reason, to avoid battle is not injustice, but cowardice. But he that enrolleth himself a soldier, or taketh imprest money, taketh away the excuse of a timorous nature; and is obliged not only to go to the battle, but also not run from it, without his captain's leave. And when the defense of the commonwealth requireth at once the help of all that are able to bear arms, everyone is obliged; because otherwise the institution of the commonwealth, which they have not the purpose or courage to preserve, was in vain. . . .

The obligation of subjects to the sovereign, is understood to last as long, and no longer, than the power lasteth by which he is able to protect them. For the right men have by nature to protect themselves, when none else can protect them, can by no covenant be relinquished. The sovereignty is the soul of the commonwealth; which once departed from the body, the members do no more receive their motion from it. The end of obedience is protection; which, wheresoever a man seeth it, either in his own or in another's sword, nature applieth his obedience to it, and his endeavor to maintain it. And though sovereignty, in the intention of them that make it, be immortal; yet it is in its own nature, not only subject to violent death, by foreign war; but also through the ignorance, and passions of men, it hath in it, from the very institution, many seeds of a natural mortality, by intestine discord. . . .

If a monarch shall relinquish the sovereignty both for himself and his heirs, his subjects return to the absolute liberty of nature; because, though nature may declare who are his sons, and who are the nearest of his kin; yet it dependeth on his own will, as hath been said in the precedent chapter, who shall be his heir. If therefore he will have no heir, there is no sovereignty, nor subjection. The case is the same, if he die without known kindred, and without declaration of his heir. For then there can no heir be known, and consequently no subjection be due. . . .

If a monarch subdued by war, render himself subject to the victor; his subjects are delivered from their former obligation, and become obliged to the victor. If he be held prisoner, or have not the liberty of his own body, he is not understood to have given away the right of sovereignty; and therefore his subjects are obliged to yield obedience to the magistrates formerly placed, governing not in their own name, but in his. For, his right remaining, the question is only of the administration; that is to say, of the magistrates and officers; which, if he have not means to name, he is supposed to approve those which he himself had formerly appointed. . . .

Chapter XXIX

Of Those Things That Weaken, Or Tend to The Dissolution of a Commonwealth

Though nothing can be immortal, which mortals make; yet, if men had the use of reason they pretend to, their commonwealths might be secured, at least from perishing by internal diseases. For by the nature of their institution, they are designed to live, as long as mankind, or as the laws of nature, or as justice itself, which gives them life. Therefore when they come to be dissolved, not by external violence, but intestine disorder, the fault is not in men, as they are the *matter*; but as they are the makers, and orderers of them. For men, as they become at last weary of irregular jostling, and hewing one another, and desire with all their hearts, to conform themselves into one firm and lasting edifice; so for want, both of the art of making fit laws, to square their actions by, and also of humility, and patience, to suffer the rude and cumbersome points of their present greatness to be taken off, they cannot without the help of a very able architect, be compiled into any other than a crazy building, such as hardly lasting out their own time, must assuredly fall upon the heads of their posterity. . . .

Chapter XLIII

Of What Is Necessary for a Man's Reception Into the Kingdom of Heaven

The most frequent pretext of sedition, and civil war, in Christian commonwealths, hath a long time proceeded from a difficulty, not yet sufficiently resolved, of obeying at once both God and man, then when their commandments are one contrary to the other. It is manifest enough, that when a man receiveth two contrary commands, and knows that one of them is God's, he ought to obey that, and not the other, though it be the command even of his lawful sovereign (whether a monarch, or a sovereign assembly), or the command of his father. The difficulty therefore consisteth in this, that men, when they are commanded in the name of God, know not in divers cases, whether the command be from God, or whether he that commandeth do but abuse God's name for some private ends of his own. For as there were in the Church of the Jews, many false prophets, that sought reputation with the people, by feigned dreams and visions; so there have been in all times in the Church of Christ, false teachers, that seek reputation with the people, by fantastical and false doctrines; and by such reputation (as is the nature of ambition) to govern them for their private benefit.

But this difficulty of obeying both God and the civil sovereign on earth, to those that can distinguish between what is *necessary*, and what is not *necessary for their reception into the kingdom of God*, is of no moment. For if the command of the civil sovereign be such, as that it may be obeyed without the forfeiture of life eternal; not to obey it is unjust; and the precept of the apostle takes place: *Servants obey your masters in all things*; and *Children obey your parents in all things*; and the precept of our Saviour, *The Scribes and Pharisees sit in Moses' chair; all therefore they shall say, that observe and do.* But if the command be such as cannot be obeyed, without being damned to eternal death; then it were madness to obey it, and the council of our Saviour takes place, (Matth. x. 28), *Fear not those that kill the body, but cannot kill the soul.* All men therefore that would avoid, both the punishments that are to be in this world inflicted, for disobedience to their earthly sovereign, and those that shall be inflicted in the world to come, for disobedience to God, have need be taught to distinguish well between what is, and what is not necessary to eternal salvation.

All that is necessary to salvation, is contained in two virtues, *faith in Christ*, and *obedience to laws*. The latter of these, if it were perfect, were enough to us. But because we are all guilty of disobedience to God's law, not only originally in Adam, but also actually by our own transgressions, there is required at our hands now, not only *obedience* for the rest of our time, but also a *remission of sins* for the time past; which remission is the reward of our faith in Christ. That nothing else is necessarily required to salvation, is manifest from this, that the kingdom of heaven is shut to none but to sinners; that is to say, to the disobedient, or transgressors of the law; nor to them, in case they repent, and believe all the articles of Christian faith necessary to salvation. . . .

But what commandments are those that God hath given us? Are all those laws which were given to the Jews by the hand of Moses, the commandments of God? If they be, why are not Christians taught to obey them? If they be not, what others are so, besides the law of nature? For our Saviour Christ hath not given us new laws, but counsel to observe those we are subject to; that is to say, the laws of nature, and the laws of our several sovereigns: nor did he make any new law to the Jews in his Sermon on the Mount, but only expounded the law of Moses, to which they were subject before. The laws of God therefore are none but the laws of nature, whereof the principal is, that we should not violate our faith, that is, a commandment to obey our civil sovereigns, which we constituted over us by mutual pact one with another. And this law of God, that commandeth obedience to the law civil, commandeth by consequence obedience to all the precepts of the Bible; which, as I have proved in the precedent chapter, is there only law, where the civil sovereign hath made it so; and in other places, but counsel; which a man at his own peril may without injustice refuse to obey. . . .

Having thus shown what is necessary to salvation; it is not hard to reconcile our obedience to God, with our obedience to the civil sovereign; who is either Christian, or infidel. If he be a Christian, he alloweth the belief of this article, that *Jesus is the Christ*; and of all the articles that are contained in, or are by evident consequence deduced from it: which is all the faith necessary to salvation. And because he is a sovereign, he requireth obedience to all his own, that is, to all the civil laws; in which also are contained all the laws of nature, that is all the laws of God: for besides the laws of nature, and the laws of the Church, which are part of the civil law (for the Church that can make laws is the commonwealth), there be no other laws divine. ...

And when the civil sovereign is an infidel, every one of his own subjects that resisteth him, sinneth against the laws of God (for such are the laws of nature), and rejecteth the counsel of the apostles, that admonisheth all Christians to obey their princes, and all children and servants to obey their parents and masters in all things. And for their *faith*, it is internal, and invisible; they have the license that Naaman had, and need not put themselves into danger for it. But if they do, they ought to expect their reward in heaven, and not complain of their lawful sovereign; much less make war upon him. ...

And thus much shall suffice, concerning the kingdom of God, and policy ecclesiastical. Wherein I pretend not to advance any position of my own, but only to show what are the consequences that seem to me deducible from the principles of Christian politics (which are the Holy Scriptures), in confirmation of the power of civil sovereigns, and the duty of their subjects. And in the allegation of Scripture, I have endeavored to avoid such texts as are of obscure or controverted interpretation; and to allege none, but in such sense as is most plain, and agreeable to the harmony and scope of the whole Bible; which was written for the re-establishment of the kingdom of God in Christ. For it is not the bare words, but the scope of the writer, that giveth the true light, by which any writing is to be interpreted; and they that insist upon single texts, without considering the main design, can derive nothing from them clearly; but rather by casting atoms of Scripture, as dust before men's eyes, make everything more obscure than it is; an ordinary artifice of those that seek not the truth, but their own advantage. ...

Conclusion

To conclude, there is nothing in this whole discourse, nor in that I writ before of the same subject in Latin, as far as I can perceive, contrary either to the Word of God, or to good manners; or to the disturbance of the public tranquillity. Therefore I think it may be profitably printed, and more profitably taught in the Universities, in case they also think so, to whom the judgment of the same belongeth. For seeing the Universities are the fountains of civil and moral doctrine, from whence the preachers, and the gentry, drawing such water as they find, use to sprinkle the same (both from the pulpit and in their conversation), upon the people, there ought certainly to be great care taken, to have it pure, both from the venom of heathen politicians, and from the incantation of deceiving spirits. And by that means the most men, knowing their duties, will be the less subject to serve the ambition of a few discontented persons, in their purposes against the state; and be the less grieved with the contributions necessary for their peace, and defense; and the governors themselves have the less cause, to maintain at the common charge any greater army, than is necessary to make good the public liberty, against the invasions and encroachments of foreign enemies.

And thus I have brought to an end my discourse of civil and ecclesiastical government, occasioned by the disorders of the present time, without partiality, without application, and without other design than to set before men's eyes the mutual relation between protection and obedience; of which the condition of human nature, and the laws divine, both natural and positive, require an inviolable observation. And though in the revolution of states, there can be no very good constellation for truths of this nature to be born under (as having an angry aspect from the dissolvers of an old government, and seeing but the backs of them that erect a new), yet I cannot think it will be condemned at this time, either by the public judge of doctrine, or by any that desires the continuance of public peace. And in this hope I return to my interrupted speculation of bodies natural; wherein, if God give me health to finish it, I hope the novelty will as much please, as in the doctrine of this artificial body it useth to offend. For such truth, as opposeth no man's profit, nor pleasure, is to all men welcome.

Review Questions

1. Discuss Hobbes' intention to deduce a philosophical system beginning with motion or, more precisely, matter-in-motion.
2. Describe the natural state of man according to Hobbes.
3. For Hobbes, what reasons do human beings have to seek society?
4. What, for Hobbes, is the nature of the Contract pre-requisite to society?
5. In Hobbes' view, why is there a need for a Commonwealth, or State?
6. As Hobbes describes it, do individuals have rights in a Commonwealth? Do sovereigns?
7. Why is Hobbes so concerned with squaring his views on the State with the Bible?

CHAPTER 14

John Locke (1632–1704)

Introduction

The word *empiricism,* or the adjectival forms *empiric* and *empirical,* come from the Greek word *empeirikos,* which refers to an experiment or trial. Today it generally means "based on direct observation or experimentation," such as in the statement "the natural sciences are empirical" or "One of the branches of psychology is empirical psychology." When used in philosophy, it still bears the idea of directness inasmuch as it refers to knowledge gained directly from *experience,* but it refers mainly to *sense* experience. Pure positions, however, are seldom, if ever, held in philosophy because they represent such extremes that they become untenable; if, therefore, rationalism and empiricism are opposed to each other, it does not follow that the rationalist is so committed to the deductive method that he discounts sense experience entirely, or that the empiricist is so committed to sense experience that he rejects the deductive method entirely. The difference between them is rather a question of emphasis: the more the sense aspect is stressed to the exclusion of the deductive, the more empirical the position is; the more the deductive aspect is stressed to the exclusion of the sense, the more rationalist the position is. The position taken, therefore, is considered extreme or moderate depending on the degree of emphasis.

John Locke's rejection of innate ideas, his reliance on sense experience as the beginning of all knowledge, and his hesitancy regarding the metaphysical tendency of the mind clearly remove him from continental rationalism and indicate his role in the shaping of modern empiricism.

He was born in 1632 near Bristol, England, the son of a country attorney and heir to a Puritan background. His formal schooling at the prestigious Westminster School was thoroughly classical, though its solemn rigor and the meanness of school life, in later reflections on education, were repudiated by him in favor of education by a private tutor. In 1652 he went to Christ Church, Oxford, where a long preparation for a bachelor of arts degree ensued, consisting chiefly of logic, metaphysics, and classical languages. He never appears to have read a great deal, at least in philosophy, having developed a profound dislike for Aristotle and scholastic philosophy as taught there. Instead, he grew enthusiastic over the new scientific spirit and engaged in some experiments in chemistry and observation in astronomy. The Royal Society was founded while he was at Oxford, and though it embraced a wide assortment of intellectuals, it came to number, among its scientific members, Robert Boyle and Isaac Newton, who later were to become close friends of Locke; he himself was elected a fellow in 1668. Though never a medical doctor, Locke had a lifelong interest in the art of healing, which he often practiced, collaborated for a time with Thomas Sydenham, the great English physician, and finally, in 1674, received the degree of bachelor of medicine and the right to practice as a physician.

From time to time, as a young man, Locke entertained the possibility of becoming a clergyman, which he never did, perhaps because of his aversion to orthodox religion; but he was always a religious man and maintained a fondness for theology, stressing the importance of individuality, of a liberal approach to religion, and the political toleration of religious differences. As a devout Christian he professed the existence of God, Jesus as Messiah, and biblical morality.

In 1666, as a result of a chance meeting in which he was called upon to extend him some medical services, Locke met Anthony Ashley Cooper, later the first Earl of Shaftesbury, who, impressed with Locke and indebted to him, became his patron and friend. Locke's entire future was influenced by this relationship, for because of Shaftesbury, in his rise to prominence before falling into utter disfavor, Locke became engaged in civil service, met many important politicians and scientists, and traveled to France and Holland.

When, with the help of Shaftesbury, Locke was appointed by the king's warrant as a student of Christ Church, he was ensured an income, which enabled him to stop teaching grammar and philosophy and to devote his time to his own pursuits. Among these was the reading of Descartes, whose clarity and logic fascinated him, and though he reacted against some basic tenets of Cartesianism, such as innate ideas, he subscribed to others, and it may well be that his consequent interest in knowledge, which culminated in his masterwork on human understanding, began with his study of Descartes.

Probably for health reasons, as well as the uncertain future of his patron, Locke went for several years to Montpellier, France, where, among other activities, his chief philosophical occupation was to continue working on his *Essay*, which he had begun years before. He then returned to England and renewed his relationship with Shaftesbury, but when his patron's political star began falling, Locke wisely made off to Holland as a voluntary exile, remaining there until after the accession of King William in 1688. Naturally Locke fell under suspicion too, and when King Charles II stripped him of his studentship at Christ Church, he was even obliged to go into hiding. Meanwhile he was developing his thoughts on government, political liberty, and religious tolerance, for which he was achieving public recognition, so that upon his return to London in 1689, he was acknowledged and esteemed as a defender of William's ascendancy.

After his return, for the sake of the peace and quiet his health required, he accepted the invitation of Sir Francis and Lady Masham to retire to their family home at Oates, about twenty miles outside London, where he lived from 1691 on. He never stopped working. He edited the unfinished manuscript of his longtime friend Robert Boyle under the title *General History of the Air*; he gave more attention to theological questions, which he had always enjoyed but which was given impetus by his friendship in Holland with the liberal theologian Philip von Limborch; finally, he became involved in a now famous controversy with Bishop Edward Stillingfleet over his philosophical-theological views.

Locke died in 1704. His epitaph, which he himself had written, reads in part: "Stay, Traveller. Nearby lies John Locke. If you ask what kind of man he was, he answers that he lived contentedly in his modest way. He gave himself to learning for one purpose only, to pursue the truth. This you may learn from his writings, which will tell you about him more faithfully than the suspect praise of an epitaph." Locke's more important works are *Two Treatises of Civil Government* (1689), *An Essay concerning Human Understanding* (1690), *Letters on Toleration* (1689–93), and *The Reasonableness of Christianity* (1695).

The questions of *what* we know and *how* we know are focal points of entire philosophies from pre-Socratic times, through the Middle Ages, and down to the seventeenth century. At this point the consideration of knowledge again achieves primary importance, and Descartes' preoccupation with certitude becomes the point at which modern philosophy's steady exploration of epistemological problems begins to take hold. In this exploration, Locke's attention was given to the kind of inquiry that later became known as *criticism*. Certainly Locke saw the problem inherent in the Cartesian position of how, given mind and body as the two constituents of reality, mind comes to know things outside itself, and Locke had enough common sense to avoid the same pitfall. He began his study of knowledge in an informal way. In one of his many discussions with friends, the subject of knowledge came up and led to some perplexities that, as Locke tells his readers, made it "necessary to examine our own abilities, and see what *objects* our understandings were, or were not, fitted to deal with." He thought that all he would have to say on the subject could be "contained in one sheet of paper," but "new discoveries led me still on, and so it grew insensibly to the bulk it now appears in." The "bulk" is, of course, *An Essay concerning Human Understanding*, on which the author spent twenty years of his life. Though he himself was aware that it was overwritten and not at every point thought through, it is a monument in the history of epistemology and, in the end, a testimony to the mystery of human knowledge. Locke was convinced that the human mind could arrive at an understanding of things sufficient for man to be human: the "candle" in us, he says, "shines light enough for all our purposes." And if we lack certitude in some respects, we have sufficient probability "to govern all our concernments."

Locke's goal is stated succinctly in the opening line of the introduction: "Since it is the *understanding* that sets men above the rest of sensible beings, and gives them all the advantage and dominion which he has has over them, it is certainly a subject, even for its nobleness, worth our labour to inquire into." The plan of the *Essay*, spelled out in four books, centers on three main considerations: the origin of ideas, the use of language, and the different kinds of assent given by the mind. The first of these considerations is handled negatively in Book I, inasmuch as innate ideas must be rejected; therefore, a method is laid out in Book II to discover how our ideas originate. Book III is committed to language, the analysis of words, terms, and names that "the mind makes use of for the understanding of things, or conveying its knowledge to others." The assent of the mind is founded on evidence, so that the first half of Book IV is devoted to the basis and limits of knowledge that warrant certitude; the second half considers other warrants for assent, namely, faith and opinion.

Locke uses the term *idea* in its broadest possible sense to stand for whatever the mind thinks about; it is the term that "serves best to stand for whatsoever is the *object* of the understanding when a man thinks"; Locke therefore uses it "to express whatever is meant by *phantasm, notion, species,* or *whatever it is which the mind can be employed about in thinking.*" He later hesitatingly refers to ideas as "instruments, or materials of our knowledge."

In holding that these "objects" *cannot be innate*, Locke comes down strongly on the side of the empiricist against the widely received doctrine of Descartes; knowledge simply does not originate in ideas already possessed by man *before* experience. If any truths were innate, they would be universal. But speculative truths are not universal: children do not know them, nor people of unsound mind, nor the uneducated; this fact alone would disavow innate knowledge. Even more dramatic is the situation of moral principles, for there are individuals who show very little moral sense, and indeed, there are whole nations whose moral posture is, in some matters, completely reprehensible to the Western mind; these opposing positions cannot both be right: "Whatever practical principle is innate, cannot but be known to every one to be just and good. It is therefore little less than a contradiction to suppose, that whole nations of men should, both in their professions and practice, unanimously and universally give the lie to what, by the most invincible evidence, every one of them knew to be true, right, and good."

The mind, as Locke goes on to describe in Book II, comes into the world as an "empty cabinet" waiting to be filled, or a "white paper" (in other terminology, a *tabula rasa*, a clean slate) to be written upon: "Whence has [the mind] all the *materials* of reason and knowledge? To this I answer, in one word, from *experience*." Experience is had by way of sensation and reflection, the two "fountains of knowledge." The senses convey to the mind whatever it requires to produce perceptions of sensible qualities like yellow, heat, soft, and bitter: "This great source of most of the ideas we have, depending wholly upon our senses, and derived by them to the understanding, I call *sensation*." Inward operations such as perception, thinking, doubting, believing, reasoning, knowing and willing the mind is aware of itself as having, and is aware that they are different from, though follow upon, ideas of sensation: "I call this *reflection*, the ideas it affords being such only as the mind gets by reflecting on its own operations within itself."

Locke's analysis of the kinds of ideas we have is extensive and leads to many distinctions and divisions, but the chief division is into *simple* and *complex* ideas. Simple ideas are those that are "passively received," that is, ideas the mind receives, or is passive in—*passive* meaning involuntary or spontaneous: "In this part the understanding is merely passive; and whether or no it will have these beginnings, and as it were materials of knowledge, is not in its own power." Simple ideas are "unmixed" or "uncompounded," each being but "one uniform appearance, or conception in the mind." Such ideas are supplied either by sensation or reflection and are characterized by the unmistakable impressions their objects make upon us. If supplied by sensation, they can come through one sense only, "ideas of one sense," such as white, sour, solid, and so on; or through two senses, namely, sight and touch, such as space, figure, rest, and motion. If supplied by reflection, the simple ideas are those of perception or thinking (understanding) and volition or willing (will), such as remembrance, discerning, reasoning, knowledge, and faith. Lastly, simple ideas can originate from sensation and reflection together, as in pleasure or delight, pain or uneasiness, power, existence, and unity. Simple ideas, taken all in all, are original and unanalyzable and are therefore the basic materials from which *all other knowledge* the mind has "is made." No wonder Locke referred to sensation and reflection, the sources of simple ideas, as the two fountains of knowledge.

Complex ideas enter as ideas that are made, for the mind, contrary to its passive posture in receiving simple ideas, is active in producing them. The mind produces them out of simple ideas and does so in one of three ways: by combining several simple ideas, by separating them from other ideas accompanying them in their real existence (abstraction), or by placing them, as it were, side by side (relationship). Although there is an infinite variety of complex ideas, they can be classified into ideas of modes, substances, or relations—for example, beauty, gratitude, number, infinity, cause and effect, identity and diversity, and moral relations. It is clear that Locke's account of the origin of our ideas is painstaking and thorough, though there are some aspects of his analysis that will be subject to further discussion later inasmuch as they have a special bearing on empiricism.

Any philosopher who talks about ideas must talk about words as well. As he moves to Book III, Locke tells us "that there is so close a connection between ideas and words ... that it is impossible to speak clearly and distinctly of our knowledge, which all consists in propositions, without considering, first, the nature, use, and signification of Language." When Locke later evaluates the importance of signs, he ascribes the major role to words that "the mind makes use of for the understanding of things."

As *signs*, words may well stand for things, but their first signification is of ideas; if ideas are "invisible," words are "sensible" and are referred to as *marks*: words are "sensible marks of ideas; and the ideas they stand for are their proper and immediate signification." Inasmuch as ideas represent things, or may represent them, so do words. Things, however, exist "in particular," not "in general," and so if we were to use, for ourselves or for others when we try to communicate, different words for each thing that exists, we would speak only with great difficulty or not at all. To get around this problem beyond using particular words, the mind uses *general* words, like *horse*, by collecting individual things into "bundles" according to their similarities and not according to anything *real* represented by them; the mind simply makes "for the easier and readier improvement, and communication" of knowledge. These considerations not only show the ingenuity of language, along with its imperfections and abuse, but also, for Locke, how much more work had to be done on the doctrine of signs, including both ideas and words, which would perhaps "afford us another sort of logic and critic, than what we have been hitherto acquainted with."

The first half of Book IV takes up at last the question of *knowledge*, which, of course, is directly tied in with ideas and which Locke defines as "the perception of the connexion of and agreement, or disagreement and repugnancy of any of our ideas." Though there are several kinds of agreement and disagreement, there are only three *degrees of knowledge*: intuitive, demonstrative, and sensitive. *Intuitive* knowledge is the perception of the "agreement of two ideas *immediately by themselves*, without the intervention of any other"; thus, we know that three is greater than two and that a circle is not a triangle. This degree of knowledge is basic; the certainty of all knowledge depends on it. *Demonstrative* knowledge is achieved when the agreement or disagreement is not immediately apparent but requires the intervention of other ideas, such as the idea that three angles of a triangle are equal to two right angles. Demonstrative knowledge is certain, but its certainty is not as readily available as that of intuitive knowledge. *Sensitive* knowledge offers a special problem to Locke to which we shall return. It is the perception of "the particular existence of finite being" outside us; that is, we are certain that the idea we receive from an external object is in our minds, and to that extent sensitive knowledge shares the intuitive; but that is the end of our certainty here, for we do not know what they are. When the dimension of real existence is added, Locke wants to extend "certain knowledge" (agreement of ideas among themselves) to "*real* and certain knowledge" when there is an agreement between ideas and reality.

Other philosophers might stop here in saying that what we know is true, but Locke makes another distinction in holding that *truth* lies in the propositions that express agreement or disagreement; and when we perceive the relationship, it is knowledge of the truth. Here again, the idea of animal and the idea of the mythical centaur agree with one another, and the proposition "centaur is animal" is *not really* true, only verbally so. Real truth exists only where there is an agreement between the ideas in proposition and existence in nature.

Whatever falls short of knowledge, and yet is embraced by us with assurance, is called *faith* or *opinion*. At work is probability, not proof, and the more probable the grounds are, the more persuasive they are for our assent; probability supplies the defect of our knowledge. If the probability is solidly grounded on our experience or the experience of others, our confidence is produced and our assent is warranted, but in no case can faith and reason be applied to each other, and in every case faith must be reasonable. To that extent, to believe in the word of God is reasonable.

It was previously indicated that more ought to be said about certain points of Locke's epistemology, one of which turns on the question of the *objectivity* of the simple ideas of sensation, that is, those ideas we gain through one or more of our senses, like color, taste, figure, and rest. As described in Chapter Eight, Book II, Locke distinguishes between ideas and *qualities:* qualities in bodies have the power to produce ideas of themselves in us. When these qualities are inseparable from the body they are found in, they are called *primary* qualities, and the corresponding ideas of solidity, extension, figure, motion, and number they cause in us are "ideas of primary qualities"; regardless of the changes a body undergoes, it will still have solidity, extension, and so on. These qualities *really* reside in the object, and our ideas are faithful resemblances of them. But *secondary* qualities are vastly different, for though they produce sensations (color, taste, etc.) in us, they are *not really* found in the objects that cause them, and therefore do not resemble them.

The distinction between primary and secondary qualities was not original with Locke, but others who had used it, like Galileo and Boyle, did so in a scientific sense, and no particular problem occurred. When, however, Locke defines idea as "the immediate object of perception, thought or understanding," the question naturally arises, how do we know what connection ideas have with things in order to make a valid distinction between primary and secondary qualities, or even whether there is a connection *at all* between ideas and things? Two reactions to this question are possible: either to move in the direction of idealism, as Berkeley did, or to advance a relentless brand of empiricism, as Hume did. In either case, the response is precisely to a soft spot in Locke's epistemology as to how sense experience causes the mind to achieve a satisfactory relationship with real existence.

Locke's further distinction between simple and complex ideas was, as we have seen, necessary to his philosophy of knowledge. In assigning a basic role to sensation, he joined many other philosophers of the past, but he went beyond them in letting it preside over a domain hitherto reserved to metaphysics. He maintained, we should recall, that ideas contain *real truth* when they agree with something *existing in nature*, and when he proceeded to speak of "our threefold knowledge of existence," he was speaking of our knowledge of man, God, and "other things": "I say, then, that we have knowledge of our *own* existence by intuition; of the existence of *God* by demonstration; and of *other things* by sensation". My own existence is so clear that it needs no proof, and is established even in doubting. With regard to God, the fact that there is at least one actual being that had a beginning is evidence of an eternal Being. Knowledge of other things is obtained by sensation. Note that the order of discovering the entities man, God, and other things is exactly that of Descartes.

But it is precisely here that an important part of Locke's empiricism is located. The knowledge of ourselves by intuition and of God by demonstration is not peculiar to Locke, but the knowledge of other things by sensation is. Take *substance*, for example; Locke writes extensively on its meaning, showing that where there is "white" there must be "something white," even though we do not sense it. Locke *knows* that God exists and that man exists; however, he does not *know* that substance exists because it is not an object of sensation — it simply cannot be one of those "other things." Yet there is reason to *suppose* substance to be real. In a now famous hypothesis, Locke tries to show the limitations of our knowledge by offering the possibility that *matter* can *think*: "it is not harder to conceive how thinking should exist without matter, than how matter should think." Later on, in talking of God's power, Locke writes, "We have the ideas of *matter* and *thinking*, but possibly shall never be able to know whether any mere material being thinks or no," and then says that God, in His omnipotence, may be able to bring it about. The human mind, then, cannot move with certainty to the conclusion that the existence of substance is required by the existence of qualities, a conclusion that lies at the heart of metaphysics. Locke did not push this line of reasoning to its ultimate, as David Hume later did; but it is clear that he is already paving the way for the disenfranchisement of metaphysics, which, through Hume, culminates in the antimetaphysical stance of Immanuel Kant and generations of philosophers after him.

So, for Locke, the scope of knowledge is to be seen in the high, though not absolute, priority given to sensation, which causes the mind, already in sure possession of the knowledge of God's existence and its own, to be unknowing before those things whose existence it may suppose but that sense experience does not support.

By comparing rationalism and empiricism in general terms, the meaning of Locke's commitment to sensation becomes clearer. Epistemologically, rationalism and empiricism can be differentiated by the *direction of movement* in the process of knowing. When we come to know something, there is a movement involved, a process whereby we go from one state to another, from not knowing to knowing. Rationalism sees this movement as flowing from the mind to things; that is, the mind tells us, prior to experience, what things are. But for empiricism, the movement flows in the reverse direction, from things to mind; that is, in our experience, things tell us what they are. The rationalist tends to construct reality, to favor the deductive method, to think more speculatively, to sponsor ideals, to build utopias, to generate an idealistic ethics, and to suspect the body in its performance. The empiricist, on the other hand, tends to accept reality as it is given in sense experience, to favor induction, to think more pragmatically, to foster politics, to see ethics as utilitarian or behaviorist, and to hold the intellect's claims at bay. We have seen how Descartes, the exemplar of all rationalists, turned to the mind first and followed its movement mathematically to the nature of man, the existence of God, and the external world, employing thereby an epistemology that alienated sense knowledge. However faithful Descartes thought he was to the claims of his rational side, he rejected the immediate claims of his sensitive side and could never, therefore, develop a vehicle to prove the validity of knowledge as a whole. With Locke, the pendulum started to swing the other way and completed its arc in the next generation with Hume; thus, as we have seen, the claims of metaphysics were finally held to be without merit.

John Locke's influence on the philosophy of government is no less profound than his wide-ranging influence on the philosophy of knowledge. Even though his *Two Treatises of Civil Government* were issued in part to justify the ascendancy of King William after the Glorious Revolution of 1688, they stand on their own among the great documents of modern times, supporting the notion that there is no power to govern without the consent of the governed, a concept that was politically alive for some years before Locke and given earlier expression by Thomas Hobbes. Just as the political situation in England a generation before Hobbes prompted him to publish *Leviathan*, so the political situation at the time of Locke prompted him to publish the *Treatises* in 1689, stating in the preface his desire to "establish the throne of our great restorer, our present King William; to make good his title in consent of the people . . . and to justify to the world the people of England, whose love of their just and natural rights, with their resolution to preserve them, saved the nation, when it was on the very brink of slavery and ruin."

Locke's political genius lay in organizing ideas currently abroad and honing them, according to his own insights, into a persuasive essay on government *by choice* on the part of the people. Though there is much to be found in the first of the *Two Treatises*, it resembles more closely a tract for the times, and so it is the *Second Treatise* one turns to as the main source of his political philosophy. If people arrive, by consent, at a new state of affairs for themselves, Locke first wants to clarify the prior state, and so he begins, like Hobbes, with a discussion of the *state of nature*. The state of nature is a state of perfect freedom in which men may do as they are wont, "within the bounds of the law of nature," independent of other men. All men are equal by nature, no one having more power or jurisdiction than any other, unless, Locke adds, by some clearly defined divine appointment; this equality of men is the absolute foundation of mutual love from which all maxims of justice and charity are derived.

Yet the state of nature as the state of freedom is not a state of license, of "uncontrollable liberty," for all of our actions are governed by the law of nature, which is *reason* itself: "and reason, which is that law, teaches all mankind who will but consult it, that, being all equal and independent, no one ought to harm another in his life, health, liberty or possessions." What is reasonable is in accordance with the law; what is unreasonable is not. Under this rubric anyone may mete out punishment and reparation against a criminal, whose crime is to act contrary to the law of nature by invading the life of the other.

So described, Locke, who has Hobbes clearly in mind without naming him, does not share his predecessor's pessimism regarding the natural state of man and refuses to liken the state of nature to the state of war. Yet, the state of nature, not being paradise, requires a political society to uplift it: "civil government is the proper remedy for the inconveniences of the state of nature"; the word _inconveniences_ is a disingenuous understatement, for, as Locke shows later on, a political society of some kind is necessary if only to restrain the willfulness of men in trying to overreach each other.

In extending his remarks to the family, Locke affirms, again contrary to Hobbes, that society is natural to man. Even though the family requires a "voluntary compact" between a man and a woman to begin with, it is a society given by nature and one into which a person is born. Man in society is part of man's experience, and, for Locke, so much so that he opens his discussions on civil society by remarking, "God having made man such a creature, that in his own judgment it was not good for him to be alone, put him under strong obligations of necessity, convenience, and inclination to drive him into society, as well as fitted him with understanding and language to continue and enjoy it."

When it comes to a civil society, because by nature all men are free, equal, and independent, there can be no subjection to a political power except by consent, by the _common consent_ of all those who agree, not so much to surrender their individual liberty of the state of nature as to carry it over into a new state. If Locke looks to an "original compact," it is not to be taken in a chronological sense but rather in a conceptual sense, for he is trying to establish a rational basis for empowering a government. The power so consented to is not absolute, for absolute power can wreak incalculable harm, but just so much as allows men "the mutual preservation of their lives, liberties, and estates, which I call by the general name, property." Consent is a contract between person and person, not between person and king; between person and king is the relationship of _trust_, that is, the community entrusts the government with the duty to work for the good of the community; the government is the trustee of of the community: "To this end it is that men give up all their natural power to the society which they enter into, and the community put the legislative power into such hands as they think fit, with this trust, that they shall be governed by declared laws, or else their peace, quiet, and property will still be at the same uncertainty as it was in the state of nature."

There many points of government that Locke does not consider, such as the rights of minorities, or does not satisfactorily cover, such as how successive generations of people give their consent, but all the ideas just discussed, together with further ideas on majority rule, the separation of powers, the right to change governments, the right to depose a government bent on enslavement, and separation of church and state, became part of common political thinking in the eighteenth century and created a rich legacy for those who would establish constitutional governments, especially the founding fathers of the United States.

Readings

From Essay Concerning Human Understanding

Introduction

1. Since it is the *understanding* that sets man above the rest of sensible beings, and gives him all the advantage and dominion which he has over them; it is certainly a subject, even for its nobleness, worth our labour to inquire into. The understanding, like the eye, whilst it makes us see and perceive all other things, takes no notice of itself; and it requires art and pains to set it at a distance and make it its own object. But whatever be the difficulties that lie in the way of this inquiry; whatever it be that keeps us so much in the dark to ourselves; sure I am that all the light we can let in upon our minds, all the acquaintance we can make with our own understandings, will not only be very pleasant, but bring us great advantage, in directing our thoughts in the search of other things.

2. This, therefore, being my purpose—to inquire into the original, certainty, and extent of *human knowledge*, together with the grounds and degrees of *belief, opinion, and assent;*—I shall not at present meddle with the physical consideration of the mind; or trouble myself to examine wherein its essence consists; or by what motions of our spirits or alterations of our bodies we come to have any *sensation* by our organs, or any *ideas* in our understandings; and whether those ideas do in their formation, any or all of them, depend on matter or not. These are speculations which, however curious and entertaining, I shall decline, as lying out of my way in the design I am now upon. It shall suffice to my present purpose, to consider the discerning faculties of a man, as they are employed about the objects which they have to do with. And I shall imagine I have not wholly misemployed myself in the thoughts I shall have on this occasion, if, in this historical, plain meth-

od, I can give any account of the ways whereby our understandings come to attain those notions of things we have; and can set down any measures of the certainty of our knowledge; or the grounds of those persuasions which are to be found amongst men, so various, different, and wholly contradictory; and yet asserted somewhere or other with such assurance and confidence, that he that shall take a view of the opinions of mankind, observe their opposition, and at the same time consider the fondness and devotion wherewith they are embraced, the resolution and eagerness wherewith they are maintained, may perhaps have reason to suspect, that either there is no such thing as truth at all, or that mankind hath no sufficient means to attain a certain knowledge of it.

3. It is therefore worth while to search out the bounds between opinion and knowledge; and examine by what measures, in things whereof we have no certain knowledge, we ought to regulate our assent and moderate our persuasion. In order whereunto I shall pursue this following method:—

First, I shall inquire into the original of those *ideas*, notions, or whatever else you please to call them, which a man observes, and is conscious to himself he has in his mind; and the ways whereby the understanding comes to be furnished with them.

Secondly, I shall endeavour to show what *knowledge* the understanding hath by those ideas; and the certainty, evidence, and extent of it.

Thirdly, I shall make some inquiry into the nature and grounds of *faith or opinion*: whereby I mean that assent which we give to any proposition as true, of whose truth yet we have no certain knowledge. And here we shall have occasion to examine the reasons and degrees of *assent*.

Book I

Chapter I
No Innate Speculative Principles

1. It is an established opinion amongst some men, that there are in the understanding certain *innate principles*; some primary notions, κοιναι εννοιαι, characters, as it were stamped upon the mind of man; which the soul receives in its very first being, and brings into the world with it. It would be sufficient to convince unprejudiced readers of the falseness of this supposition, if I should only show (as I hope I shall in the following parts of this Discourse) how men, barely by the use of their natural faculties, may attain to all the knowledge they have, without the help of any innate impressions; and may arrive at certainty, without any such original notions or principles. For I imagine any one will easily grant that it would be impertinent to suppose the ideas of

colours innate in a creature to whom God hath given sight, and a power to receive them by the eyes from external objects: and no less unreasonable would it be to attribute several truths to the impressions of nature, and innate characters, when we may observe in ourselves faculties fit to attain as easy and certain knowledge of them as if they were originally imprinted on the mind.

But because a man is not permitted without censure to follow his own thoughts in the search of truth, when they lead him ever so little out of the common road, I shall set down the reasons that made me doubt of the truth of that opinion, as an excuse for my mistake, if I be in one; which I leave to be considered by those who, with me, dispose themselves to embrace truth wherever they find it.

2. There is nothing more commonly taken for granted than that there are certain *principles*, both *speculative* and *practical*, (for they speak of both), universally agreed upon by all mankind: which therefore, they argue, must needs be the constant impressions which the souls of men receive in their first beings, and which they bring into the world with them, as necessarily and really as they do any of their inherent faculties.

3. This argument, drawn from universal consent, has this misfortune in it, that if it were true in matter of fact, that there were certain truths wherein all mankind agreed, it would not prove them innate, if there can be any other way shown how men may come to that universal agreement, in the things they do consent in, which I presume may be done.

4. But, which is worse, this argument of universal consent, which is made use of to prove innate principles, seems to me a demonstration that there are none such: because there are none to which all mankind give an universal assent. I shall begin with the speculative, and instance in those magnified principles of demonstration, 'Whatsoever is, is,' and 'It is impossible for the same thing to be and not to be'; which, of all others, I think have the most allowed title to innate. These have so settled a reputation of maxims universally received, that it will no doubt be thought strange if any one should seem to question it. But yet I take liberty to say, that these propositions are so far from having an universal assent, that there are a great part of mankind to whom they are not so much as known.

5. For, first, it is evident, that all children and idiots have not the least apprehension or thought of them. And the want of that is enough to destroy that universal assent which must needs be the necessary concomitant of all innate truths: it seeming to me near a contradiction to say, that there are truths imprinted on the soul, which it perceives or understands not: imprinting, if it signify anything, being nothing el~ ~ut the making certain truths to be perceived. For to imprint any-

thing on the mind without the mind's perceiving it, seems to me hardly intelligible. If therefore children and idiots have souls, have minds, with those impressions upon them, *they* must unavoidably perceive them, and necessarily know and assent to these truths; which since they do not, it is evident that there are no such impressions. For if they are not notions naturally imprinted, how can they be innate? and if they are notions imprinted, how can they be unknown? To say a notion is imprinted on the mind, and yet at the same time to say, that the mind is ignorant of it, and never yet took notice of it, is to make this impression nothing. No proposition can be said to be in the mind which it never yet knew, which it was never yet conscious of. For if any one may, then, by the same reason, all propositions that are true, and the mind is capable ever of assenting to, may be said to be in the mind, and to be imprinted: since, if any one can be said to be in the mind, which it never yet knew, it must be only because it is capable of knowing it; and so the mind is of all truths it ever shall know. Nay, thus truths may be imprinted on the mind which it never did, nor ever shall know; for a man may live long, and die at last in ignorance of many truths which his mind was capable of knowing, and that with certainty. . . .

Chapter II

No Innate Practical Principles

1. If those speculative Maxims, whereof we discoursed in the foregoing chapter, have not an actual universal assent from all mankind, as we there proved, it is much more visible concerning practical Principles, that they come short of an universal reception: and I think it will be hard to instance any one moral rule which can pretend to so general and ready an assent as, 'What is, is'; or to be so manifest a truth as this, that 'It is impossible for the same thing to be and not to be.' Whereby it is evident that they are further removed from a title to be innate; and the doubt of their being native impressions on the mind is stronger against those moral principles than the other. Not that it brings their truth at all in question. They are equally true, though not equally evident. Those speculative maxims carry their own evidence with them: but moral principles require reasoning and discourse, and some exercise of the mind, to discover the certainty of their truth. They lie not open as natural characters engraven on the mind; which, if any such were, they must needs be visible by themselves, and by their own light be certain and known to everybody. But this is no derogation to their truth and certainty; no more than it is to the truth or certainty of the three angles of a triangle being equal to two right ones: because it is not so evident as 'the whole is bigger than a part,' nor so

apt to be assented to at first hearing. It may suffice that these moral rules are capable of demonstration: and therefore it is our own faults if we come not to a certain knowledge of them. But the ignorance wherein many men are of them, and the slowness of assent wherewith others receive them, are manifest proofs that they are not innate, and such as offer themselves to their view without searching.

2. Whether there be any such moral principles, wherein all men do agree, I appeal to any who have been but moderately conversant in the history of mankind, and looked abroad beyond the smoke of their own chimneys. Where is that practical truth that is universally received, without doubt or question, as it must be if innate? *Justice*, and keeping of contracts, is that which most men seem to agree in. This is a principle which is thought to extend itself to the dens of thieves, and the confederacies of the greatest villains; and they who have gone furthest towards the putting off of humanity itself, keep faith and rules of justice one with another. I grant that outlaws themselves do this one amongst another: but it is without receiving these as the innate laws of nature. They practise them as rules of convenience within their own communities: but it is impossible to conceive that he embraces justice as a practical principle, who acts fairly with his fellow-highwayman, and at the same time plunders or kills the next honest man he meets with. Justice and truth are the common ties of society; and therefore even outlaws and robbers, who break with all the world besides, must keep faith and rules of equity amongst themselves; or else they cannot hold together. But will any one say, that those that live by fraud or rapine have innate principles of truth and justice which they allow and assent to?

Book II

Chapter I

Of Ideas in General and Their Original

1. Every man being conscious to himself that he thinks; and that which his mind is applied about whilst thinking being the ideas that are there, it is past doubt that men have in their minds several ideas,—such as are those expressed by the words *whiteness, hardness, sweetness, thinking, motion, man, elephant, army, drunkenness,* and others: it is in the first place then to be inquired, *How he comes by them?*

2. Let us then suppose the mind to be, as we say, white paper, void of all characters, without any ideas:—How comes it to be furnished? Whence comes it by that vast store which the busy and boundless fancy of man has painted on it with an almost endless variety? Whence

has it all the *materials* of reason and knowledge? To this I answer, in one word, from EXPERIENCE. In that all our knowledge is founded; and from that it ultimately derives itself. Our observation employed either, about external sensible objects, or about the internal operations of our minds perceived and reflected on by ourselves, is that which supplies our understandings with all the *materials* of thinking. These two are the fountains of knowledge, from whence all the ideas we have, or can naturally have, do spring.

3. First, our Senses, conversant about particular sensible objects, do convey into the mind several distinct perceptions of things, according to those various ways wherein those objects do affect them. And thus we come by those *ideas* we have of *yellow, white, heat, cold, soft, hard, bitter, sweet,* and all those which we call sensible qualities; which when I say the senses convey into the mind, I mean, they from external objects convey into the mind what produces there those perceptions. This great source of most of the ideas we have, depending wholly upon our senses, and derived by them to the understanding, I call SENSATION.

4. Secondly, the other fountain from which experience furnisheth the understanding with ideas is,—the perception of the operations of our own mind within us, as it is employed about the ideas it has got;— which operations, when the soul comes to reflect on and consider, do furnish the understanding with another set of ideas, which could not be had from things without. And such are *perception, thinking, doubting, believing, reasoning, knowing, willing,* and all the different actings of our own minds;—which we being conscious of, and observing in ourselves, do from these receive into our understandings as distinct ideas as we do from bodies affecting our senses. This source of ideas every man has wholly in himself; and though it be not sense, as having nothing to do with external objects, yet it is very like it, and might properly enough be called internal sense. But as I call the other Sensation, so I call this REFLECTION, the ideas it affords being such only as the mind gets by reflecting on its own operations within itself. By reflection then, in the following part of this discourse, I would be understood to mean, that notice which the mind takes of its own operations, and the manner of them, by reason whereof there come to be ideas of these operations in the understanding. These two, I say, viz. external material things, as the objects of SENSATION, and the operations of our own minds within, as the objects of REFLECTION, are to me the only originals from whence all our ideas take their beginnings. The term *operations* here I use in a large sense, as comprehending not barely the actions of the mind about its ideas, but some sort of passions arising sometimes from them, such as is the satisfaction or uneasiness arising from any thought.

Chapter II

Of Simple Ideas

1. The better to understand the nature, manner, and extent of our knowledge, one thing is carefully to be observed concerning the ideas we have; and that is, that some of them are *simple* and some *complex*.

Though the qualities that affect our senses are, in the things themselves, so united and blended, that there is no separation, no distance between them; yet it is plain, the ideas they produce in the mind enter by the senses simple and unmixed. For, though the sight and touch often take in from the same object, at the same time, different ideas;— as a man sees at once motion and colour; the hand feels softness and warmth in the same piece of wax: yet the simple ideas thus united in the same subject, are as perfectly distinct as those that come in by different senses. The coldness and hardness which a man feels in a piece of ice being as distinct ideas in the mind as the smell and whiteness of a lily; or as the taste of sugar, and smell of a rose. And there is nothing can be plainer to a man than the clear and distinct perception he has of those simple ideas; which, being each in itself uncompounded, contains in it nothing but *one uniform appearance, or conception in the mind*, and is not distinguishable into different ideas.

2. These simple ideas, the materials of all our knowledge, are suggested and furnished to the mind only by those two ways above mentioned, Viz. sensation and reflection

Chapter III

Of Simple Ideas of Sense

1. The better to conceive the ideas we receive from sensation, it may not be amiss for us to consider them, in reference to the different ways whereby they make their approaches to our minds, and make themselves perceivable by us.

First, then, There are some which come into our minds *by one sense only*.

Secondly, There are others that convey themselves into the mind *by more senses than one*.

Thirdly, Others that are had from *reflection only*.

Fourthly, There are some that make themselves way, and are suggested to the mind *by all the ways of sensation and reflection*.

We shall consider them apart under these several heads.

There are some ideas which have admittance only through one sense, which is peculiarly adapted to receive them. Thus light and colours, as white, red, yellow, blue; with their several degrees or shades and mixtures, as green, scarlet, purple, sea-green, and the rest, come in only by the eyes. All kinds of noises, sounds, and tones, only by the ears. The several tastes and smells, by the nose and palate. And if these organs, or the nerves which are the conduits to convey them from without to their audience in the brain,—the mind's presence-room (as I may so call it)—are any of them so disordered as not to perform their functions, they have no postern to be admitted by; no other way to bring themselves into view, and be perceived by the understanding.

The most considerable of those belonging to the touch, are heat and cold, and solidity: all the rest, consisting almost wholly in the sensible configuration, as smooth and rough; or else, more or less firm adhesion of the parts, as hard and soft, tough and brittle, are obvious enough.

Chapter V

Of Simple Ideas of Divers Senses

The ideas we get by more than one sense are, of *space* or *extension, figure, rest, and motion.* For these make perceivable impressions, both on the eyes and touch; and we can receive and convey into our minds the ideas of the extension, figure, motion, and rest of bodies, both by seeing and feeling. But having occasion to speak more at large of these in another place, I here only enumerate them.

Chapter VI

Of Simple Ideas of Reflection

The mind receiving the ideas mentioned in the foregoing chapters from without, when it turns its view inward upon itself, and observes its own actions about those ideas it has, takes from thence other ideas, which are as capable to be the objects of its contemplation as any of those it received from foreign things.

The two great and principal actions of the mind, which are most frequently considered, and which are so frequent that every one that pleases may take notice of them in himself, are these two:—

Perception, or *Thinking*; and *Volition,* or *Willing.*

[The power of thinking is called the *Understanding,* and the power of volition is called the *Will*; and these two powers or abilities in the mind are denominated faculties.]

Of some of the *modes* of these simple ideas of reflection, such as are *remembrance, discerning, reasoning, judging, knowledge, faith,* &c., I shall have occasion to speak hereafter.

Chapter VII

Of Simple Ideas of Both Sensation and Reflection

1. There be other simple ideas which convey themselves into the mind by all the ways of sensation and reflection, viz. *pleasure* or *delight,* and its opposite, *pain,* or *uneasiness; power; existence; unity.*

2. Delight or uneasiness, one or other of them, join themselves to almost all our ideas both of sensation and reflection: and there is scarce

any affection of our senses from without, any retired thought of our mind within, which is not able to produce in us pleasure or pain. By pleasure and pain, I would be understood to signify, whatsoever delights or molests us; whether it arises from the thoughts of our minds, or anything operating on our bodies. For, whether we call it satisfaction, delight, pleasure, happiness, &c., on the one side, or uneasiness, trouble, pain, torment, anguish, misery, &c., on the other, they are still but different degrees of the same thing, and belong to the ideas of pleasure and pain, delight or uneasiness; which are the names I shall most commonly use for those two sorts of ideas.

3. The infinite wise Author of our being, having given us the power over several parts of our bodies, to move or keep them at rest as we think fit; and also, by the motion of them, to move ourselves and other contiguous bodies, in which consist all the actions of our body: having also given a power to our minds, in several instances, to choose, amongst its ideas, which it will think on, and to pursue the inquiry of this or that subject with consideration and attention, to excite us to these actions of thinking and motion that we are capable of,—has been pleased to join to several thoughts, and several sensations a perception of delight. If this were wholly separated from all our outward sensations, and inward thoughts, we should have no reason to prefer one thought or action to another; negligence to attention, or motion to rest. And so we should neither stir our bodies, nor employ our minds, but let our thoughts (if I may so call it) run adrift, without any direction or design, and suffer the ideas of our minds, like unregarded shadows, to make their appearances there, as it happened, without attending to them. In which state man, however furnished with the faculties of understanding and will, would be a very idle, inactive creature, and pass his time only in a lazy, lethargic dream. It has therefore pleased our wise Creator to annex to several objects, and the ideas which we receive from them, as also to several of our thoughts, a concomitant pleasure, and that in several objects, to several degrees, that those faculties which he had endowed us with might not remain wholly idle and unemployed by us.

7. *Existence* and *Unity* are two other ideas that are suggested to the understanding by every object without, and every idea within. When ideas are in our minds, we consider them as being actually there, as well as we consider things to be actually without us;—which is, that they exist, or have existence. And whatever we can consider as one thing, whether a real being or idea, suggests to the understanding the idea of unity.

8. *Power* also is another of those simple ideas which we receive from sensation and reflection. For, observing in ourselves that we do and can think, and that we can at pleasure move several parts of our bodies

which were at rest; the effects, also, that natural bodies are able to produce in one another, occurring every moment to our senses,—we both these ways get the idea of power. . . .

10. These, if they are not all, are at least (as I think) the most considerable of those simple ideas which the mind has, and out of which is made all its other knowledge; all which it receives only by the two forementioned ways of sensation and reflection.

Nor let any one think these too narrow bounds for the capacious mind of man to expatiate in, which takes its flight further than the stars, and cannot be confined by the limits of the world; that extends its thoughts often even beyond the utmost expansion of Matter, and makes excursions into that incomprehensible Inane. I grant all this, but desire any one to assign any *simple idea* which is not received from one of those inlets before mentioned, or *any complex* idea not made out of those simple ones. Nor will it be so strange to think these few simple ideas sufficient to employ the quickest thought, or largest capacity; and to furnish the materials of all that various knowledge, and more various fancies and opinions of all mankind, if we consider how many words may be made out of the various composition of twenty-four letters; or if, going one step further, we will but reflect on the variety of combinations that may be made with barely one of the above-mentioned ideas, viz. number, whose stock is inexhaustible and truly infinite: and what a large and immense field doth extension alone afford the mathematicians?

Chapter VIII

Some Further Considerations Concerning Our Simple Ideas of Sensation

7. To discover the nature of our ideas the better, and to discourse of them intelligibly, it will be convenient to distinguish them *as they are ideas or perceptions in our minds*; and *as they are modifications of matter in the bodies that cause such perceptions in us*: that so we may not think (as perhaps usually is done) that they are exactly the images and resemblances of something inherent in the subject; most of those of sensation being in the mind no more the likeness of something existing without us, than the names that stand for them are the likeness of our ideas, which yet upon hearing they are apt to excite in us.

8. Whatsoever the mind perceives *in itself*, or is the immediate object of perception, thought, or understanding, that I call *idea*; and the power to produce any idea in our mind, I call *quality* of the subject wherein that power is. Thus a snowball having the power to produce in us the ideas of white, cold, and round,—the power to produce those ideas in us, as they are in the snowball, I call qualities; and as they are sensations or perceptions in our understandings, I call them ideas;

which *ideas*, if I speak of sometimes as in the things themselves, I would be understood to mean those qualities in the objects which produce them in us.

9. Qualities thus considered in bodies are,

First, such as are utterly inseparable from the body, in what state soever it be; and such as in all the alterations and changes it suffers, all the force can be used upon it, it constantly keeps; and such as sense constantly finds in every particle of matter which has bulk enough to be perceived; and the mind finds inseparable from every particle of matter, though less than to make itself singly be perceived by our senses: v.g. Take a grain of wheat, divide it into two parts; each part has still solidity, extension, figure, and mobility: divide it again, and it retains still the same qualities; and so divide it on, till the parts become insensible; they must retain still each of them all those qualities. For division (which is all that a mill, or pestle, or any other body, does upon another, in reducing it to insensible parts) can never take away either solidity, extension, figure, or mobility from any body, but only makes two or more distinct separate masses of matter, of that which was but one before; all which distinct masses, reckoned as so many distinct bodies, after division, make a certain number.

These I call *original* or *primary qualities* of body, which I think we may observe to produce simple ideas in us, viz. solidity, extension, figure, motion or rest, and number.

10. *Secondly*, such qualities which in truth are nothing in the objects themselves but powers to produce various sensations in us by their primary qualities, i.e. by the bulk, figure, texture, and motion of their insensible parts, as colours, sounds, tastes, &c. These I call *secondary qualities*. . . .

15. From whence I think it easy to draw this observation,—that the ideas of primary qualities of bodies are resemblances of them, and their patterns do really exist in the bodies themselves, but the ideas produced in us by these secondary qualities have no resemblance of them at all. There is nothing like our ideas, existing in the bodies themselves. They are, in the bodies we denominate from them, only a power to produce those sensations in us: and what is sweet, blue, or warm in idea, is but the certain bulk, figure, and motion of the insensible parts, in the bodies themselves, which we call so.

16. Flame is denominated hot and light; snow, white and cold; and manna, white and sweet, from the ideas they produce in us. Which qualities are commonly thought to be the same in those bodies that those ideas are in us, the one the perfect resemblance of the other, as they are in a mirror, and it would by most men be judged very extravagant if one should say otherwise. And yet he that will consider that the same fire that, at one distance produces in us the sensation of warmth,

does, at a nearer approach, produce in us the far different sensation of pain, ought to bethink himself what reason he has to say—that this idea of warmth, which was produced in him by the fire, is *actually in the fire*; and his idea of pain, which the same fire produced in him the same way, is *not* in the fire. Why are whiteness and coldness in snow, and pain not, when it produces the one and the other idea in us; and can do neither, but by the bulk, figure, number, and motion of its solid parts?

17. The particular bulk, number, figure, and motion of the parts of fire or snow are really in them,—whether any one's senses perceive them or no: and therefore they may be called real qualities, because they really exist in those bodies. But light, heat, whiteness, or coldness, are no more really in them than sickness or pain is in manna. Take away the sensation of them; let not the eyes see light or colours, nor the ears hear sounds; let the palate not taste, nor the nose smell, and all colours, tastes, odours, and sounds, *as they are such particular ideas*, vanish and cease, and are reduced to their causes, i.e. bulk, figure, and motion of parts.

Chapter XII

Of Complex Ideas

1. We have hitherto considered those ideas, in the reception whereof the mind is only passive, which are those simple ones received from sensation and reflection before mentioned, whereof the mind cannot make one to itself, nor have any idea which does not wholly consist of them. But as the mind is wholly passive in the reception of all its simple ideas, so it exerts several acts of its own, whereby out of its simple ideas, as the materials and foundations of the rest, the others are framed. The acts of the mind, wherein it exerts its power over its simple ideas, are chiefly these three: (1) Combining several simple ideas into one compound one; and thus all *complex ideas* are made. (2) The second is bringing two ideas, whether simple or complex, together, and setting them by one another, so as to take a view of them at once, without uniting them into one; by which way it gets all its *ideas of relations*. (3) The third is separating them from all other ideas that accompany them in their real existence: this is called abstraction: and thus all its *general ideas* are made. This shows man's power, and its ways of operation, to be much the same in the material and intellectual world. For the materials in both being such as he has no power over, either to make or destroy, all that man can do is either to unite them together, or to set them by one another, or wholly separate them. I shall here begin with the first of these in the consideration of complex ideas, and come to the other two in their due places. As simple ideas are observed to exist in several combinations united together, so the

mind has a power to consider several of them united together as one idea; and that not only as they are united in external objects, but as itself has joined them together. Ideas thus made up of several simple ones put together, I call *complex*;—such as are beauty, gratitude, a man, an army, the universe; which, though complicated of various simple ideas, or complex ideas made up of simple ones, yet are, when the mind pleases, considered each by itself, as one entire thing, and signified by one name.

2. In this faculty of repeating and joining together its ideas, the mind has great power in varying and multiplying the objects of its thoughts, infinitely beyond what sensation or reflection furnished it with: but all this still confined to those simple ideas which it received from those two sources, and which are the ultimate materials of all its compositions. For simple ideas are all from things themselves, and of these the mind *can* have no more, nor other than what are suggested to it. It can have no other ideas of sensible qualities than what come from without by the senses; nor any ideas of other kind of operations of a thinking substance, than what it finds in itself. But when it has once got these simple ideas, it is not confined barely to observation, and what offers itself from without; it can, by its own power, put together those ideas it has, and make new complex ones, which it never received so united.

3. *Complex ideas*, however compounded and decompounded, though their number be infinite, and the variety endless, wherewith they fill and entertain the thoughts of men; yet I think they may be all reduced under these three heads:—

1. Modes.
2. Substances.
3. Relations.

4. First, *Modes* I call such complex ideas which, however compounded, contain not in them the supposition of subsisting by themselves, but are considered as dependences on, or affections of substances;—such as are the ideas signified by the words triangle, gratitude, murder, &c. And if in this I use the word mode in somewhat a different sense from its ordinary signification, I beg pardon; it being unavoidable in discourses, differing from the ordinary received notions, either to make new words, or to use old words in somewhat a new signification; the later whereof, in our present case, is perhaps the more tolerable of the two.

5. Of these *modes*, there are two sorts which deserve distinct consideration:—

First, there are some which are only variations, or different combinations of the same simple idea, without the mixture of any other;—as a dozen, or score; which are nothing but the ideas of so many distinct units added together, and these I call *simple modes* as being contained within the bounds of one simple idea.

Secondly, there are others compounded of simple ideas of several kinds, put together to make one complex one;—v.g. beauty, consisting of a certain composition of colour and figure, causing delight to the beholder; theft, which being the concealed change of the possession of anything, without the consent of the proprietor, contains, as is visible, a combination of several ideas of several kinds: and these I call *mixed modes*.

6. Secondly, the ideas of *substances* are such combinations of simple ideas as are taken to represent distinct *particular* things subsisting by themselves; in which the supposed or confused idea of substance, such as it is, is always the first and chief. Thus if to substance be joined the simple idea of a certain dull whitish colour, with certain degrees of weight, hardness, ductility, and fusibility, we have the idea of lead; and a combination of the ideas of a certain sort of figure, with the powers of motion, thought and reasoning, joined to substance, make the ordinary idea of a man. Now of substances also, there are two sorts of ideas:—one of single substances, as they exist separately, as of a man or a sheep; the other of several of those put together, as an army of men, or flock of sheep—which collective ideas of several substances thus put together are as much each of them one single idea as that of a man or an unit.

7. Thirdly, the last sort of complex ideas is that we call *relation*, which consists in the consideration and comparing one idea with another.

Of these several kinds we shall treat in their order.

8. If we trace the progress of our minds, and with attention observe how it repeats, adds together, and unites its simple ideas received from sensation or reflection, it will lead us further than at first perhaps we should have imagined. And, I believe, we shall find, if we warily observe the originals of our notions, that *even the most abstruse ideas*, how remote soever they may seem from sense, or from any operations of our own minds, are yet only such as the understanding frames to itself, by repeating and joining together ideas that it had either from objects of sense, or from its own operations about them: so that those even large and abstract ideas are derived from sensation or reflection, being no other than what the mind, by the ordinary use of its own faculties, employed about ideas received from objects of sense, or from the operations it observes in itself about them, may, and does, attain unto.

This I shall endeavour to show in the ideas we have of space, time, and infinity, and some few others that seem the most remote, from those originals.

Chapter XXIII

Of Our Complex Ideas of Substances

1. The mind being, as I have declared, furnished with a great number of the simple ideas, conveyed in by the senses as they are found in exterior things, or by reflection on its own operations, takes notice also that a certain number of these simple ideas go constantly together; which being presumed to belong to one thing, and words being suited to common apprehensions, and made use of for quick dispatch, are called, so united in one subject, by one name; which, by inadvertency, we are apt afterward to talk of and consider as one simple idea, which indeed is a complication of many ideas together: because, as I have said, not imagining how these simple ideas *can* subsist by themselves, we accustom ourselves to suppose some *substratum* wherein they do subsist, and from which they do result, which therefore we call *substance*.

2. So that if any one will examine himself concerning his notion of pure substance in general, he will find he has no other idea of it at all, but only a supposition of he knows not what *support* of such qualities which are capable of producing simple ideas in us; which qualities are commonly called accidents. If any one should be asked, what is the subject wherein colour or weight inheres, he would have nothing to say, but the solid extended parts. ... The idea then we have, to which we give the *general* name substance, being nothing but the supposed, but unknown, support of those qualities we find existing, which we imagine cannot subsist *sine re substante*, without something to support them, we call that support *substantia*; which, according to the true import of the word, is, in plain English, standing under or upholding.

3. An obscure and relative idea of *substance in general* being thus made we come to have the ideas of *particular sorts of substances*, by collecting *such* combinations of simple ideas as are, by experience and observation of men's senses, taken notice of to exist together; and are therefore supposed to flow from the particular internal constitution, or unknown essence of that substance. Thus we come to have the ideas of a man, horse, gold, water, &c.; of which substances, whether any one has any other *clear* idea, further than of certain simple ideas co-existent together, I appeal to every one's own experience. It is the ordinary qualities observable in iron, or a diamond, put together, that make the true complex idea of those substances, which a smith or a jeweller commonly knows better than a philosopher; who, whatever *substantial forms* he may talk of, has no other idea of those substances, than what is framed by a collection of those simple ideas which are to be found in them: only we must take notice, that our complex ideas of substances, besides all those simple ideas they are made up of, have always the confused idea of something to which they belong, and in which they subsist: and therefore when we speak of any

sort of substance, we say it is a thing having such or such qualities; as body is a thing that is extended, figured, and capable of motion; spirit, a thing capable of thinking; and so hardness, friability, and power to draw iron, we say, are qualities to be found in a loadstone. These, and the like fashions of speaking, intimate that the substance is supposed always *something besides* the extension, figure, solidity, motion, thinking, or other observable ideas, though we know not what it is.

4. Hence, when we talk or think of any particular sort of corporeal substances, as horse, stone, &c., though the idea we have of either of them be but the complication or collection of those several simple ideas of sensible qualities, which we used to find united in the thing called horse or stone; yet, *because we cannot conceive how they should subsist alone, nor one in another*, we suppose them existing in and supported by some common subject; which support we denote by the name substance, though it be certain we have no clear or distinct idea of that thing we suppose a support.

5. The same thing happens concerning the operations of the mind, viz. thinking, reasoning, fearing, &c., which we concluding not to subsist of themselves, nor apprehending how they can belong to body, or be produced by it, we are apt to think these the actions of some other *substance*, which we call *spirit*; whereby yet it is evident that, having no other idea or notion of matter, but something wherein those many sensible qualities which affect our senses do subsist; by supposing a substance wherein thinking, knowing, doubting, and a power of moving, &c., do subsist, we have as clear a notion of the substance of spirit, as we have of body; the one being supposed to be (without knowing what it is) the *substratum* to those simple ideas we have from without; and the other supposed (with a like ignorance of what it is) to be the *substratum* to those operations we experiment in ourselves within. . . .

29. To conclude. Sensation convinces us that there are solid extended substances; and reflection, that there are thinking ones: experience assures us of the existence of such beings, and that the one hath a power to move body by impulse, the other by thought; this we cannot doubt of. Experience, I say, every moment furnishes us with the clear ideas both of the one and the other. But beyond these ideas, as received from their proper sources, our faculties will not reach. If we would inquire further into their nature, causes, and manner, we perceive not the nature of extension clearer than we do of thinking. If we would explain them any further, one is as easy as the other; and there is no more difficulty to conceive how *a substance we know not* should, by thought, set body into motion, than how *a substance we know not* should, by impulse, set body into motion. So that we are no more able to discover wherein the ideas belonging to body consist, than those belonging to spirit. From whence it seems probable to me, that the sim-

ple ideas we receive from sensation and reflection are the boundaries of our thoughts; beyond which the mind, whatever efforts it would make, is not able to advance one jot; nor can it make any discoveries, when it would pry into the nature and hidden causes of these ideas.

Book IV

Chapter I

Of Knowledge in General

1. Since the mind, in all its thoughts and reasonings, hath no other immediate object but its own ideas, which it alone does or can contemplate, it is evident that our knowledge is only conversant about them.

2. *Knowledge* then seems to me to be nothing but *the perception of the connexion of and agreement, or disagreement and repugnancy of any of our ideas.* In this alone it consists. Where this perception is, there is knowledge, and where it is not, there, though we may fancy, guess, or believe, yet we always come short of knowledge. For when we know that white is not black, what do we else but perceive, that these two ideas do not agree? When we possess ourselves with the utmost security of the demonstration, that the three angles of a triangle are equal to two right ones, what do we more but perceive, that equality to two right ones does necessarily agree to, and is inseparable from, the three angles of a triangle?

3. But to understand a little more distinctly wherein this agreement or disagreement consists, I think we may reduce it all to these four sorts:

    I. *Identity, or diversity.*
    II. *Relation.*
    III. *Co-existence, or necessary connexion.*
    IV. *Real existence.*

4. *First,* As to the first sort of agreement or disagreement, viz. *identity or diversity.* It is the first act of the mind, when it has any sentiments or ideas at all, to perceive its ideas; and so far as it perceives them, to know each what it is, and thereby also to perceive their difference, and that one is not another. This is so absolutely necessary, that without it there could be no knowledge, no reasoning, no imagination, no distinct thoughts at all. By this the mind clearly and infallibly perceives each idea to agree with itself, and to be what it is; and all distinct ideas to disagree, i.e. the one not to be the other: and this it does without pains, labour, or deduction; but at first view, by its natural

power of perception and distinction. And though men of art have reduced this into those general rules, *What is, is,* and *It is impossible for the same thing to be and not to be,* for ready application in all cases, wherein there may be occasion to reflect on it: yet it is certain that the first exercise of this faculty is about particular ideas. A man infallibly knows, as soon as ever he has them in his mind, that the ideas he calls *white* and *round* are the very ideas they are; and that they are not other ideas which he calls *red* or *square*. Nor can any maxim or proposition in the world make him know it clearer or surer than he did before, and without any such general rule. This then is the first agreement or disagreement which the mind perceives in its ideas; which it always perceives at first sight: and if there ever happen any doubt about it, it will always be found to be about the names, and not the ideas themselves, whose identity and diversity will always be perceived, as soon and clearly as the ideas themselves are; nor can it possibly be otherwise.

5. *Secondly,* the next sort of agreement or disagreement the mind perceives in any of its ideas may, I think, be called *relative,* and is nothing but the perception of the *relation* between any two ideas, of what kind soever, whether substances, modes, or any other. For, since all distinct ideas must eternally be known not to be the same, and so be universally and constantly denied one of another, there could be no room for any positive knowledge at all, if we could not perceive any relation between our ideas, and find out the agreement or disagreement they have one with another, in several ways the mind takes of comparing them.

6. *Thirdly,* The third sort of agreement or disagreement to be found in our ideas, which the perception of the mind is employed about, is *co-existence* or *non-co-existence* in the *same subject*; and this belongs particularly to substances. Thus when we pronounce concerning gold, that it is fixed, our knowledge of this truth amounts to no more but this, that fixedness, or a power to remain in the fire unconsumed, is an idea that always accompanies and is joined with that particular sort of yellowness, weight, fusibility, malleableness, and solubility in *aqua regia*, which make our complex idea signified by the word gold.

7. *Fourthly,* The fourth and last sort is that of *actual real existence* agreeing to any idea.

Within these four sorts of agreement or disagreement is, I suppose, contained all the knowledge we have, or are capable of. For all the inquiries we can make concerning any of our ideas, all that we know or can affirm concerning any of them, is, That it is, or is not, the same with some other; that it does or does not always co-exist with some other idea in the same subject; that it has this or that relation with some other idea; or that it has a real existence without the mind. Thus, 'blue is not yellow,' is of identity. 'Two triangles upon equal bases between two parallels are equal,' is of relation. 'Iron is susceptible of magnetical impressions,' is of coexistence. 'God is,' is of real existence. Though identity and co-existence are truly nothing but relations, yet they are such peculiar ways of agreement or disagreement of our ideas, that they deserve well to be considered as distinct heads, and not under relation in general; since they are so different grounds of affirmation and negation, as will easily appear to any one, who will but reflect on what is said in several places of this *Essay.*

I should now proceed to examine the several degrees of our knowledge, but that it is necessary first, to consider the different acceptations of the word *knowledge.*

Chapter II

Of The Degrees of Our Knowledge

1. All our knowledge consisting, as I have said, in the view the mind has of its own ideas, which is the utmost light and greatest certainty we, with our faculties, and in our way of knowledge, are capable of, it may not be amiss to consider a little the degrees of its evidence. The different clearness of our knowledge seems to me to lie in the different way of perception the mind has of the agreement or disagreement of any of its ideas. For if we will reflect on our own ways of thinking, we will find, that sometimes the mind perceives the agreement or disagreement of two ideas *immediately by themselves*, without the intervention of any other: and this I think we may call *intuitive knowledge.* For in this the mind is at no pains of proving or examining, but perceives the truth as the eye doth light, only by being directed towards it. Thus the mind perceives that *white* is not *black*, that a *circle* is not a *triangle*, that *three* are more than *two* and equal to *one and two.* Such kinds of truths the mind perceives at the first sight of the ideas together, by bare intuition; without the intervention of any other idea: and this kind of knowledge is the clearest and most certain that human frailty is capable of. This part of knowledge is irresistible, and, like bright sunshine, forces itself immediately to be perceived, as soon as ever the mind turns its view that way; and leaves no room for hesitation, doubt, or examination, but the mind is presently filled with the clear light of it. *It is on this intuition that depends all the certainty and evidence of all our knowledge*; which certainty every one finds to be so great, that he cannot imagine, and therefore not require a greater: for a man cannot conceive himself capable of a greater certainty than to know that any idea in his mind is such as he perceives it to be; and that two ideas, wherein he perceives a difference, are different and not precisely the same. He that demands a greater certainty than this, demands he knows not what, and shows only that he has a mind to be

a sceptic, without being able to be so. Certainty depends so wholly on this intuition, that, in the next degree of knowledge which I call demonstrative, this intuition is necessary in all the connexions of the intermediate ideas, without which we cannot attain knowledge and certainty.

2. The next degree of knowledge is, where the mind perceives the agreement or disagreement of any ideas, but not immediately. Though wherever the mind perceives the agreement or disagreement of any of its ideas, there be certain knowledge; yet it does not always happen, that the mind sees that agreement or disagreement, which there is between them, even where it is discoverable; and in that case remains in ignorance, and at most gets no further than a probable conjecture. The reason why the mind cannot always perceive presently the agreement or disagreement of two ideas, is, because those ideas, concerning whose agreement or disagreement the inquiry is made, cannot by the mind be so put together as to show it. In this case then, when the mind cannot so bring its ideas together as by their immediate comparison, and as it were juxta-position or application one to another, to perceive their agreement or disagreement, it is fain, *by the intervention of other ideas* (one or more, as it happens) to discover the agreement or disagreement which it searches; and this is that which we call *reasoning*. Thus, the mind being willing to know the agreement or disagreement in bigness between the three angles of a triangle and two right ones, cannot by an immediate view and comparing them do it: because the three angles of a triangle cannot be brought at once, and be compared with any other one, or two, angles; and so of this the mind has no immediate, no intuitive knowledge. In this case the mind is fain to find out some other angles, to which the three angles of a triangle have an equality; and, finding those equal to two right ones, comes to know their equality to two right ones.

3. Those intervening ideas, which serve to show the agreement of any two others, are called *proofs*; and where the agreement and disagreement is by this means plainly and clearly perceived, it is called *demonstration*; it being *shown* to the understanding, and the mind made to see that it is so. A quickness in the mind to find out these intermediate ideas, (that shall discover the agreement or disagreement of any other,) and to apply them right, is, I suppose, that which is called *sagacity*.

4. This knowledge, by intervening proofs, though it be certain, yet the evidence of it is not altogether so clear and bright, nor the assent so ready, as in intuitive knowledge. For, though in demonstration the mind does at last perceive the agreement or disagreement of the ideas it considers; yet it is not without pains and attention: there must be more than one transient view to find it. A steady application and pur-

suit are required to this discovery: and there must be a progression by steps and degrees, before the mind can in this way arrive at certainty, and come to perceive the agreement or repugnancy between two ideas that need proofs and the use of reason to show it. . . .

14. These two, viz. intuition and demonstration, are the degrees of our *knowledge*; whatever comes short of one of these, with what assurance soever embraced, is but *faith* or *opinion*, but not knowledge, at least in all general truths. There is, indeed, another perception of the mind, employed about *the particular existence of finite beings without us*, which, going beyond bare probability, and yet not reaching perfectly to either of the foregoing degrees of certainty, passes under the name of *knowledge*. There can be nothing more certain than that the idea we receive from an external object is in our minds: this is intuitive knowledge. But whether there be anything more than barely that idea in our minds; whether we can thence certainly infer the existence of anything without us, which corresponds to that idea, is that whereof some men think there may be a question made; because men may have such ideas in their minds, when no such thing exists, no such object affects their senses. But yet here I think we are provided with an evidence that puts us past doubting. For I ask any one, Whether he be not invincibly conscious to himself of a different perception, when he looks on the sun by day, and thinks on it by night; when he actually tastes wormwood, or smells a rose, or only thinks on that savour or odour? We as plainly find the difference there is between any idea revived in our minds by our own memory, and actually coming into our minds by our senses, as we do between any two distinct ideas. If any one say, a dream may do the same thing, and all these ideas may be produced in us without any external objects; he may please to dream that I make him this answer:—1. That it is no great matter, whether I remove his scruple or no: where all is but dream, reasoning and arguments are of no use, truth and knowledge nothing. 2. That I believe he will allow a very manifest difference between dreaming of being in the fire, and being actually in it. But yet if he be resolved to appear so skeptical as to maintain, that what I call being actually in the fire is nothing but a dream; and that we cannot thereby certainly know, that any such thing as fire actually exists without us: I answer, That we certainly finding that pleasure or pain follows upon the application of certain objects to us, whose existence we perceive, or dream that we perceive, by our senses; this certainty is as great as our happiness or misery, beyond which we have no concernment to know or to be. So that, I think, we may add to the two former sorts of knowledge this also, of the existence of particular external objects, by that perception and consciousness we have of the actual entrance of ideas from them, and allow these three degrees of knowledge, viz. *intuitive*, *demonstrative*,

and *sensitive*: in each of which there are different degrees and ways of evidence and certainty.

Chapter III

Of the Extent of Human Knowledge

1. Knowledge, as has been said, lying in the perception of the agreement or disagreement of any of our ideas, it follows from hence, That,
    First, we can have knowledge no further than we have *ideas*.

2. Secondly, That we can have no knowledge further than we can have *perception* of that agreement or disagreement. Which perception being: 1. Either by *intuition*, or the immediate comparing any two ideas; or, 2. By *reason*, examining the agreement or disagreement of two ideas, by the intervention of some others; or, 3. By *sensation*, perceiving the existence of particular things: hence it also follows:

3. Thirdly, That we cannot have an *intuitive knowledge* that shall extend itself to all our ideas, and all that we would know about them; because we cannot examine and perceive all the relations they have one to another, by juxta-position, or an immediate comparison one with another. Thus, having the ideas of an obtuse and an acute angled triangle, both drawn from equal bases, and between parallels, I can, by intuitive knowledge, perceive the one not to be the other, but cannot that way know whether they be equal or no; because their agreement or disagreement in equality can never be perceived by an immediate comparing them: the difference of figure makes their parts incapable of an exact immediate application; and therefore there is need of some intervening qualities to measure them by, which is demonstration, or rational knowledge.

4. Fourthly, It follows, also, from what is above observed, that our *rational knowledge* cannot reach to the whole extent of our ideas: because between two different ideas we would examine, we cannot always find such mediums as we can connect one to another with an intuitive knowledge in all the parts of the deduction; and wherever that fails, we come short of knowledge and demonstration.

5. Fifthly, *Sensitive knowledge* reaching no further than the existence of things actually present to our senses, is yet much narrower than either of the former.

6. Sixthly, From all which it is evident, that the *extent of our knowledge* comes not only short of the reality of things, but even of the extent of our own ideas. Though our knowledge be limited to our ideas, and cannot exceed them either in extent or perfection; and though these be very narrow bounds, in respect of the extent of All-being, and far short of what we may justly imagine to be in some even created understandings, not tied down to the dull and narrow information that is to be received from some few, and not very acute, ways of perception,

such as are our senses; yet it would be well with us if our knowledge were but as large as our ideas, and there were not many doubts and inquiries *concerning the ideas we have*, whereof we are not, nor I believe ever shall be in this world resolved. Nevertheless, I do not question but that human knowledge, under the present circumstances of our beings and constitutions, may be carried much further than it has hitherto been, if men would sincerely, and with freedom of mind, employ all that industry and labour of thought, in improving the means of discovering truth, which they do for the colouring or support of falsehood, to maintain a system, interest, or party they are once engaged in. But yet after all, I think I may, without injury to human perfection, be confident, that our knowledge would never reach to all we might desire to know concerning those ideas we have; nor be able to surmount all the difficulties, and resolve all the questions that might arise concerning any of them. We have the ideas of a *square*, a *circle*, and *equality*; and yet, perhaps, shall never be able to find a circle equal to a square, and certainly know that it is so. We have the ideas of *matter* and *thinking*, but possibly shall never be able to know whether [any mere material being] thinks or no; it being impossible for us, by the contemplation of our own ideas, without revelation, to discover whether Omnipotency has not given to some systems of matter, fitly disposed, a power to perceive and think, or else joined and fixed to matter, so disposed, a thinking immaterial substance: it being, in respect of our notions, not much more remote from our comprehension to conceive that God can, if he pleases, superadd to matter a *faculty of thinking*, than that he should superadd to it *another substance with a faculty of thinking*; since we know not wherein thinking consists, nor to what sort of substances the Almighty has been pleased to give that power, which cannot be in any created being, but merely by the good pleasure and bounty of the Creator.

Chapter IV

Of The Reality of Knowledge

1. I doubt not but my reader, by this time, may be apt to think that I have been all this while only building a castle in the air; and be ready to say to me:—

'To what purpose all this stir? Knowledge, say you, is only the perception of the agreement or disagreement of our own ideas: but who knows what those ideas may be? Is there anything so extravagant as the imaginations of men's brains? Where is the head that has no chimeras in it? Or if there be a sober and a wise man, what difference will there be, by your rules, between his knowledge and that of the most extravagant fancy in the world? They both have their ideas, and perceive their agreement and disagreement one with another. If there be any difference between them, the advantage will be on the warm-headed man's side, as having the more ideas, and the more lively. And so, by your rules, he will be the more knowing. If it be true, that all knowledge lies only in the perception of the agreement or disagreement of our own ideas, the visions of an enthusiast and the reasonings of a sober man will be equally certain. It is no matter how things are: so a man observe but the agreement of his own imaginations, and talk conformably, it is all truth, all certainty. Such castles in the air will be as strongholds of truth, as the demonstrations of Euclid. That an harpy is not a centaur is by this way as certain knowledge, and as much a truth, as that a square is not a circle.

'But of what use is all this fine knowledge of *men's own imaginations*, to a man that inquires after the reality of things? It matters not what men's fancies are, it is the knowledge of things that is only to be prized: it is this alone gives a value to our reasonings, and preference to one man's knowledge over another's, that it is of things as they really are, and not of dreams and fancies.'

2. To which I answer, That if our knowledge of our ideas terminate in them, and reach no further, where there is something further intended, our most serious thoughts will be of little more use than the reveries of a crazy brain; and the truths built thereon of no more weight than the discourses of a man who sees things clearly in a dream, and with great assurance utters them. But I hope, before I have done, to make it evident, that this way of certainty, by the knowledge of our own ideas, goes a little further than bare imagination: and I believe it will appear that all the certainty of general truths a man has lies in nothing else.

3. It is evident the mind knows not things immediately, but only by the intervention of the ideas it has of them. Our knowledge, therefore, is real only so far as there is a *conformity* between our ideas and the reality of things. But what shall be here the criterion? How shall the mind, when it perceives nothing but its own ideas, know that they agree with things themselves? This, though it seems not to want difficulty, yet, I think, there be two sorts of ideas that we may be assured agree with things.

4. *First*, The first are simple ideas, which since the mind, as has been showed, can by no means make to itself, must necessarily be the product of things operating on the mind, in a natural way, and producing therein those perceptions which by the Wisdom and Will of our Maker they are ordained and adapted to. From whence it follows, that simple ideas are not fictions of our fancies, but the natural and regular productions of things without us, really operating upon us; and so carry with them all the conformity which is intended; or which our state requires: for they represent to us things under those appearances which

they are fitted to produce in us: whereby we are enabled to distinguish the sorts of particular substances, to discern the states they are in, and so to take them for our necessities, and apply them to our uses. Thus the idea of whiteness, or bitterness, as it is in the mind, exactly answering that power which is in any body to produce it there, has all the real conformity it can or ought to have, with things without us. And this conformity between our simple ideas and the existence of things, is sufficient for real knowledge.

5. *Secondly*, All our complex ideas, *except those of substances*, being archetypes of the mind's own making, not intended to be the copies of anything, nor referred to the existence of anything, as to their originals, cannot want any conformity necessary to real knowledge. For that which is not designed to represent anything but itself, can never be capable of a wrong representation, nor mislead us from the true apprehension of anything, by its dislikeness to it: and such, excepting those of substances, are all our complex ideas. Which, as I have showed in another place, are combinations of ideas, which the mind, by its free choice, puts together, without considering any connexion they have in nature. And hence it is, that in all these sorts the ideas themselves are considered as the archetypes, and things no otherwise regarded, but as they are conformable to them. So that we cannot but be infallibly certain, that all the knowledge we attain concerning these ideas is real, and reaches things themselves. Because in all our thoughts, reasonings, and discourses of this kind, we intend things no further than as they are conformable to our ideas. So that in these we cannot miss of a certain and undoubted reality.

6. I doubt not but it will be easily granted, that the knowledge we have of mathematical truths is not only certain, but real knowledge; and not the bare empty vision of vain, insignificant chimeras of the brain: and yet, if we will consider, we shall find that it is only of our own ideas. The mathematician considers the truth and properties belonging to a rectangle or circle only as they are in idea in his own mind. For it is possible he never found either of them existing mathematically, i.e. precisely true, in his life. But yet the knowledge he has of any truths or properties belonging to a circle, or any other mathematical figure, are nevertheless true and certain, even of real things existing: because real things are no further concerned, nor intended to be meant by any such propositions, than as things really agree to those archetypes in his mind. Is it true of the *idea* of a triangle, that its three angles are equal to two right ones? It is true also of a triangle, wherever it *really exists*. Whatever other figure exists, that it is not exactly answerable to that idea of a triangle in his mind, is not at all concerned in that proposition. And therefore he is certain all his knowledge concerning such ideas is real knowledge: because, intending things no fur-

ther than they agree with those his ideas, he is sure what he knows concerning those figures, when they have *barely an ideal existence* in his mind, will hold true of them also when they have *a real existence* in matter: his consideration being barely of those figures, which are the same wherever or however they exist.

Chapter V

Of Truth in General

1. What is truth? was an inquiry many ages since; and it being that which all mankind either do, or pretend to search after, it cannot but be worth our while carefully to examine wherein it consists; and so acquaint ourselves with the nature of it, as to observe how the mind distinguishes it from falsehood.

2. Truth, then, seems to me, in the proper import of the word, to signify nothing but *the joining or separating of Signs, as the Things signified by them do agree or disagree one with another*. The joining or separating of signs here meant, is what by another name we call *proposition*. So that truth properly belongs only to propositions: whereof there are two sorts, viz. mental and verbal; as there are two sorts of signs commonly made use of, viz. ideas and words.

3. To form a clear notion of truth, it is very necessary to consider truth of thought, and truth of words, distinctly one from another: but yet it is very difficult to treat of them asunder. Because it is unavoidable, in treating of mental propositions, to make use of words: and then the instances given of mental propositions cease immediately to be barely mental, and become verbal. For a *mental proposition* being nothing but a bare consideration of the ideas, as they are in our minds, stripped of names, they lose the nature of purely mental propositions as soon as they are put into words.

5. But to return to the consideration of truth: we must, I say, observe two sorts of propositions that we are capable of making:—

First, *mental*, wherein the ideas in our understandings are without the use of words put together, or separated, by the mind perceiving or judging of their agreement or disagreement.

Secondly, *Verbal* propositions, which are words, the signs of our ideas, put together or separated in affirmative or negative sentences. By which way of affirming or denying, these signs, made by sounds, are, as it were, put together or separated one from another. So that proposition consists in joining or separating signs; and truth consists in the putting together or separating those signs, according as the things which they stand for agree or disagree.

6. Every one's experience will satisfy him, that the mind, either by perceiving, or supposing, the agreement or disagreement of any of its ideas, does tacitly within itself put them into a kind of proposition af-

firmative or negative; which I have endeavoured to express by the terms putting together and separating. But this action of the mind, which is so familiar to every thinking and reasoning man, is easier to be conceived by reflecting on what passes in us when we affirm or deny, than to be explained by words. When a man has in his head the idea of two lines, viz. the side and diagonal of a square, whereof the diagonal is an inch long, he may have the idea also of the division of that line into a certain number of equal parts; v.g. into five, ten, a hundred, a thousand, or any other number, and may have the idea of that inch line being divisible, or not divisible, into such equal parts, as a certain number of them will be equal to the sideline. Now, whenever he perceives, believes, or supposes such a kind of divisibility to agree or disagree to his idea of that line, he, as it were, joins or separates those two ideas, viz. the idea of that line, and the idea of that kind of divisibility; and so makes a mental proposition, which is true or false, according as such a kind of divisibility, a divisibility into such *aliquot* parts, does really agree to that line or no. When ideas are so put together, or separated in the mind, as they or the things they stand for do agree or not, that is, as I may call it, *mental truth*. But *truth of words* is something more; and that is the affirming or denying of words one of another, as the ideas they stand for agree or disagree: and this again is two-fold; either purely verbal and trifling, which I shall speak of, (chap. viii.,) or real and instructive; which is the object of that real knowledge which we have spoken of already.

7. But here again will be apt to occur the same doubt about truth, that did about knowledge: and it will be objected, that if truth be nothing but the joining and separating of words in propositions, as the ideas they stand for agree or disagree in men's minds, the knowledge of truth is not so valuable a thing as it is taken to be, nor worth the pains and time men employ in the search of it: since by this account it amounts to no more than the conformity of words to the chimeras of men's brains. Who knows not what odd notions many men's heads are filled with, and what strange ideas all men's brains are capable of? But if we rest here, we know the truth of nothing by this rule, but of the visionary words in our own imaginations; nor have other truth, but what as much concerns harpies and centaurs, as men and horses. For those, and the like, may be ideas in our heads, and have their agreement or disagreement there, as well as the ideas of real beings, and so have as true propositions made about them. And it will be altogether as true a proposition to say *all centaurs are animals*, as that *all men are animals*; and the certainty of one as great as the other. For in both the propositions, the words are put together according to the agreement of the ideas in our minds: and the agreement of the idea of animal with that of centaur is as clear and visible to the mind, as the

agreement of the idea of animal with that of man; and so these two propositions are equally true, equally certain. But of what use is all such truth to us?

8. Though what has been said in the foregoing chapter to distinguish real from imaginary knowledge might suffice here, in answer to this doubt, to distinguish real truth from chimerical, or (if you please) barely nominal, they depending both on the same foundation; yet it may not be amiss here again to consider, that though our words signify nothing but our ideas, yet being designed by them to signify things, the truth they contain when put into propositions will be only verbal, when they stand for ideas in the mind that have not an agreement with the reality of things. And therefore truth as well as knowledge may well come under the distinction of verbal and real; that being only verbal truth, wherein terms are joined according to the agreement or disagreement of the ideas they stand for; without regarding whether our ideas are such as really have, or are capable of having, an existence in nature. But then it is they contain *real truth*, when these signs are joined, as our ideas agree; and when our ideas are such as we know are capable of having an existence in nature: which in substances we cannot know, but by knowing that such have existed.

9. Truth is the marking down in words the agreement or disagreement of ideas as it is. Falsehood is the marking down in words the agreement or disagreement of ideas otherwise than it is. And so far as these ideas, thus marked by sounds, agree to their archetypes, so far only is the truth real. The knowledge of this truth consists in knowing what ideas the words stand for, and the perception of the agreement or disagreement of those ideas, according as it is marked by those words.

Chapter IX

Of Our Threefold Knowledge of Existence

1. Hitherto we have only considered the essences of things; which being only abstract ideas, and thereby removed in our thoughts from particular existence, (that being the proper operation of the mind, in abstraction, to consider an idea under no other existence but what it has in the understanding,) gives us no knowledge of real existence at all. Where, by the way, we may take notice, that universal propositions of whose truth or falsehood we can have certain knowledge concern not existence: and further, that all particular affirmations or negations that would not be certain if they were made general, are only concerning existence; they declaring only the accidental union or separation of ideas in things existing, which, in their abstract natures, have no known necessary union or repugnancy.

2. But, leaving the nature of propositions, and different ways of predication to be considered more at large in another place, let us pro-

ceed now to inquire concerning our knowledge of the *existence of things*, and how we come by it. I say, then, that we have the knowledge of *our own* existence by intuition; of the existence of *God* by demonstration; and of *other things* by sensation.

3. As for our *own existence*, we perceive it so plainly and so certainly, that it neither needs nor is capable of any proof. For nothing can be more evident to us than our own existence. I think, I reason, I feel pleasure and pain: can any of these be more evident to me than my own existence? If I doubt of all other things, that very doubt makes me perceive my own existence, and will not suffer me to doubt of that. For if I know I feel pain, it is evident I have as certain perception of my own existence, as of the existence of the pain I feel: or if I know I doubt, I have as certain perception of the existence of the thing doubting, as of that thought which I *call doubt*. Experience then convinces us, that we have an *intuitive knowledge* of our own existence, and an internal infallible perception that we are. In every act of sensation, reasoning, or thinking, we are conscious to ourselves of our own being; and, in this matter, come not short of the highest degree of certainty.

Chapter X

Of Our Knowledge of the Existence of a God

1. Though God has given us no innate ideas of himself; though he has stamped no original characters on our minds, wherein we may read his being; yet having furnished us with those faculties our minds are endowed with, he hath not left himself without witness: since we have sense, perception, and reason, and cannot want a clear proof of him, as long as we carry *ourselves* about us. Nor can we justly complain of our ignorance in this great point; since he has so plentifully provided us with the means to discover and know him; so far as is necessary to the end of our being, and the great concernment of our happiness. But, though this be the most obvious truth that reason discovers, and though its evidence be (if I mistake not) equal to mathematical certainty: yet it requires thought and attention; and the mind must apply itself to a regular deduction of it from some part of our intuitive knowledge, or else we shall be as uncertain and ignorant of this as of other propositions, which are in themselves capable of clear demonstration. To show, therefore, that we are capable of *knowing*, i.e. *being certain* that there is a God, and *how we may come by* this certainty, I think we need go no further than ourselves, and that undoubted knowledge we have of our own existence.

2. I think it is beyond question, that man has a clear idea of his own being; he knows certainly he exists, and that he is something. He that can doubt whether he be anything or no, I speak not to; no more than I would argue with pure nothing, or endeavour to convince nonentity

that it were something. If any one pretends to be so sceptical as to deny his own existence, (for really to doubt of it is manifestly impossible,) let him for me enjoy his beloved happiness of being nothing, until hunger or some other pain convince him of the contrary. This, then, I think I may take for a truth, which every one's certain knowledge assures him of, beyond the liberty of doubting, viz. that he is *something that actually exists.*

3. In the next place, man knows, by an intuitive certainty, that bare *nothing can no more produce any real being, than it can be equal to two right angles.* If a man knows not that nonentity, or the absence of all being, cannot be equal to two right angles, it is impossible he should know any demonstration in Euclid. If, therefore, we know there is some real being, and that nonentity cannot produce any real being, it is an evident demonstration, that *from eternity there has been something*; since what was not from eternity had a beginning; and what had a beginning must be produced by something else. . . .

From what has been said, it is plain to me we have a more certain knowledge of the existence of a God, than of anything our senses have not immediately discovered to us. Nay, I presume I may say, that we more certainly know that there is a God, than that there is anything else without us. When I say we *know*, I mean there is such a knowledge within our reach which we cannot miss, if we will but apply our minds to that, as we do to several other inquiries. . . .

7. How far the *idea* of a most perfect being, which a man may frame in his mind, does or does not prove the *existence* of a God, I will not here examine. For in the different make of men's tempers and application of their thoughts, some arguments prevail more on one, and some on another, for the confirmation of the same truth. But yet, I think, this I may say, that it is an ill way of establishing this truth, and silencing atheists, to lay the whole stress of so important a point as this upon that sole foundation: and take some men's having that idea of God in their minds, (for it is evident some men have none, and some worse than none, and the most very different,) for the only proof of a Deity; and out of an over fondness of that darling invention, cashier, or at least endeavour to invalidate all other arguments; and forbid us to hearken to those proofs, as being weak or fallacious, which our own existence, and the sensible parts of the universe offer so clearly and cogently to our thoughts, that I deem it impossible for a considering man to withstand them. For I judge it as certain and clear a truth as can anywhere be delivered, that 'the invisible things of God are clearly seen from the creation of the world, being understood by the things that are made, even his eternal power and Godhead.' Though our own being furnishes us, as I have shown, with an evident and incontestible proof of a Deity; and I believe nobody can avoid the cogency of it, who will

but as carefully attend to it, as to any other demonstration of so many parts: yet this being so fundamental a truth, and of that consequence, that all religion and genuine morality depend thereon, I doubt not but I shall be forgiven by my reader if I go over some parts of this argument again, and enlarge a little more upon them.

Chapter XI

Of Our Knowledge of the Existence of Other Things

1. The knowledge of our own being we have by intuition. The existence of a God, reason clearly makes known to us, as has been shown.

The knowledge of the existence of *any other thing* we can have only by *sensation*: for there being no necessary connexion of real existence with any *idea* a man hath in his memory; nor of any other existence but that of God with the existence of any particular man: no particular man can know the existence of any other being, but only when, by actual operating upon him, it makes itself perceived by him. For, the having the idea of anything in our mind, no more proves the existence of that thing, than the picture of a man evidences his being in the world, or the visions of a dream make thereby a true history.

2. It is therefore the *actual receiving* of ideas from without that gives us notice of the existence of other things, and makes us know, that something doth exist at that time without us, which causes that idea in us; though perhaps we neither know nor consider how it does it. For it takes not from the certainty of our senses, and the ideas we receive by them, that we know not the manner wherein they are produced: v.g. whilst I write this, I have, by the paper affecting my eyes, that idea produced in my mind, which, whatever object causes, I call *white*; by which I know that that quality or accident (i.e. whose appearance before my eyes always causes that idea) doth really exist, and hath a being without me. And of this, the greatest assurance I can possibly have, and to which my faculties can attain, is the testimony of my eyes, which are the proper and sole judges of this thing; whose testimony I have reason to rely on as so certain, that I can no more doubt, whilst I write this, that I see white and black, and that something really exists that causes that sensation in me, than that I write or move my hand; which is a certainty as great as human nature is capable of, concerning the existence of anything, but a man's self alone, and of God.

From The Second Treatise of Civil Government

Chapter I

The Introduction

3. Political power, then I take to be a right of making laws with penalties of death, and consequently all less penalties, for the regulating

and preserving of property, and of employing the force of the community in the execution of such laws, and in the defense of the commonwealth from foreign injury, and all this only for the public good.

Chapter II

Of The State of Nature

4. To understand political power aright, and derive it from its original, we must consider what state all men are naturally in, and that is a state of perfect freedom to order their actions and dispose of their possessions and persons as they think fit, within the bounds of the law of nature, without asking leave, or depending upon the will of any other man.

A state also of equality, wherein all the power and jurisdiction is reciprocal, no one having more than another; there being nothing more evident than that creatures of the same species and rank, promiscuously born to all the same advantages of nature, and the use of the same faculties, should also be equal one amongst another without subordination or subjection, unless the Lord and Master of them all should by any manifest declaration of His will set one above another, and confer on him by an evident and clear appointment an undoubted right to dominion and sovereignty.

5. This equality of men by nature the judicious Hooker looks upon as so evident in itself and beyond all question, that he makes it the foundation of that obligation to mutual love amongst men on which he builds the duties they owe one another, and from whence he derives the great maxims of justice and charity. His words are:—

"The like natural inducement hath brought men to know that it is no less their duty to love others than themselves; for seeing those things which are equal must needs all have one measure, if I cannot but wish to receive good, even as much at every man's hands as any man can wish unto his own soul, how should I look to have any part of my desire herein satisfied, unless myself be careful to satisfy the like desire, which is undoubtedly in other men weak, being of one and the same nature? To have anything offered them repugnant to this desire, must needs in all respects grieve them as much as me, so that, if I do harm, I must look to suffer, there being no reason that others should show greater measures of love to me than they have by me showed unto them. My desire, therefore, to be loved of my equals in nature as much as possible may be, imposeth upon me a natural duty of bearing to themward fully the like affection; from which relation of equality between ourselves and them that are as ourselves, what several rules and canons natural reason hath drawn for direction of life no man is ignorant."—(Eccl. Pol., lib. i).

6. But though this be a state of liberty, yet it is not a state of license; though man in that state have an uncontrollable liberty to dispose of

his person or possessions, yet he has not liberty to destroy himself, or so much as any creature in his possession, but where some nobler use than its bare preservation calls for it. The state of nature has a law of nature to govern it, which obliges everyone; and reason, which is that law, teaches all mankind who will but consult it, that, being all equal and independent, no one ought to harm another in his life, health, liberty, or possessions. For men being all the workmanship of one omnipotent and infinitely wise Maker—all the servants of one sovereign Master, sent into the world by His order, and about His business— they are His property, whose workmanship they are, made to last during His, not one another's pleasure; and being furnished with like faculties, sharing all in one community of nature, there cannot be supposed any such subordination among us, that may authorize us to destroy one another, as if we were made for one another's uses, as the inferior ranks of creatures are for ours. Everyone, as he is bound to preserve himself, and not to quit his station willfully, so, by the like reason, when his own preservation comes not in competition, ought he, as much as he can, to preserve the rest of mankind, and not, unless it be to do justice on an offender, take away or impair the life, or what tends to the preservation of the life, the liberty, health, limb, or goods of another.

7. And that all men may be restrained from invading others' rights, and from doing hurt to one another, and the law of nature be observed, which willeth the peace and preservation of all mankind, the execution of the law of nature is in that state put into every man's hand, whereby everyone has a right to punish the transgressors of that law to such a degree as may hinder its violation. For the law of nature would, as all other laws that concern men in this world, be in vain if there were nobody that, in the state of nature, had a power to execute that law, and thereby preserve the innocent and restrain offenders. And if anyone in the state of nature may punish another for any evil he has done, everyone may do so. For in that state of perfect equality, where naturally there is no superiority or jurisdiction of one over another, what any may do in prosecution of that law, everyone must needs have a right to do.

8. And thus in the state of nature one man comes by a power over another; but yet no absolute or arbitrary power, to use a criminal, when he has got him in his hands, according to the passionate heats or boundless extravagance of his own will; but only to retribute to him so far as calm reason and conscience dictate what is proportionate to his transgression, which is so much as may serve for reparation and restraint. For these two are the only reasons why one man may lawfully do harm to another, which is that we call punishment. In transgressing the law of nature, the offender declares himself to live by another rule

than that of common reason and equity, which is that measure God has set to the actions of men, for their mutual security; and so he becomes dangerous to mankind, the tie which is to secure them from injury and violence being slighted and broken by him. Which, being a trespass against the whole species, and the peace and safety of it, provided for by the law of nature, every man upon this score, by the right he hath to preserve mankind in general, may restrain, or, where it is necessary, destroy things noxious to them, and so may bring such evil on anyone who hath transgressed that law, as may make him repent the doing of it, and thereby deter him, and by his example others, from doing the like mischief. And in this case, and upon this ground, every man hath a right to punish the offender, and be executioner of the law of nature.

9. I doubt not but this will seem a very strange doctrine to some men: but before they condemn it, I desire them to resolve me by what right any prince or state can put to death or punish an alien, for any crime he commits in their country. 'Tis certain their laws, by virtue of any sanction they receive from the promulgated will of the legislative, reach not a stranger: they speak not to him, nor, if they did, is he bound to hearken to them. The legislative authority, by which they are in force over the subjects of that commonwealth, hath no power over him. Those who have the supreme power of making laws in England, France, or Holland, are to an Indian but like the rest of the world—men without authority. And, therefore, if by the law of nature every man hath not a power to punish offenses against it, as he soberly judges the case to require, I see not how the magistrates of any community can punish an alien of another country; since in reference to him they can have no more power than what every man naturally may have over another.

10. Besides the crime which consists in violating the law, and varying from the right rule of reason, whereby a man so far becomes degenerate, and declares himself to quit the principles of human nature, and to be a noxious creature, there is commonly injury done, and some person or other, some other man receives damage by his transgression, in which case he who hath received any damage, has, besides the right of punishment common to him with other men, a particular right to seek reparation from him that has done it. And any other person who finds it just, may also join with him that is injured, and assist him in recovering from the offender so much as may make satisfaction for the harm he has suffered.

11. From these two distinct rights—the one of punishing the crime for restraint and preventing the like offense, which right of punishing is in everybody; the other of taking reparation, which belongs only to the injured party—comes it to pass that the magistrate, who by being

magistrate hath the common right of punishing put into his hands, can often, where the public good demands not the execution of the law, remit the punishment of criminal offenses by his own authority, but yet cannot remit the satisfaction due to any private man for the damage he has received. That he who has suffered the damage has a right to demand in his own name, and he alone can remit. The damnified person has this power of appropriating to himself the goods or service of the offender, by right of self-preservation, as every man has a power to punish the crime, to prevent its being committed again, by the right he has of preserving all mankind, and doing all reasonable things he can in order to that end. And thus it is that every man in the state of nature has a power to kill a murderer, both to deter others from doing the like injury, which no reparation can compensate, by the example of the punishment that attends it from everybody, and also to secure men from the attempts of a criminal who having renounced reason, the common rule and measure God hath given to mankind, hath by the unjust violence and slaughter he hath committed upon one, declared war against all mankind, and therefore may be destroyed as a lion or a tiger, one of those wild savage beasts with whom men can have no society nor security. And upon this is grounded that great law of nature. "Whoso sheddeth man's blood, by man shall his blood be shed." And Cain was so fully convinced that everyone had a right to destroy such a criminal, that after the murder of his brother he cries out, "Every one that findeth me shall slay me;" so plain was it writ in the hearts of mankind.

12. By the same reason may a man in the state of nature punish the lesser breaches of that law. It will perhaps be demanded, With death? I answer, each transgression may be punished to that degree, and with so much severity, as will suffice to make it an ill bargain to the offender, give him cause to repent, and terrify others from doing the like. Every offense that can be committed in the state of nature, may in the state of nature be also punished equally, and as far forth as it may, in a commonwealth. For though it would be beside my present purpose to enter here into the particulars of the law of nature, or its measures of punishment, yet it is certain there is such a law, and that, too, as intelligible and plain to a rational creature and a studier of that law as the positive laws of commonwealths; nay, possibly plainer, as much as reason is easier to be understood than the fancies and intricate contrivances of men, following contrary and hidden interests put into words; for truly so are a great part of the municipal laws of countries, which are only so far right as they are founded on the law of nature, by which they are to be regulated and interpreted.

13. To this strange doctrine—viz., that in the state of nature everyone has the executive power of the law of nature—I doubt not but it

will be objected that it is unreasonable for men to be judges in their own cases, that self-love will make men partial to themselves and their friends. And on the other side, that ill-nature, passion, and revenge will carry them too far in punishing others; and hence nothing but confusion and disorder will follow; and that therefore God hath certainly appointed government to restrain the partiality and violence of men. I easily grant that civil government is the proper remedy for the inconveniences of the state of nature, which must certainly be great where men may be judges in their own case, since 'tis easy to be imagined that he who was so unjust as to do his brother an injury, will scarce be so just as to condemn himself for it. But I shall desire those who make this objection, to remember that absolute monarchs are but men, and if government is to be the remedy of those evils which necessarily follow from men's being judges in their own cases, and the state of nature is therefore not to be endured, I desire to know what kind of government that is, and how much better it is than the state of nature, where one man commanding a multitude, has the liberty to be judge in his own case, and may do to all his subjects whatever he pleases, without the least question or control of those who execute his pleasure; and in whatsoever he doth, whether led by reason, mistake, or passion, must be submitted to, which men in the state of nature are not bound to do one to another? And if he that judges, judges amiss in his own or any other case, he is answerable for it to the rest of mankind.

14. 'Tis often asked as a mighty objection, Where are, or ever were there, any men in such a state of nature? To which it may suffice as an answer at present: That since all princes and rulers of independent governments all through the world are in a state of nature, 'tis plain the world never was, nor ever will be, without numbers of men in that state. I have named all governors of independent communities, whether they are or are not in league with others. For 'tis not every compact that puts an end to the state of nature between men, but only this one of agreeing together mutually to enter into one community, and make one body politic; other promises and compacts men may make one with another, and yet still be in the state of nature. The promises and bargains for truck, etc., between the two men in Soldania, in or between a Swiss and an Indian, in the woods of America, are binding to them, though they are perfectly in a state of nature in reference to one another. For truth and keeping of faith belong to men as men, and not as members of society.

15. To those that say there were never any men in the state of nature, I will not only oppose the authority of the judicious Hooker— (Eccl. Pol., lib. i., sect. 10), where he says, "The laws which have been hitherto mentioned," i.e., the laws of nature, "do bind men absolutely, even as they are men, although they have never any settled fellowship,

and never any solemn agreement amongst themselves what to do or not to do; but forasmuch as we are not by ourselves sufficient to furnish ourselves with competent store of things needful for such a life as our nature doth desire—a life fit for the dignity of man—therefore to supply those defects and imperfections which are in us, as living single and solely by ourselves, we are naturally induced to seek communion and fellowship with others; this was the cause of men's uniting themselves at first in politic societies"—but I moreover affirm that all men are naturally in that state, and remain so, till by their own consents they make themselves members of some politic society; and I doubt not, in the sequel of this discourse, to make it very clear.

Chapter VII

Of Political or Civil Society

77. God having made man such a creature, that in his own judgment it was not good for him to be alone, put him under strong obligations of necessity, convenience, and inclination to drive him into society, as well as fitted him with understanding and language to continue and enjoy it. The first society was between man and wife, which gave beginning to that between parents and children; to which, in time, that between master and servant came to be added; and though all these might, and commonly did meet together, and make up but one family, wherein the master or mistress of it had some sort of rule proper to a family; each of these, or all together, came short of political society, as we shall see, if we consider the different ends, ties, and bounds of each of these.

78. Conjugal society is made by a voluntary compact between man and woman, and though it consist chiefly in such a communion and right in one another's bodies as is necessary to its chief end, procreation, yet it draws with it mutual support and assistance, and a communion of interests too, as necessary not only to unite their care and affection, but also necessary to their common offspring, who have a right to be nourished and maintained by them till they are able to provide for themselves. . . .

84. The society betwixt parents and children, and the distinct rights and powers belonging respectively to them, I have treated of so largely in the foregoing chapter that I shall not here need to say anything of it; and I think it is plain that it is far different from a politic society. . . .

89. Wherever, therefore, any number of men so unite into one society, as to quit everyone his executive power of the law of nature, and to resign it to the public, there, and there only, is a political, or civil society. And this is done wherever any number of men, in the state of nature, enter into society to make one people, one body politic, under

one supreme government, or else when anyone joins himself to, and incorporates with, any government already made. For hereby he authorises the society, or, which is all one, the legislative thereof, to make laws for him, as the public good of the society shall require, to the execution whereof his own assistance (as to his own decrees) is due. And this puts men out of a state of nature into that of a commonwealth, by setting up a judge on earth with authority to determine all the controversies and redress the injuries that may happen to any member of the commonwealth; which judge is the legislative, or magistrates appointed by it. And wherever there are any number of men, however associated, that have no such decisive power to appeal to, there they are still in the state of nature.

Review Questions

1. What is Locke's role in the history of British empiricism?
2. What goals did Locke have in mind in his exploration of human knowledge? Are they the same as Descartes'?
3. If, for Locke, ideas are not innate, how do they originate?
4. Differentiate Locke's three kinds of knowledge: intuitive, demonstrative, and sensitive.
5. What problem does Locke have with the idea of substance?
6. Distinguish between rationalism and empiricism.
7. Compare the views of Locke and Hobbes on the state of nature.
8. Discuss Locke's view that common consent in civil society is based on trust.

CHAPTER 15

George Berkeley
(1685–1753)

Introduction

In the previous chapter, mention was made of the idealism of Berkeley as one of the possible consequences of Locke's view of the relationship of ideas to material things, yet Berkeley is also seen as a link between the moderate empiricism of Locke and the extreme empiricism of Hume. And so, we have an interesting description of Berkeley as an idealist and an empiricist at the same time. A plausible way to understand this is by attending to Berkeley's reference to himself as an "immaterialist" rather than an idealist, which means that he thought of himself as a realist inasmuch as things perceived are real even though they do not attach to material things outside the mind. The very being of sense objects is their being perceived, and if in the past there were philosophers who insisted on a substance called *matter*, to which our ideas refer, it was the result of an errant metaphysics. Berkeley's philosophy of immaterialism, summarized in the phrase "to be is to be perceived" (*esse est percipi*), is a gauntlet thrown down in the face of common sense and is an event in the history of philosophy that commands our examination.

George Berkeley was born in 1685 in Kilkenny, Ireland, and, though of an English family and in contrast to others of similar birth, he thought of himself as Irish. His family, though not rich, was comfortable enough to see to his early education at the prestigious Kilkenny School and to send him later to Trinity College, Dublin, where, besides studying Latin, Greek, French, and Hebrew, he read programmatically in philosophy, with a special focus on his older French contemporary Malebranche, whose doctrine was as arresting as his own budding immaterialism, and on Locke, whose *Essay* had appeared only ten years earlier. After brilliantly taking his B.A. degree in 1704, an academic career seemed to be in his future. Accordingly, in 1707, he became a fellow of Trinity College; several years later, he was ordained a priest, as required by the statutes. Around this time, he began keeping his notebooks, known in recent years as *Philosophical Commentaries*, a personal diary with random jottings, comments, and thoughts, some of which he subsequently developed into major works.

Berkeley's first visit to London in 1713 was the beginning of an eight-year period that, at various stages, took him to France and Italy as chaplain and tutor. When in London, he was made welcome at the royal court and in literary circles, where he was befriended by such well-known figures as Addison, Steele, Pope, and Swift, among whom he achieved a reputation as a man of charm and character, as well as learning. During a visit to Paris in 1715, he went to see Malebranche, who was sick and confined to his bed. As the story goes — if it's not true, it's still fun to pass on — they got into a heated argument which brought on such a "violent increase of his disorder" that the old man died a few days later, perhaps the first recorded case of death by metaphysics!

On his return to Dublin in 1721, Berkeley was awarded a doctorate of divinity and lectured in divinity at Trinity. During the next few years, however, he tried to give some realistic shape to a project for the New World he had been considering, the founding of a college in Bermuda, which in the popular mind was a highly romanticized island, where English youth might be educated to supply the churches with "pastors of good morals and good learning" and where "a number of young American savages may also be educated till they have taken their degree of Master of Arts." Needing funds for this ambitious venture, he was required to enlist public support as well as to invest his own money and, to augment his income for that end, he resigned his post at Trinity and accepted the higher-salaried appointment as Dean of Derry in 1724.

Perhaps to give himself the opportunity to reevaluate the feasibility of a college in Bermuda, now that he had come to realize its inaccessibility from the mainland, he set sail, with his new wife, for Newport, Rhode Island, in 1728; here, as the highest-ranking visiting ecclesiastic yet, he was warmly welcomed, and he settled in until the time was ripe to undertake his project. He had already been given a charter to establish St. Paul's College as its first president, but the promised funding was never forthcoming; disillusioned, he returned to England in 1731. However, during the time of his stay in the colonies, he was active in matters of education; he visited William and Mary College in Virginia; his advice was sought on the founding of Columbia University (then King's College) and the University of Pennsylvania; he became a benefactor of Harvard and Yale. Many years later, as a remembrance of his interest in early college education in America, California's Berkeley was named after him, a fitting complement to the verse he wrote on his hopes for education in America: "Westward the Course of Empire takes its way."

Back in Ireland, Berkeley was installed as the Bishop of Cloyne in 1734, a post he held for the next two decades. He was a beloved churchman, filled with concern for the welfare of his people; he kept on writing, but none of his major works were done at this time. However, because of the inadequacy of medical services in his diocese, he wrote a widely read book entitled *Siris*, in which he encouraged the use of a liquid he had learned of in America known as *tar-water*, a mixture of water and pine resin; he referred to it as a "medicine that cures or relieves all different species of distempers." The book, whose subtitle is "Philosophical Reflexions and Inquiries concerning the Virtues of Tar Water," is an enthusiastic, curious work in which the author, seriously committed to both medicine and religion, attempts to link the health properties of tar-water, through the great chain of being, with the triune God. In this work, as in his others, the learned bishop desired to see God as the end of all his labors. He died in Oxford in 1753.

His chief works are *An Essay towards a New Theory of Vision* (1709), *A Treatise concerning the Principles of Human Knowledge* (1710), and *Three Dialogues between Hylas and Philonous* (1713).

If there is any guiding principle that runs through all of Berkeley's works, it is the presence of God to the universe, but especially to man, who therefore, out of duty and love, must find ways to reaffirm His existence, put down skepticism, and rout the free thinkers. The *Principles*, for example, begins in God's name: "What I here make public has, after a long and scrupulous inquiry, seemed to me evidently true, and not unuseful to be known, particularly to those who are tainted with scepticism, or want a demonstration of the existence and immateriality of God, or the natural immortality of the soul." It also ends in God's name: "For after all, what serves the first place in our studies is the consideration of *God*, and our *duty*; which to promote, as it was the main drift and design of my labours, so shall I esteem them altogether useless and ineffectual, if by what I have said I cannot inspire my readers with a pious sense of the presence of God."

But if God has equipped man for a human journey through life, man's mind must be suitable to the task, so it is not the mind's incapacity that has led to confusion and difficulties in assenting to the divine; it is only when man uses his mind incorrectly that absurdities of all kinds begin to arise. So Berkeley's purpose, he tells us, is to remove all absurdities that philosophy has become encrusted with and, like so many philosophers before him, to sweep clean, uproot the confusion, and start anew.

Berkeley's first contention, then, is that confusion abounds because of the abuse of language, words being so carelessly used as to be assigned meaning when they have none — the same fear that Hobbes and Locke had before him. The main culprit in the abuse of language is *abstraction*, a power some falsely believe we possess to "frame abstract ideas," which then leads to a use of words matching these abstract ideas and endowing them with meaning they do not have. Berkeley arrives at this conclusion by beginning with "qualities" that traditionally belong, in one way or another, to the thing they are qualities of, such as "white" paper. But qualities of things never exist on their own, apart from other qualities with which they are "mixed," so, for example, "white" and "extended" are found together in the paper; "we are told" by some philosophers, complains Berkeley, that the mind is able to consider each quality apart from the others, and so to "abstract." Then the power of abstraction is enlarged to include triangles and triangularity, animal and animality, man and humanity, and so on, separating something common to all instances of triangle, animal, and man from all the particular features with which these objects are found in reality. Berkeley will allow the separation of particular parts from other particular parts of the same object, but that is as far as he will go; to separate by abstraction what is "general" can in no way refer to what is "particular." Regarding the "doctrine" of abstraction, Berkeley is at a loss to understand what it is "that inclines the men of speculation to embrace an opinion so remote from common sense as that seems to be." If anyone says that abstract ideas really refer to things, that is bad enough, but it is worse if he assigns words to these ideas and pretends that the assigned words have meaning in referring to real things. That, for Berkeley, is the abuse of words.

Yet there is an obvious "universal" content implied when we use the same word or notion of many things, as "man" of Peter, James, and John. This is accounted for not because there is a common nature among the particulars, which is impossible, but because our imagination enables us to hold together the similarities among things and so to use a word "universally," knowing full well that only particulars exist. Because it would be impossible to assign a word or name to every particular thing that exists, Berkeley suggests that universal words or names are a convenient way to refer to particulars, but they do so "indifferently" by not taking into account the differences that make things particular. David Hume, who succeeds Berkeley in the English empirical tradition, praised him on this point when he wrote, "A great philosopher has disputed the received opinion ... and has asserted that all general ideas are nothing but particular ones. ... As I look upon this to be one of the greatest and most valuable discoveries that has been made of late years in the republic of letters, I shall here endeavour to confirm it by some arguments, which I hope will put it beyond all doubt and controversy."

Berkeley's foray against abstraction is total: qualities, whether primary or secondary, are not abstracted; there is no externally existing nature common to particular things; there is no substance "out there" to act as a support for qualities, and he even reprimands Locke for wavering on the question he declared that we simply do not know if there is such an entity as material substance or not.

Further, it is clear for Berkeley that it is a *mind* (spirit, soul, my self) that works at various objects of knowledge which, if they are "ideas imprinted on the sense," are sensory objects, and which, if they are ideas coming from within the mind itself, are mental objects. In either case, it is the *perceiving* mind at work. Relying on this fundamental distinction, Berkeley gets to the heart of the thesis for which he is remembered in the history of philosophy: sensible objects have a mental existence only. No one ever had any problem with the fact that sensing is in the sensing subject, but Berkeley was the first to hold that the very things sensed are *in* the subject: the mind's sense objects are in the mind itself; sense *is* the sensing mind. To show the absolute correlation between the *existence* of sensed things and the *perception* of them, Berkeley invites us to attend to "what is meant by the term *exist* when applied to sensible things." To take his example, when I say that the table is in my study, I *mean* that by sight, touch, or smell, I *perceive* it; the *existence* of the table means nothing more than my *perception* of it: *to be is to be perceived* (*esse est percipi*). It is a mistake, brought about by abstraction, to think that sensible objects have an existence beyond being perceived; sensible objects, or ideas, are what they are and cannot be taken as signs of anything else.

An immediate corollary to the doctrine that "to be is to be perceived" as it applies to material things is that *no* "unthinking thing" exists outside the mind; the only thing that exists is the thinking thing, the "perceiver." The world is a spiritual world, for only spirits exist. In Berkeley's view, the demonstration that only the spiritual world exists is the trump card against materialism, for, with matter gone, the prejudices of the materialists are gone too. Berkeley's effort was a bit more philosophical than the storied demonstration of Dr. Samuel Johnson who said, "I refute materialism thus" as he kicked a stone with his foot. Historically, Berkeley represents one extreme of the mind–body duality created by Descartes: all mind, no body; others represent the other extreme: all body, no mind. The irony here is that Berkeley arrived at this extreme on the strength of a position that ranks him among the bold empiricists of modern philosophy.

Having come thus far with Berkeley in his firm emphasis on ideas, spirit, and mind, one might think that his affirmation of God would take on the coloration of the Cartesian argument, moving from the idea of the all-perfect to the existence of the all-perfect. But this is never advanced by him, and in *Alciphron*, a beautifully written Christian apologetic against the free-thinking "minute philosophers" personified by Alciphron, when the ontological argument is mentioned, Berkeley's sentiment appears to be against it. Rather, he hews to the causal argument by pointing out that the ideas in us must be caused: "yet it is evident to everyone, that those things which are called the works of Nature, that is, the far greater part of the ideas or sensations perceived by us, are not produced by, or dependent on the wills of men. There is therefore some other spirit that causes them, since it is repugnant that they should subsist by themselves." For Berkeley, the argument is clear, evident, and immediate: "Hence it is evident, that God is known as certainly and immediately as any other mind or spirit whatsoever, distinct from ourselves." His argument is consistent with his philosophy of immaterialism.

Both in answering the objections that might be raised against immaterialism and in refuting the arguments against God's existence, benignity, or providence made by the skeptics, Berkeley unhesitatingly maintainsthe primacy of his new principles of knowledge, or "the great advantages that arise from the belief of immaterialism." One is able to see the advantages of physics and mathematics, now that phenomena are nothing more than ideas and are free from endless disputes concerning gravity, extension, divisibility, and so on; in metaphysics, questions like abstraction and substance are put to rest; and above all, in morality, for now the mind is immediately present to God and not through the mediation of unthinking second causes. However, the goal of understanding the immediate presence of God is not itself given immediately, for it takes the unyielding steadiness of the pilgrim to get there. In the last lines of his last work, we see that Berkeley thought of himself as just such a pilgrim: "The eye by long use comes to see even in the darkest cavern: and there is no subject so obscure but we may discern some glimpse of truth by long poring on it. Truth is the cry of all, but the game of few. . . . He that would make a real progress in knowledge must dedicate his age as well as youth, the later growth as well as first fruits, at the altar of Truth."

Readings

From A Treatise Concerning the Principles of Human Knowledge

Preface

What I here make public has, after a long and scrupulous inquiry, seemed to me evidently true, and not unuseful to be known, particularly to those who are tainted with scepticism, or want a demonstration of the existence and immateriality of God, or the natural immortality of the soul. Whether it be so or no, I am content the reader should impartially examine; since I do not think myself any further concerned for the success of what I have written than as it is agreeable to truth. But to the end this may not suffer, I make it my request that the reader suspend his judgment till he has once, at least, read the whole through with that degree of attention and thought which the subject matter shall seem to deserve. For as there are some passages that, taken by themselves, are very liable (nor could it be remedied) to gross misinterpretation, and to be charged with most absurd consequences, which, nevertheless, upon an entire perusal will appear not to follow from them: so likewise, though the whole should be read over, yet if this be done transiently, it is very probable my sense may be mistaken; but to a thinking reader, I flatter myself, it will be throughout clear and obvious. As for the characters of novelty and singularity, which some of the following notions may seem to bear, it is, I hope, needless to make any apology on that account. He must surely be either very weak, or very little acquainted with the sciences, who shall reject a truth that is capable of demonstration, for no other reason but because it is newly known and contrary to the prejudices of mankind. Thus much I thought fit to premise, in order to prevent, if possible, the hasty censures of a sort of men, who are too apt to condemn an opinion before they rightly comprehend it.

Introduction

Philosophy being nothing else but the study of wisdom and truth, it may with reason be expected that those who have spent most time and pains in it should enjoy a greater calm and serenity of mind, a greater clearness and evidence of knowledge, and be less disturbed with doubts and difficulties than other men. Yet so it is, we see the illiterate bulk of mankind that walk the highroad of plain common sense, and are governed by the dictates of nature, for the most part easy and undisturbed. To them nothing that is familiar appears unaccountable or difficult to comprehend. They complain not of any want of evidence in their senses, and are out of all danger of becoming sceptics. But no sooner do we depart from sense and instinct to follow the light of a superior principle, to reason, meditate, and reflect on the nature of things, but a thousand scruples spring up in our minds concerning those things which before we seemed fully to comprehend. Prejudices and errors of sense do from all parts discover themselves to our view; and, endeavoring to correct these by reason, we are insensibly drawn into uncouth paradoxes, difficulties, and inconsistencies, which multiply and grow upon us as we advance in speculation, till at length, having wandered through many intricate mazes, we find ourselves just where we were, or, which is worse, sit down in a forlorn scepticism.

2. The cause of this is thought to be the obscurity of things, or the natural weakness and imperfection of our understandings. It is said the faculties we have are few, and those designed by nature for the support and comfort of life, and not to penetrate into the inward essence and constitution of things. Besides, the mind of man being finite, when it treats of things which partake of infinity it is not to be wondered at if it run into absurdities and contradictions, out of which it is impossible it should ever extricate itself, it being of the nature of infinite not to be comprehended by that which is finite.

3. But perhaps we may be too partial to ourselves in placing the fault originally in our faculties, and not rather in the wrong use we make of them. It is a hard thing to suppose that right deductions from true principles should ever end in consequences which cannot be maintained or made consistent. We should believe that God has dealt more bountifully with the sons of men than to give them a strong desire for that knowledge which he had placed quite out of their reach. This were not agreeable to the wonted indulgent methods of Providence, which whatever appetites it may have implanted in the creatures, doth usually furnish them with such means as, if rightly made use of, will not fail to satisfy them. Upon the whole, I am inclined to think that the far greater part, if not all, of those difficulties which have hitherto amused philosophers, and blocked up the way to knowledge, are entirely owing to ourselves—that we have first raised a dust and then complain we cannot see.

4. My purpose therefore is, to try if I can discover what those principles are which have introduced all that doubtfulness and uncertainty, those absurdities and contradictions, into the several sects of philosophy: insomuch that the wisest men have thought our ignorance incurable, conceiving it to arise from the natural dullness and limitation of our faculties. And surely it is a work well deserving our pains to make a strict inquiry concerning the first principles of human knowledge, to sift and examine them on all sides, especially since there may be some grounds to suspect that those lets and difficulties, which stay and embarrass the mind in its search after truth, do not spring from any darkness and intricacy in the objects, or natural defect in the understanding so much as from false principles which have been insisted on, and might have been avoided.

5. How difficult and discouraging soever this attempt may seem, when I consider how many great and extraordinary men have gone before me in the like designs, yet I am not without some hopes, upon the consideration that the largest views are not always the clearest, and that he who is short-sighted will be obliged to draw the object nearer,

and may, perhaps, by a close and narrow survey, discern that which had escaped far better eyes.

6. In order to prepare the mind of the reader for the easier conceiving what follows, it is proper to premise somewhat, by way of introduction, concerning the nature and abuse of language. But the unraveling this matter leads me in some measure to anticipate my design, by taking notice of what seems to have had a chief part in rendering speculation intricate and perplexed, and to have occasioned innumerable errors and difficulties in almost all parts of knowledge. And that is the opinion that the mind hath a power of framing *abstract ideas* or notions of things. He who is not a perfect stranger to the writings and disputes of philosophers must needs acknowledge that no small part of them are spent about abstract ideas. These are in a more especial manner thought to be the object of those sciences which go by the name of *logic* and *metaphysics,* and of all that which passes under the notion of the most abstracted and sublime learning, in all which one shall scarce find any question handled in such a manner as does not suppose their existence in the mind, and that it is well acquainted with them.

7. It is agreed on all hands, that the qualities or modes of things do never really exist each of them apart by itself, and separated from all others, but are mixed, as it were, and blended together, several in the same object. But we are told, the mind being able to consider each quality singly, or abstracted from those other qualities with which it is united, does by that means frame to itself abstract ideas. For example, there is perceived by sight an object extended, coloured, and moved: this mixed or compound idea the mind resolving into its simple, constituent parts, and viewing each by itself, exclusive of the rest, does frame the abstract ideas of extension, colour, and motion. Not that it is possible for colour or motion to exist without extension: but only that the mind can frame to itself by *abstraction* the idea of colour exclusive of extension, and of motion exclusive of both colour and extension.

8. Again, the mind having observed that in the particular extensions perceived by sense, there is something common and alike in all, and some other things peculiar, as this or that figure or magnitude, which distinguish them one from another; it considers apart or singles out by itself that which is common, making thereof a most abstract idea of extension, which is neither line, surface, nor solid, nor has any figure or magnitude but is an idea entirely prescinded from all these. So likewise the mind by leaving out of the particular colours perceived by sense, that which distinguishes them one from another, and retaining that only which is common to all, makes an idea of colour in abstract which is neither red, nor blue, nor white, nor any other determinate colour. And in like manner by considering motion abstractedly not only from

the body moved, but likewise from the figure it describes, and all particular directions and velocities, the abstract idea of motion is framed; which equally corresponds to all particular motions whatsoever that may be perceived by sense.

9. And as the mind frames to itself abstract ideas of qualities or modes, so does it, by the same precision or mental separation, attain abstract ideas of the more compounded beings, which include several coexistent qualities. For example, the mind having observed that Peter, James, and John, resemble each other, in certain common agreements of shape and other qualities, leaves out of the complex or compounded idea it has of Peter, James, and any other particular man, that which is peculiar to each, retaining only what is common to all; and so makes an abstract idea wherein all the particulars equally partake, abstracting entirely from and cutting off all those circumstances and differences which might determine it to any particular existence. And after this manner it is said we come by the abstract idea of man or, if you please, humanity or human nature; wherein it is true, there is included colour, because there is no man but has some colour, but then it can be neither white, nor black, nor any particular colour; because there is no one particular colour wherein all men partake. So likewise there is included stature, but then it is neither tall stature nor low stature, nor yet middle stature, but something abstracted from all these. And so of the rest. Moreover, there being a great variety of other creatures that partake in some parts, but not all, of the complex idea of *man,* the mind leaving out those parts which are peculiar to men, and retaining those only which are common to all the living creatures, frameth the idea of *animal,* which abstracts not only from all particular men, but also all birds, beasts, fishes, and insects. The constituent parts of the abstract idea of animal are body, life, sense and spontaneous motion. By *body* is meant, body without any particular shape or figure, there being no one shape or figure common to all animals, without covering, either of hair or feathers, or scales etc. nor yet naked: hair, feathers, scales, and nakedness being the distinguishing properties of particular animals, and for that reason left out of the *abstract idea.* Upon the same account the spontaneous motion must be neither walking, nor flying, nor creeping, it is nevertheless a motion; but what that motion is, it is not easy to conceive.

10. Whether others have this wonderful faculty of *abstracting their ideas,* they best can tell: for myself I find indeed I have a faculty of imagining, or representing to myself the ideas of those particular things I have perceived and of variously compounding and dividing them. I can imagine a man with two heads or the upper parts of a man joined to the body of a horse. I can consider the hand, the eye, the nose, each by itself abstracted or separated from the rest of the body.

But then whatever hand or eye I imagine, it must have some particular shape and colour. Likewise the idea of man that I frame to myself, must be either of a white, or a black, or a tawny, a straight, or a crooked, a tall, or a low, or a middle-sized man. I cannot by any effort of thought conceive the abstract idea above described. And it is equally impossible for me to form the abstract idea of motion distinct from the body moving, and which is neither swift nor slow, curvilinear nor rectilinear; and the like may be said of all other abstract general ideas whatsoever. To be plain, I own myself able to abstract in one sense, as when I consider some particular parts or qualities separated from others, with which though they are united in some object, yet it is possible they may really exist without them. But I deny that I can abstract one from another, or conceive separately, those qualities which it is impossible should exist so separated; or that I can frame a general notion by abstracting from particulars in the manner aforesaid. Which two last are the proper acceptations of *abstraction*. And there are grounds to think most men will acknowledge themselves to be in my case. The generality of men which are simple and illiterate never pretend to *abstract notions*. It's said they are difficult and not to be attained without pains and study. We may therefore reasonably conclude that, if such there be, they are confined only to the learned.

11. I proceed to examine what can be alleged in defence of the doctrine of abstraction, and try if I can discover what it is that inclines the men of speculation to embrace an opinion so remote from common sense as that seems to be. There has been a late deservedly esteemed philosopher [Locke], who, no doubt, has given it very much countenance by seeming to think the having of abstract general ideas is what puts the widest difference in point of understanding betwixt man and beast. 'The having of general ideas', saith he, 'is that which puts a perfect distinction betwixt man and brutes, and is an excellency which the faculties of brutes do by no means attain unto. For it is evident we observe no footsteps in them of making use of general signs for universal ideas; from which we have reason to imagine that they have not the faculty of *abstracting* or making general ideas, since they have no use of words or any other general signs.' And a little after: 'Therefore, I think we may suppose that it is in this that the species of brutes are discriminated from men, and 'tis that proper difference wherein they are wholly separated, and which at last widens to so wide a distance. For if they have any ideas at all, and are not bare machines (as some would have them) we cannot deny them to have some reason. It seems as evident to me that they do some of them in certain instances reason as that they have sense, but it is only in particular ideas, just as they receive them from their senses. They are the best of them tied up within those narrow bounds, and have not (as I think) the faculty to en-

large them by any kind of *abstraction*.' (*Essay*, Bk. II, C. 11, Sects. 10 and 11). I readily agree with this learned author, that the faculties of brutes can by no means attain to *abstraction*. But then if this be made the distinguishing property of that sort of animals, I fear a great many of those that pass for men must be reckoned into their number. The reason that is here assigned why we have no grounds to think brutes have abstract general ideas is that we observe in them no use of words or any other general signs; which is built on this supposition, to wit, that the making use of words implies the having general ideas. From which it follows, that men who use language are able to abstract or generalise their ideas. That this is the sense and arguing of the author will further appear by his answering the question he in another place puts. 'Since all things that exist are only particulars, how come we by general terms?' His answer is, 'Words become general by being made the signs of general ideas' (*Essay*, Bk. III, C. 3, Sect. 6). But it seems that a word becomes general by being made the sign, not of an abstract general idea, but of several particular ideas, any one of which it indifferently suggests to the mind. For example, when it is said *the change of motion is proportional to the impressed force*, or that *whatever has extension is divisible*; these propositions are to be understood of motion and extension in general, and nevertheless it will not follow that they suggest to my thoughts an idea of motion without a body moved, or any determinate direction and velocity, or that I must conceive an abstract general idea of extension, which is neither line, surface nor solid, neither great nor small, black, white, nor red, nor of any other determinate colour. It is only implied that whatever motion I consider, whether it be swift or slow, perpendicular, horizontal or oblique, or in whatever object, the axiom concerning it holds equally true. As does the other of every particular extension, it matters not whether line, surface or solid, whether of this or that magnitude or figure.

Part One

1. It is evident to anyone who takes a survey of the objects of human knowledge, that they are either ideas actually imprinted on the senses, or else such as are perceived by attending to the passions and operations of the mind, or lastly ideas formed by help of memory and imagination, either compounding, dividing, or barely representing those originally perceived in the aforesaid ways. By sight I have the ideas of light and colours with their several degrees and variations. By touch I perceive, for example, hard and soft, heat and cold, motion and resistance, and of all these more and less either as to quantity or degree. Smelling furnishes me with odours, the palate with tastes, and hearing conveys sounds to the mind in all their variety of tone and composi-

tion. And as several of these are observed to accompany each other, they come to be marked by one name, and so to be reputed as one thing. Thus, for example, a certain colour, taste, smell, figure and consistence having been observed to go together, are accounted one distinct thing, signified by the name *apple*. Other collections of ideas constitute a stone, a tree, a book, and the like sensible things; which, as they are pleasing or disagreeable, excite the passions of love, hatred, joy, grief, and so forth.

2. But besides all that endless variety of ideas or objects of knowledge, there is likewise something which knows or perceives them, and exercises divers operations, as willing, imagining, remembering about them. This perceiving, active being is what I call *mind, spirit, soul* or *my self*. By which words I do not denote any one of my ideas, but a thing entirely distinct from them, wherein they exist, or, which is the same thing, whereby they are perceived; for the existence of an idea consists in being perceived.

3. That neither our thoughts, nor passions, nor ideas formed by the imagination, exist without the mind, is what everybody will allow. And it seems no less evident that the various sensations or ideas imprinted on the sense, however blended or combined together (that is, whatever objects they compose) cannot exist otherwise than in a mind perceiving them. I think an intuitive knowledge may be obtained of this by anyone that shall attend to what is meant by the term *exist* when applied to sensible things. The table I write on, I say, exists, that is, I see and feel it; and if I were out of my study I should say it existed, meaning thereby that if I was in my study I might perceive it, or that some other spirit actually does perceive it. There was an odour, that is, it was smelled; there was a sound, that is to say, it was heard; a colour or figure, and it was perceived by sight or touch. This is all that I can understand by these and the like expressions. For as to what is said of the absolute existence of unthinking things without any relation to their being perceived, that seems perfectly unintelligible. Their *esse* is *percipi*, nor is it possible they should have any existence out of the minds or thinking things which perceive them.

4. It is indeed an opinion strangely prevailing amongst men, that houses, mountains, rivers, and in a word all sensible objects, have an existence natural or real, distinct from their being perceived by the understanding. But with how great an assurance and acquiescence soever this principle may be entertained in the world; yet whoever shall find in his heart to call it in question may, if I mistake not, perceive it to involve a manifest contradiction. For what are the forementioned objects but the things we perceive by sense, and what do we perceive besides our own ideas or sensations; and is it not plainly repugnant that any one of these or any combination of them should exist unperceived?

5. If we thoroughly examine this tenet, it will, perhaps, be found at bottom to depend on the doctrine of *abstract ideas*. For can there be a nicer strain of abstraction than to distinguish the existence of sensible objects from their being perceived, so as to conceive them existing unperceived? Light and colours, heat and cold, extension and figures, in a word the things we see and feel, what are they but so many sensations, notions, ideas or impressions on the sense; and is it possible to separate, even in thought, any of these from perception? For my part I might as easily divide a thing from itself. I may indeed divide in my thoughts or conceive apart from each other those things which, perhaps, I never perceived by sense so divided. Thus I imagine the trunk of a human body without the limbs, or conceive the smell of a rose without thinking on the rose itself. So far I will not deny I can abstract, if that may properly be called *abstraction*, which extends only to the conceiving separately such objects as it is possible may really exist or be actually perceived asunder. But my conceiving or imagining power does not extend beyond the possibility of real existence or perception. Hence as it is impossible for me to see or feel anything without an actual sensation of that thing, so is it impossible for me to conceive in my thoughts any sensible thing or object distinct from the sensation or perception of it.

6. Some truths there are so near and obvious to the mind that a man need only open his eyes to see them. Such I take this important one to be, to wit, that all the choir of heaven and furniture of the earth, in a word all those bodies which compose the mighty frame of the world, have not any subsistence without a mind, that their being is to be perceived or known; that consequently so long as they are not actually perceived by me, or do not exist in my mind or that of any other created spirit, they must either have no existence at all, or else subsist in the mind of some eternal spirit: it being perfectly unintelligible and involving all the absurdity of abstraction, to attribute to any single part of them an existence independent of a spirit. To be convinced of which, the reader need only reflect and try to separate in his own thoughts the being of a sensible thing from its being perceived.

7. From what has been said, it follows, there is not any other substance than spirit, or that which perceives. But for the fuller proof of this point, let it be considered, the sensible qualities are colour, figure, motion, smell, taste, and such like, that is, the ideas perceived by sense. Now for an idea to exist in an unperceiving thing is a manifest contradiction; for to have an idea is all one as to perceive: that therefore wherein colour, figure, and the like qualities exist, must perceive them; hence it is clear there can be no unthinking substance or *substratum* of those ideas.

8. But, say you, though the ideas themselves do not exist without the mind, yet there may be things like them whereof they are copies or re-

semblances, which things exist without the mind, in an unthinking substance. I answer, an idea can be like nothing but an idea; a colour or figure can be like nothing but another colour or figure. If we look but ever so little into our thoughts, we shall find it impossible for us to conceive a likeness except only between our ideas. Again, I ask whether those supposed originals or external things, of which our ideas are the pictures or representations, be themselves perceivable or no? If they are, then they are ideas, and we have gained our point; but if you say they are not, I appeal to anyone whether it be sense to assert a colour is like something which is invisible; hard or soft, like something which is intangible; and so of the rest.

9. Some there are who make a distinction betwixt *primary* and *secondary* qualities: by the former, they mean extension, figure, motion, rest, solidity or impenetrability, and number: by the latter they denote all other sensible qualities, as colours, sounds, tastes, and so forth. The ideas we have of these they acknowledge not to be the resemblances of any thing existing without the mind or unperceived; but they will have our ideas of the primary qualities to be patterns or images of things which exist without the mind, in an unthinking substance which they call *matter*. By matter therefore we are to understand an inert, senseless substance, in which extension, figure, and motion do actually subsist. But it is evident from what we have already shown, that extension, figure and motion are only ideas existing in the mind, and that an idea can be like nothing but another idea, and that consequently neither they nor their archetypes can exist in an unperceiving substance. Hence it is plain that the very notion of what is called *matter* or *corporeal substance* involves a contradiction in it.

10. They who assert that figure, motion, and the rest of the primary or original qualities do exist without the mind, in unthinking substances, do at the same time acknowledge that colours, sounds, heat, cold, and suchlike secondary qualities, do not, which they tell us are sensations existing in the mind alone, that depend on and are occasioned by the different size, texture and motion of the minute particles of matter. This they take for an undoubted truth, which they can demonstrate beyond all exception. Now if it be certain, that those original qualities are inseparably united with the other sensible qualities, and not even in thought capable of being abstracted from them, it plainly follows that they exist only in the mind. But I desire any one to reflect and try, whether he can by any abstraction of thought conceive the extension and motion of a body without all other sensible qualities. For my own part, I see evidently that it is not in my power to frame an idea of a body extended and moved, but I must withal give it some colour or other sensible quality which is acknowledged to exist only in the mind. In short, extension, figure, and motion, abstracted from all other

qualities, are inconceivable. Where therefore the other sensible qualities are, there must these be also, to wit, in the mind and nowhere
else. . . .

16. But let us examine a little the received opinion. It is said extension is a mode or accident of matter, and that matter is the *substratum*
that supports it. Now I desire that you would explain what is meant
by matter's *supporting* extension: say you, I have no idea of matter,
and therefore cannot explain it. I answer, though you have no positive,
yet if you have any meaning at all, you must at least have a relative
idea of matter; though you know not what it is, yet you must be supposed to know what relation it bears to accidents, and what is meant
by its supporting them. It is evident *support* cannot here be taken in
its usual or literal sense, as when we say that pillars support a building:
in what sense therefore must it be taken?

17. If we inquire into what the most accurate philosophers declare
themselves to mean by *material substance*, we shall find them acknowledge, they have no other meaning annexed to those sounds, but
the idea of being in general, together with the relative notion of its
supporting accidents. The general idea of being appeareth to me the
most abstract and incomprehensible of all other; and as for its supporting accidents, this, as we have just now observed, cannot be understood
in the common sense of those words; it must therefore be taken in
some other sense, but what that is they do not explain. So that when
I consider the two parts or branches which make the signification of
the words *material substance* I am convinced there is no distinct
meaning annexed to them. But why should we trouble ourselves any
farther, in discussing this material *substratum* or support of figure and
motion, and other sensible qualities? Does it not suppose they have an
existence without the mind? And is not this a direct repugnancy, and
altogether inconceivable?

18. But though it were possible that solid, figured, movable substances may exist without the mind, corresponding to the ideas we
have of bodies, yet how is it possible for us to know this? Either we
must know it by sense, or by reason. As for our senses, by them we
have the knowledge only of our sensations, ideas, or those things that
are immediately perceived by sense, call them what you will: but they
do not inform us that things exist without the mind, or unperceived,
like to those which are perceived. This the materialists themselves acknowledge. It remains therefore that if we have any knowledge at all
of external things, it must be by reason, inferring their existence from
what is immediately perceived by sense. But what reason can induce
us to believe the existence of bodies without the mind, from what we
perceive, since the very patrons of matter themselves do not pretend
there is any necessary connexion betwixt them and our ideas? I say it

is granted on all hands (and what happens in dreams, frenzies, and the like, puts it beyond dispute) that it is possible we might be affected with all the ideas we have now, though no bodies existed without, resembling them. Hence it is evident the supposition of external bodies is not necessary for the producing our ideas, since it is granted they are produced sometimes, and might possibly be produced always in the same order we see them in at present, without their concurrence. . . .

23. But say you, surely there is nothing easier than to imagine trees, for instance, in a park, or books existing in a closet, and nobody by to perceive them. I answer, you may so, there is no difficulty in it: but what is all this, I beseech you, more than framing in your mind certain ideas which you call books and trees, and at the same time omitting to frame the idea of anyone that may perceive them? But do not you yourself perceive or think of them all the while? This therefore is nothing to the purpose: it only shows you have the power of imagining or forming ideas in your mind; but it doth not show that you can conceive it possible the objects of your thought may exist without the mind: to make out this, it is necessary that you conceive them existing unconceived or unthought of, which is a manifest repugnancy. When we do our utmost to conceive the existence of external bodies, we are all the while only contemplating our own ideas. But the mind taking no notice of itself is deluded to think it can and doth conceive bodies existing unthought of or without the mind; though at the same time they are apprehended by or exist in itself. A little attention will discover to anyone the truth and evidence of what is here said, and make it unnecessary to insist on any other proofs against the existence of material substance.

24. It is very obvious, upon the least inquiry into our own thoughts, to know whether it be possible for us to understand what is meant by the *absolute existence of sensible objects in themselves, or without the mind.* To me it is evident those words mark out either a direct contradiction, or else nothing at all. And to convince others of this, I know no readier or fairer way than to entreat they would calmly attend to their own thoughts: and if by this attention, the emptiness or repugnancy of those expressions does appear, surely nothing more is requisite for their conviction. It is on this therefore that I insist, to wit, that the absolute existence of unthinking things are words without a meaning, or which include a contradiction. This is what I repeat and inculcate, and earnestly recommend to the attentive thoughts of the reader. . . .

26. We perceive a continual succession of ideas, some are anew excited, others are changed or totally disappear. There is therefore some cause of these ideas whereon they depend, and which produces and changes them. That this cause cannot be any quality or idea or combi-

nation of ideas, is clear from the preceding section. It must therefore be a substance; but it has been shown that there is no corporeal or material substance: it remains therefore that the cause of ideas is an incorporeal active substance or spirit. . . .

29. But whatever power I may have over my own thoughts, I find the ideas actually perceived by sense have not a like dependence on my will. When in broad daylight I open my eyes, it is not in my power to choose whether I shall see or no, or to determine what particular objects shall present themselves to my view; and so likewise as to the hearing and other senses, the ideas imprinted on them are not creatures of my will. There is therefore some other will or spirit that produces them.

30. The ideas of sense are more strong, lively, and distinct than those of the imagination; they have likewise a steadiness, order, and coherence, and are not excited at random, as those which are the effects of human wills often are, but in a regular train or series, the admirable connexion whereof sufficiently testifies the wisdom and benevolence of its Author. Now the set rules or established methods, wherein the mind we depend on excites in us the ideas of sense, are called the *Laws of Nature*: and these we learn by experience, which teaches us that such and such ideas are attended with such and such other ideas, in the ordinary course of things. . . .

33. The ideas imprinted on the senses by the Author of Nature are called *real things*: and those excited in the imagination, being less regular, vivid and constant, are more properly termed *ideas*, or *images of things*, which they copy and represent. But then our sensations, be they never so vivid and distinct, are nevertheless *ideas*, that is, they exist in the mind, or are perceived by it, as truly as the ideas of its own framing. The ideas of sense are allowed to have more reality in them, that is, to be more strong, orderly, and coherent than the creatures of the mind; but this is no argument that they exist without the mind. They are also less dependent on the spirit or thinking substance which perceives them, in that they are excited by the will of another and more powerful spirit: yet still they are *ideas*, and certainly no *idea*, whether faint or strong, can exist otherwise than in a mind perceiving it.

From Three Dialogues Between Hylas and Philonous

[Note: From the Third Dialogue; Hylas is a materialist and Philonous a lover of mind who represents Berkeley]

HYLAS. But still, Philonous, you hold there is nothing in the world but spirits and ideas. And this, you must needs acknowledge, sounds very oddly.

PHILONOUS. I own the word *idea*, not being commonly used for *thing*, sounds something out of the way. My reason for using it was, because a necessary relation to the mind is understood to be implied by that term; and it is now commonly used by philosophers, to denote the immediate objects of the understanding. But however oddly the proposition may sound in words, yet it includes nothing so very strange or shocking in its sense, which in effect amounts to no more than this, to wit, that there are only things perceiving, and things perceived; or that every unthinking being is necessarily, and from the very nature of its existence, perceived by some mind; if not by any finite created mind, yet certainly by the infinite mind of God, in whom *we live, and move, and have our being*. Is this as strange as to say, the sensible qualities are not on the objects: or, that we cannot be sure of the existence of things, or know anything of their real natures, though we both see and feel them, and perceive them by all our senses?

HYLAS. And in consequence of this, must we not think there are no such things as physical or corporeal causes; but that a spirit is the immediate cause of all the phenomena in Nature? Can there be anything more extravagant than this?

PHILONOUS. Yes, it is infinitely more extravagant to say, a thing which is inert, operates on the mind, and which is unperceiving, is the cause of our perceptions. Besides, that which to you, I know not for what reason, seems so extravagant, is no more than the Holy Scriptures assert in a hundred places. In them God is represented as the sole and immediate Author of all those effects, which some heathens and philosophers are wont to ascribe to Nature, matter, fate, or the like unthinking principle. This is so much the constant language of Scripture, that it were needless to confirm it by citations.

HYLAS. You are not aware, Philonous, that in making God the immediate author of all the motions in Nature, you make him the author of murder, sacrilege, adultery, and the like heinous sins.

PHILONOUS. In answer to that, I observe first, that the imputation of guilt is the same, whether a person commits an action with or without an instrument. In case therefore you suppose God to act by the mediation of an instrument, or occasion, called *matter*, you as truly make Him the author of sin as I, who think Him the immediate agent in all those operations vulgarly ascribed to Nature. I farther observe, that sin or moral turpitude doth not consist in the outward physical action or motion, but in the internal deviation of the will from the laws of reason and religion. This is plain, in that the killing an enemy in a battle, or putting a criminal legally to death, is not thought sinful, though the outward act be the very same with that in the case of murder. Since therefore sin doth not consist in the physical action, the making God an immediate cause of all such actions, is not making him the author of sin. Lastly, I have nowhere said that God is the only agent who produces all the motions in bodies. It is true, I have denied there are any other agents beside spirits: but this is very consistent with allowing to thinking rational beings, in the production of motions, the use of limited powers, ultimately indeed derived from God, but immediately under the direction of their own wills, which is sufficient to entitle them to all the guilt of their actions. . . .

HYLAS. What say you to this? Since, according to you, men judge of the reality of things by their senses, how can a man be mistaken in thinking the moon a plain lucid surface, about a foot in diameter; or a square tower, seen at a distance, round; or an oar, with one end in the water, crooked?

PHILONOUS. He is not mistaken with regard to the ideas he actually perceives; but in the inferences he makes from his present perceptions. Thus in the case of the oar, what he immediately perceives by sight is certainly crooked; and so far he is in the right. But if he thence conclude, that upon taking the oar out of the water he shall perceive the same crookedness; or that it would affect his touch as crooked things are wont to do: in that he is mistaken. In like manner if he shall conclude from what he perceives in one station, that in case he advances toward the moon or tower, he should still be affected with the like ideas, he is mistaken. But his mistake lies not in what he perceives immediately and at present (it being a manifest contradiction to suppose he should err in respect of that) but in the wrong judgment he makes concerning the idea he apprehends to be connected with those immediately perceived; or concerning the ideas that, from what he perceives at present, he imagines would be perceived in other circumstances. The case is the same with regard to the Copernican system. We do not here perceive any motion of the earth: but it were erroneous thence to conclude, that in case we were placed at as great a distance from that, as we are now from the other planets, we should not then perceive its motion . . .

HYLAS. And now I warrant you think you have made the point very clear, little suspecting that what you advance leads directly to a contradiction. Is it not an absurdity to imagine any imperfection in God?

PHILONOUS. Without doubt.

HYLAS. To suffer pain is an imperfection.

PHILONOUS. It is.

HYLAS. Are we not sometimes affected with pain and uneasiness by some other being?

PHILONOUS. We are.

HYLAS. And have you not said that being is a spirit, and is not that spirit God?

PHILONOUS. I grant it.

HYLAS. But you have asserted, that whatever ideas we perceive from without, are in the mind which affects us. The ideas therefore of pain and uneasiness are in God; or in other words, God suffers pain: that is to say, there is an imperfection in the Divine Nature, which you acknowledged was absurd. So you are caught in a plain contradiction.

PHILONOUS. That God knows or understands all things, and that he knows among other things what pain is, even every sort of painful sensation, and what it is for his creatures to suffer pain, I make no question. But that God, though he knows and sometimes causes painful sensations in us, can himself suffer pain, I positively deny. We who are limited and dependent spirits, are liable to impressions of sense, the effects of an external agent, which being produced against our wills, are sometimes painful and uneasy. But God, whom no external being can affect, who perceives nothing by sense as we do, whose will is absolute and independent, causing all things, and liable to be thwarted or resisted by nothing; it is evident such a being as this can suffer nothing, nor be affected with any painful sensation, or indeed any sensation at all. We are chained to a body, that is to say, our perceptions are connected with corporeal motions. By the law of our nature we are affected upon every alteration in the nervous parts of our sensible body: which sensible body, rightly considered, is nothing but a complexion of such qualities or ideas as have no existence distinct from being perceived by a mind: so that this connexion of sensations with corporeal motions, means no more than a correspondence in the order of Nature between two sets of ideas, or things immediately perceivable. But God is a pure spirit, disengaged from all such sympathy or natural ties. No corporeal motions are attended with the sensations of pain or pleasure in his mind. To know everything knowable is certainly a perfection; but to endure, or suffer, or feel anything by sense, is an imperfection. The former, I say, agrees to God, but not the latter. God knows or hath ideas; but his ideas are not conveyed to him by sense, as ours are. Your not distinguishing where there is so manifest a difference, makes you fancy you see an absurdity where there is none ...

PHILONOUS. When a man is swayed, he knows not why, to one side of a question; can this, think you, be anything else but the effect of prejudice, which never fails to attend old and rooted notions? And indeed in this respect I cannot deny the belief of matter to have very much the advantage over the contrary opinion, with men of a learned education.

HYLAS. I confess it seems to be as you say.

PHILONOUS. As a balance therefore to this weight of prejudice, let us throw into the scale the great advantages that arise from the belief of immaterialism, both in regard to religion and human learning. The being of a God, and incorruptibility of the soul, those great articles of religion, are they not proved with the clearest and most immediate evidence? When I say the being of a *God*, I do not mean an obscure general cause of things, whereof we have no conception, but *God*, in the strict and proper sense of the word, a being whose spirituality, omnipresence, providence, omniscience, infinite power and goodness, are as conspicuous as the existence of sensible things, of which (notwithstanding the fallacious pretences and affected scruples of *sceptics*) there is no more reason to doubt, than of our own being. Then with relation to human sciences; in natural philosophy, what intricacies, what obscurities, what contradictions, hath the belief of matter led men into! To say nothing of the numberless disputes about its extent, continuity, homogeneity, gravity, divisibility, etc., do they not pretend to explain all things by bodies operating on bodies, according to the laws of motion? And yet, are they able to comprehend how any one body should move another? Nay, admitting there was no difficulty in reconciling the notion of an inert being with a cause; or in conceiving how an accident might pass from one body to another; yet by all their strained thoughts and extravagant suppositions, have they been able to reach the mechanical production of any one animal or vegetable body? Can they account by the laws of motion, for sounds, tastes, smells, or colours, or for the regular course of things? Have they accounted by physical principles for the aptitude and contrivance, even of the most inconsiderable parts of the universe? But laying aside matter and corporeal causes, and admitting only the efficiency of an all-perfect mind, are not all the effects of Nature easy and intelligible? If the *phenomena* are nothing else but *ideas*; God is a *spirit*, but matter an unintelligent, unperceiving being. If they demonstrate an unlimited power in their cause; God is active and omnipotent, but matter an inert mass. If the order, regularity and usefulness of them can never be sufficiently admired; God is infinitely wise and provident, but matter destitute of all contrivance and design. These surely are great advantages in *physics*. Not to mention that the apprehension of a distant Deity naturally disposes men to a negligence in their *moral* actions, which they would be more cautious of, in case they thought him immediately present, and acting on their minds without the interposition of matter, or unthinking second causes. Then in *metaphysics*; what difficulties concerning entity in abstract, substantial forms, hylarchic principles, plastic natures, substance and accident, principle of individuation, possibility of matter's thinking, origin of ideas, the manner how two independent substances, so widely different as *spirit* and *matter*, should mutually operate on each other? What difficulties, I say, and endless disquisitions concerning these and innumerable other the like points, do we escape by supposing only spirits and ideas? Even the *mathematics* themselves, if we take away the absolute existence of extended things, become much more clear and easy; the most shocking paradoxes and intricate speculations in those sciences, depending on the infinite divisibility of finite extension, which depends on that supposition. But what need is there to insist on the particular sciences? Is not that opposition to all science whatsoever, that frenzy of the ancient and modern *sceptics*, built on the same foundation? Or can you produce so much as one argument against the reality of corporeal things, or in behalf of that avowed utter ignorance of their natures, which doth not suppose their reality to consist in an external absolute existence? Upon this supposition indeed, the objections from the change of colours in a pigeon's neck, or the appearances of a broken oar in the water, must be allowed to have weight. But those and the like objections vanish, if we do not maintain the being of absolute external originals, but place the reality of things in ideas, fleeting indeed, and changeable; however, not changed at random, but according to the fixed order of Nature. For herein consists that constancy and truth of things, which secures all the concerns of life, and distinguishes that which is *real* from the irregular visions of the fancy ...

Review Questions

1. Discuss Berkeley's treatment of abstract ideas.
2. What link is there between Locke's view of substance and Berkeley's?
3. Only individual things exist, and yet we use one name, such as *tree*, for many things; what justifies such common usage for Berkeley?
4. Regarding sense knowledge, what is the meaning of Berkeley's statement that "to be is to be perceived"?
5. Why does Berkeley refer to his philosophy as *immaterialism*?
6. How does Berkeley assume that his epistemology will rout the "freethinkers"?

CHAPTER 16

David Hume (1711–1776)

Introduction

In decisively capitalizing on the empirical openings supplied by John Locke and George Berkeley, David Hume occupies a critical place in the development of British empiricism and in the emergence of the anti-metaphysical character of subsequent modern European philosophy. Hume was born in Edinburgh in 1711. As a young man he undertook, at his family's behest, the study of law, but soon abandoned it for a program of private study in literature and philosophy. To relieve himself of the depression brought on by intense study, he moved to France for several years, settling down for a time in La Flèche, a place he learned to love as suited to quiet reflection; he enjoyed conversation with the learned and hospitable Jesuits there, and must have often been reminded of Descartes, who was educated by them a century and a quarter before. La Flèche was also the place where Hume completed *A Treatise of Human Nature*, published in London in 1739–40. Though he had high expectations for its success, the *Treatise* received very little recognition, and Hume himself later referred to it as having fallen "deadborn from the press." However, this did not prevent him from revising several parts of this "juvenile work" in the years ahead.

Thoroughly committed to writing, Hume did achieve success with the appearance of *Essays Moral and Political* in 1742. With a growing reputation, and with the help of some good friends, he made a bid for the chair of philosophy at the University of Edinburgh, but because he was now beginning to be known as a person with ideas that ran contrary to the moral and religious views prevailing in Scotland, he failed. Some time later, however, he was appointed librarian to the Faculty of Advocates, a post that, though it provided practically no income, gave him the opportunity to begin his *History of England*; he soon resigned his librarianship.

After spending some time as a military attaché, Hume took up residence in Edinburgh, and with the publication of additional volumes of his history of England and various essays, he was acknowledged as a distinguished man of letters, proclaimed by some as the most polished contemporary writer in the English language. From 1763 to 1765 he was secretary to the British embassy in Paris, and his stay there was marked by a gracious welcome in intellectual circles, where he was known not only as a respected writer and philosopher but also as a charming and witty gentleman. He was esteemed by *les philosophes* Voltaire, Diderot, D'Alembert, and d'Holbach. Later he was introduced to Jean-Jacques Rousseau, whom he befriended and invited to return with him to Edinburgh; but even though Hume was acknowledged to have had an affable and sociable personality, an unhappy turn of events brought the friendship to an end. He spent his last years in Edinburgh, where he died in 1776. In addition to the works published during his lifetime, several others were published posthumously, including *Dialogues concerning Natural Religion* and his autobiography, edited by his friend Adam Smith.

Isaac Newton's huge success with the scientific method had a profound influence on the empirical Hume. If Newton startled the world by arguing, as he put it, from phenomena "without feigning hypotheses," and thus effectively uniting the work of his predecessors, then perhaps a substantial dose of empiricism in philosophy would have the same salutary results. Certainly this was Hume's intention as he tried to make his study of man as empirical as possible, and so labeled his "philosophy" of man a "science" of man; the subtitle of his main work announces it as an "attempt to introduce the experimental method" into the study of human nature.

Because Hume's approach follows that of Locke and Berkeley, the basic ingredients of his epistemology seem familiar. Experience provides the first access to knowledge for man, and whatever man knows by experience is called *perception* by Hume. Perceptions are divided into *impressions* and *ideas*, which are distinguished by the degree of *vividness* (vivacity) with which they are given to us. Impressions are the immediate data of experience; they are lively, direct, and forceful, so that they make an "impression" on us. They include not only sensations but also passions and emotions. Ideas are "copies" or "faint images" of our impressions in thinking and reasoning. Ideas, in turn, are subject to two divisions. The first division is into *ideas of memory*, which are recollections of events, as well as the order in which they took place; and *ideas of imagination*, which are free associations of perceptions with one another. The second division is into *simple* and *complex*. Simple ideas are those that permit no distinction or separation, such as a particular colors or tastes; complex ideas are those that do permit distinction or separation, such as relations, modes, and substances.

The importance of these distinctions is that impressions provide our chief access to knowledge, and the more closely our ideas correspond to our impressions, the more reliable they are. "Every simple idea has a simple impression, which resembles it," which is not the case with complex ideas, many of which have no impressions that correspond to them. In other words, if impressions are the direct consequence of our experience, they are the main vehicle for our knowledge of objects, and it is precisely here that Hume must draw up his defenses against causality and substance, the two considerations, as we saw in Locke, that lie at the heart of metaphysics.

The classical formulation of causality states that whatever comes into being requires a cause, that new existences do not explain themselves and are necessarily effects; it is a self-evident truth. But for Hume, the idea of cause and effect does not come from our experience, is not a fact of sensation, and is therefore not found among our impressions. It is only a *supposed necessity* that whatever comes into existence must have a cause. He suggests that there is no difficulty in separating the idea of cause from that of a new existence: "The separation, therefore, of the idea of a cause from that of a beginning of existence, is plainly possible for the imagination; and consequently the actual separation of these objects is so far possible, that it implies no contradiction nor absurdity."

The most Hume admits, based on his principle of the association of ideas, is that we constantly associate in our minds those objects that are constantly associated outside them: there is, for example a *constant conjunction* between flame and heat, and so our minds associate one with the other as cause and effect: "Thus we remember to have seen that species of object we call *flame*, and to have felt that species of sensation we call *heat*. We likewise call to mind their constant conjunction in all past instances. Without further ceremony, we call the one *cause* and the other *effect*, and infer the existence of the one from that of the other." The relationship between cause and effect is only mental, not real, and where there is no constant conjunction, we cannot say anything; for example, we cannot say that the next falling of a pebble will not extinguish the sun.

Having denied the knowability of causal influence, Hume still has to explain why the human mind is prone to associate two events as though they were cause and effect. To do this, he invokes what he calls *belief*. In a sense, though we do not *know* causality, we *believe* it. Again, Hume uses liveliness, or vividness, to explain belief. Characteristic of the way we react in some instances is the *feeling* we have about a relationship, such as the strong feeling I have in associating flame with heat. It is the *manner* in which we conceive a thing: "So that as belief does nothing but vary the manner, in which we conceive any object, it can only bestow on our ideas an additional force and vivacity. An opinion, therefore, or belief may be most accurately defined, *a lively idea related to or associated with a present impression*."

The treatment Hume gives to causality is similarly given to *substance*, and here too Hume exploits the opening made by Locke. In comparison with traditional metaphysics, which holds to the existence of substance as a reality we must conclude to, given the existence of qualities, substance has no further meaning than that of a mere "collection of particular qualities, nor have we any other meaning when we either talk or reason concerning it." *Substance* is simply the name used to signify that collection. Every quality has its own existence and may exist apart from every other quality and, indeed, "from that unintelligible chimera of a substance."

What is true of substance in general is true of one substance in particular, namely, the *soul*. In his tract on the soul, Hume states that there is no way of knowing that there is such a thing as immaterial substance, and he argues to the inconclusiveness of the so-called metaphysical demonstrations. Because we have no impression of a soul, Hume is prompted to ask those philosophers "who pretend that we have an idea of the substance of our minds, to point out the impression that produces it, and tell distinctly after what manner that impression operates, and from what object it is derived." That is, if we don't know it empirically through sensation, we don't know it.

As we saw earlier, the denial of the intellect's ability to get to substance and causality is a denial of metaphysics. Though the mind, even for Hume, requires sense reports to be unified in some way, this is still not sufficient to say that it *is* so; it is a mental requirement, not an existential one. Separate sense reports remain separate; separate reports, for example, of "red," "sweet," and "round" remain that way even when we call them collectively "apple" — the mind, that is, endows them with a unity they *really* do not have. Similarly, the causal influence is not sensed, though in classical metaphysics it is *understood*, and therefore real. But for Hume, our belief in causal influence does not warrant our saying that it *is* so.

These Humean positions have a remarkable corollary when it comes to the question of self-identification. What, for Hume, is the *self*? Do we have anything like *personal identity*? With Hume's insistence that distinct perceptions mean distinct existences, the mind does not perceive any real connection between them. A multiplicity of experiences, yes, but no single experience in which unity of self is perceived: "When I turn my reflection on *myself*, I never can perceive this *self* without some one or more perceptions; nor can I ever perceive any thing but the perceptions. 'Tis the composition of these, therefore, which forms the self."

Having previously rejected the soul as anything knowable, which would have grounded the unity of man, Hume is quite consistent in rejecting self and personal identity as anything knowable either, except perhaps as a succession of related objects that sometimes leads us to believe erroneously that they are one thing. The atom-like independence of our perceptions requires a vision of man as "nothing but a bundle or collection of different perceptions, which succeed each other with an inconceivable rapidity, and are in perpetual flux and movement." Or, a few lines later, "The mind is a kind of theatre, where several perceptions successively make their appearance; pass, re-pass, glide away, and mingle in an infinite variety of postures and situations." Hume never really decides what it is that *endures* throughout all this succession.

The same attitude prevails with regard to God. We have no impression of Him; we can construct no valid argument for His existence; we cannot get to know whether He exists; but we must allow some probability, on the strength of order in the world, of an existence resembling human intelligence that is the principle of order. Toward the end of *Dialogues concerning Natural Religion*, in the opinion expressed by one of the members of the dialogue, Hume seems to be setting forth his own view: "If the whole of Natural Theology, as some people seem to maintain, resolves itself into one simple, though somewhat ambiguous, at least undefined proposition, *That the cause or causes of order in the universe probably bear some remote analogy to human intelligence,*" then "what can the most inquisitive, contemplative, and religious man do more than give a plain, philosophical assent to the proposition, as often as it occurs; and believe that the arguments, on which it is established, exceed the objections, which lie against it?" It is difficult to reconcile this view of God with the rest of Hume's philosophy, but perhaps what he was trying to do was to free any belief in God from an absolute "dogmatism," that is, acceptance without justification.

In the moral sphere the empirical method still obtains, for whatever is true in the physical sphere regarding the basic propositions on cause and effect is also true of the moral sphere. The morality of an action is not the result of a will that causes the action, or of the reason that understands and judges the quality of the action; virtue and vice are the objects of *feeling*. Take vice, for example; it is not reason but feeling that reveals it: "You never can find it, till you turn your reflection into your own breast, and find a sentiment of disapprobation, which arises in you, towards this action. Here is a matter of fact; but 'tis the object of feeling, not of reason." If the terminology of traditional moral value is to be kept, *virtue* becomes a feeling of agreeableness, pleasure, and easiness, whereas *vice* becomes a feeling of disagreeableness, pain, and uneasiness: "Nothing can be more real, or concern us more, than our own sentiments of pleasure and uneasiness; and if these be favourable to virtue, and unfavourable to vice, no more can be requisite to the regulation of our conduct and behavior." Hume's philosophy is a good example of how empiricism in matters of knowledge is linked with its counterpart in matters of morality, an affiliation that runs deep in the British tradition.

Hume's views on the operation of the senses and the work of reason seem to be summed up in a phrase he uses in an appendix to the *Treatise*: the "privilege of a skeptic." Skepticism attaches to Hume just as much as it did to Montaigne, but the analysis of our knowing powers was not a project for Montaigne, as it was for Hume. After sifting through so many problems concerned with the sense and the objects of sense, and after accounting for the various activities of the mind, "knowledge," concludes Hume, "resolves itself into probability," and it is this probability, as the basis of belief, that becomes the only requirement for living humanly. If dogmatism is acceptance without justification, a healthy skepticism is its cure: "A true skeptic", he writes, "will be diffident of his philosophical doubts, as well as of his philosophical convictions," and as a consequence, "will never refuse any innocent satisfaction, which offers itself, upon account of either of them."

The human side of David Hume the philosopher is captured in the honesty and charm of the following confession: "I dine, I play a game of back-gammon, I converse, and am merry with my friends; and when after three or four hours' amusement, I wou'd return to these speculations, they appear so cold, and strain'd, and ridiculous, that I cannot find in my heart to enter into them any farther. ... I am ready to throw all my books and papers into the fire, and resolve never more to renounce the pleasures of life for the sake of reasoning and philosophy." That this is but a temptation is seen in his oft-quoted words: "Be a philosopher; but amidst all your philosophy, be still a man."

Readings

Impressions and Ideas (from *An Enquiry Concerning Human Understanding,* Section II)

11. Every one will readily allow, that there is a considerable difference between the perceptions of the mind, when a man feels the pain of excessive heat, or the pleasure of moderate warmth, and when he afterwards recalls to his memory this sensation, or anticipates it by his imagination. These faculties may mimic or copy the perceptions of the

senses; but they never can entirely reach the force and vivacity of the original sentiment. The utmost we say of them, even when they operate with greatest vigour, is, that they represent their object in so lively a manner, that we could almost say we feel or see it: But, except the mind be disordered by disease or madness, they never can arrive at such a pitch of vivacity, as to render these perceptions altogether undistinguishable. All the colours of poetry, however splendid, can never paint natural objects in such a manner as to make the description be taken for a real landskip. The most lively thought is still inferior to the dullest sensation.

We may observe a like distinction to run through all the other perceptions of the mind. A man in a fit of anger, is actuated in a very different manner from one who only thinks of that emotion. If you tell me, that any person is in love, I easily understand your meaning, and form a just conception of his situation; but never can mistake that conception for the real disorders and agitations of the passion. When we reflect on our past sentiments and affections, our thought is a faithful mirror, and copies its objects truly; but the colours which it employs are faint and dull, in comparison of those in which our original perceptions were clothed. It requires no nice discernment or metaphysical head to mark the distinction between them.

12. Here therefore we may divide all the perceptions of the mind into two classes or species, which are distinguished by their different degrees of force and vivacity. The less forcible and lively are commonly denominated *Thoughts* or *Ideas.* The other species want a name in our language, and in most others; I suppose, because it was not requisite for any, but philosophical purposes, to rank them under a general term or appellation. Let us, therefore, use a little freedom, and call them *Impressions*; employing that word in a sense somewhat different from the usual. By the term *impression,* then, I mean all our more lively perceptions, when we hear, or see, or feel, or love, or hate, or desire, or will. And impressions are distinguished from ideas, which are the less lively perceptions, of which we are conscious, when we reflect on any of those sensations or movements above mentioned.

13. Nothing, at first view, may seem more unbounded than the thought of man, which not only escapes all human power and authority, but is not even restrained within the limits of nature and reality. To form monsters, and join incongruous shapes and appearances, costs the imagination no more trouble than to conceive the most natural and familiar objects. And while the body is confined to one planet, along which it creeps with pain and difficulty; the thought can in an instant transport us into the most distant regions of the universe; or even beyond the universe, into the unbounded chaos, where nature is supposed to lie in total confusion. What never was seen, or heard of, may yet be

conceived; nor is any thing beyond the power of thought, except what implies an absolute contradiction.

But though our thought seems to possess this unbounded liberty, we shall find, upon a nearer examination, that it is really confined within very narrow limits, and that all this creative power of the mind amounts to no more than the faculty of compounding, transposing, augmenting, or diminishing the materials afforded us by the senses and experience. When we think of a golden mountain, we only join two consistent ideas, *gold,* and *mountain,* with which we were formerly acquainted. A virtuous horse we can conceive; because, from our own feeling, we can conceive virtue; and this we may unite to the figure and shape of a horse, which is an animal familiar to us. In short, all the materials of thinking are derived either from our outward or inward sentiment: the mixture and composition of these belongs alone to the mind and will. Or, to express myself in philosophical language, all our ideas or more feeble perceptions are copies of our impressions or more lively ones.

Doubts Concerning the Understanding: The Cause-and-Effect Relationship (from An Enquiry Concerning Human Understanding, Section IV)

Part I

20. All the objects of human reason or enquiry may naturally be divided into two kinds, to wit, *Relations of Ideas,* and *Matters of Fact.* Of the first kind are the sciences of Geometry, Algebra, and Arithmetic; and in short, every affirmation which is either intuitively or demonstratively certain. *That the square of the hypothenuse is equal to the square of the two sides,* is a proposition which expresses a relation between these figures. *That three times five is equal to the half of thirty,* expresses a relation between these numbers. Propositions of this kind are discoverable by the mere operation of thought, without dependence on what is anywhere existent in the universe. Though there never were a circle or triangle in nature, the truths demonstrated by Euclid would for ever retain their certainty and evidence.

21. Matters of fact, which are the second objects of human reason, are not ascertained in the same manner; nor is our evidence of their truth, however great, of a like nature with the foregoing. The contrary of every matter of fact is still possible; because it can never imply a contradiction, and is conceived by the mind with the same facility and distinctness, as if ever so conformable to reality. *That the sun will not rise tomorrow* is no less intelligible a proposition, and implies no more contradiction than the affirmation, *that it will rise.* We should in vain,

therefore, attempt to demonstrate its falsehood. Were it demonstratively false, it would imply a contradiction, and could never be distinctly conceived by the mind.

It may, therefore, be a subject worthy of curiosity, to enquire what is the nature of that evidence which assures us of any real existence and matter of fact, beyond the present testimony of our senses, or the records of our memory.

22. All reasonings concerning matter of fact seem to be founded on the relation of *Cause and Effect*. By means of that relation alone we can go beyond the evidence of our memory and senses. If you were to ask a man, why he believes any matter of fact, which is absent; for instance, that his friend is in the country, or in France; he would give you a reason; and this reason would be some other fact; as a letter received from him, or the knowledge of his former resolutions and promises. A man finding a watch or any other machine in a desert island, would conclude that there had once been men in that island. All our reasonings concerning fact are of the same nature. And here it is constantly supposed that there is a connexion between the present fact and that which is inferred from it. Were there nothing to bind them together, the inference would be entirely precarious. The hearing of an articulate voice and rational discourse in the dark assures us of the presence of some person: Why? because these are the effects of the human make and fabric, and closely connected with it. If we anatomize all the other reasonings of this nature, we shall find that they are founded on the relation of cause and effect, and that this relation is either near or remote, direct or collateral. Heat and light are collateral effects of fire, and the one effect may justly be inferred from the other.

23. If we would satisfy ourselves, therefore, concerning the nature of that evidence, which assures us of matters of fact, we must enquire how we arrive at the knowledge of cause and effect.

I shall venture to affirm, as a general proposition, which admits of no exception, that the knowledge of this relation is not, in any instance, attained by reasonings *a priori*; but arises entirely from experience, when we find that any particular objects are constantly conjoined with each other. Let an object be presented to a man of ever so strong natural reason and abilities; if that object be entirely new to him, he will not be able, by the most accurate examination of its sensible qualities, to discover any of its causes or effects. Adam, though his rational faculties be supposed, at the very first, entirely perfect, could not have inferred from the fluidity and transparency of water that it would suffocate him, or from the light and warmth of fire that it would consume him. No object ever discovers, by the qualities which appear to the senses, either the causes which produced it, or the effects which will arise from it; nor can our reason, unassisted by experience, ever draw any inference concerning real existence and matter of fact.

24. This proposition, *that causes and effects are discoverable, not by reason but by experience,* will readily be admitted with regard to such objects, as we remember to have once been altogether unknown to us; since we must be conscious of the utter inability, which we then lay under, of foretelling what would arise from them. Present two smooth pieces of marble to a man who has no tincture of natural philosophy; he will never discover that they will adhere together in such a manner as to require great force to separate them in a direct line, while they make so small a resistance to a lateral pressure. Such events, as bear little analogy to the common course of nature, are also readily confessed to be known only by experience; nor does any man imagine that the explosion of gunpowder, or the attraction of a loadstone, could ever be discovered by arguments *a priori.* In like manner, when an effect is supposed to depend upon an intricate machinery or secret structure of parts, we make no difficulty in attributing all our knowledge of it to experience. Who will assert that he can give the ultimate reason, why milk or bread is proper nourishment for a man, not for a lion or a tiger?

But the same truth may not appear, at first sight, to have the same evidence with regard to events, which have become familiar to us from our first appearance in the world, which bear a close analogy to the whole course of nature, and which are supposed to depend on the simple qualities of objects, without any secret structure of parts. We are apt to imagine that we could discover these effects by the mere operation of our reason, without experience. We fancy, that were we brought on a sudden into this world, we could at first have inferred that one Billard-ball would communicate motion to another upon impulse; and that we needed not to have waited for the event, in order to pronounce with certainty concerning it. Such is the influence of custom, that, where it is strongest, it not only covers our natural ignorance, but even conceals itself, and seems not to take place, merely because it is found in the highest degree.

25. But to convince us that all the laws of nature, and all the operations of bodies without exception, are known only by experience, the following reflections may, perhaps, suffice. Were any object presented to us, and were we required to pronounce concerning the effect, which will result from it, without consulting past observation; after what manner, I beseech you, must the mind proceed in this operation? It must invent or imagine some event, which it ascribes to the object as its effect; and it is plain that this invention must be entirely arbitrary. The mind can never possibly find the effect in the supposed cause, by the most accurate scrutiny and examination. For the effect is totally different from the cause, and consequently can never be discovered in it. Motion in the second Billiard-ball is a quite distinct event from mo-

tion in the first; nor is there anything in the one to suggest the smallest hint of the other. A stone or piece of metal raised into the air, and left without any support, immediately falls: but to consider the matter *a priori*, is there anything we discover in this situation which can beget the idea of a downward, rather than an upward, or any other motion, in the stone or metal?

And as the first imagination or invention of a particular effect, in all natural operations, is arbitrary, where we consult not experience; so must we also esteem the supposed tie or connexion between the cause and effect, which binds them together, and renders it impossible that any other effect could result from the operation of that cause. When I see, for instance, a Billiard-ball moving in a straight line towards another; even suppose motion in the second ball should by accident be suggested to me, as the result of their contact or impulse; may I not conceive, that a hundred different events might as well follow from that cause? May not both these balls remain at absolute rest? May not the first ball return in a straight line, or leap off from the second in any line or direction? All these suppositions are consistent and conceivable. Why then should we give the preference to one, which is no more consistent or conceivable than the rest? All our reasonings *a priori* will never be able to show us any foundation for this preference.

In a word, then, every effect is a distinct event from its cause. It could not, therefore, be discovered in the cause, and the first invention or conception of it, *a priori*, must be entirely arbitrary. And even after it is suggested, the conjunction of it with the cause must appear equally arbitrary; since there are always many other effects, which, to reason, must seem fully as consistent and natural. In vain, therefore, should we pretend to determine any single event, or infer any cause or effect, without the assistance of observation and experience.

26. Hence we may discover the reason why no philosopher, who is rational and modest, has ever pretended to assign the ultimate cause of any natural operation, or to show distinctly the action of that power, which produces any single effect in the universe. It is confessed, that the utmost effort of human reason is to reduce the principles, productive of natural phenomena, to a greater simplicity, and to resolve the many particular effects into a few general causes, by means of reasonings from analogy, experience, and observation. But as to the causes of these general causes, we should in vain attempt their discovery; nor shall we ever be able to satisfy ourselves, by any particular explication of them. These ultimate springs and principles are totally shut up from human curiosity and enquiry. Elasticity, gravity, cohesion of parts, communication of motion by impulse; these are probably the ultimate causes and principles which we shall ever discover in nature; and we may esteem ourselves sufficiently happy, if, by accurate enquiry and

reasoning, we can trace up the particular phenomena to, or near to, these general principles. The most perfect philosophy of the natural kind only staves off our ignorance a little longer: as perhaps the most perfect philosophy of the moral or metaphysical kind serves only to discover larger portions of it. Thus the observation of human blindness and weakness is the result of all philosophy, and meets us at every turn, in spite of our endeavours to elude or avoid it.

27. Nor is geometry, when taken into the assistance of natural philosophy, ever able to remedy this defect, or lead us into the knowledge of ultimate causes, by all that accuracy of reasoning for which it is so justly celebrated. Every part of mixed mathematics proceeds upon the supposition that certain laws are established by nature in her operations; and abstract reasonings are employed, either to assist experience in the discovery of these laws, or to determine their influence in particular instances, where it depends upon any precise degree of distance and quantity. Thus, it is a law of motion, discovered by experience, that the moment or force of any body in motion is in the compound ratio or proportion of its solid contents and its velocity; and consequently, that a small force may remove the greatest obstacle or raise the greatest weight, if, by any contrivance or machinery, we can increase the velocity of that force, so as to make it an overmatch for its antagonist. Geometry assists us in the application of this law, by giving us the just dimensions of all the parts and figures which can enter into any species of machine; but still the discovery of the law itself is owing merely to experience, and all the abstract reasonings in the world could never lead us one step towards the knowledge of it. When we reason *a priori*, and consider merely any object or cause, as it appears to the mind, independent of all observation, it never could suggest to us the notion of any distinct object, such as its effect; much less, show us the inseparable and inviolable connexion between them. A man must be very sagacious who could discover by reasoning that crystal is the effect of heat, and ice of cold, without being previously acquainted with the operation of these qualities.

Part II

28. But we have not yet attained any tolerable satisfaction with regard to the question first proposed. Each solution still gives rise to a new question as difficult as the foregoing, and leads us on to farther enquiries. When it is asked, *What is the nature of all our reasonings concerning matter of fact?* the proper answer seems to be, that they are founded on the relation of cause and effect. When again it is asked, *What is the foundation of all our reasonings and conclusions concerning that relation?* it may be replied in one word, Experience. But if we

still carry on our sifting humour, and ask, *What is the foundation of all conclusions from experience?* this implies a new question, which may be of more difficult solution and explication. Philosophers, that give themselves airs of superior wisdom and sufficiency, have a hard task when they encounter persons of inquisitive dispositions, who push them from every corner to which they retreat, and who are sure at last to bring them to some dangerous dilemma. The best expedient to prevent this confusion, is to be modest in our pretensions; and even to discover the difficulty ourselves before it is objected to us. By this means, we may make a kind of merit of our very ignorance.

I shall content myself, in this section, with an easy task, and shall pretend only to give a negative answer to the question here proposed. I say then, that, even after we have experience of the operations of cause and effect, our conclusions from that experience are *not* founded on reasoning, or any process of the understanding. This answer we must endeavour both to explain and to defend.

29. It must certainly be allowed, that nature has kept us at a great distance from all her secrets, and has afforded us only the knowledge of a few superficial qualities of objects; while she conceals from us those powers and principles on which the influence of those objects entirely depends. Our senses inform us of the colour, weight, and consistence of bread; but neither sense nor reason can ever inform us of those qualities which fit it for the nourishment and support of a human body. Sight or feeling conveys an idea of the actual motion of bodies; but as to that wonderful force or power, which would carry on a moving body for ever in a continued change of place, and which bodies never lose but by communicating it to others; of this we cannot form the most distant conception. But notwithstanding this ignorance of natural powers and principles, we always presume, when we see like sensible qualities, that they have like secret powers, and expect that effects, similar to those which we have experienced, will follow from them. If a body of like colour and consistence with that bread, which we have formerly eat, be presented to us, we make no scruple of repeating the experiment, and foresee, with certainty, like nourishment and support. Now this is a process of the mind or thought, of which I would willingly know the foundation. It is allowed on all hands that there is no known connexion between the sensible qualities and the secret powers; and consequently, that the mind is not led to form such a conclusion concerning their constant and regular conjunction, by anything which it knows of their nature. As to past *Experience,* it can be allowed to give *direct* and *certain* information of those precise objects only, and that precise period of time, which fell under its cognizance: but why this experience should be extended to future times, and to other objects, which for aught we know, may be only in appearance

similar; this is the main question on which I would insist. The bread, which I formerly eat, nourished me; that is, a body of such sensible qualities was, at that time, endued with such secret powers: but does it follow, that other bread must also nourish me at another time, and that like sensible qualities must always be attended with like secret powers? The consequence seems nowise necessary. At least, it must be acknowledged that there is here a consequence drawn by the mind; that there is a certain step taken; a process of thought, and an inference, which wants to be explained. These two propositions are far from being the same, *I have found that such an object has always been attended with such an effect,* and *I foresee, that other objects, which are, in appearance, similar, will be attended with similar effects.* I shall allow, if you please, that the one proposition may justly be inferred from the other: I know, in fact, that it always is inferred. But if you insist that the inference is made by a chain of reasoning, I desire you to produce that reasoning. The connexion between these propositions is not intuitive. There is required a medium, which may enable the mind to draw such an inference, if indeed it be drawn by reasoning and argument. What that medium is, I must confess, passes my comprehension; and it is incumbent on those to produce it, who assert that it really exists, and is the origin of all our conclusions concerning matter of fact.

30. This negative argument must certainly, in process of time, become altogether convincing, if many penetrating and able philosophers shall turn their enquiries this way and no one be ever able to discover any connecting proposition or intermediate step, which supports the understanding in this conclusion. But as the question is yet new, every reader may not trust so far to his own penetration, as to conclude, because an argument escapes his enquiry, that therefore it does not really exist. For this reason it may be requisite to venture upon a more difficult task; and enumerating all the branches of human knowledge, endeavour to show that none of them can afford such an argument.

All reasonings may be divided into two kinds, namely, demonstrative reasoning, or that concerning relations of ideas, and moral reasoning, or that concerning matters of fact and existence. That there are no demonstrative arguments in the case seems evident; since it implies no contradiction that the course of nature may change, and that an object, seemingly like those which we have experienced, may be attended with different or contrary effects. May I not clearly and distinctly conceive that a body, falling from the clouds, and which, in all other respects, resembles snow, has yet the taste of salt or feeling of fire? Is there any more intelligible proposition than to affirm, that all the trees will flourish in December and January, and decay in May and June? Now whatever is intelligible, and can be distinctly conceived, implies no contradiction, and can never be proved false by any demonstrative argument or abstract reasoning *a priori*.

If we be, therefore, engaged by arguments to put trust in past experience, and make it the standard of our future judgement, these arguments must be probable only, or such as regard matter of fact and real existence, according to the division above mentioned. But that there is no argument of this kind, must appear, if our explication of that species of reasoning be admitted as solid and satisfactory. We have said that all arguments concerning existence are founded on the relation of cause and effect; that our knowledge of that relation is derived entirely from experience; and that all our experimental conclusions proceed upon the supposition that the future will be conformable to the past. To endeavour, therefore, the proof of this last supposition by probable arguments, or arguments regarding existence, must be evidently going in a circle, and taking that for granted, which is the very point in question.

31. In reality, all arguments from experience are founded on the similarity which we discover among natural objects, and by which we are induced to expect effects similar to those which we have found to follow from such objects. And though none but a fool or madman will ever pretend to dispute the authority of experience, or to reject that great guide of human life, it may surely be allowed a philosopher to have so much curiosity at least as to examine the principle of human nature, which gives this mighty authority to experience, and makes us draw advantage from that similarity which nature has placed among different objects. From causes which appear *similar* we expect similar effects. This is the sum of all our experimental conclusions. Now it seems evident that, if this conclusion were formed by reason, it would be as perfect at first, and upon one instance, as after ever so long a course of experience. But the case is far otherwise. Nothing so like as eggs; yet no one, on account of this appearing similarity, expects the same taste and relish in all of them. It is only after a long course of uniform experiments in any kind, that we attain a firm reliance and security with regard to a particular event. Now where is that process of reasoning which, from one instance, draws a conclusion, so different from that which it *infers* from a hundred instances that are nowise different from that single one? This question I propose as much for the sake of information, as with an intention of raising difficulties. I cannot find, I cannot imagine any such reasoning. But I keep my mind still open to instruction, if any one will vouchsafe to bestow it on me.

32. Should it be said that, from a number of uniform experiments, we *infer* a connexion between the sensible qualities and the secret powers; this, I must confess, seems the same difficulty, couched in different terms. The question still recurs, on what process of argument this in-

ference is founded? Where is the medium, the interposing ideas, which join propositions so very wide of each other? It is confessed that the colour, consistence, and other sensible qualities of bread appear not, of themselves, to have any connexion with the secret powers of nourishment and support. For otherwise we could infer these secret powers from the first appearance of these sensible qualities, without the aid of experience; contrary to the sentiment of all philosophers, and contrary to plain matter of fact. Here, then, is our natural state of ignorance with regard to the powers and influence of all objects. How is this remedied by experience? It only shows us a number of uniform effects, resulting from certain objects, and teaches us that those particular objects, at that particular time, were endowed with such powers and forces. When a new object, endowed with similar sensible qualities, is produced, we expect similar powers and forces, and look for a like effect. From a body of like colour and consistence with bread we expect like nourishment and support. But this surely is a step or progress of the mind, which wants to be explained. When a man says, *I have found, in all past instances, such sensible qualities conjoined with such secret powers:* And when he says, *Similar sensible qualities will always be conjoined with similar secret powers,* he is not guilty of a tautology, nor are these propositions in any respect the same. You say that the one proposition is an inference from the other. But you must confess that the inference is not intuitive; neither is it demonstrative: Of what nature is it, then? To say it is experimental, is begging the question. For all inferences from experience suppose, as their foundation, that the future will resemble the past, and that similar powers will be conjoined with similar sensible qualities. If there be any suspicion that the course of nature may change, and that the past may be no rule for the future, all experience becomes useless, and can give rise to no inference or conclusion. It is impossible, therefore, that any arguments from experience can prove this resemblance of the past to the future; since all these arguments are founded on the supposition of that resemblance. Let the course of things be allowed hitherto ever so regular; that alone, without some new argument or inference, proves not that, for the future, it will continue so. In vain do you pretend to have learned the nature of bodies from your past experience. Their secret nature, and consequently all their effects and influence, may change, without any change in their sensible qualities. This happens sometimes, and with regard to some objects: Why may it not happen always, and with regard to all objects? What logic, what process of argument secures you against this supposition? My practice, you say, refutes my doubts. But you mistake the purport of my question. As an agent, I am quite satisfied in the point; but as a philosopher, who has some share of curiosity, I will not say scepticism, I want to learn the foundation of this inference. No reading, no enquiry has yet been able to remove my difficulty, or give me satisfaction in a matter of such importance. Can I do better than propose the difficulty to the public, even though, perhaps, I have small hopes of obtaining a solution? We shall at least, by this means, be sensible of our ignorance, if we do not augment our knowledge.

33. I must confess that a man is guilty of unpardonable arrogance who concludes, because an argument has escaped his own investigation, that therefore it does not really exist. I must also confess that, though all the learned, for several ages, should have employed themselves in fruitless search upon any subject, it may still, perhaps, be rash to conclude positively that the subject must, therefore, pass all human comprehension. Even though we examine all the sources of our knowledge, and conclude them unfit for such a subject, there may still remain a suspicion, that the enumeration is not complete, or the examination not accurate. But with regard to the present subject, there are some considerations which seem to remove all this accusation of arrogance or suspicion of mistake.

It is certain that the most ignorant and stupid peasants—nay infants, nay even brute beasts—improve by experience, and learn the qualities of natural objects, by observing the effects which result from them. When a child has felt the sensation of pain from touching the flame of a candle, he will be careful not to put his hand near any candle; but will expect a similar effect from a cause which is similar in its sensible qualities and appearance. If you assert, therefore, that the understanding of the child is led into this conclusion by any process of argument or ratiocination, I may justly require you to produce that argument; nor have you any pretence to refuse so equitable a demand. You cannot say that the argument is abstruse, and may possibly escape your enquiry; since you confess that it is obvious to the capacity of a mere infant. If you hesitate, therefore, a moment, or if, after reflection, you produce any intricate or profound argument, you, in a manner, give up the question, and confess that it is not reasoning which engages us to suppose the past resembling the future, and to expect similar effects from causes which are, to appearance, similar. This is the proposition which I intended to enforce in the present section. If I be right, I pretend not to have made any mighty discovery. And if I be wrong, I must acknowledge myself to be indeed a very backward scholar; since I cannot now discover an argument which, it seems, was perfectly familiar to me long before I was out of my cradle.

The Advantages of Scepticism (from *An Enquiry Concerning Human Understanding*, Section XII, Part III)

129. There is, indeed, a more *mitigated* scepticism or *academical* philosophy, which may be both durable and useful, and which may, in

part, be the result of this Pyrrhonism, or *excessive* scepticism, when its undistinguished doubts are, in some measure, corrected by common sense and reflection. The greater part of mankind are naturally apt to be affirmative and dogmatical in their opinions; and while they see objects only on one side, and have no idea of any counterpoising argument, they throw themselves precipitately into the principles, to which they are inclined; nor have they any indulgence for those who entertain opposite sentiments. To hesitate or balance perplexes their understanding, checks their passion, and suspends their action. They are, therefore, impatient till they escape from a state, which to them is so uneasy: and they think, that they could never remove themselves far enough from it, by the violence of their affirmations and obstinacy of their belief. But could such dogmatical reasoners become sensible of the strange infirmities of human understanding, even in its most perfect state, and when most accurate and cautious in its determinations; such a reflection would naturally inspire them with more modesty and reserve, and diminish their fond opinion of themselves, and their prejudice against antagonists. The illiterate may reflect on the disposition of the learned, who, amidst all the advantages of study and reflection, are commonly still diffident in their determinations: and if any of the learned be inclined, from their natural temper, to haughtiness and obstinacy, a small tincture of Pyrrhonism might abate their pride, by showing them, that the few advantages, which they may have attained over their fellows, are but inconsiderable, if compared with the universal perplexity and confusion, which is inherent in human nature. In general, there is a degree of doubt, and caution, and modesty, which, in all kinds of scrutiny and decision, ought for ever to accompany a just reasoner.

130. Another species of *mitigated* scepticism which may be of advantage to mankind, and which may be the natural result of the Pyrrhonian doubts and scruples, is the limitation of our enquiries to such subjects as are best adapted to the narrow capacity of human understanding. The imagination of man is naturally sublime, delighted with whatever is remote and extraordinary, and running, without control, into the most distant parts of space and time in order to avoid the objects, which custom has rendered too familiar to it. A correct *Judgement* observes a contrary method, and avoiding all distant and high enquiries, confines itself to common life, and to such subjects as fall under daily practice and experience; leaving the more sublime topics to the embellishment of poets and orators, or to the arts of priests and politicians. To bring us to so salutary a determination, nothing can be more serviceable, than to be once thoroughly convinced of the force of the Pyrrhonian doubt, and of the impossibility, that anything, but the strong power of natural instinct, could free us from it. Those who have a pro-

pensity to philosophy, will still continue their researches; because they reflect, that, besides the immediate pleasure, attending such an occupation, philosophical decisions are nothing but the reflections of common life, methodized and corrected. But they will never be tempted to go beyond common life, so long as they consider the imperfection of those faculties which they employ, their narrow reach, and their inaccurate operations. While we cannot give a satisfactory reason, why we believe, after a thousand experiments, that a stone will fall, or fire burn; can we ever satisfy ourselves concerning any determination, which we may form, with regard to the origin of worlds, and the situation of nature, from, and to eternity?

This narrow limitation, indeed, of our enquiries, is, in every respect, so reasonable, that it suffices to make the slightest examination into the natural powers of the human mind and to compare them with their objects, in order to recommend it to us. We shall then find what are the proper subjects of science and enquiry.

131. It seems to me, that the only objects of the abstract science or of demonstration are quantity and number, and that all attempts to extend this more perfect species of knowledge beyond these bounds are mere sophistry and illusion. As the component parts of quantity and number are entirely similar, their relations become intricate and involved; and nothing can be more curious, as well as useful, than to trace, by a variety of mediums, their equality or inequality, through their different appearances. But as all other ideas are clearly distinct and different from each other, we can never advance farther, by our utmost scrutiny, than to observe this diversity, and, by an obvious reflection, pronounce one thing not to be another. Or if there be any difficulty in these decisions, it proceeds entirely from the undeterminate meaning of words, which is corrected by juster definitions. That *the square of the hypothenuse is equal to the squares of the other two sides,* cannot be known, let the terms be ever so exactly defined, without a train of reasoning and enquiry. But to convince us of this proposition, that *where there is no property, there can be no injustice,* it is only necessary to define the terms, and explain injustice to be a violation of property. This proposition is, indeed, nothing but a more imperfect definition. It is the same case with all those pretended syllogistical reasonings, which may be found in every other branch of learning, except the sciences of quantity and number; and these may safely, I think, be pronounced the only proper objects of knowledge and demonstration.

132. All other enquiries of men regard only matter of fact and existence; and these are evidently incapable of demonstration. Whatever *is* may *not be.* No negation of a fact can involve a contradiction. The

non-existence of any being, without exception, is as clear and distinct an idea as its existence. The proposition, which affirms it not to be, however false, is no less conceivable and intelligible, than that which affirms it to be. The case is different with the sciences, properly so called. Every proposition, which is not true, is there confused and unintelligible. That the cube root of 64 is equal to the half of 10, is a false proposition, and can never be distinctly conceived. But that Caesar, or the angel Gabriel, or any being never existed, may be a false proposition, but still is perfectly conceivable and implies no contradiction.

The existence, therefore, of any being can only be proved by arguments from its cause or its effect; and these arguments are founded entirely on experience. If we reason *a priori*, anything may appear able to produce anything. The falling of a pebble may, for aught we know, extinguish the sun; or the wish of a man control the planets in their orbits. It is only experience, which teaches us the nature and bounds of cause and effect, and enables us to infer the existence of one object from that of another. Such is the foundation of moral reasoning, which forms the greater part of human knowledge, and is the source of all human action and behaviour.

Moral reasonings are either concerning particular or general facts. All deliberations in life regard the former; as also all disquisitions in history, chronology, geography, and astronomy.

The sciences, which treat of general facts, are politics, natural philosophy, physic, chemistry, &c. where the qualities, causes and effects of a whole species of objects are enquired into.

Divinity or Theology, as it proves the existence of a Deity, and the immortality of souls, is composed partly of reasonings concerning particular, partly concerning general facts. It has a foundation in reason, so far as it is supported by experience. But its best and most solid foundation is *faith* and divine revelation.

Morals and criticism are not so properly objects of the understanding as of taste and sentiment. Beauty, whether moral or natural, is felt, more properly than perceived. Or if we reason concerning it, and endeavour to fix its standard, we regard a new fact, to wit, the general tastes of mankind, or some such fact, which may be the object of reasoning and enquiry.

When we run over libraries, persuaded of these principles, what havoc must we make? If we take in our hand any volume; of divinity or school metaphysics, for instance; let us ask, *Does it contain any abstract reasoning concerning quantity or number?* No. *Does it contain any experimental reasoning concerning matter of fact and existence?* No. Commit it then to the flames: for it can contain nothing but sophistry and illusion.

Dialogues Concerning Natural Religion

Part II

I must own, Cleanthes, said Demea, that nothing can more surprise me, than the light, in which you have, all along, put this argument. By the whole tenor of your discourse, one would imagine that you were maintaining the being of a God, against the cavils of atheists and infidels; and were necessitated to become a champion for that fundamental principle of all religion. But this, I hope, is not by any means a question among us. No man; no man, at least, of common sense, I am persuaded, ever entertained a serious doubt with regard to a truth, so certain and self-evident. The question is not concerning the *being*, but the *nature* of God. This, I affirm, from the infirmities of human understanding, to be altogether incomprehensible and unknown to us. The essence of that supreme mind, his attributes, the manner of his existence, the very nature of his duration; these and every particular, which regards so divine a being, are mysterious to men. Finite, weak, and blind creatures, we ought to humble ourselves in his august presence, and, conscious of our frailties, adore in silence his infinite perfections, which eye hath not seen, ear hath not heard, neither hath it entered into the heart of man to conceive them. They are covered in a deep cloud from human curiosity: it is profaneness to attempt penetrating through these sacred obscurities: and next to the impiety of denying his existence, is the temerity of prying into his nature and essence, decrees and attributes.

But lest you should think, that my *piety* has here got the better of my *philosophy*, I shall support my opinion, if it needs any support, by a very great authority. I might cite all the divines almost, from the foundation of Christianity, who have ever treated of this or any other theological subject: but I shall confine myself, at present, to one equally celebrated for piety and philosophy. It is Father Malebranche, who, I remember, thus expresses himself. 'One ought not so much (says he) to call God a spirit, in order to express positively what he is, as in order to signify that he is not matter. He is a Being infinitely perfect: of this we cannot doubt. But in the same manner as we ought not to imagine, even supposing him corporeal, that he is clothed with a human body, as the Anthropomorphites asserted, under color that that figure was the most perfect of any; so neither ought we to imagine, that the spirit of God has human ideas, or bears any resemblance to our spirit; under color that we know nothing more perfect than a human mind. We ought rather to believe, that as he comprehends the perfections of matter without being material . . . he comprehends also the perfections of created spirits, without being spirit, in the manner we conceive spirit: that his true name is, *He that is*, or, in other words, Being without restriction, All Being, the Being infinite and universal.'

After so great an authority, Demea, replied Philo, as that which you have produced, and a thousand more, which you might produce, it would appear ridiculous in me to add my sentiment, or express my approbation of your doctrine. But surely, where reasonable men treat these subjects the question can never be concerning the being, but only the nature of the Deity. The former truth, as you well observe, is unquestionable and self-evident. Nothing exists without a cause; and the original cause of this universe (whatever it be) we call God; and piously ascribe to him every species of perfection. Whoever scruples this fundamental truth, deserves every punishment, which can be inflicted among philosophers, to wit, the greatest ridicule, contempt and disapprobation. But as all perfection is entirely relative, we ought never to imagine, that we comprehend the attributes of this divine Being, or to suppose, that his perfections have any analogy or likeness to the perfections of a human creature. Wisdom, thought, design, knowledge; these we justly ascribe to him; because these words are honorable among men, and we have no other language or other conceptions, by which we can express our adoration of him. But let us beware, lest we think, that our ideas any wise correspond to his perfections, or that his attributes have any resemblance to these qualities among men. He is infinitely superior to our limited view and comprehension; and is more the object of worship in the temple, than of disputation in the schools.

In reality, Cleanthes, continued he, there is no need of having recourse to that affected scepticism, so displeasing to you, in order to come at this determination. Our ideas reach no farther than our experience: we have no experience of divine attributes and operations: I need not conclude my syllogism: you can draw the inference yourself. And it is a pleasure to me (and I hope to you too) that just reasoning and sound piety here concur in the same conclusion, and both of them establish the adorably mysterious and incomprehensible nature of the Supreme Being.

Not to lose any time in circumlocutions, said Cleanthes, addressing himself to Demea, much less in replying to the pious declamations of Philo; I shall briefly explain how I conceive this matter. Look round the world: contemplate the whole and every part of it: you will find it to be nothing but one great machine, subdivided into an infinite number of lesser machines, which again admit of subdivisions, to a degree beyond what human senses and faculties can trace and explain. All these various machines, and even their most minute parts, are adjusted to each other with an accuracy, which ravishes into admiration all men, who have ever contemplated them. The curious adapting of means to ends, throughout all nature, resembles exactly, though it much exceeds, the productions of human contrivance; of human design, thought, wisdom, and intelligence. Since therefore the effects resemble each other, we are led to infer, by all the rules of analogy, that the causes also resemble; and that the Author of Nature is somewhat similar to the mind of men; though possessed of much larger faculties, proportioned to the grandeur of the work, which he has executed. By this argument *a posteriori*, and by this argument alone, do we prove at once the existence of a Deity, and his similarity to human mind and intelligence.

I shall be so free, Cleanthes, said Demea, as to tell you, that from the beginning, I could not approve of your conclusion concerning the similarity of the Deity to men; still less can I approve of the mediums, by which you endeavor to establish it. What! No demonstration of the being of a God! No abstract arguments! No proofs *a priori*! Are which have hitherto been so much insisted on by philosophers, all fallacy, all sophism? Can we reach no father in this subject than experience and probability? I will not say, that this is betraying the cause of a deity: but surely, by this affected candor, you give advantage to atheists, which they never could obtain, by the mere dint of argument and reasoning.

What I chiefly scruple in this subject, said Philo, is not so much, that all religious arguments are by Cleanthes reduced to experience, as that they appear not to be even the most certain and irrefragable of that inferior kind. That a stone will fall, that fire will burn, that the earth has solidity, we have observed a thousand and a thousand times; and when any new instance of this nature is presented, we draw without hesitation the accustomed inference. The exact similarity of the cases gives us a perfect assurance of a similar event; and a stronger evidence is never desired nor sought after. But wherever you depart, in the least, from the similarity of the cases, you diminish proportionably the evidence; and may at last bring it to a very weak *analogy*, which is confessedly liable to error and uncertainty. After having experienced the circulation of the blood in human creatures, we make no doubt that it takes place in Titius and Maevius: but from its circulation in frogs and fishes, it is only a presumption, though a strong one, from analogy, that it takes place in men and other animals. The analogical reasoning is much weaker, when we infer the circulation of the sap in vegetables from our experience, that the blood circulates in animals; and those, who hastily followed that imperfect analogy, are found, by more accurate experiments, to have been mistaken.

If we see a house, Cleanthes, we conclude, with the greatest certainty, that it had an architect or builder; because this is precisely that species of effect, which we have experienced to proceed from that species of cause. But surely you will not affirm, that the universe bears such a resemblance to a house, that we can with the same certainty infer a similar cause, or that the analogy is here entire and perfect. The dissimilitude is so striking, that the utmost you can here pretend to is a guess, a conjecture, a presumption concerning a similar cause; and how that pretension will be received in the world, I leave you to consider.

It would surely be very ill received, replied Cleanthes; and I should be deservedly blamed and detested, did I allow, that the proofs of a Deity amounted to no more than a guess or conjecture. But is the whole adjustment of means to ends in a house and in the universe so slight a resemblance? The economy of final causes? The order, proportion, and arrangement of every part? Steps of a stair are plainly contrived, that human legs may use them in mounting; and this inference is certain and infallible. Human legs are also contrived for walking and mounting; and this inference, I allow, is not altogether so certain, because of the dissimilarity which you remark; but does it, therefore, deserve the name only of presumption or conjecture?

Good God! cried Demea, interrupting him, where are we? Zealous defenders of religion allow, that the proofs of a Deity fall short of perfect evidence! And you, Philo, on whose assistance I depended, in proving the adorable mysteriousness of the Divine Nature, do you assert to all these extravagant opinions of Cleanthes? For what other name can I give them? Or why spare my censure, when such principles are advanced, supported by such an authority, before so young a man as Pamphilus?

You seem not to apprehend, replied Philo, that I argue with Cleanthes in his own way; and by showing him the dangerous consequences of his tenets, hope at last to reduce him to our opinion. But what sticks most with you, I observe, is the representation which Cleanthes has made of the argument *a posteriori*; and finding, that that argument is likely to escape your hold and vanish into air, you think it so disguised, that you can scarcely believe it to be set in its true light. Now, however much I may dissent, in other respects, from the dangerous principles of Cleanthes, I must allow, that he has fairly represented that argument; and I shall endeavor so to state the matter to you, that you will entertain no farther scruples with regard to it.

Were a man to abstract from everything which he knows or has seen, he would be altogether incapable, merely from his own ideas, to determine what kind of scene the universe must be, or to give the preference to one state or situation of things above another. For as nothing which he clearly conceives, could be esteemed impossible or implying a contradiction, every chimera of his fancy would be upon an equal footing; nor could he assign any just reason, why he adheres to one idea or system, and rejects the others, which are equally possible.

Again; after he opens his eyes, and contemplates the world, as it really is, it would be impossible for him, at first, to assign the cause of any one event; much less, of the whole of things or of the universe. He might set his fancy a rambling; and she might bring him in an infinite variety of reports and representations. These would all be possible; but being all equally possible, he would never, of himself, give a satisfactory account for his preferring one of them to the rest. Experience alone can point out to him the true cause of any phenomenon.

Now, according to this method of reasoning, Demea, it follows (and is, indeed, tacitly allowed by Cleanthes himself) that order, arrangement, or the adjustment of final causes is not, of itself, any proof of design; but only so far as it has been experienced to proceed from that principle. For aught we can know *a priori*, matter may contain the source or spring of order originally, within itself, as well as mind does; and there is no more difficulty in conceiving, that the several elements, from an internal unknown cause, may fall into the most exquisite arrangement, than to conceive that their ideas, in the great, universal mind, from a like internal, unknown cause, fall into that arrangement. The equal possibility of both these suppositions is allowed. But by experience we find (according to Cleanthes), that there is a difference between them. Throw several pieces of steel together, without shape or form; they will never arrange themselves so as to compose a watch: stone, and mortar, and wood, without an architect, never erect a house. But the ideas in a human mind, we see, by an unknown, inexplicable economy, arrange themselves so as to form the plan of a watch or house. Experience, therefore, proves, that there is an original principle of order in mind, not in matter. From similar effects we infer similar causes. The adjustment of means to ends is alike in the universe, as in a machine of human contrivance. The causes, therefore, must be resembling.

I was from the beginning scandalized, I must own, with this resemblance, which is asserted, between the Deity and human creatures; and must conceive it to imply such a degradation of the Supreme Being as no sound theist could endure. With your assistance, therefore, Demea, I shall endeavor to defend what you justly called the adorable mysteriousness of the Divine Nature, and shall refute this reasoning of Cleanthes, provided he allows, that I have made a fair representation of it.

When Cleanthes had assented, Philo, after a short pause, proceeded in the following manner.

That all inferences, Cleanthes, concerning fact, are founded on experience, and that all experimental reasonings are founded on the supposition, that similar causes prove similar effects, and similar effects similar causes; I shall not, at present, much dispute with you. But observe, I entreat you, with what extreme caution all just reasoners proceed in the transferring of experiments to similar cases. Unless the cases be exactly similar, they repose no perfect confidence in applying their past observation to any particular phenomenon. Every alteration of circumstances occasions a doubt concerning the event; and it requires new experiments to prove certainly, that the new circumstances are of no moment or importance. A change in bulk, situation, arrangement, age, disposition of the air, or surrounding bodies; any of these particulars may be attended with the most unexpected consequences: and unless the objects be quite familiar to us, it is the highest temerity to expect with assurance, after any of these changes, an event similar to that which before fell under our observation. The slow and deliberate steps of philosophers, here, if anywhere, are distinguished from the precipitate march of the vulgar, who, hurried on by the smallest similitudes, are incapable of all discernment or consideration.

But can you think, Cleanthes, that your usual phlegm and philosophy have been preserved in so wide a step as you have taken, when you compared to the universe, houses, ships, furniture, machines; and from their similarity in some circumstances inferred a similarity in their causes? Thought, design, intelligence, such as we discover in men and other animals, is no more than one of the springs and principles of the universe, as well as heat or cold, attraction or repulsion, and a hundred others, which fall under daily observation. It is an active cause, by which some particular parts of nature, we find, produce alterations on other parts. But can a conclusion, with any propriety, be transferred from parts to the whole? Does not the great disproportion bar all comparison and inference? From observing the growth of a hair, can we learn anything concerning the generation of a man? Would the manner of a leaf's blowing, even though perfectly known, afford us any instruction concerning the vegetation of a tree?

But allowing that we were to take the *operations* of one part of nature upon another for the foundation of our judgment concerning the *origin* of the whole (which never can be admitted), yet why select so minute, so weak, so bounded a principle as the reason and design of animals is found to be upon this planet? What peculiar privilege has this little agitation of the brain which we call *thought*, that we must thus make it the model of the whole universe? Our partiality in our own favor does indeed present it on all occasions; but sound philosophy ought carefully to guard against so natural an illusion.

So far from admitting, continued Philo, that the operations of a part can afford us any just conclusion concerning the origin of the whole, I will not allow any one part to form a rule for another part, if the latter be very remote from the former. Is there any reasonable ground to conclude, that the inhabitants of other planets possess thought, intelligence, reason, or anything similar to these faculties in men? When Nature has so extremely diversified her manner of operation in this small globe; can we imagine, that she incessantly copies herself throughout so immense a universe? And if thought, as we may well suppose, be confined merely to this narrow corner, and has even there so limited a sphere of action; with what propriety can we assign it for the original cause of all things? The narrow views of a peasant, who makes his domestic economy the rule for the government of kingdoms, is in comparison a pardonable sophism.

But were we ever so much assured, that a thought and reason, resembling the human, were to be found throughout the whole universe, and were its activity elsewhere vastly greater and more commanding than it appears in this globe; yet I cannot see, why the operations of a world, constituted, arranged, adjusted, can with any propriety be extended to a world, which is in its embryo state, and is advancing towards that constitution and arrangement. By observation, we know somewhat of the economy, action, and nourishment of a finished animal; but we must transfer with great caution that observation to the growth of a fetus in the womb, and still more, to the formation of an animalcule in the loins of its male parent. Nature, we find, even from our limited experience, possesses an infinite number of springs and principles, which incessantly discover themselves on every change of her position and situation. And what new and unknown principles would actuate her in so new and unknown a situation as that of the formation of a universe, we cannot, without the utmost temerity, pretend to determine.

A very small part of this great system, during a very short time, is very imperfectly discovered to us: and do we thence pronounce decisively concerning the origin of the whole?

Admirable conclusion! Stone, wood, brick, iron, brass, have not, at this time, in this minute globe of earth, an order or arrangement without human art and contrivance: therefore the universe could not originally attain its order and arrangement, without something similar to human art. But is a part of nature a rule for another part very wide of the former? Is it a rule for the whole? Is a very small part a rule for the universe? Is nature in one situation, a certain rule for nature in another situation, vastly different from the former?

And can you blame me, Cleanthes, if I here imitate the prudent reserve of Simonides, who, according to the noted story, being asked by Hiero, *What God was?* desired a day to think of it, and then two days more; and after that manner continually prolonged the term, without ever bringing in his definition or description? Could you even blame me, if I had answered at first *that I did not know*, and was sensible that this subject lay vastly beyond the reach of my faculties? You might cry out sceptic and rallier as much as you pleased: but having found, in so many other subjects, much more familiar, the imperfections and even contradictions of human reason, I never should expect any success from its feeble conjectures, in a subject, so sublime, and so remote from the sphere of our observation. When two species of objects have always been observed to be conjoined together, I can infer, by custom, the existence of one wherever I see the existence of the other: and this I call an argument from experience. But how this argument can have place, where the objects, as in the present case, are single, individual, without parallel, or specific resemblance, may be difficult to explain. And will any man tell me with a serious countenance, that an orderly universe must arise from some thought and art, like the human; because we have experience of it? To ascertain this reasoning, it were requisite, that we had experience of the origin of worlds; and it is not sufficient surely, that we have seen ships and cities arise from human art and contrivance. . . .

Philo was proceeding in this vehement manner, somewhat between jest and earnest, as it appeared to me; when he observed some signs of impatience in Cleanthes, and then immediately stopped short. What I had to suggest, said Cleanthes, is only that you would not abuse terms, or make use of popular expressions to subvert philosophical reasonings. You know, that the vulgar often distiguish reason from experience, even where the question relates only to matter of fact and existence; though it is found, where that reason is properly analyzed, that it is nothing but a species of experience. To prove by experience the origin of the universe from mind is not more contrary to common speech than to prove the motion of the earth from the same principle. And a caviler might raise all the same objections to the Copernican system, which you have urged against my reasonings. Have you other earths, might he say, which you have seen to move? Have. . . .

Yes! cried Philo, interrupting him, we have other earths. Is not the moon another earth, which we see to turn round its center? Is not Venus another earth, where we observe the same phenomenon? Are not the revolutions of the sun also a confirmation, from analogy, of the same theory? All the planets, are they not earths, which revolve about the sun? Are not the satellites moons, which move round Jupiter and Saturn, and along with these primary planets, round the sun? These analogies and resemblances, with others, which I have not mentioned, are the sole proofs of the Copernican system: and to you it belongs to consider, whether you have any analogies of the same kind to support your theory.

In reality, Cleanthes, continued he, the modern system of astronomy is now so much received by all inquirers, and has become so essential a part even of our earliest education, that we are not commonly very scrupulous in examining the reasons upon which it is founded. It is now become a matter of mere curiosity to study the first writers on that subject, who had the full force of prejudice to encounter, and were obliged to turn their arguments on every side, in order to render them popular and convincing. But if we peruse Galileo's famous Dialogues concerning the system of the world, we shall find, that that great genius, one of the sublimest that ever existed, first bent all his endeavors to prove, that there was no foundation for the distinction commonly made between elementary and celestial substances. The schools, proceeding from the illusions of sense, had carried this distinction very far; and had established the latter substances to be ingenerable, incorruptible, unalterable, impassable; and had assigned all the opposite qualities to the former. But Galileo, beginning with the moon, proved its similarity in every particular to the earth; its convex figure, its natural darkness when not illuminated, its density, its distinction into solid and liquid, the variations of its phases, the mutual illuminations of the earth and moon, their mutual eclipses, the inequalities of the lunar surface, etc. After many instances of this kind, with regard to all the planets, men plainly saw, that these bodies became proper objects of experience; and that the similarity of their nature enabled us to extend the same arguments and phenomena from one to the other.

In this cautious proceeding of the astronomers, you may read your own condemnation, Cleanthes; or rather may see, that the subject in which you are engaged exceeds all human reason and inquiry. Can you pretend to show any such similarity between the fabric of a house, and the generation of a universe? Have you ever seen nature in any such situation as resembles the first arrangement of the elements? Have worlds ever been formed under your eye? and have you had leisure to observe the whole progress of the phenomenon, from the first appearance of order to its final consummation? If you have, then cite your experience, and deliver your theory.

Review Questions

1. Explaining how Hume's empiricism derives from Locke through Berkeley.
2. In what sense is Hume a sceptic?
3. Discuss the fate of metaphysics as a science in Hume's philosophy.
4. What is the meaning of *constant conjunction* in Hume's analysis of causality?
5. Show the relationship of substance in Hume to that in Locke and Berkeley.
6. Why is personal identity a problem in Hume's philosophy?
7. Discuss Hume's general approach to the problem of moral right and wrong.

CHAPTER 17

Immanuel Kant (1724–1804)

Introduction

The skeptical soundings of human knowledge taken by Hume had a far-reaching effect on Immanuel Kant, who credited Hume with arousing him from his "dogmatic slumber"; generations of modern philosophers have shared Kant's feeling. He was born in 1724 in the small Prussian town of Königsberg in northeast Germany. His parents were religious people and, though Kant always retained a genuine regard for religion and a deep moral sense, he rejected the puritanical pietism that prevailed in his family. His life was undramatic and hardly filled with the traveling spirit of many of his predecessors; as a matter of sober fact, he never got beyond thirty miles of his native town. His schooling was all done locally, including his years at the University of Königsberg, which shared the quiet anonymity of the town. He was much influenced there by a young professor of philosophy, Martin Knutsen, who introduced him to the rationalist tradition of Leibniz and Christian Wolff, as well as to the world of Newtonian physics. For several years he was a family tutor, and then a lecturer with the title of *Privatdozent* at the university, in which capacities he broadened his intellectual interests by the number of subjects he was called upon to teach, ranging from logic to geology. In 1770 he received an appointment as professor of philosophy. Though perhaps it is not readily recognizable in his works, he is reported to have been an excellent lecturer, full of wit and good humor. His first important book was not published until he was fifty-seven years old, and then his works appeared in profusion. The three works on which his reputation chiefly rests are the *Critique of Pure Reason* (1781), *Critique of Practical Reason* (1790), and *Critique of the Faculty of Judgment* (1793).

In his famous daily routine, Kant is a perfect example of German orderliness, rising each day at the same time and performing the day's activities, whether drinking coffee, preparing class, or taking lunch, all at a fixed hour. The poet Heine wrote: "Neighbors knew that it was exactly half past three when Immanuel Kant in his grey coat, with his bamboo cane in his hand, left his house door and went to the Lime tree avenue, which is still called, in memory of him, the 'Philosopher's Walk.'" He almost always took his midday meal at a nearby inn with a friend, but even this was subject to routine; on one occasion, when a friend was late, Kant proceeded to leave just as his friend was arriving. Kant simply doffed his hat and kept going on his way!

Descartes' search for certitude as a reaction to skepticism was buoyed by his hopes for a universal mathematics, but his hopes inaugurated an entire cycle that ironically began against the skepticism of Montaigne and ended in the skepticism of Hume. Kant confronted a similar problem. He appreciated immensely what Hume was trying to do, but at the same time, he took his own path: "I openly confess my recollection of David Hume was the very thing which many years ago first interrupted my dogmatic slumber and gave my investigation in the field of speculative philosophy a quite new direction." But no progress could be made until philosophy, especially metaphysics, saw the need to reevaluate itself, to become self-critical, as the sciences had become. The sciences had indeed made progress, but only after they successfully restructured themselves in terms of method.

Hitherto, according to Kant, in the knowledge–object relationship, the *object* of knowledge was the first consideration for philosophers; with him, however, it was the *manner of knowing* the object that came first. All attempts to advance knowledge ended in failure when it was assumed that knowledge must conform to objects; therefore, "We must make trial whether we may not have more success in the tasks of metaphysics, if we suppose that objects must conform to our knowledge." For Kant, this was so drastic a change from the past that he likened it to the revolution in astronomy brought about by Copernicus. Questions like "What are our knowing faculties capable of?", "What is their internal structure?", "What are the conditions of knowledge?", and "What are the boundaries of knowledge?" became the focal questions in Kantian *criticism* and explain the presence of the word *Critique* in the titles of his chief works. The derivative terms *critical problem* and *critical philosophy*, insofar as they pertain to the exploration of our knowing faculties, stem from the legacy left by Kant.

How is this conformity of the object with the mind to be brought about? The mind has many faculties, three of which are described in the *Critique of Pure Reason*: sensibility, understanding, and (pure) reason. Relying upon the experience of sense, called *a posteriori*, the mind receives impressions of whatever exists, but it receives them on its own terms; that is, the mind imposes itself on the sensible, and its manner of imposing itself is the manner in which it knows impressions; in Kant's terms, we have knowledge of objects *a priori*, that is, we are able to "determine something in regard to them prior to their being given." If a housewife is making a batch of cookies, she "imposes" a cookie cutter on the formless dough in order to achieve the shape she wants. As far as knowledge is concerned, the sense objects to be known are formless until the mind imposes its forms on them, and the very forms it imposes are the way things *appear* to the mind, and are therefore called *appearances*, or *phenomena*. Kant was convinced of the truth of Newton's view that the two chief characteristics of the physical world, space and time, are *absolutes*; that is, their existence is independent of the human mind; Kant adapted this view so that space and time became absolutes in the very structure of the mind, coming into play in the act of sensation. Sensibility grasps the world of phenomena in two forms, space and time; because they are built-in ways of knowing and are present before sense experience takes place, they are called by Kant *a priori* forms.

Whatever is given to the mind in sensibility is subject to conceptual rendering by the *understanding*; that is, whatever is *given* in sensibility is *thought* in understanding: "If the *receptivity* of our mind, its power of receiving representations in so far as it is in any wise affected, is to be entitled sensibility, then the mind's power of producing representations from itself, the *spontaneity* of knowledge, should be called the understanding. ... Without sensibility no object would be given to us, without understanding no object would be thought." The understanding organizes the phenomena, synthesizes them, makes judgments; just as sensibility functions through *a priori* forms, the understanding functions through *a priori* concepts, whence they are called *categories* by Kant. There are twelve such categories: unity, plurality, totality; reality, negation, limitation; substance, cause, community; possibility, existence, necessity. It is under these headings that all judging or thinking takes place. Kant's view, then, is that *knowledge* is limited to the combined role of sensibility and understanding, both of which are concerned with sense experience, though in different ways.

The third of the mind's faculties, reason, has several functions, and is called *pure reason* in its functioning with objects of thought that have no connection with the sensible realm, namely, the soul, the world, and God. The word Kant uses to express these objects is *noumena*, to oppose them to phenomena. Phenomena pertain to the sensible world, noumena to the suprasensible. Phenomena are appearances because they are given in the sense; noumena are not appearances because they are not given in the sense. Phenomena are objects of experience; noumena are not objects of experience, they are transcendental. Because they are objects of experience, phenomena can be known; because they are not objects of experience, noumena cannot be known. Pure reason, by its very nature, deals with transcendentals; it *must* think the ideas of soul, world, and God. At the same time it criticizes itself, which is the "critique" of pure reason, and realizes the limitation of its own activity because the ideas it has *cannot be known* as corresponding to objects outside the mind: "all illusion consists in holding the subjective ground of our judgments to be objective." Thus metaphysics is necessary but illusory.

But do such significant ideas as soul, world, and God, unknowable in the context of pure reason, have to be dismissed? Indeed not, for their very presence in the reason indicates that they must have a role to play. That role is one of unification, the bringing together of the disparate parts of our knowledge: the sensibility endows the sense manifold with the unity of space and time; the understanding endows the phenomena with the unity of its concepts; and finally, the reason endows the concepts with the unity of its transcendental ideas. Kant calls this function of reason a "peculiar vocation": "The transcendental Ideas therefore express the peculiar vocation of reason as a principle of systematic unity in the use of understanding." The caution here is not to be misled into thinking that real objects correspond to the ideas. Their function is to "regulate"; as *regulative* ideas they are principles of unity, unifying under the rubric of "as if": as if the soul existed, as if the world existed, as if God existed. The regulative ideas of the soul give us the unity of a continuing self, or ego; the idea of the world gives us a sense of total oneness in the physical manifold; and the idea of God, in Kant's words, "directs us to look upon all connection in the world *as if* it originated from an all-sufficient necessary cause." However, the full meaning of soul, world, and God requires the consideration of the *Critique of Practical Reason* and Kant's other moral works.

Though it would be misleading to say that the *Critique of Practical Reason* takes up where the *Critique of Pure Reason* leaves off, because for Kant each of these faculties is self-contained, there is certainly a continuity between the two in terms of his intention to explore the full range of experience, which is the basis, though not the extent, of all we hold to be true. Moral experience is a new kind of experience and is totally different from the sense experience with which pure reason begins. Just as Kant analyzes one function of the reason to arrive at the critique of pure reason (more precisely, pure theoretical reason), he analyzes a second function of the reason to arrive at the critique of practical reason (more precisely, pure practical reason).

This analysis begins with a feeling of *duty,* a sense of obligation, an experience of oughtness that we recognize in ourselves in the face of certain kinds of actions we are called upon to perform. Kant considers this sense of oughtness as a given; we do not demonstrate its existence; we neither deduce it nor induce it; we have no need to prove it. Because it is a datum, and therefore does not derive from anything else, it must be understood in terms of nothing but itself. As the first step in this understanding, Kant clearly sees that oughtness entails *freedom*; That is, we must be free to do what we ought; otherwise, we risk a stark contradiction in saying that we ought to do what we cannot do. If the rest of nature is governed by necessity, the will is not. Kant's insistence on freedom is behind all of his writings on practical reason and morality; he supports it even while being unsure about how to reconcile it with the necessity of nature: "Yet for *practical purposes* the narrow footpath of freedom is the only one on which it is possible to make use of reason in our conduct; hence it is just as impossible for the subtlest philosophy as for the commonest reason of men to argue away freedom. Philosophy must then assume that no real contradiction will be found between freedom and physical necessity of the same human actions, for it cannot give up the conception of nature any more than that of freedom." No determinist view of morality can possibly make allowance for freedom, and therefore no genuine expression of what ought to be can enter the determinist's lexicon. Freedom is the basic ingredient of a human act; without it there can be no "ought."

Though the acknowledgment of duty comes from within me as an individual, it is just as clear and unmistakable, for Kant, that what is imposed on me is imposed on all, and so the binding aspect of duty is one with the binding aspect of *law,* in virtue of which it binds all; that is, duty is given to me as a law inasmuch as it binds me together with all others. The words *categorical* and *imperative* reinforce each other in emphasizing the obligatory character of law, whence the term *categorical imperative* is used by Kant to express a course of moral action whose intrinsic morality is grasped. Though Kant produces several formulations of the categorical imperative, the first one directly announces the aspect of universality: "Act only on a maxim through which you can at the same time will that it should become a universal law.""

As is true of all law, the more general its scope, the less a particular action is envisioned; the law has to be applied to the individual case. There is an analogy here with the *a priori* form of space that does not apply to any particular thing until the phenomenon is given, and only then is the phenomenon "spatialized"; so the law does not become particular until an individual action is to be placed. For example, in the case of a man beset by a series of misfortunes, Kant asks "whether it would not be contrary to his duty to himself to take his own life." Kant answers this by pointing out the contradiction involved in a system of nature whose special feature is the improvement of life to allow it to be destroyed. Suicide cannot be universalized; therefore, it is morally wrong.

At this point, several ideas flow together. Observance of the law, reflected in a person's acting out of fidelity to his will, is the basic path man has to follow to achieve the highest good, the *summum bonum*, which brings about man's happiness. Perfect accordance of the will with the moral law is a demand of a rational being, and yet perfect accordance is not possible in this life; as Kant puts it, "Perfect accordance of the will with the moral law is *holiness*, a perfection of which no rational being of the sensible world is capable at any moment of his existence." Progress toward the perfect will is endless, and only based on the supposition of the soul's endless duration, called *immortality*, can such progress be asserted. In addition, the possibility of the *summum bonum* could not be realized at all without invoking the existence of a cause, connecting happiness with morality, namely, God: "it is morally necessary to assume the existence of God."

The immortality of the soul and the existence of God are, for Kant, *postulates*, a term borrowed from mathematics, which means that although a proposition cannot be proven to be true, it must be accepted as true. That parallel lines never meet is a postulate, held to be true without being subject to proof. God and the soul must be accepted as true for the sake of maintaining the integrity of the moral order; should either one not be taken as true, the moral order would crumble, and this would be the final infidelity to our original moral experience.

Once again, it is extremely illuminating, and perhaps indicative of the unyielding claim of truth to be permanent, that Kant's movement against skepticism, which terminates in the philosophical need for the soul, God, and the world, is remarkably akin to Descartes' movement against skepticism, which terminated in the same need.

Though philosophers have many problems with Kant, his constant view of "the starry heavens above and the moral law within" has permeated modern philosophy and made him, for many fellow philosophers, the "absolutely indispensable philosopher."

Readings

Introduction to the Critique of Pure Reason

I. Of the Difference Between Pure and Empirical Knowledge

That all our knowledge begins with experience there can be no doubt. For how is it possible that the faculty of cognition should be awakened into exercise otherwise than by means of objects which affect our senses, and partly of themselves produce representations, partly rouse our powers of understanding into activity, to compare, to connect, or to separate these, and so to convert the raw material of our sensuous impressions into a knowledge of objects, which is called experience? In respect of time, therefore, no knowledge of ours is antecedent to experience, but begins with it.

But, though all our knowledge begins with experience, it by no means follows, that all arises out of experience. For, on the contrary, it is quite possible that our empirical knowledge is a compound of that which we receive through impressions, and that which the faculty of cognition supplies from itself (sensuous impressions giving merely the *occasion*), an addition which we cannot distinguish from the original element given by sense, till long practice has made us attentive to, and skilful in separating it. It is, therefore, a question which requires close investigation, and is not to be answered at first sight—whether there exists a knowledge altogether independent of experience, and even of all sensuous impressions? Knowledge of this kind is called *a priori*, in contra-distinction to empirical knowledge, which has its sources *a posteriori*, that is, in experience.

But the expression, '*a priori*,' is not as yet definite enough, adequately to indicate the whole meaning of the question above started. For, in speaking of knowledge which has its sources in experience, we are wont to say, that this or that may be known *a priori*, because we do not derive this knowledge immediately from experience, but from a general rule, which, however, we have itself borrowed from experience. Thus, if a man undermined his house, we say, 'he might know *a priori* that it would have fallen;' that is, he needed not to have waited for the experience that it did actually fall. But still, *a priori*, he could not know even this much. For, that bodies are heavy, and, consequently, that they fall when their supports are taken away, must have been known to him previously, by means of experience.

By the term 'knowledge *a priori*,' therefore, we shall in the sequel understand, not such as is independent of this or that kind of experience, but such as is absolutely so of all experience. Opposed to this is empirical knowledge, or that which is possible only *a posteriori*, that is, through experience. Knowledge *a priori* is either pure or impure. Pure knowledge *a priori* is that with which no empirical element is mixed up. For example, the proposition, 'Every change has a cause,' is a proposition *a priori*, but impure, because change is a conception which can only be derived from experience.

II. The Human Intellect, Even in an Unphilosophical State, Is In Possession of Certain Cognitions 'a Priori'

The question now is as to a *criterion*, by which we may securely distinguish a pure from an empirical cognition. Experience no doubt teaches us that this or that object is constituted in such and such a manner, but not that it could not possibly exist otherwise. Now, in the first place, if we have a proposition which contains the idea of necessity in its very conception, it is a judgment _a priori_; if, moreover, it is not derived from any other proposition, unless from one equally involving the idea of necessity, it is absolutely _a priori_. Secondly, an empirical judgment never exhibits strict and absolute, but only assumed and comparative universality (by induction); therefore, the most we can say is—so far as we have hitherto observed, there is no exception to this or that rule. If, on the other hand, a judgment carries with it strict and absolute universality, that is, admits of no possible exception, it is not derived from experience, but is valid absolutely _a priori_.

Empirical universality is, therefore, only an arbitrary extension of validity, from that which may be predicated of a proposition valid in most cases, to that which is asserted of a proposition which holds good in all; as, for example, in the affirmation, 'All bodies are heavy.' When, on the contrary, strict universality characterizes a judgment, it necessarily indicates another peculiar source of knowledge, namely, a faculty of cognition _a priori_. Necessity and strict universality, therefore, are infallible tests for distinguishing pure from empirical knowledge, and are inseparably connected with each other. But as in the use of these criteria the empirical limitation is sometimes more easily detected than the contingency of the judgment, or the unlimited universality which we attach to a judgment is often a more convincing proof than its necessity, it may be advisable to use the criteria separately, each being by itself infallible.

Now, that in the sphere of human cognition we have judgments which are necessary, and in the strictest sense universal, consequently pure _a priori_, it will be an easy matter to show. If we desire an example from the sciences, we need only take any proposition in mathematics. If we cast our eyes upon the commonest operations of the understanding, the proposition, 'Every change must have a cause,' will amply serve our purpose. In the latter case, indeed, the conception of a cause so plainly involves the conception of a necessity of connection with an effect, and of a strict universality of the law, that the very notion of a cause would entirely disappear, were we to derive it, like Hume, from a frequent association of what happens with that which precedes, and the habit thence originating of connecting representations—the necessity inherent in the judgment being therefore merely subjective. Besides, without seeking for such examples of principles existing _a priori_ in cognition, we might easily show that such principles are the indispensable basis of the possibility of experience itself, and consequently prove their existence _a priori_. For whence could our experience itself acquire certainty, if all the rules on which it depends were themselves empirical, and consequently fortuitous? No one, therefore, can admit the validity of the use of such rules as first principles. But, for the present, we may content ourselves with having established the fact, that we do possess and exercise a faculty of pure *a priori* cognition; and, secondly, with having pointed out the proper tests of such cognition, namely, universality and necessity.

Not only in judgments, however, but even in conceptions, is an *a priori* origin manifest. For example, if we take away by degrees from our conceptions of a body all that can be referred to mere sensuous experience—colour, hardness or softness, weight, even impenetrability—the body will then vanish; but the space which it occupied still remains, and this it is utterly impossible to annihilate in thought. Again, if we take away, in like manner, from our empirical conception of any object, corporeal or incorporeal, all properties which mere experience has taught us to connect with it, still we cannot think away those through which we cogitate it as substance, or adhering to substance, although our conception of substance is more determined than that of an object. Compelled, therefore, by that necessity with which the conception of substance forces itself upon us, we must confess that it has its seat in our faculty of cognition *a priori*.

III. Philosophy Stands in Need of a Science Which Shall Determine the Possibility, Principles, and Extent of Human Knowledge 'a Priori'

Of far more importance than all that has been above said, is the consideration that certain of our cognitions rise completely above the sphere of all possible experience, and by means of conceptions, to which there exists in the whole extent of experience no corresponding object, seem to extend the range of our judgments beyond its bounds. And just in this transcendental or supersensible sphere, where experience affords us neither instruction nor guidance, lie the investigations of *Reason*, which, on account of their importance, we consider far preferable to, and as having a far more elevated aim than, all that the understanding can achieve within the sphere of sensuous phenomena. So high a value do we set upon these investigations, that even at the risk of error, we persist in following them out, and permit neither doubt nor disregard nor indifference to restrain us from the pursuit. These unavoidable problems of mere pure reason are GOD, FREEDOM (of will), and IMMORTALITY. The science which, with all its preliminaries, has for its especial object the solution of these problems is named metaphysics—a science which is at the very outset dogmatical, that is, it confidently takes upon itself the execution of this task without any previous investigation of the ability or inability of reason for such an undertaking.

Now the safe ground of experience being thus abandoned, it seems nevertheless natural that we should hesitate to erect a building with the cognitions we possess, without knowing whence they come, and on the strength of principles, the origin of which is undiscovered. Instead of thus trying to build without a foundation, it is rather to be expected that we should long ago have put the question, how the understanding can arrive at these *a priori* cognitions and what is the extent, validity, and worth which they may possess? We say, this is natural enough, meaning by the word natural, that which is consistent with a just and reasonable way of thinking; but if we understand by the term, that which usually happens, nothing indeed could be more natural and more comprehensible than that this investigation should be left long unattempted. For one part of our pure knowledge, the science of mathematics, has been long firmly established, and thus leads us to form flattering expectations with regard to others, though these may be of quite a different nature. Besides, when we get beyond the bounds of experience, we are of course safe from opposition in that quarter; and the charm of widening the range of our knowledge is so great, that unless we are brought to a standstill by some evident contradiction, we hurry on undoubtingly in our course. This, however, may be avoided, if we are sufficiently cautious in the construction of our fictions, which are not the less fictions on that account.

Mathematical science affords us a brilliant example, how far, independently of all experience, we may carry our *a priori* knowledge. Is it true that the mathematician occupies himself with objects and cognitions only in so far as they can be represented by means of intuition. But this circumstance is easily overlooked, because the said intuition can itself be given *a priori*, and therefore is hardly to be distinguished from a mere pure conception. Deceived by such a proof of the power of reason, we can perceive no limits to the extension of our knowledge. The light dove cleaving in free flight the thin air, whose resistance it feels, might imagine that her movements would be far more free and rapid in airless space. Just in the same way did Plato, abandoning the world of sense because of the narrow limits it sets to the understanding, venture upon the wings of ideas beyond it, into the void space of pure intellect. He did not reflect that he made no real progress by all his efforts; for he met with no resistance which might serve him for a support, as it were, whereon to rest, and on which he might apply his powers, in order to let the intellect acquire momentum for its progress. It is, indeed, the common fate of human reason in speculation, to finish the imposing edifice of thought as rapidly as possible, and then for the first time to begin to examine whether the foundation is a solid one or no. Arrived at this point, all sorts of excuses are sought after, in order to console us for its want of stability, or rather, indeed, to enable us to dispense altogether with so late and dangerous an investigation. But what frees us during the process of building from all apprehension or suspicion, and flatters us into the belief of its solidity, is this. A great part, perhaps the greatest part, of the business of our reason consists in the analysation of the conceptions which we already possess of objects. By this means we gain a multitude of cognitions, which although really nothing more than elucidations or explanations of that which (though in a confused manner) was already thought in our conceptions, are, at least in respect of their form, prized as new introspections; whilst, so far as regards their matter or content, we have really made no addition to our conceptions, but only disinvolved them. But as this process does furnish real *a priori* knowledge, which has a sure progress and useful results, reason, deceived by this, slips in, without being itself aware of it, assertions of a quite different kind; in which, to given conceptions it adds others, *a priori* indeed, but entirely foreign to them, without our knowing how it arrives at these, and, indeed, without such a question ever suggesting itself. I shall therefore at once proceed to examine the difference between these two modes of knowledge.

IV. Of the Difference Between Analytical and Synthetical Judgments

In all judgments wherein the relation of a subject to the predicate is cogitated (I mention affirmative judgments only here; the application to negative will be very easy), this relation is possible in two different ways. Either the predicate B belongs to the subject A, as somewhat which is contained (though covertly) in the conception A; or the predicate B lies completely out of the conception A, although it stands in connection with it. In the first instance, I term the judgment analytical, in the second, synthetical. Analytical judgments (affirmative) are therefore those in which the connection of the predicate with the subject is cogitated through identity; those in which this connection is cogitated without identity, are called synthetical judgments. The former may be called *explicative*, the latter *augmentative* judgments; because the former add in the predicate nothing to the conception of the subject, but only analyse it into its constituent conceptions, which were thought already in the subject, although in a confused manner; the latter add to our conceptions of the subject a predicate which was not contained in it, and which no analysis could ever have discovered therein. For example, when I say, 'All bodies are extended,' this is an analytical judgment. For I need not go beyond the conception of *body* in order to find extension connected with it, but merely analyse the conception, that is, become conscious of the manifold properties which I think in that conception, in order to discover this predicate in it: it is therefore an analytical judgment. On the other hand, when I say, 'All bodies are heavy,' the predicate is something totally different from that which I think in the mere conception of a body. By the addition of such a predicate, therefore, it becomes a synthetical judgment.

Judgments of experience, as such, are always synthetical. For it would be absurd to think of grounding an analytical judgment on experience, because in forming such a judgment I need not go out of the sphere of my conceptions, and therefore recourse to the testimony of experience is quite unnecessary. That 'bodies are extended' is not an empirical judgment, but a proposition which stands firm *a priori*. For before addressing myself to experience, I already have in my conception all the requisite conditions for the judgment, and I have only to extract the predicate from the conception, according to the principle of contradiction, and thereby at the same time become conscious of the necessity of the judgment, a necessity which I could never learn from experience. On the other hand, though at first I do not at all include the predicate of weight in my conception of body in general, that conception still indicates an object of experience, a part of the totality of experience, to which I can still add other parts; and this I do when I recognize by observation that bodies are heavy. I can cognize beforehand by analysis the conception of body through the characteristics of extension, impenetrability, shape, etc., all which are cogitated in this conception. But now I extend my knowledge, and looking back on experience from which I had derived this conception of body, I find weight at all times connected with the above characteristics, and therefore I synthetically add to my conceptions this as a predicate, and say, 'All bodies are heavy.' Thus it is experience upon which rests the possibility of the synthesis of the predicate of weight with the conception of body, because both conceptions, although the one is not contained in the other, still belong to one another (only contingently, however), as parts of a whole, namely, of experience, which is itself a synthesis of intuitions.

But to synthetical judgments *a priori*, such aid is entirely wanting. If I go out of and beyond the conception A, in order to recognize another B as connected with it, what foundation have I to rest on, whereby to render the synthesis possible? I have here no longer the advantage of looking out in the sphere of experience for what I want. Let us take, for example, the proposition, 'Everything that happens has a cause.' In the conception of *something that happens*, I indeed think an existence which a certain time antecedes, and from this I can derive analytical judgments. But the conception of a cause lies quite out of the above conception, and indicates something entirely different from 'that which happens,' and is consequently not contained in that conception. How then am I able to assert concerning the general conception—'that which happens'—something entirely different from that conception, and to recognize the conception of cause although not contained in it, yet as belonging to it, and even necessarily? what is here the unknown = X, upon which the understanding rests when it believes it has found, out of the conception A a foreign predicate B, which it nevertheless considers to be connected with it? It cannot be experience, because the principle adduced annexes the two representations, cause and effect, to the representation existence, not only with universality, which experience cannot give, but also with the expression of necessity, therefore completely *a priori* and from pure conceptions. Upon such synthetical, that is augmentative propositions, depends the whole aim of our speculative knowledge *a priori*; for although analytical judgments are indeed highly important and necessary, they are so, only to arrive at that clearness of conceptions which is requisite for a sure and extended synthesis, and this alone is a real acquisition.

V. In All Theoretical Sciences of Reason, Synthetical Judgments 'a Priori' Are Contained as Principles

1. Mathematical judgments are always synthetical. Hitherto this fact, though incontestably true and very important in its consequences, seems to have escaped the analysts of the human mind, nay, to be in complete opposition to all their conjectures. For as it was found that mathematical conclusions all proceed according to the principle of contradiction (which the nature of every apodeictic certainty requires), people became persuaded that the fundamental principles of the science also were recognized and admitted in the same way. But the notion is fallacious; for although a synthetical proposition can certainly be discerned by means of the principle of contradiction, this is possible only when another synthetical proposition precedes, from which the latter is deduced, but never of itself.

Before all, be it observed, that proper mathematical propositions are always judgments *a priori*, and not empirical, because they carry along with them the conception of necessity, which cannot be given by experience. If this be demurred to, it matters not; I will then limit my assertion to *pure* mathematics, the very conception of which implies that it consists of knowledge altogether non-empirical and *a priori*.

We might, indeed, at first suppose that the proposition $7 + 5 = 12$ is a merely analytical proposition, following (according to the principle of contradiction) from the conception of a sum of seven and five. But if we regard it more narrowly, we find that our conception of the sum of seven and five contains nothing more than the uniting of both sums into one, whereby it cannot at all be cogitated what this single number is which embraces both. The conception of twelve is by no means obtained by merely cogitating the union of seven and five; and we may analyse our conception of such a possible sum as long as we will, still we shall never discover in it the notion of twelve. We must go beyond these conceptions, and have recourse to an intuition which corresponds to one of the two—our five fingers, for example, or like Segner in his *Arithmetic* five points, and so by degrees, add the units contained in the five given in the intuition, to the conception of seven. For I first take the number 7, and, for the conception of 5 calling in the aid of the fingers of my hand as objects of intuition, I add the units, which I before took together to make up the number 5, gradually now by means of the material image my hand, to the number 7, and by this process, I at length see the number 12 arise. That 7 should be added to 5, I have certainly cogitated in my conception of a sum $= 7 + 5$, but not that this sum was equal to 12. Arithmetical propositions are therefore always synthetical, of which we may become more clearly convinced by trying large numbers. For it will thus become quite evident, that turn and twist our conceptions as we may, it is impossible, without having recourse to intuition, to arrive at the sum total or product by means of the mere analysis of our conceptions. Just as little is any principle of pure geometry analytical. 'A straight line between two points is the shortest,' is a synthetical proposition. For my conception of *straight* contains no notion of *quantity*, but is merely *qualitative*. The conception of the *shortest* is therefore wholly an addition, and by no analysis can it be extracted from our conception of a straight line. Intuition must therefore here lend its aid, by means of which and thus only, our synthesis is possible.

Some few principles preposited by geometricians are, indeed, really analytical, and depend on the principle of contradiction. They serve, however, like identical propositions, as links in the chain of method, not as principles—for example, $a = a$, the whole is equal to itself, or $(a + b) > a$, the whole is greater than its part. And yet even these principles themselves, though they derive their validity from pure conceptions, are only admitted in mathematics because they can be presented in intuition. What causes us here commonly to believe that the predicate of such apodeictic judgments is already contained in our conception, and that the judgment is therefore analytical, is merely the equivocal nature of the expression. We must join in thought a certain predicate to a given conception, and this necessity cleaves already to the conception. But the question is, not what we must join in thought to the given conception, but what we really think therein, though only obscurely, and then it becomes manifest, that the predicate pertains to these conceptions, necessarily indeed, yet not as thought in the conception itself, but by virtue of an intuition, which must be added to the conception.

2. The science of Natural Philosophy (Physics) contains in itself synthetical judgments *a priori*, as principles. I shall adduce two propositions. For instance, the proposition, 'In all changes of the material world, the quantity of matter remains unchanged'; or, that, 'In all communication of motion, action and reaction must always be equal.' In both of these, not only is the necessity, and therefore their origin *a pri-*

ori clear, but also that they are synthetical propositions. For in the conception of matter, I do not cogitate its permanency, but merely its presence in space, which it fills. I therefore really go out of and beyond the conception of matter, in order to think on to it something *a priori*, which I did not think in it. The proposition is therefore not analytical, but synthetical, and nevertheless conceived *a priori*; and so it is with regard to the other propositions of the pure part of natural philosophy.

3. As to Metaphysics, even if we look upon it merely as an attempted science, yet, from the nature of human reason, an indispensable one, we find that it must contain synthetical propositions *a priori*. It is not merely the duty of metaphysics to dissect, and thereby analytically to illustrate the conceptions which we form *a priori* of things; but we seek to widen the range of our *a priori* knowledge. For this purpose, we must avail ourselves of such principles as add something to the original conception—something not identical with, nor contained in it, and by means of synthetical judgments *a priori*, leave far behind us the limits of experience; for example, in the proposition, 'the world must have a beginning,' and such like. Thus metaphysics, according to the proper aim of the science, consists merely of synthetical propositions a priori.

VI. The Universal Problem of Pure Reason

It is extremely advantageous to be able to bring a number of investigations under the formula of a single problem. For in this manner, we not only facilitate our own labour, inasmuch as we define it clearly to ourselves, but also render it more easy for others to decide whether we have done justice to our undertaking. The proper problem of pure reason, then, is contained in the question: 'How are synthetical judgments *a priori* possible?'

That metaphysical science has hitherto remained in so vacillating a state of uncertainty and contradiction, is only to be attributed to the fact, that this great problem, and perhaps even the difference between analytical and synthetical judgments, did not sooner suggest itself to philosophers. Upon the solution of this problem, or upon sufficient proof of the impossibility of synthetical knowledge *a priori*, depends the existence or downfall of the science of metaphysics. Among philosophers, David Hume came the nearest of all to this problem; yet it never acquired in his mind sufficient precision, nor did he regard the question in its universality. On the contrary, he stopped short at the synthetical proposition of the connection of an effect with its cause (*principium causalitatis*), insisting that such proposition *a priori* was impossible. According to his conclusions, then, all that we term metaphysical science is a mere delusion, arising from the fancied insight of reason into that which is in truth borrowed from experience, and to which habit has given the appearance of necessity. Against this assertion, destructive to all pure philosophy, he would have been guarded, had he had our problem before his eyes in its universality. For he would then have perceived that, according to his own argument, there likewise could not be any pure mathematical science, which assuredly cannot exist without synthetical propositions *a priori*—an absurdity from which his good understanding must have saved him.

In the solution of the above problem is at the same time comprehended the possibility of the use of pure reason in the foundation and construction of all sciences which contain theoretical knowledge *a priori* of objects, that is to say, the answer to the following questions:

How is pure mathematical science possible?

How is pure natural science possible?

Respecting these sciences, as they do certainly exist, it may with propriety be asked, *how* they are possible?—for that they must be possible, is shown by the fact of their really existing. But as to metaphysics, the miserable progress it has hitherto made, and the fact that of no one system yet brought forward, as far as regards its true aim, can it be said that this science really exists, leaves any one at liberty to doubt with reason the very possibility of its existence.

Yet, in a certain sense, this kind of knowledge must unquestionably be looked upon as given; in other words, metaphysics must be considered as really existing, if not as a science, nevertheless as a natural disposition of the human mind (*metaphysica naturalis*). For human reason, without any instigations imputable to the mere vanity of great knowledge, unceasingly progresses, urged on by its own feeling of need, towards such questions as cannot be answered by any empirical application of reason, or principles derived therefrom; and so there has ever really existed in every man some system of metaphysics. It will always exist, so soon as reason awakes to the exercise of its power of speculation. And now the question arises: How is metaphysics, as a natural disposition, possible? In other words, how, from the nature of universal human reason, do those questions arise which pure reason proposes to itself, and which it is impelled by its own feeling of need to answer as well as it can?

But as in all the attempts hitherto made to answer the questions which reason is prompted by its very nature to propose to itself, for example, whether the world had a beginning, or has existed from eternity, it has always met with unavoidable contradictions, we must not rest satisfied with the mere natural disposition of the mind to metaphysics, that is, with the existence of the faculty of pure reason, whence, indeed, some sort of metaphysical system always arises; but it must be possible to arrive at certainty in regard to the question whether we know or do not know the things of which metaphysics treats. We must be able to arrive at a decision on the subjects of its questions, or on the ability or inability of reason to form any judgment respecting them;

and therefore either to extend with confidence the bounds of our pure reason, or to set strictly defined and safe limits to its action. This last question, which arises out of the above universal problem, would properly run thus: How is metaphysics possible as a science?

Thus, the critique of reason leads at last, naturally and necessarily, to science; and, on the other hand, the dogmatical use of reason without criticism leads to groundless assertions, against which others equally specious can always be set, thus ending unavoidably in scepticism.

Besides, this science cannot be of great and formidable prolixity, because it has not to do with objects of reason, the variety of which is inexhaustible, but merely with Reason herself and her problems; problems which arise out of her own bosom, and are not proposed to her by the nature of outward things, but by her own nature. And when once Reason has previously become able completely to understand her own power in regard to objects which she meets with in experience, it will be easy to determine securely the extent and limits of her attempted application to objects beyond the confines of experience.

We may and must, therefore, regard the attempts hitherto made to establish metaphysical science dogmatically as non-existent. For what of analysis, that is, mere dissection of conceptions, is contained in one or other, is not the aim of, but only a preparation for metaphysics proper, which has for its object the extension, by means of synthesis, of our *a priori* knowledge. And for this purpose, mere analysis is of course useless, because it only shows what is contained in these conceptions, but not how we arrive, *a priori*, at them; and this it is her duty to show, in order to be able afterwards to determine their valid use in regard to all objects of experience, to all knowledge in general. But little self-denial, indeed, is needed to give up these pretensions, seeing the undeniable, and in the dogmatic mode of procedure, inevitable contradictions of Reason with herself, have long since ruined the reputation of every system of metaphysics that has appeared up to this time. It will require more firmness to remain undeterred by difficulty from within, and opposition from without, from endeavouring, by a method quite opposed to all those hitherto followed, to further the growth and fruitfulness of a science indispensable to human reason—a science from which every branch it has borne may be cut away, but whose roots remain indestructible.

Transcendental Illusion (from *Critique of Pure Reason*)

We termed Dialectic in general a logic of appearance. This does not signify a doctrine of *probability*; for probability is truth, only cognized upon insufficient grounds, and though the information it gives us is imperfect, it is not therefore deceitful. Hence it must not be separated from the analytical part of logic. Still less must *phenomenon* and *appearance* be held to be identical. For truth or illusory appearance does not reside in the object, in so far as it is intuited, but in the judgment upon the object, in so far as it is thought. It is therefore quite correct to say that the senses do not err, not because they always judge correctly, but because *they do not* judge at all. Hence truth and error, consequently also, illusory appearance as the cause of error, are only to be found in a judgment, that is, in the relation of an object to our understanding. In a cognition, which completely harmonizes with the laws of the understanding, no error can exist. In a representation of the senses—as not containing any judgment—there is also no error. But no power of nature can of itself deviate from its own laws. Hence neither the understanding *per se* (without the influence of another cause), nor the senses *per se*, would fall into error; the former could not, because, if it acts only according to its own laws, the effect (the judgment) must necessarily accord with these laws. But in accordance with the laws of the understanding consists the formal element in all truth. In the senses there is no judgment—neither a true nor a false one. But, as we have no source of cognition besides these two, it follows that error is caused solely by the unobserved influence of the sensibility upon the understanding. And thus it happens that the subjective grounds of a judgment blend and are confounded with the objective, and cause them to deviate from their proper determination, just as a body in motion would always of itself proceed in a straight line, but if another impetus gives to it a different direction, it will then start off into a curvilinear line of motion. To distinguish the peculiar action of the understanding from the power which mingles with it, it is necessary to consider an erroneous judgment as the diagonal between two forces, that determine the judgment in two different directions, which, as it were, form an angle, and to resolve this composite operation into the simple ones of the understanding and the sensibility. In pure *a priori* judgments this must be done by means of transcendental reflection, whereby, as has been already shown, each representation has its place appointed in the corresponding faculty of cognition, and consequently the influence of the one faculty upon the other is made apparent.

It is not at present our business to treat of empirical illusory appearance (for example, optical illusion), which occurs in the empirical application of otherwise correct rules of the understanding, and in which the judgment is misled by the influence of imagination. Our purpose is to speak of *transcendental illusory appearance*, which influences principles—that are not even applied to experience, for in this case we should possess a sure test of their correctness—but which leads us, in disregard of all the warnings of criticism, completely beyond the empirical employment of the categories, and deludes us with the chimera of an extension of the sphere of the *pure understanding*. We shall term those principles, the application of which is confined entirely within the limits of possible experience, *immanent*; those, on the other hand, which transgress these limits, we shall call *transcendent* principles. But by these latter I do not understand principles of the *transcendental* use or misuse of the categories, which is in reality a mere fault of the judgment when not under due restraint from criticism, and therefore not paying sufficient attention to the limits of the sphere in which the pure understanding is allowed to exercise its functions; but real principles which exhort us to break down all those barriers, and to lay claim to a perfectly new field of cognition, which recognizes no line of demarcation. Thus *transcendental* and *transcendent* are not identical terms. The principles of the pure understanding, which we have already propounded, ought to be of empirical and not of transcendental use, that is, they are not applicable to any object beyond the sphere of experience. A principle which removes these limits, nay, which authorizes us to overstep them, is called *transcendent*. If our criticism can succeed in exposing the illusion in these pretended principles, those which are limited in their employment to the sphere of experience, may be called, in opposition to the others, *immanent* principles of the pure understanding.

Logical illusion, which consists merely in the imitation of the form of reason (the illusion in sophistical syllogism), arises entirely from a want of due attention to logical rules. So soon as the attention is awakened to the case before us, this illusion totally disappears. Transcendental illusion, on the contrary, does not cease to exist, even after it has been exposed, and its nothingness clearly perceived by means of transcendental criticism. Take, for example, the illusion in the proposition: 'The world must have a beginning in time.' The cause of this is as follows. In our reason, subjectively considered as a faculty of human cognition, there exist fundamental rules and maxims of its exercise, which have completely the appearance of objective principles. Now from this cause it happens, that the subjective necessity of a certain connection of our conceptions, is regarded as an objective necessity of the determination of things in themselves. This illusion it is impossible to avoid, just as we cannot avoid perceiving that the sea appears to be higher at a distance than it is near the shore, because we see the former by means of higher rays than the latter, or, which is a still stronger case, as even the astronomer cannot prevent himself from seeing the moon larger at its rising than some time afterwards, although he is not deceived by this illusion.

Transcendental dialectic will therefore content itself with exposing the illusory appearance in transcendental judgments, and guarding us against it; but to make it, as in the case of logical illusion, entirely disappear and cease to be illusion, is utterly beyond its power. For we have here to do with a natural and unavoidable illusion, which rests upon subjective principles, and imposes these upon us as objective, while logical dialectic, in the detection of sophisms, has to do merely with an error in the logical consequence of the propositions, or with an artificially constructed illusion, in imitation of the natural error. There is, therefore, a natural and unavoidable dialectic of pure reason—not that in which the bungler, from want of the requisite knowledge, involves himself, nor that which the sophist devises for the purpose of misleading, but that which is an inseparable adjunct of human reason, and which, even after its illusions have been exposed, does not cease to deceive, and continually to lead reason into momentary errors, which it becomes necessary continually to remove.

The Paralogism of Rational Psychology (from *Critique of Pure Reason*)

The logical paralogism consists in the falsity of an argument in respect of its form, be the content what it may. But a transcendental paralogism has a transcendental foundation, and concludes falsely, while the form is correct and unexceptionable. In this manner the paralogism has its foundation in the nature of human reason, and is the parent of an unavoidable, though not insoluble, mental illusion.

We now come to a conception which was not inserted in the general list of transcendental conceptions, and yet must be reckoned with them, but at the same time without in the least altering, or indicating a deficiency in that table. This is the conception, or, if the term is preferred, the judgment, *I think*. But it is readily perceived that this thought is as it were the vehicle of all conceptions in general, and consequently of transcendental conceptions also, and that it is therefore regarded as a transcendental conception, although it can have no peculiar claim to be so ranked, inasmuch as its only use is to indicate that all thought is accompanied by consciousness. At the same time, pure as this conception is from all empirical content (impressions of the senses), it enables us to distinguish two different kinds of objects. *I*, as thinking, am an object of the internal sense, and am called soul. That which is an object of the external senses is called body. Thus the expression, I, as a thinking being, designates the object-matter of psychology, which may be called the rational doctrine of the soul, inasmuch as in this science I desire to know nothing of the soul but what, independently of all experience (which determines me *in concreto*), may be concluded from this conception *I*, in so far as it appears in all thought.

Now, the *rational* doctrine of the soul is really an undertaking of this kind. For if the smallest empirical element of thought, if any particular perception of my internal state, were to be introduced among the grounds of cognition of this science, it would not be a rational, but an *empirical* doctrine of the soul. We have thus before us a pretended science, raised upon the single proposition, *I think*, whose foundation or want of foundation we may very properly, and agreeably with the nature of a transcendental philosophy, here examine. It ought not to be objected that in this proposition, which expresses the perception of one's self, an internal experience is asserted, and that consequently the rational doctrine of the soul which is founded upon it, is not pure, but partly founded upon an empirical principle. For this internal perception is nothing more than the mere apperception, *I think*, which in fact renders all transcendental conceptions possible, in which we say, I think substance, cause, etc. For internal experience in general and its possibility, or perception in general, and its relation to other perceptions, unless some particular distinction or determination thereof is empirically given, cannot be regarded as empirical cognition, but as cognition of the empirical, and belongs to the investigation of the possibility of every experience, which is certainly transcendental. The smallest object of experience (for example, only pleasure or pain), that should be included in the general representation of self-consciousness, would immediately change the rational into an empirical psychology.

I think is therefore the only text of rational psychology, from which it must develop its whole system. It is manifest that this thought, when applied to an object (myself), can contain nothing but transcendental predicates thereof; because the least empirical predicate would destroy the purity of the science and its independence of all experience.

. . .

Now, as the proposition *I think* (in the problematical sense) contains the form of every judgment in general, and is the constant accompaniment of all the categories; it is manifest, that conclusions are drawn from it only by a transcendental employment of the understanding. This use of the understanding excludes all empirical elements; and we cannot, as has been shown above, have any favourable conception beforehand of its procedure. We shall therefore follow with a critical eye this proposition through all the predicaments of pure psychology; but we shall, for brevity's sake, allow this examination to proceed in an uninterrupted connection.

Before entering on this task, however, the following general remark may help to quicken our attention to this mode of argument. It is not merely through my thinking that I cognize an object, but only through my determining a given intuition in relation to the unity of consciousness in which all thinking consists. It follows that I cognize myself, not through my being conscious of myself as thinking, but only when I am conscious of the intuition of myself as determined in relation to the function of thought. All the modi of self-consciousness in thought are hence not conceptions of objects (conceptions of the understanding—categories); they are mere logical functions, which do not present to thought an object to be cognized, and cannot therefore present my Self as an object. Not the consciousness of the *determining*, but only that of the *determinable* self, that is, of my internal intuition (in so far as the manifold contained in it can be connected conformably with the general condition of the unity of apperception in thought), is the object.

1. In all judgments I am the *determining* subject of that relation which constitutes a judgment. But that the I which thinks, must be considered as in thought always a *subject*, and as a thing which cannot be a predicate to thought, is an apodeictic and *identical* proposition. But this proposition does not signify that I, as an object, am, for myself, a *self-subsistent being* or *substance*. This latter statement—an ambitious one—requires to be supported by data which are not to be discovered in thought; and are perhaps (in so far as I consider the thinking self merely *as such*) not to be discovered in the thinking self at all.

2. That the *I* or *Ego* of apperception, and consequently in all thought, is *singular* or simple, and cannot be resolved into a plurality of subjects, and therefore indicates a logically simple subject—this is self-evident from the very conception of an Ego, and is consequently an analytical proposition. But this is not tantamount to declaring that the thinking Ego is a simple *substance*—for this would be a synthetical proposition. The conception of substance always relates to intuitions, which with me cannot be other than sensuous, and which consequently lie completely out of the sphere of the understanding and its thought: but to this sphere belongs the affirmation that the Ego is simple in thought. It would indeed be surprising, if the conception of substance, which in other cases requires so much labour to distinguish from the other elements presented by intuition—so much trouble, too, to discover whether it can be simple (as in the case of the parts of matter), should be presented immediately to me, as if by revelation, in the poorest mental representation of all.

3. The proposition of the identity of my Self amidst all the manifold representations of which I am conscious, is likewise a proposition lying in the conceptions themselves, and is consequently analytical. But this identity of the subject, of which I am conscious in all its representations, does not relate to or concern the intuition of the subject, by which it is given as an object. This proposition cannot therefore enounce the identity of the person, by which is understood the consciousness of the identity of its own substance as a thinking being in all change and variation of circumstances. To prove this, we should re-

quire not a mere analysis of the proposition, but synthetical judgments based upon a given intuition.

4. I distinguish my own existence, as that of a thinking being, from that of other things external to me—among which my body also is reckoned. This is also an analytical proposition, for *other* things are exactly those which I think as different or *distinguished* from myself. But whether this consciousness of myself is possible *without* things external to me; and whether therefore I can exist merely as a thinking being (without being man)—cannot be known or inferred from this proposition.

Thus we have gained nothing as regards the cognition of myself as object, by the analysis of the consciousness of my Self in thought. The logical exposition of thought in general is mistaken for a metaphysical determination of the object.

Our *Critique* would be an investigation utterly superfluous, if there existed a possibility of proving a priori, that all thinking beings are in themselves simple substances, as such, therefore, possess the inseparable attribute of personality, and are conscious of their existence apart from and unconnected with matter. For we should thus have taken a step beyond the world of sense, and have penetrated into the sphere of *noumena*; and in this case the right could not be denied us of extending our knowledge in this sphere, of establishing ourselves, and, under a favouring star, appropriating to ourselves possessions in it. For the proposition: 'Every thinking being, as such, is simple substance,' is an *a priori* synthetical proposition; because in the first place it goes beyond the conception which is the subject of it, and adds to the mere notion of a thinking being the *mode of its existence*, and in the second place annexes a predicate (that of simplicity) to the latter conception—a predicate which it could not have discovered in the sphere of experience. It would follow that *a priori* synthetical propositions are possible and legitimate, not only, as we have maintained, in relation to objects of possible experience, and as principles of the possibility of this experience itself, but are applicable to things as things in themselves—an inference which makes an end of the whole of this *Critique*, and obliges us to fall back on the old mode of metaphysical procedure. But indeed the danger is not so great, if we look a little closer into the question.

There lurks in the procedure of rational psychology a paralogism, which is represented in the following syllogism:

That which cannot be cogitated otherwise than as subject, does not exist otherwise than as subject, and is therefore substance.

A thinking being, considered merely as such, cannot be cogitated otherwise than as subject.

Therefore it exists also as such, that is, as substance.

In the major we speak of a being that can be cogitated generally and in every relation, consequently as it may be given in intuition. But in the minor we speak of the same being only in so far as it regards itself as subject, relatively to thought and the unity of consciousness, but not in relation to intuition, by which it is presented as an object to thought. Thus the conclusion is here arrived at by a *Sophisma figurae dictionis*.

That this famous argument is a mere paralogism, will be plain to any one who will consider the general remark which precedes our exposition of the principles of the pure understanding, and the section on noumena. For it was there proved that the conception of a thing, which can exist *per se*—only as a subject and never as a predicate, possesses no objective reality; that is to say, we can never know whether there exists any object to correspond to the conception; consequently, the conception is nothing more than a conception, and from it we derive no proper knowledge. If this conception is to indicate by the term *substance*, an object that can be given, if it is to become a cognition, we must have at the foundation of the cognition a permanent intuition, as the indispensable condition of its objective reality. For through intuition alone can an object be given. But in internal intuition there is nothing permanent, for the Ego is but the consciousness of my thought. If, then, we appeal merely to thought, we cannot discover the necessary condition of the application of the conception of substance—that is, of a subject existing *per se*—to the subject as a thinking being. And thus the conception of the simple nature of substance, which is connected with the objective reality of this conception, is shown to be also invalid, and to be, in fact, nothing more than the logical qualitative unity of self-consciousness in thought; whilst we remain perfectly ignorant whether the subject is composite or not.

Conclusion of the Solution of the Psychological Paralogism

The dialectical illusion in rational psychology arises from our confounding an idea of reason (of a pure intelligence) with the conception—in every respect undetermined—of a thinking being in general. I cogitate myself in behalf of a possible experience, at the same time making abstraction of all actual experience; and infer therefrom that I can be conscious of myself apart from experience and its empirical conditions. I consequently confound the possible *abstraction* of my empirically determined existence with the supposed consciousness of a possible *separate* existence of my thinking self; and I believe that I cognize what is substantial in myself as a transcendental subject, when I have nothing more in thought than the unity of consciousness, which lies at the basis of all determination of cognition.

The task of explaining the community of the soul with the body does not properly belong to the psychology of which we are here speaking;

because it proposes to prove the personality of the soul apart from this communion (after death), and is therefore *transcendent* in the proper sense of the word, although occupying itself with an object of experience—only in so far, however, as it ceases to be an object of experience. But a sufficient answer may be found to the question in our system. The difficulty which lies in the execution of this task consists, as is well known, in the presupposed heterogeneity of the object of the internal sense (the soul) and the objects of the external senses; inasmuch as the formal condition of the intuition of the one is time, and of that of the other space also. But if we consider that both kinds of objects do not differ internally, but only in so far as the one *appears* externally to the other—consequently, that what lies at the basis of phenomena, as a thing in itself, may not be heterogeneous; this difficulty disappears. There then remains no other difficulty than is to be found in the question—how a community of substances is possible; a question which lies out of the region of psychology, and which the reader, after what in our Analytic has been said of primitive forces and faculties, will easily judge to be also beyond the region of human cognition.

The Three Regulative Ideas of Pure Reason (from *Critique of Pure Reason*)

And now we can clearly perceive the result of our transcendental dialectic, and the proper aim of the ideas of pure reason—which become dialectical solely from misunderstanding and inconsiderateness. Pure reason is, in fact, occupied with itself, and not with any object. Objects are not presented to it to be embraced in the unity of an empirical conception; it is only the cognitions of the understanding that are presented to it, for the purpose of receiving the unity of a rational conception, that is, of being connected according to a principle. The unity of reason is the unity of system; and this systematic unity is not an objective principle, extending its dominion over objects, but a subjective maxim, extending its authority over the empirical cognition of objects. The systematic connection which reason gives to the empirical employment of the understanding, not only advances the extension of that employment, but ensures its correctness, and thus the principle of a systematic unity of this nature is also objective, although only in an indefinite respect (*principium vagum*). It is not, however, a constitutive principle, determining an object to which it directly relates; it is merely a regulative principle or maxim, advancing and strengthening the empirical exercise of reason, by the opening up of new paths of which the understanding is ignorant, while it never conflicts with the laws of its exercise in the sphere of experience.

But reason cannot cogitate this systematic unity, without at the same time cogitating an object of the idea—an object that cannot be presented in any experience, which contains no concrete example of a complete systematic unity. This being (*ens rationis ratiocinatae*) is therefore a mere idea, and is not assumed to be a thing which is real absolutely and in itself. On the contrary, it forms merely the problematical foundation of the connection which the mind introduces among the phenomena of the sensuous world. We look upon this connection, in the light of the above-mentioned idea, as if it drew its origin from the supposed being which corresponds to the idea. And yet all we aim at is the possession of this idea as a secure foundation for the systematic unity of experience—a unity indispensable to reason, advantageous to the understanding, and promotive of the interests of empirical cognition.

We mistake the true meaning of this idea, when we regard it as an enouncement, or even as a hypothetical declaration of the existence of a real thing, which we are to regard as the origin or ground of a systematic constitution of the universe. On the contrary, it is left completely undetermined what the nature or properties of this so-called ground may be. The idea is merely to be adopted as a point of view, from which this unity, so essential to reason and so beneficial to the understanding, may be regarded as radiating. In one word, this transcendental thing is merely the schema of a regulative principle, by means of which Reason, so far as in her lies, extends the dominion of systematic unity over the whole sphere of experience.

The first object of an idea of this kind is the Ego, considered merely as a thinking nature or soul. If I wish to investigate the properties of a thinking being, I must interrogate experience. But I find that I can apply none of the categories to this object, the schema of these categories, which is the condition of their application, being given only in sensuous intuition. But I cannot thus attain to the cognition of a systematic unity of all the phenomena of the internal sense. Instead, therefore, of an empirical conception of what the soul really is, reason takes the conception of the empirical unity of all thought, and, by cogitating this unity as unconditioned and primitive, constructs the rational conception or idea of a simple substance which is in itself unchangeable, possessing personal identity, and in connection with other real things external to it; in one word, it constructs the idea of a simple self-subsistent intelligence. But the real aim of reason in this procedure is the attainment of principles of systematic unity for the explanation of the phenomena of the soul. That is, reason desires to be able to represent all the determinations of the internal sense, as existing in one subject, all powers as deduced from one fundamental power, all changes as mere varieties in the condition of a being which is permanent and always the same, and all *phenomena* in space as entirely different in their nature from the procedure of thought. Essential simplicity (with the other attributes predicated of the Ego) is regarded as the mere schema of this regulative principle; it is not assumed that it is the actual ground of the properties of the soul. For these properties may rest upon quite different grounds, of which we are completely ignorant; just as the above predicates could not give us any knowledge of the soul as it is in itself, even if we regarded them as valid in respect of it, inasmuch as they constitute a mere idea, which cannot be represented *in concreto*. Nothing but good can result from a psychological idea of this kind, if we only take proper care not to consider it as more than an idea; that is, if we regard it as valid merely in relation to the employment of reason, in the sphere of the phenomena of the soul. Under the guidance of this idea, or principle, no empirical laws of corporeal phenomena are called in to explain that which is a phenomenon of the *internal sense* alone; no windy hypotheses of the generation, annihilation, and palingenesis of souls are admitted. Thus the consideration of this object of the internal sense is kept pure, and unmixed with heterogenous elements; while the investigation of reason aims at reducing all the grounds of explanation employed in this sphere of knowledge to a single principle. All this is best effected, nay, cannot be effected otherwise than by means of such a schema, which requires us to regard this ideal thing as an actual existence. The psychological idea is therefore meaningless and inapplicable, except as the schema of a regulative conception. For, if I ask whether the soul is not really of a spiritual nature—it is a question which has no meaning. From such a conception has been abstracted, not merely all corporeal nature, but all nature, that is, all the predicates of a possible experience; and consequently, all the conditions which enable us to cogitate an object to this conception have disappeared. But, if these conditions are absent, it is evident that the conception is meaningless.

The second regulative idea of speculative reason is the conception of the universe. For nature is properly the only object presented to us, in regard to which reason requires regulative principles. Nature is twofold—thinking and corporeal nature. To cogitate the latter in regard to its internal possibility, that is, to determine the application of the categories to it, no idea is required—no representation which transcends experience. In this sphere, therefore, an idea is impossible, sensuous intuition being our only guide; while, in the sphere of psychology, we require the fundamental idea (I), which contains *a priori* a certain form of thought, namely, the unity of the Ego. Pure reason has therefore nothing left but nature in general, and the completeness of conditions in nature in accordance with some principle. The absolute totality of the series of these conditions is an idea, which can never be fully realized in the empirical exercise of reason, while it is serviceable as a rule for the procedure of reason in relation to that totality. It requires us, in the explanation of given phenomena (in the regress or ascent in the series), to proceed as if the series were infinite in itself, that is, were prolonged *in indefinitum*; while, on the other hand, where reason is regarded as itself the determining cause (in the region of freedom), we are required to proceed as if we had not before us an object of sense, but of the pure understanding. In this latter case, the conditions do not exist in the series of phenomena, but may be placed quite out of and beyond it, and the series of conditions may be regarded as if it had an absolute beginning from an intelligible cause. All this proves that the cosmological ideas are nothing but regulative principles, and not constitutive; and that their aim is not to realize an actual totality in such series. The full discussion of this subject will be found in its proper place in the chapter on the antinomy of pure reason.

The third idea of pure reason, containing the hypothesis of a being which is valid merely as a relative hypothesis, is that of the one and all-sufficient cause of all cosmological series, in other words, the idea of God. We have not the slightest ground absolutely to admit the existence of an object corresponding to this idea; for what can empower or authorize us to affirm the existence of a being of the highest perfection—a being whose existence is absolutely necessary, merely because we possess the conception of such a being? The answer is—it is the existence of the world which renders this hypothesis necessary. But this answer makes it perfectly evident, that the idea of this being, like all other speculative ideas, is essentially nothing more than a demand upon reason that it shall regulate the connection which it and its subordinate faculties introduce into the phenomena of the world by principles of systematic unity, and consequently, that it shall regard all phenomena as originating from one all embracing being, as the supreme and all-sufficient cause. From this it is plain that the only aim of reason in this procedure is the establishment of its own formal rule for the extension of its dominion in the world of experience; that it does not aim at an extension of its cognition *beyond the limits of experience*; and that, consequently, this idea does not contain any constitutive principle.

The highest formal unity, which is based upon ideas alone, is the unity of all things—a unity in accordance with an aim or purpose; and the speculative interest of reason renders it necessary to regard all order in the world as if it originated from the intention and design of a supreme reason. This principle unfolds to the view of reason in the sphere of experience new and enlarged prospects, and invites it to connect the phenomena of the world according to teleological laws, and in this way to attain to the highest possible degree of systematic unity. The hypothesis of a supreme intelligence, as the sole cause of the universe—an intelligence which has for us no more than an ideal existence, is accordingly always of the greatest service to reason. Thus, if we presuppose, in relation to the figure of the earth (which is round, but somewhat flattened at the poles), or that of mountains or seas, wise designs on the part of an author of the universe, we cannot fail to make, by the light of this supposition, a great number of interesting discoveries. If we keep to this hypothesis, as a principle which is purely regulative, even error cannot be very detrimental. For, in this case, error can have no more serious consequences than that, where we expected to discover a teleological connection (*nexus finalis*), only a mechanical or physical connection appears. In such a case, we merely fail to find the additional form of unity we expected, but we do not lose the rational unity which the mind requires in its procedure in experience. But even a miscarriage of this sort cannot affect the law in its general and teleological relations. For although we may convict an anatomist of an error, when he connects the limb of some animal with a certain purpose; it is quite impossible to *prove* in a single case, that any arrangement of nature, be it what it may, is entirely without aim or design. And thus medical physiology, by the aid of a principle presented to it by pure reason, extends its very limited empirical knowledge of the purposes of the different parts of an organized body so far, that it may be asserted with the utmost confidence, and with the approbation of all reflecting men, that every organ or bodily part of an animal has its use and answers a certain design. Now, this is a supposition, which, if regarded as of a constitutive character, goes much farther than any experience or observation of ours can justify. Hence it is evident that it is nothing more than a regulative principle of reason, which aims at the highest degree of systematic unity, by the aid of the idea of a causality according to design in a supreme cause—a cause which it regards as the highest intelligence.

(Trans. J. M. D. Meiklejohn)

The Categorical Imperative (from *Foundations of the Metaphysics of Morals*)

Everything in nature works according to laws. Only a rational being has the capacity of acting according to the conception of laws, i.e., according to principles. This capacity is will. Since reason is required for the derivation of actions from laws, will is nothing else than practical reason. If reason infallibly determines the will, the actions which such a being recognizes as objectively necessary are also subjectively necessary. That is, the will is a faculty of choosing only that which reason, independently of inclination, recognizes as practically necessary, i.e., as good. But if reason of itself does not sufficiently determine the will, and if the will is subjugated to subjective conditions (certain incentives) which do not always agree with objective conditions; in a word, if the will is not of itself in complete accord with reason (the actual case of men), then the actions which are recognized as objectively necessary are subjectively contingent, and the determination of such a will according to objective laws is constraint. That is, the relation of objective laws to a will which is not completely good is conceived as the determination of the will of a rational being by principles of reason to which this will is not by nature necessarily obedient.

The conception of an objective principle, so far as it constrains a will, is a command (of reason), and the formula of this command is called an *imperative*.

All imperatives are expressed by an "ought" and thereby indicate the relation of an objective law of reason to a will which is not in its subjective constitution necessarily determined by this law. This relation is that of constraint. Imperatives say that it would be good to do or to refrain from doing something, but they say it to a will which does not always do something simply because it is presented to it as a good thing to do. Practical good is what determines the will by means of the conception of reason and hence not by subjective causes but, rather, objectively, i.e., on grounds which are valid for every rational being as such. It is distinguished from the pleasant, as that which has an influence on the will only by means of a sensation from merely subjective causes, which hold only for the senses of this or that person and not as a principle of reason which holds for everyone.

A perfectly good will, therefore, would be equally subject to objective laws (of the good), but it could not be conceived as constrained by them to act in accord with them, because, according to its own subjective constitution, it can be determined to act only through the conception of the good. Thus no imperatives hold for the divine will or, more generally, for a holy will. The "ought" is here out of place, for the volition of itself is necessarily in unison with the law. Therefore imperatives are only formulas expressing the relation of objective laws of volition in general to the subjective imperfection of the will of this or that rational being, e.g., the human will.

All imperatives command either hypothetically or categorically. The former present the practical necessity of a possible action as a means to achieving something else which one desires (or which one may possibly desire). The categorical imperative would be one which presented an action as of itself objectively necessary, without regard to any other end.

. . .

If I think of a hypothetical imperative as such, I do not know what it will contain until the condition is stated [under which it is an imperative]. But if I think of a categorical imperative, I know immediately what it contains. For since the imperative contains besides the law only the necessity of the maxim of acting in accordance with this law, while the law contains no condition to which it is restricted, there is nothing remaining in it except the universality of law as such to which the maxim of the action should conform; and in effect this conformity alone is represented as necessary by the imperative.

There is, therefore, only one categorical imperative. It is: Act only according to that maxim by which you can at the same time will that it should become a universal law.

Now if all imperatives of duty can be derived from this one imperative as a principle, we can at least show what we understand by the concept of duty and what it means, even though it remain undecided whether that which is called duty is an empty concept or not.

The universality of law according to which effects are produced constitutes what is properly called nature in the most general sense (as to form), i.e., the existence of things so far as it is determined by universal laws. [By analogy], then, the universal imperative of duty can be expressed as follows: Act as though the maxim of your action were by your will to become a universal law of nature.

We shall now enumerate some duties, adopting the usual division of them into duties to ourselves and to others and into perfect and imperfect duties.

1. A man who is reduced to despair by a series of evils feels a weariness with life but is still in possession of his reason sufficiently to ask whether it would not be contrary to his duty to himself to take his own life. Now he asks whether the maxim of his action could become a universal law of nature. His maxim, however, is: For love of myself, I make it my principle to shorten my life when by a longer duration it threatens more evil than satisfaction. But it is questionable whether this principle of self-love could become a universal law of nature. One immediately sees a contradiction in a system of nature, whose law would be to destroy life by the feeling whose special office is to impel the improvement of life. In this case it would not exist as nature; hence that maxim cannot obtain as a law of nature, and thus it wholly contradicts the supreme principle of all duty.

2. Another man finds himself forced by need to borrow money. He well knows that he will not be able to repay it, but he also sees that nothing will be loaned him if he does not firmly promise to repay it at a certain time. He desires to make such a promise, but he has enough conscience to ask himself whether it is not improper and opposed to duty to relieve his distress in such a way. Now, assuming he does decide to do so, the maxim of his action would be as follows: When I believe myself to be in need of money, I will borrow money and promise to repay it, although I know I shall never do so. Now this principle of self-love or of his own benefit may very well be compatible with his whole future welfare, but the question is whether it is right. He changes the pretension of self-love into a universal law and then puts the question: How would it be if my maxim became a universal law? He immediately sees that it could never hold as a universal law of nature and be consistent with itself; rather it must necessarily contradict itself. For the universality of a law which says that anyone who believes himself to be in need could promise what he pleased with the intention of not fulfilling it would make the promise itself and the end to be accomplished by it impossible; no one would believe what was promised to him but would only laugh at any such assertion as vain pretense.

3. A third finds in himself a talent which could, by means of some cultivation, make him in many respects a useful man. But he finds himself in comfortable circumstances and prefers indulgence in pleasure to troubling himself with broadening and improving his fortunate natural gifts. Now, however, let him ask whether his maxim of neglecting his gifts, besides agreeing with his propensity to idle amusement, agrees also with what is called duty. He sees that a system of nature could indeed exist in accordance with such a law, even though man (like the inhabitants of the South Sea Islands) should let his talents rust and resolve to devote his life merely to idleness, indulgence, and propagation—in a word, to pleasure. But he cannot possibly will that this should become a universal law of nature or that it should be implanted in us by a natural instinct. For, as a rational being, he necessarily wills that all his faculties should be developed, inasmuch as they are given to him for all sorts of possible purposes.

4. A fourth man, for whom things are going well, sees that others (whom he could help) have to struggle with great hardships, and he asks, "What concern of mine is it? Let each one be as happy as heaven wills, or as he can make himself; I will not take anything from him or even envy him; but to his welfare or to his assistance in time of need I have no desire to contribute." If such a way of thinking were a universal law of nature, certainly the human race could exist, and without doubt even better than in a state where everyone talks of sympathy and good will or even exerts himself occasionally to practice them

while, on the other hand, he cheats when he can and betrays or otherwise violates the rights of man. Now although it is possible that a universal law of nature according to that maxim could exist, it is nevertheless impossible to will that such a principle should hold everywhere as a law of nature. For a will which resolved this would conflict with itself, since instances can often arise in which he would need the love and sympathy of others, and in which he would have robbed himself, by such a law of nature springing from his own will, of all hope of the aid he desires.

Postulates of Pure Practical Reason (from *Critique of Practical Reason*)

IV. The Immortality of the Soul as a Postulate of Pure Practical Reason

The achievement of the highest good in the world is the necessary object of a will determinable by the moral law. In such a will, however, the complete fitness of intentions to the moral law is the supreme condition of the highest good. This aptness, therefore, must be just as possible as its object, because it is contained in the command that requires us to promote the latter. But complete fitness of the will to the moral law is holiness, which is a perfection of which no rational being in the world of sense is at any time capable. But since it is required as practically necessary, it can be found only in an endless progress to that complete fitness; on principles of pure practical reason, it is necessary to assume such a practical progress as the real object of our will.

This infinite progress is possible, however, only under the presupposition of an infinitely enduring existence and personality of the same rational being; this is called the immortality of the soul. Thus the highest good is practically possible only on the supposition of the immortality of the soul, and the latter, as inseparably bound to the moral law, is a postulate of pure practical reason. By a postulate of pure practical reason I understand a theoretical proposition which is not as such demonstrable, but which is an inseparable corollary of an *a priori* unconditionally valid practical law.

The thesis of the moral destiny of our nature, viz., that it is able only in an infinite progress to attain complete fitness to the moral law, is of great use, not merely for the present purpose of supplementing the impotence of speculative reason, but also with respect to religion. Without it, either the moral law is completely degraded from its holiness, by being made out as lenient (indulgent) and thus compliant to our convenience, or our notions of our vocation and our expectation are strained to an unattainable destination, i.e., a hoped-for complete attainment of holiness of will, thus losing themselves in fanatical theosophical dreams which completely contradict our knowledge of ourselves. In either case, we are only hindered in the unceasing striving toward and precise and persistent obedience to a command of reason which is stern, unindulgent, truly commanding, really and not just ideally possible. Only endless progress from lower to higher stages of moral perfection is possible to a rational but finite being. The Infinite Being, to whom the temporal condition is nothing, sees in this series, which is for us without end, a whole conformable to the moral law; holiness, which His law inexorably commands in order to be true to His justice in the share He assigns to each in the highest good, is to be found in a single intellectual intuition of the existence of rational beings. All that can be granted to a creature with respect to hope for this share is consciousness of his tried character. And on the basis of his previous progress from the worse to the morally better, and of the immutability of intention which thus becomes known to him, he may hope for a further uninterrupted continuation of this progress, however long his existence may last, even beyond this life. But he cannot hope here or at any foreseeable point of his future existence to be fully adequate to God's will, without indulgence or remission which would not harmonize with justice. This he can do only in the infinity of his duration which God alone can survey.

V. The Existence of God as a Postulate of Pure Practical Reason

The moral law led, in the foregoing analysis, to a practical problem which is assigned solely by pure reason and without any concurrence of sensuous incentives. It is the problem of the completeness of the first and principal part of the highest good, viz., morality; since this problem can be solved only in eternity, it led to the postulate of immortality. The same law must also lead us to affirm the possibility of the second element of the highest good, i.e., happiness proportional to that morality; it must do so just as disinterestedly as heretofore, by a purely impartial reason. This it can do on the supposition of the existence of a cause adequate to this effect, i.e., it must postulate the existence of God as necessarily belonging to the possibility of the highest good (the object of our will which is necessarily connected with the moral legislation of pure reason). We proceed to exhibit this connection in a convincing manner.

Happiness is the condition of a rational being in the world, in whose whole existence everything goes according to wish and will. It thus rests on the harmony of nature with his entire end and with the essential determining ground of his will. But the moral law commands, as a law of freedom, by grounds of determination which are wholly independent of nature and its harmony with our faculty of desire (as incentives). Still, the acting rational being in the world is not at the same time the cause of the world and of nature itself. Hence there is not the slightest ground in the moral law for a necessary connection between the morality and proportionate happiness of a being which belongs to the world as one of its parts and as thus dependent on it. Not being nature's cause, his will cannot by its own strength bring nature, as it touches on his happiness, into complete harmony with his practical principles. Nevertheless, in the practical task of pure reason, i.e., in the necessary endeavor after the highest good, such a connection is postulated as necessary: we should seek to further the highest good (which therefore must be at least possible). Therefore also the existence is postulated of a cause of the whole of nature, itself distinct from nature, which contains the ground of the exact coincidence of happiness with morality. This supreme cause, however, must contain the ground of the agreement of nature not merely with a law of the will of rational beings but with the idea of this law so far as they make it the supreme ground of determination of the will. Thus it contains the ground of the agreement of nature not merely with actions moral in their form but also with their morality as the motive to such actions, i.e., with their moral intention. Therefore, the highest good is possible in the world only on the supposition of a supreme cause of nature which has a causality corresponding to the moral intention. Now a being which is capable of actions by the idea of laws is an intelligence (a rational being), and the causality of such a being according to this idea of laws is his will. Therefore, the supreme cause of nature, in so far as it must be presupposed for the highest good, is a being which is the cause (and consequently the author) of nature through understanding and will, i.e., God. As a consequence, the postulate of the possibility of a highest derived good (the best world) is at the same time the postulate of the reality of a highest original good, namely, the existence of God. Now it was our duty to promote the highest good; and it is not merely our privilege but a necessity connected with duty as a requisite to presuppose the possibility of this highest good. This presupposition is made only under the condition of the existence of God, and this condition inseparably connects this supposition with duty. Therefore, it is morally necessary to assume the existence of God.

Review Questions

1. Kant's "criticism" of knowledge occupies an important place in modern philosophy. What does it mean, and how does it tie in with the work of his predecessors like Descartes, Locke, Berkeley and Hume?
2. Would you say that Kant's several *Critiques* are an attempt to refute scepticism?

3. Describe the genesis of sense knowledge for Kant; in what way is it _a priori_? In what way _a posteriori_?
4. Why does Kant call _pure reason_ pure? _Practical reason_ practical?
5. Relate the fate of metaphysics in modern philosophy to Kant and Hume.
6. According to Kant, must the metaphysical entities unknown to reason be rejected in every sense?
7. According to Kant, how do we arrive at moral judgments?
8. How does Kant relate moral law to holiness?

18

Georg Wilhelm Friedrich Hegel (1770–1831)

Introduction

Georg Wilhelm Friedrich Hegel was one of the philosophers of the next generation who, while acknowledging Kant as an indispensable philosopher, was bound by his own vision of absolute unity to reject the dichotomy introduced by Kant in separating the practical from the speculative order and sensibility from reason. As a consequence, Hegel launched a gigantic effort to establish unity and reconciliation at the heart of reality.

He was born in Stuttgart in 1770 and died in Berlin in 1831. He was a student in theology at the University of Tübingen, together with Schelling the philosopher and Holderlin the poet. He was not a brilliant student, and his leaving certificate indicated that his knowledge of philosophy wa inadequate — a much needed source of comfort for all students of philosophy. Upon leaving the university he became a tutor for several families, first in Berne and later in Frankfurt. In 1801 he received an appointment at the University of Jena as *Privatdozent* and a few years later as professor. His first great work, and the one that sets forth the prevailing lines of his thought despite the haste with which it was brought to completion — on the eve of the Battle of Jena between the French and Prussian troops — was *The Phenomenology of Mind* in 1807. Because of the battle the university was closed, and Hegel, in order to make a living, removed first to Bamberg to edit a paper and later to Nürnberg, where he was appointed director of the gymnasium. He married in 1811. He left Nürnberg to accept a post at the University of Heidelberg for a year, after which he went to the University of Berlin, where he remained until his death. At Berlin he was hailed as a brilliant lecturer, and his lectures became the basis of his works on history, art, nature, and religion. Besides the *Phenomenology*, Hegel's other chief works include *The Science of Log-*

ic (1816), *The Encyclopedia of the Philosophical Sciences* (1817), and *Outlines of the Philosophy of Right* (1821).

Unity in reality is a constant theme in philosophy, but at certain times the need to articulate it is more pressing than at others, and thus the systems of thinkers like Pythagoras, Plotinus, Nicholas of Cusa, Leibniz, Spinoza, and now Hegel arise. Though there are many problems attaching to the question of unity, there is one in modern philosophy which we have already seen: the mind–body problem. We will recall that Descartes' reaction to skepticism involved an elaboration of a new philosophical method powerful enough to overcome the haunting lack of certitude that some attributed to the human mind. Methodic doubt led to the discovery of the *cogito* as the first truth in the Cartesian scheme, which, by a deductive process inspired by mathematics, led to the definition of man as spirit only. The body, never *essentially* united with the spirit, enjoyed its own separate existence as a substance, and thus the Cartesian picture of reality presented two substances, entirely separate from each other.

What Descartes accepted as certain became, in turn, a problem for succeeding philosophers who were unhappy with the tenuous relationship he delineated between mind and body. Leibniz, maintaining that his monads were separate substances, accounted for their unity by a marvelous harmony established by God among them and their mind and body components. Spinoza rejected any separability whatsoever, holding to a one-substance reality of which mind and body were attributes.

In a manner of speaking, Descartes, Leibniz and Spinoza faced the mind–body problem ontologically; that is, inasmuch as they were concerned with the knowability of extramental (objective) reality, the question of the unity of substance, vis-à-vis mind and body, was real (objective). Locke, Hume, and Kant, however, faced the same problem epistemologically; that is, inasmuch as they were concerned with *how* we know, the question of unity was more subjective (mental) than real (objective, extramental).

We have, then, in Descartes and Kant, two widely divergent reactions to skepticism, each of which, following its own inner logic, terminated in a sundered view of reality. Descartes' reaction led to a reality whose two component substances were divorced from each other, while Kant's led to a cleavage between sensibility and reason — a division no less significant than Descartes', but on the subject side.

A divided reality was a scandal to Hegel; his fundamental purpose, therefore, was to overcome division, separateness, opposition, and even contradiction by seeing reality *as a whole* and by following the implications of wholeness down to the smallest detail. The whole of reality, in its very totality, is called the *Absolute* by Hegel; other names are variously used depending on the context: *Idea, Nature, Spirit, Mind, God.* Inasmuch as movement, for Hegel, is constitutive of reality, the Absolute cannot be considered simply as being *there*, as though static and immobile, one of the difficulties with Spinoza's concept of the Absolute. No, the Absolute is being on the move, pushing forward, dynamic, with an activity reminiscent of the constant flux of Heraclitus. This dynamism is not the motion of blind, unconscious forces, for consciousness is the very life of the Absolute; yet the notion of consciousness, if modeled after Aristotle's designation of God as Self-thinking Thought, is not enough, for it remains entirely subjective. In order to account for objects in the world, the nature of Spirit has to account for both subject and object at the same time and in the same activity; the self-consciousness of Spirit looks both ways, to subjectivity and objectivity, and its *objectifying* is the *process* whereby Spirit becomes more fully itself while creating objects. To the notion of *Self*-thinking Thought, the notion of *externalizing* has to be added; the realm of objects is the emergence of appearances as the "making known" of the Mind, whence the phrase *phenomenology of Mind.*

For Hegel, the difficulty with Kant was the cul-de-sac in knowledge caused by so overloading the subject side of the subject–object relationship that there was no obvious vehicle for reaching the object. To overcome this problem, Hegel looked upon the process of objectification from the epistemological point of view, holding that the Spirit, conscious of the emergence of objects from itself, knows itself in an act of self-consciousness, so that the one activity, as previously indicated, accounts for both subject and object in the knowledge equation: in one activity Spirit knows subjectively what it produces objectively. Subject and object are two sides of the same coin, both essential to Spirit in the process of unfolding.

A further look at this process discloses the *necessary opposition*, or *contradiction*, from which the unfolding takes place; Being has to be itself, while opposed to itself; to be identical with itself, while different from itself; its "very self-identity is internal distinction." The Absolute's difference in its own identity, its *identity in difference*, is an affirmation of its being and not-being at the same time and is the reason why becoming is possible at all within the Absolute. The processive movement, a "self-producing course of activity, maintaining its advance by returning back into itself," is called the *dialectical movement*, or simply the *dialectic* (from the Greek, meaning back and forth, as in conversation).

Though the terminology of *thesis, antithesis*, and *synthesis* is not that of Hegel, it has often been used to explain the concept of dialectic, particularly as it has taken a permanent place in the Marxist tradition of modern philosophy. Hegel often speaks of things in threes, in triads, so that an interaction between the first two will produce the third. In the highest triad, the Absolute, as it is actually posited — that is, in its positive affirmation of being — is called *thesis*; its contradiction, the element of not-being, is called *antithesis*; the interaction between these two is the dialectical movement of becoming, the issue of which is called *synthesis*. Recalling that Idea is also a word used by Hegel for the totality, the process is often referred to as *dialectical idealism*, to be compared later with Marx's use of the dialectic, for which he employed the term *dialectical materialism*.

But expressions of the Spirit can vary insofar as they bear a remote or close similarity to it. The realm of nature, because it is matter, is of the first type; it is the realm of mechanics, physics, and organics, where particularity holds sway and a lack of freedom is the common denominator. Because matter stands in opposition to idea, deduction is impossible and things have to be known *empirically*, a grudging admission on Hegel's part that natural sciences have a legitimate role and their own method, for he had gone so far as to deny that Newton's physics was a *true* physics. Still, the world of matter somehow belongs to the life of the Spirit and shares the dialectical process, and it is interesting to see to what lengths Hegel is willing to go to make them fit. For example, an acid and a base are so called only in relation to each other, and the fact that they enter into a process whereby they neutralize each other "makes their existence lie in being cancelled and superseded, or makes it into a universal; and acid and base possess truth merely *qua* universal."

It is, however, in the realm of *ethical action* that the Spirit finds itself more sympathetically expressed and, following the rule of process, even this expression is subject to increasing levels of kinship with pure Spirit. The individual at first feeds his own individuality with every kind of self-satisfaction, without taking into account the universal aspect of his action. This aspect begins to assert itself among many individuals who, while trying to act together, still act as individuals — a kind of herd of animals. Stark individuality gradually gives way to the recognition that true individualism has meaning only in *social* life, and with this recognition individuals enter the sphere of spritual existence. The life of the Spirit in the socialized individual ranges in degree from the simplest society of the family to the complex society of state government.

With social life there immediately arises a course of action called *law*, which reason perceives as the fulcrum balancing individuality with universality so that one is not achieved without the other. The individual, thus seeing himself endowed with universality through the laws of the social order, sees himself as possessing a whole spectrum of rights that constitute him as a *person*. This progression is not any easy one, for the Spirit as individual in working its way to the Spirit as universal is conscious of this *estrangement* and must overcome the struggles imposed by various cultures and civilizations, even though the highest levels of finite life are found in society.

Human life, as finite Spirit, reaches its highest level in morality, for here, with Hegel following the lead of Kant, society mediates universal law for the individual, in virtue of which the moral will is the one that is conscious of, and does, its Duty; this is what constitutes freedom. Conscience, then, is the self-legislating individual will, conscious of the universality flowing into it from society; and this activity of the will is the supreme achievement of the finite Spirit.

But the finite Spirit is the Spirit conscious of itself in finite modes only, not yet having achieved the consciousness of itself as Infinite. This last consciousness requires two more stages. The first stage is Religion, conceived by Hegel as a kind of gathering up of all previous modes of the finite into a single totality and expressed in a variety of art forms and religious terms. In the final stage, however, all "forms" and "terms" and every other type of *representation* are put aside because they are finite, and the Spirit comes to know itself *through itself*, in the perfect act of what Hegel calls *Absolute Knowledge*.

Hegel's system of metaphysical idealism, in all its minute abstraction, stands as one of the greatest efforts philosophers have made to reach the interconnections of all reality and to grasp being, finite and infinite, as a seamless garment. The observation that there are today few formal Hegelians does not do justice to the towering influence Hegel once had. In Germany, Britain, Italy, and the United States in the nineteenth and early twentieth centuries, there were many philosophers who considered themselves followers and interpreters of the master. And in nonphilosophical fields there is no way of measuring the influence of the man who offered a fresh scheme to theologians for the reinterpretation of Christianity, a primer of subjective analysis for phenomenologists, a basic terminology for psychologists, and a dialectical framework for Marxian philosophy, to say nothing of his influence on the study of history, sociology, and law.

Readings

The Absolute as Process of Self-Becoming (from *Phenomenology of Spirit, Preface*)

17. In my view, which can be justified only by the exposition of the system itself, everything turns on grasping and expressing the True,

not only as *Substance*, but equally as *Subject*. At the same time, it is to be observed that substantiality embraces the universal, or the *immediacy of knowledge* itself, as well as that which is *being* or immediacy *for* knowledge. If the conception of God as the one Substance shocked the age in which it was proclaimed, the reason for this was on the one hand an instinctive awareness that, in this definition, self-consciousness was only submerged and not preserved. On the other hand, the opposite view, which clings to thought as thought, to *universality* as such, is the very same simplicity, is undifferentiated, unmoved substantiality. And if, thirdly, thought does unite itself with the being of Substance, and apprehends immediacy or intuition as thinking, the question is still whether this intellectual intuition does not again fall back into inert simplicity, and does not depict actuality itself in a non-actual manner.

18. Further, the living Substance is being which is in truth *Subject*, or, what is the same, is in truth actual only in so far as it is the movement of positing itself, or is the mediation of its self-othering with itself. This Substance is, as Subject, pure, *simple negativity*, and is for this very reason the bifurcation of the simple; it is the doubling which sets up opposition, and then again the negation of this indifferent diversity and of its antithesis [the immediate simplicity]. Only this self-*restoring* sameness, or this reflection in otherness within itself— not an *original* or *immediate* unity as such—is the True. It is the process of its own becoming, the circle that presupposes its end as its goal, having its end also as its beginning; and only by being worked out to its end, is it actual.

19. Thus the life of God and divine cognition may well be spoken of as a disporting of Love with itself; but this idea sinks into mere edification, and even insipidity, if it lacks the seriousness, the suffering, the patience, and the labour of the negative. *In itself*, that life is indeed one of untroubled equality and unity with itself, for which otherness and alienation, and the overcoming of alienation, are not serious matters. But this *in-itself* is abstract universality, in which the nature of the divine life *to be for itself*, and so too the self-movement of the form, are altogether left out of account. If the form is declared to be the same as the essence, then it is *ipso facto* a mistake to suppose that cognition can be satisfied with the in-itself or the essence, but can get along without the form—that the absolute principle or absolute intuition makes the working-out of the former, or the development of the latter, superfluous. Just because the form is as essential to the essence as the essence is to itself, the divine essence is not to be conceived and expressed merely as essence, i.e. as immediate substance or pure self-contemplation of the divine, but likewise as *form*, and in the whole wealth of the developed form. Only then is it conceived and expressed as an actuality.

20. The True is the whole. But the whole is nothing other than the essence consummating itself through its development. Of the Absolute it must be said that it is essentially a *result*, that only in the *end* is it what it truly is; and that precisely in this consists its nature, viz. to be actual, subject, the spontaneous becoming of itself. Though it may seem contradictory that the Absolute should be conceived essentially as a result, it needs little pondering to set this show of contradiction in its true light. The beginning, the principle, or the Absolute, as at first immediately enunciated, is only the universal. Just as when I say '*all* animals', this expression cannot pass for a zoology, so it is equally plain that the words, 'the Divine', 'the Absolute', 'the Eternal', etc., do not express what is contained in them; and only such words, in fact, do express the intuition as something immediate. Whatever is more than such a word, even the transition to a mere proposition, contains a *becoming-other* that has to be taken back, or is a mediation. But it is just this that is rejected with horror, as if absolute cognition were being surrendered when more is made of mediation than in simply saying that it is nothing absolute, and is completely absent in the Absolute.

21. But this abhorrence in fact stems from ignorance of the nature of mediation, and of absolute cognition itself. For mediation is nothing beyond self-moving selfsameness, or is reflection into self, the moment of the 'I' which is for itself pure negativity or, when reduced to its pure abstraction, *simple becoming*. The 'I', or becoming in general, this mediation, on account of its simple nature, is just immediacy in the process of becoming, and is the immediate itself. Reason is, therefore, misunderstood when reflection is excluded from the True, and is not grasped as a positive moment of the Absolute. It is reflection that makes the True a result, but it is equally reflection that overcomes the antithesis between the process of its becoming and the result, for this becoming is also simple, and therefore not different from the form of the True which shows itself as *simple* in its result; the process of becoming is rather just this return into simplicity. Though the embryo is indeed *in itself* a human being, it is not so *for itself*; this it only is as cultivated Reason, which has *made* itself into what it is *in itself*. And that is when it for the first time is actual. But this result is itself a simple immediacy, for it is self-conscious freedom at peace with itself, which has not set the antithesis on one side and left it lying there, but has been reconciled with it.

22. What has just been said can also be expressed by saying that Reason is *purposive activity*. The exaltation of a supposed Nature over a misconceived thinking, and especially the rejection of external teleology, has brought the form of purpose in general into discredit. Still, in the sense in which Aristotle, too, defines Nature as purposive activity, purpose is what is immediate and *at rest*, the unmoved which is also

self-moving, and as such is Subject. Its power to move, taken abstractly, is *being-for-self* or pure negativity. The result is the same as the beginning, only because the *beginning* is the *purpose*; in other words, the actual is the same as its Notion only because the immediate, as purpose, contains the self or pure actuality within itself. The realized purpose, or the existent actuality, is movement and unfolded becoming; but it is just this unrest that is the self; and the self is like that immediacy and simplicity of the beginning because it is the result, that which has returned into itself, the latter being similarly just the self. And the self is the sameness and simplicity that relates itself to itself.

23. The need to represent the Absolute as *Subject* has found expression in the propositions: *God* is the eternal, the moral world-order, love, and so on. In such propositions the True is only posited *immediately* as Subject, but is not presented as the movement of reflecting itself into itself. In a proposition of this kind one begins with the word 'God'. This by itself is a meaningless sound, a mere name; it is only the predicate that says *what God is*, gives Him content and meaning. Only in the end of the proposition does the empty beginning become actual knowledge. This being so, it is not clear why one does not speak merely of the eternal, of the moral world-order, and so on, or, as the ancients did, of pure notions like 'being', 'the One', and so on, in short, of that which gives the meaning without adding the *meaningless* sound as well. But it is just this word that indicates that what is posited is not a being [i.e. something that merely is], or essence, or a universal in general, but rather something that is reflected into itself, a Subject. But at the same time this is only anticipated. The Subject is assumed as a fixed point to which, as their support, the predicates are affixed by a movement belonging to the knower of this Subject, and which is not regarded as belonging to the fixed point itself; yet it is only through this movement that the content could be represented as Subject. The way in which this movement has been brought about is such that it cannot belong to the fixed point; yet, after this point has been presupposed, the nature of the movement cannot really be other than what it is, it can only be external. Hence, the mere anticipation that the Absolute is Subject is not only *not* the actuality of this Notion, but it even makes the actuality impossible; for the anticipation posits the subject as an inert point, whereas the actuality is self-movement.

24. Among the various consequences that follow from what has just been said, this one in particular can be stressed, that knowledge is only actual, and can only be expounded, as Science or as *system*; and furthermore, that a so-called basic proposition or principle of philosophy, if true, is also false, just because it is *only* a principle. It is, therefore, easy to refute it. The refutation consists in pointing out its defect; and

it is defective because it is only the universal or principle, is only the beginning. If the refutation is thorough, it is derived and developed from the principle itself, not accomplished by counter-assertions and random thoughts from outside. The refutation would, therefore, properly consist in the further development of the principle, and in thus remedying the defectiveness, if it did not mistakenly pay attention solely to its *negative* action, without awareness of its progress and result on their *positive* side too—The genuinely *positive* exposition of the beginning is thus also, conversely, just as much a negative attitude towards it, viz. towards its initially one-sided form of being *immediate* or *purpose*. It can therefore be taken equally well as a refutation of the principle that constitutes the *basis* of the system, but it is more correct to regard it as a demonstration that the *basis* or principle of the system is, in fact, only its *beginning*.

25. That the True is actual only as system, or that Substance is essentially Subject, is expressed in the representation of the Absolute as *Spirit*—the most sublime Notion and the one which belongs to the modern age and its religion. The spiritual alone is the *actual*; it is essence, or that which has *being in itself*; it is that which *relates itself to itself* and is *determinate*, it is *other-being* and *being-for-self*, and in this determinateness, or in its self-externality, abides within itself; in other words, it is *in and for itself.*—But this being-in-and-for-itself is at first only for us, or *in itself*, it is spiritual *Substance*. It must also be this *for itself*, it must be the knowledge of the spiritual, and the knowledge of itself as Spirit, i.e. it must be an *object* to itself, but just as immediately a sublated object, reflected into itself. It is *for itself* only for *us*, in so far as its spiritual content is generated by itself. But in so far as it is also for itself for its own self, this self-generation, the pure Notion, is for it the objective element in which it has its existence, and it is in this way, in its existence for itself, an object reflected into itself. The Spirit that, so developed, knows itself as Spirit, is *Science*; Science is its actuality and the realm which it builds for itself in its own element.

The Introduction to Phenomenology of Spirit: Consciousness and the Dialectical Process

73. It is a natural assumption that in philosophy, before we start to deal with its proper subject-matter, viz. the actual cognition of what truly is, one must first of all come to an understanding about cognition, which is regarded either as the instrument to get hold of the Absolute, or as the medium through which one discovers it. A certain uneasiness seems justified, partly because there are different types of cognition, and one of them might be more appropriate than another for the at-

tainment of this goal, so that we could make a bad choice of means; and partly because cognition is a faculty of a definite kind and scope, and thus, without a more precise definition of its nature and limits, we might grasp clouds of error instead of the heaven of truth. This feeling of uneasiness is surely bound to be transformed into the conviction that the whole project of securing for consciousness through cognition what exists in itself is absurd, and that there is a boundary between cognition and the Absolute that completely separates them. For, if cognition is the instrument for getting hold of absolute being, it is obvious that the use of an instrument on a thing certainly does not let it be what it is for itself, but rather sets out to reshape and alter it. If, on the other hand, cognition is not an instrument of our activity but a more or less passive medium through which the light of truth reaches us, then again we do not receive the truth as it is in itself, but only as it exists through and in this medium. Either way we employ a means which immediately brings about the opposite of its own end; or rather, what is really absurd is that we should make use of a means at all.

It would seem, to be sure, that this evil could be remedied through an acquaintance with the way in which the *instrument* works; for this would enable us to eliminate from the representation of the Absolute which we have gained through it whatever is due to the instrument, and thus get the truth in its purity. But this 'improvement' would in fact only bring us back to where we were before. If we remove from a reshaped thing what the instrument has done to it, then the thing—here the Absolute—becomes for us exactly what it was before this [accordingly] superfluous effort. On the other hand, if the Absolute is supposed merely to be brought nearer to us through this instrument, without anything in it being altered, like a bird caught by a lime-twig, it would surely laugh our little ruse to scorn, if it were not with us, in and for itself, all along, and of its own volition. For a ruse is just what cognition would be in such a case, since it would, with its manifold exertions, be giving itself the air of doing something quite different from creating a merely immediate and therefore effortless relationship. Or, if by testing cognition, which we conceive of as a *medium*, we get to know the law of its refraction, it is again useless to subtract this from the end result. For it is not the refraction of the ray, but the ray itself whereby truth reaches us, that is cognition; and if this were removed, all that would be indicated would be a pure direction or a blank space.

74. Meanwhile, if the fear of falling into error sets up a mistrust of Science, which in the absence of such scruples gets on with the work itself, and actually cognizes something, it is hard to see why we should not turn round and mistrust this very mistrust. Should we not be concerned as to whether this fear of error is not just the error itself? Indeed, this fear takes something—a great deal in fact—for granted as

truth, supporting its scruples and inferences on what is itself in need of prior scrutiny to see if it is true. To be specific, it takes for granted certain ideas about cognition as an *instrument* and as a *medium*, and assumes that there is a *difference between ourselves and this cognition.* Above all, it presupposes that the Absolute stands on one side and cognition on the other, independent and separated from it, and yet is something real; or in other words, it presupposes that cognition which, since it is excluded from the Absolute, is surely outside of the truth as well, is nevertheless true, an assumption whereby what calls itself fear of error reveals itself rather as fear of the truth.

75. This conclusion stems from the fact that the Absolute alone is true, or the truth alone is absolute. One may set this aside on the grounds that there is a type of cognition which, though it does not cognize the Absolute as Science aims to, is still true, and that cognition in general, though it be incapable of grasping the Absolute, is still capable of grasping other kinds of truth. But we gradually come to see that this kind of talk which goes back and forth only leads to a hazy distinction between an absolute truth and some other kind of truth, and that words like 'absolute', 'cognition', etc. presuppose a meaning which has yet to be ascertained.

76. Instead of troubling ourselves with such useless ideas and locutions about cognition as 'an instrument for getting hold of the Absolute', or as 'a medium through which we view the truth' (relationships which surely, in the end, are what all these ideas of a cognition cut off from the Absolute, and an Absolute separated from cognition, amount to); instead of putting up with excuses which create the incapacity of Science by assuming relationships of this kind in order to be exempt from the hard work of Science, while at the same time giving the impression of working seriously and zealously; instead of bothering to refute all these ideas, we could reject them out of hand as adventitious and arbitrary, and the words associated with them like 'absolute', 'cognition', 'objective' and 'subjective', and countless others whose meaning is assumed to be generally familiar, could even be regarded as so much deception. For to give the impression that their meaning is generally well known, or that their Notion is comprehended, looks more like an attempt to avoid the main problem, which is precisely to provide this Notion. We could, with better justification, simply spare ourselves the trouble of paying any attention whatever to such ideas and locutions; for they are intended to ward off Science itself, and constitute merely an empty appearance of knowing, which vanishes immediately as soon as Science comes on the scene. But Science, just because it comes on the scene, is itself an appearance: in coming on the scene it is not yet Science in its developed and unfolded truth. In this connection it makes no difference whether we think of Science as the appearance be-

cause it comes on the scene alongside another mode of knowledge, or whether we call that other untrue knowledge its manifestation. In any case Science must liberate itself from this semblance, and it can do so only by turning against it. For, when confronted with a knowledge that is without truth, Science can neither merely reject it as an ordinary way of looking at things, while assuring us that its Science is a quite different sort of cognition for which that ordinary knowledge is of no account whatever; nor can it appeal to the vulgar view for the intimations it gives us of something better to come. By the former *assurance*, Science would be declaring its power to lie simply in its *being*; but the untrue knowledge likewise appeals to the fact that *it is*, and *assures* us that for it Science is of no account. *One* bare assurance is worth just as much as another. Still less can Science appeal to whatever intimations of something better it may detect in the cognition that is without truth, to the signs which point in the direction of Science. For one thing, it would only be appealing again to what merely *is*; and for another, it would only be appealing to itself, and to itself in the mode in which it exists in the cognition that is without truth. In other words, it would be appealing to an inferior form of its being, to the way it appears, rather than to what it is in and for itself. It is for this reason that an exposition of how knowledge makes its appearance will here be undertaken.

77. Now, because it has only phenomenal knowledge for its object, this exposition seems not to be Science, free and self-moving in its own peculiar shape; yet from this standpoint it can be regarded as the path of the natural consciousness which presses forward to true knowledge; or as the way of the Soul which journeys through the series of its own configurations as though they were the stations appointed for it by its own nature, so that it may purify itself for the life of the Spirit, and achieve finally, through a completed experience of itself, the awareness of what it really is in itself.

78. Natural consciousness will show itself to be only the Notion of knowledge, or in other words, not to be real knowledge. But since it directly takes itself to be real knowledge, this path has a negative significance for it, and what is in fact the realization of the Notion, counts for it rather as the loss of its own self; for it does lose its truth on this path. The road can therefore be regarded as the pathway of *doubt*, or more precisely as the way of despair. For what happens on it is not what is ordinarily understood when the word 'doubt' is used: shilly-shallying about this or that presumed truth, followed by a return to that truth again, after the doubt has been appropriately dispelled—so that at the end of the process the matter is taken to be what it was in the first place. On the contrary, this path is the conscious insight into the untruth of phenomenal knowledge, for which the supreme reality

is what is in truth only the unrealized Notion. Therefore this thorough-going scepticism is also not the scepticism with which an earnest zeal for truth and Science fancies it has prepared and equipped itself in their service: the *resolve*, in Science, not to give oneself over to the thoughts of others, upon mere authority, but to examine everything for oneself and follow only one's own conviction, or better still, to produce everything oneself, and accept only one's own deed as what is true.

The series of configurations which consciousness goes through along this road is, in reality, the detailed history of the *education* of con-sciousness itself to the standpoint of Science. That zealous resolve rep-resents this education simplistically as something directly over and done with in the making of the resolution; but the way of the Soul is the actual fulfilment of the resolution, in contrast to the untruth of that view. Now, following one's own conviction is, of course, more than giving oneself over to authority; but changing an opinion accepted on authority into an opinion held out of personal conviction, does not nec-essarily alter the content of the opinion, or replace error with truth. The only difference between being caught up in a system of opinions and prejudices based on personal conviction, and being caught up in one based on the authority of others, lies in the added conceit that is innate in the latter position. The scepticism that is directed against the whole range of phenomenal consciousness, on the other hand, renders the Spirit for the first time competent to examine what truth is. For it brings about a state of despair about all the so-called natural ideas, thoughts, and opinions, regardless of whether they are called one's own or someone else's, ideas with which the consciousness that sets about the examination [of truth] *straight away* is still filled and hampered, so that it is, in fact, incapable of carrying out what it wants to under-take.

79. The necessary progression and interconnection of the forms of the unreal consciousness will by itself bring to pass the *completion* of the series. To make this more intelligible, it may be remarked, in a pre-liminary and general way, that the exposition of the untrue conscious-ness in its untruth is not a merely negative procedure. The natural consciousness itself normally takes this one-sided view of it; and a knowledge which makes this one-sidedness its very essence is itself one of the patterns of incomplete consciousness which occurs on the road itself, and will manifest itself in due course. This is just the scepticism which only ever sees pure nothingness in its result and abstracts from the fact that this nothingness is specifically the nothingness of that *from which it results*. For it is only when it is taken as the result of that from which it emerges, that it is, in fact, the true result; in that case it is itself a *determinate* nothingness, one which has a *content*. The scepticism that ends up with the bare abstraction of nothingness

or emptiness cannot get any further from there, but must wait to see whether something new comes along and what it is, in order to throw it too into the same empty abyss. But when, on the other hand, the result is conceived as it is in truth, namely, as a *determinate* negation, a new form has thereby immediately arisen, and in the negation the transition is made through which the progress through the complete series of forms comes about of itself.

80. But the *goal* is as necessarily fixed for knowledge as the serial progression; it is the point where knowledge no longer needs to go beyond itself, where knowledge finds itself, where Notion corresponds to object and object to Notion. Hence the progress towards this goal is also unhalting, and short of it no satisfaction is to be found at any of the stations on the way. Whatever is confined within the limits of a natural life cannot by its own efforts go beyond its immediate existence; but it is driven beyond it by something else, and this uprooting entails its death. Consciousness, however, is explicitly the *Notion* of itself. Hence it is something that goes beyond limits, and since these limits are its own, it is something that goes beyond itself. With the positing of a single particular the beyond is also established for consciousness, even if it is only *alongside* the limited object as in the case of spatial intuition. Thus consciousness suffers this violence at its own hands: it spoils its own limited satisfaction. When consciousness feels this violence, its anxiety may well make it retreat from the truth, and strive to hold on to what it is in danger of losing. But it can find no peace. If it wishes to remain in a state of unthinking inertia, then thought troubles its thoughtlessness, and its own unrest disturbs its inertia. Or, if it entrenches itself in sentimentality, which assures us that it finds everything to be *good in its kind*, then this assurance likewise suffers violence at the hands of Reason, for, precisely in so far as something is merely a kind, Reason finds it *not* to be good. Or, again, its fear of the truth may lead consciousness to hide, from itself and others, behind the pretension that its burning zeal for truth makes it difficult or even impossible to find any other truth but the unique truth of vanity—that of being at any rate cleverer than any thoughts that one gets by oneself or from others. This conceit which understands how to belittle every truth, in order to turn back into itself and gloat over its own understanding, which knows how to dissolve every thought and always find the same barren Ego instead of any content—this is a satisfaction which we must leave to itself, for it flees from the universal, and seeks only to be for itself.

81. In addition to these preliminary general remarks about the manner and the necessity of the progression, it may be useful to say something about the *method of carrying out the inquiry*. If this exposition is viewed as a way of *relating Science* to *phenomenal* knowledge, and

as an investigation and *examination of the reality of cognition*, it would seem that it cannot take place without some presupposition which can serve as its underlying *criterion*. For an examination consists in applying an accepted standard, and in determining whether something is right or wrong on the basis of the resulting agreement or disagreement of the thing examined; thus the standard as such (and Science likewise if it were the criterion) is accepted as the *essence* or as the *in-itself*. But here, where Science has just begun to come on the scene, neither Science nor anything else has yet justified itself as the essence or the in-itself; and without something of the sort it seems that no examination can take place.

82. This contradiction and its removal will become more definite if we call to mind the abstract determinations of truth and knowledge as they occur in consciousness. Consciousness simultaneously *distinguishes* itself from something, and at the same time *relates* itself to it, or, as it is said, this something exists *for* consciousness; and the determinate aspect of this *relating*, or of the *being* of something for a consciousness, is *knowing*. But we distinguish this being-for-another from *being-in-itself*; whatever is related to knowledge or knowing is also distinguished from it, and posited as existing outside of this relationship; this *being-in-itself* is called *truth*. Just what might be involved in these determinations is of no further concern to us here. Since our object is phenomenal knowledge, its determinations too will at first be taken directly as they present themselves; and they do present themselves very much as we have already apprehended them.

83. Now, if we inquire into the truth of knowledge, it seems that we are asking what knowledge is *in itself*. Yet in this inquiry knowledge is *our* object, something that exists *for us*; and the *in-itself* that would supposedly result from it would rather be the being of knowledge *for us*. What we asserted to be its essence would be not so much its truth but rather just our knowledge of it. The essence or criterion would lie within ourselves, and that which was to be compared with it and about which a decision would be reached through this comparison would not necessarily have to recognize the validity of such a standard.

84. But the dissociation, or this semblance of dissociation and presupposition, is overcome by the nature of the object we are investigating. Consciousness provides its own criterion from within itself, so that the investigation becomes a comparison of consciousness with itself; for the distinction made above falls within it. In consciousness one thing exists *for* another, i.e. consciousness regularly contains the determinateness of the moment of knowledge; at the same time, this other is to consciousness not merely *for it*, but is also outside of this relationship, or exists *in itself*: the moment of truth. Thus in what consciousness affirms from within itself as *being-in-itself* or the *True* we have

the standard which consciousness itself sets up by which to measure what it knows. If we designate *knowledge* as the Notion, but the essence or the *True* as what exists, or the *object,* then the examination consists in seeing whether the Notion corresponds to the object. But if we call the *essence* or in-itself of the *object* the *Notion,* and on the other hand understand by the *object* the Notion itself as *object*, viz. as it exists *for an other,* then the examination consists in seeing whether the object corresponds to its Notion. It is evident, of course, that the two procedures are the same. But the essential point to bear in mind throughout the whole investigation is that these two moments, 'Notion' and 'object', 'being-for-another' and 'being-in-itself', both fall *within* that knowledge which we are investigating. Consequently, we do not need to import criteria, or to make use of our own bright ideas and thoughts during the course of the inquiry; it is precisely when we leave these aside that we succeed in contemplating the matter in hand as it is *in and for itself.*

85. But not only is a contribution by us superfluous, since Notion and object, the criterion and what is to be tested, are present in consciousness itself, but we are also spared the trouble of comparing the two and really *testing* them, so that, since what consciousness examines is its own self, all that is left for us to do is simply to look on. For consciousness is, on the one hand, consciousness of the object, and on the other, consciousness of itself; consciousness of what for it is the True, and consciousness of its knowledge of the truth. Since both are *for* the same consciousness, this consciousness is itself their comparison; it is for this same consciousness to know whether its knowledge of the object corresponds to the object or not. The object, it is true, seems only to be for consciousness in the way that consciousness knows it; it seems that consciousness cannot, as it were, get behind the object as it exists for consciousness so as to examine what the object is *in itself*, and hence, too, cannot test its own knowledge by that standard. But the distinction between the in-itself and knowledge is already present in the very fact that consciousness knows an object at all. Something is *for it* the *in-itself*; and knowledge, or the being of the object for consciousness, is, *for it,* another moment. Upon this distinction, which is present as a fact, the examination rests. If the comparison shows that these two moments do not correspond to one another, it would seem that consciousness must alter its knowledge to make it conform to the object. But, in fact, in the alteration of the knowledge, the object itself alters for it too, for the knowledge that was present was essentially a knowledge of the object: as the knowledge changes, so too does the object, for it essentially belonged to this knowledge. Hence it comes to pass for consciousness that what it previously took to be the *in-itself* is not an *in-itself*, or that it was only an in-itself *for consciousness.*

Since consciousness thus finds that its knowledge does not correspond to its object, the object itself does not stand the test; in other words, the criterion for testing is altered when that for which it was to have been the criterion fails to pass the test; and the testing is not only a testing of what we know, but also a testing of the criterion of what knowing is.

86. *Inasmuch as the new true object issues from it*, this *dialectical* movement which consciousness exercises on itself and which affects both its knowledge and its object, is precisely what is called *experience* [*Erfahrung*]. In this connection there is a moment in the process just mentioned which must be brought out more clearly, for through it a new light will be thrown on the exposition which follows. Consciousness knows *something*; this object is the essence or the *in-itself*; but it is also for consciousness the in-itself. This is where the ambiguity of this truth enters. We see that consciousness now has two objects: one is the first *in-itself*, the second is the *being-for-consciousness of this in-itself*. The latter appears at first sight to be merely the reflection of consciousness into itself, i.e. what consciousness has in mind is not an object, but only its knowledge of that first object. But, as was shown previously, the first object, in being known, is altered for consciousness; it ceases to be the in-itself, and becomes something that is the *in-itself* only *for consciousness*. And this then is the True: the being-for-consciousness of this in-itself. Or, in other words, this is the *essence*, or the *object* of consciousness. This new object contains the nothingness of the first, it is what experience has made of it.

87. This exposition of the course of experience contains a moment in virtue of which it does not seem to agree with what is ordinarily understood by experience. This is the moment of transition from the first object and the knowledge of it, to the other object, which experience is said to be about. Our account implied that our knowledge of the first object, or the being-*for*-consciousness of the first in-itself, itself becomes the second object. It usually seems to be the case, on the contrary, that our experience of the untruth of our first notion comes by way of a second object which we come upon by chance and externally, so that our part in all this is simply the pure *apprehension* of what is in and for itself. From the present viewpoint, however, the new object shows itself to have come about through a *reversal of consciousness itself*. This way of looking at the matter is something contributed by *us*, by means of which the succession of experiences through which consciousness passes is raised into a scientific progression—but it is not known to the consciousness that we are observing. But, as a matter of fact, we have here the same situation as the one discussed in regard to the relation between our exposition and scepticism, viz. that in every case the result of an untrue mode of knowledge must not be allowed

to run away into an empty nothing, but must necessarily be grasped as the nothing *of that from which it results*—a result which contains what was true in the preceding knowledge. It shows up here like this: since what first appeared as the object sinks for consciousness to the level of its way of knowing it, and since the in-itself becomes a *being-for-consciousness* of the in-itself, the latter is now the new object. Herewith a new pattern of consciousness comes on the scene as well, for which the essence is something different from what it was at the preceding stage. It is this fact that guides the entire series of the patterns of consciousness in their necessary sequence. But it is just this necessity itself, or the *origination* of the new object, that presents itself to consciousness without its understanding how this happens, which proceeds for us, as it were, behind the back of consciousness. Thus in the movement of consciousness there occurs a moment of *being-in-itself* or *being-for-us* which is not present to the consciousness comprehended in the experience itself. The *content*, however, of what presents itself to us does exist *for it*; we comprehend only the formal aspect of that content, or its pure origination. *For it,* what has thus arisen exists only as an object; *for us,* it appears at the same time as movement and a process of becoming.

88. Because of this necessity, the way to Science is itself already *Science,* and hence, in virtue of its content, is the Science of the *experience of consciousness.*

89. The experience of itself which consciousness goes through can, in accordance with its Notion, comprehend nothing less than the entire system of consciousness, or the entire realm of the truth of Spirit. For this reason, the moments of this truth are exhibited in their own proper determinateness, viz. as being not abstract moments, but as they are for consciousness, or as consciousness itself stands forth in its relation to them. Thus the moments of the whole are *patterns of consciousness.* In pressing forward to its true existence, consciousness will arrive at a point at which it gets rid of its semblance of being burdened with something alien, with what is only for it, and some sort of 'other', at a point where appearance becomes identical with essence, so that its exposition will coincide at just this point with the authentic Science of Spirit. And finally, when consciousness itself grasps this its own essence, it will signify the nature of absolute knowledge itself.

Time and the Self-Realization of Spirit (From Phenomenology of Spirit)

801. Now, in actuality, the substance that knows exists earlier than its form or its Notion-determined 'shape'. For substance is the as yet undeveloped *in-itself,* or the Ground and Notion in its still unmoved

simplicity, and therefore the *inwardness* or the Self of the Spirit that does not yet *exist*. What *is there*, exists as the still undeveloped simple and immediate, or as the object of the *picture-thinking* consciousness in general. Cognition, because it is the spiritual consciousness for which what *is in itself* only *is,* in so far as it is a *being for* the Self and a being of the *Self* or Notion, has for this reason at first only a meagre object, in contrast with which substance and the consciousness of this substance are richer. The disclosure or revelation which substance has in this consciousness is in fact concealment, for substance is still *self-less being* and what is disclosed to it is only the certainty of itself. At first, therefore, only the *abstract moments* of substance belong to *self*-consciousness; but since these, as pure movements, spontaneously impel themselves onward, self-consciousness enriches itself till it has wrested from consciousness the entire substance and has absorbed into itself the entire structure of the essentialities of substance. And, since this negative attitude to objectivity is just as much positive, it is a positing, it has produced them out of itself, and in so doing has at the same time restored them for consciousness. In the Notion that knows itself as Notion, the *moments* thus appear earlier than the *filled* [or *fulfilled*] whole whose coming-to-be is the movements of those moments. In *consciousness*, on the other hand, the whole, though uncomprehended, is prior to the moments. Time is the Notion itself that *is there* and which presents itself to consciousness as empty intuition; for this reason, Spirit necessarily appears in Time, and it appears in Time just so long as it has not *grasped* its pure Notion, i.e. has not annulled Time. It is the *outer,* intuited pure Self which is *not grasped* by the Self, the merely intuited Notion; when this latter grasps itself it sets aside its Time-form, comprehends this intuiting, and is a comprehended and comprehending intuiting. Time, therefore, appears as the destiny and necessity of Spirit that is not yet complete within itself, the necessity to enrich the share which self-consciousness has in consciousness, to set in motion the *immediacy of the in-itself,* which is the form in which substance is present in consciousness; or conversely, to realize and reveal what is at first only *inward* (the in-itself being taken as what is *inward),* i.e. to vindicate it for Spirit's certainty of itself.

802. For this reason it must be said that nothing is *known* that is not in *experience,* or, as it is also expressed, that is not *felt to be true,* not given as an *inwardly revealed* eternal verity, assomething sacred that is *believed,* or whatever other expressions have been used. For experience is just this, that the content—which is Spirit—is *in itself* substance, and therefore an *object* of *consciousness.* But this substance which is Spirit is the process inwhich Spirit *becomes* what it is *in itself;* and it is only asthis process of reflecting itself into itself that it is in itself truly *Spirit.* It is in itself the movement which is cogni

tion—the transform ing of that in-itself into that which is *for itself,* of Substance into Subject, of the object of *consciousness* into an object of *self-consciousness,* i.e. into an object that is just as much superseded, or into the *Notion.* The movement is the circle that returns into itself, the circle that presupposes its beginning and reaches it only at the end. Hence, so far as Spirit is necessarily this immanent differentiation, its intuited whole appears over against its simple self-consciousness, and since, then, the former is what is differentiated, it is differentiated into its intuited pure Notion, into *Time* and into the content or into the *in-itself.* Substance is charged, as Subject, with the *at first only inward* necessity of setting forth within itself what it is *in itself,* of exhibiting itself *as Spirit.* Only when the objective presentation is complete is it at the same time the reflection of substance or the process in which substance becomes Self. Consequently, until Spirit has completed itself *in itself,* until it has completed itself as world-spirit, it cannot reach its consummation as *self-conscious* Spirit. Therefore, the content of religion proclaims earlier in time than does Science, what *Spirit is,* but only Science is its true knowledge of itself.

(From Hegel, *Phenomenology of Spirit.* Trans. A. V. Millers Oxford: Clarendon Press, 1977. Reprinted by permission of Oxford University Press.)

Review Questions

1. Explain how Hegel attempts to overcome all separation and division in reality.
2. Compare Hegel's view of reality-as-a-whole with that of Spinoza.
3. How does Hegel tackle the problem of Spirit as absolute being, yet becoming at the same time?
4. Explain what Hegel means by the dialectical movement.
5. How does the individual maintain his individuality in Hegel's view of reality-as-one-Substance?

CHAPTER 19

John Stuart Mill (1806–1873)

Introduction

In his timely, sensitive, and clear-headed analyses of moral and political life, John Stuart Mill bridges the contemporary and classical
modern periods. He can be seen as a contemporary philosopher inasmuch as he championed personal value in his advocacy of individuality, sought for some way to ground humanity in view of a declining
Christianity, and tried to improve the conditions of the working class
of England. But perhaps he can be seen more clearly as working in the
empirical tradition of Locke, Berkeley, and Hume: his view of man was
sympathetic to that tradition; he elaborated its moral implications
anew as utilitarianism; and his thoughts on government reach back to
Locke.

He was born in London in 1806, the oldest child of James and Harriet Mill. His father was a Scotsman who, in pursuing an intellectual career in London, became a respected author and a devoted follower of
the utilitarian philosopher Jeremy Bentham. In the opening pages of
his *Autobiography*, the younger Mill describes how his father became
the principal shaper of his early life by putting him through one of the
most exacting programs of home education ever recorded. As a child he
learned Greek at age three and read Greek authors in their own language before he was seven (Plato at age eight); he did arithmetic as
well and commenced the study of Latin. He read extensively, and each
morning he had to give an account to his father of his previous day's
reading. Such an intense intellectual regime, coupled with his father's
inability to show any "signs of feeling," took its toll on the child's development, for the normal playfulness, feelings, and friendships of
childhood were not his: "I never was a boy," he wrote. His education
was completely areligious, which was surprising only in that his father,
who embraced a humanistic religion, had once studied for the ministry.
On the eve of his son's visit to France at age thirteen, James Mill
thought it wise to advise his intellectually superior offspring that he

was not like other young men of his own age. From the beginning, John Stuart Mill was destined for a life of the mind.

Though Mill was well schooled in Bentham's philosophy, it was only after reading a treatise on his teaching by a Swiss disciple that the full force of the "greatest happiness" doctrine struck him. In "one of the turning points in [his] mental history," he saw the futility of past speculation on morality, and in its place he "had a grand conception" laid before him "of changes to be effected in the condition of mankind through that doctrine." In the next few years this ardent apostle began writing on his own, contributing, as a reformer and radical, articles to the newly founded *Westminster Review*.

Mill was never an academician, but did his studying and writing in conjunction with his work as a civil servant in the East India Company. Though the job itself was not demanding, young Mill's self-imposed regimen was a heavy one and led to a mental overload that ended in a breakdown and a depression lasting for several months. He had thought that, with a Benthamite outlook, he had a satisfying object in life, and his conception of his own happiness "was entirely identified with this object." The depression did not abate until he was able to allow sentiments earlier denied him grow into a larger and warmer sense of humanity than he had previously possessed; this was occasioned by the reading of Wordsworth's poetry. He did not cease believing in Benthamism, whose principles he clung to permanently, but he was now able to see them less formalistically and more humanly, and to realize that there were more levels of happiness than Bentham was ready to admit; this vision henceforth supported him. The vision was given an additional and unexpected personal dimension when he formed a lasting friendship with Harriet Taylor, who became his wife when her husband died. Her inspiration was such, according to Mill's account, that she must be credited as co-author of several of his most important works. During those years he completed *A System of Logic* (1843), *The Principles of Political Economy* (1848), and *On Liberty* (1859). A few years after his wife's death, he published *Considerations on Representative Government* (1861), and edited some earlier essays under the title of *Utilitarianism* (1863).

Surprised by an invitation to run for Parliament, and after weighing the pros and cons of the active political life versus the theoretical, Mill agreed to run and was elected in 1865. During his few years as a member of Parliament, he fought for the exploited Negroes in Jamaica, for reform to enfranchise the working class in England, and for the redistribution of land in Ireland. His last original work was *An Examination of Sir William Hamilton's Philosophy* (1865). His *Autobiography* and *Three Essays on Religion* were published posthumously. At his death in 1873, looking back on a life devoted to the cause of human happiness and the alleviation of human misery, he said to his step-daughter, "You know that I have done my work."

We have already seen what constituted Mill's work, for, from his early years on, he addressed himself to the "condition of mankind" by applying the principles of utilitarianism. For the maturing Mill, however, Bentham's utilitarian formulation became far too narrow, although it was never as ludicrously gross as its opponents often made it out to be. Mill argued the fundamental soundness of Bentham's insight but tried to depart from a too quantitative analysis of pleasure and pain. Toward the beginning of *Utilitarianism* he states: "The creed which accepts as the foundation of morals, Utility, or the Greatest Happiness Principle, holds that actions are right in proportion as they tend to promote happiness, wrong as they tend to promote the reverse of happiness. By happiness is intended pleasure, and the absence of pain; by unhappiness, pain, and the privation of pleasure." Mill immediately amplifies the meaning of pleasure and happiness by insisting that "some *kinds* of pleasure are more desirable and more valuable than others" — quality too must enter into one's judgment. Once one understands the level of dignity that attaches to the human being over other beings, and understands that there are different levels of value in the human being itself, one understands, as Mill puts it, that "It is better to be a human being dissatisfied than a pig satisfied; better to be Socrates dissatisfied than a fool satisfied."

Simple as this statement sounds, Mill knew it was complex, particularly regarding the need to make a moral judgment. Is there moral rightness to begin with? How do we estimate right and wrong? By intuition, deduction, reason, trial and error, our feelings? On these questions Mill brings his empiricism to bear. We do not have direct knowledge of the moral or ethical value of an act; there is no place for intuition in morality, no special faculty of immediate moral apprehension. Yet Mill did not want to deny the role of moral feelings, for even early in his career he expostulated against those who denied their existence. Feelings are not innate; they are acquired, brought about by education and experience and subject to rational control: "the moral faculty, if not part of our nature, is a natural outgrowth from it; capable ... in a small degree, of springing up spontaneously; and susceptible of being brought by cultivation to a high degree of development."

As Mill asserts in *A System of Logic*, the study of moral sciences which include ethics, politics, character analysis, psychology, and sociology, has not achieved the scientific exactness of the physical sciences and it will be a long time before it does. "Bad generalizations" (empiricism in Mill's use of the word) regarding human behavior are totally unacceptable, but that does not mean that human behavior is not subject to the *law of causation*, as everything in nature is; it is simply that we do not know enough about the causes at work. Though in some respects more detailed in Mill, the law of causation is pure Hume and means that "every consequent has an invariable antecedent," or, more exactly, "the cause of a phenomenon" is defined "to be the antecedent, or the concurrence of antecedents, on which it is invariably and *unconditionally* consequent." Mill's view is that the uniformity prevailing in nature, and embodied in its laws, prevails in man too, but those causes for the most part remain to be discovered. He had hopes for the positivist enterprise of Auguste Comte in his discovery of the laws of man's social development, and for the associationist psychology of David Hartley in which particular experiences associated with pleasure and pain lead to moral conclusions. If we were able to know *all* the antecedents of a given action, on the basis of the law of causation, we could predict it, but the human being is so complex that our present state of science disallows prediction.

But this belief completely negates free will, and thus Mill finds himself in the classical nutcracker between freedom and determinism; how this "Philosophical Necessity" weighed on his mind like an incubus is movingly told in the *Autobiography*: if one is free, the whole law of causation collapses; if one is determined, one becomes "the helpless slave of antecedent circumstances." Is there any way of saying that we have real control over our character formation and still are subject to the law of causation? Mill believed that he had finally made a breakthrough by admitting, on the one hand, that "our character is formed by circumstances" and, on the other, that "our own desires can do much to shape those circumstances." Thus there is a midway point between determinism–fatalism and the doctrine propounding free will as a special undetermined causal agency in man. Laying aside any question as to the objective satisfactoriness of Mill's treatment, it did settle matters for him; he indicated in the chapter's concluding words that his resolution was "sufficiently established for the purposes of this treatise."

The last book of the *Logic* is entitled "On the Logic of the Moral Sciences," and inasmuch as the consideration of moral science is not necessary for the study of logic proper, it may not unreasonably be asked whether, over a ten–year period, Mill wrote his principal opus for the sake of the last book. The principles of induction he painstakingly elaborates in the *Logic* are precisely the ones he uses to substantiate most of his writing on the moral sciences. But long before the last chapter is reached, Mill's monumental logic unfolds. It was his set purpose to do for inductive reasoning what Aristotle did for deductive reasoning, and in the opinion of many he succeeded. The syllogism, proper to deduction, is valid but, for Mill, does not give very much, if any, new knowledge; new knowledge is the domain of induction. In reality, all inference is from particulars to particulars: from a number of particular instances, I draw a general truth or proposition that, relying on the uniformity of nature, I apply to any future instance of the same. I do not, therefore, deduce that "the Duke of Wellington is mortal" from the proposition "All men are mortal," as though it were a given major proposition; rather, I deduce it only in the sense that "a general truth is but an aggregate of particular truths," and so it is really from the particular instances of the death of John and Thomas and others that I infer the generalization (make the conclusion) that "All men are mortal," in which the particular man, the Duke of Wellington, is included. It is on this basis that the law of causation, Mill's golden thread, rests and becomes applicable to the activities of the universe as a whole and those of man in particular. .

The moral sciences are theoretical and practical at the same time, so a philosopher like John Stuart Mill, in turning his attention to social problems, does so in the best tradition of the speculative-cum-practical. Social problems, always connected with some kind of injustice, require a social philosophy, and a social philosophy, in turn, requires a philosophy of political economy, hence the subtitle of Mill's *Principles of Political Economy* is "with Some of Their Applications to Social Philosophy." It appeared in 1848, the same year as the *Communist Manifesto*, although there is scant evidence that Mill knew of the writings of Karl Marx laboring in the British Museum. Mill, at home with economics since childhood, often reflected on the link between wealth and freedom; this theme was brought to a head with the Irish potato famine of 1846–47, "when the stern necessities of the time seemed to afford a chance of gaining attention for what appeared to me the only mode of combining relief to immediate destitution with permanent improvement of the social and economical condition of the Irish people." He had already been working on his huge *Political Economy*, culling raw material from hundreds of examples the world over, not least from the impoverished working class in England, but it was the Irish problem that prompted him to finish it in less than two years so that it could be published as soon as possible. And since an overall philosophy was necessary to have political economy make any sense at all, it was, of course, the utilitarian philosophy of greatest happiness that he once again put to work.

The inductive pattern discussed above covers the whole range in political economy from the production of wealth to its distribution, though the laws governing each are significantly different. On the production side Mill analyzes the relationship of capital and labor, and on the distribution side the roles of wages, property, slavery, profits, and rent, along with the options of communism and socialism; the flows of money, trade, taxes, debts, and government functions are considered as part of the production–distribution cycle. All this is done with the ultimate goal of improving the condition of mankind by first changing modes of thought: "I am now convinced, that no great improvements in the lot of mankind are possible, until a great change takes place in the fundamental constitution of their modes of thought."

A further contribution to this work is Mill's espousal of human freedom as stated in his essay *On Liberty*, a work published in 1859 and that he predicted had a better chance of survival than anything else he had written; his prediction has been amply supported. The subject of this work, as stated in its opening sentence, is "Civil, or Social Liberty: the nature and limits of the power which can be legitimately exercised by society over the individual." Society will always have its defenders and its champions, but not the individual; so, *On Liberty* is a ringing proclamation of individual freedom, which historically has been buffeted by two forces, the state and "prevailing opinion"; it is therefore indispensable to find the limit of legitimate interference between state and collective opinion on one side and individual independence on the other. There is one very simple principle, Mill asserts, that governs the dealings of society with the individual in terms of the use of power: "That principle is, that the sole end for which mankind are warranted, individually or collectively, in interfering with the liberty of action of any of their number, is self-protection. That the only purpose for which power can be rightfully exercised over any member of a civilised community, against his will, is to prevent harm to others."

This general principle safeguards the individual in his pursuit of good as he sees it, his "inward domain of consciousness," his liberty to unite with others for any reason not involving harm to others, and his freedom of thought and discussion. If anyone wishes to look for historical personifications of these ideals, let him consider Socrates and Jesus, both of whom were put down by state and public opinion, and the Roman emperor Marcus Aurelius, who, despite his tragic persecution of the Christians, was still a man of "unblemished justice" and "tenderest heart."

Mill delicately tries to delineate the boundaries between the individual and the state, and he sees the state's obligation in restraining an individual if his actions are injurious to others. He formulates two maxims, two principles, which he says form the entire doctrine of *On Liberty*: "The maxims are, first, that the individual is not accountable to society for his actions, in so far as these concern the interests of no person but himself. Advice, instruction, persuasion, and avoidance by other people if thought necessary by them for their own good, are the only measures by which society can justifiably express its dislike or disapprobation of his conduct. Secondly, that for such actions as are prejudicial to the interests of others, the individual is accountable, and may be subjected either to social or to legal punishment, if society is of opinion that the one or the other is requisite for its protection." Mill's application of the greatest happiness doctrine, this time in his concern for the individual and for minorities, is evidenced again, and the liberty of which he speaks bids the state to exert itself in fostering it, for anything else will result in a state that dwarfs its men, and "with small men no great thing can really be accomplished."

We have stated that one of Mill's goals in philosophy was to find ground for humanity in view of a declining Christianity. This statement was not meant to imply a conscious goal on Mill's part, for it must be recognized, as Mill did, that he never shed religious beliefs because he never had any. Rather, this statement was meant to indicate the situation of a philosopher straining after the human dimension, and doing so without any palpable support of religion. Yet, published posthumously by his stepdaughter were _Three Essays on Religion_, which she says were withheld not "on account of reluctance to encounter whatever odium might result from the free expression of his opinions on religion"; rather, it "was in accord with the Author's habit in regard to the public utterance of his religious opinions." Be that as it may, these essays indicate Mill's willingness to accept at least the argument from the design of Nature towards the probability of the world's being created but not by an omnipotent intelligence, and perhaps a pragmatic defense of believing in God inasmuch as such belief is conducive to good. On the other hand, religion as "supernatural" must be eschewed in the present stage of man's development, regardless of how necessary its services were in the early stages; immortality is "utterly opposed to every presumption that can be deduced from the light of Nature"; and the supernatural origin of the "received maxims of morality" entails a "very real evil" because it consecrates them and puts them beyond discussion or criticism. In sum, religion has its utility, but whatever recommendation is found in supernatural religion is found eminently in the "Religion of Humanity," for it is able to direct the emotions and desires toward an ideal object and to fulfill the functions of religion by a sense of unity with mankind and a deep feeling for the general good. The Religion of Humanity "is not only capable of fulfilling these functions, but would fulfill them better than any form whatever of supernaturalism ... it is a better religion than any of those which are ordinarily called by that title."

In this grand conception of the Religion of Humanity, the figure of Christ has a preeminent place; consider the following passage written by Mill shortly before he died: "But about the life and sayings of Jesus there is a stamp of personal originality combined with profundity of insight, which if we abandon the idle expectation of finding scientific precision where something very different was aimed at, must place the

Prophet of Nazareth, even in the estimation of those who have no belief in his inspiration, in the very first rank of the men of sublime genius of whom our species can boast ... it remains a possibility that Christ actually was what he supposed himself to be — not God, for he never made the smallest pretense to that character ... — but a man charged with a special, express and unique commission from God to lead mankind to truth and virtue."

Readings

What Utilitarianism Is (from *Utilitarianism*)

A passing remark is all that needs be given to the ignorant blunder of supposing that those who stand up for utility as the test of right and wrong, use the term in that restricted and merely colloquial sense in which utility is opposed to pleasure. An apology is due to the philosophical opponents of utilitarianism, for even the momentary appearance of confounding them with anyone capable of so absurd a misconception; which is the more extraordinary, inasmuch as the contrary accusation, of referring everything to pleasure, and that too in its grossest form, is another of the common charges against utilitarianism: and, as has been pointedly remarked by an able writer, the same sort of persons, and often the very same persons, denounce the theory "as impracticably dry when the word utility precedes the word pleasure, and as too practicably voluptuous when the word pleasure precedes the word utility." Those who know anything about the matter are aware that every writer, from Epicurus to Bentham, who maintained the theory of utility, meant by it, not something to be contradistinguished from pleasure, but pleasure itself, together with exemption from pain; and instead of opposing the useful to the agreeable or the ornamental, have always declared that the useful means these, among other things. Yet the common herd, including the herd of writers, not only in newspapers, and periodicals, but in books of weight and pretension, are perpetually falling into this shallow mistake. Having caught up the word 'utilitarian,' while knowing nothing whatever about it but its sound, they habitually express by it the rejection, or the neglect, of pleasure in some of its forms: of beauty, of ornament, or of amusement. Nor is the term thus ignorantly misapplied solely in disparagement, but occasionally in compliment; as though it implied superiority to frivolity and the mere pleasures of the moment. And this perverted use is the only one in which the word is popularly known, and the one from which the new generation are acquiring their sole notion of its meaning. Those who introduced the word, but who had for many years discontinued it as a distinctive appellation, may well feel themselves called upon to resume it, if by doing so they can hope to contribute anything towards rescuing it from this utter degradation.[1]

The creed which accepts as the foundation of morals *utility*, or the *greatest happiness principle*, holds that actions are right in proportion as they tend to promote happiness, wrong as they tend to produce the reverse of happiness. By 'happiness' is intended pleasure, and the absence of pain; by 'unhappiness,' pain, and the privation of pleasure. To give a clear view of the moral standard set up by the theory, much more requires to be said; in particular, what things it includes in the ideas of pain and pleasure; and to what extent this is left an open question. But these supplementary explanations do not affect the theory of life on which this theory of morality is grounded—namely, that pleasure, and freedom from pain, are the only things desirable as ends; and that all desirable things (which are as numerous in the utilitarian as in any other scheme) are desirable either for the pleasure inherent in themselves, or as means to the promotion of pleasure and the prevention of pain.

Now such a theory of life excites in many minds, and among them in some of the most estimable in feeling and purpose, inveterate dislike. To suppose that life has (as they express it) no higher end than pleasure—no better and nobler object of desire and pursuit—they designate as utterly mean and groveling; as a doctrine worthy only of swine, to whom the followers of Epicurus were, at a very early period, contemptuously likened; and modern holders of the doctrine are occasionally made the subject of equally polite comparisons by its German, French, and English assailants.

When thus attacked, the Epicureans have always answered that it is not they but their accusers who represent human nature in a degrading light; since the accusation supposes human beings to be capable of no pleasures except those of which swine are capable. If this supposition were true, the charge could not be gainsaid, but would then be no longer an imputation; for if the sources of pleasure were precisely the

---

[1] The author of this essay has reason for believing himself to be the first person who brought the word 'utilitarian' into use. He did not invent it, but adopted it from a passing expression in Mr. Galt's *Annals of the Parish*. After using it as a designation for several years, he and others abandoned it from a growing dislike to anything resembling a badge or watchword of sectarian distinction. But as a name for one single opinion, not a set of opinions—to denote the recognition of utility as a standard, not any particular way of applying it—the term supplies a want in the language, and offers, in many cases, a convenient mode of avoiding tiresome circumlocution.

same to human beings and to swine, the rule of life which is good enough for the one would be good enough for the other. The comparison of the Epicurean life to that of beasts is felt as degrading, precisely because a beast's pleasures do not satisfy a human being's conceptions of happiness. Human beings have faculties more elevated than the animal appetites, and when once made conscious of them, do not regard anything as happiness which does not include their gratification. I do not, indeed, consider the Epicureans to have been by any means faultless in drawing out their scheme of consequences from the utilitarian principle. To do this in any sufficient manner, many Stoic, as well as Christian elements require to be included. But there is no known Epicurean theory of life which does not assign to the pleasures of the intellect, of the feelings and imagination, and of the moral sentiments, a much higher value as pleasures than to those of mere sensation. It must be admitted, however, that utilitarian writers in general have placed the superiority of mental over bodily pleasures chiefly in the greater permanency, safety, uncostliness, etc., of the former—that is, in their circumstantial advantages rather than in their intrinsic nature. And on all these points utilitarians have fully proved their case; but they might have taken the other, and, as it may be called, higher ground, with entire consistency. It is quite compatible with the principle of utility to recognize the fact, that some _kinds_ of pleasure are more desirable and more valuable than others. It would be absurd that while, in estimating all other things, quality is considered as well as quantity, the estimation of pleasures should be supposed to depend on quantity alone.

If I am asked what I mean by difference of quality in pleasures, or what makes one pleasure more valuable than another merely as a pleasure, except its being greater in amount, there is but one possible answer. Of two pleasures, if there be one to which all or almost all who have experience of both give a decided preference, irrespective of any feeling of moral obligation to prefer it, that is the more desirable pleasure. If one of the two is, by those who are competently acquainted with both, placed so far above the other that they prefer it, even though knowing it to be attended with a greater amount of discontent, and would not resign it for any quantity of the other pleasure which their nature is capable of, we are justified in ascribing to the preferred enjoyment a superiority in quality, so far outweighing quantity as to render it, in comparison, of small account.

Now it is an unquestionable fact that those who are equally acquainted with, and equally capable of appreciating and enjoying, both, do give a most marked preference to the manner of existence which employs their higher faculties. Few human creatures would consent to be changed into any of the lower animals, for a promise of the fullest allowance of a beast's pleasures; no intelligent human being would consent to be a fool, no instructed person would be an ignoramus, no person of feeling and conscience would be selfish and base, even though they should be persuaded that the fool, the dunce, or the rascal is better satisfied with his lot than they are with theirs. They would not resign what they possess more than he for the most complete satisfaction of all the desires which they have in common with him. If they ever fancy they would, it is only in cases of unhappiness so extreme, that to escape from it they would exchange their lot for almost any other, however undesirable in their own eyes. A being of higher faculties requires more to make him happy, is capable probably of more acute suffering, and certainly accessible to it at more points, than one of an inferior type; but in spite of these liabilities, he can never really wish to sink into what he feels to be a lower grade of existence. We may give what explanation we please of this unwillingness: we may attribute it to pride, a name which is given indiscriminately to some of the most and to some of the least estimable feelings of which mankind are capable; we may refer it to the love of liberty and personal independence, an appeal to which was with the Stoics one of the most effective means for the inculcation of it; to the love of power, or to the love of excitement, both of which do really enter into and contribute to it: but its most appropriate appellation is a sense of dignity, which all human beings possess in one form or other, and in some, though by no means in exact, proportion to their higher faculties, and which is so essential a part of the happiness of those in whom it is strong, that nothing which conflicts with it could be, otherwise than momentarily, an object of desire to them. Whoever supposes that this preference takes place at a sacrifice of happiness—that the superior being, in anything like equal circumstances, is not happier than the inferior—confounds the two very different ideas, of *happiness* and *content*. It is indisputable that the being whose capacities of enjoyment are low, has the greatest chance of having them fully satisfied; and a highly endowed being will always feel that any happiness which he can look for, as the world is constituted, is imperfect. But he can learn to bear its imperfections, if they are at all bearable; and they will not make him envy the being who is indeed unconscious of the imperfections, but only because he feels not at all the good which those imperfections qualify. It is better to be a human being dissatisfied than a pig satisfied; better to be Socrates dissatisfied than a fool satisfied. And if the fool, or the pig, are of a different opinion, it is because they only know their own side of the question. The other party to the comparison knows both sides.

It may be objected that many who are capable of the higher pleasures, occasionally, under the influence of temptation, postpone them to the lower. But this is quite compatible with a full appreciation of the intrinsic superiority of the higher. Men often, from infirmity of character, make their election for the nearer good, though they know it to be the less valuable; and this no less when the choice is between two bodily pleasures, than when it is between bodily and mental. They pursue sensual indulgences to the injury of health, though perfectly aware that health is the greater good. It may be further objected that many who begin with youthful enthusiasm for everything noble, as they advance in years sink into indolence and selfishness. But I do not believe that those who undergo this very common change, voluntarily choose the lower description of pleasures in preference to the higher. I believe that before they devote themselves exclusively to the one, they have already become incapable of the other. Capacity for the nobler feelings is in most natures a very tender plant, easily killed, not only by hostile influences, but by mere want of sustenance; and in the majority of young persons it speedily dies away if the occupations to which their position in life has devoted them, and the society into which it has thrown them, are not favorable to keeping that higher capacity in exercise. Men lose their high aspirations as they lose their intellectual tastes, because they have not time or opportunity for indulging them; and they addict themselves to inferior pleasures not because they deliberately prefer them, but because they are either the only ones to which they have access or the only ones which they are any longer capable of enjoying. It may be questioned whether anyone who has remained equally susceptible to both classes of pleasures, ever knowingly and calmly preferred the lower; though many, in all ages, have broken down in an ineffectual attempt to combine both.

From this verdict of the only competent judges I apprehend there can be no appeal. On a question which is the best worth having of two pleasures, or which of two modes of existence is the most grateful to the feelings, apart from its moral attributes and from its consequences, the judgment of those who are qualified by knowledge of both, or, if they differ, that of the majority among them, must be admitted as final. And there need be the less hesitation to accept this judgment respecting the quality of pleasures, since there is no other tribunal to be referred to even on the question of quantity. What means are there of determining which is the acutest of two pains, or the intensest of two pleasurable sensations, except the general suffrage of those who are familiar with both? Neither pains nor pleasures are homogeneous, and pain is always heterogeneous with pleasure. What is there to decide whether a particular pleasure is worth purchasing at the cost of a particular pain, except the feelings and judgment of the experienced? When, therefore, those feelings and judgment declare the pleasures derived from the higher faculties to be preferable *in kind*, apart from the question of intensity, to those of which the animal nature, disjoined from the higher faculties, is suspectible, they are entitled on this subject to the same regard.

I have dwelt on this point, as being a necessary part of a perfectly just conception of utility, or happiness, considered as the directive rule of human conduct. But it is by no means an indispensable condition to the acceptance of the utilitarian standard; for that standard is not the agent's own greatest happiness, but the greatest amount of happiness altogether; and if it may possibly be doubted whether a noble character is always the happier for its nobleness, there can be no doubt that it makes other people happier, and that the world in general is immensely a gainer by it. Utilitarianism, therefore, could only attain its end by the general cultivation of nobleness of character, even if each individual were only benefited by the nobleness of others, and his own, so far as happiness is concerned, were a sheer deduction from the benefit. But the bare enunciation of such an absurdity as this last renders refutation superfluous.

Of the Law of Universal Causation (from *A System of Logic*)

1. [*The universal law of successive phenomena is the Law of Causation*] The phenomena of nature exist in two distinct relations to one another; that of simultaneity, and that of succession. Every phenomenon is related, in an uniform manner, to some phenomena that coexist with it, and to some that have preceded and will follow it.

Of the uniformities which exist among synchronous phenomena, the most important, on every account, are the laws of number; and next to them those of space, or, in other words, of extension and figure. The laws of number are common to synchronous and successive phenomena. That two and two make four, is equally true whether the second two follow the first two or accompany them. It is as true of days and years as of feet and inches. The laws of extension and figure (in other words, the theorems of geometry, from its lowest to its highest branches) are, on the contrary, laws of simultaneous phenomena only. The various parts of space, and of the objects which are said to fill space, coexist; and the unvarying laws which are the subject of the science of geometry, are an expression of the mode of their coexistence.

This is a class of laws, or in other words, of uniformities, for the comprehension and proof of which it is not necessary to suppose any lapse of time, any variety of facts or events succeeding one another. The propositions of geometry are independent of the succession of events. All things which possess extension, or, in other words, which fill space, are subject to geometrical laws. Possessing extension, they possess figure; possessing figure, they must possess some figure in particular, and have all the properties which geometry assigns to that figure.

If one body be a sphere and another a cylinder, of equal height and diameter, the one will be exactly two-thirds of the other, let the nature and quality of the material be what it will. Again, each body, and each point of a body, must occupy some place or position among other bodies; and the position of two bodies relatively to each other, of whatever nature the bodies be, may be unerringly inferred from the position of each of them relatively to any third body.

In the laws of number, then, and in those of space, we recognise in the most unqualified manner, the rigorous universality of which we are in quest. Those laws have been in all ages the type of certainty, the standard of comparison for all inferior degrees of evidence. Their invariability is so perfect, that it renders us unable even to conceive any exception to them; and philosophers have been led, though (as I have endeavoured to show) erroneously, to consider their evidence as lying not in experience, but in the original constitution of the intellect. If, therefore, from the laws of space and number, we were able to deduce uniformities of any other description, this would be conclusive evidence to us that those other uniformities possessed the same rigorous certainty. But this we cannot do. From laws of space and number alone, nothing can be deduced but laws of space and number.

Of all truths relating to phenomena, the most valuable to us are those which relate to the order of their succession. On a knowledge of these is founded every reasonable anticipation of future facts, and whatever power we possess of influencing those facts to our advantage. Even the laws of geometry are chiefly of practical importance to us as being a portion of the premises from which the order of the succession of phenomena may be inferred. Inasmuch as the motion of bodies, the action of forces, and the propagation of influences of all sorts, take place in certain lines and over definite spaces, the properties of those lines and spaces are an important part of the laws to which those phenomena are themselves subject. Again, motions, forces, or other influences, and times, are numerable quantities; and the properties of number are applicable to them as to all other things. But though the laws of number and space are important elements in the ascertainment of uniformities of succession, they can do nothing towards it when taken by themselves. They can only be made instrumental to that purpose when we combine with them additional premises, expressive of uniformities of succession already known. By taking, for instance, as premises these propositions, that bodies acted upon by an instantaneous force move with uniform velocity in straight lines; that bodies acted upon by a continuous force move with accelerated velocity in straight lines; and that bodies acted upon by two forces in different directions move in the diagonal of a parallelogram, whose sides represent the direction and quantity of those forces; we may by combining these truths with propositions relating to the properties of straight lines and of parallelograms, (as that a triangle is half a parallelogram of the same base and altitude,) deduce another important uniformity of succession, viz., that a body moving round a centre of force describes areas proportional to the times. But unless there had been laws of succession in our premises, there could have been no truths of succession in our conclusions. A similar remark might be extended to every other class of phenomena really peculiar; and, had it been attended to, would have prevented many chimerical attempts at demonstrations of the indemonstrable, and explanations which do not explain.

It is not, therefore, enough for us that the laws of space, which are only laws of simultaneous phenomena, and the laws of number, which though true of successive phenomena do not relate to their succession, possess the rigorous certainty and universality of which we are in search. We must endeavour to find some law of succession which has those same attributes, and is therefore fit to be made the foundation of processes for discovering, and of a test for verifying, all other uniformities of succession. This fundamental law must resemble the truths of geometry in their most remarkable peculiarity, that of never being, in any instance whatever, defeated or suspended by any change of circumstances.

Now among all those uniformities in the succession of phenomena, which common observation is sufficient to bring to light, there are very few which have any, even apparent, pretension to this rigorous indefeasibility: and of those few, one only has been found capable of completely sustaining it. In that one, however, we recognise a law which is universal also in another sense; it is coextensive with the entire field of successive phenomena, all instances whatever of succession being examples of it. This law is the Law of Causation. The truth that every fact which has a beginning has a cause, is coextensive with human experience.

This generalization may appear to some minds not to amount to much, since after all it asserts only this: "it is a law, that every event depends on some law:" "it is a law, that there is a law for everything." We must not, however, conclude that the generality of the principle is merely verbal; it will be found on inspection to be no vague or unmeaning assertion, but a most important and really fundamental truth.

6. [*The cause is not the invariable antecedent, but the* unconditional *invariable antecedent*] It now remains to advert to a distinction which is of first-rate importance both for clearing up the notion of cause, and for obviating a very specious objection often made against the view which we have taken of the subject.

When we define the cause of anything (in the only sense in which the present inquiry has any concern with causes) to be "the antecedent which it invariably follows," we do not use this phrase as exactly synonymous with "the antecedent which it invariably *has* followed in our past experience." Such a mode of conceiving causation would be liable to the objection very plausibly urged by Dr. Reid, namely, that according to this doctrine night must be the cause of day, and day the cause of night; since these phenomena have invariably succeeded one another from the beginning of the world. But it is necessary to our using the word cause, that we should believe not only that the antecedent always *has* been followed by the consequent, but that, as long as the present constitution of things endures, it always *will* be so. And this would not be true of day and night. We do not believe that night will be followed by day under all imaginable circumstances, but only that it will be so *provided* the sun rises above the horizon. If the sun ceased to rise, which, for aught we know, may be perfectly compatible with the general laws of matter, night would be, or might be, eternal. On the other hand, if the sun is above the horizon, his light not extinct, and no opaque body between us and him, we believe firmly that unless a change takes place in the properties of matter, this combination of antecedents will be followed by the consequent, day; that if the combination of antecedents could be indefinitely prolonged, it would be always day; and that if the same combination had always existed, it would always have been day, quite independently of night as a previous condition. Therefore is it that we do not call night the cause, nor even a condition, of day. The existence of the sun (or some such luminous body), and there being no opaque medium in a straight line between that body and the part of the earth where we are situated, are the sole conditions; and the union of these, without the addition of any superfluous circumstance, constitutes the cause. This is what writers mean when they say that the notion of cause involves the idea of necessity. If there be any meaning which confessedly belongs to the term necessity, it is *unconditionalness.* That which is necessary, that which *must* be, means that which will be, whatever supposition we may make in regard to all other things. The succession of day and night evidently is not necessary in this sense. It is conditional on the occurrence of other antecedents. That which will be followed by a given consequent when, and only when, some third circumstance also exists, is not the cause, even though no case should ever have occurred in which the phenomenon took place without it.

Invariable sequence, therefore, is not synonymous with causation, unless the sequence, besides being invariable, is unconditional. There are sequences, as uniform in past experience as any others whatever, which yet we do not regard as cases of causation, but as conjunctions in some sort accidental. Such, to an accurate thinker, is that of day and night. The one might have existed for any length of time, and the other not have followed the sooner for its existence; it follows only if certain other antecedents exist; and where those antecedents existed, it would follow in any case. No one, probably, ever called night the cause of day; mankind must so soon have arrived at the very obvious generalization, that the state of general illumination which we call day would follow from the presence of a sufficiently luminous body, whether darkness had preceded or not.

We may define, therefore, the cause of a phenomenon, to be the antecedent, or the concurrence of antecedents, on which it is invariably and *unconditionally* consequent. Or if we adopt the convenient modification of the meaning of the word cause, which confines it to the assemblage of positive conditions without the negative, then instead of "unconditionally," we must say, "subject to no other than negative conditions."

To some it may appear, that the sequence between night and day being invariable in our experience, we have as much ground in this case as experience can give in any case, for recognising the two phenomena as cause and effect; and that to say that more is necessary—to require a belief that the succession is unconditional, or in other words that it would be invariable under all changes of circumstances, is to acknowledge in causation an element of belief not derived from experience. The answer to this is, that it is experience itself which teaches us that one uniformity of sequence is conditional and another unconditional. When we judge that the succession of night and day is a derivative sequence, depending on something else, we proceed on grounds of experience. It is the evidence of experience which convinces us that day could equally exist without being followed by night, and that night could equally exist without being followed by day. To say that these beliefs are "not generated by our mere observation of sequence," is to forget that twice in every twenty-four hours, when the sky is clear, we have an *experimentum crucis* that the cause of day is the sun. We have an experimental knowledge of the sun which justifies us on experimental grounds in concluding, that if the sun were always above the horizon there would be day, though there had been no night, and that if the sun were always below the horizon there would be night, though there had been no day. We thus know from experience that the succession of night and day is not unconditional. Let me add, that the antecedent which is only conditionally invariable, is not the invariable antecedent. Though a fact may, in experience, have always been followed by another fact, yet if the remainder of our experience teaches us that it might not always be so followed, or if the experience itself is such as leaves room for a possibility that the known cases may not correctly represent all possible cases, the hitherto invariable antecedent is not accounted the cause; but why? Because we are not sure that it *is* the invariable antecedent. . . .

Of Liberty and Necessity (from *A System of Logic*)

1. [*Are human actions subject to the law of causality*?] The question, whether the law of causality applies in the same strict sense to human actions as to other phenomena, is the celebrated controversy concerning the freedom of the will: which, from at least as far back as the time of Pelagius, has divided both the philosophical and the religious world. The affirmative opinion is commonly called the doctrine of Necessity, as asserting human volitions and actions to be necessary and inevitable. The negative maintains that the will is not determined, like other phenomena, by antecedents, but determines itself; that our volitions are not, properly speaking, the effects of causes, or at least have no causes which they uniformly and implicitly obey.

I have already made it sufficiently apparent that the former of these opinions is that which I consider the true one; but the misleading terms in which it is often expressed, and the indistinct manner in which it is usually apprehended, have both obstructed its reception, and perverted its influence when received. The metaphysical theory of free will, as held by philosophers, (for the practical feeling of it, common in a greater or less degree to all mankind, is in no way inconsistent with the contrary theory,) was invented because the supposed alternative of admitting human actions to be *necessary*, was deemed inconsistent with every one's instinctive consciousness, as well as humiliating to the pride and even degrading to the moral nature of man. Nor do I deny that the doctrine, as sometimes held, is open to these imputations; for the misapprehension in which I shall be able to show that they originate, unfortunately is not confined to the opponents of the doctrine, but is participated in by many, perhaps we might say by most, of its supporters.

2. [*The doctrine commonly called Philosophical Necessity, in what sense true*?] Correctly conceived, the doctrine called Philosophical Necessity is simply this: that, given the motives which are present to an individual's mind, and given likewise the character and disposition of the individual, the manner in which he will act might be unerringly inferred: that if we knew the person thoroughly, and knew all the inducements which are acting upon him, we could foretell his conduct with as much certainty as we can predict any physical event. This proposition I take to be a mere interpretation of universal experience, a statement in words of what every one is internally convinced of. No one who believed that he knew thoroughly the circumstances of any case, and the characters of the different persons concerned, would hesitate to foretell how all of them would act. Whatever degree of doubt he may in fact feel, arises from the uncertainty whether he really knows the circumstances, or the character of some one or other of the persons, with the degree of accuracy required: but by no means from thinking

that if he did know these things, there could be any uncertainty what the conduct would be. Nor does this full assurance conflict in the smallest degree with what is called our feeling of freedom. We do not feel ourselves the less free, because those to whom we are intimately known are well assured how we shall will to act in a particular case. We often, on the contrary, regard the doubt what our conduct will be, as a mark of ignorance of our character, and sometimes even resent it as an imputation. The religious metaphysicians who have asserted the freedom of the will, have always maintained it to be consistent with divine foreknowledge of our actions: and if with divine, then with any other foreknowledge. We may be free, and yet another may have reason to be perfectly certain what use we shall make of our freedom. It is not, therefore, the doctrine that our volitions and actions are invariable consequents of our antecedent states of mind, that is either contradicted by our consciousness, or felt to be degrading.

But the doctrine of causation, when considered as obtaining between our volitions and their antecedents, is almost universally conceived as involving more than this. Many do not believe, and very few practically feel, that there is nothing in causation but invariable, certain, and unconditional sequence. There are few to whom mere constancy of succession appears a sufficiently stringent bond of union for so peculiar a relation as that of cause and effect. Even if the reason repudiates, the imagination retains, the feeling of some more intimate connexion, of some peculiar tie, or mysterious constraint exercised by the antecedent over the consequent. Now this it is which, considered as applying to the human will, conflicts with our consciousness, and revolts our feelings. We are certain that, in the case of our volitions, there is not this mysterious constraint. We know that we are not compelled, as by a magical spell, to obey any particular motive. We feel, that if we wished to prove that we have the power of resisting the motive, we could do so, (that wish being, it needs scarcely be observed, a *new antecedent*;) and it would be humiliating to our pride, and (what is of more importance) paralysing to our desire of excellence, if we thought otherwise. But neither is any such mysterious compulsion now supposed, by the best philosophical authorities, to be exercised by any other cause over its effect. Those who think that causes draw their effects after them by a mystical tie, are right in believing that the relation between volitions and their antecedents is of another nature. But they should go farther, and admit that this is also true of all other effects and their antecedents. If such a tie is considered to be involved in the word necessity, the doctrine is not true of human actions; but neither is it then true of inanimate objects. It would be more correct to say that matter is not bound by necessity, than that mind is so.

That the free-will metaphysicians, being mostly of the school which rejects Hume's and Brown's analysis of Cause and Effect, should miss

their way for want of the light which that analysis affords, cannot surprise us. The wonder is, that the necessitarians, who usually admit that
philosophical theory, should in practice equally lose sight of it. The
very same misconception of the doctrine called Philosophical Necessity, which prevents the opposite party from recognising its truth, I believe to exist more or less obscurely in the minds of most necessitarians, however they may in words disavow it. I am much mistaken if
they habitually feel that the necessity which they recognise in actions
is but uniformity of order, and capability of being predicted. They
have a feeling as if there were at bottom a stronger tie between the volitions and their causes: as if, when they asserted that the will is governed by the balance of motives, they meant something more cogent
than if they had only said, that whoever knew the motives, and our habitual susceptibilities to them, could predict how we should will to act.
They commit, in opposition to their own scientific system, the very
same mistake which their adversaries commit in obedience to theirs;
and in consequence do really in some instances suffer those depressing
consequences, which their opponents erroneously impute to the doctrine itself.

3. [*Inappropriateness and pernicious effect of the term Necessity*]
I am inclined to think that this error is almost wholly an effect of the
associations with a word; and that it would be prevented, by forbearing
to employ, for the expression of the simple fact of causation, so extremely inappropriate a term as Necessity. That word, in its other acceptations, involves much more than mere uniformity of sequence: it
implies irresistibleness. Applied to the will, it only means that the giv-
en cause will be followed by the effect, subject to all possibilities of
counteraction by other causes: but in common use it stands for the operation of those causes exclusively, which are supposed too powerful to
be counteracted at all. When we say that all human actions take place
of necessity, we only mean that they will certainly happen if nothing
prevents:—when we say that dying of want, to those who cannot get
food, is a necessity, we mean that it will certainly happen whatever
may be done to prevent it. The application of the same term to the
agencies on which human actions depend, as is used to express those
agencies of nature which are really uncontrollable, cannot fail, when
habitual, to create a feeling of uncontrollableness in the former also.
This however is a mere illusion. There are physical sequences which we
call necessary, as death for want of food or air; there are others which,
though as much cases of causation as the former, are not said to be
necessary, as death from poison, which an antidote, or the use of the
stomach-pump, will sometimes avert. It is apt to be forgotten by people's feelings, even if remembered by their understandings, that human
actions are in this last predicament: they are never (except in some

cases of mania) ruled by any one motive with such absolute sway, that there is no room for the influence of any other. The causes, therefore, on which action depends, are never uncontrollable; and any given effect is only necessary provided that the causes tending to produce it are not controlled. That whatever happens, could not have happened otherwise unless something had taken place which was capable of preventing it, no one surely needs hesitate to admit. But to call this by the name necessity is to use the term in a sense so different from its primitive and familiar meaning, from that which it bears in the common occasions of life, as to amount almost to a play upon words. The associations derived from the ordinary sense of the term will adhere to it in spite of all we can do: and though the doctrine of Necessity, as stated by most who hold it, is very remote from fatalism, it is probable that most necessitarians are fatalists, more or less, in their feelings.

A fatalist believes, or half believes (for nobody is a consistent fatalist), not only that whatever is about to happen, will be the infallible result of the causes which produce it, (which is the true necessitarian doctrine), but moreover that there is no use in struggling against it; that it will happen however we may strive to prevent it. Now, a necessitarian, believing that our actions follow from our characters, and that our characters follow from our organization, our education, and our circumstances, is apt to be, with more or less of consciousness on his part, a fatalist as to his own actions, and to believe that his nature is such, or that his education and circumstances have so moulded his character, that nothing can now prevent him from feeling and acting in a particular way, or at least that no effort of his own can hinder it. In the words of the sect which in our own day has most perseveringly inculcated and most perversely misunderstood this great doctrine, his character is formed *for* him, and not *by* him; therefore his wishing that it had been formed differently is of no use; he has no power to alter it. But this is a grand error. He has, to a certain extent, a power to alter his character. Its being, in the ultimate resort, formed for him, is not inconsistent with its being, in part, formed *by* him as one of the intermediate agents. His character is formed by his circumstances (including among these his particular organization); but his own desire to mould it in a particular way, is one of those circumstances, and by no means one of the least influential. We cannot, indeed, directly will to be different from what we are. But neither did those who are supposed to have formed our characters, directly will that we should be what we are. Their will had no direct power except over their own actions. They made us what they did make us, by willing, not the end, but the requisite means; and we, when our habits are not too inveterate, can, by similarly willing the requisite means, make ourselves different. If they could place us under the influence of certain circumstances, we, in like manner, can place ourselves under the influence of other circumstances. We are exactly as capable of making our own character, *if we will*, as others are of making it for us.

Yes (answers the Owenite), but these words, "if we will," surrender the whole point: since the will to alter our own character is given us, not by any efforts of ours, but by circumstances which we cannot help; it comes to us either from external causes, or not at all. Most true: if the Owenite stops here, he is in a position from which nothing can expel him. Our character is formed by us as well as for us; but the wish which induces us to attempt to form it is formed for us; and how? Not, in general, by our organization, nor wholly by our education, but by our experience; experience of the painful consequences of the character we previously had: or by some strong feeling of admiration or aspiration, accidentally aroused. But to think that we have no power of altering our character, and to think that we shall not use our power unless we desire to use it, are very different things, and have a very different effect on the mind. A person who does not wish to alter his character, cannot be the person who is supposed to feel discouraged or paralysed by thinking himself unable to do it. The depressing effect of the fatalist doctrine can only be felt where there *is* a wish to do what that doctrine represents as impossible. It is of no consequence what we think forms our character, when we have no desire of our own about forming it; but it is of great consequence that we should not be prevented from forming such a desire by thinking the attainment impracticable, and that if we have the desire, we should know that the work is not so irrevocably done as to be incapable of being altered.

And indeed, if we examine closely, we shall find that this feeling, of our being able to modify our own character *if we wish*, is itself the feeling of moral freedom which we are conscious of. A person feels morally free who feels that his habits or his temptations are not his masters, but he theirs: who even in yielding to them knows that he could resist; that were he desirous of altogether throwing them off, there would not be required for that purpose a stronger desire than he knows himself to be capable of feeling. It is of course necessary, to render our consciousness of freedom complete, that we should have succeeded in making our character all we have hitherto attempted to make it; for if we have wished and not attained, we have, to that extent, not power over our own character, we are not free. Or at least, we must feel that our wish, if not strong enough to alter our character, is strong enough to conquer our character when the two are brought into conflict in any particular case of conduct. And hence it is said with truth, that none but a person of confirmed virtue is completely free.

The application of so improper a term as Necessity to the doctrine of cause and effect in the matter of human character, seems to me one of the most signal instances in philosophy of the abuse of terms, and its practical consequences one of the most striking examples of the power of language over our associations. The subject will never be generally understood, until that objectionable term is dropped. The free-will doctrine, by keeping in view precisely that portion of the truth which the word Necessity puts out of sight, namely the power of the mind to co-operate in the formation of its own character, has given to its adherents a practical feeling much nearer to the truth than has generally (I believe) existed in the minds of necessitarians. The latter may have had a stronger sense of the importance of what human beings can do to shape the characters of one another; but the free-will doctrine has, I believe, fostered in its supporters a much stronger spirit of self-culture.

4. [*A motive not always the anticipation of a pleasure or pain*]. There is still one fact which requires to be noticed (in addition to the existence of a power of self-formation) before the doctrine of the causation of human actions can be freed from the confusion and misapprehensions which surround it in many minds. When the will is said to be determined by motives, a motive does not mean always, or solely, the anticipation of a pleasure or of a pain. I shall not here inquire whether it be true that, in the commencement, all our voluntary actions are mere means consciously employed to obtain some pleasure, or avoid some pain. It is at least certain that we gradually, through the influence of association, come to desire the means without thinking of the end: the action itself becomes an object of desire, and is performed without reference to any motive beyond itself. Thus far, it may still be objected, that, the action having through association become pleasurable, we are, as much as before, moved to act by the anticipation of a pleasure, namely, the pleasure of the action itself. But granting this, the matter does not end here. As we proceed in the formation of habits, and become accustomed to will a particular act or a particular course of conduct because it is pleasurable, we at last continue to will it without any reference to its being pleasurable. Although, from some change in us or in our circumstances, we have ceased to find any pleasure in the action, or perhaps to anticipate any pleasure as the consequence of it, we still continue to desire the action, and consequently to do it. In this manner it is that habits of hurtful excess continue to be practised although they have ceased to be pleasurable; and in this manner also it is that the habit of willing to persevere in the course which he has chosen, does not desert the moral hero, even when the reward, however real, which he doubtless receives from the consciousness of well-doing, is anything but an equivalent for the sufferings he undergoes, or the wishes which he may have to renounce.

A habit of willing is commonly called a purpose; and among the causes of our volitions, and of the actions which flow from them, must be reckoned not only likings and aversions, but also purposes. It is only when our purposes have become independent of the feelings of pain or pleasure from which they originally took their rise, that we are said to have a confirmed character. "A character," says Novalis, "is a completely fashioned will:" and the will, once so fashioned, may be steady and constant, when the passive susceptibilities of pleasure and pain are greatly weakened, or materially changed.

With the corrections and explanations now given, the doctrine of the causation of our volitions by motives, and of motives by the desirable objects offered to us, combined with our particular susceptibilities of desire, may be considered, I hope, as sufficiently established for the purposes of this treatise.

Of the Logic of Practice, or Art; Including Morality and Policy (from *A System of Logic*)

1. [*Morality not a Science, but an Art*] In the preceding chapters we have endeavoured to characterize the present state of those among the branches of knowledge called Moral, which are sciences in the only proper sense of the term, that is, inquiries into the course of nature. It is customary, however, to include under the term moral knowledge, and even (though improperly) under that of moral science, an inquiry the results of which do not express themselves in the indicative, but in the imperative mood, or in periphrases equivalent to it; what is called the knowledge of duties; practical ethics, or morality.

Now, the imperative mood is the characteristic of art, as distinguished from science. Whatever speaks in rules, or precepts, not in assertions respecting matters of fact, is art: and ethics, or morality, is properly a portion of the art corresponding to the sciences of human nature and society.

The Method, therefore, of Ethics, can be no other than that of Art, or Practice, in general: and the portion yet uncompleted, of the task which we proposed to ourselves in the concluding Book, is to characterize the general Method of Art, as distinguished from Science.

2. [*Relation between rules of art and the theorems of the corresponding science*] In all branches of practical business, there are cases in which individuals are bound to conform their practice to a pre-established rule, while there are others in which it is part of their task to find or construct the rule by which they are to govern their conduct. The first, for example, is the case of a judge, under a definite written code. The judge is not called upon to determine what course would be intrinsically the most advisable in the particular case in hand, but only within what rule of law it falls; what the legislature has ordained to be done in the kind of case, and must therefore be pre-

sumed to have intended in the individual case. The method must here be wholly and exclusively one of ratiocination, or syllogism; and the process is obviously, what in our analysis of the syllogism we showed that all ratiocination is, namely the interpretation of a formula.

In order that our illustration of the opposite case may be taken from the same class of subjects as the former, we will suppose, in contrast with the situation of the judge, the position of the legislator. As the judge has laws for his guidance, so the legislator has rules, and maxims of policy; but it would be a manifest error to suppose that the legislator is bound by these maxims in the same manner as the judge is bound by the laws, and that all he has to do is to argue down from them to the particular case, as the judge does from the laws. The legislator is bound to take into consideration the reasons or grounds of the maxim; the judge has nothing to do with those of the law, except so far as a consideration of them may throw light upon the intention of the law-maker, where his words have left it doubtful. To the judge, the rule, once positively ascertained, is final; but the legislator, or other practitioner, who goes by rules rather than by their reasons, like the old-fashioned German tacticians who were vanquished by Napoleon, or the physician who preferred that his patients should die by rule rather than recover contrary to it, is rightly judged to be a mere pedant, and the slave of his formulas.

Now, the reasons of a maxim of policy, or of any other rule of art, can be no other than the theorems of the corresponding science.

The relation in which rules of art stand to doctrines of science may be thus characterized. The art proposes to itself an end to be attained, defines the end, and hands it over to the science. The science receives it, considers it as a phenomenon or effect to be studied, and having investigated its causes and conditions, sends it back to art with a theorem of the combinations of circumstances by which it could be produced. Art then examines these combinations of circumstances, and according as any of them are or are not in human power, pronounces the end attainable or not. The only one of the premises, therefore, which Art supplies, is the original major premise, which asserts that the attainment of the given end is desirable. Science then lends to Art the proposition (obtained by a series of inductions or of deductions) that the performance of certain actions will attain the end. From these premises Art concludes that the performance of these actions is desirable, and finding it also practicable, converts the theorem into a rule or precept.

On the Probable Futurity of the Labouring Classes (from Principles of Political Economy)

1. [*The theory of dependence and protection is no longer applicable to the condition of modern society*] The observations in the preceding

chapter had for their principal object to deprecate a false ideal of human society. Their applicability to the practical purposes of present times, consists in moderating the inordinate importance attached to the mere increase of production, and fixing attention upon improved distribution, and a large remuneration of labour, as the two desiderata. Whether the aggregate produce increases absolutely or not, is a thing in which, after a certain amount has been obtained, neither the legislator nor the philanthropist need feel any strong interest: but, that it should increase relatively to the number of those who share in it, is of the utmost possible importance; and this, (whether the wealth of mankind be stationary, or increasing at the most rapid rate ever known in an old country,) must depend on the opinions and habits of the most numerous class, the class of manual labourers.

When I speak, either in this place or elsewhere, of "the labouring classes," or of labourers as a "class," I use those phrases in compliance with custom, and as descriptive of an existing, but by no means a necessary or permanent, state of social relations. I do not recognise as either just or salutary, a state of society in which there is any "class" which is not labouring; any human beings, exempt from bearing their share of the necessary labours of human life, except those unable to labour, or who have fairly earned rest by previous toil. So long, however, as the great social evil exists of a non-labouring class, labourers also constitute a class, and may be spoken of, though only provisionally, in that character.

Considered in its moral and social aspect, the state of the labouring people has latterly been a subject of much more speculation and discussion than formerly; and the opinion that it is not now what it ought to be, has become very general. The suggestions which have been promulgated, and the controversies which have been excited, on detached points rather than on the foundations of the subject, have put in evidence the existence of two conflicting theories, respecting the social position desirable for manual labourers. The one may be called the theory of dependence and protection, the other that of self-dependence.

According to the former theory, the lot of the poor, in all things which affect them collectively, should be regulated *for* them, not *by* them. They should not be required or encouraged to think for themselves, or give to their own reflection or forecast an influential voice in the determination of their destiny. It is supposed to be the duty of the higher classes to think for them, and to take the responsibility of their lot, as the commander and officers of an army take that of the soldiers composing it. This function, it is contended, the higher classes should prepare themselves to perform conscientiously, and their whole demeanour should impress the poor with a reliance on it, in order that, while yielding passive and active obedience to the rules prescribed for them, they may resign themselves in all other respects to a trustful *insouciance*, and repose under the shadow of their protectors. The relation between rich and poor, according to this theory (a theory also applied to the relation between men and women) should be only partly authoritative; it should be amiable, moral, and sentimental: affectionate tutelage on the one side, respectful and grateful deference on the other. The rich should be *in loco parentis* to the poor, guiding and restraining them like children. Of spontaneous action on their part there should be no need. They should be called on for nothing but to do their day's work, and to be moral and religious. Their morality and religion should be provided for them by their superiors, who should see them properly taught it, and should do all that is necessary to ensure their being, in return for labour and attachment, properly fed, clothed, housed, spiritually edified, and innocently amused.

This is the ideal of the future, in the minds of those whose dissatisfaction with the present assumes the form of affection and regret towards the past. Like other ideals, it exercises an unconscious influence on the opinions and sentiments of numbers who never consciously guide themselves by any ideal. It has also this in common with other ideals, that it has never been historically realized. It makes its appeal to our imaginative sympathies in the character of a restoration of the good times of our forefathers. But no times can be pointed out in which the higher classes of this or any other country performed a part even distantly resembling the one assigned to them in this theory. It is an idealization, grounded on the conduct and character of here and there an individual. All privileged and powerful classes, as such, have used their power in the interest of their own selfishness, and have indulged their self-importance in despising, and not in lovingly caring for, those who were, in their estimation, degraded, by being under the necessity of working for their benefit. I do not affirm that what has always been must always be, or that human improvement has no tendency to correct the intensely selfish feelings engendered by power; but though the evil may be lessened, it cannot be eradicated, until the power itself is withdrawn. This, at least, seems to me undeniable, that long before the superior classes could be sufficiently improved to govern in the tutelary manner supposed, the inferior classes would be too much improved to be so governed.

I am quite sensible of all that is seductive in the picture of society which this theory presents. Though the facts of it have no prototype in the past, the feelings have. In them lies all that there is of reality in the conception. As the idea is essentially repulsive of a society only held together by the relations and feelings arising out of pecuniary interests, so there is something naturally attractive in a form of society abounding in strong personal attachments and disinterested self-devotion. Of such feelings it must be admitted that the relation of protector and protected has hitherto been the richest source. The strongest attachments of human beings in general, are towards the things or the persons that stand between them and some dreaded evil. Hence, in an age of lawless violence and insecurity, and general hardness and roughness of manners, in which life is beset with dangers and sufferings at every step, to those who have neither a commanding position of their own, nor a claim on the protection of some one who has—a generous giving of protection, and a grateful receiving of it, are the strongest ties which connect human beings; the feelings arising from that relation are their warmest feelings; all the enthusiasm and tenderness of the most sensitive natures gather round it; loyalty on the one part and chivalry on the other are principles exalted into passions. I do not desire to depreciate these qualities. The error lies in not perceiving, that these virtues and sentiments, like the clanship and the hospitality of the wandering Arab, belong emphatically to a rude and imperfect state of the social union; and that the feelings between protector and protected, whether between kings and subjects, rich and poor, or men and women, can no longer have this beautiful and endearing character, where there are no longer any serious dangers from which to protect. What is there in the present state of society to make it natural that human beings, of ordinary strength and courage, should glow with the warmest gratitude and devotion in return for protection? The laws protect them, wherever the laws do not criminally fail in their duty. To be under the power of some one, instead of being as formerly the sole condition of safety, is now, speaking generally, the only situation which exposes to grievous wrong. The so-called protectors are now the only persons against whom, in any ordinary circumstances, protection is needed. The brutality and tyranny with which every police report is filled, are those of husbands to wives, of parents to children. That the law does not prevent these atrocities, that it is only now making a first timid attempt to repress and punish them, is no matter of necessity, but the deep disgrace of those by whom the laws are made and administered. No man or woman who either possesses or is able to earn an independent livelihood, requires any other protection than that which the law could and ought to give. This being the case, it argues great ignorance of human nature to continue taking for granted that relations founded on protection must always subsist, and not to see that the assumption of the part of protector, and of the power which belongs to it, without any of the necessities which justify it, must engender feelings opposite to loyalty.

Of the working men, at least in the more advanced countries of Europe, it may be pronounced certain, that the patriarchal or paternal system of government is one to which they will not again be subject.

That question was decided, when they were taught to read, and allowed access to newspapers and political tracts; when dissenting preachers were suffered to go among them, and appeal to their faculties and feelings in opposition to the creeds professed and countenanced by their superiors; when they were brought together in numbers, to work socially under the same roof; when railways enabled them to shift from place to place, and change their patrons and employers as easily as their coats; when they were encouraged to seek a share in the government, by means of the electoral franchise. The working classes have taken their interests into their own hands, and are perpetually showing that they think the interests of their employers not identical with their own, but opposite to them. Some among the higher classes flatter themselves that these tendencies may be counteracted by moral and religious education: but they have let the time go by for giving an education which can serve their purpose. The principles of the Reformation have reached as low down in society as reading and writing, and the poor will not much longer accept morals and religion of other people's prescribing. I speak more particularly of this country, especially the town population, and the districts of the most scientific agriculture or the highest wages, Scotland and the north of England. Among the more inert and less modernized agricultural population of the southern counties, it might be possible for the gentry to retain, for some time longer, something of the ancient deference and submission of the poor, by bribing them with high wages and constant employment; by insuring them support, and never requiring them to do anything which they do not like. But these are two conditions which never have been combined, and never can be, for long together. A guarantee of subsistence can only be practically kept up, when work is enforced and superfluous multiplication restrained by at least a moral compulsion. It is then, that the would-be revivers of old times which they do not understand, would feel practically in how hopeless a task they were engaged. The whole fabric of patriarchal or seignorial influence, attempted to be raised on the foundation of caressing the poor, would be shattered against the necessity of enforcing a stringent Poor-law.

2. [*The future well-being of the labouring classes is principally dependent on their own mental cultivation*]. It is on a far other basis that the well-being and well-doing of the labouring people must henceforth rest. The poor have come out of leading-strings, and cannot any longer be governed or treated like children. To their own qualities must now be commended the care of their destiny. Modern nations will have to learn the lesson, that the well-being of a people must exist by means of the justice and self-government, the δικαιοσυνη and σωφροσυνη, of the individual citizens. The theory of dependence attemps to dispense with the necessity of these qualities in the dependent classes.

But now, when even in position they are becoming less and less dependent, and their minds less and less acquiescent in the degree of dependence which remains, the virtues of independence are those which they stand in need of. Whatever advice, exhortation, or guidance is held out to the labouring classes, must henceforth be tendered to them as equals, and accepted by them with their eyes open. The prospect of the future depends on the degree in which they can be made rational beings.

There is no reason to believe that prospect other than hopeful. The progress indeed has hitherto been, and still is, slow. But there is a spontaneous education going on in the minds of the multitude, which may be greatly accelerated and improved by artificial aids. The instruction obtained from newspapers and political tracts may not be the most solid kind of instruction, but it is an immense improvement upon none at all. What it does for a people, has been admirably exemplified during the cotton crisis, in the case of the Lancashire spinners and weavers, who have acted with the consistent good sense and forbearance so justly applauded, simply because, being readers of newspapers, they understood the causes of the calamity which had befallen them, and knew that it was in no way imputable either to their employers or to the Government. It is not certain that their conduct would have been as rational and exemplary, if the distress had preceded the salutary measure of fiscal emancipation which gave existence to the penny press. The institutions for lectures and discussion, the collective deliberations on questions of common interest, the trades unions, the political agitation, all serve to awaken public spirit, to diffuse variety of ideas among the mass, and to excite thought and reflection in the more intelligent. Although the too early attainment of political franchises by the least educated class might retard, instead of promoting, their improvement, there can be little doubt that it has been greatly stimulated by the attempt to acquire them. In the meantime, the working classes are now part of the public; in all discussions on matters of general interest they, or a portion of them, are now partakers; all who use the press as an instrument may, if it so happens, have them for an audience; the avenues of instruction through which the middle classes acquire such ideas as they have, are accessible to, at least, the operatives in the towns. With these resources, it cannot be doubted that they will increase in intelligence, even by their own unaided efforts; while there is reason to hope that great improvements both in the quality and quantity of school education will be effected by the exertions either of government or of individuals, and that the progress of the mass of the people in mental cultivation, and in the virtues which are dependent on it, will take place more rapidly, and with fewer intermittences and aberrations, than if left to itself.

From this increase of intelligence, several effects may be confidently anticipated. First: that they will become even less willing than at present to be led and governed, and directed into the way they should go, by the mere authority and *prestige* of superiors. If they have not now, still less will they have hereafter, any deferential awe, or religious principle of obedience, holding them in mental subjection to a class above them. The theory of dependence and protection will be more and more intolerable to them, and they will require that their conduct and condition shall be essentially self-governed. It is, at the same time, quite possible that they may demand, in many cases, the intervention of the legislature in their affairs, and the regulation by law of various things which concern them, often under very mistaken ideas of their interest. Still, it is their own will, their own ideas and suggestions, to which they will demand that effect should be given, and not rules laid down for them by other people. It is quite consistent with this, that they should feel respect for superiority of intellect and knowledge, and defer much to the opinions, on any subject, of those whom they think well acquainted with it. Such deference is deeply grounded in human nature; but they will judge for themselves of the persons who are and are not entitled to it.

3. [*Probable effects of improved intelligence in causing a better adjustment of population—Would be promoted by the social independence of women*] It appears to me impossible but that the increase of intelligence, of education, and of the love of independence among the working classes, must be attended with a corresponding growth of the good sense which manifests itself in provident habits of conduct, and that population, therefore, will bear a gradually diminishing ratio to capital and employment. This most desirable result would be much accelerated by another change, which lies in the direct line of the best tendencies of the time; the opening of industrial occupations freely to both sexes. The same reasons which make it no longer necessary that the poor should depend on the rich, make it equally unnecessary that women should depend on men; and the least which justice requires is that law and custom should not enforce dependence (when the correlative protection has become superfluous) by ordaining that a woman, who does not happen to have a provision by inheritance, shall have scarcely any means open to her of gaining a livelihood, except as a wife and mother. Let women who prefer that occupation, adopt it; but that there should be no option, no other *carrière* possible for the great majority of women, except in the humbler departments of life, is a flagrant social injustice. The ideas and institutions by which the accident of sex is made the groundwork of an inequality of legal rights, and a forced dissimilarity of social functions, must ere long be recognized as the greatest hindrance to moral, social, and even intellectual improve-

ment. On the present occasion I shall only indicate, among the probable consequences of the industrial and social independence of women, a great diminution of the evil of over-population. It is by devoting one-half of the human species to that exclusive function, by making it fill the entire life of one sex, and interweave itself with almost all the objects of the other, that the animal instinct in question is nursed into the disproportionate preponderance which it has hitherto exercised in human life.

Liberty (from *On Liberty*)

Chapter I

Introductory

The subject of this essay is not the so-called liberty of the will, so unfortunately opposed to the misnamed doctrine of philosophical necessity; but civil, or social liberty: the nature and limits of the power which can be legitimately exercised by society over the individual. A question seldom stated and hardly ever discussed in general terms, but which profoundly influences the practical controversies of the age by its latent presence, and is likely soon to make itself recognized as the vital question of the future. It is so far from being new, that, in a certain sense, it has divided mankind almost from the remotest ages; but in the stage of progress into which the more civilized portions of the species have now entered, it presents itself under new conditions, and requires a different and more fundamental treatment. . . .

But in political and philosophical theories, as well as in persons, success discloses faults and infirmities which failure might have concealed from observation. The notion that the people have no need to limit their power over themselves, might seem axiomatic when popular government was a thing only dreamed about, or read of as having existed at some distant period of the past. Neither was that notion necessarily disturbed by such temporary aberrations as those of the French Revolution, the worst of which were the work of a usurping few, and which, in any case, belonged not to the permanent working of popular institutions, but to a sudden and convulsive outbreak against monarchical and aristocratic despotism. In time, however, a democratic republic came to occupy a large portion of the earth's surface, and made itself felt as one of the most powerful members of the community of nations; and elective and responsible government became subject to the observations and criticisms which wait upon a great existing fact. It was now perceived that such phrases as 'self-government,' and 'the power of the people over themselves,' do not express the true state of the case. The 'people' who exercise the power are not always the same people with those over whom it is exercised; and the 'self-government' spoken of is not the government of each by himself, but of each by all the rest. The will of the people, moreover, practically means the will of the most numerous or the most active *part* of the people; the majority, or those who succeed in making themselves accepted as the majority: the people, consequently *may* desire to oppress a part of their number, and precautions are as much needed against this as against any other abuse of power. The limitation, therefore, of the power of government over individuals loses none of its importance when the holders of power are regularly accountable to the community, that is, to the strongest party therein. This view of things, recommending itself equally to the intelligence of thinkers and to the inclination of those important classes in European society to whose real or supposed interests democracy is adverse, has had no difficulty in establishing itself; and in political speculations 'the tyranny of the majority' is now generally included among the evils against which society requires to be on its guard.

Like other tyrannies, the tyranny of the majority was at first, and is still vulgarly, held in dread chiefly as operating through the acts of the public authorities. But reflecting persons perceived that when society is itself the tyrant—society collectively over the separate individuals who compose it—its means of tyrannizing are not restricted to the acts which it may do by the hands of its political functionaries. Society can and does execute its own mandates; and if it issues wrong mandates instead of right, or any mandates at all in things with which it ought not to meddle, it practices a social tyranny more formidable than many kinds of political oppression, since, though not usually upheld by such extreme penalties, it leaves fewer means of escape, penetrating much more deeply into the details of life, and enslaving the soul itself. Protection, therefore, against the tyranny of the magistrate is not enough: there needs protection also against the tyranny of the prevailing opinion and feeling; against the tendency of society to impose, by other means than civil penalties, its own ideas and practices as rules of conduct on those who dissent from them; to fetter the development, and, if possible, prevent the formation, of any individuality not in harmony with its ways, and compels all characters to fashion themselves upon the model of its own. There is a limit to the legitimate interference of collective opinion with individual independence; and to find that limit, and maintain it against encroachment, is as indispensable to a good condition of human affairs, as protection against political despotism.

But though this proposition is not likely to be contested in general terms, the practical question, where to place the limit—how to make the fitting adjustment between individual independence and social control—is a subject on which nearly everything remains to be done. All that makes existence valuable to anyone, depends on the enforcement of restraints upon the actions of other people. Some rules of conduct, therefore, must be imposed, by law in the first place, and by opinion on many things which are not fit subjects for the operation of law. What these rules should be is the principal question in human affairs; but if we except a few of the most obvious cases, it is one of those which least progress has been made in resolving. No two ages, and scarcely any two countries, have decided it alike; and the decision of one age or country is a wonder to another. Yet the people of any given age and country no more suspect any difficulty in it, than if it were a subject on which mankind had always been agreed. The rules which obtain among themselves appear to them self-evident and self-justifying. This all but universal illusion is one of the examples of the magical influence of custom, which is not only, as the proverb says, a second nature, but is continually mistaken for the first. The effect of custom, in preventing any misgiving respecting the rules of conduct which mankind impose on one another, is all the more complete because the subject is one on which it is not generally considered necessary that reasons should be given, either by one person to others or by each to himself. . . . Wherever there is an ascendant class, a large portion of the morality of the country emanates from its class interests, and its feelings of class superiority. The morality between Spartans and Helots, between planters and Negroes, between princes and subjects, between nobles and roturiers, between men and women, has been for the most part the creation of these class interests and feelings; and the sentiments thus generated react in turn upon the moral feelings of the members of the ascendant class, in their relations among themselves. Where, on the other hand, a class, formerly ascendant, has lost its ascendancy, or where its ascendancy is unpopular, the prevailing moral sentiments frequently bear the impress of an impatient dislike of superiority. Another grand determining principle of the rules of conduct, both in act and forbearance, which have been enforced by law or opinion, has been the servility of mankind towards the supposed preferences or aversions of their temporal masters or of their gods. This servility, though essentially selfish, is not hypocrisy; it gives rise to perfectly genuine sentiments of abhorrence; it made men burn magicians and heretics. Among so many baser influences, the general and obvious interests of society have of course had a share, and a large one, in the direction of the moral sentiments; less, however, as a matter of reason, and on their own account, than as a consequence of the sympathies and antipathies which grew out of them; and sympathies and antipathies which had little or nothing to do with the interests of society, have made themselves felt in the establishment of moralities with quite as great force.

The likings and dislikings of society, or of some powerful portion of it, are thus the main thing which has practically determined the rules laid down for general observance, under the penalties of law or opinion. And in general, those who have been in advance of society in thought and feeling, have left this condition of things unassailed in principle, however they may have come into conflict with it in some of its details. They have occupied themselves rather in inquiring what things society ought to like or dislike, than in questioning whether its likings or dislikings should be a law to individuals. They preferred endeavoring to alter the feelings of mankind on the particular points on which they were themselves heretical, rather than make common cause in defense of freedom, with heretics generally. The only case in which the higher ground has been taken on principle and maintained with consistency, by any but an individual here and there, is that of religious belief: a case instructive in many ways, and not least so as forming a most striking instance of the fallibility of what is called the moral sense; for the *odium theologicum*, in a sincere bigot, is one of the most unequivocal cases of moral feeling. Those who first broke the yoke of what called itself the Universal Church, were in general as little willing to permit difference of religious opinion as that church itself. But when the heat of the conflict was over, without giving a complete victory to any party, and each church or sect was reduced to limit its hopes to retaining possession of the ground it already occupied; minorities, seeing that they had no chance of becoming majorities, were under the necessity of pleading to those whom they could not convert, for permission to differ. It is accordingly on this battlefield, almost solely, that the rights of the individual against society have been asserted on broad grounds of principle, and the claim of society to exercise authority over dissentients openly controverted. The great writers to whom the world owes what religious liberty it possesses, have mostly asserted freedom of conscience as an indefeasible right, and denied absolutely that a human being is accountable to others for his religious belief. Yet so natural to mankind is intolerance in whatever they really care about, that religious freedom has hardly anywhere been practically realized, except where religious indifference, which dislikes to have its peace disturbed by theological quarrels, has added its weight to the scale. In the minds of almost all religious persons, even in the most tolerant countries, the duty of toleration is admitted with tacit reserves. One person will bear with dissent in matters of church government, but not of dogma; another can tolerate everybody, short of a Papist or a Unitarian; another everyone who believes in revealed religion; a few extend their charity a little further, but stop at the belief in a God and in a future state. Wherever the sentiment of the majority is still genuine and intense, it is found to have abated little of its claim to be obeyed. . . .

The object of this essay is to assert one very simple principle, as entitled to govern absolutely the dealings of society with the individual in the way of compulsion and control, whether the means used be physical force in the form of legal penalties, or the moral coercion of public opinion. That principle is, that the sole end for which mankind are warranted, individually or collectively, in interfering with the liberty of action of any of their number, is self-protection. That the only purpose for which power can be rightfully exercised over any member of a civilized community, against his will, is to prevent harm to others. His own good, either physical or moral, is not a sufficient warrant. He cannot rightfully be compelled to do or forbear because it will be better for him to do so, because it will make him happier, because, in the opinions of others, to do so would be wise, or even right. These are good reasons for remonstrating with him, or reasoning with him, or persuading him, or entreating him, but not for compelling him, or visiting him with any evil in case he do otherwise. To justify that, the conduct from which it is desired to deter him must be calculated to produce evil to someone else. The only part of the conduct of anyone, for which he is amenable to society, is that which concerns others. In the part which merely concerns himself, his independence is, of right, absolute. Over himself, over his own body and mind, the individual is sovereign.

It is perhaps hardly necessary to say that this doctrine is meant to apply only to human beings in the maturity of their faculties. We are not speaking of children, or of young persons below the age which the law may fix as that of manhood or womanhood. Those who are still in a state to require being taken care of by others, must be protected against their own actions as well as against external injury. For the same reason, we may leave out of consideration those backward states of society in which the race itself may be considered as in its nonage. The early difficulties in the way of spontaneous progress are so great, and there is seldom any choice of means for overcoming them; and a ruler full of the spirit of improvement is warranted in the use of any expedients that will attain an end, perhaps otherwise unattainable. Despotism is a legitimate mode of government in dealing with barbarians, provided the end be their improvement, and the means justified by actually effecting that end. Liberty, as a principle, has no application to any state of things anterior to the time when mankind have become capable of being improved by free and equal discussion. Until then, there is nothing for them but implicit obedience to an Akbar or a Charlemagne, if they are so fortunate as to find one. But as soon as mankind have attained the capacity of being guided to their own improvement by conviction or persuasion (a period long since reached in all nations with whom we need here concern ourselves), compulsion, either in the direct form or in that of pains and penalties for non-compliance, is no longer admissible as a means to their own good, and justifiable only for the security of others.

It is proper to state that I forego any advantage which could be derived to my argument from the idea of abstract right, as a thing independent of utility. I regard utility as the ultimate appeal on all ethical questions; but it must be utility in the largest sense, grounded on the permanent interests of a man as a progressive being. Those interests, I contend, authorized the subjection of individual spontaneity to external control, only in respect to those actions of each which concern the interest of other people. If anyone does an act hurtful to others, there is a _prima facie_ case for punishing him, by law, or, where legal penalties are not safely applicable, by general disapprobation. There are also many positive acts for the benefit of others, which he may rightfully be compelled to perform: such as to give evidence in a court of justice; to bear his fair share in the common defense, or in any other joint work necessary to the interest of the society of which he enjoys the protection; and to perform certain acts of individual beneficence, such as saving a fellow-creature's life, or interposing to protect the defenseless against ill-usage, things which whenever it is obviously a man's duty to do, he may rightfully be made responsible to society for not doing. A person may cause evil to others not only by his actions but by his inaction, and in either case he is justly accountable to them for the injury. The latter case, it is true, requires a much more cautious exercise of compulsion than the former. To make anyone answerable for doing evil to others is the rule; to make him answerable for not preventing evil is, comparatively speaking, the exception. Yet there are many cases clear enough and grave enough to justify that exception. In all things which regard the external relations of the individual, he is _de jure_ amenable to those whose interests are concerned, and, if need be, to society as their protector. There are often good reasons for not holding him to the responsibility; but these reasons must arise from the special expediencies of the case: either because it is a kind of case in which he is on the whole likely to act better, when left to his own discretion, than when controlled in any way in which society have it in their power to control him; or because the attempt to exercise control would produce other evils, greater than those which it would prevent. When such reasons as these preclude the enforcement of responsibility, the conscience of the agent himself should step into the vacant judgment seat, and protect those interests of others which have no external protection; judging himself all the more rigidly, because the case does not admit of his being made accountable to the judgment of his fellow-creatures.

But there is a sphere of action in which society, as distinguished from the individual, has, if any, only an indirect interest; comprehending all that portion of a person's life and conduct which affects only himself, or if it also affects others, only with their free, voluntary, and undeceived consent and participation. When I say only himself, I mean directly, and in the first instance; for whatever affects himself, may affect others through himself; and the objection which may be grounded on this contingency, will receive consideration in the sequel. This, then, is the appropriate region of human liberty. It comprises, *first*, the inward domain of consciousness; demanding liberty of conscience in the most comprehensive sense; liberty of thought and feeling; absolute freedom of opinion and sentiment on all subjects, practical or speculative, scientific, moral, or theological. The liberty of expressing and publishing opinions may seem to fall under a different principle, since it belongs to that part of the conduct of an individual which concerns other people; but, being almost of as much importance as the liberty of thought itself, and resting in great part on the same reasons, is practically inseparable from it. *Secondly*, the principle requires liberty of tastes and pursuits; of framing the plan of our life to suit our own character; of doing as we like, subject to such consequences as may follow: without impediment from our fellow-creatures, so long as what we do does not harm them, even though they should think our conduct foolish, perverse, or wrong. *Thirdly*, from this liberty of each individual, follows the liberty, within the same limits, of combination among individuals; freedom to unite, for any purpose not involving harm to others: the persons combining being supposed to be of full age, and not forced or deceived,

No society in which these liberties are not, on the whole, respected, is free, whatever may be its form of government; and none is completely free in which they do not exist absolute and unqualified. The only freedom which deserves the name, is that of pursuing our own good in our own way, so long as we do not attempt to deprive others of theirs, or impede their efforts to obtain it. Each is the proper guardian of his own health, whether bodily, or mental and spiritual. Mankind are greater gainers by suffering each other to live as seems good to themselves, than by compelling each to live as seems good to the rest. ...

It will be convenient for the argument, if, instead of at once entering upon the general thesis, we confine ourselves in the first instance to a single branch of it, on which the principle here stated is, if not fully, yet to a certain point, recognized by the current opinions. This one branch is the *liberty of thought*: from which it is impossible to separate the cognate liberty of speaking and of writing. Although these liberties, to some considerable amount, form part of the political morality of all countries which profess religious toleration and free institutions, the grounds, both philosophical and practical, on which they rest, are perhaps not so familiar to the general mind, nor so thoroughly appreciated by many even of the leaders of opinion, as might have been expected. Those grounds, when rightly understood, are of much wider application than to only one division of the subject, and a thorough consideration of this part of the question will be found the best introduction to the remainder.

Review Questions

1. What is the basic idea of Mill's utilitarianism?
2. Explain the meaning of the law of causation in Mill; does it differ from Hume's? How does it apply to living in society? How is it reconciled to freedom?
3. Describe Mill's defense of the individual and the minority in the face of a capitalist economy.
4. Describe Mill's view of the individual's claim to liberty while still a member of society.
5. The true religion is the Religion of Humanity; explain what Mill means.

PART IV

The Contemporary Period

The Spirit of Contemporary Philosophy: The Ascendancy of the Person

Continuity with the past allows the time of any given age to be fixed differently by different authors. Thus, the "contemporary period" can be set at an earlier or later time depending on the author's purpose. So if, among the many features of contemporary philosophy, concern for the *human person* is seen as giving it its unique coloring, then the three mid-nineteenth-century philosophers Kierkegaard, Nietzsche, and Marx are the ones to begin with, and the philosophical humanism they espoused must be seen as part of the historical context in which they appeared.

The year 1848, as a prism of the political and cultural forces at work, is the most significant year of the nineteenth century in Europe. This was the year in which the dissatisfaction of the masses, smoldering for decades, erupted all over Europe with such power that it is often referred to as the Revolution of 1848. Except for some concessions to liberalism in England, France, and Belgium, most of mid- nineteenth-century Europe lived under political repression. The hope for freedom generated by the French Revolution was dashed by the personal goals and final defeat of Napoleon and sealed at the Congress of Vienna in 1815 when the monarchical claims of the Old Regime were reasserted in central Europe. But the masses still longed for change: they wanted social reform, economic improvement, and a role in determining how they were to be governed; many ethnic groups yearned for their rights as independent peoples. Longings that could not find expression in politics were embodied in the activity of young university students, writers, artists, and musicians — Chopin composing one polonaise after another out of compassion for his suffering Poland and

Byron fighting for Greek independence from Turkey — "romantics" all because they yearned for the unfulfilled. Throughout 1848, beginning in Paris, there were demonstrations, uprisings, and insurrections across the continent, massive efforts to proclaim a variety of rights and freedoms. For a short time, these movements appeared to be on the verge of success, but within three years the Old Regime prevailed and the longing for human dignity went unfulfilled.

The invention of new machines to speed production and transportation took a horrible toll of humanity during the Industrial Revolution, when the absence of social conscience drove thousands of workers into a subhuman existence and robbed children of their childhood. Poverty and crisis, the lot of too many in the years immediately preceding 1848, were symbolized in the great bread riots of 1847 that broke out in several European cities. That the *Communist Manifesto* of Marx and Engels should have appeared in 1848 was no coincidence.

Science, begun so enthusiastically in the seventeenth century, continued to make a steady stream of contributions in the nineteenth. The laboratory of Justus Liebig was world famous; Faraday's name became one with electricity; organic chemistry was discovered and the way paved for the creation of synthetic substances; Louis Pasteur made medical history; and towards the turn of the century the names of Roentgen, Curie, Einstein, and Planck gained a permanent place in the history of physics. But it was the science of biology, which up to then had been mainly the classification of types, that revealed the transcendent nature of the living body, for Gregor Mendel's experiments revealed the laws of heredity whereby characteristics are transmitted from one generation to another, and Charles Darwin's discovery of natural selection established the evolution of living beings, including man. Evolution corroborated the conclusion of geologists that the age of the earth far exceeded the biblical 4004 years—once again, as in the seventeenth century, causing religious believers to readjust their interpretation of the Bible.

Toward the end of the nineteenth century, another revolution took place that extended well into the twentieth: the revolution in psychology led by Sigmund Freud. In this discovery of the subconscious, and of how the subconscious becomes the unknown source of human activity, Freud was searching for the key to restore wholeness in those persons in whom it had been shattered. In the context of the nineteenth century, an individual so in need of help was seen as another example of the struggle for human personhood; the forces of suppression were viewed as never really overcome but only temporarily driven into the subconscious, to resurface later with the same power to destroy; such an individual is still struggling for freedom, for dignity, and for personhood.

It is clear, then, that the overarching concern of the contemporary period, especially in its initial phases, was the human person, and thinkers and activists in general were bent on either probing or expressing the concepts of human value and dignity. But the main philosophical problem was how to ground human value: is human dignity self-contained? Is human value a value unto itself? Is there anything "higher," in virtue of which the person is to be understood? The responses to these questions were clearly divided into a humanism that was God centered or not — a theistc humanism or an atheistic humanism. But the responses were not the result of academic argumentation for the existence or nonexistence of God; they were the result of reactions to the God of tradition, and in this struggle the opponents of institutionalized religion, particularly Christianity, carried the day. The areligious humanist saw the church, Protestant or Catholic, as concerned with institutions and empty formulas, not the humanness of its members. And precisely because the church professed to stand for the ultimate good of man, it was to be ultimately blamed for man's sorry plight.

This is the background to the distinctive change that took place in philosophy, heralding a new age and called by some a "Copernican revolution." The course of philosophy in the hundred years preceding the mid-nineteenth century was focused on the object: with *objective* questions asked about what we know and how we know it; if man was considered a proper object of philosophy, it was precisely as an object rather than as a human being, with personhood in danger of being lost in the abstractions of transcendentalism. As we previously cautioned ourselves in regard to the emergence of new ideas, it is not as though, up to this time, no attention at all had been given to the individual as a human being; now, however, there is a definite change in the texture of inquiry: the human being in his *lived existence* becomes the focus of concern. Existence is not abstract; it pertains to the *concrete* individual, whose very condition of existence is the experience with which a philosopher should begin.

Man thus became the subject of philosophy and, though Kierkegaard, Nietzsche, and Marx approached man from different viewpoints, their hope was to rediscover human values and human dignity. The point of contact with human existence for Kierkegaard was the *religious* man, for Nietzsche the *cultural* man, and for Marx the *laboring* man; although their paths led through different terrains, the unmistakable common horizon was humanity. This was the key to the "Copernican revolution."

The importance of humanist themes continued unabated, and in the next generation, Bergson and James, following their lifelong interest in biology and psychology, felt humanity was under an imperative to perfect itself in holiness. In the immediate past, Russell and Wittgenstein, in their commitment to the analysis of language, developed insights permitting a deeper understanding of the human person; and Sartre, probing the depths of intersubjectivity, paved the way for a deeper appreciation of human freedom.

What contemporary philosophy has done is to show that lived existence puts in proper perspective any claim that human nature is fixed or static by making clear the dynamic and unfolding character of the human being; it has generated an insight into the individual that abstractions cannot do.

CHAPTER 20

Søren Kierkegaard (1813–1855)

Introduction

As a philosopher totally responding to the personal dimension of life, Søren Kierkegaard understandably reacted against the abstractions of Hegel, which he saw as hardly touching the real world — without place for the being whose meaning is our only real concern, the individual person. He spent his brief life trying to rectify this neglect.

Kierkegaard was born in Copenhagen, Denmark, in 1813 into a rigidly pietistic family. His father was a good man but endowed with a somber sense of God as a severe demander of righteous behavior, with misbehavior likely to be punished by a proportionate displeasure. He was a successful businessman and an influential figure, though he had a moody and melancholy disposition. The personality traits of his father contributed heavily to the psychological burden the already introspective young man had to carry, and he did the only thing he could to free himself, revolting against religion and, indeed, life in general. He enrolled at the University of Copenhagen in theology, though his main interests were always philosophy and literature; he read enthusiastically the works of Plato, Shakespeare, and the romantic authors. He led a rather free-spirited life as a student, and gradually his earlier cynicism wore off as he came to see the importance of personal commitment to ethical and religious values. He wrote of a moment of "indescribable joy" in May 1838, "a joy which cools and refreshes us like a breath of wind, a wave of air, from the trade wind which blows from the plains of Mamre to the everlasting habitations." So strong did this feeling of commitment become that he broke his engagement to a girl he loved because he felt that the requirements of married life would detract from his self-appointed mission, which was to establish the individual as the centerpiece of philosophy. One of the elements of this mission was a profound distrust of institutions, which, by their

539

own inner logic, tend to manipulate, if not absorb, the individual. This is why Kierkegaard, though he fervently held that one's authentic individuality is measured by how one stands before God, declaimed against the Danish state church, and every institutionalized religion, as inimical to the true interests of the individual. He died in 1855. Though he died young, he had written voluminously and passionately. His chief works are *Fear and Trembling* (1843), *Either/Or* (1843), *Philosophical Fragments* (1844), and *Concluding Scientific Postscript to the Philosophical Fragments* (1846).

Kierkegaard is an intensely personal philosopher because, for him, philosophy is nothing more than a personal reflection on one's lived experience. Life is too precious and mysterious to be entrusted to a system of abstract logic, which is why, while not oblivious to Hegel's undoubted merits, Kierkegaard rejected his idealism as the vehicle capable of destroying the individual. The human being must be fully aware of his individuality; it is his prized possession and unshared by any other creature. But the temptation to lose oneself is all too great, particularly among the masses of people whom the individual must live with; the *crowd*, by its very nature, is a destroyer of the individual: "a crowd in its very concept is the untruth, by reason of the fact that it renders the individual completely impenitent and irresponsible."

If the individual person is primary in Kierkegaard's thought, and if authentic personhood resides in one's relationship with God, then the first question to be asked is, how does one, for Kierkegaard, come to know God? His personalism precludes a systematic, reasoned approach to God's existence, for this would narrow down the infinite God to the very argument used to prove His existence and would make it impossible for God to be thought of as being any different from the categories used to know Him. I therefore do not *prove* that God exists; yet, it must be acknowledged that, whatever method reason uses to increase its understanding, it comes up against what is unknown, and it is this very fact that compels me to recognize His existence *as* the Unknown. I am, according to Kierkegaard, driven by a troubled kind of certainty to assent to this Unknown, to the very God who blesses the *leap* I have made toward Him. In Kierkegaard's own words: "So also with the proof for God's existence. As long as I keep my hold on the proof, i.e., continue to demonstrate, the existence does not come out, if for no other reason than that I am engaged in proving it; but when I let the proof go, the existence is there." He goes on: "Must not this also be taken into account, this little moment, brief as it may be — it need not be long, for it is a *leap*." So, the intellectual commitment I make to the existence of God is profoundly personal and touches the mystery of the person-to-person relationship that, though reasonable, is not a matter of reason: because God is in every sense believable and welcoming, I, by my personal choice, believe in Him; I make, in Kierkegaard's unusual expression, a "leap" toward Him, confident that the very meaning of my personhood requires it.

Kierkegaard's description of his awareness of God's existence and his response to that awareness is the immediate background of his notion of *self-actualization*, which, of all notions, is the one that summarizes his thought. *Crowd* existence, previously mentioned, violates self-identity, personhood, and human dignity, whereas the goal of self-actualization is the affirmation of the individual as an individual, the making actual of the true self within. Self-actualization is a summons, not only to my rational life, for man is much more than reason, but to my affective and emotional life as well. The individual, in the process of realizing himself, becomes a measure of himself, of society, and of mankind; he even measures God in the sense that a God–*man* relationship has no meaning for *me*, but a God–*me* relationship has. The relationship I have with God is the *ultimate* form of self-actualization because it represents the deepest level of *commitment to the truth* I can discover in myself. Truth is not impersonal, for it is what draws me to commit myself to it. I am not personally committed, let us say, to a mathematical truth, but I am committed to those conditions, circumstances, ideas, things, actions, and individuals that touch the living me. In Kierkegaard's own words, written as early as 1835, he said, "What I really need is to get clear about *what I must do*, not what I must know, except insofar as knowledge must precede every act. What matters is to find a purpose, to see what it really is that God wills that *I* shall do; the crucial thing is to find a truth which is truth *for me*, to find *the idea for which I am willing to live and die*. Of what use would it be to me to discover a so-called objective truth, to work through the philosophical systems so that I could, if asked, make critical judgments about them, could point out the fallacies in each system; of what use would it be to me to be able to develop a theory of the state, getting details from various sources and combining them into a whole, and constructing a world I did not live in but merely held up for others to see; of what use would it be to me to be able to formulate the meaning of Christianity, to be able to explain many specific points — if it had no deeper meaning *for me and for my life?*"

Throughout many of his works, Kierkegaard presents us with a description of self-actualization as a movement through several stages or levels in which the self is progressively realized. It is a growth, or even a dialectical development of sorts, in which the person mounts to the highest level of existence possible to him. He describes three such stages: the esthetic, the ethical, and the religious. Recalling that the word *esthetic* means "pertaining to the sense," the first stage is marked by its saturation with sense experience; the individual acts not out of any moral standard or firm religious faith, but out of pleasure or impulse or emotion, without care for accountability. Because life is seemingly without restraints, the esthetic man equates his carefree ways with freedom. However, this kind of life cannot continue without grave consequences because, like a stone skimming over the water and suddenly going down beneath the surface, the esthetic man sees the dispersion of his unanchored life amid an empty feeling of self-lessness and *despair*, a category that Kierkegaard acutely and poignantly analyzes. Such despair signifies the moment when a person recognizes that his emptiness is in fact a beckoning to a higher level of life; it is a "despair in truth," the boundary between the esthetic stage and the ethical. This is also the moment of choice; the esthetic man must choose to ascend to the ethical stage or to stay in the esthetic: either-or. Kierkegaard selects literary or real-life figures to typify these stages; the examplar of the esthetic man is Don Juan, the legendary lover. Here is a man who refuses to make the choice to go higher. As depicted in Mozart's opera, Don Giovanni is a lover of wine, women, and song, and as he sings of the carefree life he has led and refuses to give up, he is consumed in the flames of the burning palace, symbolic of the fires of hell.

The second, or ethical, stage is characterized by the effort to conquer the dispersion of life by the primacy of duty. A person accepts *morality* as the reponse of one's own inwardness and a further step in the actualization of the self. Though moral standards are universal and pertain to all men, they oblige me personally to choose a life of consistency and seriousness that were absent in the first stage. A person lays aside the "freedom" of the first stage and accepts his new state with all of its obligations; he lays aside, for example, the sexual carelessness of the esthetic life and, in taking a wife, accepts marriage in its full consequences. Socrates represented this kind of seriousness in his attitude toward universal obligation inasmuch as the firm stand he took before his accusers led to the surrender of his life; he is, in Kierkegaard's eyes, a "tragic hero" who renounced his life to "express the universal."

Yet, even if it is true that the universal pertains to me as an individual — for "the ethical quality is jealous for its own integrity" — it may fail to provide me, as an individual, with support in certain exceptional instances. So, it is possible, in those instances, for the universal to be transcended, and this possibility leads to the next stage.

The transition to the third stage is not an easy one. A person has to see himself "before God," to see himself as he really is, with a chasm between himself and God because of the sins he has committed and the fear he has of opening himself to the ultimate Goodness. This point, for Kierkegaard, is a higher point than the acceptance of the moral law because it marks the highest personal transformation whereby the self can become fully actualized in its relationship with God. It is the highest of *either-or* choices, for it requires the highest commitment a person can make; and because no human can measure the demands of God, the choice, for all of its sureness, is blind; this is the *leap* a person may be called upon to make, a leap from time to eternity, from the finite to the infinite, from human to divine — a movement of *faith* accompanied by all the passion befitting a critical juncture in one's life. As the paragon of faith, Kierkegaard chooses the Old Testament patriarch Abraham, singled out in the Bible as the "father of all those who believe." Heeding God's command, addressed to him as an individual, Abraham, with all the reluctance a human being can experience at surrendering his greatest love, was willing to sacrifice his son Isaac, until his hand was stayed by the admonition of an angel. The example of Abraham, Kierkegaard tells us, offers two salient points of instruction. The first is that the leap of faith is *absurd*: on the one side, a person is sure that he must believe; on the other side is the vast uncertainty of what faith leads him to. To that extent the leap of faith is absurd, reminiscent of the paradox of faith as stated by the ancient Christian, Tertullian: "I believe because it is absurd." The second point of instruction is that Abraham's stance before God is the stance of an *individual,* answering to no one but God, and inasmuch as Abraham is not following the universal standard of morality, he is *breaking through the universal*: "The paradox of faith," writes Kierkegaard, "is this, that the individual is higher than the universal."

This third stage, the religious, is the final stage of self-actualization. It is a freedom, a freedom first of all from the *dread* that haunts a person who takes life seriously but who feels life's meaning to be so elusive, so inconsistent, so absurd as to bring him to the verge of annihilation. Dread is the companion of death, which is itself a universal phenomenon. It is the point at which the human being must ask whether life is an enduring value or, when all the votes are counted, nothing more than a dance on the edge of nothingness. We saw, with Socrates, that the response we make to the problem of death is the key to the meaning of life: death is not primarily a biological problem, but a value problem. For Kierkegaard, it is in the context of a life-giving faith that the fear of death is met and dread, which gnaws away at the substance of life at every level, is overcome. This is especially true of the person who experiences a profound sense of guilt at the prospect and actuality of sin. Dread, however, recedes at the coming of faith; guilt is assuaged with the saving love of God: "Here is the reason for joy: at every moment both present and future it is eternally certain that nothing invented by the most morbid imagination and translated into fact, which can shake the belief that God is love."

Kierkegaard, as a committed but noninstitutionalized Christian, sees complete freedom and complete selfhood as realizable in Christ; it is

He, by His incarnation, who entered the "zone of the existential," thus creating the hoped-for bridge between time and eternity. For Kierkegaard, love of Christ is translated into the fundamental understanding of reality: "Christ says: I will manifest myself to him who loves me . . . and the lover . . . himself is transformed into the likeness of the thing beloved, and to become what one loves is the only fundamental way of understanding." Having possessed a "troubled truth," the man of faith now possesses the assurance that all absurdity dissolves when he says "*I* believe."

Kierkegaard's philosophy places him in the forefront of the personalist tradition. Eschewing the academic because it would restrict him to its categories, he delves into the unlit regions to discover the wellsprings of the human person. This aspect of his thought has worked its way into contemporary appreciation of personhood and left an indelible impression on existentialism; it has given fresh insights to the psychologist and the theologian, as well as to the philosopher.

Readings

The Search for Personal Meaning (from *Journals*)

What I really need is to get clear about what I must do, not what I must know, except insofar as knowledge must precede every act. What matters is to find a purpose, to see what it really is that God wills that I shall do; the crucial thing is to find a truth which is truth for me, to find the idea for which I am willing to live and die. Of what use would it be to me to discover a so-called objective truth, to work through the philosophical systems so that I could, if asked, make critical judgments about them, could point out the fallacies in each system; of what use would it be to me to be able to develop a theory of the state, getting details from various sources and combining them into a whole, and constructing a world I did not live in but merely held up for others to see; of what use would it be to me to be able to formulate the meaning of Christianity, to be able to explain many specific points—if it had no deeper meaning for me and for my life? And the better I was at it, the more I saw others appropriate the creations of my mind, the more tragic my situation would be, not unlike that of parents who in their poverty are forced to send their children out into the world and turn them over to the care of others. Of what use would it be to me for truth to stand before me, cold and naked, not caring whether or not I acknowledged it, making me uneasy rather than trustingly receptive. I certainly do not deny that I still accept an imperativeof knowledge and that through it men may be influenced, but then it must come alive in me, and this is what I now recognize as the most important of all. This is what my soul thirsts for as the African deserts thirst for water. This is what is lacking, and this is why I am like a man who has collected furniture, rented an apartment, but as yet has not found the beloved to share life's ups and downs with him. But in order to find that idea—or, to put it more correctly—to find myself, it does no good to plunge still farther into the world. That was just what I did before. The reason I thought it would be good to throw myself into law was that I believed I could develop my keenness of mind in the many muddles and messes of life. Here, too, was offered a whole mass of details in which I could lose myself; here, perhaps, with the given facts, I could construct a totality, an organic view of criminal life, pursue it in all its dark aspects (here, too, a certain fraternity of spirit is very evident). I also wanted to become a lawyer so that by putting myself in another's role I could, so to speak, find a substitute for my own life and by means of this external change find some diversion.

This is what I needed to lead a *completely human life* and not merely one of *knowledge*, so that I could base the development of my thought not on—yes, not on something called objective—something which in any case is not my own, but upon something which is bound up with the deepest roots of my existence [*Existents*], through which I am, so to speak, grafted into the divine, to which I cling fast even though the whole world may collapse. *This is what I need, and this is what I strive for.* I find joy and refreshment in contemplating the great men who have found that precious stone for which they sell all, even their lives, whether I see them becoming vigorously engaged in life, confidently proceeding on their chosen course without vacillating, or discover them off the beaten path, absorbed in themselves and in working toward their high goal. I even honor and respect the by-path which lies so close by. It is this inward action of man, this God-side of man, which is decisive, not a mass of data, for the latter will no doubt follow and will not then appear as accidental aggregates or as a succession of details, one after the other, without a system, without a focal point. I, too, have certainly looked for this focal point. I have vainly sought an anchor in the boundless sea of pleasure as well as in the depths of knowledge. I have felt the almost irresistible power with which one pleasure reaches a hand to the next; I have felt the counterfeit enthusiasm it is capable of producing. I have also felt the boredom, the shattering, which follows on its heels. I have tasted the fruits of the tree of knowledge and time and again have delighted in their savoriness. But this joy was only in the moment of cognition and did not leave a deeper mark on me. It seems to me that I have not drunk from the cup of wisdom but have fallen into it. I have sought to find the principle for my life through resignation [_Resignation_], by supposing that since everything proceeds according to inscrutable laws it could not be otherwise, by blunting my ambitions and the antennae of my vanity. Because I could not get everything to suit me, I abdicated with a consciousness of my own competence, somewhat the way decrepit clergymen resign with pension. What did I find? Not my self [_Jeg_], which is what I did seek to find in that way (I imagined my soul, if I may say so, as shut up in a box with a spring lock, which external surroundings would release by pressing the spring). —Consequently the seeking and finding of the Kingdom of Heaven was the first thing to be resolved. But it is just as useless for a man to want first of all to decide the externals and after that the fundamentals as it is for a cosmic body, thinking to form itself, first of all to decide the nature of its surface, to what bodies it should turn its light, to which its dark side, without first letting the harmony of centrifugal and centripetal forces realize [_realisere_] its existence [_Existents_] and letting the rest come of itself. One must first learn to know himself before knowing anything else (γνωθι σέαυτον). Not until a man has inwardly understood _himself_ and then sees the course he is to take does his life gain peace and meaning; only then is he free of that irksome, sinister traveling companion—that irony of life which manifests itself in the sphere of knowledge and invites true knowing to begin with a not-knowing (Socrates), just as God created the world from nothing. But in the waters of morality it is especially at home to those who still have not entered the tradewinds of virtue. Here it tumbles a person about in a horrible way, for a time lets him feel happy and content in his resolve to go ahead along the right path, then hurls him into the abyss of despair. Often it lulls a man to sleep with the thought, "After all, things cannot be otherwise," only to awaken him suddenly to a rigorous interrogation. Frequently it seems to let a veil of forgetfulness fall over the past, only to make every single trifle appear in a strong light again. When he struggles along the right path, rejoicing in having overcome temptation's power, there may come at almost the same time, right on the heels of perfect victory, an apparently insignificant external circumstance which pushes him down, like Sisyphus, from the height of the crag. Often when a person has concentrated on something, a minor external circumstance arises which destroys everything. (As in the case of a man who, weary of life, is about to throw himself into the Thames and at the crucial moment is halted by the sting of a mosquito.) Frequently a person feels his very best when the illness is the worst, as in tuberculosis. In vain he tries to resist it but he has not sufficient strength, and it is no help to him that he has gone through the same thing many times; the kind of practice acquired in this way does not apply here. Just as no one who has been taught a great deal about swimming is able to keep afloat in a storm, but only the man who is intensely convinced and has experienced that he is actually lighter than water, so a person who lacks this inward point of poise is unable to keep afloat in life's storms.—Only when a man has understood himself in this way is he able to maintain an independent existence and thus avoid surrendering his own I. How often we see (in a period when we extol that Greek historian because he knows how to appropriate an unfamiliar style so delusively like the original author's, instead of censuring him, since the first prize always goes to an author for having his own style—that is, a mode of expression and presentation qualified by his own individuality)—how often we see people who either out of mental-spiritual laziness live on the crumbs that fall from another's table or for more egotistical reasons seek to identify themselves with others, until eventually they believe it all, just like the liar through frequent repetition of his stories. Although I am still far from this kind of interior understanding of myself, with profound respect for its significance I have sought to preserve my individuality—worshipped the unknown God. With a premature anxiety I have tried to avoid coming in close contact with those things whose force of attraction might be too powerful for me. I have sought to appropriate much from them, studied their distinctive characteristics and meaning in human life, but at the same time guarded against coming, like the moth, too close to the flame. I have had little to win or to lose in association with the ordinary run of men, partly because what they do—so-called practical life—does not interest me much, partly because their coldness and indifference to the spiritual and deeper currents in man alienate me even more from them. With few exceptions my companions have had no special influence upon me. A life that has not arrived at clarity about itself must necessarily exhibit an uneven side-surface; confronted by certain facts [_Facta_] and their apparent disharmony, they simply halted there, for, as I see it, they did not have sufficient interest to seek a resolution in a higher harmony or to recognize the necessity of it. Their opinion of me was always one-sided, and I have vacillated between putting too much or too little weight on what they said. I have now withdrawn from their influence and the potential variations of my life's compass resulting from it. Thus I am again standing at the point where I must begin again in another way. I shall now calmly attempt to look at myself and begin to initiate inner action; for only thus will I be able, like a child calling itself "I" in its first consciously undertaken act, be able to call myself "I" in a profounder sense.

But that takes stamina, and it is not possible to harvest immediately what one has sown. I will remember that philosopher's method of having his disciples keep silent for three years; then I dare say it will come. Just as one does not begin a feast at sunrise but at sundown, just so in the spiritual world one must first work forward for some time before the sun really shines for us and rises in all its glory; for although it is true as it says that God lets his sun shine upon the good and the evil and lets the rain fall on the just and the unjust, it is not so in the spiritual world. So let the die be cast—I am crossing the Rubicon! No doubt this road takes me into battle, but I will not renounce it. I will not lament the past—why lament? I will work energetically and not waste time in regrets, like the person stuck in a bog and first calculating how far he has sunk without recognizing that during the time he spends on that he is sinking still deeper. I will hurry along the path I have found and shout to everyone I meet: Do not look back as Lot's wife did, but remember that we are struggling up a hill.

(From *Søren Kierkegaard's Journals and Papers,* Vol. 5, ed. by Howard V. Hong and Edna H. Hong. Bloomington: Indiana University Press, 1978. Reprinted by permission of Indiana University Press.)

Abraham and "Breaking Through the Universal" (from *Fear and Trembling*)

It was early in the morning when Abraham arose: he embraced Sarah, the bride of his old age, and Sarah kissed Isaac, who took away her disgrace, Isaac her pride, her hope for all the generations to come. They rode along the road in silence, and Abraham stared continuously and fixedly at the ground until the fourth day, when he looked up and saw Mount Moriah far away, but once again he turned his eyes toward the ground. Silently he arranged the firewood and bound Isaac; silently he drew the knife — then he saw the ram that God had selected. This he sacrificed and went home. — — — From that day henceforth, Abraham was old; he could not forget that God had ordered him to do this. Isaac flourished as before, but Abraham's eyes were darkened, and he saw joy no more. . . .

The ethical as such is the universal, and as the universal it applies to everyone, which from another angle means that it applies at all times. It rests immanent in itself, has nothing outside itself that is its $\tau\epsilon\lambda o\varsigma$ [end, purpose] but it is itself the $\tau\epsilon\lambda o\varsigma$ for everything outside itself, and when the ethical has absorbed this into itself, it goes not further. The single individual, sensately and psychically qualified in immediacy, is the individual who has his $\tau\epsilon\lambda o\varsigma$ in the universal, and it is his ethical task continually to express himself in this, to annul his singularity in order to become the universal. As soon as the single individual asserts himself in his singularity before the universal, he sins, and only by acknowledging this can he be reconciled again with the universal. Every time the single individual, after having entered the universal, feels an impulse to assert himself as the single individual, he is in a spiritual trial [*Anfaegtelse*], from which he can work himself only by repentently surrendering as the single individual in the universal. If this is the highest that can be said of man and his existence, then the ethical is of the same nature as a person's eternal salvation, which is his τέλος forevermore and at all times, since it would be a contradiction for this to be capable of being surrendered (that is, teleologically suspended), because as soon as this is suspended it is relinquished, whereas that which is suspended is not relinquished but is preserved in the higher, which is its τέλος. . .

Faith is precisely the paradox that the single individual as the single individual is higher than the universal, is justified before it, not as inferior to it but as superior—yet in such a way, please note, that it is the single individual who, after being subordinate as the single individual to the universal, now by means of the universal becomes the single individual who as the single individual is superior, that the single individual as the single individual stands in an absolute relation to the absolute. This position cannot be mediated, for all mediation takes place only by virtue of the universal; it is and remains for all eternity a paradox, impervious to thought. And yet faith is this paradox, or else (and I ask the reader to bear these consequences *in mente* [in mind] even though it would be too prolix for me to write them all down) or else faith has never existed simply because it has always existed, or else Abraham is lost.

It is certainly true that the single individual can easily confuse this paradox with spiritual trial, but it ought not to be concealed for that reason. It is certainly true that many persons may be so constituted that they are repulsed by it, but faith ought not therefore to be made into something else to enable one to have it, but one ought rather to admit to not having it, while those who have faith ought to be prepared to set forth some characteristics whereby the paradox can be distinguished from a spiritual trial.

The story of Abraham contains just such a teleological suspension of the ethical. There is no dearth of keen minds and careful scholars who have found analogies to it. What their wisdom amounts to is the beautiful proposition that basically everything is the same. If one looks more closely, I doubt very much that anyone in the whole wide world will find one single analogy, except for a later one, which proves nothing if it is certain that Abraham represents faith and that it is manifested normatively in him, whose life not only is the most paradoxical that can be thought but is also so paradoxical that it simply cannot be thought. He acts by virtue of the absurd, for it is precisely the absurd that he as the single individual is higher than the universal. This paradox cannot be mediated, for as soon as Abraham begins to do so, he has to confess that he was in a spiritual trial, and if that is the case, he will never sacrifice Isaac, or if he did sacrifice Isaac, then in repentance he must come back to the universal. He gets Isaac back again by virtue of the absurd. Therefore, Abraham is at no time a tragic hero but is something entirely different, either a murderer or a man of faith. Abraham does not have the middle term that saves the tragic hero. This is why I can understand a tragic hero but cannot understand Abraham, even though in a certain demented sense I admire him more than all others.

In ethical terms, Abraham's relation to Isaac is quite simply this: the father shall love the son more than himself. But within its own confines the ethical has various gradations. We shall see whether this story contains any higher expression for the ethical that can ethically explain his behavior, can ethically justify his suspending the ethical obligation to the son, but without moving beyond the teleology of the ethical. . . .

The paradox of faith, then, is this: that the single individual is higher than the universal, that the single individual—to recall a distinction in dogmatics rather rare these days—determines his relation to the universal by his relation to the absolute, not his relation to the absolute by his relation to the universal. The paradox may also be expressed in this way: that there is an absolute duty to God, for in this relationship of duty the individual relates himself as the single individual absolutely to the absolute. In this connection, to say that it is a duty to love God means something different from the above, for if this duty is absolute, then the ethical is reduced to the relative. From this it does not follow that the ethical should be invalidated; rather, the ethical receives a completely different expression, a paradoxical expression, such as, for example, that love to God may bring the knight of faith to give his love to the neighbor—an expression opposite to that which, ethically speaking, is duty.

If this is not the case, then faith has no place in existence, then faith is a spiritual trial and Abraham is lost, inasmuch as he gave in to it. . . .

Now we are face to face with the paradox. Either the single individual as the single individual can stand in an absolute relation to the absolute, and consequently the ethical is not the highest, or Abraham is lost: he is neither a tragic hero nor an esthetic hero.

Here again it may seem that the paradox is the simplest and easiest of all. May I repeat, however, that anyone who remains convinced of this is not a knight of faith, for distress and anxiety are the only justification conceivable, even if it is not conceivable in general, for then the paradox is canceled.

Abraham remains silent—*but he cannot speak.* Therein lies the distress and anxiety. Even though I go on talking night and day without interruption, if I cannot make myself understood when I speak, then

I am not speaking. This is the case with Abraham. He can say everything, but one thing he cannot say, and if he cannot say that—that is, say it in such a way that the other understands it—then he is not speaking. The relief provided by speaking is that it translates me into the universal. Now, Abraham can describe his love for Isaac in the most beautiful words to be found in any language. But this is not what is on his mind; it is something deeper, that he is going to sacrifice him because it is an ordeal. No one can understand the latter, and thus everyone can only misunderstand the former.

Socrates can be used as an example. He was an intellectual tragic hero. His death sentence is announced to him. At that moment he dies, for anyone who does not understand that it takes the whole power of the spirit to die and that the hero always dies before he dies will not advance very far in his view of life. As a hero Socrates is now required to be calm and collected, but as an intellectual tragic hero he is required to have enough spiritual strength in the final moment to consummate himself. He cannot, as does the ordinary tragic hero, concentrate on self-control in the presence of death, but he must make this movement as quickly as possible so that he is instantly and consciously beyond this struggle and affirms himself. Thus, if Socrates had been silent in the crisis of death, he would have diminished the effect of his life and aroused a suspicion that the elasticity of irony in him was not a world power but a game, the resilience of which had to be used on an inverted scale in order to sustain him in pathos at the crucial moment.

These brief suggestions are indeed not applicable to Abraham if one expects to be able to find by means of some analogy an appropriate final word for Abraham, but they do apply if one perceives the necessity for Abraham to consummate himself in the final moment, not to draw the knife silently but to have a word to say, since as the father of faith he has absolute significance oriented to spirit. . . .

And what was the contemporary age's verdict on the tragic hero? That he was great and that it admired him. And that honorable assembly of noble-minded men, the jury that every generation sets up to judge the past generation—it gave the same verdict. But there was no one who could understand Abraham. And yet what did he achieve? He remained true to his love. But anyone who loves God needs no tears, no admiration; he forgets the suffering in the love. Indeed, so completely has he forgotten it that there would not be the slightest trace of his suffering left if God himself did not remember it, for he sees in secret and recognizes distress and counts the tears and forgets nothing.

Thus, either there is a paradox, that the single individual as the single individual stands in an absolute relation to the absolute, or Abraham is lost.

(From *Fear and Trembling*, trans. by Howard V. Hong and Edna H. Hong. In: *Fear and Trembling/Repetition.* Princeton, Princeton University Press, 1983).

The Subjective Truth, Inwardness; Truth Is Subjectivity (from Concluding Unscientific Postscript)

If an existing individual were really able to transcend himself, the truth would be for him something final and complete; but where is the point at which he is outside himself? The I-am-I is a mathematical point which does not exist, and in so far there is nothing to prevent everyone from occupying this standpoint; the one will not be in the way of the other. It is only momentarily that the particular individual is able to realize existentially a unity of the infinite and the finite which transcends existence. This unity is realized in the moment of passion. Modern philosophy has tried anything and everything in the effort to help the individual to transcend himself objectively, which is a wholly impossible feat; existence exercises its restraining influence, and if philosophers nowadays had not become mere scribblers in the service of a fantastic thinking and its preoccupation, they would long ago have perceived that suicide was the only tolerable practical interpretation of its striving. But the scribbling modern philosophy holds passion in contempt; and yet passion is the culmination of existence for an existing individual—and we are all of us existing individuals. In passion the existing subject is rendered infinite in the eternity of the imaginative representation, and yet he is at the same time most definitely himself. The fantastic I-am-I is not an identity of the infinite and the finite, since neither the one nor the other is real; it is a fantastic rendezvous in the clouds, an unfruitful embrace, and the relationship of the individual self to this mirage is never indicated.

All essential knowledge relates to existence, or only such knowledge as has an essential relationship to existence is essential knowledge. All knowledge which does not inwardly relate itself to existence, in the reflection of inwardness, is, essentially viewed, accidental knowledge; its degree and scope is essentially indifferent. That essential knowledge is essentially related to existence does not mean the above-mentioned identity which abstract thought postulates between thought and being; nor does it signify, objectively, that knowledge corresponds to something existent as its object. But it means that knowledge has a relationship to the knower, who is essentially an existing individual, and that for this reason all essential knowledge is essentially related to existence. Only ethical and ethico-religious knowledge has an essential relationship to the existence of the knower. . . .

In an attempt to make clear the difference of way that exists between an objective and a subjective reflection, I shall now proceed to show how a subjective reflection makes its way inwardly in inwardness. Inwardness in an existing subject culminates in passion; corresponding to passion in the subject the truth becomes a paradox; and the fact that the truth becomes a paradox is rooted precisely in its having a relationship to an existing subject. Thus the one corresponds to the other. By forgetting that one is an existing subject, passion goes by the board and the truth is no longer a paradox; the knowing subject becomes a fantastic entity rather than a human being, and the truth becomes a fantastic object for the knowledge of this fantastic entity.

When the question of truth is raised in an objective manner, reflection is directed objectively to the truth, as an object to which the knower is related. Reflection is not focussed upon the relationship, however, but upon the question of whether it is the truth to which the knower is related. If only the object to which he is related is the truth, the subject is accounted to be in the truth. When the question of the truth is raised subjectively, reflection is directed subjectively to the nature of the individual's relationship; if only the mode of this relationship is in the truth, the individual is in the truth even if he should happen to be thus related to what is not true. Let us take as an example the knowledge of God. Objectively, reflection is directed to the problem of whether this object is the true God; subjectively, reflection is directed to the question whether the individual is related to a something in such a manner that his relationship is in truth a God-relationship. On which side is the truth now to be found? Ah, may we not here resort to a mediation, and say: It is on neither side, but in the mediation of both? Excellently well said, provided we might have it explained how an existing individual manages to be in a state of mediation. For to be in a state of mediation is to be finished, while to exist is to become. Nor can an existing individual be in two places at the same time—he cannot be an identity of subject and object. When he is nearest to being in two places at the same time he is in passion; but passion is momentary, and passion is also the highest expression of subjectivity.

The existing individual who chooses to pursue the objective way enters upon the entire approximation-process by which it is proposed to bring God to light objectively. But this is in all eternity impossible, because God is a subject, and therefore exists only for subjectivity in inwardness. The existing individual who chooses the subjective way apprehends instantly the entire dialectical difficulty involved in having to use some time, perhaps a long time, in finding God objectively; and he

---

* The reader will observe that the question here is about essential truth, or about the truth which is essentially related to existence, and that it is precisely for the sake of clarifying it as inwardness or as subjectivity that this contrast is drawn.

feels this dialectical difficulty in all its painfulness, because every moment is wasted in which he does not have God.* That very instant he
has God, not by virtue of any objective deliberation, but by virtue of
the infinite passion of inwardness. The objective inquirer, on the other
hand, is not embarrassed by such dialectical difficulties as are involved
in devoting an entire period of investigation to finding God—since it
is possible that the inquirer may die tomorrow; and if he lives he can
scarcely regard God as something to be taken along if convenient, since
God is precisely that which one takes *a tout prix,* which in the understanding of passion constitutes the true inward relationship to God.

It is at this point, so difficult dialectically, that the way swings off
for everyone who knows what it means to think, and to think existentially; which is something very different from sitting at a desk and
writing about what one has never done, something very different from
writing *de omnibus dubitandum* and at the same time being as credu-
lous existentially as the most sensuous of men. Here is where the way
swings off, and the change is marked by the fact that while objective
knowledge rambles comfortably on by way of the long road of approximation without being impelled by the urge of passion, subjective
knowledge counts every delay a deadly peril, and the decision so infinitely important and so instantly pressing that it is as if the opportunity had already passed.

Now when the problem is to reckon up on which side there is most
truth, whether on the side of one who seeks the true God objectively,
and pursues the approximate truth of the God-idea; or on the side of
one who, driven by the infinite passion of his need of God, feels an infinite concern for his own relationship to God in truth (and to be at
one and the same time on both sides equally, is as we have noted not
possible for an existing individual, but is merely the happy delusion of
an imaginary I-am-I): the answer cannot be in doubt for anyone who
has not been demoralized with the aid of science. If one who lives in
the midst of Christendom goes up to the house of God, the house of
the true God, with the true conception of God in his knowledge, and
prays, but prays in a false spirit; and one who lives in an idolatrous
community prays with the entire passion of the infinite, although his
eyes rest upon the image of an idol: where is there most truth? The one

---

* In this manner God certainly becomes a postulate, but not in the otiose manner
in which this word is commonly understood. It becomes clear rather that the only
way in which an existing individual comes into relation with God, is when the dialectical contradiction brings his passion to the point of despair, and helps him to
embrace God with the "category of despair" (faith). Then the postulate is so far
from being arbitrary that it is precisely a life-necessity. It is then not so much
that God is a postulate, as that the existing individual's postulation of God is a
necessity.

prays in truth to God though he worships an idol; the other prays falsely to the true God, and hence worships in fact an idol.

When one man investigates objectively the problem of immortality, and another embraces an uncertainty with the passion of the infinite: where is there most truth, and who has the greater certainty? The one has entered upon a never-ending approximation, for the certainty of immortality lies precisely in the subjectivity of the individual; the other is immortal, and fights for his immortality by struggling with the uncertainty. Let us consider Socrates. Nowadays everyone dabbles in a few proofs; some have several such proofs, others fewer. But Socrates! He puts the question objectively in a problematic manner: *if* there is an immortality. He must therefore be accounted a doubter in comparison with one of our modern thinkers with the three proofs? By no means. On this "if" he risks his entire life, he has the courage to meet death, and he has with the passion of the infinite so determined the pattern of his life that it must be found acceptable—if there is an immortality. Is any better proof capable of being given for the immortality of the soul? But those who have the three proofs do not at all determine their lives in conformity therewith; if there is an immortality it must feel disgust over their manner of life: can any better refutation be given of the three proofs? The bit of uncertainty that Socrates had, helped him because he himself contributed the passion of the infinite; the three proofs that the others have do not profit them at all, because they are dead to spirit and enthusiasm, and their three proofs, in lieu of proving anything else, prove just this.

The objective accent falls on WHAT is said, the subjective accent on HOW it is said. . . .Objectively the interest is focussed merely on the thought-content, subjectively on the inwardness. At its maximum this inward "how" is the passion of the infinite, and the passion of the infinite is the truth. But the passion of the infinite is precisely subjectivity, and thus subjectivity becomes the truth. Objectively there is no infinite decisiveness, and hence it is objectively in order to annul the difference between good and evil, together with the principle of contradiction, and therewith also the infinite difference between the true and the false. Only in subjectivity is there decisiveness, to seek objectivity is to be in error. It is the passion of the infinite that is the decisive factor and not its content, for its content is precisely itself. In this manner subjectivity and the subjective "how" constitute the truth.

But the "how" which is thus subjectively accentuated precisely because the subject is an existing individual, is also subject to a dialectic with respect to time. In the passionate moment of decision, where the road swings away from objective knowledge, it seems as if the infinite decision were thereby realized. But in the same moment the existing individual finds himself in the temporal order, and the subjective "how" is transformed into a striving, a striving which receives indeed its impulse and a repeated renewal from the decisive passion of the infinite, but is nevertheless a striving.

When subjectivity is the truth, the conceptual determination of the truth must include an expression for the antithesis to objectivity, a memento of the fork in the road where the way swings off; this expression will at the same time serve as an indication of the tension of the subjective inwardness. Here is such a definition of truth: *An objective uncertainty held fast in an appropriation-process of the most passionate inwardness is the truth,* the highest truth attainable for an *existing* individual. At the point where the way swings off (and where this is cannot be specified objectively, since it is a matter of subjectivity), there objective knowledge is placed in abeyance. Thus the subject merely has, objectively, the uncertainty; but it is this which precisely increases the tension of that infinite passion which constitutes his inwardness. The truth is precisely the venture which chooses an objective uncertainty with the passion of the infinite. I contemplate the order of nature in the hope of finding God, and I see omnipotence and wisdom; but I also see much else that disturbs my mind and excites anxiety. The sum of all this is an objective uncertainty. But it is for this very reason that the inwardness becomes as intense as it is, for it embraces this objective uncertainty with the entire passion of the infinite. In the case of a mathematical proposition the objectivity is given, but for this reason the truth of such a proposition is also an indifferent truth.

But the above definition of truth is an equivalent expression for faith. Without risk there is no faith. Faith is precisely the contradiction between the infinite passion of the individual's inwardness and the objective uncertainty. If I am capable of grasping God objectively, I do not believe, but precisely because I cannot do this I must believe. If I wish to preserve myself in faith I must constantly be intent upon holding fast the objective uncertainty, so as to remain out upon the deep, over seventy thousand fathoms of water, still preserving my faith.

In the principle that subjectivity, inwardness, is the truth, there is comprehended the Socratic wisdom, whose everlasting merit it was to have become aware of the essential significance of existence, of the fact that the knower is an existing individual. For this reason Socrates was in the truth by virtue of his ignorance, in the highest sense in which this was possible within paganism. . . .

When subjectivity, inwardness, is the truth, the truth becomes objectively a paradox; and the fact that the truth is objectively a paradox shows in its turn that subjectivity is the truth. For the objective situation is repellent; and the expression for the objective repulsion constitutes the tension and the measure of the corresponding inwardness.

The paradoxical character of the truth is its objective uncertainty; this uncertainty is an expression for the passionate inwardness, and this passion is precisely the truth. So far the Socratic principle. The eternal and essential truth, the truth which has an essential relationship to an existing individual because it pertains essentially to existence (all other knowledge being from the Socratic point of view accidental, its scope and degree a matter of indifference), is a paradox. But the eternal essential truth is by no means in itself a paradox; but it becomes paradoxical by virtue of its relationship to an existing individual. The Socratic ignorance gives expression to the objective uncertainty attaching to the truth, while his inwardness in existing is the truth. To anticipate here what will be developed later, let me make the following remark. The Socratic ignorance is an analogue to the category of the absurd, only that there is still less of objective certainty in the absurd, and in the repellent effect that the absurd exercises. It is certain only that it is absurd, and precisely on that account it incites to an infinitely greater tension in the corresponding inwardness. The Socratic inwardness in existing is an analogue to faith; only that the inwardness of faith, corresponding as it does, not to the repulsion of the Socratic ignorance, but to the repulsion exerted by the absurd, is infinitely more profound. . . .

The infinite merit of the Socratic position was precisely to accentuate the fact that the knower is an existing individual, and that the task of existing is his essential task. Making an advance upon Socrates by failing to understand this, is quite a mediocre achievement. This Socratic principle we must therefore bear in mind, and then inquire whether the formula may not be so altered as really to make an advance beyond the Socratic position.

Subjectivity, inwardness, has been posited as the truth; can any expression for the truth be found which has a still higher degree of inwardness? Aye, there is such an expression, provided the principle that subjectivity or inwardness is the truth begins by positing the opposite principle: that subjectivity is untruth. Let us not at this point succumb to such haste as to fail in making the necessary distinctions. Speculative philosophy also says that subjectivity is untruth, but says it in order to stimulate a movement in precisely the opposite direction, namely, in the direction of the principle that objectivity is the truth. Speculative philosophy determines subjectivity negatively as tending toward objectivity. This second determination of ours, however, places a hindrance in its own way while proposing to begin, which has the effect of making the inwardness far more intensive. Socratically speaking, subjectivity is untruth if it refuses to understand that subjectivity is truth, but, for example, desires to become objective. Here, on the other hand, subjectivity in beginning upon the task of becoming the truth through a subjectifying process, is in the difficulty that it is already untruth. Thus, the labor of the task is thrust backward, backward, that is, in inwardness. So far is it from being the case that the way tends in the direction of objectivity, that the beginning merely lies still deeper in subjectivity. . . .

The paradox emerges when the eternal truth and existence are placed in juxtaposition with one another; each time the stamp of existence is brought to bear, the paradox becomes more clearly evident. Viewed Socratically the knower was simply an existing individual, but now the existing individual bears the stamp of having been essentially altered by existence.

Let us now call the untruth of the individual Sin. Viewed eternally he cannot be sin, nor can he be eternally presupposed as having been in sin. By coming into existence therefore (for the beginning was that subjectivity is untruth), he becomes a sinner. He is not born as a sinner in the sense that he is presupposed as being a sinner before he is born, but he is born in sin and as a sinner. This we might call Original Sin. But if existence has in this manner acquired a power over him, he is prevented from taking himself back into the eternal by way of recollection. If it was paradoxical to posit the eternal truth in relationship to an existing individual, it is now absolutely paradoxical to posit it in relationship to such an individual as we have here defined. But the more difficult it is made for him to take himself out of existence by way of recollection, the more profound is the inwardness that his existence may have in existence; and when it is made impossible for him, when he is held so fast in existence that the back door of recollection is forever closed to him, then his inwardness will be the most profound possible. But let us never forget that the Socratic merit was to stress the fact that the knower is an existing individual; for the more difficult the matter becomes, the greater the temptation to hasten along the easy road of speculation, away from fearful dangers and crucial decisions, to the winning of renown and honors and property, and so forth. If even Socrates understood the dubiety of taking himself speculatively out of existence back into the eternal, although no other difficulty confronted the existing individual except that he existed, and that existing was his essential task, now it is impossible. Forward he must, backward he cannot go.

Subjectivity is the truth. By virtue of the relationship subsisting between the eternal truth and the existing individual, the paradox came into being. Let us now go further, let us suppose that the eternal essential truth is itself a paradox. How does the paradox come into being? By putting the eternal essential truth into juxtaposition with existence. Hence when we posit such a conjunction within the truth itself, the truth becomes a paradox. The eternal truth has come into being in time: this is the paradox. If in accordance with the determinations just posited, the subject is prevented by sin from taking himself back into the eternal, now he need not trouble himself about this; for now the eternal essential truth is not behind him but in front of him, through its being in existence or having existed, so that if the individual does not existentially and in existence lay hold of the truth, he will never lay hold of it. . . .

When Socrates believed that there was a God, he held fast to the objective uncertainty with the whole passion of his inwardness, and it is precisely in this contradiction and in this risk, that faith is rooted. Now it is otherwise. Instead of the objective uncertainty, there is here a certainty, namely, that objectively it is absurd; and this absurdity, held fast in the passion of inwardness, is faith. The Socratic ignorance is as a witty jest in comparison with the earnestness of facing the absurd; and the Socratic existential inwardness is as Greek lightmindedness in comparison with the grave strenuosity of faith.

What now is the absurd? The absurd is—that the eternal truth has come into being in time, that God has come into being, has been born, has grown up, and so forth, precisely like any other individual human being, quite indistinguishable from other individuals. . . . The absurd is precisely by its objective repulsion the measure of the intensity of faith in inwardness. Suppose a man who wishes to acquire faith; let the comedy begin. He wishes to have faith, but he wishes also to safeguard himself by means of an objective inquiry and its approximation-process. What happens? With the help of the approximation-process the absurd becomes something different; it becomes probable, it becomes increasingly probable, it becomes extremely and emphatically probable. Now he is ready to believe it, and he ventures to claim for himself that he does not believe as shoemakers and tailors and simple folk believe, but only after long deliberation. Now he is ready to believe it; and lo, now it has become precisely impossible to believe it. Anything that is almost probable, or probable, or extremely and emphatically probable, is something he can almost know, or as good as know, or extremely and emphatically almost *know*—but it is impossible to *believe*. For the absurd is the object of faith, and the only object that can be believed. . . .

If speculative philosophy wishes to take cognizance of this, and say as always, that there is no paradox when the matter is viewed eternally, divinely, theocentrically—then I admit that I am not in a position to determine whether the speculative philosopher is right, for I am only a poor existing human being, not competent to contemplate the eternal either eternally or divinely or theocentrically, but compelled to content myself with existing. So much is certain, however, that speculative philosophy carries everything back, back past the Socratic position, which at least comprehended that for an existing individual existence is essential; to say nothing of the failure of speculative philosophy to take time to grasp what it means to be so critically situated in existence as the existing individual in the experiment. . . .

Christianity has declared itself to be the eternal essential truth which has come into being in time. It has proclaimed itself as the Paradox, and it has required of the individual the inwardness of faith in relation to that which stamps itself as an offense to the Jews and a folly to the Greeks—and an absurdity to the understanding. It is impossible more strongly to express the fact that subjectivity is truth, and that the objectivity is repellent, repellent even by virtue of its absurdity. And indeed it would seem very strange that Christianity should have come into the world merely to receive an explanation; as if it had been somewhat bewildered about itself, and hence entered the world to consult that wise man, the speculative philosopher, who can come to its assistance by furnishing the explanation. It is impossible to express with more intensive inwardness the principle that subjectivity is truth, than when subjectivity is in the first instance untruth, and yet subjectivity is the truth. . . .

If the speculative philosopher explains the paradox so as to remove it, and now in his knowledge knows that it is removed, that the paradox is not the essential relationship that the eternal essential truth bears to an existing individual in the extremity of his existence, but only an accidental relative-relationship to those of limited intelligence: in that case there is established an essential difference between the speculative philosopher and the plain man, which confounds existence from the foundations. God is affronted by getting a group of hangers-on, an intermediary staff of clever brains; and humanity is affronted because the relationship to God is not identical for all men. The godly formula set up above for the difference between the plain man's knowledge of the simple, and the simple wise man's knowledge of the same, that the difference consists in the insignificant trifle that the wise man knows that he knows, or knows that he does not know, what the plain man knows—this formula is by no means respected by speculative philosophy, nor does it respect the likeness involved in this distinction between the plain man and the wise man, namely, that both know the same thing. For the speculative philosopher and the plain man do not by any means know the same thing, when the plain man believes the paradox, and the speculative philosopher knows it to be abrogated. According to the above-mentioned formula, however, which honors God and loves men, the difference is that the wise man also knows that it must be a paradox, this paradox that he himself believes. Hence they both know essentially the same thing; the wise man does not know everything else about the paradox, but knows that he knows this about the paradox. The simple wise man will thus seek to apprehend the paradox more and more profoundly as a paradox, and will not engage in the business of explaining the paradox by understanding that there is none. . . .

Faith has in fact two tasks: to take care in every moment to discover the improbable, the paradox; and then to hold it fast with the passion of inwardness. The common conception is that the improbable, the paradoxical, is something to which faith is related only passively; it must provisionally be content with this relationship, but little by little things will become better, as indeed seems probable. O miraculous creation of confusions in speaking about faith! One is to begin believing, in reliance upon the probability that things will soon become better. In this way probability is after all smuggled in, and one is prevented from believing; so that it is easy to understand that the fruit of having been for a long time a believer is, that one no longer believes, instead of, as one might think, that the fruit is a more intensive inwardness in faith. No, faith is self-active in its relation to the improbable and the paradoxical, self-active in the discovery, and self-active in every moment holding it fast—in order to believe. Merely to lay hold of the improbable requires all the passion of the infinite and its concentration in itself; for the improbable and the paradoxical are not to be reached by the understanding's quantitative calculation of the more and more difficult. Where the understanding despairs, faith is already present in order to make the despair properly decisive, in order that the movement of faith may not become a mere exchange within the bargaining sphere of the understanding. But to believe against the understanding is martyrdom; to begin to get the understanding a little in one's favor, is temptation and retrogression. This martyrdom is something that the speculative philosopher is free from. That he must pursue his studies, and especially that he must read many modern books, I admit is burdensome; but the martyrdom of faith is not the same thing. What I therefore fear and shrink from, more than I fear to die and to lose my sweetheart, is to say about Christianity that it is to a certain degree true. If I lived to be seventy years old, if I shortened the night's sleep and increased the day's work from year to year, inquiring into Christianity—how insignificant such a little period of study, viewed as entitling me to judge in so lofty a fashion about Christianity! For to be so embittered against Christianity after a casual acquaintance with it, that I declared it to be false: that would be far more pardonable, far more human. But this lordly superiority seems to me the true corruption, making every saving relationship impossible—and it may possibly be the case, that Christianity is the truth. . . .

My principal thought was that in our age, because of the great increase of knowledge, we had forgotten what it means to *exist,* and what *inwardness* signifies, and that the misunderstanding between speculative philosophy and Christianity was explicable on that ground. I now resolved to go back as far as possible, in order not to reach the religious mode of existence too soon, to say nothing of the specifically Christian mode of religious existence, in order not to leave difficulties unexplored behind me. If men had forgotten what it means to exist religiously, they had doubtless also forgotten what it means to exist as human beings; this must therefore be set forth. But above all it must not be done in a dogmatizing manner, for then the misunderstanding would instantly take the explanatory effort to itself in a new misunderstanding, as if existing consisted in getting to know something about this or that. If communicated in the form of knowledge, the recipient is led to adopt the misunderstanding that it is knowledge he is to receive, and then we are again in the sphere of knowledge.

(From Soren Kierkegaard, *Concluding Unscientific Postscript,* trans. David F. Swenson and Walter Lowrie. Copyright 1941, © 1969 renewed by Princeton University Press. Excerpts reprinted by permission by Princeton University Press.)

Review Questions

1. In what way does Kierkegaard mark a turning point in nineteenth-century philosophy?
2. Can Kierkegaard's philosophy be seen as a reaction to the impersonalism of Hegel's philosophy?
3. Can the leap, which is beyond reason, be called reasonable?
4. Discuss the individual versus the crowd.
5. Explain Kierkegaardian self-actualization.
6. Compare the personal dimension of truth in Kierkegaard with that of St. Augustine.
7. Discuss the story of Abraham and explain why it is, for Kierkegaard, the example par excellence of breaking through the universal.

CHAPTER 21

Friedrich Nietzsche
(1844-1900)

Introduction

Although unlike Kierkegaard in many respects, especially regarding the ultimate meaning of individuality, Friedrich Nietzsche is very much like him in his intense personalism, in rejecting a systematic approach to man, in positioning the subject of man as the true object of philosophy, and in literary style. He was born in 1844 near Leipzig. His father was a Lutheran minister who died young, leaving his son to grow up in a society of women including his mother, sister, grandmother, and two aunts. After normal schooling at the local gymnasium, he briefly attended the University of Bonn, where he studied theology, but gave it up once he lost the faith he was born in, beginning a separation from religion which grew more entrenched over the years. From 1864 to 1869 he attended the University of Leipzig, where he gained a reputation as a brilliant student in classical philology. In a most unusual move, he was appointed professor of philology at the University of Basel, Switzerland, at the age of twenty-four, without having completed the formal requirement of the doctorate, whereupon the University of Leipzig conferred it on him without an examination. For a short time during the Franco-Prussian War he served with the ambulance corps, but illness forced him to resign and to return to his professorial duties.

While at Basel he developed a disciple-like friendship with the great composer Richard Wagner and helped him to establish the famous Bayreuth Festival. He accepted Wagner not only as a musical genius but also as a cultural hero who would become the longed-for messiah destined to save a retrograde German culture and lead it to new heights; these themes he put forward as early as 1872 in his first book, *The Birth of Tragedy*. After 1876, however, he broke with Wagner, becoming disillusioned with him not only for personal reasons but also because of what he felt was Wagner's abuse of the art of music. Along with this disillusionment went his despair at ever seeing the rescue of German culture. Offering ill health as a reason, he resigned his chair at Basel in 1879, but no doubt felt that continuing in an academic career would hamper his development as a writer. From then on he led a lonely life, but his writing increased apace until he had fairly well expended himself by 1889, when, having shown signs of mental instability and after being treated clinically, he lived out his remaining days with his sister at Weimar until he died in 1900. For most of his life, his work was not seriously received; ironically, acceptance and fame came in the last ten years of his life, at a time when he could not know, let alone enjoy, the reputation his works had finally won him. His main books include *Thus Spoke Zarathustra* (1883), *Beyond Good and Evil* (1886), *The Gay Science* (1882–87), *The Genealogy of Morals* (1887), and *Twilight of the Idols* (1888).

If it is not true that style makes the man, it at least announces who he is. Nietzsche's style is an immediate reflection of how human life is actually lived — personal, nonsystematic, emotionally charged, and full of peaks and valleys. He writes now in aphorisms and epigrams, now in story form, now in poetry, now in essays, but never in any methodical or scientific way; where necessary, he creates new words and phrases: his writing can never be more confined than his thought. His writings reflect a lived existence, a style of flesh and blood, sometimes pungent and acidulous; it is not designed to persuade by charm, but by its direct, prophetic tone.

His style, however, befits a philosopher who is disturbed about man's state and who is searching for new ways to arrive at a humanism without the constraints of the past that have, in his view, sorrowfully brought man to where he is today. Nietzsche punctured the membrane of contemporary life as often as possible in the hope of releasing the forces and energy of life, which could then be creatively reassembled into a new humanism.

As a young man, Nietzsche began to probe the possibilities of a renewed humanism through the dimension of culture. As we have stated, *The Birth of Tragedy* was his first book; in it he expressed an apprehension that in its culture, particularly German culture, Western man was headed for a new barbarism, and some way had to be found to divert it from the impending cataclysm. Greek culture was, for Nietzsche, the model of all cultures, and when he tried to resolve the elements that made it so, he discovered they were two, the Apollonian and the Dionysian. The Apollonian, after the god Apollo, whose prophetic voice was often heard in the oracle of Delphi, is the formal element, giving measure, restraint, form, and individuality to life, supplying the opportunity to share in the ideal world. In art form, it is expressed in the epic and the plastic arts. The Dionysian is the element of enthusiasm, after the god Dionysus (the Roman god Bacchus), in whose honor wild revelry was held at grape-gathering, wine-drinking time; this element is an unplanned, uncharted insertion into the stream of life without concern about where it might lead, the acceptance of dark and shadow as well as joy, the blind affirmation of existence; here the individual tends to dissolve and merge with primordial unity. In art form, the Dionysian is expressed in tragedy and music.

When either of these two elements gains the ascendancy and overrides the other, the imbalance spells the doom of culture and of the life of man. There is a clear need for a savior, for someone who, as a creative genius, can stave off the wild forces at work, transforming existence and giving it meaning. Though the original need for a creative genius stemmed mainly from a decaying culture, as time went on the role became more and more enlarged to involve every important aspect of life, thus developing a still greater demand for such a genius, now called *Superman* (Overman; *Übermensch*).

The center of this transformation is the individual, who has to be free to create new values. In the moral sphere, for example, *universal* morality has to be rejected because it destroys the individual's freedom to act according to his own creative insights. Universal morality, compelling everyone to behave the same way, is absolute, closed — a torturous straightjacket preventing the individual from asserting himself. The same rigorous individualism occurs in Nietzsche's division of morality into *master morality* and *slave morality*; the former stresses independence, self-approbation, action flowing out of strength or power; the latter bespeaks a herd mentality, behavior unsure of itself, action born out of resentment, whence its emphasis on virtues like humility and patience. In these terms, morality has to be transformed from the self-defeating, absolute precepts of slave morality that, in the course of history invaded all of Europe, into the independence of creative action characteristic of master morality.

The transformation of moral values is the first consequence of the longed-for renunciation of God — a confident proclamation that *God is dead*. Belief in God, as history abundantly shows, destroys man, closes in on him, denies him his freedom, and generates a morality inimical to human dignity. Only atheism, which pits man against all external powers, can encourage him to return to his inner strength, there to find the source of true moral values and indeed all human value. The transcendence of man can come only with the emergence of the individual, and not in any appeal to the cosmic evolution of Hegel, or the biological evolution of Darwin, or the mystical transcendence of the theologian. In the opening pages of *Thus Spoke Zarathustra*, Nietzsche proclaims the death of God, as well as the advent of the Superman. Having come down from his mountain, the prophet Zarathustra meets a holy man who has spent long years in the forest praising God in his prayers and songs, and then the prophet asks himself, "Could it be possible? This old saint in the forest has not yet heard anything of this, that *God is dead!*" More explicitly, it is the Christian God who is dead: "The greatest recent event — that 'God is dead', that the belief in the Christian god has become unbelievable — is already beginning to cast its first shadows over Europe." With the fall of God, values dependent on Him will also fall.

When the term *nihilism* is used of Nietzsche's philosophy, what is usually referred to is the destruction of values following the death of God. But the destruction of these God-dependent values does not mean for him the absolute destruction of value, for value as such seems to be a permanent given in human existence. Granted that it is not always easy to determine his meaning, by the *revaluation of values* or the *transvaluation of values*, Nietzsche looks forward primarily to the imminent obliteration of traditional values. Philosophers have to oppose their "today" while looking forward to their "tomorrow," and they have to be "the bad conscience of their time. By putting the vivisectionist's knife to the *virtues of their time*, they revealed their own secret: they knew a *new* magnitude of man, a new un-worn path to his magnification." It may be that Nietzsche, in his prophetic style, is simply calling for courage to stand up against accepted values, come what may, but a plain reading shows more; it shows that, even though he does not have in mind a whole spectrum of new values ready to take over once the old ones are gone, he passionately expects a new order of things without knowing its specifics. This is an integral part of the role of Superman, whose "strength of will, hardness, and ability to make far-reaching decisions" refer not only to putting down the intolerable present but also to the fearless charting of the unseen future.

With the death of God and the transvaluation of values, the task of Superman is huge. The word *super-man* appears several times in classical literature and in German literature before Nietzsche, but with him the concept of Superman becomes an essential part of his philosophy. He is that person (whether one person or a member of a class) who represents the high point of human existence, combining in himself the highest of human traits; in that sense, he is man beyond man. Zarathustra tells the people of a town gathered in the marketplace, "*I teach you the overman.* Man is something that shall be overcome. . . . All beings so far have created something beyond themselves; and do you want to be the ebb of this great flood and even go back to the beasts rather than overcome man?"

Because Superman is strong-willed, independent, and the apex of master morality, he becomes the force through whom values will be recreated; and because God is dead and expectations from the "other-world" are futile, his nourishment comes from "this world": "The over-man is the meaning of the earth. Let your will say: the overman *shall be* the meaning of the earth. I beseech you, my brothers, remain faithful to the earth, and do not believe those who speak to you of other-worldy hopes!" Glimpses of Superman are given us in certain figures of history, such as Caesar, whom Nietzsche refers to as the "Roman Caesar with Christ's soul"; Napoleon, with whom he had a love–hate relationship; and Goethe. But there are no examples of the ideal Superman as the one who integrates all variations of human power under the free mastery of the will and faces the future with a sense of boundless time. Furthermore, because Nietzsche sees the meaning of humanity in terms of its "highest specimens", Superman is the value-creative genius who, savior-like, refracts the light of a new order for the rest of us.

Whether it is the primacy of the will, the revaluation of value, the death of God, or Superman, all of Nietzsche's thoughts are so interwoven that an insight into one is an insight into the others. This is particularly true of the concept of the *will to power*, which, in the view of some commentators on Nietzsche, is the central thought of his later writings. On first hearing the phrase, there is a suggestion of power for the sake of power, might as right, or naked force; however, this is far from Nietzsche's meaning, since his thought carries with it no sense of domination or hurt. Nietzsche himself became worried over the way some of his ideas were taken up and wanted to dissociate himself, for example, from the concept of Bismarck's *Reich*, a *Deutschland Über Alles*. Basically what Nietzsche had in mind was an extension of the very strength that made for Superman, the strength first and foremost of overcoming the fear one has of himself, of overcoming weakness, or simply of *self-overcoming*. In the chapter entitled "On Self - overcoming" in *Thus Spoke Zarathustra*, Nietzsche has the prophet say, "That is your whole will, you who are wisest: a will to power — when you speak of good and evil, too, and of valuations. You still want to create the world before which you can kneel: that is your ultimate hope and intoxication. ... Whatever lives, obeys ... he who cannot obey himself is commanded. That is the nature of the living. ... Where I found the living, there I found will to power; and even in the will of those who serve I found the will to be master. ... And life itself confided this secret to me. 'Behold', it said, 'I am *that which must always overcome itself*. Indeed, you call it a will to procreate or a drive to an end, to something higher, farther, more manifold: but all this is one, and one secret'." The will to power underlies all human activities — knowledge, politics, pursuit of virtue, emotions of pleasure and pain: "all driving force is will to power ... there is no other physical, dynamic, or psychic force except this." Value is decisive for life, not truth. The will to power is life itself. It is no surprise, then, that for Superman it is the basis of his exhilaration.

But Superman's exhilaration requires one more test; otherwise, it would be short-lived. The test is a test of strength, of the final surge of the will to power in what Nietzsche calls *eternal recurrence*. As previously indicated, Nietzsche's meaning is sometimes difficult to understand; the doctrine of eternal recurrence is one such difficulty, although its importance for Nietzsche is clear. Given the unlimited amount of time involved in eternity, and given the limited number of things in this world that exist in time, we can imaginatively suppose that amid the countless shufflings and reshufflings of the world's elements, there must be repeated configurations of things as they are at this moment. Eternal recurrence is the "unconditional and infinitely repeated circulations of all things." In *Thus Spoke Zarathustra* Nietzsche describes the present moment as a "gateway," and if the lane leading to it is eternal and the lane leading away is eternal, then "From this gateway, Moment, a long, eternal lane leads *backwards*: behind us lies an eternity. Must not whatever *can* walk have walked on this lane before? . . . And are not all things knotted together so firmly that this moment draws after it *all* that is to come? . . . whatever *can* walk — in this long lane out *there* too, it *must* walk once more."

Eternal recurrence seems to be a bleak doctrine for one who looks forward to eternal joy. Perhaps Nietzsche espoused it as a hypothesis fitting in nicely with his atheism which could not permit a deity to preside over the course of the world's events; a universe self-contained, self-enclosed, that always was and always will be, was the only answer. Also, Nietzsche saw in eternal recurrence the ultimate exercise of Superman's will to power, for it is the final trial in his saying "yes" to life regardless of where it would lead him; and it it leads Superman, and in him all humanity, to the state where he would never again rest "in endless trust"; then he would have to say "yes" and rejoice in accepting it. Or, using the imagery of the poet Heinrich Heine, Nietzsche has a demon say, "This life as you now live it and have lived it, you have to live once more and innumerable times more; and there will be nothing new in it, but every pain and every joy and every thought and sigh and everything unutterably small or great in your life will have to return to you, all in the same succession . . . how well disposed would you have to become to yourself and to life *to crave nothing more fervently* than this ultimate confirmation and seal?" Therein lies the profound strength of Superman, for if eternal recurrence is true, the new world he fought so hard to create would be fated to go under and the entire scenario to be replayed as though it had never happened before. This is the paragon of the Dionysian man who throws himself gladly into the primal stream of life.

If the success of a philosophy is measured by the insights it opens up for others, Nietzsche has been truly successful. Philosophers, theologians, and psychologists have long since been pursuing the leads supplied by him; art critics have been given a new awareness of the subleties of artistic expression and political scientists astringent lessons in politics and government. At least one of Nietzsche's recent admirerers, in the person of Walter Kaufman, Nietzsche's competent translator and interpreter, feels that Nietzsche is the most creative mind since Plato.

Readings

The Death of God and the Ascendancy of the Overman (from Thus Spoke Zarathustra)

1

When Zarathustra was thirty years old he left his home and the lake of his home and went into the mountains. Here he enjoyed his spirit and his solitude, and for ten years did not tire of it. But at last a change came over his heart, and one morning he rose with the dawn, stepped before the sun, and spoke to it thus:

"You great star, what would your happiness be had you not those for whom you shine?

"For ten years you have climbed to my cave: you would have tired of your light and of the journey had it not been for me and my eagle and my serpent.

"But we waited for you every morning, took your overflow from you, and blessed you for it.

"Behold, I am weary of my wisdom, like a bee that has gathered too much honey; I need hands outstretched to receive it.

"I would give away and distribute, until the wise among men find joy once again in their folly, and the poor in their riches.

"For that I must descend to the depths, as you do in the evening when you go behind the sea and still bring light to the underworld, you overrich star.

"Like you, I must go under—go down, as is said by man, to whom I want to descend.

"So bless me then, you quiet eye that can look even upon an all-too-great happiness without envy!

"Bless the cup that wants to overflow, that the water may flow from it golden and carry everywhere the reflection of your delight.

"Behold, this cup wants to become empty again, and Zarathustra wants to become man again."

Thus Zarathustra began to go under.

2

Zarathustra descended alone from the mountains, encountering no one. But when he came into the forest, all at once there stood before him an old man who had left his holy cottage to look for roots in the woods. And thus spoke the old man to Zarathustra:

"No stranger to me is this wanderer: many years ago he passed this way. Zarathustra he was called, but he has changed. At that time you carried your ashes to the mountains; would you now carry your fire into the valleys? Do you not fear to be punished as an arsonist?

"Yes, I recognize Zarathustra. His eyes are pure, and around his mouth there hides no disgust. Does he not walk like a dancer?

"Zarathustra has changed, Zarathustra has become a child, Zarathustra is an awakened one; what do you now want among the sleepers? You lived in your solitude as in the sea, and the sea carried you. Alas, would you now climb ashore? Alas, would you again drag your own body?"

Zarathustra answered: "I love man."

"Why," asked the saint, "did I go into the forest and the desert? Was it not because I loved man all-too-much? Now I love God; man I love not. Man is for me too imperfect a thing. Love of man would kill me."

Zarathustra answered: "Did I speak of love? I bring men a gift."

"Give them nothing!" said the saint. "Rather, take part of their load and help them to bear it—that will be best for them, if only it does you good! And if you want to give them something, give no more than alms, and let them beg for that!"

"No," answered Zarathustra. "I give no alms. For that I am not poor enough."

The saint laughed at Zarathustra and spoke thus: "Then see to it that they accept your treasures. They are suspicious of hermits and do not believe that we come with gifts. Our steps sound too lonely through the streets. And what if at night, in their beds, they hear a man walk by long before the sun has risen—they probably ask themselves, Where is the thief going?

"Do not go to man. Stay in the forest! Go rather even to the animals! Why do you not want to be as I am—a bear among bears, a bird among birds?"

"And what is the saint doing in the forest?" asked Zarathustra.

The saint answered: "I make songs and sing them; and when I make songs, I laugh, cry, and hum: thus I praise God. With singing, crying, laughing, and humming, I praise the god who is my god. But what do you bring us as a gift?"

When Zarathustra had heard these words he bade the saint farewell and said: "What could I have to give you? But let me go quickly lest I take something from you!" And thus they separated, the old one and the man, laughing as two boys laugh.

But when Zarathustra was alone he spoke thus to his heart: "Could it be possible? This old saint in the forest has not yet heard anything of this, that *God is dead!*"

3

When Zarathustra came into the next town, which lies on the edge of the forest, he found many people gathered together in the market place; for it had been promised that there would be a tightrope walker. And Zarathustra spoke thus to the people:

"*I teach you the overman.* Man is something that shall be overcome. What have you done to overcome him?

"All beings so far have created something beyond themselves; and do you want to be the ebb of this great flood and even go back to the beasts rather than overcome man? What is the ape to man? A laughingstock or a painful embarrassment. And man shall be just that for the overman: a laughingstock or a painful embarrassment. You have made your way from worm to man, and much in you is still worm. Once you were apes, and even now, too, man is more ape than any ape.

"Whoever is the wisest among you is also a mere conflict and cross between plant and ghost. But do I bid you become ghosts or plants?

"Behold, I teach you the overman. The overman is the meaning of the earth. Let your will say: the overman *shall be* the meaning of the earth! I beseech you, my brothers, *remain faithful to the earth,* and do not believe those who speak to you of otherworldly hopes! Poison-mixers are they, whether they know it or not. Despisers of life are they, decaying and poisoned themselves, of whom the earth is weary: so let them go.

"Once the sin against God was the greatest sin; but God died, and these sinners died with him. To sin against the earth is now the most dreadful thing, and to esteem the entrails of the unknowable higher than the meaning of the earth.

"Once the soul looked contemptuously upon the body, and then this contempt was the highest: she wanted the body meager, ghastly, and starved. Thus she hoped to escape it and the earth. Oh, this soul herself was still meager, ghastly, and starved: and cruelty was the lust of this soul. But you, too, my brothers, tell me: what does your body proclaim of your soul? Is not your soul poverty and filth and wretched contentment?

"Verily, a polluted stream is man. One must be a sea to be able to receive a polluted stream without becoming unclean. Behold, I teach you the overman: he is this sea; in him your great contempt can go under.

"What is the greatest experience you can have? It is the hour of the great contempt. The hour in which your happiness, too, arouses your disgust, and even your reason and your virtue.

"The hour when you say, 'What matters my happiness? It is poverty and filth and wretched contentment. But my happiness ought to justify existence itself.'

"The hour when you say, 'What matters my reason? Does it crave knowledge as the lion his food? It is poverty and filth and wretched contentment.'

"The hour when you say, 'What matters my virtue? As yet it has not made me rage. How weary I am of my good and my evil! All that is poverty and filth and wretched contentment.'

"The hour when you say, 'What matters my justice? I do not see that I am flames and fuel. But the just are flames and fuel.'

"The hour when you say, 'What matters my pity? Is not pity the cross on which he is nailed who loves man? But my pity is no crucifixion.'

"Have you yet spoken thus? Have you yet cried thus? Oh, that I might have heard you cry thus!

"Not your sin but your thrift cries to heaven; your meanness even in your sin cries to heaven.

"Where is the lightning to lick you with its tongue? Where is the frenzy with which you should be inoculated?

"Behold, I teach you the overman: he is this lightning, he is this frenzy."

When Zarathustra had spoken thus, one of the people cried: "Now we have heard enough about the tightrope walker; now let us see him too!" And all the people laughed at Zarathustra. But the tightrope walker, believing that the word concerned him, began his performance.

Fearlessness (from *The Gay Science*)

343

The meaning of our cheerfulness. — The greatest recent event—that "God is dead," that the belief in the Christian god has become unbelievable—is already beginning to cast its first shadows over Europe. For the few at least, whose eyes—the *suspicion* in whose eyes is strong and subtle enough for this spectacle, some sun seems to have set and some ancient and profound trust has been turned into doubt; to them our old world must appear daily more like evening, more mistrustful, stranger, "older." But in the main one may say: The event itself is far too great, too distant, too remote from the multitude's capacity for comprehension even for the tidings of it to be thought of as having *arrived* as yet. Much less may one suppose that many people know as yet *what* this event really means—and how much must collapse now that this faith has been undermined because it was built upon this faith, propped up by it, grown into it; for example, the whole of our European morality. This long plenitude and sequence of breakdown, destruction, ruin, and cataclysm that is now impending—who could guess enough of it today to be compelled to play the teacher and advance proclaimer of this monstrous logic of terror, the prophet of a gloom and an eclipse of the sun whose like has probably never yet occurred on earth?

Even we born guessers of riddles who are, as it were, waiting on the mountains, posted between today and tomorrow, stretched in the contradiction between today and tomorrow, we firstlings and premature births of the coming century, to whom the shadows that must soon envelop Europe really *should* have appeared by now—why is it that even we look forward to the approaching gloom without any real sense of involvement and above all without any worry and fear for *ourselves*? Are we perhaps still too much under the impression of the *initial consequences* of this event—and these initial consequences, the consequences for *ourselves,* are quite the opposite of what one might perhaps expect: They are not at all sad and gloomy but rather like a new and scarcely describable kind of light, happiness, relief, exhilaration, encouragement, dawn.

Indeed, we philosophers and "free spirits" feel, when we hear the news that "the old god is dead," as if a new dawn shone on us; our heart overflows with gratitude, amazement, premonitions, expectation. At long last the horizon appears free to us again, even if it should not be bright; at long last our ships may venture out again, venture out to face any danger; all the daring of the lover of knowledge is permitted again; the sea, *our* sea, lies open again; perhaps there has never yet been such an "open sea."—

344

How we, too, are still pious.— In science convictions have no rights of citizenship, as one says with good reason. Only when they decide to descend to the modesty of hypotheses, of a provisional experimental point of view, of a regulative fiction, they may be granted admission and even a certain value in the realm of knowledge—though always with the restriction that they remain under police supervision, under the police of mistrust. —But does this not mean, if you consider it more precisely, that a conviction may obtain admission to science only when it ceases to be a conviction? Would it not be the first step in the discipline of the scientific spirit that one would not permit oneself any more convictions?

Probably this is so; only we still have to ask: *To make it possible for this discipline to begin,* must there not be some prior conviction—even one that is so commanding and unconditional that it sacrifices all other convictions to itself? We see that science also rests on a faith; there simply is no science "without presuppositions." The question whether *truth* is needed must not only have been affirmed in advance, but affirmed to such a degree that the principle, the faith, the conviction finds expression: *"Nothing* is needed *more* than truth, and in relation to it everything else has only second-rate value."

This unconditional will to truth—what is it? Is it the will *not to allow oneself to be deceived*? Or is it the will *not to deceive*? For the will to truth could be interpreted in the second way, too—if only the special case "I do not want to deceive myself" is subsumed under the generalization "I do not want to deceive." But why not deceive? But why not allow oneself to be deceived?

Note that the reasons for the former principle belong to an altogether different realm from those for the second. One does not want to allow oneself to be deceived because one assumes that it is harmful, dangerous, calamitous to be deceived. In this sense, science would be a long-range prudence, a caution, a utility; but one could object in all fairness: How is that? Is wanting not to allow oneself to be deceived really less harmful, less dangerous, less calamitous? What do you know in advance of the character of existence to be able to decide whether the greater advantage is on the side of the unconditionally mistrustful or of the unconditionally trusting? But if both should be required, much trust *as well as* much mistrust, from where would science then be permitted to take its unconditional faith or conviction on which it rests, that truth is more important than any other thing, including every other conviction? Precisely this conviction could never have come into being if both truth and untruth constantly proved to be useful, which is the case. Thus—the faith in science, which after all exists undeniably, cannot owe its origin to such a calculus of utility; it must have originated *in spite of* the fact that the disutility and dangerousness of "the will to truth," of "truth at any price" is proved to it constantly. "At any price": how well we understand these words once we have offered and slaughtered one faith after another on this altar!

Consequently, "will to truth" does *not* mean "I will not allow myself to be deceived" but—there is no alternative—"I will not deceive, not even myself"; *and with that we stand on moral ground.* For you only have to ask yourself carefully, "Why do you not want to deceive?" especially if it should seem—and it does seem!—as if life aimed at semblance, meaning error, deception, simulation, delusion, self-delusion, and when the great sweep of life has actually always shown itself to be on the side of the most unscrupulous *polytropoi.* Charitably interpreted, such a resolve might perhaps be a quixotism, a minor slightly mad enthusiasm; but it might also be something more serious, namely, a principle that is hostile to life and destructive. —"Will to truth"—that might be a concealed will to death.

Thus the question "Why science?" leads back to the moral problem: *Why have morality at all* when life, nature, and history are "not moral"? No doubt, those who are truthful in that audacious and ultimate sense that is presupposed by the faith in science *thus affirm another world* than the world of life, nature, and history; and insofar as they affirm this "other world"—look, must they not by the same token negate its counterpart, this world, *our* world?—But you will have gathered what I am driving at, namely, that it is still a *metaphysical faith* upon which our faith in science rests—that even we seekers after knowledge today, we godless anti-metaphysicians still take our fire, too, from the flame lit by a faith that is thousands of years old, that Christian faith which was also the faith of Plato, that God is the truth, that truth is divine. —But what if this should become more and more incredible, if nothing should prove to be divine any more unless it were error, blindness, the lie—if God himself should prove to be our most enduring lie?—

Anti-Christ And Revaluation (from *The Anti-Christ*)

Preface

Revaluation of All Values

This book belongs to the very few. Perhaps not one of them is even living yet. Maybe they will be the readers who understand my *Zarathustra:* how could I mistake myself for one of those for whom there are ears even now? Only the day after tomorrow belongs to me. Some are born posthumously.

The conditions under which I am understood, and then of *necessity*—I know them only too well. One must be honest in matters of the spirit to the point of hardness before one can even endure my seriousness and my passion. One must be skilled in living on mountains—seeing the wretched ephemeral babble of politics and national self-seeking *beneath* oneself. One must have become indifferent; one must never ask if the truth is useful or if it may prove our undoing. The predilection of strength for questions for which no one today has the courage; the courage for the *forbidden;* the predestination to the labyrinth. An experience of seven solitudes. New ears for new music. New eyes for what is most distant. A new conscience for truths that have so far remained mute. *And* the will to the economy of the great style: keeping our strength, our *enthusiasm* in harness. Reverence for oneself; love of oneself; unconditional freedom before oneself.

Well then! Such men alone are my readers, my right readers, my predestined readers: what matter the rest? The rest—that is merely mankind. One must be above mankind in strength, in *loftiness* of soul—in contempt.

First Book: The Antichrist

Attempt at a Critique Of Christianity

1

Let us face ourselves. We are Hyperboreans; we know very well how far off we live. "Neither by land nor by sea will you find the way to the Hyperboreans"—Pindar already knew this about us. Beyond the north, ice, and death—*our* life, *our* happiness. We have discovered happiness, we know the way, we have found the exit out of the labyrinth of thousands of years. Who else has found it? Modern man perhaps? "I have got lost; I am everything that has got lost," sighs modern man.

This modernity was our sickness: lazy peace, cowardly compromise, the whole virtuous uncleanliness of the modern Yes and No. This tolerance and *largeur* of the heart, which "forgives" all because it "understands" all, is *sirocco* for us. Rather live in the ice than among modern virtues and other south winds!

We were intrepid enough, we spared neither ourselves nor others; but for a long time we did not know where to turn with our intrepidity. We became gloomy, we were called fatalists. *Our fatum*—the abundance, the tension, the damming of strength. We thirsted for lightning and deeds and were most remote from the happiness of the weakling, "resignation." In our atmosphere was a thunderstorm; the nature we are became dark—*for we saw no way*. Formula for our happiness: a Yes, a No, a straight line, a goal.

2

What is good? Everything that heightens the feeling of power in man, the will to power, power itself.

What is bad? Everything that is born of weakness.

What is happiness? The feeling that power is growing, that resistance is overcome.

Not contentedness but more power; not peace but war; not virtue but fitness (Renaissance virtue, *virtù*, virtue that is moraline-free).

The weak and the failures shall perish: first principle of our love of man. And they shall even be given every possible assistance.

What is more harmful than any vice? Active pity for all the failures and all the weak: Christianity.

3

The problem I thus pose is not what shall succeed mankind in the sequence of living beings (man is an *end*), but what type of man shall be *bred*, shall be *willed*, for being higher in value, worthier of life, more certain of a future.

Even in the past this higher type has appeared often—but as a fortunate accident, as an exception, never as something *willed*. In fact, this has been the type most dreaded—almost *the* dreadful—and from dread the opposite type was willed, bred, and *attained:* the domestic animal, the herd animal, the sick human animal—the Christian.

4

Mankind does *not* represent a development toward something better or stronger or higher in the sense accepted today. "Progress" is merely a modern idea, that is, a false idea. The European of today is vastly inferior in value to the European of the Renaissance: further development is altogether not according to any necessity in the direction of elevation, enhancement, or strength.

In another sense, success in individual cases is constantly encountered in the most widely different places and cultures: here we really do find a *higher type,* which is, in relation to mankind as a whole, a kind of overman. Such fortunate accidents of great success have always been possible and *will* perhaps always be possible. And even whole families, tribes, or peoples may occasionally represent such a *bull's-eye.*

5

Christianity should not be beautified and embellished: it has waged deadly war against this higher type of man; it has placed all the basic instincts of this type under the ban; and out of these instincts it has distilled evil and the Evil One: the strong man as the typically reprehensible man, the "reprobate." Christianity has sided with all that is weak and base, with all failures; it has made an ideal of whatever *contradicts* the instinct of the strong life to preserve itself; it has corrupted the reason even of those strongest in spirit by teaching men to consider the supreme values of the spirit as something sinful, as something that leads into error—as temptations. The most pitiful example: the corruption of Pascal, who believed in the corruption of his reason through original sin when it had in fact been corrupted only by his Christianity.

6

It is a painful, horrible spectacle that has dawned on me: I have drawn back the curtain from the *corruption* of man. In my mouth, this word is at least free from one suspicion: that it might involve a moral accusation of man. It is meant—let me emphasize this once more—*moraline-free*. So much so that I experience this corruption most strongly precisely where men have so far aspired most deliberately to "virtue" and "godliness." I understand corruption, as you will guess, in the sense of decadence: it is my contention that all the values in which mankind now sums up its supreme desiderata are *decadence-values*.

I call an animal, a species, or an individual corrupt when it loses its instincts, when it chooses, when it prefers, what is disadvantageous for it. A history of "lofty sentiments," of the "ideals of mankind"—and it is possible that I shall have to write it—would almost explain too *why* man is so corrupt. Life itself is to my mind the instinct for growth, for durability, for an accumulation of forces, for *power:* where the will to power is lacking there is decline. It is my contention that all the supreme values of mankind *lack* this will—that the values which are symptomatic of decline, *nihilistic* values, are lording it under the holiest names.

7

Christianity is called the religion of *pity*. Pity stands opposed to the tonic emotions which heighten our vitality: it has a depressing effect. We are deprived of strength when we feel pity. That loss of strength which suffering as such inflicts on life is still further increased and multiplied by pity. Pity makes suffering contagious. Under certain circumstances, it may engender a total loss of life and vitality out of all proportion to the magnitude of the cause (as in the case of the death of the Nazarene). That is the first consideration, but there is a more important one.

Suppose we measure pity by the value of the reactions it usually produces; then its perilous nature appears in an even brighter light. Quite in general, pity crosses the law of development, which is the law of selection. It preserves what is ripe for destruction; it defends those who have been disinherited and condemned by life; and by the abundance of the failures of all kinds which it keeps alive, it gives life itself a gloomy and questionable aspect.

Some have dared to call pity a virtue (in every *noble* ethic it is considered a weakness); and as if this were not enough, it has been made *the* virtue, the basis and source of all virtues. To be sure—and one should always keep this in mind—this was done by a philosophy that was nihilistic and had inscribed the *negation of life* upon its shield. Schopenhauer was consistent enough: pity negates life and renders it *more deserving of negation*.

Pity is the *practice* of nihilism. To repeat: this depressive and contagious instinct crosses those instincts which aim at the preservation of life and at the enhancement of its value. It multiplies misery and conserves all that is miserable, and is thus a prime instrument of the advancement of decadence: pity persuades men to *nothingness!* Of course, one does not say "*nothingness*" but "beyond" or "God," or "*true* life," or Nirvana, salvation, blessedness.

This innocent rhetoric from the realm of the religious-moral idiosyncrasy appears much less innocent as soon as we realize which tendency it is that here shrouds itself in sublime words: *hostility against life.* Schopenhauer was hostile to life; therefore pity became a virtue for him.

Aristotle, as is well known, considered pity a pathological and dangerous condition, which one would be well advised to attack now and then with a purge: he understood tragedy as a purge. From the standpoint of the instinct of life, a remedy certainly seems necessary for such a pathological and dangerous accumulation of pity as is represented by the case of Schopenhauer (and unfortunately by our entire literary and artistic decadence from St. Petersburg to Paris, from Tolstoi to Wagner)—to puncture it and make it *burst.*

In our whole unhealthy modernity there is nothing more unhealthy than Christian pity. To be physicians *here,* to be inexorable *here,* to wield the scalpel *here*—that is *our* part, that is *our* love of man, that is how we are philosophers, we *Hyperboreans.*

48

Has the famous story that stands at the beginning of the Bible really been understood? the story of God's hellish fear of *science*? It has not been understood. This priestly book par excellence begins, as is fitting, with the great inner difficulty of the priest: he knows only one great danger, consequently "God" knows only one great danger.

The old God, all "spirit," all high priest, all perfection, takes a stroll in his garden; but he is bored. Against boredom even gods struggle in vain. What does he do? He invents man—man is entertaining. But lo and behold! Man too is bored. God's compassion with the sole distress that distinguishes all paradises knows no limits: soon he creates other animals as well. God's *first* mistake: man did not find the animals entertaining; he ruled over them, he did not even want to be "animal." Consequently God created woman. And indeed, that was the end of boredom—but of other things too! Woman was God's *second* mistake. "Woman is by nature a snake, Heve"[1] —every priest knows that; "from woman comes all calamity in the world"—every priest knows that, too. "Consequently, it is from her too that science comes." Only from woman did man learn to taste of the tree of knowledge.

What had happened? The old God was seized with hellish fear. Man himself had turned out to be his *greatest* mistake; he had created a rival for himself; science makes godlike—it is all over with priests and gods when man becomes scientific. Moral: science is the forbidden as such—it alone is forbidden. Science is the *first* sin, the seed of all sin, the *original* sin. *This alone is morality.* "Thou shalt not know"—the rest follows.

God's hellish fear did not prevent him from being clever. How does one resist science? This became his main problem for a long time. Answer: out of paradise with man! Happiness, idleness, give rise to ideas—all ideas are bad ideas. Man *shall* not think. And the "priest-as-such" invents distress, death, the mortal danger of pregnancy, every kind of misery, old age, trouble, and, above all, *sickness*—all means in the fight against science. Distress does not permit man to think. And yet—horrible!—the edifice of knowledge begins to tower, heaven-storming, suggesting twilight to the gods. What is to be done? The old God invents *war,* he divides the peoples, he fixes it so men will annihilate each other (priests have always required wars). War—among other things a great disrupter of science! Incredible! Knowledge, the *emancipation from the priest,* continues to grow in spite of wars. And the old God makes a final decision: "Man has become scientific—*there is no other way, he has to be drowned.*"

---

[1] Although Nietzsche seems to have in mind a well-known etymology of the Hebrew "Havvah" ("Eva" in German), not one of the Hebrew words for snake resembles this name. Genesis 3:20 links the name with life, and the only other verse in which it figures is Genesis 4:1.

Review Questions

1. Compare the notion of humanism in Nietzsche with that of Kierkegaard.
2. In what way is the cultural man the point of contact with human existence for Nietzsche?
3. Why is traditional morality found wanting by Nietzsche?
4. What does Nietzsche mean by his announcement that God is dead?
5. Is Nietzsche truly a nihilist? What does he mean by *transvaluation of values*?
6. What is the role of Overman (Superman) in evolving a new set of values?
7. What does Nietzsche mean by *eternal recurrence*?

CHAPTER 22

Karl Marx (1816–1883)

Introduction

Kierkegaard and Nietzsche highlighted the direction taken by philosophy in the mid-nineteenth century by searching for the roots of a true humanism; Karl Marx did the same, but took as his starting point the experience of the laboring man, alienated by the demands put upon him in a capitalist society. His was a practical philosophy designed to resolve the tension between the capitalist and working classes, paving the way for the restoration of man to his true dignity.

Marx was born in Trier, Germany, in 1816, of Jewish descent, though he was baptized a Christian at the age of six, when his father, not unquestionably for religious reasons, was converted. For a short time he attended the University of Bonn, where he began the study of law, but left Bonn for Berlin, where he studied a variety of subjects, settling finally on philosophy; he was awarded a doctorate for his dissertation on the atomism of the Greek philosophers Democritus and Epicurus. After giving up his intention of teaching philosophy, he joined a group of young radical Hegelians in Berlin who believed that philosophy, conceived in terms of the dialectic, must have a practical political end; however, before long, Marx left the group, feeling that it was far too theoretical. He took on the editorship of the *Rheinische Zeitung*, an activist paper in Cologne that was soon discovered to be uncongenial to the public authorities, who clamped such tight censorship on it that Marx resigned. In one year, 1843, he got married, moved to Paris, helped to found the short-lived *Deutsch-Französische Jahrbücher*, joined an active socialist group, and took up a detailed study of political economy. Earlier he had met Friedrich Engels, the son of a wealthy industrialist living in England, who was actively involved in socialism; the two worked in close collaboration for the rest of their lives. Banished now from Paris, he went to Brussels, where he continued to deepen his affiliation with the Communist League and to collaborate with Engels, principally on the *Communist Manifesto*, published in 1848. One last government crackdown brought him to London, where he was allowed to remain. His dedication to his work resulted in poverty for himself and his family, who barely survived with help from Engels and from articles he wrote for the *New York Tribune*.

He carried on his research at the British Museum, where he became a familiar figure, and while he continued writing, he remained active in his support of the cause of the working man, founding, for example, the First International Workingmen's Association in 1864. He had designed three volumes for his major work, *Das Kapital*, the first of which he published in 1867; though he never lived to complete it, Engels was able to do so from the extensive preparation already done. Marx died in 1883; his wife and two of his children predeceased him. In addition to the *Communist Manifesto* and *Das Kapital*, some of his other works include *The Holy Family* (with Engels, 1845), *German Ideology* (with Engels, 1846), *Poverty of Philosophy* (1847), and the *Critique of Political Economy* (1859); in addition to his books, he wrote a vast number of articles for various magazines and journals.

As pointed out in an earlier chapter, every segment of reality invites reflection and response; yet, though man had always been a laborer, man the laborer had never been brought to the forefront of human consciousness as it was by Marx. In one sense, the world of the Industrial Revolution that Marx saw, everyone saw; in another sense, no one did. Surrounding him were thousands of human beings who endured a life completely determined by an inhuman labor system. The worker rose before dawn, sweated out the day, had supper as the last event before sleep, and awoke to the same unbroken, day-by-day routine in a grind that made him behave like the machine he worked on. Often no meal, often no sleep, always squalid. The chapter on "The Working Day" in *Capital* is a catalog of the brutal conditions prevailing throughout the industrialized world — a system of exploitation, thought Marx, tantamount to slavery.

What chance, asked Marx, did such people or their families have for education, cultural growth, self-reliance, leisure, or the whole range of pursuits that enlarge one's humanity? How could they escape the feeling of being embattled? Of being strangers to life? Of alienation? Thoughts like these activated Marx, who, very early in life, appreciated the fact that if ideas are to live they should not remain idle but must be dressed in the clothes of practical action and enter the real world as living philosophy. In the phrase of Ernst Bloch, the young Marx developed a "*public* self-consciousness," and would never entertain any but a philosophy directed to action.

Marx touches on three main points: the loss of man's meaning, the philosophical framework of loss and gain, and the recovery of man's meaning. Every window Marx looked through opened on to a human landscape as frightful as the one previously described, and it seemed to him that all the forces that should have supported man — economy, politics, culture, religion — conspired to destroy him. Marx followed a fellow German philosopher, Ludwig Feuerbach, in his analysis of *alienation*, the loss of meaning for man. Take religion, for example; even though it may be argued that religion, in the beginning, was a revolt against human degradation, it gradually developed as a force in its own interest, to which it sacrificed the good of man. In a strangely psychological but understandable way, under the oppression of religion, man surrendered his own attributes, one by one, to an external divinity, and in the process lost them for himself. So man, in this state of alienation, accepted religion as a solace for his oppression, as a drug to deaden the pain from so much suffering, or, in Marx's oft-quoted phrase, as the opium of the people: "Religion is the sigh of the oppressed creature, the sentiment of a heartless world, and the soul of soulless conditions. It is the *opium* of the people." Man, as Marx sees it, has finally become conscious of this destructive relationship and owes it to his humanity to purge God radically from his life.

The situation is exactly the same in the social order, for man has alienated himself from *his own labor*; his *productive activity* is not for himself. In this he has become enslaved, with little hope for emancipation. If his needs as a human being are to be satisfied by his productive capacity, then truly he has been indentured by the capitalist, who, in defrauding him of his labor, defrauds him of his humanity. Though valuation will vary from age to age, in the age of capitalism human values are seen to be a function of labor; that is, a just return to the worker for his labor means a respect for him as a human being and an opportunity, as previously mentioned, to engage in humanizing pursuits; to the extent that justice is denied, human values are lessened or even extinguished. For Marx, inasmuch as labor endows a thing with value, value is crystallized human labor: "When looked at as crystals of this social substance (i.e. human labor), common to them all, they are — Values."

The framework of Marx's philosophy is most often referred to as *dialectical materialism*, a term that, though not used by Marx himself, aptly designates his meaning. It is an amalgam of the dialectic of Hegel and the materialism of Feuerbach. For Hegel, dialectical idealism is the process whereby the Idea, or Spirit, unfolds itself in the course of time. For Marx, consistent with his atheism, reality is not to be conceived of in terms of Idea, or Spirit, but in terms of matter, that is, in terms of a materialism that departs from the old "billiard ball" kind, as found in Democritus, whose luckless atoms enter into chance configurations, but of the kind that admits free will, mind, value, virtue —

in short, all the attributes one would like to welcome in the name of what is "natural", yet remaining on the side of what is "supernatural." In comparing his use of the dialectic with that of Hegel, whom he regarded as a mighty thinker, Marx writes: "My dialectic method is not only different from the Hegelian, but is its direct opposite. To Hegel, the life-process of the human brain, i.e. the process of thinking, which, under the name of 'the Idea', he even transforms into an independent subject, is the demiurgos of the real world, and the real world is only the external, phenomenal form of 'the Idea'. With me, on the contrary, the ideal is nothing else than the material world reflected by the human mind, and translated into forms of thought." In Hegel, the dialectic is "standing on its head" and has to be turned right side up again; this is accomplished by Marx in giving primacy to matter over mind rather than to mind over matter.

The philosophical path to be taken to recover man's meaning is now clear. In the course of history, society has always developed a class structure on the basis of productive activity, whether it be freeman and slave, lord and serf, or capitalist and worker. More than the social strata themselves, the forces of production govern the entire shape of society, determining its culture, morality, and indeed all social relations: "Social relations are closely bound up with productive forces. In acquiring new productive forces men change their mode of production; and in changing their mode of production, in changing the way of earning their living, they change all their social relations. The handmill gives you society with the feudal lord; the steam-mill, society with the industrial capitalist. The same men who establish their social relations in conformity with their material productivity, produce also principles, ideas and categories, in conformity with their social relations."

The recovery of man's meaning, therefore, takes on an inevitable social thrust in terms of the classes of society, which are, in the nature of social reality, subject to the dialectic and must resolve the tension between them. Using the terminology introduced in the discussion of Hegel, the capitalist (bourgeois) class as thesis necessarily contradicts and reacts to the proletariat class as antithesis, thus transforming a two-class society into a classless society as synthesis. A *social revolution* is underway and historically inevitable, and all the productive forces hitherto consigned to private property will meld into the common good as the communist society, the next stage in the process of human emancipation and recovery, emerges.

For Marx, man is determined by the social structure in which he lives, or, more precisely, the kind of productive/economic structure in which he exists creates his very existence. At times this idea is expressed in the terms *substructure* and *superstructure*: the substructure is the productive/economic structure, which serves as a foundation for the legal, political, and social superstructures. If the substructure is antipathetic to humanity, so is the superstructure, and the only way to make the superstructure sympathetic to humanity is to change the substructure radically. In Marx's own words: "In the social production of their life, men enter into definite relations that are indispensable and independent of their will, relations of production which correspond to a definite stage of development of their material productive forces. The sum total of these relations of production constitutes the economic structure of society, the real foundation, on which rises a legal, political superstructure and to which correspond definite forms of social consciousness. The mode of production of material life conditions the social, political and intellectual life process in general." This is followed by a single sentence that summarizes Marx's whole philosophy: "It is not the consciousness of men that determines their being, but, on the contrary, their social being that determines their consciousness."

With the transformation of economic and productive forces, values as a whole are transformed; they are transformed into a truly human configuration, for the expropriation of man's labor will be done away with and the recovery of man's dignity will be achieved: Communism is "the *positive* transcendence of *private property*, or human *self-estrangement*, and therefore . . . the real *appropriation of the human* essence by and for man; . . . the complete return of man to himself as a *social* (i.e. human) being — a return become conscious, and accomplished within the entire wealth of previous development."

It is true that ideas have consequences, and Marx's ideas have had immediate practical consequences for countless millions of people throughout the world living under a Marx-inspired social philosophy. However, without trying to evaluate Marxian philosophy quantitatively or politically, it must be seen as a personalist philosophy, in the guise of an ethical revolt, an attempt to discover a human life for human beings.

Readings

A chapter in the Exploitation of The Working Man (from *Das Kapital*)

SECTION 3

Branches of English Industry without Legal Limits to Exploitation

We have hitherto considered the tendency to the extension of the working day, the were-wolf's hunger for surplus-labour in a department where the monstrous exactions, not surpassed, says an English bourgeois economist, by the cruelties of the Spaniards to the American red-skins, caused capital at last to be bound by the chains of legal regulations. Now, let us cast a glance at certain branches of production in which the exploitation of labour is either free from fetters to this day, or was so yesterday.

Mr. Broughton Charlton, county magistrate, declared as chairman of a meeting held at the Assembly Rooms, Nottingham, on the 14th of January, 1860, "that there was an amount of privation and suffering among that portion of the population connected with the lace trade, unknown in other parts of the kingdom, indeed, in the civilized world. ... Children of nine or ten years are dragged from their squalid beds at two, three, or four o'clock in the morning and compelled to work for a bare subsistence until ten, eleven, or twelve at night, their limbs wearing away, their frames-dwindling, their faces whitening, and their humanity absolutely sinking into a stone-like torpor, utterly horrible to contemplate. ... We are not surprised that Mr. Mallett, or any other manufacturer, should stand forward and protest against discussion. ... The system, as the Rev. Montagu Valpy describes it, is one of unmitigated slavery, socially, physically, morally, and spiritually. ... What can be thought of a town which holds a public meeting to petition that the period of labour for men shall be diminished to eighteen hours a day?. ... We declaim against the Virginian and Carolina cotton-planters. Is their black-market, their lash, and their barter of human flesh more detestable than this slow sacrifice of humanity which takes place in order that veils and collars may be fabricated for the benefit of capitalists?"

William Wood, 9 years old, was 7 years and 10 months when he began to work. He "ran moulds" (carried ready-moulded articles into the drying room, afterwards bringing back the empty mould) from the beginning. He came to work every day in the week at 6 a.m., and left off about 9 p.m. "I work till 9 o'clock at night six days in the week. I have done so seven or eight weeks." Fifteen hours of labour for a child of 7 years old! J. Murray, 12 years of age, says: "I turn jigger, and run moulds. I come at 6. Sometimes I come at 4. I worked all last night, till 6 o'clock this morning. I have not been in bed since the night before last. There were eight or nine other boys working last night. All but one have come this morning. I get 3 shillings and sixpence. I do not get any more for working at night. I worked two nights last week." Fernyhough, a boy of ten: "I have not always an hour (for dinner). I have only half an hour sometimes; on Thursday, Friday, and Saturday."

From the report of the Commissioners in 1863, the following: Dr. J. T. Arledge, senior physician of the North Staffordshire Infirmary, says: "The potters as a class, both men and women, represent a degenerated population, both physically and morally. They are, as a rule, stunted in growth, ill-shaped, and frequently ill-formed in the chest; they become prematurely old, and are certainly short-lived; they are phlegmatic and bloodless, and exhibit their debility of constitution by obstinate attacks of dyspepsia, and disorders of the liver and kidneys, and by rheumatism. But of all diseases they are especially prone to chest-disease, to pneumonia, phthisis, bronchitis, and asthma. One form would appear peculiar to them, and is known as potter's asthma, or potter's consumption. Scrofula attacking the glands, or bones, or other parts of the body, is a disease of two-thirds or more of the potters. ... That the 'degenerescence' of the population of this district is not even greater than it is, is due to the constant recruiting from the adjacent country, and intermarriages with more healthy races."

J. Leach deposes: "Last winter six out of nineteen girls were away from ill-health at one time from over-work. I have to bawl at them to keep them awake." W. Duffy: "I have seen when the children could none of them keep their eyes open for the work; indeed, none of us could." J. Lightbourne: "Am 13 ... We worked last winter till 9 (evening), and the winter before till 10. I used to cry with sore feet every night last winter." G. Apsden: "That boy of mine ... when he was 7 years old I used to carry him on my back to and from through the snow, and he used to have 16 hours a day ... I have often knelt down to feed him as he stood by the machine, for he could not leave it or stop." Smith, the managing partner of a Manchester factory: "We (he means his "hands" who work for "us") work on, with no stoppage for meals, so that the day's work of 10 1/2 hours is finished by 4.30. p.m., and all after that is overtime." (Does this Mr. Smith take no meals himself during 10 1/2 hours?) "We (this same Smith) seldom leave off working before 6 p.m. (he means leave off the consumption of 'our' labour-power machines), so that we (iterum Crispinus) are really working overtime the whole year round. ...

No branch of industry in England (we do not take into account the making of bread by machinery recently introduced) has preserved up to the present day a method of production so archaic, so—as we see from the poets of the Roman Empire—pre-christian, as baking. But capital, as was said earlier, is at first indifferent as to the technical character of the labour-process; it begins by taking it just as it finds it.

The incredible adulteration of bread, especially in London, was first revealed by the House of Commons Committee "on the adulteration of articles of food" (1855–56), and Dr. Hassall's work, "Adulterations detected." The consequence of these revelations was the Act of August 6th, 1860, "for preventing the adulteration of articles of food and drink," an inoperative law, as it naturally shows the tenderest consideration for every free-trader who determines by the buying or selling of adulterated commodities "to turn an honest penny." The Committee itself formulated more or less naively its conviction that free-trade meant essentially trade with adulterated, or as the English ingeniously put it, "sophisticated" goods. In fact this kind of sophistry knows better than Protagoras how to make white black, and black white, and better than the Eleatics how to demonstrate *ad oculos* that everything is only appearance.

At all events the committee had directed the attention of the public to its "daily bread," and therefore to the baking trade. At the same time in public meetings and in petitions to Parliament rose the cry of the London journeymen bakers against their over-work, &c. The cry was so urgent that Mr. H. S. Tremenheere, also a member of the Commission of 1863 several times mentioned, was appointed Royal Commissioner of Inquiry. His report, together with the evidence given, roused not the heart of the public but its stomach. Englishmen, always well up in the Bible, knew well enough that man, unless by elective grace a capitalist, or landlord, or sinecurist, is commanded to eat his bread in the sweat of his brow, but they did not know that he had to eat daily in his bread a certain quantity of human perspiration mixed with the discharge of abcesses, cobwebs, dead black-beetles, and putrid German yeast, without counting alum, sand, and other agreeable mineral ingredients. Without any regard to his holiness, Freetrade, the free baking-trade was therefore placed under the supervision of the State inspectors (Close of the Parliamentary session of 1863), and by the same Act of Parliament, work from 9 in the evening to 5 in the morning was forbidden for journeymen bakers under 18. The last clause speaks volumes as to the over-work in this old-fashioned, homely line of business.

"The work of a London journeyman baker begins, as a rule, at about eleven at night. At that hour he 'makes the dough,'—a laborious process, which lasts from half-an-hour to three quarters of an hour, according to the size of the batch or the labour bestowed upon it. He then lies down upon the kneading-board, which is also the covering of the trough in which the dough is 'made;' and with a sack under him, and another rolled up as a pillow, he sleeps for about a couple of hours. He is then engaged in a rapid and continuous labour for about five hours—throwing out the dough, 'scaling it off,' moulding it, putting it into the oven, preparing and baking rolls and fancy bread, taking the batch bread out of the oven, and up into the shop, &c., &c. The temperature of a bakehouse ranges from about 75 to upwards of 90 degrees, and in the smaller bakehouses approximates usually to the higher rather than to the lower degree of heat. When the business of making the bread, rolls, &c., is over, that of its distribution begins, and a considerable proportion of the journeymen in the trade, after working hard in the manner described during the night, are upon their legs for many hours during the day, carrying baskets, or wheeling hand-carts, and sometimes again in the bakehouse, leaving off work at various hours between 1 and 6 p.m. according to the season of the year, or the amount and nature of their master's business; while others are again engaged in the bakehouse in 'bringing out' more batches until late in the afternoon. ... During what is called 'the London season,' the operatives belonging to the 'full-priced' bakers at the West End of the town, generally begin work at 11 p.m., and are engaged in making the bread, with one or two short (sometimes very short) intervals of rest, up to 8 o'clock the next morning. They are then engaged all day long, up to 4, 5, 6, and as late as 7 o'clock in the evening carrying out bread, or sometimes in the afternoon in the bakehouse again, assisting in the biscuit-baking. They may have, after they have done their work, sometimes five or six, sometimes only four or five hours' sleep before they begin again. On Fridays they always begin sooner, some about ten o'clock, and continue in some cases, at work, either in making or delivering the bread up to 8 p.m. on Saturday night, but more generally up to 4 or 5 o'clock, Sunday morning. On Sundays the men must attend twice or three times during the day for an hour or two to make preparations for the next day's bread. ... The men employed by the underselling masters (who sell their bread under the 'full price,' and who, as already pointed out, comprise three-fourths of the London bakers) have not only to work on the average longer hours, but their work is almost entirely confined to the bakehouse. The underselling masters generally sell their bread ... in the shop. If they send it out, which is not common, except as supplying chandlers' shops, they usually employ other hands for that purpose. It is not their practice to deliver bread from house to house. Towards the end of the week. ... the men begin on Thursday night at 10 o'clock, and continue on with only slight intermission until late on Saturday evening."

Even the bourgeois intellect understands the position of the "underselling" masters. "The unpaid labour of the men was made the source whereby the competition was carried on." And the "full-priced" baker denounces his underselling competitors to the Commission of Inquiry as thieves of foreign labour and adulterators. "They only exist now by first defrauding the public, and next getting 18 hours work out of their men for 12 hours' wages."

The adulteration of bread and the formation of a class of bakers that sells the bread below the full price, date from the beginning of the 18th century, from the time when the corporate character of the trade was lost, and the capitalist in the form of the miller or flour-factor, rises behind the nominal master baker. Thus was laid the foundation of capitalistic production in this trade, of the unlimited extension of the working day and of night labour, although the latter only since 1824 gained a serious footing, even in London.

After what has just been said, it will be understood that the Report of the Commission classes journeymen bakers among the short-lived labourers, who, having by good luck escaped the normal decimation of the children of the working-class, rarely reach the age of 42. Nevertheless, the baking trade is always overwhelmed with applicants. The sources of the supply of these labour-powers to London are Scotland, the western agricultural districts of England, and Germany.

. . .

In the last week of June, 1863, all the London daily papers published a paragraph with the "sensational" heading "Death from simple over-work." It dealt with the death of the milliner, Mary Anne Walkley, 20 years of age, employed in a highly-respectable dressmaking establishment, exploited by a lady with the pleasant name of Elise. The old, often-told story, was once more recounted. This girl worked, on an average, 16 1/2 hours, during the season often 30 hours, without a break, whilst her failing labour-power was revived by occasional supplies of sherry, port, or coffee. It was just now the height of the season. It was necessary to conjure up in the twinkling of an eye the gorgeous dresses for the noble ladies bidden to the ball in honour of the newly-imported Princess of Wales. Mary Anne Walkley had worked without intermission for 26 1/2 hours, with 60 other girls, 30 in one room, that only afforded 1/3 of the cubic feet of air required for them. At night, they slept in pairs in one of the stifling holes into which the bedroom was divided by partitions of board. And this was one of the best millinery establishments in London. Mary Anne Walkley fell ill on the Friday, died on Sunday, without, to the astonishment of Madame Elise, having previously completed the work in hand. The doctor, Mr. Keys, called too late to the death-bed, duly bore witness before the coroner's jury that "Mary Anne Walkley had died from long hours of work in an over-crowded workroom, and a too small and badly-ventilated bedroom." In order to give the doctor a lesson in good manners, the coroner's jury thereupon brought in a verdict that "the deceased had died of apoplexy, but there was reason to fear that her death had been accelerated by over-work in an overcrowded workroom, &c." "Our white slaves," cried the "Morning Star," the organ of the free-traders, Cobden and Bright, "our white slaves, who are toiled into the grave, for the most part silently pine and die."

"It is not in dressmakers' rooms that working to death is the order of the day, but in a thousand other places; in every place I had almost said, where 'a thriving business' has to be done. . . . We will take the blacksmith as a type. If the poets were true, there is no man so hearty, so merry, as the blacksmith; he rises early and strikes his sparks before the sun; he eats and drinks and sleeps as no other man. Working in moderation, he is, in fact, in one of the best of human positions, physically speaking. But we follow him into the city or town, and we see the stress of work on that strong man, and what then is his position in the death-rate of his country. In Marylebone, blacksmiths die at the rate of 31 per thousand per annum, or 11 above the mean of the male adults of the country in its entirety. The occupation, instinctive almost as a portion of human art, unobjectionable as a branch of human industry, is made by mere excess of work, the destroyer of the man. He can strike so many blows per day, walk so many steps, breathe so many breaths, produce so much work, and live an average, say of fifty years; he is made to strike so many more blows, to walk so many more steps, to breathe so many more breaths per day, and to increase altogether a fourth of his life. He meets the effort; the result is, that producing for a limited time a fourth more work, he dies at 37 for 50."

(From *Capital*, Vol. I, Chap. X, Sect. 3, translated from 3rd German edition by Samuel Moore and Edward Aveling, edited by Frederick Engels, 1887. Republished by Allen and Unwin, 1957.)

On the Alienation of Man (from *Economic And Philosophical Manuscripts*)

We shall begin from a *contemporary* economic fact. The worker becomes poorer the more wealth he produces and the more his production increases in power and extent. The worker becomes an ever cheaper commodity the more goods he creates. The *devaluation* of the human world increases in direct relation with the *increase in value* of the world of things. Labour does not only create goods; it also produces itself and the worker as a *commodity*, and indeed in the same proportion as it produces goods.

This fact simply implies that the object produced by labour, its product, now stands opposed to it as an *alien being,* as a *power independent* of the producer. The product of labour is labour which has been embodied in an object and turned into a physical thing; this product is an *objectification* of labour. The performance of work is at the same time its objectification. The performance of work appears in the sphere of political economy as a *vitiation* of the worker, objectification as a *loss* and as *servitude to the object,* and appropriation as *alienation.*

So much does the performance of work appear as vitiation that the worker is vitiated to the point of starvation. So much does objectification appear as loss of the object that the worker is deprived of the most essential things not only of life but also of work. Labour itself becomes an object which he can acquire only by the greatest effort and with unpredictable interruptions. So much does the appropriation of the object appear as alienation that the more objects the worker produces the fewer he can possess and the more he falls under the domination of his product, of capital.

All these consequences follow from the fact that the worker is related to the *product of his labour* as to an *alien* object. For it is clear on this presupposition that the more the worker expends himself in work the more powerful becomes the world of objects which he creates in face of himself, the poorer he becomes in his inner life, and the less he belongs to himself. It is just the same as in religion. The more of himself man attributes to God the less he has left in himself. The worker puts his life into the object, and his life then belongs no longer to himself but to the object. The greater his activity, therefore, the less he possesses. What is embodied in the product of his labour is no longer his own. The greater this product is, therefore, the more he is diminished. The *alienation* of the worker in his product means not only that his labour becomes an object, assumes an *external* existence, but that it exists independently, *outside himself,* and alien to him, and that it stands opposed to him as an autonomous power. The life which he has given to the object sets itself against him as an alien and hostile force. ...

Let us now examine more closely the phenomenon of *objectification;* the worker's production and the *alienation* and *loss* of the object it produces, which is involved in it. The worker can create nothing without *nature,* without the *sensuous external world.* The latter is the material in which his labour is realized, in which it is active, out of which and through which it produces things.

But just as nature affords the *means of existence* of labour, in the sense that labour cannot *live* without objects upon which it can be exercised, so also it provides the *means of existence* in a narrower sense; namely the means of physical existence for the *worker* himself. Thus, the more the worker *appropriates* the external world of sensuous nature by his labour the more he deprives himself of *means of existence,* in two respects: first, that the sensuous external world becomes progressively less an object belonging to his labour or a means of existence of his labour, and secondly, that it becomes progressively less a means of existence in the direct sense, a means for the physical subsistence of the worker.

In both respects, therefore, the worker becomes a slave of the object; first, in that he receives an *object of work,* i.e. receives *work,* and secondly, in that he receives *means of subsistence.* Thus the object enables him to exist, first as a *worker* and secondly, as a *physical subject.* The culmination of this enslavement is that he can only maintain himself as a *physical subject* so far as he is a *worker,* and that it is only as a *physical subject* that he is a worker.

(The alienation of the worker in his object is expressed as follows in the laws of political economy: the more the worker produces the less he has to consume; the more value he creates the more worthless he becomes; the more refined his product the more crude and misshapen the worker; the more civilized the product the more barbarous the worker; the more powerful the work the more feeble the worker; the more the work manifests intelligence the more the worker declines in intelligence and becomes a slave of nature.)

Political economy conceals the alienation in the nature of labour in so far as it does not examine the direct relationship between the worker (work) and production. Labour certainly produces marvels for the rich but it produces privation for the worker. It produces palaces, but hovels for the worker. It produces beauty, but deformity for the worker. It replaces labour by machinery, but it casts some of the workers back into a barbarous kind of work and turns the others into machines. It produces intelligence, but also stupidity and cretinism for the workers.

The direct relationship of labour to its products is the relationship of the worker to the objects of his production. The relationship of property owners to the objects of production and to production itself is merely a *consequence* of this first relationship and confirms it. We shall consider this second aspect later.

Thus, when we ask what is the important relationship of labour, we are concerned with the relationship of the *worker* to production.

So far we have considered the alienation of the worker only from one aspect; namely, *his relationship with the products of his labour.* However, alienation appears not merely in the result but also in the *process of production*, within *productive activity* itself. How could the worker stand in an alien relationship to the product of his activity if he did not alienate himself in the act of production itself? The product is indeed only the résumé of activity, of production. Consequently, if the product of labour is alienation, production itself must be active alienation—the alienation of activity and the activity of alienation. The alienation of the object of labour merely summarizes the alienation in the work activity itself.

What constitutes the alienation of labour? First, that the work is *external* to the worker, that it is not part of his nature; and that, consequently, he does not fulfil himself in his work but denies himself, has a feeling of misery rather than well-being, does not develop freely his mental and physical energies but is physically exhausted and mentally debased. The worker, therefore, feels himself at home only during his leisure time, whereas at work he feels homeless. His work is not voluntary but imposed, *forced labour*. It is not the satisfaction of a need, but only a *means* for satisfying other needs. Its alien character is clearly shown by the fact that as soon as there is no physical or other compulsion it is avoided like the plague. External labour, labour in which man alienates himself, is a labour of self-sacrifice, of mortification. Finally, the external character of work for the worker is shown by the fact that it is not his own work but work for someone else, that in work he does not belong to himself but to another person.

Just as in religion the spontaneous activity of human fantasy, of the human brain and heart, reacts independently as an alien activity of gods or devils upon the individual, so the activity of the worker is not his own spontaneous activity. It is another's activity and a loss of his own spontaneity.

We arrive at the result that man (the worker) feels himself to be freely active only in his animal functions—eating, drinking and procreating, or at most also in his dwelling and in personal adornment—while in his human functions he is reduced to an animal. The animal becomes human and the human becomes animal.

Eating, drinking and procreating are of course also genuine human functions. But abstractly considered, apart from the environment of human activities, and turned into final and sole ends, they are animal functions.

We have now considered the act of alienation of practical human activity, labour, from two aspects: (1) the relationship of the worker to the *product of labour* as an alien object which dominates him. This relationship is at the same time the relationship to the sensuous external world, to natural objects, as an alien and hostile world; (2) the relationship of labour to the *act of production* within *labour*. This is the relationship of the worker to his own activity as something alien and not belonging to him, activity as suffering (passivity), strength as powerlessness, creation as emasculation, the *personal* physical and mental energy of the worker, his personal life (for what is life but activity?), as an activity which is directed against himself, independent of him and not belonging to him. This is *self-alienation* as against the above-mentioned alienation of the *thing*. ... We have now to infer a third characteristic of *alienated labour* from the two we have considered.

Man is a species-being not only in the sense that he makes the community (his own as well as those of other things) his object both practically and theoretically, but also (and this is simply another expression for the same thing) in the sense that he treats himself as the present, living species, as a *universal* and consequently free being.

Species-life, for man as for animals, has its physical basis in the fact that man (like animals) lives from inorganic nature, and since man is more universal than an animal so the range of inorganic nature from which he lives is more universal. Plants, animals, minerals, air, light, etc. constitute, from the theoretical aspect, a part of human consciousness as objects of natural science and art; they are man's spiritual inorganic nature, his intellectual means of life, which he must first prepare for enjoyment and perpetuation. So also, from the practical aspect, they form a part of human life and activity. In practice man lives only from these natural products, whether in the form of food, heating, clothing, housing, etc. The universality of man appears in practice in the universality which makes the whole of nature into his inorganic body: (1) as a direct means of life; and equally (2) as the material object and instrument of his life activity. Nature is the inorganic body of man; that is to say nature, excluding the human body itself. To say that man *lives* from nature means that nature is his *body* with which he must remain in a continuous interchange in order not to die. The statement that the physical and mental life of man, and nature, are interdependent means simply that nature is interdependent with itself, for man is a part of nature.

Since alienated labour: (1) alienates nature from man; and (2) alienates man from himself, from his own active function, his life activity; so it alienates him from the species. It makes *species-life* into a means of individual life. In the first place it alienates species-life and individual life, and secondly, it turns the latter, as an abstraction, into the purpose of the former, also in its abstract and alienated form.

For labour, *life activity, productive life,* now appear to man only as *means* for the satisfaction of a need, the need to maintain his physical existence. Productive life is, however, species-life. It is life creating life. In the type of life activity resides the whole character of a species, its species-character; and free, conscious activity is the species-character of human beings. Life itself appears only as a *means of life.*

The animal is one with its life activity. It does not distinguish the activity from itself. It is *its activity.* But man makes his life activity itself an object of his will and consciousness. He has a conscious life activity. It is not a determination with which he is completely identified. Conscious life activity distinguishes man from the life activity of animals. Only for this reason is he a species-being. Or rather, he is only a self-conscious being, i.e. his own life is an object for him, because he is a species-being. Only for this reason is his activity free activity. Alienated labour reverses the relationship, in that man because he is a self-conscious being makes his life activity, his *being,* only a means for his *existence.* ...

We began with an economic fact, the alienation of the worker and his production. We have expressed this fact in conceptual terms as *alienated labour,* and in analysing the concept we have merely analysed an economic fact.

Let us now examine further how this concept of alienated labour must express and reveal itself in reality. If the product of labour is alien to me and confronts me as an alien power, to whom does it belong? If my own activity does not belong to me but is an alien, forced activity, to whom does it belong? To a being *other* than myself. And who is this being? The *gods?* It is apparent in the earliest stages of advanced production, e.g. temple building, etc. in Egypt, India, Mexico, and in the service rendered to gods, that the product belonged to the gods. But the gods alone were never the lords of labour. And no more was *nature*. What a contradiction it would be if the more man subjugates nature by his labour, and the more the marvels of the gods are rendered superfluous by the marvels of industry, the more he should abstain from his joy in producing and his enjoyment of the product for love of these powers.

The *alien* being to whom labour and the product of labour belong, to whose service labour is devoted, and to whose enjoyment the product of labour goes, can only be man himself. If the product of labour does not belong to the worker, but confronts him as an alien power, this can only be because it belongs to *a man other than the worker*. If his activity is a torment to him it must be a source of *enjoyment* and pleasure to another. Not the gods, nor nature, but only man himself can be this alien power over men.

Consider the earlier statement that the relation of man to himself is first *realized, objectified*, through his relation to other men. If he is related to the product of his labour, his objectified labour, as to an alien, hostile, powerful and independent object, he is related in such a way that another *alien*, hostile, powerful and independent man is the lord of this object. If he is related to his own activity as to unfree activity, then he is related to it as activity in the service, and under the domination, coercion and yoke, of another man.

Every self-alienation of man, from himself and from nature, appears in the relation which he postulates between other men and himself and nature. Thus religious self-alienation is necessarily exemplified in the relation between laity and priest, or, since it is here a question of the spiritual world, between the laity and a mediator. In the real world of practice this self-alienation can only be expressed in the real, practical relation of man to his fellow men. The medium through which alienation occurs is itself a *practical* one. Through alienated labour, therefore, man not only produces his relation to the object and to the process of production as to alien and hostile men; he also produces the relation of other men to his production and his product, and the relation between himself and other men. Just as he creates his own production as a vitiation, a punishment, and his own product as a loss, as a product which does not belong to him, so he creates the domination of the non-producer over production and its product. As he alienates his own activity, so he bestows upon the stranger an activity which is not his own.

Review Questions

1. Show how Marx's philosophy begins with the experience of the laboring man.
2. How does a philosophy centering on one class of mankind enlarge one's conception of humanity as a whole?
3. How is Marx's philosophy a foray against alienation?
4. Explain the phrase *dialectical materialism* and show how it differs from the *dialectical idealism* of Hegel.
5. Marx is dead set against religion. Why?
6. How is man, in our time, to recover his true meaning, according to Marx?

CHAPTER 23

Henri Bergson (1859–1941)

Introduction

At any given time, several traditions in the history of ideas exist side by side, and alongside the history of philosophy is that of science, a realm of fresh discovery that has expanded since the time of the Renaissance. The revolutionary view of the heavenly bodies created by Copernicus, Galileo, and Newton created not only a new understanding of the cosmos but also a new understanding of man. A new physics led to a new metaphysics because it moved to ever-broadening horizons in terms of which man's universe must be grasped. The advancing front of science disclosed another dimension — not in the direction of the infinite but in the direction of the infinitesimal; just as astronomy was taking man to measureless heights, chemistry, following the insights of Lavoisier, Priestly, and Dalton, was taking him to measureless depths, proclaiming that the irreducibility of matter was only apparent, not real. In actuality, matter too was an endless world of atoms, subatoms, and a dazzling array of interlocking energies just as exciting as the planets and stars. Add to this the increasing acceptance of evolution, as a result of Darwin's studies, and we have a picture of man as microcosm unimagined by the ancients.

As we have seen, the success of any discipline is its own burden, for it bears within itself the inevitable tendency to overreach and extend its method to other areas. Thus, it is to be expected that science would be offered by its enthusiasts as the ultimate arbiter of what man is really like and, postulating the machine as model, that man is to be understood in terms of scientific principles only. Henri Bergson's philosophy of human freedom at the turn of the century was a magnificent protest against such a view, though he stoutly maintained that truth required a friendly holding of hands between science and philosophy.

Bergson was born in Paris in 1859, of Jewish descent, the son of a Polish father and an English mother. As a young student he distinguished himself in mathematics and later, at the École Normale

Supérieure, became a passionate reader in science and philosophy. At age twenty-two he began his teaching career at Angers and continued at other places until 1900, during which time he enjoyed a growing reputation, especially with the publication of his doctoral dissertation on the immediate data of consciousness. In 1900 he was invited to take the chair of modern philosophy at the Collège de France in Paris, where his prestige as a lecturer was steadily enhanced and filled the hall with avid students — a cross section of men and women, even from the fashionable world, all eager to hear him defend the claims of human freedom and spirituality against scientific determinism. In the same year he published *Laughter*, on the role of the comic in human life. The best insight into his method is found in *An Introduction to Metaphysics*, published in 1903. On the strength of *Creative Evolution*, published in 1907, Bergson was recognized the world over not only as an outstanding philosopher, but as by far the most engaging stylist writing in any language; William James was prompted to call his book "a pure classic in point of form." At the peak of his reputation, Bergon's ill health forced him to retreat from teaching and finally to resign from academic life in 1921, and practically from public life, with the exception of his service as president of the League of Nations committee for intellectual cooperation for several years. In 1928 he won the Nobel Prize for literature. Just when it seemed that his writing years were over, Bergson astonished the intellectual world in 1932 with the publication of *The Two Sources of Morality and Religion*, in which he developed the concepts of open morality and dynamic religion as opposed to closed morality and static religion. Bergson's waning years were wracked not only with pain but also with sorrow at the occupation of France early in World War II and the anti-Jewish measures of the regime. To declare his solidarity with the Jewish people, he refused to let his fame exempt him from the repressive laws against them, and for the same reason he postponed making public his wish to espouse Christianity until he knew he was dying in 1941.

Bergson belongs to that group of philosophers who see reality as a whole, though not with the determinate wholeness of mathematics or science. Quite the contrary, Bergson's vision of wholeness comes from a living, undetermined reality whose universal impulse is to create human beings who are free to reach their full humanity by entering, beyond all rationality, into a mystical union with the ultimate. However, the mind in its relationship with reality begins its work almost with the reverse effect. When we say we know a thing, we abstract it or cut it out of its setting, thereby separating it from the whole in which it is presented. We call this thing a table, a chair, a dog, and in doing so sort out this parcel of sensible qualities from all others and give it a name. The sense of continuity, of oneness with all else, is not immediately seized and is, at least for the present, relegated to the sidelines. The same is true of the sciences, which, by analysis, pursue objects as though they were detached from a larger whole. Biology, for example, is concerned with organs, cells, tissues, and such like without once considering what life itself is in the whole living organism, thereby losing the sense of continuity.

Accordingly, Bergson makes a distinction between *intelligence* and *intuition*. Intelligence, which functions as analysis, separates or detaches the object from its setting; analysis "goes around" the object. Intuition, on the other hand, is the power of the mind to grasp a thing in its wholeness, to see it in its relatedness, and therefore to seize its meaning; it "gets inside" the object. Intelligence creates isolated parcels; it does not consider movement as a continuity, but measures it as "successive location"; intelligence is the faculty of "man as maker," *homo faber*. Intuition, in its vision of wholeness, is not satisfied with the piecemeal and seeks to lay hold of the unity and continuity in the stream of existence; intuition is the faculty of "man as wise," *homo sapiens*.

This notion of continuous existence, called *duration*, is the most important single notion in Bergson, for it involves the mysterious fact that things endure through time; they do not exist from moment to moment, as though moments are discrete measures of existence; no, their duration means their existence, not parceled out, but as one with the stream of becoming in which they are immersed. This is especially true of man, whose awareness of duration gives him the awareness of himself as a *self*, and as the ultimate goal of the larger duration of all living things under the grand movement of *creative evolution*.

The concept of creative evolution was born of Bergson's intensive studies in biology and of his firm belief that life is not subject to mechanical laws determining events beforehand, or to teleology in the sense of an already established evolutionary plan. If what we see around us is a great unfolding of life, such unfolding is possible because there is at the foundation of living things a throbbing surge to life that Bergson calls the *life impulse*, the *élan vital*. Reality, as recognized from ancient days on, is constantly becoming, and for Bergson there is more in becoming than there is in being. The *élan vital*, in this stream of reality, can move upward or downward, ascend or descend; as it ascends it creates more living, more consciousness, more freedom; as it descends, by becoming more and more tied to matter, life diminishes, exhausts itself. It is as though the *élan vital*, given in such profusion, is creatively experimenting, trying to discover how much less of an obstacle matter might become as it gropes for higher expressions of life. In the course of its evolution, as the *élan vital* fractioned off into the animal and plant worlds, it discovered a higher level of life in the former, and as it further probed its way through animal life, it pushed on to two yet higher levels, insect and human life, differentiated by the former's high development of instinct, particularly with regard to the use of certain of its organs as tools, and the latter's development of its own tools, characteristic of *homo faber*.

But man, now possessed not only of intellect but also of intuition, is the highest stage of life on our planet and lies open to further evolution *as a human being* on the basis of his own humanity, that is, of his consciousness and freedom. To "lie open" is the all-important factor. Man's moral life can be a closed affair, a *closed morality*, meaning an unfree social conformism, acting under pressure or stereotyped obligation; or an *open morality*, which stands for what is truly human and personal, and for the sensitivity with which a person becomes attuned to the boundary-less possibilities of his humanity, following the many examples given by moral heroes and saints. Religion, the second great arena of man's life, is the practical stance man takes toward the higher powers, or, in Bergson's words, "that element which, in beings endowed with reason, is called upon to make good any deficiency of attachment to life." Religion is *static* insofar as it is a defense against nature and its necessity, but it is *dynamic* when looked upon as springing forth from the depths of the life impulse in its struggle toward an unseen though strongly felt goal, exemplified in mysticism, whose ultimate end is "the establishment of a contact, consequently of a partial coincidence, with the creative efforts which life itself manifests. This effort is of God, if it is not God himself."

For Bergson, then, the living universe has brought about the phenomenon of man, who is phenomenon precisely because he expresses what is highest in the universe, because he is the culmination of the *élan vital's* struggle to ascend from necessity to freedom. With increasing freedom comes increasing joy, "diffused throughout the world by an ever-spreading mystic intuition," and, yes, even by the "furtherance of scientific experiment." But freedom carries with it a charge and a hope: "Mankind lies groaning, half crushed beneath the weight of its own progress. Men do not sufficiently realize that their future is in their own hands. Theirs is the task of determining first of all whether they want to go on living or not. Theirs the responsibility, then, for deciding if they want merely to live, or intend to make just the extra effort required for fulfilling, even on their refractory planet, the essential function of the universe, which is a machine for the making of gods."

William James, quoted earlier in this section, had a very high opinion of Bergson's works, but the publication of *Two Sources* occurred long after James died. However, upon the publication of *Creative Evolution*, he wrote to Bergson, "And if your next book proves to be as great an advance on this one as this is on its two predecessors, your name will surely go down as one of the great creative names in philosophy." The future turned out to be true to his prophecy. Bergson's popularity today is hardly what it was when James wrote those words, but his works remain a permanent testimony to the legitimacy of metaphysics, a metaphysics, in his case, rooted in experience and expanded by the insight afforded him by science and mysticism; it enabled him to produce a philosophy in which we can seek the meaning of the universe, not among the dead, but among the living.

Readings

From *Creative Evolution*

1. Creative Evolution
The history of the evolution of life, incomplete as it yet is, already reveals to us how the intellect has been formed, by an uninterrupted progress, along a line which ascends through the vertebrate series up to man. It shows us in the faculty of understanding an appendage of the faculty of acting, a more and more precise, more and more complex and supple adaptation of the consciousness of living beings to the conditions of existence that are made for them. Hence should result this consequence that our intellect, in the narrow sense of the word, is intended to secure the perfect fitting of our body to its environment, to represent the relations of external things among themselves—in short, to think matter. Such will indeed be one of the conclusions of the present essay. We shall see that the human intellect feels at home among inanimate objects, more especially among solids, where our action finds its fulcrum and our industry its tools; that our concepts have been formed on the model of solids; that our logic is, pre-eminently, the logic of solids; that, consequently, our intellect triumphs in geometry, wherein is revealed the kinship of logical thought with unorganized matter, and where the intellect has only to follow its natural movement, after the lightest possible contact with experience, in order to go from discovery to discovery, sure that experience is following behind it and will justify it invariably.

But from this it must also follow that our thought, in its purely logical form, is incapable of presenting the true nature of life, the full meaning of the evolutionary movement. Created by life, in definite circumstances, to act on definite things, how can it embrace life, of which it is only an emanation or an aspect? ...

In fact, we do indeed feel that not one of the categories of our thought—unity, multiplicity, mechanical causality, intelligent finality, etc.—applies exactly to the things of life: who can say where individuality begins and ends, whether the living being is one or many, whether it is the cells which associate themselves into the organism or the organism which dissociates itself into cells? In vain we force the living into this or that one of our moulds. All the moulds crack. They are too narrow, above all too rigid, for what we try to put into them. Our reasoning, so sure of itself among things inert, feels ill at ease on this new ground. It would be difficult to cite a biological discovery due to pure reasoning. And most often, when experience has finally shown us how life goes to work to obtain a certain result, we find its way of working is just that of which we should never have thought.

Yet evolutionist philosophy does not hesitate to extend to the things of life the same methods of explanation which have succeeded in the case of unorganized matter. It begins by showing us in the intellect a local effect of evolution, a flame, perhaps accidental, which lights up the coming and going of living beings in the narrow passage open to their action; and lo! forgetting what it has just told us, it makes of this lantern glimmering in a tunnel a Sun which can illuminate the world. Boldly it proceeds, with the powers of conceptual thought alone, to the ideal reconstruction of all things, even of life. ...

Must we then give up fathoming the depths of life? Must we keep to that mechanistic idea of it which the understanding will always give us—an idea necessarily artificial and symbolical, since it makes the total activity of life shrink to the form of a certain human activity which is only a partial and local manifestation of life, a result or by-product of the vital process? We should have to do so, indeed, if life had employed all the psychical potentialities it possesses in producing pure understandings—that is to say, in making geometricians. But the line of evolution that ends in man is not the only one. On other paths, divergent from it, other forms of consciousness have been developed, which have not been able to free themselves from external constraints or to regain control over themselves, as the human intellect has done, but which, none the less, also express something that is immanent and essential in the evolutionary movement. Suppose these other forms of consciousness brought together and amalgamated with intellect: would not the result be a consciousness as wide as life? And such a consciousness, turning around suddenly against the push of life which it feels behind, would have a vision of life complete—would it not?—even though the vision were fleeting.

It will be said that, even so, we do not transcend our intellect, for it is still with our intellect, and through our intellect, that we see the other forms of consciousness. And this would be right if we were pure intellects, if there did not remain, around our conceptual and logical thought, a vague nebulosity, made of the very substance out of which has been formed the luminous nucleus that we call the intellect. Therein reside certain powers that are complementary to the understanding, powers of which we have only an indistinct feeling when we remain shut up in ourselves, but which will become clear and distinct when they perceive themselves at work, so to speak, in the evolution of nature. They will thus learn what sort of effort they must make to be intensified and expanded in the very direction of life.

This amounts to saying that *theory of knowledge* and *theory of life* seem to us inseparable. A theory of life that is not accompanied by a criticism of knowledge is obliged to accept, as they stand, the concepts which the understanding puts at its disposal: it can but enclose the facts, willing or not, in pre-existing frames which it regards as ultimate. It thus obtains a symbolism which is convenient, perhaps even necessary to positive science, but not a direct vision of its object. On the other hand, a theory of knowledge which does not replace the intellect in the general evolution of life will teach us neither how the frames of knowledge have been constructed nor how we can enlarge or go beyond them. It is necessary that these two inquiries, theory of knowledge and theory of life, should join each other, and, by a circular process, push each other on unceasingly.

Together, they may solve by a method more sure, brought nearer to experience, the great problems that philosophy poses. For, if they should succeed in their common enterprise, they would show us the formation of the intellect, and thereby the genesis of that matter of which our intellect traces the general configuration. They would dig to the very root of nature and of mind. They would substitute for the false evolutionism of Spencer—which consists in cutting up present reality, already evolved, into little bits no less evolved, and then recomposing it with these fragments, thus positing in advance everything that is to be explained—a true evolutionism, in which reality would be followed in its generation and its growth.

But a philosophy of this kind will not be made in a day. Unlike the philosophical systems properly so called, each of which was the individual work of a man of genius and sprang up as a whole, to be taken or left, it will only be built up by the collective and progressive effort of many thinkers, of many observers also, completing, correcting and improving one another. So the present essay does not aim at resolving at once the greatest problems. It simply desires to define the method and to permit a glimpse, on some essential points, of the possibility of its application.

2. Duration

The existence of which we are most assured and which we know best is unquestionably our own, for of every other object we have notions which may be considered external and superficial, whereas, of ourselves, our perception is internal and profound. What, then, do we find? In this privileged case, what is the precise meaning of the word "exist"? Let us recall here briefly the conclusions of an earlier work.

I find, first of all, that I pass from state to state. I am warm or cold, I am merry or sad, I work or I do nothing, I look at what is around me or I think of something else. Sensations, feelings, volitions, ideas—such are the changes into which my existence is divided and which colour it in turns. I change, then, without ceasing. But this is not saying enough. Change is far more radical than we are at first inclined to suppose.

For I speak of each of my states as if it formed a block and were a separate whole. I say indeed that I change, but the change seems to me to reside in the passage from one state to the next: of each state, taken separately, I am apt to think that it remains the same during all the time that it prevails. Nevertheless, a slight effort of attention would reveal to me that there is no feeling, no idea, no volition which is not undergoing change every moment: if a mental state ceased to vary, its duration would cease to flow. Let us take the most stable of internal states, the visual perception of a motionless external object. The object may remain the same, I may look at it from the same side, at the same angle, in the same light; nevertheless the vision I now have of it differs from that which I have just had, even if only because the one is an instant older than the other. ... The truth is that we change without ceasing, and that the state itself is nothing but change.

This amounts to saying that there is no essential difference between passing from one state to another and persisting in the same state. If the state which "remains the same" is more varied than we think, on the other hand the passing from one state to another resembles, more than we imagine, a single state being prolonged; the transition is continuous. But, just because we close our eyes to the unceasing variation of every psychical state, we are obliged, when the change has become so considerable as to force itself on our attention, to speak as if a new state were placed alongside the previous one. Of this new state we assume that it remains unvarying in its turn, and so on endlessly. The apparent discontinuity of the psychical life is then due to our attention being fixed on it by a series of separate acts: actually there is only a gentle slope; but in following the broken line of our acts of attention, we think we perceive separate steps. ... Now, states thus defined cannot be regarded as distinct elements. They continue each other in an endless flow.

But, as our attention has distinguished and separated them artificially, it is obliged next to reunite them by an artificial bond. It imagines, therefore, a formless *ego*, indifferent and unchangeable, on which it threads the psychic states which it has set up as independent enti-

ties. . . . If our existence were composed of separate states with an impassive ego to unite them, for us there would be no duration. For an
ego which does not change does not *endure,* and a psychic state which
remains the same so long as it is not replaced by the following state
does not *endure* either. Vain, therefore, is the attempt to range such
states beside each other on the ego supposed to sustain them: never
can these solids strung upon a solid make up that duration which
flows. What we actually obtain in this way is an artificial imitation of
the internal life, a static equivalent which will lend itself better to the
requirements of logic and language, just because we have eliminated
from it the element of real time. But, as regards the psychical life unfolding beneath the symbols which conceal it, we readily perceive that
time is just the stuff it is made of.

3. Continuity of Life

But then, we must no longer speak of *life in general* as an abstraction, or as a mere heading under which all living beings are inscribed.
At a certain moment, in certain points of space, a visible current has
taken rise; this current of life, traversing the bodies it has organized
one after another, passing from generation to generation, has become
divided amongst species and distributed amongst individuals without
losing anything of its force, rather intensifying in proportion to its advance. . . .

Regarded from this point of view, *life is like a current passing from
germ to germ through the medium of a developed organism.* It is as
if the organism itself were only an excrescence, a bud caused to sprout
by the former germ endeavouring to continue itself in a new germ. The
essential thing is the *continuous progress* indefinitely pursued, an invisible progress, on which each visible organism rides during the short
interval of time given it to live.

Now, the more we fix our attention on this continuity of life, the
more we see that organic evolution resembles the evolution of a consciousness, in which the past presses against the present and causes the
upspringing of a new form of consciousness, incommensurable with its
antecedents. . . . Of the future, only that is foreseen which is like the
past or can be made up again with elements like those of the past.
Such is the case with astronomical, physical and chemical facts, with
all facts which form part of a system in which elements supposed to be
unchanging are merely put together, in which the only changes are
changes of position, in which there is no theoretical absurdity in imagining that things are restored to their place; in which, consequently,
the same total phenomenon, or at least the same elementary phenomena, can be repeated. But an original situation, which imparts something of its own originality to its elements, that is to say, to the partial
views that are taken of it, how can such a situation be pictured as giv-

en before it is actually produced? All that can be said is that, once produced, it will be explained by the elements that analysis will then carve out of it. .... In this sense it might be said of life, as of consciousness, that at every moment it is creating something.

4. Divergent Tendencies

The evolution movement would be a simple one, and we should soon have been able to determine its direction, if life had described a single course, like that of a solid ball shot from a cannon. But it proceeds rather like a shell, which suddenly bursts into fragments, which fragments, being themselves shells, burst in their turn into fragments destined to burst again, and so on for a time incommensurably long. We perceive only what is nearest to us, namely, the scattered movements of the pulverized explosions. From them we have to go back, stage by stage, to the original movement.

When a shell bursts, the particular way it breaks is explained both by the explosive force of the powder it contains and by the resistance of the metal. So of the way life breaks into individuals and species. It depends, we think, on two series of causes: the resistance life meets from inert matter, and the explosive force—due to an unstable balance of tendencies—which life bears within itself.

The resistance of inert matter was the obstacle that had first to be overcome. Life seems to have succeeded in this by dint of humility, by making itself very small and very insinuating, bending to physical and chemical forces, consenting even to go a part of the way with them, like the switch that adopts for a while the direction of the rail it is endeavouring to leave. Of phenomena in the simplest forms of life, it is hard to say whether they are still physical and chemical or whether they are already vital. Life had to enter thus into the habits of inert matter, in order to draw it little by little, magnetized, as it were, to another track. The animate forms that first appeared were therefore of extreme simplicity. They were probably tiny masses of scarcely differentiated protoplasm, outwardly resembling the amoeba observable to-day, but possessed of the tremendous internal push that was to raise them even to the highest forms of life. That in virtue of this push the first organisms sought to grow as much as possible, seems likely. But organized matter has a limit of expansion that is very quickly reached; beyond a certain point it divides instead of growing. Ages of effort and prodigies of subtlety were probably necessary for life to get past this new obstacle. It succeeded in inducing an increasing number of elements, ready to divide, to remain united. By the division of labour it knotted between them an indissoluble bond. The complex and quasi-discontinuous organism is thus made to function as would a continuous living mass which had simply grown bigger.

But the real and profound causes of division were those which life bore within its bosom. For life is tendency, and the essence of a tendency is to develop in the form of a sheaf, creating, by its very growth, divergent directions among which its impetus is divided. . . .

So our study of the evolution movement will have to unravel a certain number of divergent directions, and to appreciate the importance of what has happened along each of them—in a word, to determine the nature of the dissociated tendencies and estimate their relative proportion. Combining these tendencies, then, we shall get an approximation, or rather an imitation, of the indivisible motor principle whence their impetus proceeds. Evolution will thus prove to be something entirely different from a series of adaptations to circumstances, as mechanism claims; entirely different also from the realization of a plan of the whole, as maintained by the doctrine of finality.

5. Animal and Human Consciousness

Radical therefore, also, is the difference between animal consciousness, even the most intelligent, and human consciousness. For consciousness corresponds exactly to the living being's power of choice; it is co-extensive with the fringe of possible action that surrounds the real action: consciousness is synonymous with invention and with freedom. Now, in the animal, invention is never anything but a variation on the theme of routine. Shut up in the habits of the species, it succeeds, no doubt, in enlarging them by its individual initiative; but it escapes automatism only for an instant, for just the time to create a new automatism. The gates of its prison close as soon as they are opened; by pulling at its chain it succeeds only in stretching it. With man, consciousness breaks the chain. In man, and in man alone, it sets itself free. The whole history of life until man has been that of the effort of consciousness to raise matter, and of the more or less complete overwhelming of consciousness by the matter which has fallen back on it. The enterprise was paradoxical, if, indeed, we may speak here otherwise than by metaphor of enterprise and of effort. It was to create with matter, which is necessity itself, an instrument of freedom, to make a machine which should triumph over mechanism, and to use the determinism of nature to pass through the meshes of the net which this very determinism had spread. But, everywhere except in man, consciousness has let itself be caught in the net whose meshes it tried to pass through: it has remained the captive of the mechanisms it has set up. . . . But our brain, our society, and our language are only the external and various signs of one and the same internal superiority. They tell, each after its manner, the unique, exceptional success which life has won at a given moment of its evolution. They express the difference of kind, and not only of degree, which separates man from the rest of the animal world. They let us guess that, while at the end of the vast spring-board from which life has taken its leap, all the others have stepped down, finding the cord stretched too high, man alone has cleared the obstacle.

6. Philosophy and the Life of the Spirit

Philosophy introduces us thus into the spiritual life. And it shows us at the same time the relation of the life of the spirit to that of the body. The great error of the doctrines on the spirit has been the idea that by isolating the spiritual life from all the rest, by suspending it in space as high as possible above the earth, they were placing it beyond attack, as if they were not thereby simply exposing it to be taken as an effect of mirage! Certainly they are right to listen to conscience when conscience affirms human freedom; but the intellect is there, which says that the cause determines its effect, that like conditions like, that all is repeated and that all is given. They are right to believe in the absolute reality of the person and in his independence toward matter; but science is there, which shows the interdependence of conscious life and cerebral activity. They are right to attribute to man a privileged place in nature, to hold that the distance is infinite between the animal and man; but the history of life is there, which makes us witness the genesis of species by gradual transformation, and seems thus to reintegrate man in animality. When a strong instinct assures the probability of personal survival, they are right not to close their ears to its voice; but if there exist "souls" capable of an independent life, whence do they come? When, how and why do they enter into this body which we see arise, quite naturally, from a mixed cell derived from the bodies of its two parents? All these questions will remain unanswered, a philosophy of intuition will be a negation of science, will be sooner or later swept away by science, if it does not resolve to see the life of the body just where it really is, on the road that leads to the life of the spirit. . . .

Thus, to the eyes of a philosophy that attempts to reabsorb intellect in intuition, many difficulties vanish or become light. But such a doctrine does not only facilitate speculation; it gives us also more power to act and to live. For, with it, we feel ourselves no longer isolated in humanity, humanity no longer seems isolated in the nature that it dominates. As the smallest grain of dust is bound up with our entire solar system, drawn along with it in that undivided movement of descent which is materiality itself, so all organized beings, from the humblest to the highest, from the first origins of life to the time in which we are, and in all places as in all times, do but evidence a single impulsion, the inverse of the movement of matter, and in itself indivisible. All the living hold together, and all yield to the same tremendous push. The animal takes its stand on the plant, man bestrides animality, and the whole of humanity, in space and in time, is one immense army galloping beside and before and behind each of us in an overwhelming charge able to beat down every resistance and clear the most formidable obstacles, perhaps even death.

(From *Creative Evolution* by Henri Bergson. Translated by Arthur Mitchell. Copyright 1911, 1939 by Holt, Rinehart and Winston.)

Open Morality and Dynamic Religion (from *The Two Sources of Morality and Religion*)

One of the results of our analysis has been to draw a sharp distinction, in the sphere of society, between the closed and the open. The closed society is that whose members hold together, caring nothing for the rest of humanity, on the alert for attack or defence, bound, in fact, to a perpetual readiness for battle. Such is human society fresh from the hands of nature. Man was made for this society, as the ant was made for the ant-heap. We must not overdo the analogy; we should note, however, that the hymenopterous communities are at the end of one of the two principal lines of animal evolution, just as human societies are at the end of the other, and that they are in this sense counterparts of one another. True, the first are stereotyped, whereas the others vary; the former obey instinct, the latter intelligence. But if nature, and for the very reason that she has made us intelligent, has left us to some extent with freedom of choice in our type of social organization, she has at all events ordained that we should live in society. A force of unvarying direction, which is to the soul what force of gravity is to the body, ensures the cohesion of the group by bending all individual wills to the same end. That force is moral obligation. We have shown that it may extend its scope in societies that are becoming open, but that it was made for the closed society. And we have shown also how a closed society can live, resist this or that dissolving action of intelligence, preserve and communicate to each of its members that confidence which is indispensable, only through a religion born of the myth-making function. This religion, which we have called static, and this obligation, which is tantamount to a pressure, are the very substance of closed society.

Never shall we pass from the closed society to the open society, from the city to humanity, by any mere broadening out. The two things are not of the same essence. The open society is the society which is deemed in principle to embrace all humanity. A dream dreamt, now and again, by chosen souls, it embodies on every occasion something of itself in creations, each of which, through a more or less far-reaching transformation of man, conquers difficulties hitherto unconquerable. But after each occasion the circle that has momentarily opened closes again. Part of the new has flowed into the mould of the old; individual aspiration has become social pressure; and obligation covers the whole. . . .

This impetus is thus carried forward through the medium of certain men, each of whom thereby constitutes a species composed of a single individual. If the individual is fully conscious of this, if the fringe of intuition surrounding his intelligence is capable of expanding sufficiently to envelop its object, that is the mystic life. The dynamic religion which thus springs into being is the very opposite of the static religion born of the myth-making function, in the same way as the open society is the opposite of the closed society. But just as the new moral aspiration takes shape only by borrowing from the closed society its natural form, which is obligation, so dynamic religion is propagated only through images and symbols supplied by the myth-making function. There is no need to go back over these different points. I wanted simply to emphasize the distinction I have made between the open and the closed society. . . .

Joy indeed would be that simplicity of life diffused throughout the world by an ever-spreading mystic intuition; joy, too, that which would automatically follow a vision of the life beyond attained through the furtherance of scientific experiment. Failing so throughgoing a spiritual reform, we must be content with shifts and submit to more and more numerous and vexatious regulations, intended to provide a means of circumventing each successive obstacle that our nature sets up against our civilization. But, whether we go bail for small measures or great, a decision is imperative. Mankind lies groaning, half crushed beneath the weight of its own progress. Men do not sufficiently realize that their future is in their own hands. Theirs is the task of determining first of all whether they want to go on living or not. Theirs the responsibility, then, for deciding if they want merely to live, or intend to make just the extra effort required for fulfilling, even on their refractory planet, the essential function of the universe, which is a machine for the making of gods.

(From The Two Sources of Morality and Religion. Translated by R. Ashley Audra and Cloudesley Brereton. London: Macmillan, 1935.)

Review Questions

1. Some philosophers rely heavily on the findings of science; show how this is true of Bergson.
2. Explain how Bergson's concern for totality is based on life.
3. Discuss Bergson's notion of *life impulse* together with his notion of creative evolution.
4. What is the meaning of intuition for Bergson?
5. If biological evolution is over, where does man go from here, according to Bergson?
6. What does Bergson mean by *open morality*? *Dynamic religion*?

CHAPTER 24

William James (1842–1910)

Introduction

There are many affinities between the philosophies of Henri Bergson and William James: they are both firmly rooted in an empirical base, allow for the role of the nonrational in arriving at truth, and are totally centered on the value of human life. While Bergson, however, was emerging from a European matrix, James, although quite at home in the European tradition, was emerging from an American matrix: he knew the works of the early divines like Cotton Mather and Jonathan Edwards; through his father, a thinker in his own right, he came to know Ralph Waldo Emerson; he had, as colleagues or friends, Charles Sanders Peirce, Josiah Royce, and George Santayana; he respected the work of John Dewey; and, while lamenting America's huge defects, James could still write in 1882 that his recent experience made him "quieter with my home-lot and readier to believe that it is one of the chosen places of the Earth." In a sense, the study of James is the study of American philosophy in capsule form, which is borne out by the fact that the force already poised to produce pragmatism as a truly American contribution to philosophy did so in the philosopher whose name is most directly connected with it.

William James was born in 1842 in New York City into a family of four brothers and a sister. His father was a wealthy gentleman, widely traveled in Europe and a deeply religious person. His brother Henry was a famous novelist. His early schooling occurred both in America and abroad, giving him the opportunity to learn French and German fluently. He gave up the study of art to pursue science for the next eight years at Harvard University, first at the Lawrence Scientific School and then at the Medical School, interrupting his medical education in 1865 to accompany the famed Louis Agassiz in an expedition to the Amazon. Though frail in health, he continued his medical studies in Germany in 1867 and began to develop his deep interest in psychology, perhaps as a result of a long-standing internal conflict between freedom and religion on the one hand and science and mechanism on the other. At one point, he fell into a sudden depression at the "horrible fear of my own existence" and found comforting support in the writings of the French philosopher-psychologist Charles Renouvier, who reaffirmed for James the actuality of freedom and the strength of the will. In 1869 he received his medical degree from Harvard, which, after several years, appointed him as an instructor in physiology and later in psychology. He married in 1878. From the 1880s on, he taught and wrote in the fields of philosophy, religion, and ethics. He died in 1910. His chief works include *Principles of Psychology* (1891), *The Will to Believe* (1897), *Varieties of Religious Experience* (1902), *Pragmatism* (1907), *A Pluralistic Universe* and *The Meaning of Truth* (1909), and posthumously *Essays in Radical Empiricism* (1912).

We have seen several times that philosophical attitudes in human knowing reduce to two, empiricism and rationalism, and that even though pure empiricism or pure rationalism is hard to find, there is a wide range of mixtures between them, often with a tendency to lean in one direction or the other. In describing these two kinds of mental makeup, James uses vest-pocket terminology in referring to the first type as "tough-minded" and the second as "tender-minded"; the empirical mind "goes by facts," the rationalist mind "goes by principles." When James writes, "Never were as many men of a decidedly empiricist proclivity in existence as there are at the present day," he is not counting noses but expressing the temper of the time in which he lived and considering himself as an example. The touchstone of truth is experience, for only through experience can any position be verified; what is beyond experience can never enter into our consciousness and can never compel us to admit its existence. By prefixing the word *radical* to *empiricism*, James elaborates his own position as a "radical empiricist" and proclaims his brand of empiricism as going more to the root of things than even that of Hume, whose philosophy he criticized for not being radical enough. Yet, when surveyed, his empiricism seems to be more tender than Hume's, for Hume could only bring himself to see experiences as atomistic, mirroring an atomistic world where one fact had no connection with any other. For James, however, interrelation and interconnection are themselves *facts of experience*, so that the immense difficulty Hume had, for example, in managing causality is not a difficulty for James. This loosening up of empiricism, even though he calls it radical, helps James to achieve a more satisfactory posture regarding the universe than Hume, whose hands were empty when the unifying questions were asked.

A further consideration shows that, for James, experience is the event in which mind and object hold together, so that there is no duality between them; prior to experience, there is no subject, as *knowing*, which exists independently, and no object, as *known*, which exists independently. No, they are two sides of the one experience, momentarily snatched from reality, which itself must be understood as the "immediate flux of life which furnishes the material to our later reflection with its conceptual categories." So, the distinction between knower and known, subject and object, matter and mind, consciousness and content is subsequent to experience.

Empiricism, as an attitude, seeks the method best adapted to its nature and, for James, that method is *pragmatism*. Its characteristics existed long before James, even in Socrates and Aristotle, but only at the turn of the twentieth century, beginning with James and the group familiar with his work, did it "generalize itself" and "become conscious of a universal mission." Historically, though it was given its popular shape by James, pragmatism was actually introduced by Charles Peirce. It is a way of arriving at the meaning of a thought by determining the conduct or action it was "fitted to produce," a way of attaining as much clarity as possible in our ideas from the practical effects we believe them to have. Pragmatism for James represents the empiricist attitude, and "in a more radical and in a less objectionable form than it has ever yet assumed." It looks away from the fixity of things — from supposed necessities, tight categories and stiff theories — which arrests the freely searching mind and it looks to consequences, action, fruits, facts. The pragmatist's interest is in how an idea can be converted into an empirical return, or in James' favorite expression, into "cash value." An idea has worth only insofar as it can be translated into the facts of experience; if it cannot be translated, it has no value. As a method, it can presumably be used by the scientist, the metaphysician, the ethician, or even by persons of opposite persuasion such as the theist and the atheist.

It is obvious that, if the disclosures of pragmatism are taken as true, pragmatism is more than a method; it is also a *theory of truth*. But it is a theory of truth with a difference. The popular notion of truth requires agreement between an idea and a thing, as though the idea were a copy of the thing, thus creating a static, fixed relationship between them. For the pragmatist, however, the agreement is not a copy but rather the harmonious entrance of an idea into the total fabric of one's life in response to the questions, "What concrete difference will its being true make in anyone's life?" "What is the truth's cash value in experiential terms?" For James, "True ideas are those we can assimilate, validate, corroborate and verify. False ideas are those we can not."

Truth, then, is not a stagnant property inherent in an idea, nor a static relationship between subject and object, for the dynamics of experience account only for reality as flux. As a consequence, truth *happens*; truth is *made*, not discovered: "Truth *happens* to an idea. It *becomes* true, is *made* true by events. Its verity *is* in fact an event, a process: the process namely of its verifying itself, its veri-*fication.* Its validity is the process of its valid-*ation.*" Whether dealing with concrete objects or abstractions, matters of fact or mental ideas, the notion of verification by agreement still holds, with the expectation that the more abstract the idea, the more complicated the network into which the idea must successfully, and therefore, truthfully, *lead* us.

The work of James is, of course, replete with the *application* of pragmatism to a variety of questions. Reflection on the simple example of blackboard chalk shows that the so-called attributes of whiteness, friability, and insolubility indeed exist, but there is no practical consideration that points to the existence of a *substance* lying beneath them; the very coherence of the attributes themselves is sufficient to warrant calling the group *chalk*, without looking any further. Likewise in the matter of consciousness: because experience itself is undivided, there is no need to invoke a faculty that, as subject, is conscious of another as object, so that consciousness as an "entity is fictitious, while thoughts in the concrete are fully real. But thoughts in the concrete are made of the same stuff as things are." To the question of whether the world is of one substance (monism) or of many substances (pluralism), which James felt was the most central of all philosophical questions because the designation "monist" or "pluralist" reveals more about a philosopher than any other label, pragmatism, by her criterion of practical differences, "must obviously range herself upon the pluralist side."

In concerns that come close to the center of life, namely, morality, religion, and God, James, without giving in to what he believed to be the presumptions of metaphysics, weighs the practical implications of all three in nurturing a personal life, and avers in page after page of broadening insights that, pragmatically, their role is indispensable for human meaning and value. Proceeding on a pragmatic basis, James finds no use whatsoever for the classical arguments for God's existence, which "are not solid enough to serve as religion's all-sufficient foundation." The arguments themselves prove nothing; they only strengthen one's "preexistent partialities": "If you have a God already whom you believe in, these arguments confirm you. If you are atheistic, they fail to set you right."

What then? Speaking in general terms, James writes: "On pragmatistic principles, if the hypothesis of God works satisfactorily in the widest sense of the word, it is true ... but when I tell you that I have written a book on men's religious experience, which on the whole has been regarded as making for the reality of God, you will perhaps exempt my own pragmatism from the charge of being an atheistic system." So, belief in God changes the way a person looks at the world: "Theism always stands ready with the most practically rational solution it is possible to conceive. Not an energy of our active nature to which it does not authoritatively appeal, not an emotion of which it does not normally and naturally release the springs. At a single stroke, it changes the dead blank *it* of the world into a living *thou*, with whom the whole man may have dealings." Further, if it is true that the "need for an eternal moral order is one of the deepest needs of our breast," then religion takes the form of a living correspondence with the higher powers to bring about a world bettered by our actions, indeed, to bring about the salvation of the world.

Several years after writing these words, William James died — but not the philosopher, who has been inscribed in his works as a thinker of vision, of sensitivity, of learning, and of literary style. His broad interest in timeless themes makes him a permanent contemporary. No less a thinker than Alfred North Whitehead praises James as one of history's great "assemblers," along with Plato, Aristotle, and Leibniz.

Readings

The Meaning of Pragmatism (from *What Is Pragmatism?*)

A glance at the history of the idea will show you still better what pragmatism means. The term is derived from the same Greek word Greek $\pi\rho\alpha\gamma\mu\alpha$, meaning action, from which our words 'practice' and 'practical' come. It was first introduced into philosophy by Mr. Charles Peirce in 1878. In an article entitled 'How to Make Our Ideas Clear,' in the 'Popular Science Monthly' for January of that year Mr. Peirce, after pointing out that our beliefs are really rules for action, said that, to develop a thought's meaning, we need only determine what conduct it is fitted to produce: that conduct is for us its sole significance. And the tangible fact at the root of all our thought-distinctions, however subtle, is that there is no one of them so fine as to consist in anything but a possible difference of practice. To attain perfect clearness in our thoughts of an object, then, we need only consider what conceivable effects of a practical kind the object may involve—what sensations we are to expect from it, and what reactions we must prepare. Our conception of these effects, whether immediate or remote, is then for us the whole of our conception of the object, so far as that conception has positive significance at all.

This is the principle of Peirce, the principle of pragmatism. It lay entirely unnoticed by any one for twenty years, until I, in an address before Professor Howison's philosophical union at the University of California, brought it forward again and made a special application of it to religion. By that date (1898) the times seemed ripe for its reception. The word 'pragmatism' spread, and at present it fairly spots the pages of the philosophic journals. On all hands we find the 'pragmatic movement' spoken of, sometimes with respect, sometimes with contumely, seldom with clear understanding. It is evident that the term applies itself conveniently to a number of tendencies that hitherto have lacked a collective name, and that it has 'come to stay.'

To take in the importance of Peirce's principle, one must get accustomed to applying it to concrete cases. I found a few years ago that Ostwald, the illustrious Leipzig chemist, had been making perfectly distinct use of the principle of pragmatism in his lectures on the philosophy of science, though he had not called it by that name.

"All realities influence our practice," he wrote me, "and that influence is their meaning for us. I am accustomed to put questions to my classes in this way: In what respects would the world be different if this alternative or that were true? If I can find nothing that would become different, then the alternative has no sense."

That is, the rival views mean practically the same thing, and meaning, other than practical, there is for us none. Ostwald in a published lecture gives this example of what he means. Chemists have long wrangled over the inner constitution of certain bodies called 'tautomerous.' Their properties seemed equally consistent with the notion that an instable hydrogen atom oscillates inside of them, or that they are instable mixtures of two bodies. Controversy raged, but never was decided. "It would never have begun," says Ostwald, "if the combatants had asked themselves what particular experimental fact could have been made different by one or the other view being correct. For it would then have appeared that no difference of fact could possibly ensue; and the quarrel was as unreal as if, theorizing in primitive times about the raising of dough by yeast, one party should have invoked a 'brownie,' while another insisted on an 'elf' as the true cause of the phenomenon."

It is astonishing to see how many philosophical disputes collapse into insignificance the moment you subject them to this simple test of tracing a concrete consequence. There can be no difference anywhere that doesn't make a difference elsewhere—no difference in abstract truth that doesn't express itself in a difference in concrete fact and in conduct consequent upon that fact, imposed on somebody, somehow, somewhere, and somewhen. The whole function of philosophy ought to be to find out what definite difference it will make to you and me, at definite instants of our life, if this world-formula or that world-formula be the true one.

There is absolutely nothing new in the pragmatic method. Socrates was an adept at it. Aristotle used it methodically. Locke, Berkeley, and Hume made momentous contributions to truth by its means. Shad-

worth Hodgson keeps insisting that realities are only what they are
'known as.' But these forerunners of pragmatism used it in fragments:
they were preluders only. Not until in our time has it generalized itself,
become conscious of a universal mission, pretended to a conquering
destiny. I believe in that destiny, and I hope I may end by inspiring
you with my belief.

Pragmatism represents a perfectly familiar attitude in philosophy,
the empiricist attitude, but it represents it, as it seems to me, both in
a more radical and in a less objectionable form than it has ever yet assumed. A pragmatist turns his back resolutely and once for all upon a
lot of inveterate habits dear to professional philosophers. He turns
away from abstraction and insufficiency, from verbal solutions, from
bad *a priori* reasons, from fixed principles, closed systems, and pretended absolutes and origins. He turns towards concreteness and ade-
quacy, towards facts, towards action and towards power. That means
the empiricist temper regnant and the rationalist temper sincerely giv-
en up. It means the open air and possibilities of nature, as against dogma, artificiality, and the pretence of finality in truth.

At the same time it does not stand for any special results. It is a
method only. But the general triumph of that method would mean an
enormous change in what I called in my last lecture the 'temperament'
of philosophy. Teachers of the ultra-rationalistic type would be frozen
out, much as the courtier type is frozen out in republics, as the ultra-
montane type of priest is frozen out in protestant lands. Science and
metaphysics would come much nearer together, would in fact work absolutely hand in hand.

The Pragmatic Method Applied to the Problem of Substance (from *What is Pragmatism?*)

I am now to make the pragmatic method more familiar by giving you
some illustrations of its application to particular problems. I will begin
with what is driest, and the first thing I shall take will be the problem
of *Substance*. Every one uses the old distinction between substance
and attribute, enshrined as it is in the very structure of human language, in the difference between grammatical subject and predicate.
Here is a bit of blackboard crayon. Its modes, attributes, properties,
accidents, or affections,—use which term you will,—are whiteness, friability, cylindrical shape, insolubility in water, etc., etc. But the bearer
of these attributes is so much *chalk*, which thereupon is called the substance in which they inhere. So the attributes of this desk inhere in the
substance 'wood,' those of my coat in the substance 'wool,' and so
forth. Chalk, wood and wool, show again, in spite of their differences,
common properties, and in so far forth they are themselves counted as

modes of a still more primal substance, *matter*, the attributes of which are space-occupancy and impenetrability. Similarly our thoughts and feelings are affections or properties of our several *souls*, which are substances, but again not wholly in their own right, for they are modes of the still deeper substance 'spirit.'

Now it was very early seen that all *we know* of the chalk is the whiteness, friability, etc., all *we know* of the wood is the combustibility and fibrous structure. A group of attributes is what each substance here is known-as, they form its sole cash-value for our actual experience. The substance is in every case revealed through *them*; if we were cut off from *them* we should never suspect its existence; and if God should keep sending them to us in an unchanged order, miraculously annihilating at a certain moment the substance that supported them, we never could detect the moment, for our experiences themselves would be unaltered. Nominalists accordingly adopt the opinion that substance is a spurious idea due to our inveterate human trick of turning names into things. Phenomena come in groups—the chalk-group, the wood-group, etc.,—and each group gets its name. The name we then treat as in a way supporting the group of phenomena. The low thermometer to-day, for instance, is supposed to come from something called the 'climate.' Climate is really only the name for a certain group of days, but it is treated as if it lay *behind* the day, and in general we place the name, as if it were a being, behind the facts it is the name of. But the phenomenal properties of things, nominalists say, surely do not really inhere in names, and if not in names then they do not inhere in anything. They *a*dhere, or *c*ohere, rather, *with each other*, and the notion of a substance inaccessible to us, which we think accounts for such cohesion by supporting it, as cement might support pieces of mosaic, must be abandoned. The fact of the bare cohesion itself is all that the notion of the substance signifies. Behind that fact is nothing.

The Pragmatic Method Applied to the Problem of Religion (from *What is Pragmatism?*)

I fear that my previous lectures, confined as they have been to human and humanistic aspects, may have left the impression on many of you that pragmatism means methodically to leave the superhuman out. I have shown small respect indeed for the Absolute, and I have until this moment spoken of no other superhuman hypothesis but that. But I trust that you see sufficiently that the Absolute has nothing but its superhumanness in common with the theistic God. On pragmatistic principles, if the hypothesis of God works satisfactorily in the widest sense of the word, it is true. Now whatever its residual difficulties may be, experience shows that it certainly does work, and that the problem is to build it out and determine it so that it will combine satisfactorily with all the other working truths. I can not start upon a whole theology at the end of this last lecture; but when I tell you that I have written a book on men's religious experience, which on the whole has been regarded as making for the reality of God, you will perhaps exempt my own pragmatism from the charge of being an atheistic system. I firmly disbelieve, myself, that our human experience is the highest form of experience extant in the universe. I believe rather that we stand in much the same relation to the whole of the universe as our canine and feline pets do to the whole of human life. They inhabit our drawing-rooms and libraries. They take part in scenes of whose significance they have no inkling. They are merely tangent to curves of history the beginnings and ends and forms of which pass wholly beyond their ken. So we are tangent to the wider life of things. But, just as many of the dog's and cat's ideals coincide with our ideals, and the dogs and cats have daily living proof of the fact, so we may well believe, on the proofs that religious experience affords, that higher powers exist and are at work to save the world on ideal lines similar to our own.

You see that pragmatism can be called religious, if you allow that religion can be pluralistic or merely melioristic in type. But whether you will finally put up with that type of religion or not is a question that only you yourself can decide. Pragmatism has to postpone dogmatic answer, for we do not yet know certainly which type of religion is going to work best in the long run. The various overbeliefs of men, their several faith-ventures, are in fact what are needed to bring the evidence in. You will probably make your own ventures severally. If radically tough, the hurly-burly of the sensible facts of nature will be enough for you, and you will need no religion at all. If radically tender, you will take up with the more monistic form of religion: the pluralistic form, with its reliance on possibilities that are not necessities, will not seem to afford you security enough.

But if you are neither tough nor tender in an extreme and radical sense, but mixed as most of us are, it may seem to you that the type of pluralistic and moralistic religion that I have offered is as good a religious synthesis as you are likely to find. Between the two extremes of crude naturalism on the one hand and transcendental absolutism on the other, you may find that what I take the liberty of calling the pragmatistic or melioristic type of theism is exactly what you require.

The Will to Believe[1]

I have brought with me to-night something like a sermon on justification by faith to read to you, — I mean an essay in justification *of* faith, a defence of our right to adopt a believing attitude in religious matters, in spite of the fact that our merely logical intellect may not have been coerced. 'The Will to Believe,' accordingly, is the title of my paper.

I have long defended to my own students the lawfulness of voluntarily adopted faith; but as soon as they have got well imbued with the logical spirit, they have as a rule refused to admit my contention to be lawful philosophically, even though in point of fact they were personally all the time chock-full of some faith or other themselves. I am all the while, however, so profoundly convinced that my own position is correct, that your invitation has seemed to me a good occasion to make my statements more clear. Perhaps your minds will be more open than those with which I have hitherto had to deal. I will be as little technical as I can, though I must begin by setting up some technical distinctions that will help us in the end.

I

Let us give the name of *hypothesis* to anything that may be proposed to our belief; and just as the electricians speak of live and dead wires, let us speak of any hypothesis as either *live* or *dead*. A live hypothesis is one which appeals as a real possibility to him to whom it is proposed. If I ask you to believe in the Mahdi, the notion makes no electric connection with your nature, — it refuses to scintillate with any credibility at all. As an hypothesis it is completely dead. To an Arab, however (even if he be not one of the Mahdi's followers), the hypothesis is among the mind's possibilities: it is alive. This shows that deadness and liveness in an hypothesis are not intrinsic properties, but relations to the individual thinker. They are measured by his willingness to act. The maximum of liveness in an hypothesis means willingness to act irrevocably. Practically, that means belief; but there is some believing tendency wherever there is willingness to act at all.

Next, let us call the decision between two hypotheses an *option*. Options may be of several kinds. They may be — 1, *living* or *dead*; 2, *forced* or *avoidable*; 3, *momentous* or *trivial*; and for our purposes we may call an option a *genuine* option when it is of the forced, living, and momentous kind.

[1] An Address to the Philosophical Clubs of Yale and Brown Universities. Published in the *New World*, June, 1896.

1. A living option is one in which both hypotheses are live ones. If I say to you: "Be a theosophist or be a Mohammedan," it is probably a dead option, because for you neither hypothesis is likely to be alive. But if I say: "Be an agnostic or be a Christian," it is otherwise: trained as you are, each hypothesis makes some appeal, however small, to your belief.

2. Next, if I say to you: "Choose between going out with your umbrella or without it," I do not offer you a genuine option, for it is not forced. You can easily avoid it by not going out at all. Similarly, if I say, "Either love me or hate me," "Either call my theory true or call it false," your option is avoidable. You may remain indifferent to me, neither loving nor hating, and you may decline to offer any judgment as to my theory. But if I say, "Either accept this truth or go without it," I put on you a forced option, for there is no standing place outside of the alternative. Every dilemma based on a complete logical disjunction, with no possibility of not choosing, is an option of this forced kind.

3. Finally, if I were Dr. Nansen and proposed to you to join my North Pole expedition, your option would be momentous; for this would probably be your only similar opportunity, and your choice now would either exclude you from the North Pole sort of immortality altogether or put at least the chance of it into your hands. He who refuses to embrace a unique opportunity loses the prize as surely as if he tried and failed. *Per contra*, the option is trivial when the opportunity is not unique, when the stake is insignificant, or when the decision is reversible if it later prove unwise. Such trivial options abound in the scientific life. A chemist finds an hypothesis live enough to spend a year in its verification: he believes in it to that extent. But if his experiments prove inconclusive either way, he is quit for his loss of time, no vital harm being done.

It will facilitate our discussion if we keep all these distinctions well in mind.

II

The next matter to consider is the actual psychology of human opinion. When we look at certain facts, it seems as if our passional and volitional nature lay at the root of all our convictions. When we look at others, it seems as if they could do nothing when the intellect had once said its say. Let us take the latter facts up first.

Does it not seem preposterous on the very face of it to talk of our opinions being modifiable at will? Can our will either help or hinder our intellect in its perceptions of truth? Can we, by just willing it, believe that Abraham Lincoln's existence is a myth, and that the portraits of him in McClure's Magazine are all of some one else? Can we, by any effort of our will, or by any strength of wish that it were true, believe ourselves well and about when we are roaring with rheumatism in bed, or feel certain that the sum of the two one-dollar bills in our pocket must be a hundred dollars? We can say any of these things, but we are absolutely impotent to believe them; and of just such things is the whole fabric of the truths that we do believe in made up, — matters of fact, immediate or remote, as Hume said, and relations between ideas, which are either there or not there for us if we see them so, and which if not there cannot be put there by any action of our own.

In Pascal's Thoughts there is a celebrated passage known in literature as Pascal's wager. In it he tries to force us into Christianity by reasoning as if our concern with truth resembled our concern with the stakes in a game of chance. Translated freely his words are these: You must either believe or not believe that God is — which will you do? Your human reason cannot say. A game is going on between you and the nature of things which at the day of judgment will bring out either heads or tails. Weigh what your gains and your losses would be if you should stake all you have on heads, or God's existence: if you win in such case, you gain eternal beatitude; if you lose, you lose nothing at all. If there were an infinity of chances, and only one for God in this wager, still you ought to stake your all on God; for though you surely risk a finite loss by this procedure, any finite loss is reasonable, even a certain one is reasonable, if there is but the possibility of infinite gain.

The talk of believing by our volition seems, then, from one point of view, simply silly. From another point of view it is worse than silly, it is vile. When one turns to the magnificent edifice of the physical sciences, and sees how it was reared; what thousands of disinterested moral lives of men lie buried in its mere foundations; what patience and postponement, what choking down of preference, what submission to the icy laws of outer fact are wrought into its very stones and mortar; how absolutely impersonal it stands in its vast augustness, — then how besotted and contemptible seems every little sentimentalist who comes blowing his voluntary smoke-wreaths, and pretending to decide things from out of his private dream! Can we wonder if those bred in the rugged and manly school of science should feel like spewing such subjectivism out of their mouths? The whole system of loyalties which grow up in the schools of science go dead against its toleration; so that it is only natural that those who have caught the scientific fever should pass over to the opposite extreme, and write sometimes as if the incorruptibly truthful intellect ought positively to prefer bitterness and unacceptableness to the heart in its cup.

> It fortifies my soul to know
> That, though I perish, Truth is so —

sings Clough, while Huxley exlaims: "My only consolation lies in the reflection that, however bad our posterity may become, so far as they hold by the plain rule of not pretending to believe what they have no reason to believe, because it may be to their advantage so to pretend [the word 'pretend' is surely here redundant], they will not have reached the lowest depth of immorality." And that delicious *enfant terrible* Clifford writes: "Belief is desecrated when given to unproved and unquestioned statements for the solace and private pleasure of the believer. ... Whoso would deserve well of his fellows in this matter will guard the purity of his belief with a very fanaticism of jealous care, lest at any time it should rest on an unworthy object, and catch a stain which can never be wiped away. ... If [a] belief has been accepted on insufficient evidence [even though the belief be true, as Clifford on the same page explains] the pleasure is a stolen one. ... It is sinful because it is stolen in defiance of our duty to mankind. That duty is to guard ourselves from such beliefs as from a pestilence which may shortly master our own body and then spread to the rest of the town. ... It is wrong always, everywhere, and for every one, to believe anything upon insufficient evidence."

III

All this strikes one as healthy, even when expressed, as by Clifford, with somewhat too much of robustious pathos in the voice. Free-will and simple wishing do seem, in the matter of our credences, to be only fifth wheels to the coach. Yet if any one should thereupon assume that intellectual insight is what remains after wish and will and sentimental preference have taken wing, or that pure reason is what then settles our opinions, he would fly quite as directly in the teeth of the facts.

It is only our already dead hypotheses that our willing nature is unable to bring to life again. But what has made them dead for us is for the most part a previous action of our willing nature of an antagonistic kind. When I say 'willing nature,' I do not mean only such deliberate volitions as may have set up habits of belief that we cannot now escape from, — I mean all such factors of belief as fear and hope, prejudice and passion, imitation and partisanship, the circumpressure of our caste and set. As a matter of fact we find ourselves believing, we hardly know how or why. Mr. Balfour gives the name of 'authority' to all those influences, born of the intellectual climate, that make hypotheses possible or impossible for us, alive or dead. Here in this room, we all of us believe in molecules and the conservation of energy, in democracy and necessary progress, in Protestant Christianity and the duty of fighting for 'the doctrine of the immortal Monroe,' all for no reasons worthy of the name. We see into these matters with no more inner clearness, and probably with much less, than any disbeliever in them might possess. His unconventionality would probably have some grounds to show for its conclusions; but for us, not insight, but the *prestige* of the opinions, is what makes the spark shoot from them and light up our sleeping magazines of faith. Our reason is quite satisfied, in nine hundred and ninety-nine cases out of every thousand of us, if it can find a few arguments that will do to recite in case our credulity is criticised by some one else. Our faith is faith in some one else's faith, and in the greatest matters this is most the case. Our belief in truth itself, for instance, that there is a truth, and that our minds and it are made for each other, — what is it but a passionate affirmation of desire, in which our social system backs us up? We want to have a truth; we want to believe that our experiments and studies and discussions must put us in a continually better and better position towards it; and on this line we agree to fight out our thinking lives. But if a pyrrhonistic sceptic asks us *how we know* all this, can our logic find a reply? No! certainly it cannot. It is just one volition against another, — we willing to go in for life upon a trust or assumption which he, for his part, does not care to make. . . .

Evidently, then, our non-intellectual nature does influence our convictions. There are passional tendencies and volitions which run before and others which come after belief, and it is only the latter that are too late for the fair; and they are not too late when the previous passional work has been already in their own direction. Pascal's argument, instead of being powerless, then seems a regular clincher, and is the last stroke needed to make our faith in masses and holy water complete. The state of things is evidently far from simple; and pure insight and logic, whatever they might do ideally, are not the only things that really do produce our creeds.

IV

Our next duty, having recognized this mixed-up state of affairs, is to ask whether it be simply reprehensible and pathological, or whether, on the contrary, we must treat it as a normal element in making up our minds. The thesis I defend is, briefly stated, this: *Our passional nature not only lawfully may, but must, decide an option between propositions, whenever it is a genuine option that cannot by its nature be decided on intellectual grounds; for to say, under such circumstances,*

"Do not decide, but leave the question open," is itself a passional de-cision, — just like deciding yes or no, — and is attended with the same risk of losing the truth. The thesis thus abstractly expressed will, I trust, soon become quite clear. But I must first indulge in a bit more of preliminary work.

V

It will be observed that for the purposes of this discussion we are on 'dogmatic' ground, — ground, I mean, which leaves systematic philo-sophical scepticism altogether out of account. The postulate that there is truth, and that it is the destiny of our minds to attain it, we are de-liberately resolving to make, though the sceptic will not make it. We part company with him, therefore, absolutely, at this point. But the faith that truth exists, and that our minds can find it, may be held in two ways. We may talk of the *empiricist* way and of the *absolutist* way of believing in truth. The absolutists in this matter say that we not only can attain to knowing truth, but we can *know when* we have at-tained to knowing it; while the empiricists think that although we may attain it, we cannot infallibly know when. To *know* is one thing, and to know for certain *that* we know is another. One may hold to the first being possible without the second; hence the empiricists and the abso-lutists, although neither of them is a sceptic in the usual philosophic sense of the term, show very different degrees of dogmatism in their lives.

If we look at the history of opinions, we see that the empiricist ten-dency has largely prevailed in science, while in philosophy the absolut-ist tendency has had everything its own way. The characteristic sort of happiness, indeed, which philosophies yield has mainly consisted in the conviction felt by each successive school or system that by it bot-tom-certitude had been attained. . . .

Scholastic orthodoxy, to which one must always go when one wishes to find perfectly clear statement, has beautifully elaborated this abso-lutist conviction in a doctrine which it calls that of 'objective evidence.' If, for example, I am unable to doubt that I now exist before you, that two is less than three, or that if all men are mortal then I am mortal too, it is because these things illumine my intellect irresistibly. . . . When the Cliffords tell us how sinful it is to be Christians on such 'in-sufficient evidence,' insufficiency is really the last thing they have in mind. For them the evidence is absolutely sufficient, only it makes the other way. They believe so completely in an anti-christian order of the universe that there is no living option: Christianity is a dead hypothe-sis from the start.

VI

But now, since we are all such absolutists by instinct, what in our quality of students of philosophy ought we to do about the fact? Shall we espouse and indorse it? Or shall we treat it as a weakness of our nature from which we must free ourselves, if we can?

I sincerely believe that the latter course is the only one we can follow as reflective men. Objective evidence and certitude are doubtless very fine ideals to play with, but where on this moonlit and dream-visited planet are they found? I am, therefore, myself a complete empiricist so far as my theory of human knowledge goes. I live, to be sure, by the practical faith that we must go on experiencing and thinking over our experience, for only thus can our opinions grow more true; but to hold any one of them — I absolutely do not care which — as if it never could be reinterpretable or corrigible, I believe to be a tremendously mistaken attitude, and I think that the whole history of philosophy will bear me out. There is but one indefectibly certain truth, and that is the truth that pyrrhonistic scepticism itself leaves standing, — the truth that the present phenomenon of consciousness exists. That, however, is the bare starting-point of knowledge, the mere admission of a stuff to be philosophized about. The various philosophies are but so many attempts at expressing what this stuff really is. And if we repair to our libraries what disagreement do we discover! Where is a certainly true answer found? Apart from abstract propositions of comparison (such as two and two are the same as four), propositions which tell us nothing by themselves about concrete reality, we find no proposition ever regarded by any one as evidently certain that has not either been called a falsehood, or at least had its truth sincerely questioned by some one else. . . .

No concrete test of what is really true has ever been agreed upon. Some make the criterion external to the moment of perception, putting it either in revelation, the *consensus gentium*, the instincts of the heart, or the systematized experience of the race. Others make the perceptive moment its own test, — Descartes, for instance, with his clear and distinct ideas guaranteed by the veracity of God; Reid with his 'common-sense;' and Kant with his forms of synthetic judgment *a priori*. The inconceivability of the opposite; the capacity to be verified by sense; the possession of complete organic unity or self-relation, realized when a thing is its own other, — are standards which, in turn, have been used. The much lauded objective evidence is never triumphantly there; it is a mere aspiration or *Grenzbegriff*, marking the infinitely remote ideal of our thinking life. To claim that certain truths now possess it, is simply to say that when you think them true and they *are* true, then their evidence is objective, otherwise it is not. But practically one's conviction that the evidence one goes by is of the real objective brand, is only one more subjective opinion added to the lot. For what a contradictory array of opinions have objective evidence and absolute certitude been claimed! The world is rational through and through, — its existence is an ultimate brute fact; there is a personal God, — a personal God is inconceivable; there is an extra-mental physical world immediately known, — the mind can only know its own ideas; a moral imperative exists, — obligation is only the resultant of desires; a permanent spiritual principle is in every one, — there are only shifting states of mind; there is an endless chain of causes, — there is an absolute first cause; an eternal necessity, — a freedom; a purpose, — no purpose; a primal One, — a primal Many; a universal continuity, — an essential discontinuity in things; an infinity, — no infinity. There is this, — there is that; there is indeed nothing which some one has not thought absolutely true, while his neighbor deemed it absolutely false; and not an absolutist among them seems ever to have considered that the trouble may all the time be essential, and that the intellect, even with truth directly in its grasp, may have no infallible signal for knowing whether it be truth or no. When, indeed, one remembers that the most striking practical application to life of the doctrine of objective certitude has been the conscientious labors of the Holy Office of the Inquisition, one feels less tempted than ever to lend the doctrine a respectful ear.

But please observe, now, that when as empiricists we give up the doctrine of objective certitude, we do not thereby give up the quest or hope of truth itself. We still pin our faith on its existence, and still believe that we gain an ever better position towards it by systematically continuing to roll up experiences and think. Our great difference from the scholastic lies in the way we face. The strength of his system lies in the principles, the origin, the *terminus a quo* of his thought; for us the strength is in the outcome, the upshot, the *terminus ad quem*. Not where it comes from but what it leads to is to decide. It matters not to an empiricist from what quarter an hypothesis may come to him: he may have acquired it by fair means or by foul; passion may have whispered or accident suggested it; but if the total drift of thinking continues to confirm it, that is what he means by its being true.

VII

One more point, small but important, and our preliminaries are done. There are two ways of looking at our duty in the matter of opinion, — ways entirely different, and yet ways about whose difference the theory of knowledge seems hitherto to have shown very little concern. *We must know the truth*; and *we must avoid error*, — these are our first and great commandments as would-be knowers; but they are not two ways of stating an identical commandment, they are two separable laws. Although it may indeed happen that when we believe the truth *A*, we escape as an incidental consequence from believing the falsehood *B*, it hardly ever happens that by merely disbelieving *B* we necessarily believe *A*. We may in escaping *B* fall into believing other falsehoods, *C* or *D*, just as bad as *B*; or we may escape *B* by not believing anything at all, not even *A*.

Believe truth! Shun error! — these, we see, are two materially different laws; and by choosing between them we may end by coloring differently our whole intellectual life. We may regard the chase for truth as paramount, and the avoidance of error as secondary; or we may, on the other hand, treat the avoidance of error as more imperative, and let truth take its chance. Clifford, in the instructive passage which I have quoted, exhorts us to the latter course. Believe nothing, he tells us, keep your mind in suspense forever, rather than by closing it on insufficient evidence incur the awful risk of believing lies. You, on the other hand, may think that the risk of being in error is a very small matter when compared with the blessings of real knowledge, and be ready to be duped many times in your investigation rather than postpone indefinitely the chance of guessing true. I myself find it impossible to go with Clifford. . . .

VIII

And now, after all this introduction, let us go straight at our question. I have said, and now repeat it, that not only as a matter of fact do we find our passional nature influencing us in our opinions, but that there are some options between opinions in which this influence must be regarded both as an inevitable and as a lawful determinant of our choice.

I fear here that some of you my hearers will begin to scent danger, and lend an inhospitable ear. Two first steps of passion you have indeed had to admit as necessary, — we must think so as to avoid dupery, and we must think so as to gain truth; but the surest path to those ideal consummations, you will probably consider, is from now onwards to take no further passional step.

Well, of course, I agree as far as the facts will allow. Wherever the option between losing truth and gaining it is not momentous, we can throw the chance of *gaining truth* away, and at any rate save ourselves from any chance of *believing falsehood*, by not making up our minds at all till objective evidence has come. In scientific questions, this is almost always the case; and even in human affairs in general, the need of acting is seldom so urgent that a false belief to act on is better than no belief at all. Law courts, indeed, have to decide on the best evidence attainable for the moment, because a judge's duty is to make law as well as to ascertain it, and (as a learned judge once said to me) few cases are worth spending much time over: the great thing is to have them decided on *any* acceptable principle, and got out of the way. But in our dealings with objective nature we obviously are recorders, not makers, of the truth; and decisions for the mere sake of deciding promptly and getting on to the next business would be wholly out of place. Throughout the breadth of physical nature facts are what they are quite independently of us, and seldom is there any such hurry about them that the risks of being duped by believing a premature theory need be faced. . . .

I speak, of course, here of the purely judging mind. For purposes of discovery such indifference is to be less highly recommended, and science would be far less advanced than she is if the passionate desires of individuals to get their own faiths confirmed had been kept out of the game. . . . The most useful investigator, because the most sensitive observer, is always he whose eager interest in one side of the question is balanced by an equally keen nervousness lest he become deceived. Science has organized this nervousness into a regular *technique*, her so-called method of verification; and she has fallen so deeply in love with the method that one may even say she has ceased to care for truth by itself at all. It is only truth as technically verified that interests her. The truth of truths might come in merely affirmative form, and she would decline to touch it. Such truth as that, she might repeat with Clifford, would be stolen in defiance of her duty to mankind. Human passions, however, are stronger than technical rules. "Le coeur a ses raisons," as Pascal says, "que la raison ne connait pas;" and however indifferent to all but the bare rules of the game the umpire, the abstract intellect, may be, the concrete players who furnish him the materials to judge of are usually, each of them, in love with some pet 'live hypothesis' of his own. Let us agree, however, that wherever there is no forced option, the dispassionately judicial intellect with no pet hypothesis, saving us, as it does, from dupery at any rate, ought to be our ideal.

The question next arises: Are there not somewhere forced options in our speculative questions, and can we (as men who may be interested at least as much in positively gaining truth as in merely escaping dupery) always wait with impunity till the coercive evidence shall have arrived? It seems *a priori* improbable that the truth should be so nicely adjusted to our needs and powers as that. In the great boarding-house of nature, the cakes and the butter and the syrup seldom come out so even and leave the plates so clean. Indeed, we should view them with scientific suspicion if they did.

IX

Moral questions immediately present themselves as questions whose solution cannot wait for sensible proof. A moral question is a question not of what sensibly exists, but of what is good, or would be good if it did exist. Science can tell us what exists; but to compare the *worths*, both of what exists and of what does not exist, we must consult not science, but what Pascal calls our heart. Science herself consults her heart when she lays it down that the infinite ascertainment of fact and correction of false belief are the supreme goods for man. Challenge the statement, and science can only repeat it oracularly, or else prove it by showing that such ascertainment and correction bring man all sorts of other goods which man's heart in turn declares. The question of having moral beliefs at all or not having them is decided by our will. Are our moral preferences true or false, or are they only odd biological phenomena, making things good or bad for *us*, but in themselves indifferent? How can your pure intellect decide? If your heart does not *want* a world of moral reality, your head will assuredly never make you believe in one. Mephistophelian scepticism, indeed, will satisfy the head's play-instincts much better than any rigorous idealism can. Some men (even at the student age) are so naturally cool-hearted that the moralistic hypothesis never has for them any pungent life, and in their supercilious presence the hot young moralist always feels strangely ill at ease. The appearance of knowingness is on their side, of *naiveté* and gullibility on his. Yet, in the inarticulate heart of him, he clings to it that he is not a dupe, and that there is a realm in which (as Emerson says) all their wit and intellectual superiority is no better than the cunning of a fox. Moral scepticism can no more be refuted or proved by logic than intellectual scepticism can. When we stick to it that there *is* truth (be it of either kind), we do so with our whole nature, and resolve to stand or fall by the results. The sceptic with his whole nature adopts the doubting attitude; but which of us is the wiser, Omniscience only knows.

Turn now from these wide questions of good to a certain class of questions of fact, questions concerning personal relations, states of mind between one man and another. *Do you like me or not?*—for example. Whether you do or not depends, in countless instances, on whether I meet you half-way, am willing to assume that you must like me, and show you trust and expectation. The previous faith on my part in your liking's existence is in such cases what makes your liking come. But if I stand aloof, and refuse to budge an inch until I have objective evidence, until you shall have done something apt, as the absolutists say, *ad extorquendum assensum meum*, ten to one your liking never comes. How many women's hearts are vanquished by the mere sanguine insistence of some man that they *must* love him! he will not consent to the hypothesis that they cannot. The desire for a certain kind of truth here brings about that special truth's existence; and so it is in innumerable cases of other sorts. Who gains promotions, boons, appointments, but the man in whose life they are seen to play the part of live hypotheses, who discounts them, sacrifices other things for their sake before they have come, and takes risks for them in advance? His faith acts on the powers above him as a claim, and creates its own verification.

A social organism of any sort whatever, large or small, is what it is because each member proceeds to his own duty with a trust that the other members will simultaneously do theirs. Wherever a desired result is achieved by the co-operation of many independent persons, its existence as a fact is a pure consequence of the precursive faith in one another of those immediately concerned. A government, an army, a commercial system, a ship, a college, an athletic team, all exist on this condition, without which not only is nothing achieved, but nothing is even attempted. A whole train of passengers (individually brave enough) will be looted by a few highwaymen, simply because the latter can count on one another, while each passenger fears that if he makes a movement of resistance, he will be shot before any one else backs him up. If we believed that the whole car-full would rise at once with us, we should each severally rise, and train-robbing would never even be attempted. There are, then, cases where a fact cannot come at all unless a preliminary faith exists in its coming. *And where faith in a fact can help create the fact*, that would be an insane logic which should say that faith running ahead of scientific evidence is the 'lowest kind of immorality' into which a thinking being can fall. Yet such is the logic by which our scientific absolutists pretend to regulate our lives!

X

In truths dependent on our personal action, then, faith based on desire is certainly a lawful and possibly an indispensable thing.

But now, it will be said, these are all childish human cases, and have nothing to do with great cosmical matters, like the question of religious faith. Let us then pass on to that. Religions differ so much in their accidents that in discussing the religious question we must make it very generic and broad. What then do we now mean by the religious hypothesis? Science says things are; morality says some things are better than other things; and religion says essentially two things.

First, she says that the best things are the more eternal things, the overlapping things, the things in the universe that throw the last stone, so to speak, and say the final word. "Perfection is eternal,"—this phrase of Charles Secretan seems a good way of putting this first affirmation of religion, an affirmation which obviously cannot yet be verified scientifically at all.

The second affirmation of religion is that we are better off even now if we believe her first affirmation to be true.

Now, let us consider what the logical elements of this situation are *in case the religious hypothesis in both its branches be really true.* (Of course, we must admit that possibility at the outset. If we are to discuss the question at all, it must involve a living option. If for any of you religion be a hypothesis that cannot, by any living possibility be true, then you need go no farther. I speak to the 'saving remnant' alone.) So proceeding, we see, first, that religion offers itself as a *momentous* option. We are supposed to gain, even now, by our belief, and to lose by our non-belief, a certain vital good. Secondly, religion is a *forced* option, so far as that good goes. We cannot escape the issue by remaining sceptical and waiting for more light, because although we do avoid error in that way *if religion be untrue*, we lose the good, *if it be true*, just as certainly as if we positively chose to disbelieve. It is as if a man should hesitate indefinitely to ask a certain woman to marry him because he was not perfectly sure that she would prove an angel after he brought her home. Would he not cut himself off from that particular angel-possibility as decisively as if he went and married some one else? Scepticism, then, is not avoidance of option; it is option of a certain particular kind of risk. *Better risk loss of truth than chance of error,* — that is your faith-vetoer's exact position. He is actively playing his stake as much as the believer is; he is backing the field against the religious hypothesis, just as the believer is backing the religious hypothesis against the field. To preach scepticism to us as a duty until 'sufficient evidence' for religion be found, is tantamount therefore to telling us, when in presence of the religious hypothesis, that to yield to our fear of its being error is wiser and better than to yield to our hope that it may be true. It is not intellect against all passions, then; it is only intellect with one passion laying down its law. And by what, forsooth, is the supreme wisdom of this passion warranted? Dupery for dupery, what proof is there that dupery through hope is so much worse than dupery through fear? I, for one, can see no proof; and I simply refuse obedience to the scientist's command to imitate his kind of option, in a case where my own stake is important enough to give me the right to choose my own form of risk. If religion be true and the evidence for it be still insufficient, I do not wish, by putting your extinguisher upon my nature (which feels to me as if it had after all some business in this matter), to forfeit my sole chance in life of getting upon the winning side, — that chance depending, of course, on my willingness to run the risk of acting as if my passional need of taking the world religiously might be prophetic and right.

All this is on the supposition that it really may be prophetic and right, and that, even to us who are discussing the matter, religion is a live hypothesis which may be true. Now, to most of us religion comes in a still further way that makes a veto on our active faith even more illogical. The more perfect and more eternal aspect of the universe is represented in our religions as having personal form. The universe is no longer a mere *It* to us, but a *Thou*, if we are religious; and any relation that may be possible from person to person might be possible here. For instance, although in one sense we are passive portions of the universe, in another we show a curious autonomy, as if we were small active centres on our own account. We feel, too, as if the appeal of religion to us were made to our own active good-will, as if evidence might be forever withheld from us unless we met the hypothesis half-way. To take a trivial illustration: just as a man who in a company of gentlemen made no advances, asked a warrant for every concession, and believed no one's word without proof, would cut himself off by such churlishness from all the social rewards that a more trusting spirit would earn, — so here, one who should shut himself up in snarling logicality and try to make the gods extort his recognition willy-nilly, or not get it at all, might cut himself off forever from his only opportunity of making the gods' acquaintance. This feeling, forced on us we know not whence, that by obstinately believing that there are gods (although not to do so would be so easy both for our logic and our life) we are doing the universe the deepest service we can, seems part of the living essence of the religious hypothesis. If the hypothesis *were* true in all its parts, including this one, then pure intellectualism, with its veto on our making willing advances, would be an absurdity; and some participation of our sympathetic nature would be logically required. I, therefore, for one, cannot see my way to accepting the agnostic rules for truth-seeking, or wilfully agree to keep my willing nature out of the game. I cannot do so for this plain reason, that *a rule of thinking which would absolutely prevent me from acknowledging certain kinds of truth if those kinds of truth were really there, would be an irrational rule.* That for me is the long and short of the formal logic of the situation, no matter what the kinds of truth might materially be.

I confess I do not see how this logic can be escaped. But sad experience makes me fear that some of you may still shrink from radically saying with me, *in abstracto*, that we have the right to believe at our own risk any hypothesis that is live enough to tempt our will. I suspect, however, that if this is so, it is because you have got away from the abstract logical point of view altogether, and are thinking (perhaps without realizing it) of some particular religious hypothesis which for you is dead. The freedom to 'believe what we will' you apply to the case of some patent superstition; and the faith you think of is the faith defined by the schoolboy when he said, "Faith is when you believe something that you know ain't true." I can only repeat that this is misapprehension. *In concreto*, the freedom to believe can only cover living options which the intellect of the individual cannot by itself resolve; and living options never seem absurdities to him who has them to consider. When I look at the religious question as it really puts itself to concrete men, and when I think of all the possibilities which both practically and theoretically it involves, then this command that we shall put a stopper on our heart, instincts, and courage, and *wait* — acting of course meanwhile more or less as if religion were *not* true[2] — till doomsday, or till such time as our intellect and senses working together may have raked in evidence enough, — this command, I say, seems to me the queerest idol ever manufactured in the philosophic cave. Were we scholastic absolutists, there might be more excuse. If we had an infallible intellect with its objective certitudes, we might feel ourselves disloyal to such a perfect organ of knowledge in not trusting to it exclusively, in not waiting for its releasing word. But if we are empiricists, if we believe that no bell in us tolls to let us know for certain when truth is in our grasp, then it seems a piece of idle fantasticality to preach so solemnly our duty of waiting for the bell. Indeed we *may* wait if we will, — I hope you do not think that I am denying that, — but if we do so, we do so at our peril as much as if we believed. In either case we *act*, taking our life in our hands. No one of us ought to issue vetoes to the other, nor should we bandy words of abuse. We ought, on the contrary, delicately and profoundly to respect one another's mental freedom: then only shall we bring about the intellectual republic; then only shall we have that spirit of inner tolerance without which all our outer tolerance is soulless, and which is empiricism's glory; then only shall we live and let live, in speculative as well as in practical things.

---

[2] Since belief is measured by action, he who forbids us to believe religion to be true, necessarily also forbids us to act as we should if we did believe it to be true. The whole defence of religious faith hinges upon action. If the action required or inspired by the religious hypothesis is in no way different from that dictated by the naturalistic hypothesis, then religious faith is a pure superfluity, better pruned away, and controversy about its legitimacy is a piece of idle trifling, unworthy of serious minds. I myself believe, of course, that the religious hypothesis gives to the world an expression which specifically determines our reactions, and makes them in a large part unlike what they might be on a purely naturalistic scheme of belief.

Review Questions

1. Explain what is meant by the *radical* empiricism of James.
2. In what way is pragmatism a method?
3. As a method for clarifying ideas, is pragmatism a totally new approach, or does it have some traditional forebears?
4. Show how, for example, James applies the pragmatic method to the notion of substance; to God.

CHAPTER 25

Bertrand Russell (1872–1970)

Introduction

James' aversion to idealism paralleled a similar sentiment in England, where philosophy seemed to have taken temporary leave of its empirical and scientific tradition. Francis H. Bradley, Bernard Bosanquet, and John M. E. McTaggart were a trio of outstanding and influential idealists who would have liked to create in a generation of budding philosophers a sympathy for idealism — for a world in which the Absolute reigned supreme and the particular did not gain easy admittance. But this adventure in idealism was short-lived because the new generation, counting among its members George E. Moore, Bertrand Russell, and Samuel Alexander, reacted strongly against it in favor of a realism that hewed closely to the main line of British empiricism. At first, this reaction took the form of a "common sense" appeal made by Moore, to the effect that I, by common sense, am able to formulate statements or propositions concerning my own existence and the existence of sense objects. However, his emphasis on propositions resulted in the propositions themselves becoming the object of succeeding British philosophers. This began with Russell's treatment of propositions, called *analysis*, and continued with Ludwig Wittgenstein's fascinating approach to philosophical language, followed by the school of *logical positivism* with its concern with the problem of meaning as empirical verifiability. The figure, then, who stands out at the critical juncture, bidding farewell to idealism and welcome to the logical-language path to realism, was Bertrand Russell.

He was born in 1872 in Monmouthshire, England, the son of Lord and Lady Amberley, both of whom died when he was a child. He was brought up by his grandmother and his grandfather, Lord John Russell. His parents had been liberal thinkers — John Stuart Mill was his informal godfather — but his grandparents had a sternly religious home. As a young man, however, he abandoned the basic beliefs of religion, namely, free will, immortality, and God. At Cambridge University, which he entered in 1890, he took up the study of mathematics and philosophy, becoming an early devotee of Hegel through Bradley's influence. Upon leaving Cambridge, he became attached to the British Embassy in Paris for a year before going on to Berlin for the purpose of studying economics and German political science; this experience resulted in his first book, *German Social Democracy*, in 1896. In 1898 he rejected Hegelianism and every kind of idealism, being led by his friend Moore to the position that whatever common sense held to be real *is* real. In 1900 he wrote a book on Leibniz, considering areas of that thinker's logic hitherto neglected. In the same year, his attendance at the International Congress of Philosophy gave him the impetus to pursue his interest in the foundation of mathematics, which brought him to the publication of *The Principles of Mathematics* in 1903, and, years later, to his epoch-making opus with Alfred North Whitehead, *Principia Mathematica* (1910–13).

From 1910 to 1916 he lectured at Cambridge, having Wittgenstein as one of his students. Wittgenstein, in his turn, influenced Russell in several important aspects of the philosophy of language and the nature of mathematics. Russell thought so much of Wittgenstein's innovative ideas that he offered to write the introduction to his now famous work, *Tractatus Logico-Philosophicus* (1922). During this time Russell became involved in social issues, mainly as a result of World War I, and embraced a pacificism that made him exceedingly unpopular and caused the university to dismiss him; he maintained his record of pacificism, with the exception of his approval of World War II as the only means of repelling Nazi aggression. After the war he resumed his pacificism, highlighted by the position he assumed against the nuclear bomb and the activities of the United States in Vietnam. From 1938 on, he taught in several places in the United States, but had an appointment to the City College of New York canceled after a stormy and discreditable reaction to his liberal views on sexual morality. In 1950 he was awarded the Nobel Prize for literature.

Despite his extremely active life of traveling and of espousing social causes, his literary output never abated; he wrote many articles, pamphlets, and books, ranging from the popular to the professional. He died in 1970. Among his chief works, besides those mentioned already, are *The Problems of Philosophy* (1912), *Our Knowledge of the External World* (1914), *The Analysis of Mind* (1921), *An Inquiry into Meaning and Truth* (1940), *A History of Western Philosophy* (1945), and *My Philosophical Development* (1959).

In the context of Russell's belief that philosophy should be scientific, and perhaps even more rigorous than the sciences themselves, his philosophical method, which, as previously noted, is called *analysis*, is addressed first of all to the analysis of empirical data, that is, to an analysis of things as they are given in experience; sense data are realities, they are trans-subjective. But things of the outside world are not given to us directly; they are given to us through their properties and their relations to each other, which Russell refers to as *facts*, so that analysis is principally a method for evaluating facts. Adopting as a basic part of his method a principle adopted from the fourteenth-century philosopher William of Ockham, which states that "entities are not to be multiplied without necessity"—appropriately called *Ockham's razor* — Russell attempts to eliminate as many complexities, postulates, and entities as possible to arrive at the "last residue" of what is "uneliminable." We therefore cannot *infer* the existence of entities not known empirically to exist, and because the mind constructs *logical* relations within the sense field in which facts are given, "wherever possible logical constructions are to be substituted for inferred entities."

The most fruitful source of logical construction is *language*, and it is by the *analysis of language* that we are brought to a knowledge of the reality beyond it. Although he does not try to state precisely why there is a connection between language and reality, it is essential for him to hold that there is some kind of connection between the way the mind *works* and the way reality *is*, or between "the laws of syntax and the laws of physics."

Facts are stated in the form of propositions, and, by analysis, the simplest proposition would be one like "John is tall," that is, a proposition composed of a proper name and a simple predicate; or, because we do not assign proper names to every single thing, a similar proposition would be "This is red." These propositions Russell calls *atomic propositions*; they signify *atomic facts*. Where several atomic propositions are put together, as in "This is red and sweet" (i.e., "This is red" and "This is sweet"), the proposition is called a *molecular proposition*. But, by the application of Ockham's razor, molecular propositions do not signify *molecular facts* because the truth of a molecular proposition depends on, or is a function of, the atomic propositions it is composed of; therefore, the atomic fact is all that is necessary. This is true even of a fact that refers to an entire class, such as "All trees are green"; even if it is a *general* fact, it is still atomic because it is irreducible. Russell refers to this view of things — a view very much in keeping with the British tradition of analyzing the given down to its simplest elements — as *logical atomism*, although he disagrees in several important respects with the views of Locke and Hume.

The enormous contribution Russell, together with Whitehead, made to the study of the nature of mathematics can be left to mathematicians. Here we simply want to point out that Russell's interest in making language as precise an instrument as possible urged him to develop a vehicle that would avoid the limitations of ordinary language. A new language, to be logically perfect, would use symbols and symbolic expressions, transcend national languages, avert the pitfalls of grammar, and make it easier to deal with abstractions and deductions than words allow. Accordingly, Russell and Whitehead, furthering the work of their predecessors, fine-tuned mathematical or symbolic logic to such an extent that serious students in this field must familiarize themselves with *Principia Mathematica*, "one of the most influential works of European thought in the twentieth century."

It is not difficult to see how logical atomism inclines favorably toward the sciences and, because philosophy is to be built on an empirical foundation, the obvious source of hard knowledge is the natural sciences. It is sometimes difficult to see how, for Russell, philosophy differs from the sciences, for philosophy consists of learning "principles and methods and general conceptions" from science. Philosophy, even though it is focused more on organizing principles and less on detail, still has the same objective as science: "Philosophy involves a criticism of scientific knowledge, not from a point of view ultimately different from that of science, but from a point of view less concerned with details and more concerned with the harmony of the whole body of special sciences." The laws and language of the sciences must themselves be subject to logical analysis in order to clarify their meaning, which becomes one of the major tasks of philosophy.

Even with his complete devotion to the sciences, Russell does not come down as heavily on metaphysics as most of his empiricist predecessors. It is true that he sees no compelling reason for substance, self, soul, immortality, and God, yet the fact that he was looking for "harmony," or trying to find out what is "ultimate" in the universe, is a clear indication that he is not eschewing metaphysics altogether. And as previously indicated, though he did not elaborate on the link between language and things, he writes, "I am inclined to think that quite important metaphysical conclusions, of a more or less skeptical kind, can be drawn from simple considerations as to the relation between language and things."

Ambiguity in metaphysics in no way deterred Russell from holding that one of the goals of philosophy is to give an account of "daily life." This statement is borne out in a practical way, by his ardent and personal commitment to social causes for most of his life, but particularly after World War I, which he saw as a cataclysm crystallizing the evil forces in man and paving the way for endless suffering in the future. The principles behind the activities of daily life pertain to ethics, the province of general maxims and not of specific applications in specific circumstances. Morality derives meaning in a social context; as such, the common good or happiness is the fundamental consideration, so that a person's actions, "inspired by love and guided by knowledge," ought to proceed from a desire for harmony in the whole of a society. Imitating Kant's mode of formulation, Russell states the supreme moral rule as follows: "_Act so as to produce harmonious rather than discordant desires._"

Russell tells us that it was his interest in religion that urged him, as a young man, to take up the study of philosophy; he wanted "to find some satisfaction for religious impulses." In anticipation, he moved on to one philosophical system after another, seeking its religious tone, but he never found "religious satisfaction in any philosophical doctrine" he could accept. However, he attests to the agony of the philosopher whose emotions go one way while his intellect goes another: "Those who attempt to make a religion of humanism, which recognizes nothing greater than man, do not satisfy my emotions. And yet I am unable to believe that, in the world as known, there is anything that I can value outside human beings, and, to a much lesser extent, animals."

A beautiful testimony by Russell as to what life is finally all about is worth giving in full: "Three passions, simple but overwhelmingly strong, have governed my life: the longing for love, the search for knowledge, and unbearable pity for the suffering of mankind. These passions, like great winds, have blown me hither and thither in a wayward course over a deep ocean of anguish, reaching to the very verge of despair.

"I have sought love, first, because it brings ecstasy, — ecstasy so great that I would often have sacrificed all the rest of life for a few hours of this joy. I have sought it, next, because it relieves loneliness — that terrible loneliness in which one shivering consciousness looks over the rim of the world into the cold unfathomable lifeless abyss. I have sought it, finally, because in the union of love I have seen, in a mystic miniature, the prefiguring vision of the heaven that saints and poets have imagined. This is what I sought, and though it might seem too good for human life, this is what — at last — I have found.

"With equal passion I have sought knowledge. I have wished to understand the hearts of men. I have wished to know why the stars shine. A little of this, but not much, I have achieved.

"Love and knowledge, so far as they were possible, led upward toward the heavens. But always pity brought me back to earth. Echoes of cries of pain reverberate in my heart. Children in famine, victims tortured by oppressors, helpless old people a hated burden to their sons, and the whole world of loneliness, poverty, and pain make a mockery of what human life should be. I long to alleviate the evil, but I cannot, and I too suffer.

"This has been my life. I have found it worth living, and would gladly live it again if the chance were offered me."

Readings

Mathematics and Logic (from *Introduction to Mathematical Philosophy*)

Mathematics and logic, historically speaking, have been entirely distinct studies. Mathematics has been connected with science, logic with Greek. But both have developed in modern times: logic has become more mathematical and mathematics has become more logical. The consequence is that it has now become wholly impossible to draw a line between the two; in fact, the two are one. They differ as boy and man: logic is the youth of mathematics and mathematics is the manhood of logic. This view is resented by logicians who, having spent their time in the study of classical texts, are incapable of following a piece of symbolic reasoning, and by mathematicians who have learnt a technique without troubling to inquire into its meaning or justification. Both types are now fortunately growing rarer. So much of modern mathematical work is obviously on the border-line of logic, so much of modern logic is symbolic and formal, that the very close relationship of logic and mathematics has become obvious to every instructed student. The proof of their identity is, of course, a matter of detail: starting with premises which would be universally admitted to belong to logic, and arriving by deduction at results which as obviously belong to mathematics, we find that there is no point at which a sharp line can be drawn, with logic to the left and mathematics to the right. If there are still those who do not admit the identity of logic and mathematics, we may challenge them to indicate at what point, in the successive definitions and deductions of *Principia Mathematica*, they consider that logic ends and mathematics begins. It will then be obvious that any answer must be quite arbitrary.

In the earlier chapters of this book, starting from the natural numbers, we have first defined "cardinal number" and shown how to generalise the conception of number, and have then analysed the conceptions involved in the definition, until we found ourselves dealing with the fundamentals of logic. In a synthetic, deductive treatment these fundamentals come first, and the natural numbers are only reached after a long journey. Such treatment, though formally more correct than that which we have adopted, is more difficult for the reader, because the ultimate logical concepts and propositions with which it starts are remote and unfamiliar as compared with the natural numbers. Also they represent the present frontier of knowledge, beyond which is the still unknown; and the dominion of knowledge over them is not as yet very secure.

It used to be said that mathematics is the science of "quantity." "Quantity" is a vague word, but for the sake of argument we may replace it by the word "number." The statement that mathematics is the science of number would be untrue in two different ways. On the one hand, there are recognised branches of mathematics which have nothing to do with number—all geometry that does not use co-ordinates or measurement, for example: projective and descriptive geometry, down to the point at which co-ordinates are introduced, does not have to do with number, or even with quantity in the sense of _greater_ and _less_. On the other hand, through the definition of cardinals, through the theory of induction and ancestral relations, through the general theory of series, and through the definitions of the arithmetical operations, it has become possible to generalise much that used to be proved only in connection with numbers. The result is that what was formerly the single study of Arithmetic has now become divided into numbers of separate studies, no one of which is specially concerned with numbers. The most elementary properties of numbers are concerned with one-one relations, and similarity between classes. Addition is concerned with the construction of mutually exclusive classes respectively similar to a set of classes which are not known to be mutually exclusive. Multiplication is merged in the theory of "selections," _i.e._ of a certain kind of one-many relations. Finitude is merged in the general study of ancestral relations, which yields the whole theory of mathematical induction. The ordinal properties of the various kinds of number-series, and the elements of the theory of continuity of functions and the limits of functions, can be generalised so as no longer to involve any essential reference to numbers. It is a principle, in all formal reasoning, to generalise to the utmost, since we thereby secure that a given process of deduction shall have more widely applicable results; we are, therefore, in thus generalising the reasoning of arithmetic, merely following a precept which is universally admitted in mathematics. And in thus generalising we have, in effect, created a set of new deductive systems, in which traditional arithmetic is at once dissolved and enlarged; but whether any one of these new deductive systems—for example, the theory of selections—is to be said to belong to logic or to arithmetic is entirely arbitrary, and incapable of being decided rationally.

We are thus brought face to face with the question: What is this subject, which may be called indifferently either mathematics or logic? Is there any way in which we can define it?

Certain characteristics of the subject are clear. To begin with, we do not, in this subject, deal with particular things or particular properties:

we deal formally with what can be said about *any* thing or *any* property. We are prepared to say that one and one are two, but not that Socrates and Plato are two, because, in our capacity of logicians or pure mathematicians, we have never heard of Socrates and Plato. A world in which there were no such individuals would still be a world in which one and one are two. It is not open to us, as pure mathematicians or logicians, to mention anything at all, because, if we do so, we introduce something irrelevant and not formal. We may make this clear by applying it to the case of the syllogism. Traditional logic says: "All men are mortal, Socrates is a man, therefore Socrates is mortal." Now it is clear that what we *mean* to assert, to begin with, is only that the premisses imply the conclusion, not that premisses and conclusion are actually true; even the most traditional logic points out that the actual truth of the premisses is irrelevant to logic. Thus the first change to be made in the above traditional syllogism is to state it in the form: "If all men are mortal and Socrates is a man, then Socrates is mortal." We may now observe that it is intended to convey that this argument is valid in virtue of its *form*, not in virtue of the particular terms occurring in it. If we had omitted "Socrates is a man" from our premisses, we should have had a non-formal argument, only admissible because Socrates is in fact a man; in that case we could not have generalised the argument. But when, as above, the argument is *formal*, nothing depends upon the terms that occur in it. Thus we may substitute α for *men*, β for *mortals*, and x for Socrates, where α and β are any classes whatever, and x is any individual. We then arrive at the statement: "No matter what possible values x and α and β may have, if all α's are β's and x is an α, is a β"; in other words, "the propositional function 'if all α's are β and x is an α, then x is a β' is always true." Here at last we have a proposition of logic—the one which is only suggested by the traditional statement about Socrates and men and mortals.

It is clear that, if *formal* reasoning is what we are aiming at, we shall always arrive ultimately at statements like the above, in which no actual things or properties are mentioned; this will happen through the mere desire not to waste our time proving in a particular case what can be proved generally. It would be ridiculous to go through a long argument about Socrates, and then go through precisely the same argument again about Plato. If our argument is one (say) which holds of all men, we shall prove it concerning "x," with the hypothesis "if x is a man." With this hypothesis, the argument will retain its hypothetical validity even when x is not a man. But now we shall find that our argument would still be valid if, instead of supposing x to be a man, we were to suppose him to be a monkey or a goose or a Prime Minister. We shall therefore not waste our time taking as our premiss "x is a man" but shall take "x is an α," where α is any class of individuals, or "ϕx" where

ϕ is any propositional function of some assigned type. Thus the absence of all mention of particular things or properties in logic or pure mathematics is a necessary result of the fact that this study is, as we say, "purely formal."

At this point we find ourselves faced with a problem which is easier to state than to solve. The problem is: "What are the constituents of a logical proposition?" I do not know the answer, but I propose to explain how the problem arises.

Take (say) the proposition "Socrates was before Aristotle." Here it seems obvious that we have a relation between two terms, and that the constituents of the proposition (as well as of the corresponding fact) are simply the two terms and the relation, i.e. Socrates, Aristotle, and *before*. (I ignore the fact that Socrates and Aristotle are not simple; also the fact that what appear to be their names are really truncated descriptions. Neither of these facts is relevant to the present issue.) We may represent the general form of such propositions by "x R y," which may be read "x has the relation R to y." This general form may occur in logical propositions, but no particular instance of it can occur. Are we to infer that the general form itself is a constituent of such logical propositions?

Given a proposition, such as "Socrates is before Aristotle," we have certain constituents and also a certain form. But the form is not itself a new constituent; if it were, we should need a new form to embrace both it and the other constituents. We can, in fact, turn *all* the constituents of a proposition into variables, while keeping the form unchanged. This is what we do when we use such a schema as "x R y," which stands for any one of a certain class of propositions, namely, those asserting relations between two terms. We can proceed to general assertions, such as "x R y is sometimes true"—i.e. there are cases where dual relations hold. This assertion will belong to logic (or mathematics) in the sense in which we are using the word. But in this assertion we do not mention any particular things or particular relations; no particular things or relations can ever enter into a proposition of pure logic. We are left with pure forms as the only possible constituents of logical propositions.

I do not wish to assert positively that pure forms—*e.g.* the form "x R y"—do actually enter into propositions of the kind we are considering. The question of the analysis of such propositions is a difficult one, with conflicting considerations on the one side and on the other. We cannot embark upon this question now, but we may accept, as a first approximation, the view that *forms* are what enter into logical propositions as their constituents. And we may explain (though not formally define) what we mean by the "form" of a proposition as follows:—

The "form" of a proposition is that, in it, that remains unchanged when every constituent of the proposition is replaced by another.

Thus "Socrates is earlier than Aristotle" has the same form as "Napoleon is greater than Wellington," though every constituent of the two propositions is different.

We may thus lay down, as a necessary (though not sufficient) characteristic of logical or mathematical propositions, that they are to be such as can be obtained from a proposition containing no variables (*i.e.* no such words as *all*, *some*, *a*, *the*, etc.) by turning every constituent into a variable and asserting that the result is always true or sometimes true, or that it is always true in respect of some of the variables that the result is sometimes true in respect of the others, or any variant of these forms. And another way of stating the same thing is to say that logic (or mathematics) is concerned only with *forms*, and is concerned with them only in the way of stating that they are always or sometimes true—with all the permutations of "always" and "sometimes" that may occur.

There are in every language some words whose sole function is to indicate form. These words, broadly speaking, are commonest in languages having fewest inflections. Take "Socrates is human." Here "is" is not a constituent of the proposition, but merely indicates the subject-predicate form. Similarly in "Socrates is earlier than Aristotle," "is" and "than" merely indicate form; the proposition is the same as "Socrates precedes Aristotle," in which these words have disappeared and the form is otherwise indicated. Form, as a rule, can be indicated otherwise than by specific words: the order of the words can do most of what is wanted. But this principle must not be pressed. For example, it is difficult to see how we could conveniently express molecular forms of propositions (*i.e.* what we call "truth-functions") without any word at all. We saw in Chapter XIV. that one word or symbol is enough for this purpose, namely, a word or symbol expressing *incompatibility*. But without even one we should find ourselves in difficulties. This, however, is not the point that is important for our present purpose. What is important for us is to observe that form may be the one concern of a general proposition, even when no word or symbol in that proposition designates the form. If we wish to speak about the form itself, we must have a word for it; but if, as in mathematics, we wish to speak about all propositions that have the form, a word for the form will usually be found not indispensable; probably in theory it is *never* indispensable.

Assuming—as I think we may—that the forms of propositions *can* be represented by the forms of the propositions in which they are expressed without any special word for forms, we should arrive at a language in which everything formal belonged to syntax and not to vocabulary. In such a language we could express *all* the propositions of from which all the propositions mathematics even if we did not know one single word of the language. The language of mathematical logic, if it were perfected, would be such a language. We should have symbols for variables, such as "x" and "R" and "y," arranged in various ways; and the way of arrangement would indicate that something was being said to be true of all values or some values of the variables. We should not need to know any words, because they would only be needed for giving values to the variables, which is the business of the applied mathematician, not of the pure mathematician or logician. It is one of the marks of a proposition of logic that, given a suitable language, such a proposition can be asserted in such a language by a person who knows the syntax without knowing a single word of the vocabulary.

But, after all, there are words that express form, such as "is" and "than." And in every symbolism hitherto invented for mathematical logic there are symbols having constant formal meanings. We may take as an example the symbol for incompatibility which is employed in building up truth-functions. Such words or symbols may occur in logic. The question is: How are we to define them?

Such words or symbols express what are called "logical constants." Logical constants may be defined exactly as we defined forms; in fact, they are in essence the same thing. A fundamental logical constant will be that which is in common among a number of propositions, any one of which can result from any other by substitution of terms one for another. For example, "Napoleon is greater than Wellington" results from "Socrates is earlier than Aristotle" by the substitution of "Napoleon" for "Socrates," "Wellington" for "Aristotle," and "greater" for "earlier." Some propositions can be obtained in this way from the prototype "Socrates is earlier than Aristotle" and some cannot; those that can are those that are of the form "x R y," _i.e._ express dual relations. We cannot obtain from the above prototype by term-for-term substitution such propositions as "Socrates is human" or "the Athenians gave the hemlock to Socrates," because the first is of the subject-predicate form and the second expresses a three-term relation. If we are to have any words in our pure logical language, they must be such as express "logical constants," and "logical constants" will always either be, or be derived from, what is in common among a group of propositions derivable from each other, in the above manner, by term-for-term substitution. And this which is in common is what we call "form."

In this sense all the "constants" that occur in pure mathematics are logical constants. The number I, for example, is derivative from propositions of the form: "There is a term c such that ϕx is true when, and only when, x is c." This is a function of ϕ, and various different propositions result from giving different values to ϕ. We may (with a little omission of intermediate steps not relevant to our present purpose) take the above function of ϕ as what is meant by "the class determined by ϕ is a unit class" or "the class determined by ϕ is a member of I" (I being a class of classes). In this way, propositions in which I occurs acquire a meaning which is derived from a certain constant logical form. And the same will be found to be the case with all mathematical constants: all are logical constants, or symbolic abbreviations whose full use in a proper context is defined by means of logical constants.

But although all logical (or mathematical) propositions can be expressed wholly in terms of logical constants together with variables, it is not the case that, conversely, all propositions that can be expressed in this way are logical. We have found so far a necessary but not a sufficient criterion of mathematical propositions. We have sufficiently defined the character of the primitive *ideas* in terms of which all the ideas of mathematics can be *defined*, but not of the primitive *propositions* from which all the propositions of mathematics can be *deduced*. This is a more difficult matter, as to which it is not yet known what the full answer is.

We may take the axiom of infinity as an example of a proposition which, though it can be enunciated in logical terms, cannot be asserted by logic to be true. All the propositions of logic have a characteristic which used to be expressed by saying that they were analytic, or that their contradictories were self-contradictory. This mode of statement, however, is not satisfactory. The law of contradiction is merely one among logical propositions; it has no special pre-eminence; and the proof that the contradictory of some proposition is self-contradictory is likely to require other principles of deduction besides the law of contradiction. Nevertheless, the characteristic of logical propositions that we are in search of is the one which was felt, and intended to be defined, by those who said that it consisted in deducibility from the law of contradiction. This characteristic, which, for the moment, we may call *tautology*, obviously does not belong to the assertion that the number of individuals in the universe is n, whatever number n may be. But for the diversity of types, it would be possible to prove logically that there are classes of n terms, where n is any finite integer; or even that there are classes of $\aleph_0$-terms. But, owing to types, such proofs, as we saw in Chapter XIII., are fallacious. We are left to empirical observation to determine whether there are as many as n individuals in the world. Among "possible" worlds, in the Leibnizian sense, there will be worlds having one, two, three, ... individuals. There does not even seem any logical necessity why there should be even one individual[1]— why, in fact, there should be any world at all. The ontological proof of

---

[1] The primitive propositions in *Principia Mathematica* are such as to allow the inference that at least one individual exists. But I now view this as a defect in logical purity.

the existence of God, if it were valid, would establish the logical necessity of at least one individual. But it is generally recognised as invalid, and in fact rests upon a mistaken view of existence—*i.e.* it fails to realise that existence can only be asserted of something described, not of something named, so that it is meaningless to argue from "this is the so-and-so" and "the so-and-so exists" to "this exists." If we reject the ontological argument, we seem driven to conclude that the existence of a world is an accident—*i.e.* it is not logically necessary. If that be so, no principle of logic can assert "existence" except under a hypothesis, *i.e.* none can be of the form "the propositional function so-and-so is sometimes true." Propositions of this form, when they occur in logic, will have to occur as hypotheses or consequences of hypotheses, not as complete asserted propositions. The complete asserted propositions of logic will all be such as affirm that some propositional function is *always* true. For example, it is always true that if p implies q and q implies r then p implies r, or that, if all α's are β's and x is an α then x is a β. Such propositions may occur in logic, and their truth is independent of the existence of the universe. We may lay it down that, if there were no universe, *all* general propositions would be true; for the contradictory of a general proposition (as we saw in Chapter XV.) is a proposition asserting existence, and would therefore always be false if no universe existed.

Logical propositions are such as can be known *a priori*, without study of the actual world. We only know from a study of empirical facts that Socrates is a man, but we know the correctness of the syllogism in its abstract form (*i.e.* when it is stated in terms of variables) without needing any appeal to experience. This is a characteristic, not of logical propositions in themselves, but of the way in which we know them. It has, however, a bearing upon the question what their nature may be, since there are some kinds of propositions which it would be very difficult to suppose we could know without experience.

It is clear that the definition of "logic" or "mathematics" must be sought by trying to give a new definition of the old notion of "analytic" propositions. Although we can no longer be satisfied to define logical propositions as those that follow from the law of contradiction, we can and must still admit that they are a wholly different class of propositions from those that we come to know empirically. They all have the characteristic which, a moment ago, we agreed to call "tautology." This, combined with the fact that they can be expressed wholly in terms of variables and logical constants (a logical constant being something which remains constant in a proposition even when all its constituents are changed)—will give the definition of logic or pure mathematics. For the moment, I do not know how to define "tautology."[2] It would be

---

[2] The importance of "tautology" for a definition of mathematics was pointed out to me by my former pupil Ludwig Wittgenstein, who was working on the problem. I do not know whether he has solved it, or even whether he is alive or dead.

easy to offer a definition which might seem satisfactory for a while; but I know of none that I feel to be satisfactory, in spite of feeling thoroughly familiar with the characteristic of which a definition is wanted. At this point, therefore, for the moment, we reach the frontier of knowledge on our backward journey into the logical foundations of mathematics.

We have now come to an end of our somewhat summary introduction to mathematical philosophy. It is impossible to convey adequately the ideas that are concerned in this subject so long as we abstain from the use of logical symbols. Since ordinary language has no words that naturally express exactly what we wish to express, it is necessary, so long as we adhere to ordinary language, to strain words into unusual meanings; and the reader is sure, after a time if not at first, to lapse into attaching the usual meanings to words, thus arriving at wrong notions as to what is intended to be said. Moreover, ordinary grammar and syntax is extraordinarily misleading. This is the case, *e.g.*, as regards numbers; "ten men" is grammatically the same form as "white men," so that 10 might be thought to be an adjective qualifying "men." It is the case, again, wherever propositional functions are involved, and in particular as regards existence and descriptions. Because language is misleading, as well as because it is diffuse and inexact when applied to logic (for which it was never intended), logical symbolism is absolutely necessary to any exact or thorough treatment of our subject. Those readers, therefore, who wish to acquire a mastery of the principles of mathematics, will, it is to be hoped, not shrink from the labour of mastering the symbols—a labour which is, in fact, much less than might be thought. As the above hasty survey must have made evident, there are innumerable unsolved problems in the subject, and much work needs to be done. If any student is led into a serious study of mathematical logic by this little book, it will have served the chief purpose for which it has been written.

(From Bertrand Russell, *Introduction to Mathematical Philosophy.* London: Allen & Unwin. Reprinted by permission of Allen & Unwin.)

Man's Place in the Universe (from *An Outline of Philosophy*)

I want to end with a few words about man's place in the universe. It has been customary to demand of a philosopher that he should show that the world is good in certain respects. I cannot admit any duty of this sort. One might as well demand of an accountant that he should show a satisfactory balance-sheet. It is just as bad to be fraudulently optimistic in philosophy as in money matters. If the world is good, by all means let us know it; but if not, let us know that. In any case, the question of the goodness or badness of the world is one for science rather than for philosophy. We shall call the world good if it has certain characteristics that we desire. In the past philosophy professed to be able to prove that the world had such characteristics, but it is now fairly evident that the proofs were invalid. It does not, of course, follow that the world does not have the characteristics in question; it follows only that philosophy cannot decide the problem. Take for example the problem of personal immortality. You may believe this on the ground of revealed religion, but that is a ground which lies outside philosophy. You may believe it on the ground of the phenomena investigated by psychical research, but that is science, not philosophy. In former days, you could believe it on a philosophical ground, namely, that the soul is a substance and all substances are indestructible. You will find this argument, sometimes more or less disguised, in many philosophers. But the notion of substance, in the sense of permanent entity with changing states, is no longer applicable to the world. It may happen, as with the electron, that a string of events are so interconnected causally that it is practically convenient to regard them as forming one entity, but where this happens it is a scientific fact, not a metaphysical necessity. The whole question of personal immortality, therefore lies outside philosophy, and is to be decided, if at all, either by science or by revealed religion.

I will take up another matter in regard to which what I have said may have been disappointing to some readers. It is sometimes thought that philosophy ought to aim at encouraging a good life. Now, of course, I admit that it should have this effect, but I do not admit that it should have this as a conscious purpose. To begin with, when we embark upon the study of philosophy we ought not to assume that we already know for certain what the good life is; philosophy may conceivably modify our views as to what is good, in which case it will seem to the non-philosophical to have had a bad moral effect. That, however, is a secondary point. The essential thing is that philosophy is part of the pursuit of knowledge, and that we cannot limit this pursuit by insisting that the knowledge obtained shall be such as we should have thought edifying before we obtained it. I think it could be maintained with truth that *all* knowledge is edifying, provided we have a right conception of edification. When this appears to be not the case, it is because we have moral standards based upon ignorance. It may happen by good fortune that a moral standard based upon ignorance is right, but if so knowledge will not destroy it; if knowledge can destroy it, it must be wrong. The conscious purpose of philosophy, therefore, ought to be solely to *understand* the world as well as possible, not to establish this or that proposition which is thought morally desirable. Those who embark upon philosophy must be prepared to question all their preconceptions, ethical as well as scientific; if they have a determination never to surrender certain philosophic beliefs, they are not in the frame of mind in which philosophy can be profitably pursued.

But although philosophy ought not to have a moral purpose, it ought to have certain good moral effects. Any disinterested pursuit of knowledge teaches us the limits of our power, which is salutary; at the same time, in proportion as we succeed in achieving knowledge, it teaches the limits of our impotence, which is equally desirable. And philosophical knowledge, or rather philosophical thought, has certain special merits not belonging in an equal degree to other intellectual pursuits. By its generality it enables us to see human passions in their just proportions, and to realise the absurdity of many quarrels between individuals, classes, and nations. Philosophy comes as near as possible for human beings to that large, impartial contemplation of the universe as a whole which raises us for the moment above our purely personal destiny. There is a certain asceticism of the intellect which is good as a part of life, though it cannot be the whole so long as we have to remain animals engaged in the struggle for existence. The asceticism of the intellect requires that, while we are engaged in the pursuit of knowledge, we shall repress all other desires for the sake of the desire to know. While we are philosophising, the wish to prove that the world is good, or that the dogmas of this or that sect are true, must count as weaknesses of the flesh—they are temptations to be thrust on one side. But we obtain in return something of the joy which the mystic experiences in harmony with the will of God. This joy philosophy can give, but only to those who are willing to follow it to the end, through all its arduous uncertainties.

The world presented for our belief by a philosophy based upon modern science is in many ways less alien to ourselves than the world of matter as conceived in former centuries. The events that happen in our minds are part of the course of nature, and we do not know that the events which happen elsewhere are of a totally different kind. The physical world, so far as science can show at present, is perhaps less rigidly determined by causal laws than it was thought to be; one might, more or less fancifully, attribute even to the atom a kind of limited free will. There is no need to think of ourselves as powerless and small in the grip of vast cosmic forces. All measurement is conventional, and it would be possible to devise a perfectly serviceable system of measurement according to which a man would be larger than the sun. No doubt there are limits to our power, and it is good that we should recognise the fact. But we cannot say what the limits are, except in a quite abstract way, such as that we cannot create energy. From the point of view of human life, it is not important to be able to create energy; what is important is to be able to direct energy into this or that channel, and this we can do more and more as our knowledge of science increases. Since men first began to think, the forces of nature have oppressed them; earthquakes, floods, pestilences, and famines have filled them with terror. Now at last, thanks to science, mankind are discovering how to avoid much of the suffering that such events have hitherto entailed. The mood in which, as it seems to me, the modern man should face the universe is one of quiet self-respect. The universe as known to science is not in itself either friendly or hostile to man, but it can be made to act as a friend if approached with patient knowledge. Where the universe is concerned, knowledge is the one thing needful. Man, alone of living things has shown himself capable of the knowledge required to give him a certain mastery over his environment. The dangers to man in the future, or at least in any measurable future, come, not from nature, but from man himself. Will he use his power wisely? Or will he turn the energy liberated from the struggle with nature into struggles with his fellow-men? History, science, and philosophy all make us aware of the great collective achievements of mankind. It would be well if every civilised human being had a sense of these achievements and a realisation of the possibility of greater things to come, with the indifference which must result as regards the petty squabbles upon which the passions of individuals and nations are wastefully squandered.

Philosophy should make us know the ends of life, and the elements in life that have value on their own account. However our freedom may be limited in the causal sphere, we need admit no limitations to our freedom in the sphere of values: what we judge good on its own account we may continue to judge good, without regard to anything but our own feeling. Philosophy cannot itself determine the ends of life, but it can free us from the tyranny of prejudice and from distortions due to a narrow view. Love, beauty, knowledge, and joy of life: these things retain their lustre however wide our purview. And if philosophy can help us to feel the value of these things, it will have played its part in man's collective work of bringing light into a world of darkness.

(From Bertrand Russell, *An Outline of Philosophy*. London: Allen & Unwin, 1927. Reprinted by permission of Allen & Unwin.)

The Value of Philosophy (from *The Problems of Philosophy*)

Having now come to the end of our brief and very incomplete review of the problems of philosophy, it will be well to consider, in conclusion, what is the value of philosophy and why it ought to be studied. It is the more necessary to consider this question, in view of the fact that many men, under the influence of science or of practical affairs, are inclined to doubt whether philosophy is anything better than innocent but useless trifling, hair-splitting distinctions, and controversies on matters concerning which knowledge is impossible.

This view of philosophy appears to result, partly from a wrong conception of the ends of life, partly from a wrong conception of the kind of goods which philosophy strives to achieve. Physical science, through the medium of inventions, is useful to innumerable people who are wholly ignorant of it; thus the study of physical science is to be recommended, not only, or primarily, because of the effect on the student, but rather because of the effect on mankind in general. Thus utility does not belong to philosophy. If the study of philosophy has any value at all for others than students of philosophy, it must be only indirectly, through its effects upon the lives of those who study it. It is in these effects, therefore, if anywhere, that the value of philosophy must be primarily sought.

But further, if we are not to fail in our endeavour to determine the value of philosophy, we must first free our minds from the prejudices of what are wrongly called 'practical' men. The 'practical' man, as this word is often used, is one who recognizes only material needs, who realizes that men must have food for the body, but is oblivious of the necessity of providing food for the mind. If all men were well off, if poverty and disease had been reduced to their lowest possible point, there would still remain much to be done to produce a valuable society; and even in the existing world the goods of the mind are at least as important as the goods of the body. It is exclusively among the goods of the mind that the value of philosophy is to be found; and only those who are not indifferent to these goods can be persuaded that the study of philosophy is not a waste of time.

Philosophy, like all other studies, aims primarily at knowledge. The knowledge it aims at is the kind of knowledge which gives unity and system to the body of the sciences, and the kind which results from a critical examination of the grounds of our convictions, prejudices, and beliefs. But it cannot be maintained that philosophy has had any very great measure of success in its attempts to provide definite answers to its questions. If you ask a mathematician, a mineralogist, a historian, or any other man of learning, what definite body of truths has been ascertained by his science, his answer will last as long as you are willing to listen. But if you put the same question to a philosopher, he will, if he is candid, have to confess that his study has not achieved positive results such as have been achieved by other sciences. It is true that this is partly accounted for by the fact that, as soon as definite knowledge concerning any subject becomes possible, this subject ceases to be called philosophy, and becomes a separate science. The whole study of the heavens, which now belongs to astronomy, was once included in philosophy; Newton's great work was called 'the mathematical principles of natural philosophy'. Similarly, the study of the human mind, which was a part of philosophy, has now been separated from philosophy and has become the science of psychology. Thus, to a great extent, the uncertainty of philosophy is more apparent than real: those questions which are already capable of definite answers are placed in the sciences, while those only to which, at present, no definite answer can be given, remain to form the residue which is called philosophy.

This is, however, only a part of the truth concerning the uncertainty of philosophy. There are many questions—and among them those that are of the profoundest interest to our spiritual life—which, so far as we can see, must remain insoluble to the human intellect unless its powers become of quite a different order from what they are now. Has the universe any unity of plan or purpose, or is it a fortuitous concourse of atoms? Is consciousness a permanent part of the universe, giving hope of indefinite growth in wisdom, or is it a transitory accident on a small planet on which life must ultimately become impossible? Are good and evil of importance to the universe or only to man? Such questions are asked by philosophy, and variously answered by various philosophers. But it would seem that, whether answers be otherwise discoverable or not, the answers suggested by philosophy are none of them demonstrably true. Yet, however slight may be the hope of discovering an answer, it is part of the business of philosophy to continue the consideration of such questions, to make us aware of their importance, to examine all the approaches to them, and to keep alive that speculative interest in the universe which is apt to be killed by confining ourselves to definitely ascertainable knowledge.

Many philosophers, it is true, have held that philosophy could establish the truth of certain answers to such fundamental questions. They have supposed that what is of most importance in religious beliefs could be proved by strict demonstration to be true. In order to judge of such attempts, it is necessary to take a survey of human knowledge, and to form an opinion as to its methods and its limitations. On such a subject it would be unwise to pronounce dogmatically; but if the investigations of our previous chapters have not led us astray, we shall be compelled to renounce the hope of finding philosophical proofs of religious beliefs. We cannot, therefore, include as part of the value of philosophy any definite set of answers to such questions. Hence, once more, the value of philosophy must not depend upon any supposed body of definitely ascertainable knowledge to be acquired by those who study it.

The value of philosophy is, in fact, to be sought largely in its very uncertainty. The man who has no tincture of philosophy goes through life imprisoned in the prejudices derived from common sense, from the habitual beliefs of his age or his nation, and from convictions which have grown up in his mind without the co-operation or consent of his deliberate reason. To such a man the world tends to become definite, finite, obvious; common objects rouse no questions, and unfamiliar possibilities are contemptuously rejected. As soon as we begin to philosophize, on the contrary, we find, as we saw in our opening chapters, that even the most everyday things lead to problems to which only very incomplete answers can be given. Philosophy, though unable to tell us with certainty what is the true answer to the doubts which it raises, is able to suggest many possibilities which enlarge our thoughts and free them from the tyranny of custom. Thus, while diminishing our feeling of certainty as to what things are, it greatly increases our knowledge as to what they may be; it removes the somewhat arrogant dogmatism of those who have never travelled into the region of liberating doubt, and it keeps alive our sense of wonder by showing familiar things in an unfamiliar aspect.

Apart from its utility in showing unsuspected possibilities, philosophy has a value—perhaps its chief value—through the greatness of the objects which it contemplates, and the freedom from narrow and personal aims resulting from this contemplation. The life of the instinctive man is shut up within the circle of his private interests: family and friends may be included, but the outer world is not regarded except as it may help or hinder what comes within the circle of instinctive wishes. In such a life there is something feverish and confined, in comparison with which the philosophic life is calm and free. The private world of instinctive interests is a small one, set in the midst of a great and powerful world which must, sooner or later, lay our private world in ruins. Unless we can so enlarge our interests as to include the whole outer world, we remain like a garrison in a beleagured fortress, knowing that the enemy prevents escape and that ultimate surrender is inevitable. In such a life there is no peace, but a constant strife between the insistence of desire and the powerlessness of will. In one way or another, if our life is to be great and free, we must escape this prison and this strife.

One way of escape is by philosophic contemplation. Philosophic contemplation does not, in its widest survey, divide the universe into two hostile camps—friends and foes, helpful and hostile, good and bad—it views the whole impartially. Philosophic contemplation, when it is unalloyed, does not aim at proving that the rest of the universe is akin to man. All acquisition of knowledge is an enlargement of the Self, but this enlargement is best attained when it is not directly sought. It is obtained when the desire for knowledge is alone operative, by a study which does not wish in advance that its objects should have this or that character, but adapts the Self to the characters which it finds in its objects. This enlargement of Self is not obtained when, taking the Self as it is, we try to show that the world is so similar to this Self that knowledge of it is possible without any admission of what seems alien. The desire to prove this is a form of self-assertion and, like all self-assertion, it is an obstacle to the growth of Self which it desires, and of which the Self knows that it is capable. Self-assertion, in philosophic speculation as elsewhere, views the world as a means to its own ends; thus it makes the world of less account than Self, and the Self sets bounds to the greatness of its goods. In contemplation, on the contrary, we start from the not-Self, and through its greatness the boundaries of Self are enlarged; through the infinity of the universe the mind which contemplates it achieves some share in infinity.

For this reason greatness of soul is not fostered by those philosophies which assimilate the universe to Man. Knowledge is a form of union of Self and not-Self; like all union, it is impaired by dominion, and therefore by any attempt to force the universe into conformity with what we find in ourselves. There is a widespread philosophical tendency towards the view which tells us that Man is the measure of all things, that truth is man-made, that space and time and the world of universals are properties of the mind, and that, if there be anything not created by the mind, it is unknowable and of no account for us. This view, if our previous discussions were correct, is untrue; but in addition to being untrue, it has the effect of robbing philosophic contemplation of all that gives it value, since it fetters contemplation to Self. What it calls knowledge is not a union with the not-Self, but a set of prejudices, habits, and desires, making an impenetrable veil between us and the world beyond. The man who finds pleasure in such a theory of knowledge is like the man who never leaves the domestic circle for fear his word might not be law.

The true philosophic contemplation, on the contrary, finds its satisfaction in every enlargement of the not-Self, in everything that magnifies the objects contemplated, and thereby the subject contemplating. Everything, in contemplation, that is personal or private, everything that depends upon habit, self-interest, or desire, distorts the object, and hence impairs the union which the intellect seeks. By thus making a barrier between subject and object, such personal and private things become a prison to the intellect. The free intellect will see as God might see, without a *here* and *now*, without hopes and fears, without the trammels of customary beliefs and traditional prejudices, calmly, dispassionately, in the sole and exclusive desire of knowledge— knowledge as impersonal, as purely contemplative, as it is possible for man to attain. Hence also the free intellect will value more the abstract and universal knowledge into which the accidents of private history do not enter, than the knowledge brought by the senses, and dependent, as such knowledge must be, upon an exclusive and personal point of view and a body whose sense-organs distort as much as they reveal.

The mind which has become accustomed to the freedom and impartiality of philosophic contemplation will preserve something of the same freedom and impartiality in the world of action and emotion. It will view its purposes and desires as parts of the whole, with the absence of insistence that results from seeing them as infinitesimal fragments in a world of which all the rest is unaffected by any one man's deeds. The impartiality which, in contemplation, is the unalloyed desire for truth, is the very same quality of mind which, in action, is justice, and in emotion is that universal love which can be given to all, and not only to those who are judged useful or admirable. Thus contemplation enlarges not only the objects of our thoughts, but also the objects of our actions and our affections: it makes us citizens of the universe, not only of one walled city at war with all the rest. In this citizenship of the universe consists man's true freedom, and his liberation from the thraldom of narrow hopes and fears.

Thus, to sum up our discussion of the value of philosophy; Philosophy is to be studied, not for the sake of any definite answers to its questions, since no definite answers can, as a rule, be known to be true, but rather for the sake of the questions themselves; because these questions enlarge our conception of what is possible, enrich our intellectual imagination and diminish the dogmatic assurance which closes the mind against speculation; but above all because, through the greatness of the universe which philosophy contemplates, the mind also is rendered great, and becomes capable of that union with the universe which constitutes its highest good.

Review Questions

1. Explain how Russell arrived at the analysis of language as the focal point of his philosophy.
2. What is the nature of a proposition for Russell?
3. For Russell, does philosophy have any role beyond that of establishing a language for science?
4. How ought we evaluate moral action, according to Russell?
5. What relationship does Russell see between mathematics and logic?
6. What is the meaning of Russell's propositional logic?

CHAPTER 26

Ludwig Wittgenstein (1889–1951)

Introduction

Preoccupation with the problem of language in Cambridge was paralleled by a similar preoccupation in Vienna, but whereas in Cambridge the problem had a narrow setting in that it was treated by philosophers apart from the rest of the intellectual community, in Vienna the problem was considered by thinkers of diverse intellectual interests. Musicians, painters, architects, physicists, psychologists, and journalists, as well as philosophers, were all concerned with the power of language and were moved to inquire into its structure as it was employed in art, literature, and science. They tried to get inside language, inside expression, to map it from within. And so we find people like Arnold Schönberg the composer, Oskar Kokoschka the painter, Adolf Loos the architect, Ernst Mach the physicist, Karl Kraus the journalist, and Moritz Schlick the philosopher, each trying to discover the essence of expression in his own field; they were engaged in what Fritz Mauthner, the philosopher–journalist, called the "critique of language."

It is not surprising, then, that Ludwig Wittgenstein, who was thoroughly Viennese, was already caught up in the problem of language — especially the language of physics as it relates to the real world — long before he became acquainted with the work of Bertrand Russell at Cambridge.

He was born in 1889 into a family that was very much a part of the cultural life of Vienna—indeed, located at its center. Karl Wittgenstein, his father, by a combination of engineering know-how and marketing sense, developed a steel company second to none in Austria. His immense wealth enabled him to foster cultural pursuits, especially in music, so that his household became a veritable conservatory and haven for every musician in Vienna. With his father a violinist, his mother a pianist, and his older four brothers and three sisters musically or otherwise artistically talented, Ludwig was bound to play his clarinet like a virtuoso; beyond his instrumental ability, he developed a profound love of music and saw in it the epitome of nonverbal communication. From a religious point of view, though he was baptized a Roman Catholic, his heritage was Jewish, albeit for several generations of the recent past, for many reasons peculiar to central Europe, it was Jewish turned Protestant.

Educated at home until age fourteen and unattracted by a classical education, Ludwig enrolled at the _Realschule_ in Linz (just as a young student named Adolf Hitler was leaving) to study mathematics and physics. This was followed by two years of study in mechanical engineering in Berlin. In 1908 he continued his studies in engineering in England at the University of Manchester. But more and more he was being drawn to pure mathematics, and as his interests began to gravitate toward the foundations of mathematics he was directed to the work of Bertrand Russell, whose _Principles of Mathematics_ he devoured; he then decided to study with him at Cambridge in 1912–13, and was so swept up by Russell's analysis of language that in later years he occasionally referred to Russell as his "salvation." He made tremendous strides in his new undertaking and was soon able to take his own philosophical path and to discuss his ideas with Russell on equal terms.

Wittgenstein, in a situation often found among artists and intellectuals, fluctuated between a need for friendship and a need for seclusion, which reflected, on the one hand, his cheerful and sometimes charming disposition and, on the other, his depressive state of mind, which resulted in several brushes with suicide, a not uncommon situation in his family. Life was not made easier for him by his total rejection of sham and hypocrisy and his awareness that his demeanor often irritated others. At about this time, he divested himself of his portion of the fortune inherited from his father so that he could live as simple and unaffected a life as possible. A crude hut on a remote farm in Norway was congenial to his spirit, and for a time he lived there enjoying the leisure he required to work out his thoughts.

But it was not long before World War I broke out, and Wittgenstein volunteered for the Austrian army and served on the eastern front. Wherever he went he backpacked his notebooks, and from a prison camp in Italy in 1918 he completed the manuscript for the first of the two books on which his reputation rests, the _Tractatus Logico-Philosophicus_.

When the only publisher to whom he submitted the manuscript rejected it, he sent it off to Russell and, in characteristic style, told him to do whatever he wanted with it; yet when Russell offered to present it publicly with his own introduction, Wittgenstein demurred because he now had misgivings as to whether Russell really understood his main ideas. Nevertheless, it was published, first in German in 1921 and then in English/German a year later, with Russell's introduction.

The *Tractatus*, an "important event in the philosophical world," as Russell called it, is stylistically like its author — lean and reclusive; its terse, laconic form is reminiscent of Heraclitus, but its tight, mathematical-logical shape is reminiscent of Spinoza. It is a series of propositions that are the result of Wittgenstein's thinking, but the working out of the propositions, the explanation, was never put into writing except in the notebooks, previously mentioned, which he kept with him at all times and which, for the most part, were destroyed on his orders. As a result, students are forced to think through the problems for themselves and, in a sense, to retrace the steps the author himself had taken.

In the preface, Wittgenstein tells us that he is going to deal with the problems of philosophy; the reason why there are problems in the first place is that "the logic of our language is misunderstood." So, clarification of language is his main purpose and is formulated in words that have become well known: "what can be said at all can be said clearly."

Let us recall that criticism has been the concern of epistemology since Locke, and that, since Kant, the very term *critique* has meant "the exploration of the limits of"; for example, the critique of pure reason announces Kant's inquiry into the limits of that faculty. Wittgenstein, attempting a critique of language, has a similar goal in the *Tractatus*, that is, to draw a *limit to language* as the expression of thought. If such a limit can be drawn, then what lies within that limit is "sense" and what lies "on the other side of the limit" is "nonsense."

The vehicle of expression in the *Tractatus* is the *proposition*, which, as Wittgenstein puts it, is a statement of fact, and the totality of propositions — how they relate to facts and how they are interrelated among themselves — constitutes language. *How* a proposition relates to facts (i.e., combinations of things in reality, or a "state of affairs") is the key question. Wittgenstein's response to this question is that a proposition is a "picture" of reality, a "picture" of the fact it is destined to stand for, or symbolize. He did not use *picture* in the sense of a duplicate of reality, as might be found in a photograph, diagram, sketch, or image; yet there must be something in common—a kind of literalness—between the picture and the fact: "There must be something identical in a picture and what it depicts, to enable the one to be a picture of the other at all." Perhaps a better word for *picture* (*Bild*) is simply *representation*, which allows for a departure from literalness in how a fact is modeled by us in forming a proposition, while holding to a certain determinateness in the way a verbal picture actually represents: "The fact that the elements of a picture are related to one another in a determinate way represents that things are related to one another in the same way."

A discernible pattern in the way we use words enables language to be rendered in abstract form, thus making it possible to see more clearly what relationships occur among constituents of a proposition and among propositions themselves — the idea of *propositional logic*, for which Wittgenstein was indebted to Bertrand Russell. Wittgenstein then inventories *all* of the imaginable connections propositions can have: to reality, to thought, to possible states of affairs; within themselves, and to each other; and the connections they must have to be designated as true or false, meaningful or meaningless, or tautological. This inventory would reveal all the ways in which we can actually *say* something or the ways in which we can *possibly* say something. And if, as previously suggested, a proposition stands midway between thought and reality, then clarifying propositions is also clarifying thought, for "a thought is a proposition with a sense," to which Wittgenstein adds his own comment that philosophy itself is an activity that "aims at the logical clarification of thought."

Two clarifications stand out as basic to Wittgenstein's project. First, propositions are true or false and sensical or nonsensical. A proposition is true if things are the way a proposition says they are; if not, it is false: "A proposition can be true or false only in virtue of being a picture of reality." That is, a proposition, as a picture, is "attached to reality; it reaches right out to it" and "is laid against reality like a measure." Second, a proposition is sensical (has sense, makes sense) if it logically holds together and depicts a possible state of affairs; otherwise it is nonsensical (has no sense, makes no sense, is nonsense).

The tone of these distinctions is typical of much the *Tractatus* because propositions, or thoughts, or indeed knowledge appear to be concerned solely with physical reality, without allowing a viable option for the metaphysical. Statements like "The totality of true propositions is the whole of natural science" and "Superstition is nothing but belief in the causal nexus" lend some plausibility to this view, at least in the minds of the Viennese logical positivists, who regarded philosophy's role as the analysis of scientific statements in which the metaphysical had no part; indeed, when the *Tractatus* was first issued, some of them felt that they had finally found their long-sought manual of operation.

Wittgenstein, always afraid of being misunderstood or misrepresented, took pains to distance himself from this narrow interpretation of his work, and the reason why he did so is to be found in a closer look at the *Tractatus* itself. Wittgenstein consistently made the distinction between what can be *shown* and what can be *said*; the entire book is built around it. What can be said is what can be formulated in propositions, that is, what can be pictured or represented in verbal signs. However, what can be shown can never be said because it lies outside the domain of the picturable or representable. It is quite possible, then, for us to lay hold of, to "feel," to grasp, or simply to know things that cannot be said, but that show themselves: values in general, ethical values in particular, the meaning of life, soul, God — these are among the things that "cannot be put into words. They *make themselves manifest*. They are what is mystical."

The distinction between "show" and "say" shares a common thread with similar distinctions made before Wittgenstein, such as that between "to know" and "to postulate," to know through "proof" and to know through "self-evidence," to "demonstrate" and to "intuit," but in Wittgenstein's case, though it was there all along, the distinction comes with surprising force at the end of the treatise. He himself seems to have preferred the word *mystical* to refer to the domain of what cannot be shown, the nonsensical domain, and in this he is followed by Russell; others, not at all in disagreement, prefer to call the *Tractatus* a "metaphysical" or even an "ethical" work. However it is styled, its transcendental intent is clear, and the fact that "The solution of the riddle of life in space and time lies *outside* space and time" is the foundation for the remarkable conclusion to the *Tractatus*: "My propositions serve as elucidations in the following way: anyone who understands me eventually recognizes them as nonsensical, when he has used them — as steps — to climb up beyond them. (He must, so to speak, throw away the ladder after he has climbed up it.) He must transcend these propositions, and then he will see the world aright." And the very last proposition, standing there without comment, not only summarizes the book but also states the agenda operative from the outset: "What we cannot speak of we must pass over in silence."

With the *Tractatus* behind him, Wittgenstein, believing he had solved the problems of philosophy by drawing the limits of language, turned to other pursuits — pursuits that fitted his unpretentious nature and his idea of the simpleness of truly human things. He was a schoolteacher for several years in Austria, having as his charges youngsters aged nine to ten. Later, after being dissuaded by the abbot of a monastery near Vienna from becoming a monk, he served as a gardener in the monastery for a time. Meanwhile, he designed a house for one of his sisters, did some sculpting, and occasionally carried on philosophical conversations with Moritz Schlick and Friedrich Waismann.

In 1929 Wittgenstein returned to Cambridge, was awarded a doctorate on the strength of the *Tractatus*, gave lectures from 1930 to 1936, repaired for a year to his retreat in Norway, and in 1937 succeeded G. E. Moore in the chair of philosophy. He never took to the formalities of academic life and withdrew from them whenever he could. He would teach mainly in his own rooms, using no notes, and would proceed, not so much as though he were teaching, but rather "philosophizing" aloud, trying to create something new with each lecture. Between this period and the time of his death, he wrote or dictated extensively; though much of what he put down was circulated among his students, he expressly forbade the publication of his works, at least during his lifetime.

When World War II broke out, he worked as a hospital orderly and laboratory assistant. He taught at Cambridge for several more years, but in 1947 he resigned his chair and went into seclusion in Ireland. Here he tried to rework his manuscripts, but gave up his hope of reorganizing them into a whole with which he was satisfied.

The book he so struggled with appeared under the title of *Philosophical Investigations* in 1953, two years after his death; it brought together the thoughts that had occupied him for sixteen years: "the concepts of meaning, of understanding, of a proposition, of logic, the foundation of mathematics, states of consciousness, and other things." It is written in his idiosyncratic style, but is far less laconic than the *Tractatus*, and full of analogies, stories, and life situations. It is an assemblage of "remarks," or an album of "sketches of landscapes" made in the course of the long and involved journeys of thought.

During the years after the *Tractatus*, Wittgenstein was becoming gradually disenchanted with the notion of picture, which had been its mainstay, as well as with its severe logical demands. Reminiscent of the frankness displayed toward his early works by St. Augustine — the first author quoted in *Philosophical Investigations* — Wittgenstein writes, "I have been forced to recognize grave mistakes in what I wrote" in the *Tractatus*. That his mistakes were grave may not be anyone else's judgment, but it was certainly his. A key to his changing mood was given in an observation he made to Waismann in 1932: "I used to think that there was a direct link between Language and Reality." Wittgenstein highlights his new direction by a quotation from the *Confessions* in which St. Augustine describes his efforts as a child to reproduce the sounds repeatedly made by his parents to designate an object, and "I gradually learnt to understand what objects they signified." On reflection, Wittgenstein comments that Augustine is describing only *one* system of communication, but "not everything we call language is this system." So, Wittgenstein is not rejecting pictorial representation entirely, merely limiting it to one use of language.

There are, then, *many other* uses of language — ordinary language put to human use, so that meanings come from the way expressions are used in real-life situations. This view was already adumbrated in the *Tractatus* when Wittgenstein observed that "The tacit conventions on which the understanding of everyday language depends are enormously complicated." The whole of language cannot therefore be discovered in any one proposition, as maintained in the *Tractatus*, but rather in the pluralism of uses discovered in the social settings of mankind, in tribal and cultural and scientific milieus, in jobs to be done, in the simple and everyday demands of language, and in psychological contexts. The refrain is found throughout the *Philosophical Investigations* that "the meaning of a word is its use in the language." Alternatively, as another method of reaching the same goal, Wittgenstein tells us to see his remarks in the light of anthropology, "as remarks in the natural history of human beings"; or more specifically, "Commanding, questioning, recounting, chatting, are as much a part of our natural history as walking, eating, drinking, playing."

The analogy that most recommends itself to Wittgenstein to cover his new concept of language comes from his insight into the way we play games, and is therefore referred to simply as the idea of *language-games*. The shift from the *Tractatus* to the *Philosophical Investigations* is a shift from the picture notion of language to the use notion of language. A game, in Wittgenstein's explanation, is played according to the rules, yet the rules change from one kind of game to another. Given an indefinite number of games, there is also an indefinite number of rules to be used, for every game is played according to its own rules, and it becomes difficult, if not impossible, to settle on a common denominator identifying all of these activities as games, which indeed they are. Some games feature competition, others do not; some are amusing, others are not; some require skill, others do not; some are played by one person, others are not. In Wittgenstein's own words: "Consider for example the proceedings that we call 'games'. I mean board-games, card-games, ball-games, Olympic games, and so on. What is common to them all? — Don't say: "There *must* be something common, or they would not be called 'games' " — but *look and see* whether there is anything common to all. — For if you look at them you will not see something that is common to *all*, but similarities, relationships, and a whole series of them at that."

Given that nothing can be stated as common to all games, there are still similarities that "overlap" and "criss-cross"; from these Wittgenstein develops the notion of *family resemblances*: "I can think of no better expression to characterize these similarities than 'family resemblances'; for the various resemblances between members of a family: build, features, colour of eyes, gait, temperament, etc. etc. overlap and criss-cross in the same way. — And I shall say: "games" form a family." So with language. There are so many different life situations in which language is used, and used differently in each case, that the rules of language vary with each life event just as the rules of the game vary with each game event: language is a family too.

In certain ways, the *Tractatus* and the *Philosophical Investigations* are markedly different works, moving as they do from the pictorial to the descriptive, from logical atomism to linguistic pluralism. The rational certainty the mathematician-logician finds in matching pieces exactly is surrendered to the excitement of discovery the psychologist-anthropologist finds in the unshaped ways of human living. In his later book, Wittgenstein came close to adopting a position in language criticism, that of Mauthner, which he had rejected in the earlier one.

Despite the differences, there is a continuity between the earlier and the later Wittgenstein. Language is still his main concern, and the limits of language — the critique of language — is still his main goal. The work of philosophy remains constant throughout; it is, in the words of the later book, the "battle against the bewitchment of our intelligence by means of language"; it is the seeking of clarity — to show "the fly the way out of the fly-bottle."

But underlying it all is Wittgenstein's commitment to life, a commitment seen in and through himself, not unlike what he found in Kierkegaard's individualism. In his works he tried to secure the claims of the unsayable against the sayable; he kept value separate from fact, so that the meaning of life for him cannot be discovered in the realm of the rational, the scientific, or the fact-bound world — and yet it can be discovered, which is precisely what we must be "silent" about. This attitude can be summed up in the final words of a lecture on ethics Wittgenstein gave to a Cambridge society in 1929–30: "My whole tendency and I believe the tendency of all men who ever tried to write or talk on Ethics or Religion was to run against the boundaries of language. This running against the walls of our cage is perfectly, absolutely hopeless. Ethics so far as it springs from the desire to say something about the ultimate meaning of life, the absolute good, the absolute value, can be no science. What it says does not add to our knowledge in any sense. But it is a document of a tendency in the human mind which I personally cannot help respecting deeply and I would not for my life ridicule it."

Although his influence is presently declining, it is understandable why Wittgenstein, having given the philosophy of language a decisive turn, was the vogue for a generation after the appearance of *Philosophical Investigations* and why he will be remembered as one of the dominant voices of the twentieth century.

Readings

Preface to Tractatus Logico-Philosophicus

Perhaps this book will be understood only by someone who has himself already had the thoughts that are expressed in it—or at least similar thoughts.—So it is not a textbook.—Its purpose would be achieved if it gave pleasure to one person who read and understood it.

The book deals with the problems of philosophy, and shows, I believe, that the reason why these problems are posed is that the logic of our language is misunderstood. The whole sense of the book might be summed up in the following words: what can be said at all can be said clearly, and what we cannot talk about we must pass over in silence.

Thus the aim of the book is to draw a limit to thought, or rather—not to thought, but to the expression of thoughts: for in order to be able to draw a limit to thought, we should have to find both sides of the limit thinkable (i.e. we should have to be able to think what cannot be thought).

It will therefore only be in language that the limit can be drawn, and what lies on the other side of the limit will simply be nonsense.

I do not wish to judge how far my efforts coincide with those of other philosophers. Indeed, what I have written here makes no claim to novelty in detail, and the reason why I give no sources is that it is a matter of indifference to me whether the thoughts that I have had have been anticipated by someone else.

I will only mention that I am indebted to Frege's great works and to the writings of my friend Mr Bertrand Russell for much of the stimulation of my thoughts.

If this work has any value, it consists in two things: the first is that thoughts are expressed in it, and on this score the better the thoughts are expressed—the more the nail has been hit on the head—the greater will be its value.—Here I am conscious of having fallen a long way short of what is possible. Simply because my powers are too slight for the accomplishment of the task.—May others come and do it better.

On the other hand the *truth* of the thoughts that are here communicated seems to me unassailable and definitive. I therefore believe myself to have found, on all essential points, the final solution of the problems. And if I am not mistaken in this belief, then the second thing in which the value of this work consists is that it shows how little is achieved when these problems are solved.

Language as Picture (from *Tractatus Logico-Philosophicus*)

1*   The world is all that case.

1.1   The world is the totality of facts, not of things.

---

*The decimal numbers assigned to the individual propositions indicate the logical importance of the propositions, the stress laid on them in my exposition. The propositions $n.1$, $n.2$, $n.3$, etc. are comments on proposition no. n; the propositions $n.m1$, $n.m2$, etc. are comments on proposition no. $n.m$; and so on.

1.11   The world is determined by the facts, and by their being *all* the facts.

1.12   totality of facts determines what is the case, and also whatever is not the case.

1.13   The facts in logical space are the world.

1.2   The world divides into facts.

1.21   Each item can be the case or not the case while everything else remains the same.

2   What is the case—a fact—is the existence of states of affairs.

2.01   A state of affairs (a state of things) is a combination of objects (things).

2.011   It is essential to things that they should be possible constituents of states of affairs.

2.012   In logic nothing is accidental: if a thing can occur in a state of affairs, the possibility of the state of affairs must be written into the thing itself.

2.0121   It would seem to be a sort of accident, if it turned out that a situation would fit a thing that could already exist entirely on its own.

 If things can occur in states of affairs, this possibility must be in them from the beginning.

 (Nothing in the province of logic can be merely possible. Logic deals with every possibility and all possibilities are its facts.)

 Just as we are quite unable to imagine spatial objects outside space or temporal objects outside time, so too there is no object that we can imagine excluded from the possibility of combining with others.

 If I can imagine objects combined in states of affairs, I cannot imagine them excluded from the *possibility* of such combinations.

2.0122   Things are independent in so far as they can occur in all *possible* situations, but this form of independence is a form of connexion with states of affairs, a form of dependence. (It is impossible for words to appear in two different roles: by themselves, and in propositions.)

2.0123   If I know an object I also know all its possible occurrences in states of affairs.

 (Every one of these possibilities must be part of the nature of the object.)

 A new possibility cannot be discovered later.

2.01231   If I am to know an object, though I need not know its external properties, I must know all its internal properties.

2.0124   If all objects are given, then at the same time all *possible* states of affairs are also given.

2.013   Each thing is, as it were, in a space of possible states of affairs. This space I can imagine empty, but I cannot imagine the thing without the space.

2.0131   A spatial object must be situated in infinite space. (A spatial point is an argument-place.)

A speck in the visual field, though it need not be red, must have some colour: it is, so to speak, surrounded by colour-space. Notes must have *some* pitch, objects of the sense of touch *some* degree of hardness, and so on.

2.014   Objects contain the possibility of all situations.

2.0141   The possibility of its occurring in states of affairs is the form of an object.

2.02   Objects are simple.

2.0201   Every statement about complexes can be resolved into a statement about their constituents and into the propositions that describe the complexes completely.

2.021   Objects make up the substance of the world. That is why they cannot be composite.

2.0211   If the world had no substance, then whether a proposition had sense would depend on whether another proposition was true.

2.0212   In that case we could not sketch any picture of the world (true or false).

2.022   It is obvious that an imagined world, however different it may be from the real one, must have *something*—a form—in common with it.

2.023   Objects are just what constitute this unalterable form.

2.0231   The substance of the world *can* only determine a form, and not any material properties. For it is only by means of propositions that material properties are represented—only by the configuration of objects that they are produced.

2.0232   In a manner of speaking, objects are colourless.

2.0233   If two objects have the same logical form, the only distinction between them, apart from their external properties, is that they are different.

2.02331 Either a thing has properties that nothing else has, in which case we can immediately use a description to distinguish it from the others and refer to it; or, on the other hand, there are several things that have the whole set of their properties in common, in which case it is quite impossible to indicate one of them.

For if there is nothing to distinguish a thing, I cannot distinguish it, since otherwise it would be distinguished after all.

2.024   Substance is what subsists independently of what is the case.

2.025   It is form and content.

2.0251   Space, time, and colour (being coloured) are forms of objects.

2.026   There must be objects, if the world is to have an unalterable form.

2.027   Objects, the unalterable, and the subsistent are one and the same.

2.0271   Objects are what is unalterable and subsistent; their configuration is what is changing and unstable.

2.0272   The configuration of objects produces states of affairs.

2.03   In a state of affairs objects fit into one another like the links of a chain.

2.031   In a state of affairs objects stand in a determinate relation to one another.

2.032   The determinate way in which objects are connected in a state of affairs is the structure of the state of affairs.

2.033   Form is the possibility of structure.

2.034   The structure of a fact consists of the structures of states of affairs.

2.04   The totality of existing states of affairs is the world.

2.05   The totality of existing states of affairs also determines which states of affairs do not exist.

2.06   The existence and non-existence of states of affairs is reality. (We also call the existence of states of affairs a positive fact, and their non-existence a negative fact.)

2.061   States of affairs are independent of one another.

2.062   From the existence or non-existence of one state of affairs it is impossible to infer the existence or non-existence of another.

2.063   The sum-total of reality is the world.

2.1   We picture facts to ourselves.

2.11   A picture presents a situation in logical space, the existence and non-existence of states of affairs.

2.12   A picture is a model of reality.

2.13   In a picture objects have the elements of the picture corresponding to them.

2.131   In a picture the elements of the picture are the representatives of objects.

2.14   What constitutes a picture is that its elements are related to one another in a determinate way.

2.141   A picture is a fact.

2.15   The fact that the elements of a picture are related to one another in a determinate way represents that things are related to one another in the same way.

           Let us call this connexion of its elements the structure of the picture, and let us call the possibility of this structure the pictorial form of the picture.

2.151   Pictorial form is the possibility that things are related to one another in the same way as the elements of the picture.

2.1511   *That* is how a picture is attached to reality; it reaches right out to it.

2.1512   It is laid against reality like a measure.

2.15121   Only the end-points of the graduating lines actually *touch* the object that is to be measured.

2.1513   So a picture, conceived in this way, also includes the pictorial relationship, which makes it into a picture.

2.1514   The pictorial relationship consists of the correlations of the picture's elements with things.

2.1515   These correlations are, as it were, the feelers of the picture's elements, with which the picture touches reality.

2.16   If a fact is to be a picture, it must have something in common with what it depicts.

2.161   There must be something identical in a picture and what it depicts, to enable the one to be a picture of the other at all.

2.17   What a picture must have in common with reality, in order to be able to depict it—correctly or incorrectly—in the way it does, is its pictorial form.

2.171   A picture can depict any reality whose form it has.

A spatial picture can depict anything spatial, a coloured one anything coloured, etc.

2.172   A picture cannot, however, depict its pictorial form: it displays it.

2.173   A picture represents its subject from a position outside it. (Its standpoint is its representational form.) That is why a picture represents its subject correctly or incorrectly.

2.174   A picture cannot, however, place itself outside its representational form.

2.18   What any picture, of whatever form, must have in common with reality, in order to be able to depict it—correctly or incorrectly—in any way at all, is logical form, i.e. the form of reality.

2.181   A picture whose pictorial form is logical form is called a logical picture.

2.182   Every picture is *at the same time* a logical one. (On the other hand, not every picture is, for example, a spatial one.)

2.19   Logical pictures can depict the world.

2.2   A picture has logico-pictorial form in common with what it depicts.

2.201   A picture depicts reality by representing a possibility of existence and non-existence of states of affairs.

2.202   A picture represents a possible situation in logical space.

2.203   A picture contains the possibility of the situation that that it represents.

2.21   A picture agrees with reality or fails to agree; it is correct or incorrect, true or false.

2.22   What a picture represents it represents independently of its truth or falsity, by means of its pictorial form.

2.221   What a picture represents is its sense.

2.222   The agreement or disagreement of its sense with reality constitutes its truth or falsity.

2.223   In order to tell whether a picture is true or false we must compare it with reality.

2.224   It is impossible to tell from the picture alone whether it is true or false.

2.225   There are no pictures that are true a priori.

3   A logical picture of facts is a thought.

3.001   'A state of affairs is thinkable': what this means is that we can picture it to ourselves.

3.01   The totality of true thoughts is a picture of the world.

3.02   A thought contains the possibility of the situation of which it is the thought. What is thinkable is possible too.

3.03   Thought can never be of anything illogical, since, if it were, we should have to think illogically.

3.031   It used to be said that God could create anything except what would be contrary to the laws of logic.—The truth is that we could not *say* what an 'illogical' world would look like.

3.032   It is as impossible to represent in language anything that 'contradicts logic' as it is in geometry to represent by its co-ordinates a figure that contradicts the laws of space, or to give the co-ordinates of a point that does not exist.

3.0321 Though a state of affairs that would contravene the laws of physics can be represented by us spatially, one that would contravene the laws of geometry cannot.

3.04   If a thought were correct a priori, it would be a thought whose possibility ensured its truth.

3.05   A priori knowledge that a thought was true would be possible only if its truth were recognizable from the thought itself (without anything to compare it with).

3.1   In a proposition a thought finds an expression that can be perceived by the senses.

3.11   We use the perceptible sign of a proposition (spoken or written, etc.) as a projection of a possible situation.

        The method of projection is to think of the sense of the proposition.

3.12   I call the sign with which we express a thought a propositional sign.—And a proposition is a propositional sign in its projective relation to the world.

3.13   A proposition includes all that the projection includes, but not what is projected.

Therefore, though what is projected is not itself included, its possibility is.

A proposition, therefore, does not actually contain its sense, but does contain the possibility of expressing it.

('The content of a proposition' means the content of a proposition that has sense.)

A proposition contains the form, but not the content, of its sense.

3.14   What constitutes a propositional sign is that in it its elements (the words) stand in a determinate relation to one another.

A propositional sign is a fact.

3.141   A proposition is not a blend of words.—(Just as a theme in music is not a blend of notes.)

A propositional is articulate.

3.142   Only facts can express a sense, a set of names cannot.

3.143   Although a propositional sign is a fact, this is obscured by the usual form of expression in writing or print.

For in a printed proposition, for example, no essential difference is apparent between a propositional sign and a word.

(That is what made it possible for Frege to call a proposition a composite name.)

3.1431   The essence of a propositional sign is very clearly seen if we imagine one composed of spatial objects (such as tables, chairs, and books) instead of written signs.

Then the spatial arrangement of these things will express the sense of the proposition.

Beyond the Limits of Language (From *Tractatus Logico-Philosophicus*)

6.4   All propositions are of equal value.

6.41   The sense of the world must lie outside the world. In the world everything is as it is, and everything happens as it does happen: *in* it no value exists—and if it did exist, it would have no value.

If there is any value that does have value, it must lie outside the whole sphere of what happens and is the case. For all that happens and is the case is accidental.

What makes it non-accidental cannot lie *within* the world, since if it did it would itself be accidental.

It must lie outside the world.

6.42 So too it is impossible for there to be propositions of ethics. Propositions can express nothing that is higher.

6.421 It is clear that ethics cannot be put into words.

Ethics is transcendental.

(Ethics and aesthetics are one and the same.)

6.422 When an ethical law of the form, 'Thou shalt . . .', is laid down, one's first thought is, 'And what if I do not do it?' It is clear, however, that ethics has nothing to do with punishment and reward in the usual sense of the terms. So our question about the *consequences* of an action must be unimportant.—At least those consequences should not be events. For there must be something right about the question we posed. There must indeed be some kind of ethical reward and ethical punishment, but they must reside in the action itself.

(And it is also clear that the reward must be something pleasant and the punishment something unpleasant.)

6.423 It is impossible to speak about the will in so far as it is the subject of ethical attributes.

And the will as a phenomenon is of interest only to psychology.

6.43 If the good or bad exercise of the will does alter the world, it can alter only the limits of the world, not the facts—not what can be expressed by means of language.

In short the effect must be that it becomes an altogether different world. It must, so to speak, wax and wane as a whole.

The world of the happy man is a different one from that of the unhappy man.

6.431 So too at death the world does not alter, but comes to an end.

6.4311 Death is not an event in life: we do not live to experience death.

If we take eternity to mean not infinite temporal duration but timelessness, then eternal life belongs to those who live in the present.

Our life has no end in just the way in which our visual field has no limits.

6.4312 Not only is there no guarantee of the temporal immortality of the human soul, that is to say of its eternal survival after death; but, in any case, this assumption completely fails to accomplish the purpose for which it has always been intended. Or is some riddle solved by my surviving for ever? Is not this eternal life itself as much of a riddle as our present life? The solution of the riddle of life in space and time lies *outside* space and time.

(It is certainly not the solution of any problems of natural science that is required.)

6.432   *How* things are in the world is a matter of complete indiffer for what is higher. God does not reveal himself *in* the world.

6.4321   The facts all contribute only to setting the problem, not to its solution.

6.44   It is not *how* things are in the world that is mystical, but *that* it exists.

6.45   To view the world sub specie aeterni is to view it as a whole —a limited whole.

Feeling the world as a limited whole—it is this that is mystical.

6.5   When the answer cannot be put into words, neither can the question be put into words.

The riddle does not exist.

If a question can be framed at all, it is also *possible* to answer it.

6.51   Scepticism is *not* irrefutable, but obviously nonsensical when it tries to raise doubts where no questions can be asked.

For doubt can exist only where a question exists, a question only where an answer exists, and an answer only where something *can be said*.

6.52   We feel that even when all *possible* scientific questions have been answered, the problems of life remain completely untouched. Of course there are then no questions left, and this itself is the answer.

6.521   The solution of the problem of life is seen in the vanishing of the problem.

(Is not this the reason why those who have found after a long period of doubt that the sense of life became clear to them have then been unable to say what constituted that sense?)

6.522   There are, indeed, things that cannot be put into words. They *make themselves manifest*. They are what is mystical.

6.53   The correct method in philosophy would really be the following: to say nothing except what can be said, i.e. propositions of natural science—i.e. something that has nothing to do with philosophy—and then, whenever someone else wanted to say something metaphysical, to demonstrate to him that he had failed to give a meaning to certain signs in his propositions. Although it would not be satisfying to the other person—he would not have the feeling that we were teaching him philosophy—*this* method would be the only strictly correct one.

6.54   My propositions serve as elucidations in the following way: anyone who understands me eventually recognizes them as non-sensical, when he has used them—as steps—to climb up beyond them. (He must, so to speak, throw away the ladder after he has climbed up it.)

He must transcend these propositions, and then he will see the world aright.

7   What we cannot speak about we must pass over in silence.

(From *Tractatus Logico-Philosopicus*. Trans. by D. F. Pears and B. F. Mc-Guiness. London: Routledge & Regan Paul PLC, 1972. New York: Humanities Press, 1972. Reprinted by permission of Routledge & Regan Paul.)

Language as Language-Games (from *Philosophical Investigations*)

65. Here we come up against the great question that lies behind all these considerations.—For someone might object against me: "You take the easy way out! You talk about all sorts of language-games, but have nowhere said that the essence of a language-game, and hence of language, is: what is common to all these activities, and what makes them into language or parts of language. So you let yourself off the very part of the investigation that once gave you yourself most head-ache, the part about the *general form of propositions and of language.*"

And this is true.—Instead of producing something common to all that we call language, I am saying that these phenomena have no one thing in common which makes us use the same word for all,—but that they are *related* to one another in many different ways. And it is because of this relationship, or these relationships, that we call them all "language." I will try to explain this.

66. Consider for example the proceedings that we call "games". I mean board-games, card-games, ball-games, Olympic games, and so on. What is common to them all?—Don't say: "There *must* be something common, or they would not be called 'games'"—but *look and see* whether there is anything common to all.—For if you look at them you will not see something that is common to *all*, but similarities, relation-ships, and a whole series of them at that. To repeat: don't think, but look!—Look for example at board-games, with their multifarious rela-tionships. Now pass to card-games; here you find many correspon-dences with the first group, but many common features drop out, and others appear. When we pass next to ball-games, much that is common is retained, but much is lost.—Are they all 'amusing'? Compare chess with noughts and crosses. Or is there always winning and losing, or competition between players? Think of patience. In ball games there

is winning and losing; but when a child throws his ball at the wall and catches it again, this feature has disappeared. Look at the parts played by skill and luck; and at the difference between skill in chess and skill in tennis. Think now of games like ring-a-ring-a-roses; here is the element of amusement, but how many other characteristic features have disappeared! And we can go through the many, many other groups of games in the same way; can see how similarities crop up and disappear.

And the result of this examination is: we see a complicated network of similarities overlapping and criss-crossing: sometimes overall similarities, sometimes similarities of detail.

67. I can think of no better expression to characterize these similarities than "family resemblances"; for the various resemblances between members of a family: build, features, colour of eyes, gait, temperament, etc. etc. overlap and criss-cross in the same way.—And I shall say: 'games' form a family.

And for instance the kinds of number form a family in the same way. Why do we call something a "number"? Well, perhaps because it has a—direct—relationship with several things that have hitherto been called number; and this can be said to give it an indirect relationship to other things we call the same name. And we extend our concept of number as in spinning a thread we twist fibre on fibre. And the strength of the thread does not reside in the fact that some one fibre runs through its whole length, but in the overlapping of many fibres.

But if someone wished to say: "There is something common to all these constructions—namely the disjunction of all their common properties"—I should reply: Now you are only playing with words. One might as well say: "Something runs through the whole thread—namely the continuous overlapping of those fibres".

68. "All right: the concept of number is defined for you as the logical sum of these individual interrelated concepts: cardinal numbers, rational numbers, real numbers, etc.; and in the same way the concept of a game as the logical sum of a corresponding set of sub-concepts."—It need not be so. For I *can* give the concept 'number' rigid limits in this way, that is, use the word "number" for a rigidly limited concept, but I can also use it so that the extension of the concept is *not* closed by a frontier. And this is how we do use the word "game". For how is the concept of a game bounded? What still counts as a game and what no longer does? Can you give the boundary? No. You can *draw* one; for none has so far been drawn. (But that never troubled you before when you used the word "game".)

"But when the use of the word is unregulated, the 'game' we play with it is unregulated."—It is not everywhere circumscribed by rules; but no more are there any rules for how high one throws the ball in tennis, or how hard; yet tennis is a game for all that and has rules too.

69. How should we explain to someone what a game is? I imagine that we should describe *games* to him, and we might add: "This *and similar things* are called 'games'." And do we know any more about it ourselves? Is it only other people whom we cannot tell exactly what a game is?—But this is not ignorance. We do not know the boundaries because none have been drawn. To repeat, we can draw a boundary—for a special purpose. Does it take that to make the concept usable? Not at all! (Except for that special purpose.) No more than it took the definition: 1 pace = 75 cm. to make the measure of length 'one pace' usable. And if you want to say "But still, before that it wasn't an exact measure", then I reply: very well, it was an inexact one.—Though you still owe me a definition of exactness.

70. "But if the concept 'game' is uncircumscribed like that, you don't really know what you mean by a 'game'."—When I give the description: "The ground was quite covered with plants"—do you want to say I don't know what I am talking about until I can give a definition of a plant?

My meaning would be explained by, say, a drawing and the words "The ground looked roughly like this." Perhaps I even say "it looked *exactly* like this."—Then were just *this* grass and *these* leaves there, arranged just like this? No, that is not what it means. And I should not accept any picture as exact in *this* sense.

Someone says to me: "Shew the children a game." I teach them gaming with dice, and the other says "I didn't mean that sort of game." Must the exclusion of the game with dice have come before his mind when he gave me the order? (Note added by Wittgenstein — ed.)

---

71. One might say that the concept 'game' is a concept with blurred edges.—"But is a blurred concept a concept at all?"—Is an indistinct photograph a picture of a person at all? Is it even always an advantage to replace an indistinct picture by a sharp one? Isn't the indistinct one often exactly what we need?

Frege compares a concept to an area and says that an area with vague boundaries cannot be called an area at all. This presumably means that we cannot do anything with it.—But is it senseless to say: "Stand roughly there"? Suppose that I were standing with someone in a city square and said that. As I say it I do not draw any kind of boundary, but perhaps point with my hand—as if I were indicating a particular *spot*. And this is just how one might explain to someone what a game is. One gives examples and intends them to be taken in a particular way.—I do not, however, mean by this that he is supposed to see in those examples that common thing which I—for some reason—was unable to express; but that he is now to *employ* those examples in a particular way. Here giving examples is not an *indirect* means of explaining—in default of a better. For any general definition can be misunderstood too. The point is that *this* is how we play the game. (I mean the language-game with the word "game".)

72. *Seeing what is common.* Suppose I shew someone various multi-colour pictures, and say: "The colour you see in all these is called 'yellow ochre'."—This is a definition, and the other will get to understand it by looking for and seeing what is common to the pictures. Then he can look *at*, can point *to*, the common thing.

Compare with this a case in which I shew him figures of different shapes all painted the same colour, and say: "What these have in common is called 'yellow ochre'."

And compare this case: I shew him samples of different shades of blue and say: "The colour that is common to all these is what I call 'blue'."

73. When someone defines the names of colours for me by pointing to samples and saying "This colour is called 'blue', this 'green' . . . " this case can be compared in many respects to putting a table in my hands, with the words written under the colour-samples.—Though this comparison may mislead in many ways.—One is now inclined to extend the comparison: to have understood the definition means to have in one's mind an idea of the thing defined, and that is a sample or picture. So if I am shewn various different leaves and told "This is called a 'leaf'," I get an idea of the shape of a leaf, a picture of it in my mind. —But what does the picture of a leaf look like when it does not shew us any particular shape, but 'what is common to all shapes of leaf'? Which shade is the 'sample in my mind' of the colour green—the sample of what is common to all shades of green?

"But might there not be such 'general' samples? Say a schematic leaf, or a sample of *pure* green?"—Certainly there might. But for such a schema to be understood as a *schema*, and not as the shape of a particular leaf, and for a slip of pure green to be understood as a sample of all that is greenish and not as a sample of pure green—this in turn resides in the way the samples are used.

Ask yourself: what *shape* must the sample of the colour green be? Sit be rectangular? Or would it then be the sample of a green rectangle?—So should it be 'irregular' in shape? And what is to prevent us then from regarding it—that is, from using it—only as a sample of irregularity of shape?

74. Here also belongs the idea that if you see this leaf as a samp of 'leaf shape in general' you *see* it differently from someone who regards it as, say, a sample of this particular shape. Now this might well be so—though it is not so—for it would only be to say that, as a matter of experience, if you *see* the leaf in a particular way, you use it in

such-and-such a way or according to such-and-such rules. Of course, there is such a thing as seeing in *this* way or *that*; and there are also cases where whoever sees a sample like *this* will in general use it in *this* way, and whoever sees it otherwise in another way. For example, if you see the schematic drawing of a cube as a plane figure consisting of a square and two rhombi you will, perhaps, carry out the order "Bring me something like this" differently from someone who sees the picture three-dimensionally.

75. What does it mean to know what a game is? What does it mean, to know it and not be able to say it? Is this knowledge somehow equivalent to an unformulated definition? So that if it were formulated I should be able to recognize it as the expression of my knowledge? Isn't my knowledge, my concept of a game, completely expressed in the explanations that I could give? That is, in my describing examples of various kinds of game; shewing how all sorts of other games can be constructed on the analogy of these; saying that I should scarcely include this or this among games; and so on.

76. If someone were to draw a sharp boundary I could not acknowledge it as the one that I too always wanted to draw, or had drawn in my mind. For I did not want to draw one at all. His concept can then be said to be not the same as mine, but akin to it. The kinship is that of two pictures, one of which consists of colour patches with vague contours, and the other of patches similarly shaped and distributed, but with clear contours. The kinship is just as undeniable as the difference.

77. And if we carry this comparison still further it is clear that the degree to which the sharp picture *can* resemble the blurred one depends on the latter's degree of vagueness. For imagine having to sketch a sharply defined picture 'corresponding' to a blurred one. In the latter there is a blurred red rectangle: for it you put down a sharply defined one. Of course—several such sharply defined rectangles can be drawn to correspond to the indefinite one.—But if the colours in the original merge without a hint of any outline won't it become a hopeless task to draw a sharp picture corresponding to the blurred one? Won't you then have to say: "Here I might just as well draw a circle or heart as a rectangle, for all the colours merge. Anything—and nothing—is right."—And this is the position you are in if you look for definitions corresponding to our concepts in aesthetics or ethics.

In such a difficulty always ask yourself: How did we *learn* the meaning of this word ("good" for instance)? From what sort of examples? in what language-games? Then it will be easier for you to see that the word must have a family of meanings.

Review Questions

1. What is the meaning of critique as applied to the use of language?
2. Discuss the earlier position of Wittgenstein on language as picture.
3. Why did he change his position to that of language as language-games?
4. In what way can the *Tractatus* be thought of as metaphysical?
5. What significance do you attach to the exhortation that what we cannot speak about we should be silent about?

CHAPTER 27

Jean-Paul Sartre (1905–1980)

Introduction

In shifting our attention to the continental philosophy called *existentialism*, we are shifting to a philosophy that was not concerned with science or the scientific structure of language as the British philosophers were, but with the human person in the drama of the "human condition," that is, the life of human beings as it is immersed in all the vagaries of a day-by-day existence. The constant appearance of words and phrases like *absurdity, self, the other, value, freedom, anguish, consciousness, finitude, responsibility, transcendence, hate, love, death*, and *God* shows the intense personal direction such a philosophy took. Furthermore, as —e have seen, when certain philosophers want to make a personal or personalist statement, they forsake academic treatises and fall back on dialogue, metaphor, exhortation, or some style using the language of life situations. So, among the existentialists, we find a richness of literary forms including novels, short stories, plays, and even, as in the case of Marcel, music — all for the purpose of touching the center of life, which academic treatises might be ill-suited to do.

Dismay with man's low self-esteem is what prompted Kierkegard, Nietzsche, and Marx to call for the destruction of all constraints, institutional or social, which barricaded man against himself. As a result, their philosophies, especially Kierkegaard's and Nietzsche's, personalist to the core, established themselves as forebears of the age of existentialism. The movement, numbering among its better-known representatives Gabriel Marcel, Martin Heidegger, Karl Jaspers, Jean-Paul Sartre, and Albert Camus, emerged between the two world wars and achieved widespread popularity shortly after World War II. These philosophers all speak of the precarious condition of man, subject as he is to a dubious existence, fearful of death and nullity, vulnerable to the ravages of disease and chance, in danger of the thoughtless employment of scientific technology, and liable therefore to lose freedom as the essential human gift. For Sartre and Camus, there is no way to liberate man from this dead end, no way to redeem him, not from without, for God does not exist, nor from within, for man is condemned to his own absurdity. For Jaspers and Marcel, the same humanity longs for redemptive meaning, and the same human condition evidences hope in the actual presence of God.

The name that springs to mind immediately when existentialism is mentioned, and the only one who accepts the designation of himself as an existentialist, is Sartre. We can turn to him as a striking example of the philosophic mood of the time.

Jean-Paul Sartre was born in Paris in 1905. His life's dedication to words was made early, for as a child he became fascinated with the world of books, and his imagination ran free as he established his real, living world therein. His native curiosity was enhanced by his grandfather, who opened up for him the whole horizon of literature, so that Sartre says, "I had found my religion: nothing seemed to me more important than a book. I regarded the library as a temple." During his years as a lycée student, his "religion" of books nullified the hold any other religion had on him. He was brought up half Protestant, half Catholic, but as a youngster of twelve or thirteen the image of God was already becoming clouded, and he writes of the time he was awaiting the arrival of some schoolmates who were late in coming: "After a while, not knowing what else to do to occupy my mind, I decided to think of the Almighty. Immediately He tumbled into the blue and disappeared without giving any explanation. He doesn't exist, I said to myself with polite surprise, and I thought the matter was settled. In a way, it was, since never have I had the slightest temptation to bring Him back to life." Yet, the idea of God was not thereby eradicted, for, "traces of God", or "elements of the idea of God", remained with Sartre for a long time. Towards the end of his life, in an interview with Simone de Beauvoir over the course of several months, when asked what he meant by saying that atheism was a long-term task, Sartre responded:" ... moving on from idealist atheism to materialist atheism was difficult. It implied long-drawn-out work. I've told you what I meant by idealist atheism. It's the absence of an *idea*, the idea of God. Whereas materialist atheism is the world seen without God, and obviously it's a very long-term affair, passing from that absence of an idea to this new conception of the being — of the being that is left among things and is not set apart from them by a divine consciousness that contemplates them and causes them to exist."

He enrolled as a student at the École Normale Supérieure and received an academic training in philosophy. Later, after studying in

Berlin in 1934–35, he taught philosophy for several years at Le Havre and Paris, choosing finally to give up academic teaching to devote himself to writing.

Sartre was in the army in World War II, was captured, made a prisoner, and then escaped to become a leader in the resistance against the occupying forces. Earlier, in 1938, he had written his first novel, *Nausea*, and during the occupation he wrote two plays, *The Flies* and *No Exit*. In formal style, his first work in philosophy was done in 1936 as a historical study of the imagination; in 1943 his *Being and Nothingness* appeared; it has become a classic in philosophy. With the war over, Sartre became increasingly influential as a philosopher, literary figure, and political commentator, particularly after founding the journal *Les Temps Modernes*. His renewed interest in Marx culminated in the *Critique of Dialectical Reason*, in which he tries to impregnate classical Marxism with the insights of existentialism. His autobiography, *The Words*, was begun in 1964, the same year in which he declined the Nobel Prize for literature because he felt it would hamper his freedom to write. Since that time, he wrote a seemingly endless stream of works on esthetics, freedom, literature, and a host of other topics that make him a literary monument of our time. He died in 1980.

Towards the end of *The Words*, Sartre tells us that he was in fact Antoine Roquentin, the central figure of the novel *Nausea*: "I *was* Roquentin; I used him to show, without complacency, the texture of my life." In the story, Roquentin is seated on a park bench when, in a reflective mood, he notices the roots of an old chestnut tree in their huge, gnarled intertwining; in a flash, beyond the massive pressure of the roots on each other, he sees reality for what it truly is, shapeless, senseless, just *there*, and he reacts with a feeling of loathing and disgust at the absurdity of existence. Roquentin is the fictionalized personification of the philosophy Sartre explores in *Being and Nothingness*, a work so systematically detailed that it shows a Germanic intellect hovering over the Gallic emotions evident in his other works. Sartre's analysis of being is thorough, but he takes care to call it an *ontology* rather than a *metaphysics*, for ontology, even though it denotes the study of being, does not revive the ghosts of substance, soul, and God. His brand of ontology, saturated with themes adapted from Hegel and Husserl, is *phenomenological* — the study of being through its phenomena, or appearances; thus, an ontology without metaphysics.

Sartre distinguished between two categories of being, *being-in-itself* (*l'en-soi*) and *being-for-itself* (*le pour-soi*). Particular things, like Roquentin's chestnut tree, are presented to us with all their particularities, their determinate characteristics. Getting beyond these appearances (*transphenomenal*) reveals being as neither active nor passive; it does not acquire being, it does not have it, it just *is*. It harbors no potentiality, no possibility. *Being-in-itself* is completely unrelated to anything else, and without relation it is without meaning. So described, being-in-itself is reminiscent of the being of Parmenides, monolithic and unmoving, offered with the announcement that "whatever is, *is*." The second category of being, *being-for-itself*, stands in sharp contrast to the first and, in a sense, rejects it. It is the realm of the *human* being, characterized by consciousness and freedom, which enable man to decide meaning for himself by the choices he makes. By nurturing his own meaning, man gives himself his own *existence*; hence, the term *existential* pertains to the being of man, and *existentialism* to the philosophy of human existence.

Sartre's terminology often requires a readjustment in the way we normally use certain words. When, for example, he calls man "nothing," he wants to show that consciousness and freedom are open and indeterminate, the complete *opposite* of being-in-itself, which is closed and determinate; man, therefore, is nothing. Consciousness, on the same philosophical axis as freedom, is characterized by the distance it creates from being-in-itself by overcoming its passivity; in that sense, consciousness "negates" or "nihilates" being-in-itself. Freedom, however, is Sartre's main key to the understanding of man: through freedom *meaning* enters the world. Freedom brings into the zone of the real the objects man chooses or the projects (pro-jects) man sets for himself as the course for the future. Thus, man gives meaning to himself, builds up his own existence; his *ex-sistence* is the way he stands out from the meaninglessness of being-in-itself. Existence, in its ongoing creation by freedom, precedes the essence of man and therefore defines it. In page after page of his writings, Sartre never lets the notion of freedom get out of sight. Whether in his strictly philosophical essays or in his novels and plays, freedom is always seen as the meaningful force declaring the glory and misery of man.

Indeed, glory and misery, for the student of Sartre's philosophy hurtles between optimism and pessimism; he no sooner reaches the crest of the wave than he is pulled down to the trough. Man is "condemned to freedom!" Take the fact of relationship to others. It has to be. Being-for-another belongs to the very being of man. Yet the moment this relationship is analyzed, it is seen that the Other pushes against my freedom, circumscribes it. At one and the same time, the Other, who helps establish my freedom, also destroys it; being-for-itself and being-for-another shatter each other. The last line of Sartre's play *No Exit* is "Hell is other people".

There is another level that shows much more profoundly how human freedom is encircled with impossibility, so that man is truly condemned to futility. If being-for-itself seeks being, it seeks it totally and has as its "project" to become being-in-*and*-for-itself; man desires to become God: "This is why the possible is projected in general as what the for-itself lacks in order to become in-itself-for-itself. The fundamental value which presides over this project is exactly the in-itself-for-itself; that is, the ideal of a consciousness which would be the foundation of its own being-in-itself by the pure consciousness which it would have of itself. It is this ideal which can be called God. Thus the best way to conceive of the fundamental project of human reality is to say that man is the being whose project is to be God. . . . To be man means to reach toward being God. Or if you prefer, man fundamentally is the desire to be God." But the project is *impossible* because God does not exist. Like Sisyphus, man always fails. Life is irrational; being is absurd. And the human being? In an oft-quoted phrase, "Man is a useless passion."

Though Sartre never wrote a complete theory of morality, there is a distinct moral tone—better, a moral imperative—to his writings. Despite the futility that saturates man's being, *responsibility* is the correlative of freedom and therefore an indispensable ingredient of human activity. The avoidance of responsibility is Sartre's main reason for rejecting Freudian psychoanalysis: I must take seriously the fact that my being involves being-for-another. My involvement is not exhausted by this one action toward this one person, for my action has *universal* meaning and significance. There is no single activity of an atom but what affects the entire cosmos, and there is no single human activity but what affects all mankind; indeed, responsibility "extends to the entire world as a peopled-world."

Responsibility is translated into commitment. A writer, for example, has the responsibility to write for his time, to be committed to change, not to "preservation." His commitment calls for an involvement with his age; no retreat, no seclusion, no withdrawal. A philosopher's commitment must be to moral and political action, a commitment clearly exemplified in Sartre's own life and the active concern he showed toward many of humane and political causes. Expressed throughout his works, the notion of commitment reaches a final philosophical statement in one of his last, and uncompleted, works, *Critique of Dialectical Reason.* Here he espouses the view, presented earlier in an essay on method, that a philosophy is true only insofar as it speaks for the rising class, that is, for the proletariat. Though Marxism, for Sartre, is the only philosophy of the twentieth century, something has gone amiss with it; what it requires is an updating, a renewal in which the insights of existentialism are to be assimilated by the Marxian dialectic. In contemporary Marxism there is still too much acceptance of the inevitability of the dialectic working itself out, disregarding the concrete situation in actual praxis. In this matter, existentialism, alive to the demands of the existential situation, can make enormous contributions to the renewal of Marxism in meeting the needs of men in their present day struggle. Underscored here is the word *need*, or *scarcity*, which Marxism today, and even Marx himself, somehow fails to see is the basis of all human relations, and therefore of the struggle men are engaged in: "The origin of struggle always lies, in fact, in some concrete antagonism whose material condition is scarcity." The only way to understand scarcity, to understand man, is to see it against the background of *all* history, history taken as the *total* precedent to present time. So, when Sartre speaks of the *totalization* of human history, he is speaking of *all of history* seen at once as *interiorized* in me, thus explaining the scarcity in me as a "fundamental relation" of history, which in turn serves as my launching pad into the future. Thus, Sartre enrolls himself in the camp of Marx, which requires a philosophical commitment to political action to be undertaken to advance the cause of the proletariat.

At the very end of the *Critique*, Sartre again hints at the problem that lingered with him from the very beginning of his philosophical journey: the problem of God. He sees the problem in the context of history when we, in effect, ask how the vast and diverse multiplicities of history can be added up without someone to add them; totalled up without someone to total them; or, to use his terminology, how can there be totalization without a totalizer? Sartre quickly closes off the open end of his question lest he admit the need to transcend history; rather than do that, he sees history as self-enclosed so that it *totalizes itself*. Sartre is a God-conscious philosopher. This does not mean that in some inscrutable way he is "taking back" his atheism; rather, it means that, like Nietzsche, he has *consciously* organized his philosophy outside God to see what happens to man in His absence. After all, postulating that God does not exist is just as valid as postulating that He does. In company with his predecessors, Nietzsche and Marx, the denial of God is polarized by the affirmation of man: "But the being toward which human reality surpasses itself is not a transcendent God; it is at the heart of human reality; it is only human reality itself as totality." Sartre's view of man, then, is both pessimistic and optimistic. It is pessimistic inasmuch as it sees man pathetically feeling his way to the bright promise of tomorrows that never come; optimistic inasmuch as "man's destiny is within himself." This dualism is captured in the conclusion of *The Words*: "My sole concern has been to save myself — nothing in my hands, nothing up my sleeve — by work and faith. Without equipment, without tools, I set all of me to work in order to save all of me. If I relegate impossible Salvation to the prop room, what remains? A whole man, composed of all men and as good as all of them and no better than any."

Readings

The Meaning of Existentialism (from *Existentialism and Humanism*)

What then is ... existentialism?

The question is only complicated because there are two kinds of existentialists. There are, on the one hand, the Christians, amongst whom I shall name Jaspers and Gabriel Marcel, both professed Catholics; and on the other the existential atheists, amongst whom we must place Heidegger as well as the French existentialists and myself. What they have in common is simply the fact that they believe that *existence* comes before *essence*—or, if you will, that we must begin from the subjective. What exactly do we mean by that?

If one considers an article of manufacture—as, for example, a book or a paper-knife—one sees that it has been made by an artisan who had a conception of it; and he has paid attention, equally, to the conception of a paper-knife and to the pre-existent technique of production which is a part of that conception and is, at bottom, a formula. Thus the paper-knife is at the same time an article producible in a certain manner and one which, on the other hand, serves a definite purpose, for one cannot suppose that a man would produce a paper-knife without knowing what it was for. Let us say, then, of the paper-knife that its essence—that is to say the sum of the formulae and the qualities which made its production and its definition possible—precedes its existence. The presence of such-and-such a paper-knife or book is thus determined before my eyes. Here, then, we are viewing the world from a technical standpoint, and we can say that production precedes existence.

When we think of God as the creator, we are thinking of him, most of the time, as a supernal artisan. Whatever doctrine we may be considering, whether it be a doctrine like that of Descartes, or of Leibnitz himself, we always imply that the will follows, more or less, from the understanding or at least accompanies it, so that when God creates he knows precisely what he is creating. Thus, the conception of man in the mind of God is comparable to that of the paper-knife in the mind of the artisan: God makes man according to a procedure and a conception, exactly as the artisan manufactures a paper-knife, following a definition and a formula. Thus each individual man is the realisation of a certain conception which dwells in the divine understanding. In the philosophic atheism of the eighteenth century, the notion of God is suppressed, but not, for all that, the idea that essence is prior to existence; something of that idea we still find everywhere, in Diderot, in Voltaire and even in Kant. Man possesses a human nature; that "human nature," which is the conception of human being, is found in every man; which means that each man is a particular example of an universal conception, the conception of Man. In Kant, this universality goes so far that the wild man of the woods, man in the state of nature and the bourgeois are all contained in the same definition and have the same fundamental qualities. Here again, the essence of man precedes that historic existence which we confront in experience.

Atheistic existentialism, of which I am a representative, declares with greater consistency that if God does not exist there is at least one being whose existence comes before its essence, a being which exists before it can be defined by any conception of it. That being is man or, as Heidegger has it, the human reality. What do we mean by saying that existence precedes essence? We mean that man first of all exists, encounters himself, surges up in the world—and defines himself afterwards. If man as the existentialist sees him is not definable, it is because to begin with he is nothing. He will not be anything until later, and then he will be what he makes of himself. Thus, there is no human nature, because there is no God to have a conception of it. Man simply is. Not that he is simply what he conceives himself to be, but he is what he wills, and as he conceives himself after already existing—as he wills to be after that leap towards existence. Man is nothing else but that which he makes of himself. That is the first principle of existentialism. And this is what people call its "subjectivity," using the word as a reproach against us. But what do we mean to say by this, but that man is of a greater dignity than a stone or a table? For we mean to say that man primarily exists—that man is, before all else, something which propels itself towards a future and is aware that it is doing so. Man is, indeed, a project which possesses a subjective life, instead of being a kind of moss, or a fungus or a cauliflower. Before that projection of the self nothing exists; not even in the heaven of intelligence: man will only attain existence when he is what he purposes to be. Not, however, what he may wish to be. For what we usually understand by wishing or willing is a conscious decision taken—much more often than not—after we have made ourselves what we are. I may wish to join a party, to write a book or to marry—but in such a case what is usually called my will is probably a manifestation of a prior and more spontaneous decision. If, however, it is true that existence is prior to essence, man is responsible for what he is. Thus, the first effect of existentialism is that it puts every man in possession of himself as he is, and places the entire responsibility for his existence squarely upon his own shoulders. And, when we say that man is responsible for himself, we do not mean that he is responsible only for his own individuality, but that he is responsible for all men. The word "subjectivism" is to be understood in two senses, and our adversaries play upon only one of them.

Subjectivism means, on the one hand, the freedom of the individual subject and, on the other, that man cannot pass beyond human subjectivity. It is the latter which is the deeper meaning of existentialism. When we say that man chooses himself, we do mean that every one of us must choose himself; but by that we also mean that in choosing for himself he chooses for all men. For in effect, of all the actions a man may take in order to create himself as he wills to be, there is not one which is not creative, at the same time, of an image of man such as he believes he ought to be. To choose between this or that is at the same time to affirm the value of that which is chosen; for we are unable ever to choose the worse. What we choose is always the better; and nothing can be better for us unless it is better for all. If, moreover, existence precedes essence and we will to exist at the same time as we fashion our image, that image is valid for all and for the entire epoch in which we find ourselves. Our responsibility is thus much greater than we had supposed, for it concerns mankind as a whole. If I am a worker, for instance, I may choose to join a Christian rather than a Communist trade union. And if, by that membership, I choose to signify that resignation is, after all, the attitude that best becomes a man, that man's kingdom is not upon this earth, I do not commit myself alone to that view. Resignation is my will for everyone, and my action is, in consequence, a commitment on behalf of all mankind. Or if, to take a more personal case, I decide to marry and to have children, even though this decision proceeds simply from my situation, from my passion or my desire, I am thereby committing not only myself, but humanity as a whole, to the practice of monogamy. I am thus responsible for myself and for all men, and I am creating a certain image of man as I would have him to be. In fashioning myself I fashion man.

This may enable us to understand what is meant by such terms—perhaps a little grandiloquent—as anguish, abandonment and despair. As you will soon see, it is very simple. First, what do we mean by anguish? The existentialist frankly states that man is in anguish. His meaning is as follows—When a man commits himself to anything, fully realising that he is not only choosing what he will be, but is thereby at the same time a legislator deciding for the whole of mankind—in such a moment a man cannot escape from the sense of complete and profound responsibility. There are many, indeed, who show no such anxiety. But we affirm that they are merely disguising their anguish or are in flight from it. Certainly, many people think that in what they are doing they commit no one but themselves to anything: and if you ask them, "What would happen if everyone did so?" they shrug their shoulders and reply, "Everyone does not do so." But in truth, one ought always to ask oneself what would happen if everyone did as one is doing; nor can one escape from that disturbing thought except by a kind of self-deception. The man who lies in self-excuse, by saying "Everyone will not do it" must be ill at ease in his conscience, for the act of lying implies the universal value which it denies. By its very disguise his anguish reveals itself. This is the anguish that Kierkegaard called "the anguish of Abraham." You know the story: An angel commanded Abraham to sacrifice his son: and obedience was obligatory, if it really was an angel who had appeared and said, "Thou, Abraham, shalt sacrifice thy son." But anyone in such a case would wonder, first, whether it was indeed an angel and secondly, whether I am really Abraham. Where are the proofs? ... There is nothing to show that I am Abraham: nevertheless I also am obliged at every instant to perform actions which are examples. Everything happens to every man as though the whole human race had its eyes fixed upon what he is doing and regulated its conduct accordingly. So every man ought to say, "Am I really a man who has the right to act in such a manner that humanity regulates itself by what I do." If a man does not say that, he is dissembling his anguish. Clearly, the anguish with which we are concerned here is not one that could lead to quietism or inaction. It is anguish pure and simple, of the kind well known to all those who have borne responsibilities. When, for instance, a military leader takes upon himself the responsibility for an attack and sends a number of men to their death, he chooses to do it and at bottom he alone chooses. No doubt he acts under a higher command, but its orders, which are more general, require interpretation by him and upon that interpretation depends the life of ten, fourteen or twenty men. In making the decision, he cannot but feel a certain anguish. All leaders know that anguish. It does not prevent their acting, on the contrary it is the very condition of their action, for the action presupposes that there is a plurality of possibilities, and in choosing one of these, they realise that it has value only because it is chosen. Now it is anguish of that kind which existentialism describes, and moreover, as we shall see, makes explicit through direct responsibility towards other men who are concerned. Far from being a screen which could separate us from action, it is a condition of action itself.

And when we speak of "abandonment"—a favourite word of Heidegger—we only mean to say that God does not exist, and that it is necessary to draw the consequences of his absence right to the end. The existentialist is strongly opposed to a certain type of secular moralism which seeks to suppress God at the least possible expense. Towards 1880, when the French professors endeavoured to formulate a secular morality, they said something like this:—God is a useless and costly hypothesis, so we will do without it. However, if we are to have morality, a society and a law-abiding world, it is essential that certain values should be taken seriously; they must have an *a priori* existence ascribed to them. It must be considered obligatory *a priori* to be honest, not to lie, not to beat one's wife, to bring up children and so forth; so we are going to do a little work on this subject, which will enable us to show that these values exist all the same, inscribed in an intelligible heaven although, of course, there is no God. In other words—and this is, I believe, the purport of all that we in France call radicalism—nothing will be changed if God does not exist; we shall re-discover the same norms of honesty, progress and humanity, and we shall have disposed of God as an out-of-date hypothesis which will die away quietly of itself. The existentialist, on the contrary, finds it extremely embarrassing that God does not exist, for there disappears with Him all possibility of finding values in an intelligible heaven. There can no longer be any good *a priori*, since there is no infinite and perfect consciousness to think it. It is nowhere written that "the good" exists, that one must be honest or must not lie, since we are now upon the plane where there are only men. Dostoievsky once wrote "If God did not exist, everything would be permitted"; and that, for existentialism, is the starting point. Everything is indeed permitted if God does not exist, and man is in consequence forlorn, for he cannot find anything to depend upon either within or outside himself. He discovers forthwith, that he is without excuse. For if indeed existence precedes essence, one will never be able to explain one's action by reference to a given and specific human nature; in other words, there is no determinism—man is free, man *is* freedom. Nor, on the other hand, if God does not exist, are we provided with any values or commands that could legitimise our behaviour. Thus we have neither behind us, nor before us in a luminous realm of values, any means of justification or excuse. We are left alone, without excuse. That is what I mean when I say that man is condemned to be free. Condemned, because he did not create himself, yet is nevertheless at liberty, and from the moment that he is thrown into this world he is responsible for everything he does. The existentialist does not believe in the power of passion. He will never regard a grand passion as a destructive torrent upon which a man is swept into certain actions as by fate, and which, therefore, is an excuse for them. He thinks that man is responsible for his passion. Neither will an existentialist think that a man can find help through some sign being vouchsafed upon earth for his orientation: for he thinks that the man himself interprets the sign as he chooses. He thinks that every man, without any support or help whatever, is condemned at every instant to invent man.

As for "despair," the meaning of this expression is extremely simple. It merely means that we limit ourselves to a reliance upon that which is within our wills, or within the sum of the probabilities which render our action feasible. Whenever one wills anything, there are always these elements of probability. If I am counting upon a visit from a friend, who may be coming by train or by tram, I presuppose that the train will arrive at the appointed time, or that the tram will not be derailed. I remain in the realm of possibilities; but one does not rely upon any possibilities beyond those that are strictly concerned in one's action. Beyond the point at which the possibilities under consideration cease to affect my action, I ought to disinterest myself. For there is no God and no prevenient design, which can adapt the world and all its possibilities to my will. When Descartes said, "Conquer yourself rather than the world," what he meant was, at bottom, the same—that we should act without hope.

Reflections on Being and Nothingness (from *Being and Nothingness*)

1. Consciousness

Consciousness is consciousness of something. This means that transcendence is the constitutive structure of consciousness; that is, that consciousness is born *supported by* a being which is not itself. This is what we call the ontological proof. No doubt someone will reply that the existence of the demand of consciousness does not prove that this demand ought to be satisfied. But this objection can not hold up against an analysis of what Husserl calls intentionality, though, to be sure, he misunderstood its essential character. To say that consciousness is consciousness of something means that for consciousness there is no being outside of that precise obligation to be a revealing intuition of something—*i.e.*, of a transcendent being. Not only does pure subjectivity, if initially given, fail to transcend itself to posit the objective; a "pure" subjectivity disappears. What can properly be called subjectivity is consciousness (of) consciousness. But this consciousness (of being) consciousness must be qualified in some way, and it can be qualified only as revealing intuition or it is nothing. Now a revealing intuition implies something revealed. Absolute subjectivity can be established only in the face of something revealed; immanence can be defined only within the apprehension of a transcendent. It might appear that there is an echo here of Kant's refutation of problematical idealism. But we ought rather to think of Descartes. We are here on the ground of being, not of knowledge. It is not a question of showing that the phenomena of inner sense imply the existence of objective spatial phenomena, but that consciousness implies in its being a non-conscious and transphenomenal being. In particular there is no point in replying that in fact subjectivity implies objectivity and that it constitutes itself in constituting the objective; we have seen that subjectivity is powerless to constitute the objective. To say that consciousness is consciousness of something is to say that it must produce itself as a revealed-revelation of a being which is not it and which gives itself as already existing when consciousness reveals it.

Thus we have left pure appearance and have arrived at full being. Consciousness is a being whose existence posits its essence, and inversely it is consciousness of a being, whose essence implies its existence; that is, in which appearance lays claim to *being*. Being is everywhere. Certainly we could apply to consciousness the definition which Heidegger reserves for *Dasein* and say that it is a being such that in its being, its being is in question. But it would be necessary to complete the definition and formulate it more like this: *consciousness is a being such that in its being, its being is in question in so far as this being implies a being other than itself.*

We must understand that this being is no other than the transphenomenal being of phenomena and not a noumenal being which is hidden behind them. It is the being of this table, of this package of tobacco, of the lamp, more generally the being of the world which is implied by consciousness. It requires simply that the being of that which *appears* does not exist *only* in so far as it appears. The transphenomenal being of what exists *for consciousness* is itself in itself (*lui-meme en soi*).

2. Being-in-Itself

We can now form a few definite conclusions about the *phenomenon of being,* which we have considered in order to make the preceding observations. Consciousness is the revealed-revelation of existents, and existents appear before consciousness on the foundation of their being. Nevertheless the primary characteristic of the being of an existent is never to reveal itself completely to consciousness. An existent can not be stripped of its being; being is the ever present foundation of the existent; it is everywhere in it and nowhere. There is no being which is not the being of a certain mode of being, none which can not be apprehended through the mode of being which manifests being and veils it at the same time. Consciousness can always pass beyond the existent, not toward its being, but toward the *meaning of this being.* That is why we call it ontic-ontological, since a fundamental characteristic of its transcendence is to transcend the ontic toward the ontological. The meaning of the being of the existent in so far as it reveals itself to consciousness is the phenomenon of being. This meaning has itself a being, based on which it manifests itself.

A clear view of the phenomenon of being has often been obscured by a very common prejudice which we shall call "creationism." Since people supposed that God had given being to the world, being always appeared tainted with a certain passivity. But a creation *ex nihilo* can not explain the coming to pass of being; for if being is conceived in a subjectivity, even a divine subjectivity, it remains a mode of intra-subjective being. Such subjectivity can not have even the *representation* of an objectivity, and consequently it can not even be affected with the *will* to create the objective. Furthermore being, if it is suddenly placed outside the subjective by the fulguration of which Leibniz speaks, can only affirm itself as distinct from and opposed to its creator; otherwise it dissolves in him. The theory of perpetual creation, by removing from being what the Germans call *Selbständigkeit*, makes it disappear in the divine subjectivity. If being exists as over against God, it is its own support; it does not preserve the least trace of divine creation. In a word, even if it had been created, being-in-itself would be *inexplicable* in terms of creation; for it assumes its being beyond the creation.

This is equivalent to saying that being is uncreated. But we need not conclude that being creates itself, which would suppose that it is prior to itself. Being can not be *causa sui* in the manner of consciousness. Being is *itself*. This means that it is neither passivity nor activity. Both of these notions are *human* and designate human conduct or the instruments of human conduct. There is activity when a conscious being uses means with an end in view. And we call those objects passive on which our activity is exercised, in as much as they do not spontaneously aim at the end which we make them serve. In a word, man is active and the means which he employs are called passive. These concepts, put absolutely, lose all meaning. In particular, being is not active; in order for there to be an end and means, there must be being. For an even stronger reason it can not be passive, for in order to be passive, it must be. The self-consistency of being is beyond the active as it is beyond the passive.

Being is equally beyond negation as beyond affirmation. Affirmation is always affirmation of something; that is, the act of affirming is distinguished from the thing affirmed. But if we suppose an affirmation in which the affirmed comes to fulfill the affirming and is confused with it, this affirmation can not be affirmed—owing to too much of plenitude and the immediate inherence of the noema in the noesis. It is there that we find being—if we are to define it more clearly—in connection with consciousness. It is the noema in the noesis; that is, the inherence in itself without the least distance. From this point of view, we should not call it "immanence," for immanence in spite of all *connection* with self is still that very slight withdrawal which can be realized—away from the self. But being is not a connection with itself. It is *itself*. It is an immanence which can not realize itself, an affirmation which can not affirm itself, an activity which can not act, because it is glued to itself. Everything happens as if, in order to free the affirmation of self from the heart of being, there is necessary a decompression of being. Let us not, however, think that being is merely *one* undifferentiated self-affirmation; the undifferentiation of the in-itself is beyond an infinity of self-affirmations, inasmuch as there is an infinity of modes of self-affirming. We may summarize these first conclusions by saying that being is in itself.

But if being is in itself, this means that it does not refer to itself as self-consciousness does. It is this self. It is itself so completely that the perpetual reflection which constitutes the self is dissolved in an identity. That is why being is at bottom beyond the *self*, and our first formula can be only an approximation due to the requirements of language. In fact being is opaque to itself precisely because it is filled with itself. This can be better expressed by saying that *being is what it is*. This statement is in appearance strictly analytical. Actually it is far from being reduced to that principle of identity which is the unconditioned principle of all analytical judgments. First the formula designates a particular region of being, that of *being in-itself*. We shall see that the being of *for-itself* is defined, on the contrary, as being what it is not and not being what it is. The question here then is of a regional principle and is as such synthetical. Furthermore it is necessary to oppose this formula—being in-itself is what it is—to that which designates the being of consciousness. The latter in fact, as we shall see, *has to be* what it is.

3. Anguish

Kierkegaard describing anguish in the face of what one lacks characterizes it as anguish in the face of freedom. But Heidegger, whom we know to have been greatly influenced by Kierkegaard, considers anguish instead as the apprehension of nothingness. These two descriptions of anguish do not appear to us contradictory; on the contrary the one implies the other.

First we must acknowledge that Kierkegaard is right; anguish is distinguished from fear in that fear is fear of beings in the world whereas anguish is anguish before myself. Vertigo is anguish to the extent that I am afraid not of falling over the precipice, but of throwing myself over. A situation provokes fear if there is a possibility of my life being changed from without; my being provokes anguish to the extent that I distrust myself and my own reactions in that situation. The artillery preparation which precedes the attack can provoke fear in the soldier who undergoes the bombardment, but anguish is born in him when he tries to foresee the conduct with which he will face the bombardment, when he asks himself if he is going to be able to "hold up." Similarly the recruit who reports for active duty at the beginning of the war can in some instances be afraid of death, but more often he is "afraid of being afraid;" that is, he is filled with anguish before himself. Most of the time dangerous or threatening situations present themselves in facets; they will be apprehended through a feeling of fear or of anguish according to whether we envisage the situation as acting on the man or the man as acting on the situation. The man who has just received a hard blow—for example, losing a great part of his wealth in a crash—can have the fear of threatening poverty. He will experience anguish a moment later when nervously wringing his hands (a symbolic reaction to the action which is imposed but which remains still wholly undetermined), he exclaims to himself: "What am I going to do? But what am I going to do?" In this sense fear and anguish are exclusive of one another since fear is unreflective apprehension of the transcendent and anguish is reflective apprehension of the self; the one is born in the destruction of the other. The normal process in the case which I have just cited is a constant transition from the one to the other. But there exist also situations where anguish appears pure; that is, without ever being preceded or followed by fear. If, for example, I have been raised to a new dignity and charged with a delicate and flattering mission, I can feel anguish at the thought that I will not be capable perhaps of fulfilling it, and yet I will not have the least fear in the world of the consequences of my possible failure.

What is the meaning of anguish in the various examples which I have just given? Let us take up again the example of vertigo. Vertigo announces itself through fear; I am on a narrow path—without a guard-rail—which goes along a precipice. The precipice presents itself to me *as to be avoided*; it represents a danger of death. At the same time I conceive of a certain number of causes, originating in universal determinism, which can transform that threat of death into reality; I can slip on a stone and fall into the abyss; the crumbling earth of the path can give way under my steps. Through these various anticipations, I am given to myself as a thing; I am passive in relation to these possibilities; they come to me from without; in so far as I am also an object in the world, subject to gravitation, they are *my* possibilities. At this moment *fear* appears, which in terms of the situation is the apprehension of myself as a destructible transcendent in the midst of transcendents, as an object which does not contain in itself the origin of its future disappearance. My reaction will be of the reflective order; I will pay attention to the stones in the road; I will keep myself as far as possible from the edge of the path. I realize myself as pushing away the threatening situation with all my strength, and I project before myself a certain number of future conducts destined to keep the threats of the world at a distance from me. These conducts are *my* possibilities. I escape fear by the very fact that I am placing myself on a plane where *my own* possibilities are substituted for the transcendent probabilities where human action had no place.

4. Being-for-Itself

... In truth the *cogito* must be our point of departure, but we can say of it, parodying a famous saying, that it leads us only on condition that we get out of it. Our preceding study, which concerned the conditions for the possibility of certain types of conduct, had as its goal only to place us in a position to question the *cogito* about its being and to furnish us with the dialectic instrument which would enable us to find in the *cogito* itself the means of escaping from instantaneity toward the totality of being which constitutes human reality. Let us return now to description of non-thetic self-consciousness; let us examine its results and ask what it means for consciousness that it must necessarily be what it is not and not be what it is.

"The being of consciousness," we said in the Introduction, "is a being such that in its being, its being is in question." This means that the being of consciousness does not coincide with itself in a full equivalence. Such equivalence, which is that of the in-itself, is expressed by this simple formula: being is what it is. In the in-itself there is not a particle of being which is not wholly within itself without distance. When being is thus conceived there is not the slightest suspicion of duality in it; this is what we mean when we say that the density of being of the in-itself is infinite. It is a fullness. The principle of identity can be said to be synthetic not only because it limits its scope to a region of definite being, but in particular because it masses within it the infinity of density. "A is A" means that A exists in an infinite compression with an infinite density. Identity is the limiting concept of unification: it is not true that the in-itself has any need of a synthetic unification of its being; at its own extreme limit, unity disappears and passes into identity. Identity is the ideal of "one," and "one" comes into the world by human reality. The in-itself is full of itself, and no more total plenitude can be imagined, no more perfect equivalence of content to container. There is not the slightest emptiness in being, not the tiniest crack through which nothingness might slip in.

This presence to itself has often been taken for a plenitude of existence, and a strong prejudice prevalent among philosophers causes them to attribute to consciousness the highest rank in being. But this postulate can not be maintained after a more thorough description of the notion of presence. Actually *presence to* always implies duality, at least a virtual separation. The presence of being to itself implies a detachment on the part of being in relation to itself. The coincidence of identity is the veritable plenitude of being exactly because in this coincidence there is left no place for any negativity. Of course the principle of identity can involve the principle of noncontradiction as Hegel has observed. The being which is what it is must be able to be the being which is not what it is not. But in the first place this negation, like all others, comes to the surface of being through human reality, as we have shown, and not through a dialectic appropriate just to being. In addition this principle can denote only the relations of being with the *external*, exactly because it presides over the relations of being with what it is not. We are dealing then with a principle constitutive of *external relations* such that they can appear to a human reality present to being-in-itself and engaged in the world. This principle does not concern the internal relations of being; these relations, inasmuch as they would posit an otherness, do not exist. The principle of identity is the negation of every species of relation at the heart of being-in-itself.

This negative which is the nothingness of being and the nihilating power both together, is *nothingness*. Nowhere else can we grasp it in such purity. Everywhere else in one way or another we must confer on it being-in-itself as nothingness. But the nothingness which arises in the heart of consciousness is *not*. It is *made-to-be*. Belief, for example, is not the contiguity of one being with another being; it is its *own* presence to itself, its own decompression of being. Otherwise the unity of the for-itself would dissolve into the duality of two in-itselfs. Thus the for-itself must be its own nothingness. The being of consciousness qua consciousness is to exist at *a distance from itself* as a presence to itself, and this empty distance which being carries in its being is Nothingness. Thus in order for a *self* to exist, it is necessary that the unity of this being include its own nothingness as the nihilation of identity. For the nothingness which slips into belief is *its* nothingness, the nothingness of belief as belief in itself, as belief blind and full, as "simple faith." The for-itself is the being which determines itself to exist inasmuch as it can not coincide with itself.

5. Transcendence: Value and Suffering

Such is the origin of transcendence. Human reality is its own surpassing toward what it lacks; it surpasses itself toward the particular being which it would be if it were what it is. Human reality is not something which exists first in order afterwards to lack this or that; it exists first as lack and in immediate, synthetic connection with what it lacks. Thus the pure event by which human reality rises as a presence in the world is apprehended by itself as its own *lack*. In its coming into existence human reality grasps itself as an incomplete being. It apprehends itself as being in so far as it is not, in the presence of the particular totality which it lacks and which it is in the form of not being it and which is what it is. Human reality is a perpetual surpassing toward a coincidence with itself which is never given. If the *cogito reaches* toward being, it is because by its very thrust it surpasses itself toward being by qualifying itself in its being as the being to which coincidence with self is lacking in order for it to be what it is. The *cogito* is indissolubly linked to being-in-itself, not as a thought to its object—which would make the in-itself relative—but as a lack to that which defines its lack. In this sense the second Cartesian proof is rigorous. Imperfect being surpasses itself toward perfect being; the being which is the foundation only of its nothingness surpasses itself toward the being which is the foundation of its being. But the being toward which human reality surpasses itself is not a transcendent God; it is at the heart of human reality; it is only human reality itself as totality.

This totality is not the pure and simple contingent in-itself of the transcendent. If what consciousness apprehends as the being toward which it surpasses itself were the pure in-itself, it would coincide with the annihilation of consciousness. But consciousness does not surpass itself toward its annihilation; it does not want to lose itself in the in-itself of identity at the limit of its surpassing. It is for the for-itself as such that the for-itself lays claim to being-in-itself.

Thus this perpetually absent being which haunts the for-itself is itself fixed in the in-itself. It is the impossible synthesis of the for-itself and the in-itself; it would be its own foundation not as nothingness but as being and would preserve within it the necessary translucency of consciousness along with the coincidence with itself of being-in-itself. It would preserve in it that turning back upon the self which conditions every necessity and every foundation. But this return to the self would be without distance; it would not be presence to itself, but identity with itself. In short, this being would be exactly the *self* which we have shown can exist only as a perpetually evanescent relation, but it would be this self as substantial being. Thus human reality arises as such in the presence of its own totality or self as a lack of that totality. And this totality can not be given by nature, since it combines in itself the incompatible characteristics of the in-itself and the for-itself.

Let no one reproach us with capriciously inventing a being of this kind; when by a further movement of thought the being and absolute absence of this totality are hypostasized as transcendence beyond the world, it takes on the name of God. Is not God a being who is what he is—in that he is all positivity and the foundation of the world—and at the same time a being who is not what he is and who is what he is not—in that he is self-consciousness and the necessary foundation of himself? The being of human reality is suffering because it rises in being as perpetually haunted by a totality which it is without being able to be it, precisely because it could not attain the in-itself without losing itself as for-itself. Human reality therefore is by nature an unhappy consciousness with no possibility of surpassing its unhappy state.

But what exactly is the nature of this being toward which unhappy consciousness surpasses itself? Shall we say that it does not exist?

Those contradictions which we discovered in it prove only that it can not be *realized*. Nothing can hold out against this self-evident truth: consciousness can exist only as *engaged* in this being which surrounds it on all sides and which paralyzes it with its phantom presence. Shall we say that it is a being *relative* to consciousness? This would be to confuse it with the object of a *thesis*. This being is not posited through and before consciousness; there is no consciousness of this being since it haunts non-thetic self-consciousness. It points to consciousness as the meaning of its being and yet consciousness is no more conscious of it than *of* itself. Still it can not escape from consciousness; but inasmuch as consciousness enjoys being a consciousness (of) being, *this* being is there. Consciousness does not confer meaning on this being as it does for this inkwell or this pencil; but without this being, which it is in the form of not being it, consciousness would not be consciousness— *i.e.*, lack. On the contrary, consciousness derives for itself its meaning as consciousness from this being. This being comes into the world along with consciousness, at once in its heart and outside it; it is absolute transcendence in absolute immanence. It has no priority over consciousness, and consciousness has no priority over it. They *form a dyad*. Of course this being could not exist without the for-itself, but neither could the for-itself exist without it. Consciousness in relation to this being stands in the mode of *being* this being, for this being is consciousness, but as a being which consciousness can not be. It is consciousness itself, in the heart of consciousness, and yet out of reach, as an absence, an unrealizable. Its nature is to inclose its own contradiction within itself; its relation to the for-itself is a total immanence which is achieved in total transcendence.

Furthermore this being need not be conceived as present to consciousness with only the abstract characteristics which our study has established. The concrete consciousness arises in situation, and it is a unique, individualized consciousness of this situation and (of) itself in situation. It is to this concrete consciousness that the self is present, and all the concrete characteristics of consciousness have their correlates in the totality of the self. The self is individual; it is the individual completion of the self which haunts the for-itself.

A feeling, for example, is a feeling in the presence of a norm; that is, a feeling of the same type but one which would be what it is. This norm or totality of the affective self is directly present as a lack *suffered* in the very heart of suffering. One suffers and one suffers from not suffering enough. The suffering of which we speak is never exactly that which we feel. What we call "noble" or "good" or "true" suffering and what moves us is the suffering which we read on the faces of others, better yet in portraits, in the face of a statue, in a tragic mask. It is a suffering which has *being*. It is presented to us as a compact, objective whole which did not await our coming in order to be and which overflows the consciousness which we have of it; it is there in the midst of the world, impenetrable and dense, like this tree or this stone; it endures; finally it is what it is. We can speak of it—that suffering there which is expressed by that set of the mouth, by that frown. It is supported and expressed by the physiognomy but not created by it. Suffering is posited upon the physiognomy; it is beyond passivity as beyond activity, beyond negation as beyond affirmation—it is. However it can be only as consciousness of self. We know well that this mask does not express the unconscious grimace of a sleeper or the rictus of a dead man. It refers to possibilities, to a situation in the world. The suffering is the conscious relation to these possibilities, to this situation, but it is solidified, cast in the bronze of being.

Value is affected with the double character, which moralists have very inadequately explained, of both being unconditionally and not being. Qua value indeed, value has being, but this normative existent does not have to be precisely as reality. Its being is to be value; that is, not-to-be being. Thus the being of value qua value is the being of what does not have being. Value then appears inapprehensible. To take it as being is to risk totally misunderstanding its unreality and to make of it, as sociologists do, a requirement of fact among other facts. In this case the contingency of being destroys value. But conversely if one looks only at the ideality of values, one is going to extract being from them, and then for lack of being, they dissolve. Of course, as Scheler has shown, I can achieve an intuition of values in terms of concrete exemplifications; I can grasp nobility in a noble act. But value thus apprehended is not given as existing on the same level of being as the act on which it confers value—in the way, for example, that the essence "red" is in relation to a particular red. Value is given as a beyond of the acts confronted, as the limit, for example, of the infinite progression of noble acts. Value is beyond being. Yet if we are not to be taken in by fine words, we must recognize that this being which is beyond being possesses being in some way at least.

These considerations suffice to make us admit that human reality is that by which value arrives in the world. But the meaning of being for value is that it is that toward which a being surpasses its being; every value-oriented act is a wrenching away from its own being toward —. Since value is always and everywhere the beyond of all surpassings, it can be considered as the unconditioned unity of all surpassings of being. Thereby it makes a dyad with the reality which originally surpasses its being and by which surpassing comes into being—*i.e.*, with human reality. We see also that since value is the unconditioned beyond of all surpassings, it must be originally the beyond of the very being which surpasses, for that is the only way in which value can be the original beyond of all possible surpassings. If every surpassing must be able to be surpassed, it is necessary that the being which surpasses should be *a priori* surpassed *in so far* as it is the very source of surpassings. Thus value taken in its origin, or the supreme value, is the beyond and the *for* of transcendence. It is the beyond which surpasses and which provides the foundation for all my surpassings but toward which I can never surpass myself, precisely because my surpassings presuppose it.

6. Freedom

Since the intention is a choice of the end and since the world reveals itself across our conduct, it is the intentional choice of the end which reveals the world, and the world is revealed as this or that (in this or that order) according to the end chosen. The end, illuminating the world, is a state of the world to be obtained and not yet existing. The intention is a thetic consciousness of the end. But it can be so only by making itself a non-thetic consciousness of its own possibility. Thus my end can be a good meal if I am hungry. But this meal which beyond the dusty road on which I am traveling is projected as the *meaning* of this road (it goes *toward* a hotel where the table is set, where the dishes are prepared, where I am expected, *etc.*) can be apprehended only correlatively with my non-thetic project toward my own possibility of eating this meal. Thus by a double but unitary upsurge the intention illuminates the world in terms of an end not yet existing and is itself defined by the choice of its possible. My end is a certain objective state of the world, my possible is a certain structure of my subjectivity; the one is revealed to the thetic consciousness, the other flows back over the non-thetic consciousness in order to characterize it.

The free project is fundamental, for it is my being. Neither ambition nor the passion to be loved nor the inferiority complex can be considered as fundamental projects. On the contrary, they of necessity must be understood in terms of a primary project which is recognized as the project which can no longer be interpreted in terms of any other and which is total. A special phenomenological method will be necessary in order to make this initial project explicit. This is what we shall call existential psychoanalysis. We shall speak of this in the next chapter. For the present we can say that the fundamental project which I am is a project concerning not my relations with this or that particular object in the world, but my total being-in-the-world; since the world itself is revealed only in the light of an end, this project posits for its end a certain type of relation to being which the for-itself wills to adopt. This project is not instantaneous, for it can not be "in" time. Neither is it non-temporal in order to "give time to itself" afterwards. That is why we reject Kant's "choice of intelligible character." The structure of the choice necessarily implies that it be a choice in the world. A choice which would be a choice in *terms of nothing,* a choice *against nothing* would be a choice of nothing and would be annihilated as choice. There is only phenomenal choice, provided that we understand that the phenomenon is here the absolute. But in its very upsurge, the choice is temporalized since it causes a future to come to illuminate the present and to constitute it as a present by giving the meaning of *pastness* to the in-itself "data." However we need not understand by this that the fundamental project is coextensive with the entire "life" of the for-itself. Since freedom is a being-without-support and without-a-springboard, the project in order to be must be constantly renewed. I choose myself perpetually and can never be merely by virtue of having-been-chosen; otherwise I should fall into the pure and simple existence of the in-itself. The necessity of perpetually choosing myself is one with the pursued-pursuit which I am. But precisely because here we are dealing with a *choice,* this choice as it is made indicates in general other choices as possibles. The possibility of these other choices is neither made explicit nor posited, but it is lived in the feeling of unjustifiability; and it is this which is expressed by the fact of the *absurdity* of my choice and consequently of my being. Thus my freedom eats away my freedom. Since I am free, I project my total possible, but I thereby posit that I am free and that I can always nihilate this first project and make it past.

(From *Being and Nothingness.* Trans. Hazel E. Barnes. New York: Philosophical Library, 1956. Reprinted by permission of Philosophical Library.)

Reflections on Dialectical Reason (from *Critique of Dialectical Reason)*

1. The Dialectic in Marx

Marx's originality lies in the fact that, in opposition to Hegel, he demonstrated that History *is in development*, that *Being is irreducible to Knowledge*, and, also, that he preserved the dialectical movement *both in* Being *and in* Knowledge. He was correct, *practically.* But having failed *to re-think the dialectic*, Marxists have played the Positivist game. Positivists often ask Marxists how they can claim, given that Marx had the good sense to realise that 'pre-history' had not yet come to an end, to detect the 'ruses' of History, the 'secret' of the proletariat, and the direction of historical development. For Positivists, prediction is possible only to the extent that the current order of succession reenacts a previous order of succession; and so the future repeats the past. Hegel could have answered them by saying that he had only *predicted the past*, in that his history was finished and complete and that, as a matter of fact, the moment which posits itself for itself in the process of living History can only guess the future, as the truth of its own incompleteness, unknowable *for it*. The Marxist future, however, is a genuine future: it is *completely* new, and irreducible to the present. Nevertheless, Marx does make predictions, and long term rather than short term ones. But in fact, according to Positivist Rationalism, Marx had disqualified himself from doing this, and given that he himself was pre-historical and within pre-history, his judgements can have only a relative and historical significance — *even* when they concern the past. Thus Marxism *as dialectic* must reject the relativism of the positivists. Andit must be understood that relativism rejects not only vast historical syntheses, but also the most modest assertions of dialectical Reason: whatever we may say or know, however close we may be to the present or past event which we attempt to reconstitute in its totalising movement, Positivism will always deny us the right. It does not regard the synthesis of all knowledge as completely impossible (though it envisages it as an inventory rather than as an organisation of Knowledge): but it considers such a synthesis impossible *now*. It is therefore necessary to demonstrate, in opposition to Positivism, how, *at this very moment*, dialectical Reason can assert certain totalising truths — if not the whole Truth.

2. Totality and Totalization

From this point of view, and before taking the discussion any further, we must make a clear distinction between the notions of totality and totalisation. A totality is defined as a being which, while radically distinct from the sum of its parts, is present in its entirety, in one form or another, in each of these parts, and which relates to itself either through its relation to one or more of its parts or through its relation to the relations between all or some of them. If this reality is *created* (a painting or a symphony are examples, if one takes integration to an extreme), it can exist only in the imaginary *(l'imaginaire)*, that is to say, as the correlative of an act of imagination. The ontological status to which it lays claim by its very definition is that of the in-itself, the inert. The synthetic unity which produced its appearance of totality is not an activity, but only the vestige of a past action (just as the unity of a medallion is the passive remnant of its being struck). Through its being-in-exteriority, the inertia of the in-itself gnaws away at this appearance of unity; the passive totality is, in fact, eroded by infinite divisibility. Thus, as the active power of holding together its parts, the totality is only the correlative of an act of imagination: *the* symphony or *the* painting, as I have shown elsewhere, are imaginaries projected through the set of dried paints or the linking of sounds which function as their *analogon*. In the case of practical objects — machines, tools, consumer goods, etc. — our present action makes them seem like total-

ities by resuscitating, in some way, the *praxis* which attempted to totalise their inertia. We shall see below that these inert totalities are of
crucial importance and that they create the kind of relation between
men which we will refer to, later, as the practico-inert. These *human*
objects are worthy of attention in the human world, for it is there that
they attain their practico-inert statute; that is to say, they lie heavy on
our destiny because of the contradiction which opposes *praxis* (the labour which made them and the labour which utilises them) and inertia,
within them. But, as these remarks show, they are products; and the
totality, despite what one might think, is only a regulative principle of
the totalisation (and all at once disintegrates into the inert ensemble
of its provisional creations).

If, indeed, anything is to appear as the synthetic unity of the diverse,
it must be a developing unification, that is to say, an activity. The synthetic unification of a habitat is not merely the labour which has produced it, but also the activity of inhabiting it; reduced to itself, it re-
verts to the multiplicity of inertia. Thus totalisation has the same statute as the totality, for, through the multiplicities, it continues that synthetic labour which makes each part an expression of the whole and
which relates the whole to itself through the mediation of its parts. But
it is a *developing* activity, which cannot cease without the multiplici-
tyreverting to its original statute. This act delineates a practical field
which, as the undifferentiated correlative of *praxis,* is the formal unity
of the ensembles which are to be integrated; within this practical field,
the activity attempts the most rigorous synthesis of the most differentiated multiplicity. Thus, by a double movement, multiplicity is multiplied to infinity, each part is set against all the others and against the
whole which is in the process of being formed, while the totalising activity tightens all the bonds, making each differentiated element both
its immediate expression and its mediation in relation to the other elements. On this basis, it is easy to establish the intelligibility of dialectical Reason; it is the very movement of totalisation. Thus, to take only
one example, it is within the framework of totalisation that the negation of the negation becomes an affirmation. Within the practical field,
the correlative of *praxis*, every determination is a negation, for *praxis*,
in differentiating certain ensembles, excludes them from the group
formed by all the others; and the developing unification appears
simultaneously in the most differentiated products (indicating the direction of the movement), in those which are less differentiated (indicating continuities, resistances, traditions, a tighter, but more superficial, unity), and in the conflict between the two (which expresses the
present state of the developing totalisation). The new negation, which,
in determining the less differentiated ensembles, will raise them to the
level of the others, is bound to eliminate the negation which set the en-

sembles in antagonism to each other. Thus it is only within a developing unification (which has already defined the limits of its field) that a determination can be said to be a negation and that the negation of a negation is necessarily an affirmation. If dialectical Reason exists, then, from the ontological point of view, it can only be a developing totalisation, occurring where the totalisation occurs, and, from the epistemological point of view, it can only be the accessibility of that totalisation to a knowledge which is itself, in principle, totalising in its procedures. But since totalising knowledge cannot be thought of as attaining ontological totalisation as a new totalisation of it, dialectical knowledge must itself be a moment of the totalisation, or, in other words, totalisation must include within itself its own reflexive retotalisation as an essential structure and as a totalising process within the process as a whole.

... Thus the dialectic is a totalising activity. Its only laws are the rules produced by the developing totalisation, and these are obviously concerned with the relation between unification and the unified, that is to say, the modes of _effective_ presence of the totalising process in the totalised parts. And knowledge, itself totalising, is the totalisation itself in so far as it is present in particular partial structures of a definite kind. In other words, totalisation cannot be consciously present to itself if it remains a formal, faceless activity of synthetic unification, but can be so only through the mediation of differentiated realities which it unifies and which effectively embody it to the extent that they totalise _themselves_ by the very movement of the activity of totalising. These remarks enable us to define the first feature of the _critical investigation_: it takes place _inside_ the totalisation and can be neither a contemplative recognition of the totalising movement, nor a particular, autonomous totalisation of the known totalisation. Rather, it is a real moment of the developing totalisation in so far as this is embodied in all its parts and is realised as synthetic knowledge of itself through the mediation of certain of these parts. In practice, this means that the critical investigation can and must be anyone's reflexive experience.

3. Need

It should be recalled that the crucial discovery of dialectical investigation is that man is 'mediated' by things to the same extent as things are 'mediated' by man. This truth must be borne in mind in its entirety if we are to develop all its consequences. This is what is called dialectical _circularity_ and, as we shall see, it must be established by dialectical investigation. But if we were not already dialectical beings we would not even be able to comprehend this circularity. I present it at the outset not as a truth, nor even a conjecture, but as the type of thought which is necessary, _prospectively_, in order to elucidate a self-developing investigation.

On the most superficial and familiar level, the investigation *first* reveals, in the unity of dialectical connections, unification as the movement of individual *praxis*, plurality, the organisation of plurality, and the plurality of organisations. One need only open one's eyes to see this. Our problem concerns these connections. If there are individuals, *who*, or *what*, totalises?

A simple but inadequate answer is that there would not even be the beginnings of partial totalisation if the individual were not totalising *through himself. The entire historical dialectic rests on individual praxis in so far as it is already dialectical*, that is to say, to the extent that action is itself the negating transcendence of contradiction, the determination of a present totalisation in the name of a future totality, and the real effective working of matter. This much is clear, and is an old lesson of both subjective and objective investigation. Our problem is this: what becomes of *the* dialectic if there are only particular men each of whom is dialectical? As I have said, the investigation provides its own intelligibility. We must therefore see what is the real rationality of action, at the level of individual *praxis* (ignoring for the moment the collective constraints which give rise to it, limit it or make it ineffective).

Everything is to be explained through *need* (*le besoin*); need is the first totalising relation between the material being, man, and the material ensemble of which he is part. This relation is *univocal*, and *of interiority*. Indeed, it is through need that the first negation of the negation and the first totalisation appear in matter. Need is a negation of the negation in so far as it expresses itself as a *lack* within the organism; and need is a positivity in so far as the organic totality tends to preserve itself *as such* through it. The original negation, in fact, is a initial contradiction between the organic and the inorganic, in the double sense that lack is defined in relation to *a totality*, but that a *lacuna, a negativity*, has as such a *mechanical* kind of existence, an that, in the last analysis, *what is lacking* can be reduced to inorganic or less organised elements or, quite simply, to dead flesh, etc. From this point of view, the negation of this negation is achieved through the transcendence of the organic towards the inorganic: need is a link of *univocal immanence* with surrounding materiality in so far as the organism *tries to sustain itself* with it; it is already totalising, and doubly so, for it is nothing other than the living totality, manifesting itself as a totality and revealing the material environment, to infinity, as the total field of possibilities of satisfaction.

4. Labor

Man, who produces his life in the unity of the material field, is led by *praxis* itself to define zones, systems and privileged objects within this inert totality. He cannot construct his tools — and this applies to the agricultural tools of primitive peoples as much as to the practical use of atomic energy — without introducing partial determinations into the unified environment, whether this environment is the whole world or a narrow strip of land between the sea and the virgin forest. Thus he sets himself in opposition to himself through the mediation of the inert; and, conversely, the constructive power of the labourer opposes the part to the whole in the inert within the 'natural' unity. We shall come across many examples of this later. It follows, in the first place, that negation becomes internal in the very milieu of exteriority, and secondly, that it is a real opposition of forces. But this opposition comes to Nature through man in two ways, since his action constitutes both the whole and its disruption. *Labour* of any kind always exists only as a totalisation and a transcended contradiction. Once it has constituted the environment as the milieu in which the labourer produces himself, every subsequent development will be a negation precisely to the extent that it is positive. And such negations can be grasped only as moments which posit themselves for themselves, since the force of inertia increases their separation within the whole. Hence the subsequent task of labour must be to put the created object back in contact with the other sectors within the whole and to unite them from a new point of view; it negates separation.

But this new process, the negation of the negation, derives its intelligibility, once again, from the original totality. In a realist and materialist system there can be no justification for asserting, *a priori*, that the negation of a negation must give rise to a new affirmation, as long as the type of reality in which these negations occur remains undefined. Even in the human universe, the universe of totalities, there are quite definitive and classifiable situations in which the negation of the negation is a new negation, because in these special cases there is interference between totality and recurrence. But this is not our present concern. At all events, it is clear that the negation of a negation produces an indeterminate ensemble *unless* it is regarded as arising within a totality. But even within a totality the negation of the negation would be a return to the starting point if it did not involve a totality being transcended towards a totalising end. The elimination of the partial organisations of the instrumental field would simply bring us back to the original non-differentiation of the unified environment (as when one destroys the traces of an event, an experience or a construction), unless the movement to eliminate them is accompanied by an effort to preserve them — that is, unless they are regarded as a step towards a unity of *differentiation* in which a new type of subordination of the parts to the whole and a new co-ordination of the parts with one another is to be achieved. And this is what has to happen given that the aim is not to preserve the unity of the field of action in and for itself, but to find in it material elements capable of preserving or restoring the organic totality it contains. Thus, in so far as body is function, function need and need *praxis*, one can say that *human labour*, the original *praxis* by which man produces and reproduces his life, is *entirely* dialectical: its possibility and its permanent necessity rest upon the relation of interiority which unites the organism with the environment and upon the deep contradiction between the inorganic and organic orders, both of which are present in everyone. Its primary movement and its essential character are defined by a twofold contradictory transformation: the unity of the project endows the practical field with a quasi-synthetic unity, and the crucial moment of labour is that in which the organism makes itself inert (the man applies his weight to the lever, etc.) in order to transform the surrounding inertia.

5. Scarcity

Scarcity is a fundamental relation of *our* History and a contingent determination of our univocal relation to materiality.

Scarcity, as the lived relation of a practical multiplicity to surrounding materiality within that multiplicity itself, is the basis of the possibility of human history. But this calls for two explicit qualifications. First, for a historian situated in 1957, scarcity is not the basis of the possibility of *all* History. We have no way of telling whether, for different organisms on other planets — or for our descendants, if technical and social changes shatter the framework of scarcity — a different History, constituted on another basis, and with different motive forces and different internal projects, might be logically conceivable. (By this I do not simply mean that we cannot tell whether the relation of organic beings to inorganic (*inorganises*) ones might somewhere be something other than scarcity; first and foremost, I mean that it is impossible to know a *priori* whether the temporalisation of such beings would take the form of a history.) But to say that our History is a history of men is equivalent to saying that it is born and developed within the permanent framework of a field of tension produced by scarcity.

The second qualification is this. Scarcity is the basis of the possibility of human history, but not of its reality. In other words, it makes History possible, but other factors (yet to be determined) are necessary if History is to be produced. The reason for this restriction is that there are some backward societies which, in a sense, are more prone than others to famine or to seasonal depressions of food resources, but which are, nevertheless, correctly classified by ethnographers as societies with no history, societies based on repetition. This means that scarcity can exist on a very large scale. If a state of equilibrium is established within a given mode of production, and preserved from one generation to the next, it is preserved as *exis* — that is to say, as a physiological and social determination of human organisms and as a practical project of keeping institutions and physical corporate development at the same level. This corresponds ideologically to a decision about human 'nature'. *Man* is a stunted misshapen being, hardened to suffering, and he lives in order to work from dawn till dusk with *these* (primitive) technical means, on a thankless threatening earth.

Scarcity can be seen, in the abstract, as a relation of the individual to the environment. Practically and historically, that is, in so far as we exist in particular situations, the environment is a ready-constituted practical field, which relates everyone to collective structures (we shall explain what this means later). The most fundamental of these structures is scarcity as the negative unity of the multiplicity of men (of *this* concrete multiplicity). This unity is negative in relation to men because it is transmitted to man by matter *in so far as* matter is non-human (that is to say, in so far as its being human is possible *only* through struggle on this earth). This means, therefore, that the first totalisation effected by materiality manifests itself (in a given society and between independent social groups) *both* as the possibility of universal destruction *and* as the permanent possibility that this destruction through matter might come to any individual through the praxis of other men. This first aspect of scarcity *can* condition the unity of the group, in that the group, taken collectively, may organise itself to react collectively. But this dialectical and properly human aspect of *praxis* cannot possibly be contained within the relation of scarcity itself, precisely because the positive dialectical unity of a common action is the negation of negative unity as surrounding materiality turning on the individuals who have totalised it. In fact, scarcity as tension and as force-field is the expression of a quantitative fact (more or less strictly defined). There will be an insufficient quantity of a particular natural substance or manufactured product in a particular social field, given the number of members of the groups or inhabitants of the region. *There is not enough for everybody.*

6. Workers as a Class
In so far as the worker is a product of capitalism, that is to say, in so far as he works for wages and produces goods which are taken from him and uses industrial machinery which belongs to individuals or to private groups, the negative common object of the working class in the first half of the nineteenth century was, as we have seen, its total national production, that is to say, machines as capital requiring the worker to produce, through them, an expansion of capital. We have also seen that the common interest of the class can only be the negation of this negation, that is to say, the practical negation of a destiny which is suffered as common inertia. We must therefore recognise that practical organisation, *as human exigency*, is, in itself, and even in the

practico-inert field, a constitutive structure of relations amongst workers (this will become clearer in the next chapter). And this organisation is both a means and an end, since it presents itself *both* as a means of struggling against destiny (that is to say, against the men who in a particular system make *this* particular destiny out of the machine), *and* as the future reinteriorisation of the practico-inert field and its projected dissolution within a perpetually active social organisation which, as a concrete totality, will govern both the means of production and production as a whole.

The worker will be saved from his destiny only if the human multiplicity as a whole is permanently changed into a group *praxis*. His only future, therefore, is at the second degree of sociality, that is to say, in human relations as they arise in the unity of a group (and not in the disunity of the gathering-milieu). This is what Marx meant when he spoke of the sociality of the worker. Yet it should be noted that this sociality appears as the *joint* negation of two reciprocal aspects of the practical field: a negation of the common object as destiny and a connected negation of multiplicity as seriality. In other words, sociality as a still individual project of transcendence (in the organised group) of the multiplicity of individuals reveals seriality itself as a link of impotence; this seriality is the being-to-be-transcended towards an action tending to socialise the common object. On the other hand, this sociality, in so far as it was determined in everyone by the very structure of the collective in which he produced himself, and *in so far as it initially produced no result* (that is, during the first quarter of the nineteenth century and, basically, right up to the revolt of the Lyon silk-weavers) or was limited to the creation of reciprocal relations, appeared in everyone as a structure peculiar to his own project and thus decomposed into a multiplicity of identical projects, before producing active organisations through itself. Thus it emerges as a process of isolation *precisely to the extent that* it is fundamentally a transcendce of plurality towards unity. This means, quite simply, that the organising project *in everyone* begins by being negated by that which it transcends and negates, that is to say, by seriality as a link of impotence.

When we look at it more closely, we can see that the *necessity of some common action* can arise only out of an existing link between men and can present itself only as the transcendence and inversion of this fundamental link. If it were possible to conceive real (but abstract) individuals in a pure state — and I do not mean the social atoms of liberalism — in so far as they are united by bonds of reciprocity, and if one could abstract from the object's transformation of reciprocity into a link of alterity, it would be impossible to understand how the infinite dispersal of human relations could of itself produce the means of pulling itself together again. This conception is completely inapplicable to human history, but it retains some sense as a logical possibility, provided the idea mentioned above of living organisms, which depend on the universe, but are not affected by the contraction which is caused by *scarcity* as a fundamental, contingent characteristic of our History, is consistent. In the practico-inert world based on scarcity, however, the object brings men together by imposing the violent, passive unity of a seal on their multiplicity. And in the very moment where this object is a threat (for the colonised, or the exploited), in the very moment where this object, as positive interest, is threatened (for the colonists or the exploiters), the unity of impotence transforms itself into a violent contradiction: in it, *unity* opposes itself to the impotence which negates it. We shall discover the intelligibility of this moment later. For the time being, what needs to be emphasised is that impotence, as a force of alterity, is *primarily* unity in its negative form, *primarily* action in the form of passivity, and *primarily* finality in the form of counter-finality.

7. Class Struggle and History

But, in so far as the proletariat was a series, and thus affected, like all series, with impotence and with a tendency to limit action and to be satisfied with superficial, temporary advances; in so far as, in the field of appearance produced by bourgeois oppression, reality appeared to the proletariat as the impossibility of being other than it is; in so far as the concrete changes called for were always modest for everyone, the workers were affected by a spontaneous reformism. And this reformism simply expresses something which exists in everyone in his relations with every other (except for the oppressor in relation to the oppressed): the practice of conciliation (generally reinforced by the existence of mediating third parties). In a sense, the oppressed who were born into oppression, heirs of the oppressed, would be content with slight improvements: they would see these improvements as in themselves a total transformation of the situation. Obviously, in fact, they believed that they would be content with them. Nevertheless, an exploiting class which was immediately favourable to improvements (even after one or two generations) would have produced a completely different working class (with the same structures, but different internal relations, a different tension) and might perhaps have postponed revolutionary radicalisation for a time. ... capitalists in this period assumed that it was necessary for Others to be poor; and to assume the poverty of others is to acquiesce in producing it, and thus to transcend the assumed necessity by a free adoption of its laws and its themes; it is to justify this free transformation of necessity into oppression in terms of a class Manichaeism which designates the oppressed as anti-humans who deserve their oppression, and thus to condemn them to it. Lastly, it is to make this necessity-freedom even more intolerable for the oppressed, in that it presents itself as a condemnation of the exploited (a free human sentence) by things (the 'inexorable' laws of liberal economics).

... The conclusion of this investigation is that the only possible intelligibility of human relations is dialectical and that this intelligibility, in a concrete history whose true foundation is scarcity, can be manifested only as an antagonistic reciprocity. So class struggle as a practice necessarily leads to a dialectical interpretation; and, moreover, in the history of human multiplicities, class struggle is necessarily produced on the basis of historically determined conditions, as the developing realisation of dialectical rationality. Our History is intelligible to us because it is dialectical and it is dialectical because the class struggle produces us as transcending the inertia of the collective towards dialectical combat-groups.

(From *Critique of Dialectical Reason*, ed. Jonathan Ree. Trans. Alan Sheridan-Smith. London: Verso NLB, 1976. Reprinted by permission of Verso.)

Review Questions

1. In Sartre's view, what is existentialism?
2. Is there a distinction between *personalist* and *individual*?
3. Why does Sartre speak of *ontology* rather than *metaphysics*?
4. Distinguish between being-in-itself and being-for-itself.
5. Explain the notion of Freedom for Sartre.
6. What is the meaning of a *critique* of dialectical reason?
7. Are there any values in the philosophy of Sartre?
8. Is atheism an active commitment for Sartre?

Selected Bibliography

History of Philosophy: General

Copleston, F. *A History of Philosophy,* 9 vols. New York, Doubleday Image, 1946 sqq.

Edwards, P., ed. *Encyclopedia of Philosophy,* 8 vols. in 4. New York; Macmillan, 1967.

Flower, E., and Murphy, M.G. *A History of Philosophy in America,* 2 vols. New York, Capricorn Books, 1977.

Jaspers, K. *The Great Philosophers.* Ed. Arendt H., tr. Mannheim, R. New York, Harcourt, Brace, 1962.

Jordan, James N. *Western Philosophy: From Antiquity to the Middle Ages.* New York, Macmillan, 1987.

Mentor Series in Philosophy. New York, New American Library, Includes: The Age of Belief (A. Freemantle), The Age of Adventure (G. de Santillano), The Age of Reason (S. Hampshire), The Age Enlightment (I. Berlin), The Age of Ideology (H.D. Aiken), The Age of Analysis (M. White).

O'Connor, D.J. *A Critical History of Western Philosophy.* New York, Free Press, 1964.

Sorley, W.R. *History of English Philosophy to 1900.* Cambridge, Cambridge University Press, 1951.

Ancient Philosphy: General

Burnet, J. *Early Greek Philosophy.* New York, Meridian, 1960.

Cornford, F.M. *Before and After Socrates.* New York, Cambridge University Press, 1960.

Guthrie, W.R.C. *A History of Greek Philosophy,* 6 vols. Cambridge, Cambridge University Press, 1962-81.

Jaeger, W. *The Theology of the Early Greek Philosophers.* Cambridge, Cambridge University Press, 1947.

Owens, J. *A History of Ancient Philosophy.* New York, Appleton, 1957.

Chapter 1. The Pre-Socratics

Freeman, K. *Ancilla to the Pre-Socratic Philosophers.* Cambridge, Harvard University Press, 1948.

Jaeger, W. *The Theology of the Early Greek Philosophers.* Tr. Robertson,
            E.S. Westport, CT, Greenwood Press, 1980.
Kirk, G.S., Raven, J., and Schofield, M. *The Pre-Socratic Philosophers,* 2nd
            ed. Cambridge, Cambridge University Press, 1983.
Mourelatos, A.P.D. *The Pre-Socratics.* New York, Doubleday Anchor, 1974.
Nahm, M., ed. *Selections from Early Greek Philosophy.* Englewood Cliffs,
            Prentice Hall, 1964.

Chapter 2. Socrates

Levin, R., ed. *The Question of Socrates.* New York, Harcourt, Brace and
            World, 1961.
Taylor, A.E. *Socrates.* Garden City, NY, Doubleday Anchor, 1953.
Vlastos, G., ed. *The Philosophy of Socrates.* New York, Doubleday Anchor,
            1971.

Chapter 3. Plato

The Collected Dialogues of Plato. Ed. Hamilton, E., and Cairns, H.
            Princeton, Princeton University Press, 1961.
Works of Plato. Ed. Edman, I. New York Random House, 1965.
Plato Selections. Ed. Demos, R. New York, Scribners, 1927.
Gosling, J.C.B. *Plato.* London, Routledge and Kegan Paul, 1793.
Koyre, A. *Discovering Plato.* Tr. Rosenfeld, L.C. New York, Columbia
            University Press, 1945.
Randall, J.H. *Plato, Dramatist of the Life of Reason.* New York, Columbia
            University Press, 1970.
Shorey, P. *What Plato Said.* Chicago, University of Chicago Press, 1933.
Taylor, A.E. *Plato, The Man and His Work.* New York, Methuen, 1960.

Chapter 4. Aristotle

The Basic Works of Aristotle. Ed. McKeon, R.D. New York, Random
            House, 1941.
Aristotle Selections. Ed. Ross, W.D. New York, Scribners, 1938.
The Pocket Aristotle. Ed. Kaplan, J. New York, Washington Square Press,
            1983.
Edel, A. *Aristotle and His Philosophy.* Chapel Hill, University of North
            Carolina Press, 1982.
Randall, J.H. *Aristotle.* New York, Columbia University Press, 1960.
Ross, W.D. *Aristotle.* New York, Meridian, 1959.
Taylor, A.E. *Aristotle.* New York, Dover, 1955.
Veatch, H.B. *Aristotle.* Bloomington, Indiana University Press, 1974.

Part II. Medieval Philosophy, General

Ancient Christian Writers. Ed. Burghardt, W., Lawler, T.C., and Quasten, J.
    Mahwah, NJ, Paulist Press, 1946 sqq.
Fairweather, E.R. *A Scholastic Miscellany, Anselm to Ockham.*
    Philadelphia, Westminster Press, 1956.
Gilson, E. *History of Christian Philosophy in the Middle Ages.* New York,
    Random House, 1955.
The Spirit of Medieval Philosophy. Tr. Downes, A. New York, Scribners,
    1936.
Knowles, D. *The Evolution of Medieval Thought.* Baltimore, Helicon Press,
    1962.
Leff, G. *Medieval Thought, St. Augustine to Ockham.* Baltimore, Penguin,
    1958.
Maurer, A. *Medieval Philosophy.* New York, Random House, 1962.
McKeon, R.D. *Selections from Medieval Philosophers,* 2 vols. New York,
    Scribners, 1929.
Walsh, JJ, and Hyman, A., ed. *Philosophy in the Middle Ages.* Indianapolis,
    Hackett, 1983.

Chapter 5. St. Augustine

Augustine of Hippo, Selected Writings. Tr. Clark, M. Ramsey, NJ, Paulist
    Press, 1984.
City of God. Tr. Bettenson, H., ed. Knowles, D. Baltimore, Penguin, 1972.
The Essential Augustine. Ed. Bourke, V.J. Indianapolis, Hackett, 1974.
Confessions. Tr. Pine-Coffin, R.S. Baltimore, Penguin, 1961.
Brown, P. *Augustine of Hippo.* Berkeley, University of California Press,
    1967.
Gilson, E. *The Christian Philosophy of Saint Augustine.* Tr. Lynch, L. New
    York, Random House, 1961.
Markus, R.A. *Augustine.* New York, Doubleday Anchor, 1972.
Marrow, H. *Saint Augustine.* New York, Harper and Row, 1958.

Chapter 6. St. Anselm

Basic Writings, including Proslogion, Monologion and Cur Deus Homo. Tr.
    Deane, S.N. LaSalle, IN, Open Court, 1974.
St. Anselm's 'Proslogion'. Tr. Charlesworth, M.J. Oxford, Clarendon Press,
    1965.
Barth, K. *Anselm, Fides Quaerens Intellectum.* London, SCM, 1960.
Hartshorne, C. *Anselm's Discovery.* La Salle, Open Court, 1965.
McIntyre, J. *St. Anselm and His Critics.* Edinburgh, 1963.

Plantinga, A., ed. *The Ontological Argument from St. Anselm to Contemporary Philosophers.* New York, Doubleday Anchor, 1965.

Chapter 7. St. Thomas Aquinas

Basic Writings of Saint Thomas Aquinas, 2 vols. Ed. Pegis, A.C. New York, Random House, 1945.
The Pocket Aquinas. Ed. Bourke, V.J. New York, Washington Square Press, 1960.
An Aquinas Reader. Ed. Clark, M.T. New York, Doubleday Image, 1955.
Chesterton, G.K. *St. Thomas Aquinas.* New York, Doubleday Image, 1955.
Copleston, F.C. *Aquinas.* Baltimore, Penquin, 1955.
Gilson, E. *The Christian Philosophy of St. Thomas Aquinas.* Tr. Shook, L. New York, Random House, 1956.
Kenny, A. *Aquinas.* New York, Hill and Wang, 1980.
Weisheipl, J. *Friar Thomas d'Aquino.* New York, Doubleday 1974.

Chapter 8. Duns Scotus

Duns Scotus, Philosophical Writings. Tr. and ed. Wolter, A. London, Nelson, 1962.
A Treatise on God as First Principle. Tr. Wolter, A. Chicago, Forum Books, Franciscan Herald Press, 1966.
God and Creatures, The Quodlibetal Question. Tr. Alluntis, F., and Wolter, A. Princeton, Princeton University Press, 1975.
Bettoni, E. *Duns Scotus, The Basic Principles of His Philosophy.* Tr. Bonansea, B. Washington, The Catholic University Press, 1961.
Ryan, J.K., and Bonansea, B.M. *John Duns Scotus, 1265-1965.* Washington, The Catholic University Press, 1965.
Sharp, D. *Franciscan Philosophy at Oxford in the Thirteenth Century.* Oxford, Oxford University Press, 1930.

Chapter 9. Nicholas of Cusa

On Learned Ignorance. Tr. Hopkins, J. Minneapolis, AJ Bennings Press, 1981.
Unity and Reform: Selected Writings of Nicholas of Cùsa. Ed. Dolan, J. Notre Dame, Notre Dame University Press, 1962.
The Vision of God. Tr. Hopkins, J. Minneapolis, AJ Bennings Press, 1985.
Bett, H. *Nicholas of Cusa.* London, Methuen, 1932.
Hopkins, J. *A Concise Introduction to the Philosophy of Nicholas of Cusa.* Minneapolis, University of Minnesota Press, 1978.

Sigmund, P.E. *Nicholas of Cusa and Medieval Political Thought.*
    Cambridge, Harvard University Press, 1963.

Part III Modern Philosophy, General

Boas, G. *Dominant Themes of Modern Philosophy.* New York, Ronald
    Press, 1957.
Burtt, E.O. *The English Philosophers from Bacon to Mill.* New York,
    Modern Library, 1939.
Crombie, A. *Medieval and Early Modern Science,* 2 vols. Garden City,
    Doubleday Anchor, 1959.
Gilson, E., and Langan, T. *Modern Philosophy.* New York, Random House,
    1962.
Gillispie, C.C. *The Edge of Objectivity.* Princeton, Princeton University
    Press, 1960.
Kuhn, T.S. *The Copernican Revolution.* Cambridge, Havard University
    Press, 1957.
Warnock, G.J. *English Philosophy since 1900.* London, Oxford University
    Press, 1958.
Willey, B. *Seventeenth Century Background.* Garden City, Doubleday
    Anchor, 1953.

Chapter 10. Descartes

The Philosophical Works of Descartes, 2 vols. Tr. Haldane, E.S., and Ross,
    G.T.R. New York, Dover, 1955.
Descartes' Philosophical Writings. Ed. Anscombe, G.E.M., Geach, P.T., and
    Koyre, A. Indianapolis, Bobbs-Merrill, 1971.
Descartes' Philosophical Writings. Tr. and ed. Kemp Smith, N. New York,
    Modern Library, 1958.
Descartes Selections. Ed. Eaton, R.M., New York, Scribners, 1927.
Beck, L.J. *The Metaphysics of Descartes.* Oxford, Clarendon Press, 1965.
Doney, W. *Descartes.* Notre Dame, Notre Dame University Press, 1968.
Kenny, A. *Descartes, A Study of His Philosophy.* New York, Random
    House, 1968.
Roth, L. *Descartes' Discourse on Method.* Oxford, Clarendon Press, 1937.

Chapter 11. Spinoza

The Chief Works of Spinoza, 2 vols. Tr. Elwes, R.H.M. New York, Dover,
    1955.
Spinoza Selections. Ed. Wild, J. New York, Scribners, 1930.
Hampshire, S. *Spinoza.* Baltimore, Penguin, 1951.
McKeon, R. *The Philosophy of Spinoza.* New York, Longmans, 1928.

Roth, L. *Spinoza*. London, Benn, 1954.
Wolfson, H.A. *The Philosophy of Spinoza*. New York, Meridian, 1934.

Chapter 12. Leibniz

Discourse on Metaphysics, Correspondence with Arnauld, Monadology. Tr.
          Montgomery, G.R. LaSalle, IN, Open Court, 1968.
Theodicy. Tr. Huggard, E.M. and ed. Farrer, A. LaSalle, Open Court, 1952.
Leibniz Selections. Tr. Wiener, P. New York Scribners, 1951.
Carr, H.W. *Leibniz*. New York, Dover, 1960.
MacDonald, R.G. *Leibniz*. New York, Oxford University Press, 1984.
Rescher, N. *The Philosophy of Leibniz*. Englwood Cliffs, NJ, Prentice-Hall,
          1967.
Van Peursen, C.A. *Leibniz*. New York, Dutton, 1970.

Chapter 13. Hobbes

Leviathan. Ed. Oakeshott, intro. Peters, R.S. New York, Collier, 1962.
Hobbes Selections. Ed. Woodbridge, F.J.E. New York, Scribners, 1930.
Body, Mind and Citizen. Ed. Peters, R.S. New York, Collier Books, 1962.
Laird, J. *Hobbes*. London, Benn, 1934.
Oakeshott, M. *Hobbes on Civil Association*. Berkeley, University of
          California, 1975.
Richards, P. *Hobbes*. Baltimore, Penguin, 1956.
Watkins, J.W.N. *Hobbes' System of Ideas*. London, Hutchinson, 1973.

Chapter 14. Locke

An Essay Concerning Human Understanding, 2 vols. Ed. Fraser, A.C. New
          York, Dover, 1959.
The Second Treatise of Government. Ed. Macpherson, C. Indianapolis,
          Hackett, 1980.
Letter Concerning Toleration. Ed. Tully, J. Indianapolis, Hackett, 1983.
Locke Selections. Ed. Lamprecht, S. New York, Scribners, 1928.
Cranston, M. *John Locke, a Biography*. London, Longmans, 1957.
Mabbot, J.D. *John Locke*. London, Macmillan, 1973.
O'Connor, D.J. *John Locke*. Baltimore, Penguin, 1952.

Chapter 15. Berkeley

Berkeley, Philosophical Writings. Ed. Jessop, T.D. London, Nelson, 1952.
Berkeley Selections. Ed. Calkins, M.W. New York, Scribners, 1929.

A Treatise concerning the Principles of Human Knowledge. Ed. Turbayne, C.M. Indianapolis, Bobbs-Merrill, 1970.
Jessop, T.E. *George Berkeley.* London, Longmans, 1959.
Pitcher, G. *Berkeley.* London, Routledge and Kegan Paul, 1977.
Warnock, G.J. *Berkeley.* Baltimore, Penguin, 1953.

Chapter 16. Hume

An Enquiry Concerning Human Understanding. Ed. McCormack, T.J., and Calkins, M.W. LaSalle, Open Court, 1966.
Dialogues Concerning Natural Religion. Ed. Kemp Smith, N. Indianapolis, Bobbs-Merrill, 1980.
Hume Selections. Ed. Hendel, C.W. New York, Scribners, 1927.
Kemp Smith, N. *The Philosophy of David Hume,* London, Macmillian, 1949.
Mossner, E.C. *The Life of David Hume.* Oxford, Clarendon, 1980.
Norton, D.F. *David Hume.* Princeton, Princeton University Press, 1982.

Chapter 17. Kant

Critique of Pure Reason. Tr. Meiklejohn, J.M.D. London, Everyman, 1978.
Tr. Kemp Smith, N. New York, St. Martin's Press, 1969.
Critique of Practical Reason. Tr. Beck, L.W. Indianapolis, Bobbs-Merrill, 1956.
Prolegomena to Any Future Metaphysics. Tr. Carus, P. Indianapolis, Hackett, 1977.
Kant Selections. Ed. Greene, T.M. New York, Scribners, 1927.
Commentaries by L.W. Beck (*Practical Reason.* Chicago, 1960).
N. Kemp Smith (*Pure Reason.* Humanities Press, 1962).
H.W. Cassirer (*Judgment.* London, 1938).
Ewing, A.C. *A Short Commentary Kant's 'Critique of Pure Reason'.* London, Methuen, 1978.
Korner, S. *Kant.* Baltimore, Penguin, 1955.

Chapter 18. Hegel

Phenomenology of Spirit. Tr. Miller, A.V. Oxford, Clarendon, 1977.
Phenomenology of Mind. Tr. Baillie, J.B. London, Macmillan, 1931.
Hegel Selections. Ed. Loewenberg, J. New York, Scribners, 1929.
On Art, Religion and Philosophy. Tr. Gray, J.G. New York, Harper Torchbooks, 1970.
Findlay, J.N. *Hegel, A re-examination.* London, 1958.

Mure, G.R.G. *An Introduction to Hegel.* New York, Oxford Universty Press, 1940.
Stace, W.T. *The Philosophy of Hegel.* New York, Dover, 1958.

Chapter 19. Mill

On Liberty. Ed. Rapaport, E. Indianapolis, Hackett, 1978.
Utilitarianism. Baltimore, Penguin, 1982.
The Philosophy of John Stuart Mill. Ed. Cohen, M. New York, Modern Library, 1961.
Autobiography. Intro. Laski, H. Oxford, Oxford University Press, 1952.
August, E. *John Stuart Mill, A Mind at Large.* New York, Scribners, 1975.
Britton, K. *John Stuart Mill.* Baltimore, Penguin, 1953.
Packe, M. *St. John: The Life of John Stuart Mill.* 1954.

Part IV. Contemporary Philosophy. General

Ayer, A.J. *Philosophy in the Twentieth Century.* New York, Random House, 1982.
Bochenski, I.M. *Contemporary European Philosophy.* Tr. Nicholl, D., and Aschenbrenner, K. Berkeley, University of California Press, 1956.
Gilson, E., Langan, T., and Maurer, A. *Recent Philosophy.* New York, Random House, 1962.
Macquarrie, J. *Existentialism.* Baltimore, Penguin, 1973.
Passmore, J.A. *A Hundred Years of Philosophy.* London, 1959.
Warnock, G.J. *English Philosophy Since 1900.* London, 1958.
Whitehead, A.N. *Science and the Modern World.* New York, New American Library, 1949.

Chapter 20. Kierkegaard

A Kierkegaard Anthology. Ed. Bretall, R. Princeton, Princeton University Press, 1949.
Kierkegaard Selections. Tr. Hollander, L. Garden City, Doubleday Anchor, 1960.
Fear and Trembling, And Sickness Until Death. Tr. Lowrie, W. New York, Doubleday Anchor, 1954.
The Concept of Dread. Tr. Lowrie, W., and Swenson, L.M. Princeton, Princeton University Press, 1957.
Collins, J. *The Mind of Kierkegaard.* Chicago, Regnery, 1953.
Lowrie, W. *A Short Life of Kierkegaard.* Princeton, Princeton University Press, 1942.

Chapter 21. Nietzsche

The Portable Nietzsche. Tr. Kaufman, W. New York, Viking, 1968.
The Philosophy of Nietzsche. Intro. Wright, W.H. New York, Modern
        Library, 1954.
The Will to Power. Tr. Kaufman, W., and Hollingdale, R.J. New York,
        Random House, 1967.
The Gay Science. Tr. Kaufman, W. New York, Vintage, 1974.
Copleston, F. *Friedrich Nietzsche, Philosopher of Culture.* London, Burns
        Oates, 1978.
Kaufman, W. *Nietzsche.* New York, Meridian, 1956.
Hollingdale, R.J. *Nietzsche.* London, Routledge and Kegan Paul, 1973.

Chapter 22. Marx

Capital. Tr. Moore, S., and Aveling, E. Ed. Engels F. New York, Modern
        Library, 1936.
Selected Writings. Ed. McLellan, D. New York, Oxford University Press,
        1977.
Karl Marx, Early Writings. Tr. and Ed. Bottomore, T.B. London, CA
        Watts, 1963.
Communist Manifesto. With F. Engels, Baltimore, Penguin, 1968.
Berlin, I. *Karl Marx, His Life and Environment.* New York, Oxford
        University Press, 1963.
Bloch, E. *On Karl Marx.* New York, Herder and Herder, 1971.
Garaudy, R. *Marxism in the 20th Century.* New York, Scribners, 1970.

Chapter 23. Bergson

Creative Evolution. Tr. Mitchell, A. Lanham, MD, University Press of
        America, 1984.
The Two Sources of Morality and Religion. Tr. Audra, R.C., and Brereton,
        C. Notre Dame, University of Notre Dame Press,
        1977.
Alexander, I.W. *Bergson, Philosopher of Relection.* London, Bowes and
        Bowes, 1957.
Chevalier, J. *Henri Bergson.* Tr. Clare. New York, Macmillan, 1928.
Lindsay, A.D. *The Philosophy of Bergson.* New York, Dent, 1911.
Maritain, J. *Bergsonian Philosophy and Thomism.* Tr. Andison, M.L.
        Philosophical Library, 1955.

Chapter 24. James

The Writings of William James. Ed. McDermott, J. New York, Random
        House, 1967.

The Philosophy of William James. Ed. Kallen, H.M. New York, Modern
          Library, 1968.
Pragmatism. Ed. Kuklick, F. Indianapolis, Hacket, 1980.
The Varieties of Religious Experience. New York, Modern Library, 1902.
Barzun, J. *A Stroll with William James.* New York, Harper and Row, 1983.
Perry, R.B. *The Thought and Character of William James,* 2 vols. Boston,
          1935.

Chapter 25. Russell

The Problems of Philosophy. New York, Holt, 1912.
An Outline of Philosophy. London, Allen and Unwin, 1956.
Autobiography, 3 vols. London, Allen and Unwin, 1967-9.
The Basic Writings of Bertrand Russell. Ed. Egner, R.E. and Dennon, L.E.
          New York, Touchstone Books, 1967.
Bertrand Russell. Ed. Pears, D.F. New York, Doubleday Anchor, 1972.
Leggett, H.W. *Bertrand Russell.* London, 1949.
Schilpp, P.A., ed. *The Philosophy of Bertrand Russell.* New York, Harper
          and Row, 1963.
Wood, A. *Bertrand Russell, the Passionate Sceptic.* New York, Simon and
          Schuster, 1956.

Chapter 26. Wittgenstein

Tractatus Logico-Philosophicus. Tr. Pears, D.F. and McGuiness, B.F.
          London, 1961.
Philosophical Investigations. Tr. Anscombe, G.E.M. Oxford University Press,
          1953.
Janik, A., and Toulmin, S. *Wittgenstein's Vienna.* New York, Simon and
          Schuster, 1973.
Malcolm, N. *Ludwig Wittgenstein. A Memoir.* London, 1958.
McGuinness, B., ed. *Wittgenstein and His Times.* Chicago, University of
          Chicago Press, 1982.
Pitcher, G. *Wittgenstein, the Philosophical Investigations.* Garden City,
          Doubleday Anchor, 1966.

Chapter 27. Sartre

Being and Nothingness. Tr. Barnes, H.E. New York, Philosophical Library,
          1956.
Existentialism and Humanism. Tr. Mairet, P. London, Methuen, 1948.
Critique of Dialectical Reason. Tr. Sheridan-Smith, A. London, NLB, 1976.
Adieux, A Farewell to Sartre, Conversations with Simone de Beauvoir. Tr.
          O'Brian, P. New York, Pantheon, 1984.

Murdock, I. *Sartre, Romantic Rationalist.* New Haven, Yale, 1953.

Schilpp, P.A. *The Philosophy of Jean-Paul Sartre.* LaSalle, IN, Open Court, 1981.

Warnock, M. *The Philosophy of Sartre.* London, Hutchinson, 1965.

Glossary

Absolutism. A rigorously held position brooking no opposition; opposed to relativism; truth is "there" to be discovered and is not "relative" to the individual.

Abstraction. The mental process of separating one or several aspects of an object from all the others actually found in the object. The process whereby the mind, by leaving aside individuating differences, moves beyond individuals to a more inclusive level, class or category; the results thereof, e.g., humanity, animal, whiteness.

Accident. In the Aristotelian–Thomistic tradition, that which exists but only in another; exists in and through the substance of which it is a quality.

Agnosticism. The belief that is is impossible to attain certain knowledge, particularly as to God's existence.

A posteriori. Pertains to things known through experience, primarily sense experience; therefore, "based on experience."

A priori. Pertains to things known independently of experience; therefore, "prior to experience."

Argument. The total force of reasons bearing on a conclusion; another name for "reasoning."

Atheism. The belief that God does not exist.

Atomism. The view that there are small, indivisible, and irreducible quantities called atoms, and that they comprise all reality.

Becoming. Change; the process of going from one state to another, from one being to another.

Cause. That which in some way brings about the being or becoming of a thing; correlative with effect.

Concept. A term that usually refers to a general idea, or universal; e.g., "man," or "humanity" as opposed to the concrete individual, Socrates.

Conclusion. The proposition in which an argument ends.

Contradiction. The difference between two terms or two propositions that are diametrically opposed to each other, so that if one stands or is true the other does not stand or is false.

Cosmology. The study of physical reality, especially of the world as "cosmos," or unified whole.

Deduction. The act of reasoning from what is given to what necessarily follows, or from the premises to a conclusion that necessarily follows.

Determinism. The view that every event is necessarily brought about by pre-existing conditions; as a corollary, the human will is not free.

Dialectic. In its original Greek usage, a back and forth movement, as in dialogue, debate, or simple question and answer; later, the interplay among ideas, judgments, propositions in the act of reasoning; in Hegel and others, a metaphysical interplay of real opposites.

Dogmatism. The readiness to make assertions without support of proof or evidence.

Dualism. In general, the belief that there are but two substances, entities, or principles which are independent and mutually irreducible, such as, body and soul, matter and spirit, good and evil, sense and intellect, noumenal and phenomenal, actual and possible.

Empiricism. The view that all knowledge originates, and is somehow co-terminous with, experience, especially sensation; opposed to rationalism.

Epistemology. The study of knowledge; the branch of philosophy dealing with the origin, nature, and scope of knowledge.

Essence. That which makes a thing what it is; it answers the question, "what kind of thing is it?"

Esthetics (aesthetics). The philosophy of art; the study of what it is that makes a work a work of art.

Ethics. The study of moral conduct; the branch of philosophy dealing with oughtness, right and wrong, good and bad, moral value. *See* Moral philosophy.

Existentialism. A recent movement in philosophy concerned with human beings in their actual life situation, in the "human condition" of daily life in its anguish, problems, and individual choices.

Humanism. Any view that sees human dignity and values as paramount; Renaissance humanism centered on classical literature; contemporary humanism centers on human concerns apart from religious considerations.

Idealism. A term with many meanings that must be seen in context, but in general it refers to the view that reality consists mainly, or only, of ideas, spirit, mind or thought; opposed chiefly to realism, or at times, to materialism; different from its popular usage as "perfectionism."

Induction. The act of reasoning from what is given to what probably follows, or from the premises to a conclusion that probably follows.

Infinite. Not finite; without end; unlimited or unbounded in some way.

Innate. Inborn; pertains to that which is given in some way, or found in the very nature of a thing.

Intuition. Knowledge that is direct and immediate, that is, grasped without any intermediary.

Logic. The study of reasoning correctly.

Logical positivism. The view that sentences have cognitive meaning (as opposed, say, to either emotive or persuasive meaning) only when what they express is verifiable through sense-experience or is either a tautology or self-contradictory; sentences having cognitive meaning are deemed to express statements or propositions; sometimes referred to as logical empiricism.

Materialism. The view that emphasizes the priority of matter as the chief or only substance in reality.

Mechanism. The view that physical (mechanical) principles govern all activity

Metaphysics. The science of being; the study of the ultimate reasons as to why things are the way they are; the study of those things which lie "beyond physics" or "beyond the senses," traditionally, God, soul, and substance. In some recent analytical philosophy, the study of the general conceptual structure of human thought and language.

Monism. The belief that there is only one substance in reality, usually either spiritual or physical.

Moral philosophy. The branch of philosophy dealing with the irreducible aspect of human acts touching on oughtness, good or bad, right or wrong, do-able or not do-able; values of a unique nature called "moral values." In most respects, the same as ethics, but differs in that some actions may be unethical without being immoral. *See* Ethics.

Naturalism. The view that all reality can be understood in terms of what is "natural" as opposed to what is "supernatural," which it rejects; what cannot be experienced cannot be real; often associated with scientific empiricism.

Nihilism. The tendency to reject values as real, or at least the present structure of values.

Nominalism. The view that only particular things ar real, i.e., only individuals exist; therefore universal words or terms are but "names" *(nomina)* that we use only for convenience; they do not refer to anything real; opposed to "realism."

Objective. Pertaining to the object, i.e., independent of the person and personal views; opposed to subjective.

Ontology. The study of being, a word formerly used as synonomous with metaphysics; preferred by, e.g., Sartre, to avoid the overtones of God, soul, and substance as found in traditional metaphysics.

Pluralism. As opposed to either monism (one substance) or dualism (two substances), the view that there are many ultimate substances comprising reality.

Positivism. Usually refers to the view that our knowledge of reality is limited to what we can know "positively," that is, by concrete experience, mainly sensory or scientific.

Pragmatism. The method advanced by Peirce and James as a means of clarifying our ideas; the content, or truth, of an idea is measured by its practical references or consequences.

Premise. A proposition on which a conclusion is based; from which a conclusion is inferred.

Proposition. A statement; a sentence in which the predicate is affirmed or denied of the subject.

Rationalism. The belief that we can come to knowledge of the basic truths or reality first, and perhaps only, by an examination of our ideas; in this sense, opposed to empiricism.

Realism. The view that tends to hold that objects have an existence independent of the mind, or sense objects independent of the sense; opposed to idealism. In a stricter sense, opposed to nominalism; among the objects in which reality is deemed by some to be independent of mind are abstractions, universals, and numbers. Differs from the popular use of "realism" as facing facts as they are, or hard-hitting.

Relativism. The view that there is no such thing as absolute truth, for truth varies from person to person, or age to age.

Scepticism. Uncertainty or doubt concerning the very possibility of knowledge, or particular kinds of knowledge.

Scholasticism. Generally speaking, the process of education obtaining in "schools" during the Middle Ages; special reference to the philosophy taught.

Subjective. Pertaining to the subject, that is, to the person as individual; opposed to objective.

Substance. In traditional metaphysics, that which exists independently, or on its own, unlike accidents; it is not perceived by the senses but is concluded to.

Teleology. The study of purpose (end, goal, *telos* in Greek) in reality.

Transcendent. That which, or pertaining to that which, exists beyond what is given; opposed to immanent, though taken correlatively with immanent when speaking of God who is at the same time transcendent- immanent.

Utilitarianism. The view that an action is good or right or "useful" if it produces an increase of happiness or pleasure.